ܣܦܪܐ ܕܒܪܝܬܐ.

ܩܦܠܐܘܢ: ܐ.

1 ܒܪܫܝܬ ܒܪܐ ܐܠܗܐ ܝܬ ܫܡܝܐ ܘܝܬ ܐܪܥܐ.

2 ܘܐܪܥܐ ܗܘܬ ܬܘܗܐ ܘܒܘܗܝܐ ܘܚܫܘܟܐ ܥܠ ܐܦܝ ܬܗܘܡܐ: ܘܪܘܚܐ ܕܐܠܗܐ ܡܪܚܦܐ
ܥܠ ܐܦܝ ܡܝܐ.

3 ܘܐܡܪ ܐܠܗܐ: ܢܗܘܐ ܢܘܗܪܐ: ܘܗܘܐ ܢܘܗܪܐ.* ܘܚܙܐ ܐܠܗܐ ܠܢܘܗܪܐ: ܕܫܦܝܪ.

4 ܘܦܪܫ ܐܠܗܐ ܒܝܬ ܢܘܗܪܐ: ܘܒܝܬ ܚܫܘܟܐ.* ܘܩܪܐ ܐܠܗܐ ܠܢܘܗܪܐ: ܐܝܡܡܐ.

5 ܘܠܚܫܘܟܐ ܩܪܐ: ܠܠܝܐ. ܘܗܘܐ ܪܡܫܐ ܘܗܘܐ ܨܦܪܐ ܝܘܡܐ ܚܕ.

6 ܘܐܡܪ ܐܠܗܐ: ܢܗܘܐ ܪܩܝܥܐ ܒܡܨܥܬ ܡܝܐ: ܘܢܗܘܐ ܦܪܫ ܒܝܬ ܡܝܐ ܠܡܝܐ.*

7 ܘܥܒܕ ܐܠܗܐ ܪܩܝܥܐ: ܘܦܪܫ ܒܝܬ ܡܝܐ: ܕܠܬܚܬ ܡܢ ܪܩܝܥܐ ܘܒܝܬ

8 ܡܝܐ ܕܠܥܠ ܡܢ ܪܩܝܥܐ: ܘܗܘܐ ܗܟܢܐ.* ܘܩܪܐ ܐܠܗܐ ܠܪܩܝܥܐ:
ܫܡܝܐ. ܘܗܘܐ ܪܡܫܐ ܘܗܘܐ ܨܦܪܐ ܝܘܡܐ ܕܬܪܝܢ.

9 ܘܐܡܪ ܐܠܗܐ: ܢܬܟܢܫܘܢ ܡܝܐ ܕܠܬܚܬ ܡܢ ܫܡܝܐ ܠܐܬܪܐ ܚܕ: ܘܬܬܚܙܐ

10 ܝܒܝܫܬܐ: ܘܗܘܐ ܗܟܢܐ.* ܘܩܪܐ ܐܠܗܐ ܠܝܒܝܫܬܐ: ܐܪܥܐ. ܘܠܟܢܘܫܝܐ ܕܡܝܐ

11 ܩܪܐ: ܝܡܡܐ. ܘܚܙܐ ܐܠܗܐ: ܕܫܦܝܪ.* ܘܐܡܪ ܐܠܗܐ: ܬܦܩ ܐܪܥܐ ܬܕܐܐ: ܥܣܒܐ
ܕܡܙܕܪܥ ܙܪܥܐ: ܠܓܢܣܗ ܘܐܝܠܢܐ ܕܦܐܪܐ ܕܥܒܕ ܦܐܪܐ: ܠܓܢܣܗ ܕܙܪܥܗ ܒܗ

12 ܥܠܝܗ ܥܠ ܐܪܥܐ: ܘܗܘܐ ܗܟܢܐ.* ܘܐܦܩܬ ܐܪܥܐ ܬܕܐܐ: ܥܣܒܐ ܕܡܙܕܪܥ ܙܪܥܐ
ܠܓܢܣܗ: ܘܐܝܠܢܐ ܕܥܒܕ ܦܐܪܐ ܕܙܪܥܗ ܒܗ ܠܓܢܣܗ. ܘܚܙܐ

13 ܐܠܗܐ: ܕܫܦܝܪ.* ܘܗܘܐ ܪܡܫܐ ܘܗܘܐ ܨܦܪܐ ܝܘܡܐ ܕܬܠܬܐ.

14 ܘܐܡܪ ܐܠܗܐ: ܢܗܘܘܢ ܢܗܝܪܐ ܒܪܩܝܥܐ ܕܫܡܝܐ: ܠܡܦܪܫ ܒܝܬ ܐܝܡܡܐ ܘܒܝܬ

15 ܠܠܝܐ. ܘܢܗܘܘܢ ܠܐܬܘܬܐ ܘܠܙܒܢܐ: ܘܠܝܘܡܬܐ ܘܠܫܢܝܐ.* ܘܢܗܘܘܢ ܠܢܗܝܪܐ ܒܪܩܝܥܐ

16 ܕܫܡܝܐ: ܠܡܢܗܪܘ ܥܠ ܐܪܥܐ: ܘܗܘܐ ܗܟܢܐ.* ܘܥܒܕ ܐܠܗܐ ܬܪܝܢ ܢܗܝܪܐ
ܪܘܪܒܐ: ܢܗܝܪܐ ܪܒܐ ܠܫܘܠܛܢܐ ܕܐܝܡܡܐ: ܘܢܗܝܪܐ ܙܥܘܪܐ ܠܫܘܠܛܢܐ ܕܠܠܝܐ:

17 ܘܟܘܟܒܐ.* ܘܝܗܒ ܐܢܘܢ ܐܠܗܐ ܒܪܩܝܥܐ ܕܫܡܝܐ: ܠܡܢܗܪܘ ܥܠ ܐܪܥܐ.* ܘܠܡܫܠܛ

18 ܒܐܝܡܡܐ ܘܒܠܠܝܐ: ܘܠܡܦܪܫ ܒܝܬ ܢܘܗܪܐ ܘܒܝܬ ܚܫܘܟܐ. ܘܚܙܐ ܐܠܗܐ: ܕܫܦܝܪ.*

19 ܘܗܘܐ ܪܡܫܐ ܘܗܘܐ ܨܦܪܐ ܝܘܡܐ ܕܐܪܒܥܐ.

20 ܘܐܡܪ ܐܠܗܐ: ܢܪܚܫܘܢ ܡܝܐ ܪܚܫܐ ܢܦܫܐ ܚܝܬܐ: ܘܦܪܚܬܐ ܕܦܪܚܐ ܥܠ

21 ܐܪܥܐ: ܥܠ ܐܦܝ ܪܩܝܥܐ ܕܫܡܝܐ.* ܘܒܪܐ ܐܠܗܐ ܬܢܝܢܐ ܪܘܪܒܐ: ܘܟܠ

ܢܦܫܐ ܚܝܬܐ ܕܪܚܫܐ: ܕܐܪܚܫܘ ܡܝܐ ܠܓܢܣܝܗܘܢ: ܘܟܠ ܦܪܚܬܐ ܕܦܪܚܐ

22 ܠܓܢܣܗ: ܘܚܙܐ ܐܠܗܐ: ܕܫܦܝܪ.* ܘܒܪܟ ܐܢܘܢ ܐܠܗܐ ܠܡܐܡܪ: ܦܪܘ

The
Holy Bible

for the Universal Church
from the Ancient Aramaic Texts

Volume One

Genesis - II Chronicles

Translated by

Dr. George M. Lamsa

Foreword by

Dr. Gene Scott

The Aramaic Bible Society, Inc.

6195 Cherry Valley Drive, Covington, GA. 30014-3917
Telephone: 770/784-9062 Telephone/Fax: 770/385-7216

website : http://www.aramaic.org

First Aramaic Bible Society, Inc. Edition 2004.

ISBN 0-9745296-0-5

Prepress and cover design:
Third Heaven Studios
East Hampton, CT.

dmahar@snet.net

Opposite title page: The first chapter of Genesis in Assyrian script.
 Back cover: (translation) "The Holy Book - The Book of the Old Testament"
Dinkha Beth Estrangela font designed by Nicholai Seleznyov
http://silesnius.narod.ru/fonts.htm

Foreword

I first met George M Lamsa almost 40 years ago. He left an instant impression which I have never forgotten. Like the Apostle Paul he radiated a commitment to a "calling" and like Paul, he intended to finish his course. Since that time, I made the time to familiarize myself with his life and work, his passion (better, that "calling") to make the Christian world aware of the importance of the Aramaic, particularly the Syriac dialect, to the earliest New Testament writings. This translation of The Peshitta is the magnificent fruit of George Lamsa's life of sacrifice and dedication - he fought a good fight, he finished his course, he "kept the faith."

Here's the verse in the language he loved (II Tim 4:7):

ܐܓܘܢܐ ܫܦܝܪܐ ܐܬܟܬܫܬ ܘܪܗܛܝ ܛܠܡܬ ܘܗܝܡܢܘܬܝ ܢܛܪܬ ܀

George's legacy has been picked up by the Aramaic Bible Society and its president, Robert Allen, Jr.; like a "Timothy" for the Apostle Paul, Bob Allen with his associates have brought this wonderful translation of The Peshitta into English publication again. They are to be commended for this accomplishment and George Lamsa must be smiling from under his crown in the place of his rewards.

The importance of this work cannot be overstated. Cyrus H. Gordon and Gary Rendsburg in their careful study of "The Bible and the Ancient Near East" (W.W. Norton & Company, fourth edition, 1997) state on pp.21 ff.,

"The language with the widest distribution in our study is Aramaic. Although there is evidence of the Aramaic language in records of the second millennium B.C.E., the historic texts begin in the eighth century in the city-states of Aram (or inland Syria), when it displaced Phoenician as the lingua franca in Syria and nearby coastal Asia Minor. By the end of the century Aramaic had already won for itself the role of international language in official circles from at least Assyria to Judah (2 Kings 18:26; the date is 701 B.C.E.). The achievement is the more remarkable since the Arameans never forged a great empire but spread the language through relatively peaceful means, notably tribal migrations and trade. The Achaemenians used Aramaic as their inter-provincial tongue, at least for the areas west of Iran. Parts of the Bible are written in Aramaic, notably large sections of Daniel and Ezra.

. . .So great was Aramaic that it was destined to replace the native languages of all Semitic Asia outside of Arabia and it remained unchallenged until the Islamic Conquest in the seventh century C.E." (emphasis is mine)

The importance and influence of Aramaic, and particularly its Syriac (Galilean) dialect, on the New Testament is beyond dispute. Jesus and his Disciples spoke Galilean (Syriac); Paul's ministry began in Syria (Damascus). Each of Paul's missionary journeys began at Antioch in Syria - - and returned there. The first Christian City Kingdom was Edessa (Syriac), and the first harmony of the Gospel by Tatian was in Syriac. All this is well known by scholars, but most of the western Christian world has remained ignorant of this crucial Syriac role.

While writing this, I am looking at a rare copy of the <u>Aleppo Codex</u> on my desk, one of two great manuscripts on which the received text of the Hebrew Bible is based - - along the margins are notes in <u>shorthand</u> - <u>Aramaic</u>. The block letters now comprising the Biblical Hebrew alphabet were "borrowed" from the Aramaic. Christians were first called "Christians" at Antioch (Syria). Also in my collection is a copy of the ancient Bible Manuscript, the <u>Codex</u> <u>Bezae</u>, fifth in line of the Ancients, i.e., "D" after the Sinaiticus (א), the Alexandrinus (A), the Vaticanus (B) and (C) the Ephraim palimpsist. Scholars have long recognized <u>Codex Bezae</u>'s dependence on <u>Old</u> <u>Syriac</u>. Add further, the famed Dr. Edgar J. Goodspeed commented on this subject (as quoted by Dr. Lamsa himself in one of his books) by these words:

"Jesus spoke Aramaic. All his words have come down to us from that language. The first stories of his life and death were told in it. This, no serious student of the Gospels any longer denies. Most of the genuine Semiticisms of Gospels are thus fully and naturally explained." (New Chapters in the New Testament Study, MacMillan Co., New York, p.148.)

A noteworthy final point on the subject is that Armenia claims the honor of being the first kingdom (<u>Nation</u>, Edessa being a "city") to accept Christianity as its official religion. The construction of the Armenian Alphabet was first attempted by a certain Bishop Daniel - - a Syrian. The final successful alphabet by Mesrop contained <u>four</u> <u>letters</u> <u>taken</u> <u>from</u> <u>the</u> <u>Syriac</u>. According to Bruce M. Metzger (<u>The</u> <u>Early</u> <u>Versions</u> <u>of</u> <u>The</u> <u>New</u> <u>Testa-</u>

ment, Clarendon Press, Oxford, 1977, p. 157) "more manuscripts of this (Armenian) version are extant than of any other ancient version, with the exception only of the Latin Vulgate." (emphasis is mine). Metzger remarks on p.165 in his discussion of the "base" of the Armenian Version that the famous scholar J. C. "Conybeare adopted the opinion, which he held to the end of his life, that the Armenian version was made from the Syriac." (emphasis is mine).

Yes, an English translation of the Ancient Syriac Peshitta is important. Welcome to the translation of the language of the Galilean, our Lord and Savior Jesus the Christ.

Yes, indeed "something good" has come out of Galilee" (vide John 7:41, 42, 52).

And, congratulation to Robert Allen, Jr. and his associates at "The Aramaic Bible Society" for making this happen. They "kept the faith"!

Dr. Gene Scott
Ph.D. Stanford University
Pastor, the Los Angeles University
Cathedral & Teaching Voice of
"The University Network, Worldwide"

INTRODUCTION

North of the Garden of Eden in the basin of the river Tigris, in the mountain fastnesses of what is known today as Kurdistan, there lived an ancient people, the descendants of the Assyrians, the founders of the great Assyrian empire and culture in Bible days, the originators of the alphabet and many sciences which contributed so generously to the Semitic culture from which sprang our Bible. These people, the Assyrians, played an important part in the history of the Near East, of the Bible, and of religion in general.

When Nineveh was destroyed in 612 B.C., many of the princes and noblemen of this once vast empire fled northward into inaccessible mountains where they remained secluded and cut off until the dawn of the twentieth century. Nahum says: "Thy shepherds slumber, O king of Assyria: thy nobles shall dwell in the dust: thy people is scattered upon the mountains, and no man gathereth them." Nah. 3:18.

Some descendants of the Assyrians and some of the descendants of the ten tribes who were taken captive by the Assyrian kings in 721 B.C., and settled in Assyria, Babylon, Persia and other places east of the river Euphrates, were among the first converts to Christianity.

When Jesus sent seventy of his disciples to preach the gospel, he instructed them not to go in the way of the Gentiles or into any city of the Samaritans but to go to the lost sheep of the house of Israel, meaning the ten tribes who were lost from the house of Israel. Some of the descendants of these Hebrew tribes are still living in Iraq, Iran, and Turkey, and most of them still converse in Aramaic. Jesus' command was carried out. The gospel was preached to the Jews first. "Now those who had been dispersed by the persecution which occurred on account of Stephen traveled as far as Phoenicia and even to the land of Cyprus and to Antioch, preaching the word to none but to the Jews only." Acts 11:19.

The Assyrians remained dormant during the Persian, Greek, Roman and Arab conquests. Being isolated and surrounded by their enemies, they remained secluded throughout the centuries, thus preserving the Aramaic language, which was the language of the Near East, and perpetuating the ancient Biblical customs and manners which were common to all races and peoples in this part of the ancient world. Not until the Turkish reign did these isolated Assyrian tribes recognize any government or pay any taxes. During the centuries of Arab and Turkish reigns, the Assyrians retained their cultural independence, later recognizing the sympathetic Turkish rule which permitted the continuation of their institutions and their religion. Under magnanimous Turks they were ruled by their patriarchs and chiefs, paying a nominal tax to the Turkish government.

The Assyrian church, or as it is known, the ancient Apostolic and Catholic Church of the East, was one of the strongest Christian churches in the world and was noted for its missions in the Middle East, India, and China. Its missionaries carried the Christian gospel as far as China and Mongolia, Indonesia, Japan and other parts of the world. Not until the 14th century was this church rivaled by any other church in the world. It was the most powerful branch of Christen-

iii

dom in the Near East, Palestine, Arabia, Lebanon, Iran, India and elsewhere. All the literature of this church was written in literary Aramaic, the lingua franca of that time. This is corroborated by Dr. Arnold J. Toynbee in his *A Study of History* wherein he writes: " . . . Darius the Great's account of his own acts on the rock of Behistan, overhanging the Empire's great north-east road, was transcribed in triplicate in three different adaptations of the cuneiform script conveying the three imperial capitals: Elamite for Susa, Medo-Persian for Ecbatana, and Akkadian for Babylon. But the winning language within this universal state was none of the three thus officially honoured; it was Aramaic, with its handier alphabetic script. The sequel showed that commerce and culture may be more important than politics in making a language's fortune; for the speakers of Aramaic were politically of no account in the Achaemenian Empire . . . " *

The Persians used the Aramaic language because this tongue was the language of the two Semitic empires, the empire of Assyria and the empire of Babylon. Aramaic was so firmly established as the lingua franca that no government could dispense with its use as a vehicle of expression in a far-flung empire, especially in the western provinces. Moreover, without schools and other modern facilities, Aramaic could not be replaced by the speech of conquering nations. Conquerors were not interested in imposing their languages and cultures on subjugated peoples. What they wanted was taxes, spoils, and other levies.

The transition from Aramaic [1] into Arabic, a sister tongue, took place after the conquest of the Near East by the Moslem armies in the 7th century, A.D. Nevertheless, Aramaic lingered for many centuries and still is spoken in Lebanon, Syria, Iraq, and northwestern Iran, as well as among the Christian Arab tribes in northern Arabia. Its alphabet was borrowed by the Hebrews, Arabs, Iranians, and Mongols.

Dr. Philip K. Hitti, noted historian and Professor of Semitic languages at Princeton University, in his book *The History of the Arabs,* uses the terms *Aramaic* and *Syriac* interchangeably and states that Aramaic is still a living language. He says, "In country places and on their farms these dhimmis clung to their ancient cultural patterns and preserved their native languages: Aramaic and Syriac in Syria and Al-'Iraq, Iranian in Persia and Coptic in Egypt." And again, "In Al-'Iraq and Syria the transition from one Semitic tongue, the Aramaic, to another, the Arabic, was of course easier. In the out-of-the-way places, however, such as the Lebanons with their preponderant Christian population, the native Syriac put up a desperate fight and has lingered until modern times. Indeed Syriac is still spoken in Ma'lula and two other villages in Anti-Lebanon. With its disappearance, Aramaic has left in the colloquial Arabic unmistakable traces noticeable in vocabulary, accent and grammatical structure." **

The late Dr. W. A. Wigram in *The Assyrians and Their Neighbours* wrote: "One thing is certain, that the Assyrians boast with justice that they alone of all Christian nations still keep as their spoken language what is acknowledged to be the language of Palestine in the first century . . . " ***

Quoting Dr. Toynbee again from *A Study of History:* " . . . As for the Aramaic alphabet, it achieved far wider conquests. In 1599 A.D., it was adopted for the conveyance of the Manchu language on the eve of the Manchu conquest of China. The higher religions sped it on its way by taking it into their service. In its 'Square Hebrew' variant it became the vehicle of the Jewish Scriptures and liturgy; in an Arabic adaptation it became the alphabet of Islam . . . " *

As a miracle of miracles, Aramaic and most of the ancient Biblical customs which were common to Semitic people have survived in northern Iraq until today. Aramaic is still spoken in Iraq and in northwestern Iran by remnants of the Assyrian people and the Jews of the exile, and the literary Aramaic remains the same today as it was of yore. Some of the Aramaic words which are still retained in all Bible versions are still used in the Aramaic language spoken today: for

[1] The Greeks called it *Syriac* (derived from Sur, Tyre).
* By permission of Oxford University Press, Publishers, and D. C. Somervell.
** By permission of the author, the book, Macmillan & Co., Ltd. and St. Martin's Press.
*** By permission of G. Bell & Sons, Publishers, London.

Introduction

example, *Raca, Ethpatakh, Rabbuli, Lemana, Shabakthani, Talitha Koomi, Maran Etha, Manna, Khakal-Dema.*

As we have said, the survival of this small remnant of this segment of the ancient Semitic culture was due to the isolation, tenacity, and warlike character of the Assyrian people who were living isolated, now under the Parthian Empire, now under the Persian Empire, now under the Arabian Empire and now under the Turkish Empire. And because of this isolation, these ancient Christians had hardly any contact with Christians in the West. Only one of their bishops and a deacon participated in the Nicene Council in 325 A.D.

After the conversion of Emperor Constantine to Christianity in 318 A.D., Christians in the Persian Empire who hitherto had been tolerated and looked upon as the enemies of Rome, the persecutor of Christianity, now were looked upon as the friends of the Christian emperor, Constantine, and the enemies of the Persian government. Persecution of these Christians did not begin until the 4th century A.D., and lasted until the Arab conquest of Persia, 632 A.D. This is why this ancient Church was unable to establish contacts with Western Christianity.

The Scriptures in the Church of the East, from the inception of Christianity to the present day, are in Aramaic and have never been tampered with or revised, as attested by the present Patriarch of the Church of the East. The Biblical manuscripts were carefully and zealously handed down from one generation to another and kept in the massive stone walls of the ancient churches and in caves. They were written on parchment and many of them survive to the present day. When these texts were copied by expert scribes, they were carefully examined for accuracy before they were dedicated and permitted to be read in churches. Even one missing letter would render the text void. Easterners still adhere to God's commandment not to add to or omit a word from the Scriptures. The Holy Scripture condemns any addition or subtraction or modification of the Word of God.

"You shall not add to the commandment which I command you, neither shall you take from it, but you must keep the commandments of the LORD your God which I command you." Deut. 4:2.

"Everything that I command you, that you must be careful to do; you shall not add nor take from it." Deut. 12:32.

"Do not add to his words; lest he reprove you, and you be found a liar." Prov. 30:6.

"And if any man shall take away from the words of the book of this prophecy, God shall take away his portion from the tree of life and from the holy city and from the things which are written in this book." Rev. 22:19.

It is also true of the Jews and Moslems that they would not dare to alter a word of the Torah or Koran. Easterners are afraid that they may incur the curse if they make a change in the Word of God.

Some of these ancient manuscripts go back to the 5th century A.D. The oldest dated Biblical manuscript in the world is that of the four Books of Moses, 464 A.D., which now lies in the British Museum. Another one is the Codex Ambrosianus. Some of it goes back to the 7th century, some of it to the 5th century, and some of it might be earlier. This Codex is not the work of one man. Apparently some portions were written before the vowel system was invented and that would put it prior to the 5th century. The Pentateuch of the British Museum must have been written before the vowel system was invented. Aramaic documents of the 5th century and later use the vowel system, some of them fully and some in part. It is interesting to know that this vowel system was adopted by the Jews and was begun about the 5th century, A.D. In some portions of the above texts, the old Aramaic original consonantal spelling without apparatus of vowel points is well preserved. This is also true of some of the New Testament texts in the Pierpont Morgan Library, New York City.

Unfortunately many ancient and valuable Aramaic texts were lost during World War I. But printed copies of them, carefully made by American missionaries under the help and guidance of competent native scholars, are available. Moreover, a number of ancient New Testament texts, some of them going back to the 5th century A.D. are in various libraries. The New Testament texts in the Pierpont Morgan Library are among the oldest in existence.

Introduction

The translator of this work has access to the existing texts; he has spent many years comparing them in the course of translating the Bible.

Astonishingly enough, all the Peshitta texts in Aramaic agree. There is one thing of which the Eastern scribes can boast: they copied their holy books diligently, faithfully, and meticulously. Sir Frederick Kenyon, Curator of the British Museum, in his book *Textual Criticism of the New Testament,* speaks highly of the accuracy of copying and of the antiquity of Peshitta MSS.

The versions translated from Semitic languages into Greek and Latin were subject to constant revisions. Learned men who copied them introduced changes, trying to simplify obscurities and ambiguities which were due to the work of the first translators. Present translators and Bible revisers do the same when translating the Bible, treaties, and documents from one language to another. The American Constitution, written in English, will always remain the same when new copies are made, but translations into other languages will be subject to revision. Therefore, a copy of the United States Constitution published ten years ago is far more valuable than a translation made two hundred years ago. Translations are always subject to revisions and disputes over exact meaning because words and terms of speech in one language cannot be translated easily into another without loss. This is one reason why we have so many translations and revisions of the King James version.

As said before, Aramaic was the language of Semitic culture, the language of the Hebrew patriarchs and, in the older days, the lingua franca of the Fertile Crescent. The term "Hebrew" is derived from the Aramaic word *Abar* or *Habar* which means "to cross over." This name was given to the Hebrew people simply because Abraham and the people who were with him crossed the river Euphrates and went to Palestine. Therefore, they were known by those who lived east of the river Euphrates as Hebrews, that is, "the people across the river." All branches of the great Semitic people had a common speech. How could the people of Nineveh have understood Jonah, a Hebrew prophet, had the Biblical Hebrew tongue been different from Aramaic? There were some differences similar to the differences we have in English spoken in Tennessee and that spoken in New York.

This small pastoral Hebrew tribe through which God chose to reveal himself to mankind, for several generations continued to keep its paternal and racial relations with the people who lived in Padan-Aram (Mesopotamia), and preserved customs and manners which they brought with them from Padan-Aram, and the language which their fathers spoke. Jacob changed the name of Luz to Beth-el (Aramaic—the house of God). Abraham instructed his servant not to let his son, Isaac, marry a Palestinian maid but to go to Padan-Aram to his own kindred from whence to bring a maid to his son. Years later, Jacob, the grandson of Abraham, went to Padan-Aram and married his uncle's two daughters and their handmaids and lived in Haran about twenty years. Eleven of his sons were born in Padan-Aram. The first generation of the children of Jacob went to Egypt. Their sojourn in Palestine was so brief that there was no possibility of linguistic change. That is why they spoke the language which they had learned in Padan-Aram. While in Egypt, living by themselves, they continued to use names of Aramaic derivation such as Manasseh, Ephraim, Bar-Nun, Miriam, etc.

After the captivity, Aramaic became the vernacular of the Jewish people and is still used by them in their worship. Both of the Jewish Talmuds, namely, the Babylonian and Palestinian, were written in Aramaic. The later findings, especially of Jewish-Aramaic papyri which were found in Egypt in 1900, have produced many passages in Biblical Aramaic. The discovery of the Commentary on the Book of Habakkuk in the caves of Qumran in Jordan proves that Aramaic has been in constant use from early times to the present day.

It is evident that during the exile and post-exile the Hebrew writers used Aramaic. Some of the portions of their works were put into Hebrew. Daniel and Ezra were born during the captivity. Hebrew was no longer spoken and the official language of writing in Babylon was southern Aramaic and the Jewish community had already parted with their Hebrew.[1] Thus, the captivity produced the transition from Hebrew, a sister language, into Aramaic.

[1] The two languages were so close that Hebrew could not be retained in Babylon.

Introduction

Biblical Hebrew and Aramaic were very closely related, like American English and English spoken in England. Whether the Hebrew prophets wrote in Hebrew or Aramaic would make little difference. The differences would be like those between several Arabic dialects which are spoken in Arabia. Even though the vernacular speech differs because of local color and idioms, the norm of the written language remains the same. This is true today with written Arabic when compared with spoken Arabic. And such was the case with Attic Greek when compared with other Greek dialects. The grammar, verbs, nouns and other parts of speech are practically the same in the basic ancient Biblical Hebrew language and Aramaic. The structure of a sentence, in point of grammar and syntax of Biblical Hebrew and Aramaic, is the same. But this is not the case when translating from Hebrew or Aramaic into a totally alien tongue such as Greek, Latin, or English. Moreover, the alphabet in Hebrew and Aramaic is exactly the same and all letters are pronounced alike.

The Jewish Encyclopedia, Vol. II, tells us:

"In Palestinian Aramaic the dialect of Galilee was different from that of Judea, and as a result of the religious separation of the Jews and the Samaritans, a special Samaritan dialect was evolved, but its literature cannot be considered Jewish. To the eastern Aramaic, whose most distinctive point of difference is "n" in place of "y" as the prefix for the third person masculine of the imperfect tense of the verb, belong the idioms of the Babylonian Talmud, which most closely agree with the language of the Mandaean writings." *

The strongest points in ascertaining the originality of a text are the style of writing, the idioms, and the internal evidence. Words which make sense and are easily understood in one language, when translated literally into another tongue, may lose their meaning. One can offer many instances where scores of Aramaic words, some with several meanings and others with close resemblance to other words, were confused and thus mistranslated.

This is why in Jeremiah 4:10, we read in the King James:

". . . Ah, Lord God! surely thou hast greatly deceived this people . . ."

The Aramaic reads:

". . . Ah, Lord God! I have greatly deceived this people . . ." The translator's confusion is due to the position of a dot, for the position of a dot frequently determines the meaning of a word.

In Isaiah 43:28, the King James version reads:

"Therefore, I have profaned the princes of the sanctuary . . ."

The Aramaic reads:

". . . Your princes have profaned my sanctuary . . ." This error was caused by misunderstanding of a passive plural verb. The same error occurs in John 12:40, which in the Eastern Text reads:

". . . Their eyes have become blind . . ." instead of ". . . He hath blinded their eyes . . ."

In Isaiah 14:12, the Aramaic word *ailel,* to howl, is confused by the Hebrew word *helel,* light. The reference here is to the king of Babylon and not to Lucifer.

In Psalm 22:29, King James version, we read:

"All they that be fat upon earth shall eat and worship . . . and none can keep alive his own soul."

The Aramaic text reads:

"All those who are hungry (for truth) shall eat and worship . . . my soul is alive to him." The error in this instance is due to the confusion of the Aramaic words which have some resemblance. Some of these words when written by hand resemble one another. A list of words, their meanings and how they were confused one with the other will be found in this Introduction.

THE ARAMAIC PESHITTA TEXT

The term Peshitta means straight, simple, sincere and true, that is, the original. This name was given to this ancient and authoritative text to distinguish it from

---

* By special permission of Funk and Wagnalls, copyright owners, New York and London.

vii

Introduction

other Bible revisions and translations which were introduced into some of the Churches of the East (Monophysites) after the division at Ephesus and Chalcedon in 431 and 451 A.D., respectively. This ancient Peshitta is still the only authoritative text of the Old and New Testament of all Eastern Christians in the Near East and India, the Church of the East, the Roman Catholic Church in the East, the Monophysites, and Indian Christians. This is because this text was in use for 400 years before the Christian Church was divided into several sects.

The Peshitta Old Testament contains what is known as the Books of the Apocrypha, which have been handed down in the Peshitta manuscripts together with the Books of the Law and the Books of the Prophets, and since these Apocryphal books are included in the text they are looked upon as a sacred literature, even though they are not as commonly used as the others. Moreover this ancient New Testament text omits the story of the woman taken in adultery, 2 Peter, 2 and 3 John, Jude, and Revelation. (But these books are included in later Aramaic texts.) The Peshitta canon was set before the discovery of these books.

Amid persecutions, the ancient Church of the East, through God's help and protection, was able to keep these sacred writings of the Old and New Testaments in the Biblical lands in Persia and India just as the Roman Catholic Church preserved them in the West. Christianity also owes a debt to the Jewish people who preserved the Word of God amid persecution and suffering.

Therefore, Peshitta should not be confused with the 5th century Bible revisions in Aramaic and new versions which were made from Greek. None of these new revisions and versions made by the Monophysite bishops in the 5th century has ever been accepted by the Church of the East. Moreover, these bishops who left their church and joined the Greek church and produced these versions for theological reasons so that their doctrine might agree with the doctrine of the Byzantine Church, which was the powerful imperial sect, were expelled by the Patriarch of the East and their works were condemned. However, in some provinces, owing to the pressure exerted by the Byzantine emperors, these new revisions were introduced. But when the territory was occupied by the Persian government, they were destroyed.

Had the Peshitta been made by order of one of the rival churches, the others would have rejected it. But since all Christians, even the Moslems, in the Middle East accept and revere the Peshitta text, it proves beyond a doubt that it was in use many centuries before the division of the Church.

The originality of the Peshitta text is strongly supported by early evidence. Aphraates quoted it. St. Ephraim wrote a commentary on it and the doctrine of Addi placed it at the apostolic times.

According to the Peshitta text, the Semitic names of people and towns and localities, in both the New and Old Testaments, agree. The names which end with "s" are retained for the western reader. In the Peshitta text, Barnabas is Barnba, Abbas is Abba, Peter is Kepa. Then again, some of the names of localities are different but older than those in other texts. For example, Rakim is used instead of Kadesh, Mathnin instead of Bashan, Amorah for Gomorah; the error in this instance is due to close similarity between *gamel* and *ain*. A town near the city of Gomorah is called Amoriah. No doubt, the pre-exile Hebrew texts used these older names.

The late Mar-Yacob (Jacob) Eugene Manna, Chaldean Roman Catholic Metropolitan of Armenia, a distinguished Aramaic scholar whose writings are in Aramaic, says that the text which is called Peshitta is without dispute even earlier than the writings which came down from the works of Bar-Dasan, who was living in the latter part of the second century. He also states that the Aramaic speech in Mesopotamia was richer and purer than the Aramaic speech of other regions. It was the richness and the beauty of this language which was used as the lingua franca by the three great empires in the Near East and Middle East which enriched the English language. The Greek and Latin translators made literal translations of the Scriptures, keeping the Semitic rhythm and sentence structure.

Indeed, the translation of the Scriptures into the English language facilitated the work of later English writers. The style of Shakespeare, Milton, and Browning could not have been what it is without the beauty of the King James translation

Introduction

which was inherited from Semitic languages. This is true also of all languages into which the Bible has been translated.

The Septuagint is based on early Hebrew manuscripts and not on the later ones known as the Massoretic, which were made in the 6th to the 9th centuries. In other words, there are many similarities between the Septuagint and the Peshitta text but the former contains inevitable mistranslations which were due to difficulties in transmitting Hebrew or Aramaic thought and mannerisms of speech into a totally alien tongue like Greek. But as has been said, such was not the case between Biblical Aramaic and Biblical Hebrew which are of the same origin. Josephus used Aramaic and Hebrew words indiscriminately. Thus, the term "translating" from Hebrew into Aramaic or vice versa is incorrect. It would be like one stating as having translated the United States Constitution from the Pennsylvania language into the English language or from lower German to higher German. Even before the first captivity, 721 B.C., Jewish kings, scribes, and learned men understood Aramaic. 2 Kings 18:26.

The Israelites never wrote their sacred literature in any language but Aramaic and Hebrew, which are sister languages. The Septuagint was made in the 3rd century, B.C., for the Alexandrian Jews. This version was never officially read by the Jews in Palestine who spoke Aramaic and read Hebrew. Instead, the Jewish authorities condemned the work and declared a period of mourning because of the defects in the version. Evidently Jesus and his disciples used a text which came from an older Hebrew original. This is apparent because Jesus' quotations from the Old Testament agree with the Peshitta text but do not agree with the Greek text. For example, in John 12:40, the Peshitta Old Testament and New Testament agree. This is not all. Jesus and his disciples not only could not converse in Greek but they never heard it spoken.

We believe that the Scriptures were conceived and inspired by the Holy Spirit and written by Hebrew prophets who spoke and wrote, as the Holy Spirit moved them, to the people in their days, using idioms, similes, parables and metaphors in order to convey their messages. Moreover, these men of God sacrificed their lives that the Word of God might live. The Jewish race treasured these sacred writings as a priceless possession.

Writing was prevalent from the earliest days. The Israelites made more extensive use of the instrument of writing than neighboring nations such as the Ammonites, Moabites, and other kindred people round about them. Moses wrote the Ten Commandments; Joshua wrote on an altar which he built west of Jordan. The Israelites were admonished to fasten the commandments to their foreheads and necks and to write them on their doorsteps. Everything was written at the time it was revealed. God said to Moses,

"Now therefore write this song for them, and teach it to the children of Israel; and put it into their mouths; this song will be a witness for me against the children of Israel." Deut. 31:19.

"And the LORD answered me and said, Write the vision, and make it plain upon tablets, that he who reads it may understand it clearly." Hab. 2:2. Thus, the Old Testament Scriptures were written very early.

This is also true of the Gospels. They were written a few years after the resurrection and some of the portions were written by Matthew while Jesus was preaching. They were not handed down orally and then written after the Pauline Epistles, as some western scholars say; they were written many years before those Epistles. Other contemporary Jewish literature was produced at the same time the Gospels were in circulation. The Gospels, as well as the Epistles, were written in Aramaic, the language of the Jewish people, both in Palestine and in the Greco-Roman Empire.

Greek was never the language of Palestine. Josephus' book on the Jewish Wars was written in Aramaic. Josephus states that even though a number of Jews had tried to learn the language of the Greeks, hardly any of them succeeded.

Josephus wrote (42 A.D.): "I have also taken a great deal of pains to obtain the learning of the Greeks, and understand the elements of the Greek language; although I have so accustomed myself to speak our own tongue, that I cannot pronounce Greek with sufficient exactness. For our nation does not encourage

ix

those that learn the language of many nations. On this account, as there have been many who have done their endeavors, with great patience, to obtain this Greek learning, there have yet hardly been two or three that have succeeded herein, who were immediately rewarded for their pains." *Antiquities XX, XI 2.*

Indeed, the teaching of Greek was forbidden by Jewish rabbis. It was said that it was better for a man to give his child meat of swine than to teach him the language of the Greeks.

When the King James translation was made, western scholars had no access to the East as we have today. In the 16th century, A.D., the Turkish empire had extended its borders as far as Vienna. One European country after another was falling under the impact of the valiant Turkish army. Europe was almost conquered. This is not all. The reformations and controversies in the Western Church had destroyed Christian unity. Moreover, the Scriptures in Aramaic were unknown in Europe. The only recourse scholars had was to Latin and to a few portions of Greek manuscripts. This is clearly seen from the works of Erasmus. Besides, the knowledge of Greek was almost lost at this time and Christians were just emerging from the Dark Ages.

Many people have asked why the King James' translators did not use the Peshitta text from Aramaic or the Scriptures used in the East. The answer is: there were no contacts between East and West until after the conquest of India by Great Britain and the rise of the imperial power of Britain in the Near East, Middle East, and the Far East. It is a miracle that the King James' translators were able to produce such a remarkable translation from sources available in this dark period of European history. Even fifty years ago, the knowledge of Western scholars relative to the Eastern Scriptures in Aramaic and the Christian Church in the East was conjectural. Moreover, these scholars knew very little of the Eastern customs and manners in which the Biblical literature was nurtured. Thank God, today new discoveries have been made; new facts have come to light; new democratic institutions and governments have been established in the East. What in the 16th and 17th centuries was viewed at a long distance now can be seen face to face. Today, not only scholars, ministers, and Bible teachers walk on Palestinian soil but also thousands of men and women visit Biblical lands every year.

For centuries translations from Semitic languages have been subject to revision. They are, even now, subject to revision. This is why there are so many Bible versions varying each from the other. Let us just take one instance which I consider very important. In the King James version, we read in Numbers 25:4:

"And the LORD said unto Moses, Take all the heads of the people, and hang them up before the LORD against the sun, that the fierce anger of the LORD may be turned away from Israel."

The Aramaic reads:

"And the LORD said to Moses, Take all the chiefs of the people and expose them before the LORD in the daylight that the fierce anger of the LORD may be turned away from the children of Israel."

Some noted Greek scholars in recent translations have changed the word hang to execute, but this is not what the original writer said. God could not have told Moses to behead or execute all Israelites. The Lord was angry at the princes of Israel because of the sin of Baal-peor. They had been lax in enforcing the law and also guilty in joining the sensual Baal worship.

And in 1 Corinthians 7:36 and 38, King James, we read:

"But if any man think that he behaveth himself uncomely toward his virgin, if she pass the flower of her age, and needs so require, let him do what he will, he sinneth not: let them marry." "So then he that giveth her in marriage doeth well; but he that giveth her not in marriage doeth better."

The Aramaic reads:

"If any man thinks that he is shamed by the behavior of his virgin daughter because she has passed the marriage age and he has not given her in marriage and that he should give her, let him do what he will and he does not sin. Let her be married." "So then he who gives his virgin daughter in marriage does well; and he who does not give his virgin daughter in marriage does even better." Some of

Introduction

the scholars use "betrothed" instead of "virgin daughter." The American Standard Version of 1901 correctly used the term "virgin daughter." Certainly the King James' translators would have known the difference between "virgin daughter" and "betrothed." Paul, in this instance, is referring to a virgin's vow. Num. 30:16.

These discrepancies between various versions have been the cause of contentions and divisions among sincere men and women who are earnestly seeking to understand the Word of God. At times, they do not know what to believe and what not to believe. They cannot understand why the Scripture in one place says, "Love your father and mother" and in another place admonishes, "Hate your father and mother." Moreover, they are bewildered when told that Jesus on the cross cried out, "My God, my God, why hast thou forsaken me?" The King James says in John 16:32, "Behold, the hour cometh, yea, is now come, that ye shall be scattered, every man to his own, and shall leave me alone: and yet I am not alone, because the Father is with me." Then again, the Old Testament in many instances states that God does not forsake the righteous nor those who trust in him. Jesus was the son of God and entrusted his spirit to God. Jesus could not have contradicted himself.

The Peshitta text reads: "My God, my God, for this I was spared!"

After all the Bible is an Eastern Book, written primarily for the Israelites, and then for the Gentile world.

When we come to the New Testament, the new Covenant, we must not forget that Christianity grew out of Judaism. The Christian gospel was another of God's messages, first to the Jewish people and then to the Gentile world. For several centuries, the Christian movement was directed and guided by the Jews. All of the apostles and the evangelists were Jewish. These facts are strongly supported by the gospels and history.

The Pauline Epistles were letters written by Paul to small Christian congregations in Asia Minor, Greece, and Rome. These early Christians were mostly Jews of the dispersion, men and women of Hebrew origin who had been looking for the coming of the promised Messiah whose coming was predicted by the Hebrew prophets who had hailed him as a deliverer.

At the outset, the Romans were the masters of the world and the Greeks were not looking for a deliverer to rise up from among a people whom they hated and had crushed. Paul, on his journeys, always spoke in the Jewish synagogues. His first converts were Hebrews. Then came Arameans, the kindred of the Hebrews, as in the case of Timothy and Titus. Their fathers were Aramean and their mothers were Jewish.

Jesus and his disciples spoke the Galilean dialect of Aramaic, the language which the early Galileans had brought from the other side of the river Euphrates. 2 Kings 17:22–25. Mark tells us in his Gospel, 14:70 that Peter was exposed by his Galilean Aramaic speech.

Paul, in all of his Epistles, emphasizes Hebrew law, Jewish ordinances and temple rituals. He refers to Abraham, Isaac, and Jacob as "our fathers." In his letters and teaching he appeals to the Jewish people to accept Jesus as the promised Messiah. Paul's mission was first to his own people. When they refused to listen to him, he shook his garment and went out among the Gentiles. Acts 18:6. Paul preached the Christian gospel written in Aramaic. His Epistles were written years later when Christianity had spread into Syria and parts of the Near East and India. In other words, the Pauline Epistles were letters addressed to the Christian churches already established. Moreover, Paul, in nearly all of his Epistles, speaks of the Hebrew fathers, subjugation in Egypt, crossing the Red Sea, eating manna, and wandering in the desert. This proves beyond a doubt that these letters were written to members of the Hebrew race and not to the Gentile world who knew nothing of Hebrew history and divine promises made to them. The Greeks had not been persecuted in Egypt nor did they cross the Red Sea, nor did they eat manna in the desert.

Paul was educated in Jewish law in Jerusalem. He was a member of the Jewish Council. His native language was western Aramaic but he acquired his education through Hebrew and Chaldean or Palestinian Aramaic, the language spoken in

Introduction

Judea. He defended himself when on trial in his own tongue and not in Greek. Acts 22:2. Paul was converted, healed, and baptized in Damascus in Syria. Acts 9:17,18.

The Epistles were translated into Greek for the use of converts who spoke Greek. Later they were translated into Latin and other tongues.

I believe that this translation of the Bible based on the Eastern text of the Scriptures, written in a Semitic tongue which for many centuries was the lingua franca of the Near East and Palestine, will throw considerable light on many obscure passages and that it will elucidate many other passages which have lost their meaning because of mistranslations.

Many church authorities in the Near East, India, and other parts of Asia have been looking for a long time for a translation of their venerable Aramaic text of the Scriptures into the English language. Many of them, despite their religious differences, have prayed for the translation and publication of this work so that thousands of educated men and women whose second language is English might read the Word of God translated from their own ancient text rather than made from secondary sources. This is also true of thousands of educated Moslems who revere the Peshitta and look upon it as the authentic text of the Scriptures.

All the English speaking people in Asia will welcome a translation based on what they believe to be the pure original sources which have been carefully kept all these centuries without the slightest modification or revision. I firmly believe that this work will strengthen the faith in Jesus Christ of many Christians in the Near East and Far East and enhance missionary efforts in spreading the Word of God to millions of people in Asia. These were the facts which motivated me when I undertook this task, to which I have devoted my life.

Since World War I, when the Aramaic speaking people were brought to the attention of the Western world and some of their ancient books brought to America, more facts from the ancient past have come to light. *The National Geographic Magazine*, as well as British and American newspapers have touched on the question of the Aramaic speaking people. *The National Geographic Magazine* in an article on Syria and Lebanon, December, 1946, speaks of Assyrian nurses, newly trained in Christian healing, who could have understood The Sermon on the Mount as it left Jesus' lips nearly two thousand years ago. The article also mentions *The Four Gospels According to the Eastern Version*, translated by George M. Lamsa, an Assyrian, from Aramaic into English, and states that Aramaic is the still living language which Jesus spoke.

The translator wishes to express his sincerest and deepest gratitude to Dr. Walter D. Ferguson of Temple University for editorial work, for his sincere interest in this translation, for his rich knowledge and understanding of the Biblical background, and also for his inspiration and enthusiasm. I am also indebted to many others for consultation, among them my countrymen, Archdeacon Saul Neesan and the Rev. Isaac Rehana; also to a number of Jewish scholars.

The translator is also grateful to the men and women of many denominations whose generous interest and financial help enabled me to complete this work. God only can reward them for their generous part in this work.

I wish also to state that I firmly believe in the Bible as the inspired Word of God. I believe in the miracles and wonders which God wrought in the past and which are still demonstrated today. May the Holy Word of God give us faith, wisdom, and understanding to grasp the inner meaning of God's Holy Word and to make us partakers in His Kingdom. May the blessings of God rest upon the readers and students of this translation. May God's richest blessings be upon this country without whose freedom and democratic institutions, this translation could not have been made.

"Thy word is a lamp to my feet and a light to my path." Psalm 119:105.

GEORGE M. LAMSA

MAY 1957.

WORDS RESEMBLING ONE ANOTHER

The following list of Aramaic words further illustrates the difficulties of the early translators from the Aramaic into Greek, at a time when questions of punctuation, accentuation and paragraphing were unknown. This is especially true of Aramaic, which is the richest and most expressive language of the Semitic group, but having a small vocabulary when compared with the Greek and Latin. This limitation of words made necessary the use of the same words with various shades of meanings. This is because Aramaic is one of the world's most ancient languages.

Translators are well aware of these grammatical difficulties, particularly in a language like Aramaic where a single dot above or under a letter radically changes the meaning of a word. These tiny dots are made by scribes, who are not authors but mere copyists, hired for this purpose by rich and by learned men. But owing to the humidity of the climate and the nature of the ink, blots appear on the pages when pressed against each other. Again because of exposure of a manuscript and its careless handling, flies alight on the pages and leave marks. Furthermore as the lines are crowded for lack of space, a dot placed above one letter may read as though it were placed under a letter in the previous line. For example, the only difference in the words *learned man* and *stupid man* is a dot, over or under the word, respectively.

Some Aramaic words are written and pronounced alike, but their meaning differs according to the context. In other cases the differences are indicated by dots which alter the pronunciation. In yet other instances, if the translator does not speak the language from which he translates the meaning and usage of some words must be left to his knowledge and judgment.

Moreover, some Aramaic letters resemble one another especially in manuscripts. For instance, *Nun, Aey, Lamed* and *Yoth* are very close to one another when placed in certain positions. *Shilometha*, a Shilomite, in other translations reads Shunammite. 1 Kings 1:3. 2 Kings 4:12. *Gamel* is confused with *Aey*, especially when falling in the beginning of the verse. And *Nun* and *Yoth* are hard to distinguish when in the middle of a word. Some of the most important mistranslations were due to the confusion of letters and words.

The following list of words will clearly show the similarity of words and letters and how some of the mistranslations were handed down from one language into another. The confusion of letters, no doubt, was caused when the Israelites, during the time of Ezra, made a new Bible after the ancient Hebrew text was lost. See 2 Esdras, Apochrypha. The Peshitta is the only text through which we can ascertain the ancient Bible text. Dr. Joshua Block, an eminent scholar of Semitic languages, formerly head of the Department of Semitic Languages and Literature of New York University says in an article in the *American Journal* of *Semitic Languages*, April, 1919:

" . . . Owing to its great antiquity, (the Peshitta) is one of the most valuable documents in ascertaining the original text of the Bible. In fact, in point of age, the Peshitta takes precedence of every other Oriental version; and such has been the high esteem in which it has been held by men of great eminence . . . " *

* By permission of the University of Chicago Press.

Words Resembling One Another

PESHITTA TEXT	KING JAMES VERSION

Genesis 30:8

ethkashpeth, pleaded

ethkathsheth, wrestled

8 And Rachel said, I have besought the LORD, and pleaded with my sister . . .

8 And Rachel said, With great wrestlings have I wrestled with my sister . . .

Numbers 25:4

reshey, chiefs

reshey, heads

4 And the LORD said to Moses, Take all the chiefs of the people and expose them before the LORD in the daylight . . .

4 And the LORD said unto Moses, Take all the heads of the people, and hang them up before the LORD against the sun . . .

Deuteronomy 27:16

danzakhey, to revile

zimkha, radiance

16 Cursed be he who reviles his father or his mother. . . .

16 Cursed be he that setteth light by his father or his mother . . .

Deuteronomy 32:33

khimtha, venom

khamra, wine

33 Their venom is the venom of dragons, and the cruel venom of asps.

33 Their wine is the poison of dragons, and the cruel venom of asps.

2 Samuel 4:6

kheta, sinful

khetey, wheat

6 And behold, they came into the midst of the house; then those sons of wickedness took and smote him in his abdomen . . .

6 And they came thither into the midst of the house, as though they would have fetched wheat; and they smote him under the fifth rib . . .

2 Kings 4:28

tishal, to ask

teshadal, to entice

28 Then she said, Did I ask a son of my lord? Did I not say to you, Do not ask a son for me?

28 Then she said, Did I desire a son of my lord, did I not say, Do not deceive me?

Job 19:18

awaley, ungodly

eweley, babies

18 Yea, even the wicked despise me; when I rise, they speak against me.

18 Yea, young children despised me; I arose, and they spake against me.

xiv

Job 29:18   ܩܢܝܐ *kanya,* reed

        ܩܢܐ *kina,* nest

18 Then I said, I shall become straight like a reed, I shall deliver the poor and multiply my days like the sand of the seas.

18 Then I said, I shall die in my nest, and I shall multiply *my* days as the sand.

Psalm 144: 7,11   ܥܘܠܐ *awaley,* ungodly

        ܥܘܠܐ *eweley,* babies

7 Stretch forth thy hand from above; deliver me out of great waters, from the hand of the ungodly,

7 Send thine hand from above; rid me, and deliver me out of great waters, from the hand of strange children;

11 Deliver me from the hand of the wicked, whose mouths speak vanity, and their right hand is a right hand of falsehood,

11 Rid me, and deliver me from the hand of strange children, whose mouth speaketh vanity, and their right hand *is* a right hand of falsehood:

Proverbs 11:14   ܡܕܒܪܢܐ *medabrana,* leader

        ܡܠܟܢܐ *melkana,* counsellor

14 A people who have no leader shall fall; but in the multitude of counsels there is deliverance.

14 Where no counsel *is,* the people fall: but in the multitude of counselors *there is* safety.

Ecclesiastes 2:4   ܥܒܕܝ *abdey,* servants

        ܥܒܕܝ *abadey,* works

4 I multiplied my servants . . .

4 I made me great works . . .

Ecclesiastes 11:5   ܪܘܚܐ *rokha,* wind

        ܪܘܚܐ *rokha,* spirit

5 As you do not know the path of the wind, and the manner of a woman who is with child . . .

5 As thou knowest not what *is* the way of the spirit, *nor* how the bones *do grow* in the womb of her that is with child . . .

Isaiah 7:14   ܒܬܘܠܬܐ

        betholta, virgin

14 Therefore the Lord himself shall give you a sign; behold, a virgin shall conceive and bear a son, and shall call his name Immanuel.

14 Therefore the Lord himself shall give you a sign; Behold, a virgin shall conceive, and bear a son, and shall call his name Immanuel.

Isaiah 10:27   ܡܘܫܚܐ *moshkha,* bull

        ܡܫܚܐ *mishkha,* oil

27 . . . and the yoke shall be destroyed from your neck because of your strength.

27 . . . and the yoke shall be destroyed because of the anointing.

PESHITTA TEXT	KING JAMES VERSION

Isaiah 29:15

mithakmin, to act crookedly

mithamkin, to dig deep

15 Woe to them who act perversely to hide their counsel from the LORD; and their works are in the dark, and they say, Who sees us? And, Who knows what we do corruptly?

15 Woe unto them that seek deep to hide their counsel from the LORD, and their works are in the dark, and they say, Who seeth us? and who knoweth us?

Jeremiah 4:10

ataeth, I have deceived

ataith, You have deceived

10 Then I said, I beseech thee, O LORD God, surely I have greatly deceived this people and Jerusalem; for I have said . . .

10 Then said I, Ah, Lord GOD! surely thou hast greatly deceived this people and Jerusalem, saying . . .

Ezekiel 32:5

rimtha, dust

ramtha, height

5 And I will scatter your flesh upon the mountains, and fill the valleys with your dust;

5 And I will lay thy flesh upon the mountains, and fill the valleys with thy height.

Obadiah 1:21

preekey, saved

parokey, saviours

21 And those who are saved shall come up to mount Zion to judge mount Esau . . .

21 And saviours shall come up on mount Zion to judge the mount of Esau . . .

Micah 1:12

mirdath, rebellious

maroth, bitter

12 For the rebellious inhabitant is sick of waiting for good; for disaster is come down from the LORD to the gate of Jerusalem.

12 For the inhabitant of Maroth waited carefully for good: but evil came down from the LORD unto the gate of Jerusalem.

Habakkuk 3:4

keritha, town

karnatha, horns

4 And his brightness was as the light; in the city which his hands had established shall he store his power.

4 And *his* brightness was as the light; he had horns *coming* out of his hand: and there *was* the hiding of his power.

St. Matthew 19:24

gamla, rope

gamla, camel

24 Again I say to you, it is easier for a rope to go through the eye of a needle . . .

24 And again I say unto you, It is easier for a camel to go through the eye of a needle . . .

xvi

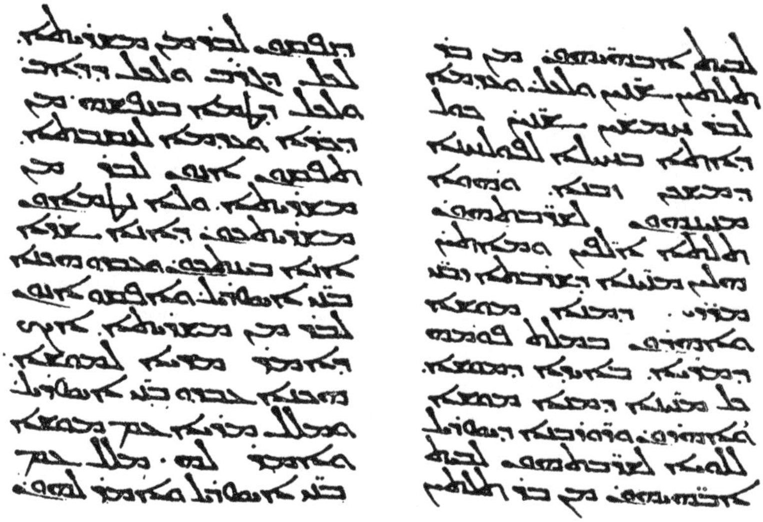

PLATE I

CODEX AMBROSIANUS — 5TH CENTURY
(Ambrosian Library, Milan, Italy.)

Punctuation, accents and breathings by original scribe.

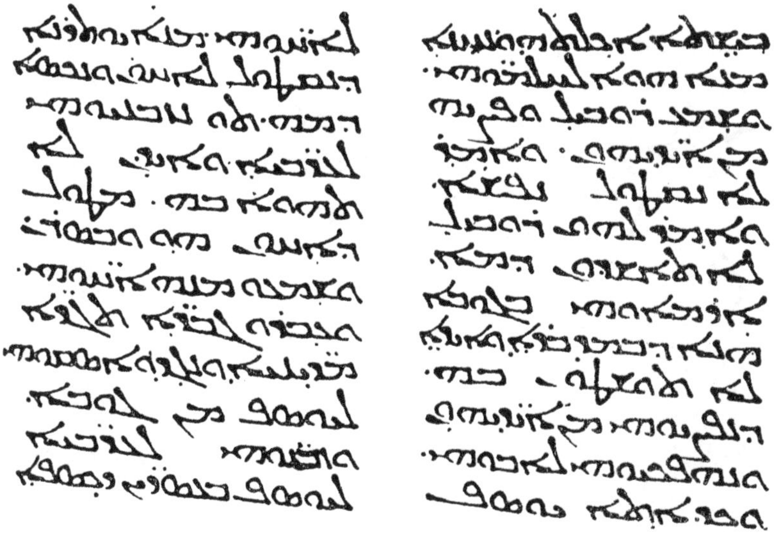

PLATE II

SYRIAC (ARAMAIC) OLD TESTAMENT MS. — A.D. 464.
(British Museum, Add. MS. 14,425.)

Oldest *dated* Biblical manuscript in existence.

xvii

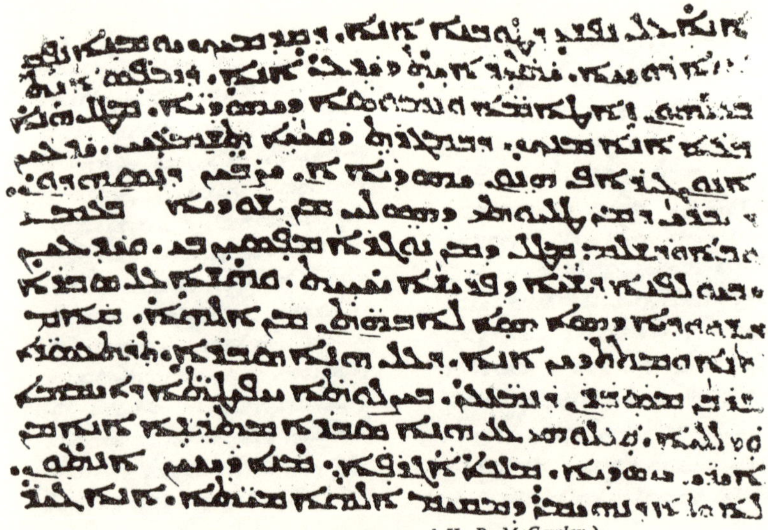

(Reproduced by courtesy of W. M. Mortimer and H. B. McCawley.)

PLATE III

ARAMAIC (SYRIAC) NEW TESTAMENT MS.
Variously identified as 6th or 7th Century.

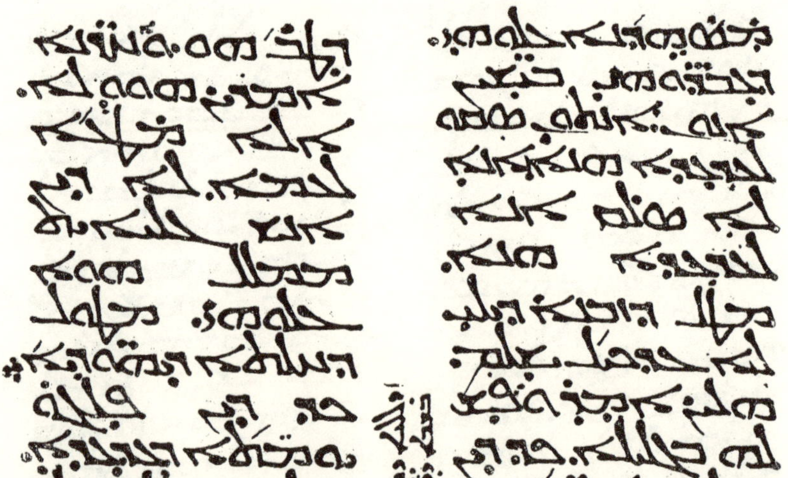

(Reproduced by courtesy of Pierpont Morgan Library.)

PLATE IV

ARAMAIC (SYRIAC) LECTIONARY — ABOUT A.D. 550.
(Pierpont Morgan Library, New York, N. Y.)

ENGLISH NAMES AND THEIR
ARAMAIC EQUIVALENTS

THE DEITY

God . . . Alaha

Lord . . . Mariah

Jesus . . . Eshoo

Messiah . . . Meshikhah

Spirit (Ghost) . . . Rohka

PATRIARCHS

Abraham . . . Oraham

Isaac . . . Eshkak

Jacob . . . Yacob

SONS OF JACOB

Reuben . . . Rubel

Simon . . . Shimun

Levi . . . Levi

Judah . . . Ehodah

Zebulun . . . Zebolun

Issachar . . . Esakhar

Dan . . . Dan

Gad . . . Gad

Asher . . . Asher

Naphtali . . . Naphtali

Joseph . . . Yosep

Benjamin . . . Benyamin

HEBREW LEADERS

Aaron . . . Ahron

Joshua . . . Eshoo Barnun

Samson . . . Shimshon

Saul . . . Shawol

David . . . Dawid

Solomon . . . Shlemon

PROPHETS

Moses . . . Moshey

Samuel . . . Shmowel

Isaiah . . . Eshaya

Jeremiah . . . Eramiah

Ezekiel . . . Khazkiel

Daniel . . . Daniel

Hosea . . . Hoshah

Joel . . . Yoel

Amos . . . Amos

Obadiah . . . Aobadiah

Jonah . . . Yonan

Micah . . . Mikha

Nahum . . . Nakhom

Habakkuk . . . Khabakuk

Zephaniah . . . Zepaniah

Haggai . . . Khagi

Zechariah . . . Zekhariah

Malachi . . . Malakhi

APOSTLES

Simon . . . Shimun Kepa

Andrew . . . Andreaos

James . . . Yacob

John . . . Yokhannan

Philip . . . Pilipus

Bartholomew . . . Bartolmi

Thomas . . . Tooma

Matthew . . . Mattai

James . . . Yacob Bar-Khalpai

Lebbaeus . . . Labai or Taddai

Simon . . . Shimun Kananaya or
Tanana

Judas . . . Ehodah Scariota

THE

Old Testament

THE NAMES AND ORDER

OF ALL THE

BOOKS OF THE OLD AND NEW TESTAMENT

WITH THE NUMBER OF THEIR CHAPTERS

THE BOOKS OF THE OLD TESTAMENT

THE FIRST BOOK OF MOSES, CALLED

GENESIS

CHAPTER 1

GOD created the heavens and the earth in the very beginning. 2 And the earth was without form, and void; and darkness was upon the face of the deep. And the Spirit of God moved upon the face of the water.

3 And God said, Let there be light; and there was light.

4 And God saw that the light was good; and God separated the light from the darkness.

5 And God called the light Day, and the darkness he called Night. And there was evening and there was morning, the first day.

6 ¶And God said, Let there be a firmament in the midst of the waters, and let it divide the waters from the waters.

7 And God made the firmament, and divided the waters that were under the firmament from the waters that were above the firmament; and it was so.

8 And God called the firmament Sky. And there was evening and there was morning, the second day.

9 ¶And God said, Let the waters that are under the sky be gathered together in one place, and let the dry land appear; and it was so.

10 And God called the dry land Earth; and the gathering together of the waters he called Seas; and God saw that it was good.

11 And God said, Let the earth bring forth vegetation, the herb yielding seed after its kind, and the fruit tree yielding fruit after its kind, wherein is their seed, upon the earth; and it was so.

12 And the earth brought forth vegetation, the herb yielding seed after its kind, and the tree bearing fruit, wherein is its seed, after its kind; and God saw that it was good.

13 And there was evening and there was morning, the third day.

14 ¶Then God said, Let there be lights in the firmament of the heaven to separate the day from the night; and let them be for signs, and for seasons, and for days, and years.

15 And let them be for lights in the firmament of the heaven to give light upon the earth; and it was so.

16 And God made two great lights, the greater light to rule the day, and the smaller light to rule the night; and the stars also.

17 And God set them in the firmament of the heavens to give light upon the earth,

18 And to rule over the day and over the night, and to separate the light from the darkness; and God saw that it was good.

19 And there was evening and there was morning, the fourth day.

20 And God said, Let the waters bring forth swarms of living creatures, and let fowl fly above the earth in the open firmament of the heaven.

21 And God created great sea monsters, and every living creature that moves, which the waters brought forth abundantly after their kind, and every winged fowl after its kind; and God saw that it was good.

22 And God blessed them, saying, Be fruitful and multiply, and fill the

waters in the seas, and let fowl multiply on the earth.

23 And there was evening and there was morning, the fifth day.

24 ¶Then God said, Let the earth bring forth living creatures after their kind, cattle, and creeping things, and beasts of the earth after their kind; and it was so.

25 And God made the beasts of the earth after their kind, and the cattle after their kind, and everything that creeps upon the earth after its kind; and God saw that it was good.

26 ¶Then God said, Let us make man in our image, after our likeness; and let them have dominion over the fish of the sea, and over the fowl of the air, and over the cattle, and over all the wild beasts of the earth, and over every creeping thing that creeps upon the earth.

27 So God created man in his own image, in the image of God he created him; male and female he created them.

28 And God blessed them, and God said to them, Be fruitful, and multiply, and fill the earth, and subdue it; and have dominion over the fish of the sea, and over the fowl of the air, and over the cattle, and over all the wild beasts that move upon the earth.

29 ¶And God said, Behold, I have given you every herb yielding seed, which is upon the face of all the earth, and every tree which bears fruit yielding seed; to you it shall be for food.

30 And to every beast of the earth, and to every fowl of the air, and to everything that creeps upon the earth, wherein there is life, I have given every green herb for food; and it was so.

31 And God saw everything that he had made, and, behold, it was very good. And there was evening and there was morning, the sixth day.

CHAPTER 2

THUS the heavens and the earth were finished, and all the host of them.

2 And on the sixth day God finished his works which he had made; and he rested on the seventh day from all his works which he had made.

3 So God blessed the seventh day, and sanctified it; because in it he had rested from all his works which God created and made.

4 ¶These are the generations of the heavens and of the earth when they were created, in the day that the LORD God made the heavens and the earth.

5 And all the trees of the field were not yet in the ground, and every herb of the field had not yet sprung up; for the LORD God had not caused it to rain upon the earth, and there was no man to till the ground.

6 But a powerful spring gushed out of the earth, and watered all the face of the ground.

7 And the LORD God formed Adam out of the soil of the earth, and breathed into his nostrils the breath of life; and man became a living being.

8 ¶And the LORD God planted a garden eastward in Eden; and there he put the man whom he had formed.

9 And out of the ground the LORD God made to grow every tree that is pleasant to the sight and good for food; the tree of life also in the midst of the garden, and the tree of the knowledge of good and evil.

10 And a river flowed out of Eden to water the garden; and from thence it divided and became into four heads.

11 The name of the first is Pishon; it is the one which encircles the whole land of Havilah, where there is gold;

12 And the gold of that land is good; there is also beryllium and the onyx stone.

13 And the name of the second river is Gihon, the one which encircles the whole land of Ethiopia.

14 And the name of the third river is Deklat (Tigris); it is the one which flows east of Assyria. And the fourth river is the Euphrates.

15 And the LORD God took the man, and put him in the garden of Eden to till it and to keep it.

16 And the LORD God commanded the man, saying, Of every tree of the garden you may freely eat;

17 But of the tree of the knowledge of good and evil, you shall not eat; for in the day that you eat of it you shall surely die.

18 ¶Then the LORD God said, It is not good that the man should be alone; I will make him a helper who is like him.

19 And out of the ground the LORD God formed every beast of the field, and every fowl of the air; and brought them to Adam to see what he would call them; and whatever Adam called every living creature, that was its name.

20 And Adam gave names to all cattle, and to all fowl of the air, and to all wild beasts; but for Adam there was not found a helper who was equal to him.

21 So the LORD God caused a deep sleep to fall upon Adam, and he slept; and he took one of his ribs, and closed up the place with flesh in its stead;

22 And of the rib which the LORD God had taken from Adam he made a woman, and brought her to Adam.

23 And Adam said, This is now bone of my bones, and flesh of my flesh; she shall be called Woman, because she was taken out of Man.

24 Therefore shall a man leave his father and his mother, and shall cleave unto his wife, and they shall be one flesh.

25 And they were both naked, Adam and his wife, and were not ashamed.

CHAPTER 3

NOW the serpent was more subtle than all the wild beasts that the LORD God had made. And the serpent said to the woman, Truly has God said that you shall not eat of any tree of the garden?

2 And the woman said to the serpent, We may eat of the fruit of all the trees of the garden;

3 But of the fruit of the tree which is in the midst of the garden, God has said, You shall not eat of it, neither shall you touch it, lest you die.

4 And the serpent said to the woman, You shall not surely die;

5 For God knows that in the day you eat of it, your eyes shall be opened, and you shall be like gods, knowing good and evil.

6 So when the woman saw that the tree was good for food, and that it was pleasant to the eyes, and that the tree was delightful to look at, she took of the fruit thereof, and did eat, and she also gave to her husband with her; and he did eat.

7 Then the eyes of them both were opened, and they knew that they were naked; and they sewed fig leaves together, and made themselves aprons.

8 And they heard the voice of the LORD God walking in the garden in the cool of the day; and Adam and his wife hid themselves from the presence of the LORD God among the trees of the garden.

9 And the LORD God called to Adam, and said to him, Where are you, Adam?

10 And he said, I heard thy voice in the garden, and when I saw that I was naked, I hid myself.

11 And the LORD God said to him, Who told you that you were naked? Have you eaten of the tree of which I commanded you that you should not eat?

12 And Adam said, The woman whom thou gavest to be with me, she gave me of the fruit of the tree, and I did eat.

13 And the LORD God said to the woman, What is this that you have done? And the woman said, The serpent beguiled me, and I did eat.

14 And the LORD God said to the serpent, Because you have done this thing, cursed are you above all cattle, and above all beasts of the field; on your belly shall you go, and dust shall you eat all the days of your life;

15 And I will put enmity between you and the woman, and between your posterity and her posterity; her posterity shall tread your head under foot, and you shall strike him in his heel.

16 To the woman he said, I will greatly multiply your pain and your conception; in pain you shall bring forth children, and you shall be de-

pendent on your husband, and he shall rule over you.

17 And to Adam he said, Because you have listened to the voice of your wife, and have eaten of the tree of which I commanded you, saying, You shall not eat of it, cursed is the ground for your sake; in sorrow shall you eat the fruits of it all the days of your life;

18 Thorns also and thistles shall it bring forth to you; and you shall eat the herb of the field;

19 In the sweat of your face shall you eat bread, until you return to the ground; out of it you were taken; for dust you are, and to dust shall you return.

20 So Adam called his wife's name Eve because she was the mother of all living.

21 And the LORD God made for Adam and for his wife coats of skin, and clothed them.

22 ¶Then the LORD God said, Behold, the man has become like one of us, to know good and evil; and now, lest he put forth his hand, and take also of the tree of life, and eat, and live forever;

23 Therefore the LORD God sent him forth from the garden of Eden, to till the ground from whence he was taken.

24 So the LORD God drove out the man; and he placed at the east of the garden of Eden Cherubim, and a flaming sword which turned every way, to guard the path to the tree of life.

CHAPTER 4

AND Adam knew Eve his wife; and she conceived, and bore Cain, and said, I have gotten a man for the LORD.

2 And she again bore his brother Abel. And Abel was a keeper of sheep, but Cain was a tiller of the ground.

3 And in the course of time it came to pass that Cain brought of the fruit of the ground an offering to the LORD.

4 And Abel also brought of the first-born of his flock and of the fatlings thereof. And the LORD was pleased with Abel and with his offering;

5 But with Cain and with his offering he was not pleased. So Cain was exceedingly displeased, and his countenance was sad.

6 And the LORD said to Cain, Why are you displeased? and why is your countenance sad?

7 Behold, if you do well, shall you not be accepted? and if you do not well, sin lies at the door. You should return to your brother, and he shall be subject to you.

8 And Cain said to Abel his brother, Let us go to the plain; and it came to pass, when they were in the field, that Cain rose up against Abel his brother, and slew him.

9 ¶And the LORD said to Cain, Where is Abel your brother? And he said, I do not know. Am I my brother's keeper?

10 And the LORD said, What have you done? The voice of your brother's blood cries to me from the ground.

11 And from henceforth, you are cursed from the earth, which has opened its mouth to receive your brother's blood from your hand;

12 When you till the ground, it shall no more yield to you its strength; a fugitive and a wanderer shall you be on the earth.

13 And Cain said to the LORD, My transgression is too great to be forgiven.

14 Behold, thou hast driven me out this day from the face of the land; and from thy face shall I be hidden; and I shall be a fugitive and a wanderer on the earth; and it shall come to pass, that whoever finds me shall slay me.

15 And the LORD said to him, It shall not be so; whoever slays Cain, vengeance shall be taken on him sevenfold. And the LORD set a mark upon Cain, so that anyone who may find him may not kill him.

16 ¶And Cain went out from the presence of the LORD, and dwelt in the land of Nod, on the east of Eden.

17 And Cain knew his wife; and she conceived, and bore Enoch; and he started to build a village, and named

the village after the name of his son, Enoch.

18 And to Enoch was born Irad; and Irad begot Mehujael; and Mehujael begot Methusael: and Methusael begot Lamech.

19 ¶And Lamech took two wives: the name of the one was Adah, and the name of the other Zillah.

20 And Adah bore Jabal, who was the father of those who dwell in tents, and are owners of cattle.

21 And his brother's name was Jubal; he was the father of all those who play the guitar and harp.

22 And Zillah also bore Tubal-cain, a craftsman in every work of brass and iron; and the sister of Tubal-cain was Naamah.

23 And Lamech said to his wives, Adah and Zillah, Hear my voice; you wives of Lamech, hearken to my speech; for I have killed a man by wounding him, and a boy by beating him.

24 For if Cain is to be avenged sevenfold, then Lamech seventy and sevenfold.

25 ¶And Adam knew his wife Eve again; and she conceived and bore a son, and called his name Seth; For God, she said, has given me another offspring instead of Abel, whom Cain slew.

26 And to Seth also there was born a son; and he called his name Enosh. Then men began to call upon the name of the LORD.

CHAPTER 5

THIS is the book of the generations of Adam. In the day that God created man, in the likeness of God created he him;

2 Male and female he created them; and God blessed them, and called their name Adam, in the day when they were created.

3 ¶And Adam lived a hundred and thirty years, and begot a son in his own likeness, after his image; and called his name Seth;

4 And Adam lived after he had begotten Seth eight hundred years; and he begot sons and daughters.

5 Thus all the days that Adam lived were nine hundred and thirty years, and he died.

6 And Seth lived a hundred and five years, and begot Enosh;

7 And Seth lived after he begot Enosh eight hundred and seven years, and begot sons and daughters;

8 And all the days of Seth were nine hundred and twelve years, and he died.

9 ¶And Enosh lived ninety years, and begot Cainan;

10 And Enosh lived after he begot Cainan eight hundred and fifteen years, and begot sons and daughters;

11 And all the days of Enosh were nine hundred and five years, and he died.

12 ¶And Cainan lived seventy years, and begot Mahlalael;

13 And Cainan lived after he begot Mahlalael eight hundred and forty years, and begot sons and daughters;

14 And all the days of Cainan were nine hundred and ten years, and he died.

15 ¶And Mahlalael lived sixty and five years, and begot Jared;

16 And Mahlalael lived after he begot Jared eight hundred and thirty years, and begot sons and daughters.

17 And all the days of Mahlalael were eight hundred ninety and five years, and he died.

18 ¶And Jared lived a hundred sixty and two years, and he begot Enoch:

19 And Jared lived after he begot Enoch eight hundred years, and begot sons and daughters;

20 And all the days of Jared were nine hundred sixty and two years, and he died.

21 ¶And Enoch lived sixty and five years, and begot Methuselah;

22 And Enoch found favor in the presence of God three hundred years after he begot Methuselah, and begot sons and daughters;

23 And all the days of Enoch were three hundred sixty-five years;

24 And Enoch found favor in the presence of God, and disappeared; for God took him away.

25 And Methuselah lived a hundred eighty-seven years, and begot Lamech;

26 And Methuselah lived after he begot Lamech seven hundred and eighty-two years, and begot sons and daughters;

27 And all the days of Methuselah were nine hundred sixty-nine years, and he died.

28 ¶And Lamech lived a hundred eighty-two years, and begot a son;

29 And he called his name Noah, saying, This one shall comfort us concerning our work and the toil of our hands, because of the ground which the LORD has cursed.

30 And Lamech lived after he begot Noah five hundred ninety-five years, and begot sons and daughters.

31 Thus all the days of Lamech were seven hundred seventy-seven years, and he died.

32 And Noah was five hundred years old, and Noah begot Shem, Ham, and Japheth.

CHAPTER 6

AND it came to pass, when men began to multiply on the face of the earth and daughters were born to them,

2 That the sons of God saw that the daughters of men were fair; so they took them wives of all whom they chose.

3 Then the LORD said, My spirit shall not dwell in man forever, because he is flesh; let his days be a hundred and twenty years.

4 There were giants on the earth in those days; and also after that, for the sons of God came in unto the daughters of men, and they bore children to them, and they became giants who in the olden days were mighty men of renown.

5 ¶And the LORD saw that the wickedness of man was great in the earth, and that every imagination of the thoughts of his heart was evil continually.

6 And the LORD was sorry that he had made man on the earth, and it grieved him in his heart.

7 So the LORD said, I will destroy men whom I have created from the face of the earth; both men and ani- mals, and the creeping things, and the fowls of the air; I am sorry that I have made them.

8 But Noah found mercy in the eyes of the LORD.

9 ¶These are the generations of Noah: Noah was a just man and innocent in his days, and God was pleased with Noah.

10 And Noah begot three sons, Shem, Ham, and Japheth.

11 The earth was corrupt in the presence of God, and the earth was filled with wickedness.

12 And God saw that the earth was corrupt; for all flesh had corrupted its way upon the earth.

13 So God said to Noah, The end of all flesh is come before me; for the earth is full of wickedness through men; and, behold, I will destroy them with the earth.

14 ¶Make yourself an ark of gopher wood; make rooms in the ark and daub it without and within with pitch.

15 And this is how you shall make it: the length of the ark shall be three hundred cubits, the breadth of it fifty cubits, and the height of it thirty cubits.

16 And you shall make a window in the ark, and to the width of a cubit shall you finish it above; and the door of the ark you shall make in its side; with lower, second, and third decks you shall make it.

17 And, behold, I will bring a flood of waters upon the earth, to destroy all flesh that has the breath of life in it from under heaven; and everything that is on the earth shall die.

18 But I will establish my covenant with you; and you shall enter into the ark, you, and your sons, and your wife, and your sons' wives with you.

19 And of every living thing of all flesh, two of every kind bring into the ark, to keep them alive with you; they shall be male and female.

20 Of fowls after their kind, and of animals after their kind, and of every creeping thing of the earth after its kind, two of every kind shall enter with you, that they may live.

21 And you must take a supply of all food that is eaten, and you shall

store it by you; and it shall be for food for you and for them.

22 Thus did Noah; according to all that God commanded him, so did he.

CHAPTER 7

THEN God said to Noah, Enter into the ark; you and all your household, for you alone have I seen righteous before me in this generation.

2 Of all clean animals you shall take with you seven pairs, both males and females; and of the beasts that are not clean two pairs, males and females.

3 Likewise, of the fowls of the air that are clean seven pairs, both males and the females; to keep their posterity alive upon the face of the earth.

4 For in seven days I will cause it to rain upon the earth forty days and forty nights; and every living thing that I have made will I destroy from off the face of the earth.

5 And Noah did according to all that the LORD commanded him.

6 And Noah was six hundred years old when the flood of waters came upon the earth.

7 ¶And Noah, with his sons and his wife and his sons' wives, went into the ark because of the waters of the flood.

8 Of clean animals, and of unclean animals, and of fowls, and of everything that creeps upon the earth,

9 There went in two and two with Noah into the ark, the males and the females, as God had commanded Noah.

10 And it came to pass after seven days that the waters of the flood came upon the earth.

11 ¶In the six hundredth year of Noah's life, in the second month, the seventeenth day of the month, on that very day all the fountains of the great deep burst forth and the windows of heaven were opened.

12 And the rain fell upon the earth for forty days and forty nights.

13 On that same day entered Noah and Shem and Ham and Japheth, the sons of Noah, and Noah's wife, and

the three wives of his sons with him, into the ark;

14 They and every beast after its kind and all the cattle after their kind and every creeping thing that creeps upon the earth after its kind and every fowl after its kind, every bird of every sort.

15 They went with Noah into the ark, two and two of all flesh in which there is the breath of life.

16 And they that entered, males and females of every living thing went in, as God had commanded him. Then the LORD shut him in.

17 And the flood lasted forty days upon the earth; and the waters increased and bore up the ark so that it was lifted up above the earth.

18 And the waters prevailed and rose higher upon the earth; and the ark floated on the face of the waters.

19 And the waters prevailed exceedingly upon the earth; so that all the high mountains under the whole heaven were covered.

20 Fifteen cubits above the mountains did the waters prevail; and the mountains were covered.

21 And all flesh died that moved upon the earth, both of fowl and of cattle and of wild beast and of every creeping thing that creeps upon the earth and every man:

22 Everything in whose nostrils was the breath of life, of all that was on the dry land, died.

23 And every living thing was destroyed that was upon the face of the ground, both man and animals and the creeping things and the fowl of the air; they were destroyed from the earth; and Noah only remained, and those who were with him in the ark.

24 And the waters prevailed upon the earth a hundred and fifty days.

CHAPTER 8

AND God remembered Noah and every living thing and all the animals and all the fowls that were with him in the ark; and God made a wind to blow over the earth, and the waters became calm;

2 The fountains of the deep and the

3

windows of heaven were closed, and the rain from the sky was restrained;

3 And the waters receded from the earth gradually; and after the end of a hundred and fifty days the waters abated.

4 And in the seventh month, on the seventeenth day of the month, the ark rested upon the mountains of Kardo.[1]

5 And the waters decreased gradually until the tenth month; on the first day of the tenth month, the tops of the mountains were seen.

6 ¶And it came to pass at the end of forty days that Noah opened the window of the ark which he had made;

7 And he sent forth a raven which went to and fro, but did not return until the waters were dried up from the face of the earth.

8 Then he sent forth a dove from the ark, to see if the waters had abated from the face of the ground;

9 But the dove found no resting place for her foot, and she returned to him in the ark, for the waters were still on the face of the whole earth. Then he put forth his hand, and took her, and brought her into the ark with him.

10 And he waited yet another seven days; and again he sent forth the dove out of the ark;

11 And the dove came back to him in the evening; and, lo, in her mouth was an olive leaf plucked off; so Noah knew that the waters had subsided from off the earth.

12 And he waited yet another seven days, and sent forth the dove; but the dove did not return again to him any more.

13 ¶And it came to pass in the six hundred and first year, in the first month, the first day of the month, the waters were dried up from off the earth; and Noah removed the covering of the ark, and looked, and, behold, the face of the ground was dry.

14 And in the second month, on the twenty-seventh day of the month, the earth was dry.

15 ¶And God spoke to Noah, saying,

16 Go forth out of the ark, you and your wife and your sons and your sons' wives with you.

17 Bring forth with you every beast of every kind that is with you, both fowl and cattle and every creeping thing that creeps on the earth; that they may breed abundantly on the earth and be fruitful and multiply upon the face of the earth.

18 So Noah went forth, and his sons and his wife and his sons' wives with him;

19 Every beast, every domestic animal, and every fowl, and whatever creeps upon the earth, after their kinds, went forth out of the ark.

20 ¶Then Noah built an altar to the LORD; and took of every clean animal and of every clean fowl, and offered burnt offerings on the altar.

21 And the LORD smelled the sweet savour; and the LORD said in his heart, I will not again curse the ground any more for man's sake; for the inclination of man's heart is evil from his youth; neither will I again destroy any more every living thing, as I have done.

22 From henceforth, while the earth remains, seedtime and harvest, and cold and heat, and summer and winter, and day and night shall not cease.

CHAPTER 9

AND God blessed Noah and his sons, and said to them, Be fruitful, and multiply, and replenish the earth.

2 And the fear of you and the dread of you shall be upon every beast of the earth, and upon every fowl of the air, upon all that moves upon the earth, and all the fish of the sea; into your hand they are delivered.

3 Every moving thing that is alive shall be food for you; even as the green herb have I given you all things.

4 Only flesh with the life thereof,

[1] A chain of mountains in northern Iraq.

that is, the blood thereof, you shall not eat.

5 And surely your lifeblood will I avenge; of every beast will I avenge it, and at the hand of man; and at the hand of a man and his brother will I avenge the life of man.

6 Whoever sheds the blood of men, by men shall his blood be shed; for man was made in the image of God.

7 As for you, be fruitful, and multiply; bring forth abundantly on the earth, and multiply in it.

8 ¶And God spoke to Noah, and to his sons with him, saying,

9 As for me, behold, I will establish my covenant with you and with your descendants after you;

10 And with every living creature that is with you, the fowl, the cattle, and every wild beast of the earth with you; with all that come out of the ark, and with every beast of the earth.

11 And I will establish my covenant with you; so that never again shall all flesh perish by the waters of a flood; neither shall there any more be a flood to destroy the earth.

12 And God said to Noah, This is the sign of the covenant which I make between me and you and every living creature that is with you, for perpetual generations:

13 I set my bow in the clouds, and it shall be for a sign of a covenant between me and the earth.

14 And it shall come to pass, when I bring clouds over the earth, that the bow shall be seen in the clouds;

15 And I will remember my covenant, which is between me and you and every living creature that is with you of all flesh; and the waters shall no more become a flood to destroy all flesh.

16 And the bow shall be in the clouds; and I will look upon it as a remembrance of the everlasting covenant between God and every living creature of all flesh that is upon the earth.

17 And God said to Noah, This is the sign of the covenant which I have established between me and all the flesh that is upon the earth.

18 ¶The sons of Noah who went forth out of the ark were Shem and Ham and Japheth; and Ham is the father of Canaan.

19 These three were the sons of Noah; and from them the people spread throughout the earth.

20 And Noah began to till the ground; and he planted a vineyard;

21 And he drank of its wine, and became drunken; and he was uncovered within his tent.

22 And Ham, the father of Canaan, saw the nakedness of his father, and he told his two brothers outside.

23 And Shem and Japheth took a mantle and laid it upon both their shoulders and walked backward and covered the nakedness of their father; and their faces were backward and they did not see their father's nakedness.

24 When Noah awoke from his wine and knew what his younger son had done to him,

25 He said, Cursed be Canaan; a servant of servants shall he be to his brothers.

26 Then he said, Blessed be the LORD God of Shem; and let Canaan be his servant.

27 God shall enrich Japheth, and he shall dwell in the tents of Shem; and Canaan shall be their servant.

28 ¶And Noah lived after the flood three hundred and fifty years.

29 And all the days of Noah were nine hundred and fifty years, and he died.

CHAPTER 10

NOW these are the descendants of the sons of Noah, Shem, Ham, and Japheth: and to them were sons born after the flood.

2 The sons of Japheth were Gomer, Mongolia, Madai, Javan, Tubal, Meshech, and Tiras.

3 And the sons of Gomer: Ashkenaz, Diphar, and Togarmah.

4 And the sons of Javan: Elishah, Tarshish, China, and Doranim.

5 It was from these that the people were divided into the Islands of the Gentiles and their main lands; every one after his language, after their families, in their nations.

6 ¶And the sons of Ham: Cush, Mizraim, Put, and Canaan.

7 And the sons of Cush: Sheba, Havilah, Sabtah, Raamah, and Sabtechah. And the sons of Raamah: Sheba, and Daran.

8 And Cush begot Nimrod; he began to be a mighty one on the earth.

9 He was a mighty hunter before the LORD; wherefore it is said, Even as Nimrod was a mighty hunter before the LORD.

10 And the beginning of his kingdom was Babylon, Erech, Akhar, and Caliah, in the land of Sinar.

11 Out of Sinar went forth the Assyrian and built Nineveh, and the city of Rehoboth, and Calah,

12 And Resen which lies between Nineveh and Calah; the same is a great city.

13 And Mizraim begot Ludim and Anamim and Lehabim and Naphtuhim

14 And Pathrusim and Casluhim (out of whom came the Philistines) and Caphtorim.

15 ¶And Canaan begot Sidon, his first-born, and Heth,

16 And the Jebusite, the Amorite, the Girgasite,

17 And the Havite, the Arkite, the Sinite,

18 And the Arvadite, the Zemarite, and the Hamathite; and afterward the families of the Canaanites spread abroad.

19 And the border of the Canaanites extended from Sidon, which is at the entrance of Gadar, as far as Gaza; which is at the entrance of Sodom, Gomorrah,[1] Admah, and Zeboim, as far as Lasha.

20 These are the sons of Ham, after their families and their languages, in their lands and in their nations.

21 ¶To Shem also, the father of all the children of Eber, the elder brother of Japheth, even to him were children born.

22 The sons of Shem: Elam, Asshur, Arphakhashar, Lud and Aram.

23 And the children of Aram: Uz, Hul, Gether, and Mash.

24 And Arphakhashar begot Shalah; and Shalah begot Eber.

25 And to Eber were born two sons: the name of the one was Peleg; for in his days the earth was divided; and his brother's name was Joktan.

26 And Joktan begot Almodad, Sheleph, Hazarmaveth, Jerah,

27 Hadoram, Uzal, Diklah,

28 Obal, Abimael, and Sheba,

29 Ophir, Havilah, and Jobab; all these were sons of Joktan.

30 The lands which they inhabited extended from Mesha, which is at the entrance of Sepharvim, a mount in the east.

31 These are the sons of Shem, after their families, their languages, in their lands, after their nations.

32 These are the descendants of the sons of Noah, according to their families, in their nations: and from these the people spread abroad on the earth after the flood.

CHAPTER 11

NOW the whole earth spoke one language and with one manner of speech.

2 And it came to pass, as men journeyed from the east, they found a plain in the land of Sinar; and they settled there.

3 And they said one to another, Come, let us make bricks and burn them with fire. And they had bricks for stone, and slime for mortar.

4 Then they said, Come, let us build ourselves a city, and a tower whose top may reach to heaven; and let us make a name for ourselves, lest we be scattered abroad upon the face of the whole earth.

5 And the LORD came down to see the city and the tower which men were building.

6 And the LORD said, Behold, they are one people, and they have all one language; and they have reasoned to do this thing; and now nothing will prevent them from doing that which they have imagined to do.

7 Come, let us go down, and there

---

[1] Aramaic Amorrah.

divide their language so that they may not understand one another's speech.

8 So the LORD scattered them abroad from there upon the face of all the earth; and they ceased from building the city.

9 Therefore they called the name of it Babel; because it was there that the LORD confounded the language of all the earth; and from there the LORD scattered them upon the face of all the earth.

10 ¶These are the descendants of Shem: Shem was a hundred years old, and begot Arphakhashar, two years after the flood;

11 And Shem lived after he begot Arphakhashar five hundred years, and begot sons and daughters.

12 And Arphakhashar lived thirty-five years, and begot Shalah;

13 And Arphakhashar lived after he begot Shalah four hundred and three years, and begot sons and daughters.

14 And Shalah lived thirty years, and begot Eber;

15 And Shalah lived after he begot Eber four hundred and three years, and begot sons and daughters.

16 And Eber lived thirty-four years, and begot Peleg;

17 And Eber lived after he begot Peleg four hundred and thirty years, and begot sons and daughters.

18 And Peleg lived thirty years, and begot Rau;

19 And Peleg lived after he begot Rau two hundred and nine years, and begot sons and daughters.

20 And Rau lived thirty-two years, and begot Serug;

21 And Rau lived after he begot Serug two hundred and seven years, and begot sons and daughters.

22 And Serug lived thirty years, and begot Nahor;

23 And Serug lived after he begot Nahor two hundred years, and begot sons and daughters.

24 And Nahor lived twenty-nine years, and begot Terah;

25 And Nahor lived after he begot Terah one hundred and nineteen years, and begot sons and daughters.

26 And Terah lived seventy-five years, and begot Abram, Nahor, and Haran.

27 ¶Now these are the descendants of Terah: Terah begot Abram, Nahor, and Haran; and Haran begot Lot.

28 And Haran died before his father Terah in his native land, in Ur of the Chaldeans.

29 And Abram and Nahor took wives for themselves; the name of Abram's wife was Sarai; and the name of Nahor's wife, Milcah, the daughter of Haran, the father of Milcah and Iscah.

30 But Sarai was barren; she had no child.

31 And Terah took Abram his son, and Lot the son of Haran, his grandson, and Sarai his daughter-in-law, his son Abram's wife; and they went forth with them from Ur of the Chaldeans to go to the land of Canaan; and they came as far as Haran, and they settled there.

32 And the days of Terah were two hundred and five years; and Terah died in Haran.

CHAPTER 12

NOW the LORD said to Abram, Depart from your country, and from the place of your nativity, and from your father's house, to a land that I will show you;

2 And I will make of you a great people, and I will bless you, and make your name great; and you shall be a blessing;

3 And I will bless those who bless you, and curse those who curse you; and in you shall all the families of the earth be blessed.

4 So Abram did as the LORD had spoken to him; and Lot went with him; and Abram was seventy-five years old when he departed from Haran.

5 And Abram took Sarai his wife and Lot his brother's son and all their possessions which they had gained and the persons that they had gotten in Haran, and they went on their way to the land of Canaan, and to the land of Canaan they came.

6 ¶And Abram passed through the land as far as the country of Shechem,

and as far as the oak of Mamre. And the Canaanites were settled then in the land.

7 Then the Lord appeared to Abram and said to him, To your descendants will I give this land; and Abram built there an altar to the Lord, for he had appeared to him.

8 And from thence he removed to a mountain on the east of Beth-el, and pitched his tent, having Beth-el on the west, and Ai on the east; and there he built an altar to the Lord and called upon the name of the Lord.

9 And Abram journeyed, going on still toward the south.

10 ¶Now there was a famine in the land; so Abram went down to Egypt to sojourn there; for the famine was severe in the land.

11 And it came to pass when he was about to enter into Egypt, he said to Sarai his wife, Behold now, I know that you are a woman beautiful to look upon;

12 And it shall come to pass, when the Egyptians see you, they will say, This is his wife; and they will kill me, but they will spare you.

13 Say, therefore, that you are my sister because I will be treated well for your sake; and my life shall be spared because of you.

14 ¶And it came to pass when Abram entered Egypt, the Egyptians saw that his wife was very beautiful.

15 The princes of Pharaoh also saw her and praised her before Pharaoh; and the woman was taken into Pharaoh's house.

16 And Abram was well treated for her sake; and he became the owner of sheep, oxen, he asses, menservants, maidservants, she asses, and camels.

17 And the Lord afflicted Pharaoh and his household with great plagues because of Sarai, Abram's wife.

18 So Pharaoh called Abram, and said to him, What is this that you have done to me? Why did you not tell me that she was your wife?

19 Why did you say, She is my sister, so that I took her for my wife? Now, therefore, here is your wife, take her, and leave the country.

20 And Pharaoh charged his men concerning him; and sent him away together with his wife, and all that he had.

CHAPTER 13

AND Abram went up from Egypt, he and his wife and all that he had, and Lot with him, into the south.

2 And Abram was very rich in cattle, in silver, and in gold.

3 And he went on his journey from the south as far as Beth-el, to the place where he had pitched his tent at first, between Beth-el and Ai;

4 To the place of the altar which he had built there at the first; and there Abram had called upon the name of the Lord.

5 ¶And Lot also, who went with Abram, had large flocks, herds, and tents.

6 And the land was not able to support them, that they might dwell together; for their herds were so large that they could not dwell together.

7 And there was a strife between the herdsmen of Abram's cattle and the herdsmen of Lot's cattle; and the Canaanites and the Perizzites dwelt then in the land.

8 And Abram said to Lot, Let there be no strife between me and you, and between my shepherds and your shepherds; for we are brethren.

9 Behold the whole land is before you, separate yourself from me; if you choose the left hand, then I will choose the right hand; or if you depart to the right hand, then I will go to the left.

10 And Lot lifted up his eyes, and saw all the land of Jordan, that it was well watered everywhere, before the Lord destroyed Sodom and Gomorrah, like the garden of God, like the land of Egypt at the entrance of Zoan.

11 Then Lot chose for himself all the land of Jordan; and Lot journeyed east; thus they separated one brother from the other.

12 Abram dwelt in the land of Canaan, and Lot dwelt in the villages of the plain, thus possessing the land as far as Sodom.

13 Now the men of Sodom were wicked and sinners in the presence of the LORD exceedingly.

14 ¶And the LORD said to Abram, after Lot had separated from him, Lift up now your eyes, and look from the place where you are, northward and southward and eastward and westward;

15 For all the land which you see, to you will I give it, and to your descendants forever.

16 And I will make your descendants like the dust of the earth; so that if you can number the dust of the earth, then shall your descendants also be numbered.

17 Arise, walk through the land in the length of it and in the breadth of it; for I will give it to you.

18 Then Abram removed his tent and came and dwelt by the oak of Mamre which is in Hebron, and built there an altar to the LORD.

CHAPTER 14

AND it came to pass in the days of Amarphel king of Sinar, Arioch king of Dalasar, Cardlaamar king of Elam, and Tarael king of Gelites

2 That these made war with Bera king of Sodom, Birsha king of Gomorrah, Shinab king of Admah, Shemer king of Zeboim, and the king of Bela, that is, Zoar.

3 All of these joined together in the valley of Siddim, which is the Salt Sea.

4 Twelve years they served Cardlaamar, and in the thirteenth year they rebelled.

5 And in the fourteenth year came Cardlaamar, and the kings that were with him, and smote the mighty men who were in Ashteroth Karnaim and the valiant men who were in the city, and the Emins in Shaveh Koriathaim,

6 And the Horites in the mountains of Seir, as far as the oak of Paran, which is in the wilderness.

7 And they returned, and came to En-dina, which is Rakim (Kadesh) and they smote all the princes of the Amalekites and also the Amorites who dwelt in En-gad.

8 And there went out the king of Sodom, the king of Gomorrah, the king of Admah, the king of Zeboim, and the king of Bela (that is, Zoar); all of these made war in the valley of Siddim,

9 With Cardlaamar, the king of Elam, Tarael the king of Gelites, Amarphel king of Sinar, and Arioch king of Dalasar; four kings against five.

10 And the valley of Siddim was full of bitumen pits; and the kings of Sodom and Gomorrah fled, and fell there; and those who survived fled to the mountain.

11 And the raiders took all the goods of Sodom and Gomorrah, and all their provisions, and went their way.

12 And they carried away Lot, Abram's brother's son, who dwelt in Sodom, and his goods, and departed.

13 ¶And there came one who escaped, and told Abram the Hebrew, who dwelt by the oak of Mamre, which belonged to the Amorite, brother of Aner and brother of Eshcol, who were allies of Abram.

14 And when Abram heard that his nephew had been taken captive, he armed his young men, born in his own house, three hundred and eighteen, and pursued the raiders as far as Dan.

15 And he divided his forces against them by night, he and his servants, and defeated them, and pursued them as far as Hobah, which is on the left hand of Damascus.

16 And he brought back all the goods, and also brought back Lot, his nephew, and his goods, and the women also, and the people.

17 ¶And the king of Sodom went out to greet him, after his return from the destruction of the forces of Cardlaamar, and the kings who were with him, at the valley of Shaveh, that is, the king's valley.

18 And Melchizedek king of Salem brought out bread and wine; he was the priest of the Most High God.

19 And he blessed him, saying, Blessed be Abram to God Most High, possessor of heaven and earth;

20 And blessed be the Most High God, who has delivered your enemies into your hands. And Abram gave him tithes of everything.

21 And the king of Sodom said to Abram, Give me the people, and take the goods for yourself.

22 And Abram said to the king of Sodom, I have lifted up my hands to the God Most High, the possessor of heaven and earth,

23 That I will not take of anything that belongs to you, from a thread to a shoestring, lest you should say, I have made Abram rich;

24 Save that which the young men have eaten and the portions of the men who went with me, Aner, Eshcol, and Mamre; let them take their portions.

CHAPTER 15

AFTER these things the word of the LORD came to Abram in a vision, saying, Fear not, Abram; I am your shield, and your reward is exceedingly great.

2 And Abram said, O LORD God, what will thou give me, for I will die childless, and Eliezer of Damascus, one of my household, will be my heir?

3 And Abram said, Behold, thou hast given me no son; and, behold, one of the members of my household will be my heir.

4 Then the LORD said to him, This man shall not be your heir; but your own son that shall come out of your own loins shall be your heir.

5 And he brought him outside, and said to him, Look now toward heaven and number the stars, if you are able to number them; and he said to him, So shall your descendants be.

6 And Abram believed in the LORD; and it was counted to him for righteousness.

7 And he said to him, I am the LORD, who brought you out of Ur of the Chaldeans, to give you this land to inherit it.

8 And Abram said, O LORD God, whereby shall I know that I shall inherit it?

9 And he said to him, Take for yourself a heifer, three years old, a three year old ram, a three year old she-goat, a pigeon, and a young dove.

10 And he took to himself all these, and cut them in two, and laid each piece against another; but the birds he did not divide.

11 And when the birds of prey came down upon the carcasses, Abram drove them away.

12 And when the sun was going down, a deep sleep fell on Abram; and, lo, fear and a great darkness fell upon him.

13 And the LORD said to Abram, Know of a surety that your descendants shall be strangers in a land that is not theirs, and shall be in servitude; and they shall afflict them for four hundred years;

14 But I will judge the nation which they shall serve; and afterward they shall come out with great wealth.

15 And you shall depart from this life and go to your fathers in peace; and you shall be buried at a good old age.

16 And after four centuries, they shall return here; for the iniquities of the Amorites are not yet full.

17 And it came to pass that when the sun had set and it was dark, behold there appeared a smoking furnace and a burning torch that passed between those pieces.

18 On that day the LORD made a covenant with Abram, saying, To your descendants have I given this land, from the river of Egypt to the great river, the river Euphrates:

19 The land of the Kenites, Kenizzites, and the Kadmonites,

20 The Hittites, the Perizzites, the Giants,

21 The Amorites, the Canaanites, the Girgashites, and the Jebusites.

CHAPTER 16

NOW Sarai, Abram's wife, bore him no children; and she had an Egyptian handmaid, whose name was Hagar.

2 And Sarai said to Abram, Behold now, the LORD has restrained me from bearing children; therefore go in unto my maid; it may be that I may be

consoled by her. And Abram hearkened to the voice of Sarai.

3 And Sarai, Abram's wife, took Hagar her Egyptian maid, and gave her to her husband Abram to be his wife. This happened after Abram had dwelt ten years in the land of Canaan.

4 ¶And he went in unto Hagar, and she conceived: and when she saw that she had conceived, her mistress was despised in her eyes.

5 And Sarai said to Abram, My wrong be upon you; I gave my maid into your bosom; and when she saw that she had conceived, I was despised in her eyes; may the LORD judge between me and you.

6 But Abram said to Sarai his wife, Behold your maid is at your disposal; do to her as it pleases you. And when Sarai dealt harshly with her, she fled from her.

7 ¶And the angel of the LORD found her by a fountain of water in the wilderness, by the fountain on the road to Gadar.

8 And he said to her, Hagar, maid of Sarai, where have you come from, and where are you going? And she said, I flee from the presence of my mistress Sarai.

9 And the angel of the LORD said to her, Return to your mistress, and submit yourself under her hands.

10 And again the angel of the LORD said to her, I will greatly multiply your descendants, that they can not be numbered because of their multitude.

11 And the angel of the LORD said to her, Behold, you are with child, and shall bear a son, and you shall call his name Ishmael; because the LORD has heard of your afflictions.

12 And he will be like a wild ass among men; with his hand against every man, and every man's hand against him, and he shall dwell on the borders of all his brethren.

13 And she called the name of the LORD who spoke to her, and said, Thou art God whom I saw; for she said, Behold, I have also seen a vision after he had seen me.

14 Therefore she called the well, Beer-di-khaya-khizan (which means, the well of the Living One who saw me). Behold, it is between Rakim and Gadar.

15 ¶And Hagar bore Abram a son; and Abram called his son's name, whom Hagar bore, Ishmael.

16 And Abram was eighty-six years old when Hagar bore Ishmael to him.

CHAPTER 17

WHEN Abram was ninety-nine years old, the LORD appeared to him, and said to him, I am the Almighty God; walk well before me, and be faultless.

2 And I will make my covenant between me and you and will multiply you exceedingly.

3 And Abram fell on his face; and God talked with him, saying,

4 As for me, behold, I am establishing my covenant with you, and you shall be a father of many peoples.

5 Neither shall your name any more be called Abram, but your name shall be Abraham; for I have made you a father of many peoples.

6 And I will make you fruitful, and multiply you exceedingly; and I will make you father of many nations, and kings shall come out of your loins.

7 And I will establish my covenant between me and you and your descendants after you throughout their generations for an everlasting covenant, and I will be God to you and to your descendants after you.

8 And I will give to you, and your descendants after you, the land in which you sojourn, all the land of Canaan, for an everlasting inheritance; and I will be their God.

9 ¶And God said to Abraham, You shall keep my covenant, you, and your descendants after you throughout their generations.

10 This is my covenant, which you shall keep between me and you and your descendants after you: Every male among you shall be circumcised.

11 And you shall circumcise the flesh of your foreskin; and it shall be a token of the covenant between me and you.

12 And he that is eight days old

shall be circumcised among you, every male throughout your generations, he that is born in the house, or bought with money of any stranger, who is not of your descendants.

13 He that is born in your house, and he that is bought with your money, shall be circumcised; and my covenant shall be in your flesh for an everlasting covenant.

14 And the uncircumcised male who is not circumcised in the flesh of his foreskin, that person shall be cut off from his people; for he has broken my covenant.

15 ¶Then God said to Abraham, As for Sarai your wife, you shall not call her name Sarai, for Sarah is her name.

16 And I will bless her, and also I will give you a son by her; yea, I will bless him and make nations of him; and the kings of the people shall come from him.

17 Then Abraham fell on his face and laughed and said in his heart, Shall a son be born to him who is a hundred years old? Or shall Sarah, who is ninety years old, bear a child?

18 And Abraham said to God, O that Ishmael might live in thy presence!

19 And God said to Abraham, Truly, Sarah your wife shall bear you a son; and you shall call his name Isaac; and I will establish my covenant with him for an everlasting covenant, and with his descendants after him.

20 And as for Ishmael, I have heard you; behold, I have blessed him, and will multiply him, and will make him exceedingly great; twelve princes shall he beget, and I will make him a great nation.

21 But I will establish my covenant with Isaac, whom Sarah shall bear to you at this set time next year.

22 And when God was through talking with him, he went up from Abraham.

23 ¶And Abraham took Ishmael his son and all of those that were born in his house and all of those that were bought with his money, every male among the men of Abraham's house-

hold, and circumcised the flesh of their foreskin in that very day, as God had said unto him.

24 And Abraham was ninety-nine years old when he was circumcised in the flesh of his foreskin.

25 And Ishmael his son was thirteen years old when he was circumcised in the flesh of his foreskin.

26 In that very day was Abraham circumcised and Ishmael his son

27 And all the men of his household, both born in the house and bought with money. He also circumcised some of the strangers with him.

CHAPTER 18

AND the Lord revealed himself to him by the oak of Mamre, as he was sitting at the door of the tent in the heat of the day;

2 And he lifted up his eyes and looked, and, behold, three men stood at a distance from him; and when he saw them, he ran from the door of the tent to meet them and bowed himself to the ground,

3 And said, O Lord, if now I have found mercy in thy sight, do not pass away from thy servant;

4 Let me bring a little water and wash your feet and rest yourselves under the tree;

5 And take a morsel of bread and sustain your hearts; after that you shall go on your way, since you have come to your servant. And they said, So do as you have said.

6 So Abraham hastened into the tent to Sarah, and said, Make ready quickly three measures of fine flour, knead it, and make cakes on a griddle.

7 And Abraham ran to the herd, and took a calf fat and good, and gave it to a servant, and he hastened to prepare it.

8 And he took butter and milk and the calf which he had prepared, and set them before them; and he stood by them under the tree, and they ate.

9 ¶And they said to him, Where is Sarah your wife? And he said, Behold, she is in the tent.

10 And the Lord said, I will cer-

tainly return to you at this time next year, and lo, Sarah your wife shall be with child, and shall have a son. And Sarah heard it in the tent door which was behind her.

11 Now Abraham and Sarah were old and well advanced in years; and Sarah was beyond the age of childbearing.

12 Therefore Sarah laughed within herself, saying, After I am grown old, shall I renew my youth, my lord being old also?

13 And the LORD said to Abraham, Why did Sarah laugh, saying, Shall I truly bear a child, when I am so old?

14 Is anything too hard for the LORD? I will return to you at this season, and Sarah your wife shall be with child, and shall have a son.

15 Then Sarah denied, saying, I did not laugh; because she was afraid. And he said, No; but you did laugh.

16 ¶And the men rose up from there and looked toward Sodom; and Abraham went with them to see them off.

17 And the LORD said, Shall I hide from my servant Abraham the thing which I am going to do,

18 Seeing that Abraham shall surely become a great and mighty nation, and all the nations of the earth shall be blessed through him?

19 For I know him well, and that he will command his children and his household after him, to keep the ways of the LORD, to do justice and righteousness; for the LORD shall fulfil for Abraham the thing that he has spoken concerning him.

20 And the LORD said, Because the cry of Sodom and Gomorrah has come before me and their sins are very grievous,

21 I will go down now and see whether they have done altogether according to their cry which has come before me; and if not, I will know.

22 So the men turned from there and went toward Sodom; but Abraham stood yet before the LORD.

23 ¶And Abraham drew near and

said, Wilt thou in thine anger destroy the righteous with the sinners?

24 Suppose there are fifty righteous within the city; wilt thou in thine anger destroy it, and not spare the place for the sake of the fifty righteous that are in it?

25 Far be it from thee to do such a thing as this, to slay the innocent with the guilty, far be it from thee, O thou Judge of the whole earth! Such a judgment should never be carried out.

26 And the LORD said, If I find in Sodom fifty righteous within the city, then I will spare the whole country for their sake.

27 And Abraham answered and said, Behold, I have ventured to speak before the LORD, and yet I am but dust and ashes;

28 Suppose there shall lack five of the fifty righteous; wilt thou destroy the whole city for the lack of five men? And he said, If I find there forty-five, I will not destroy it.

29 And Abraham spoke to him and said, Suppose there shall be forty found there? And he said, I will not destroy it, if I find there forty.

30 Then Abraham said, Oh let not the LORD be displeased and I will speak: Suppose there shall thirty be found there? And he said, I will not destroy it, if I find thirty there.

31 And he said, Behold, I have ventured to speak before the LORD; suppose there shall be twenty found there? And he said, I will not destroy it for the sake of twenty.

32 And he said, Oh, let not the LORD be displeased, and I will speak only once more; suppose ten shall be found there? And he said, I will not destroy it for the sake of ten.

33 And the LORD went his way when he had finished communing with Abraham; and Abraham returned to his place.

CHAPTER 19

AND there came two angels [1] to Sodom in the evening; and Lot was sitting at the gate of Sodom; and

¹ Aramaic: also *messengers, ministers.*

Lot saw them and rose up to meet them; and he bowed himself with his face toward the ground;

2 And he said, My lords, turn aside, I pray you, into your servant's house and spend the night and wash your feet; then rise up early in the morning and go on your way. And they said, No, we will spend the night in the street.

3 But Lot urged them greatly; and they turned in to him and entered into his house; and he made them a feast and baked unleavened cakes and they ate.

4 ¶But before they lay down, the men of the city, that is, the men of Sodom, surrounded the house, both young and old, all the people of the town;

5 And they called to Lot and said to him, Where are the men who came to you tonight? Bring them out to us that we may know them.

6 And Lot went out at the door to them; and he shut the door after him.

7 And Lot said to them, I pray you, my brethren, do not so wickedly.

8 Behold now, I have two daughters who have not known man; let me bring them out to you, and do to them whatever you please; only to these men do nothing; for they have come under the protection of my roof.

9 And they said, Get away. And they said again, This fellow came to sojourn among us, and now he tries to judge us; and they said to Lot, Now we will deal worse with you than with them. Then Lot fought desperately with them, and they drew near to break the door.

10 But the men put forth their hands and pulled Lot into the house to them and locked the door.

11 And they smote the men that were at the door of the house with blindness, from the least to the greatest, so that they became tired trying in vain to find the door.

12 ¶And the men said to Lot, What are you doing in this place? Now, your sons-in-law, your sons, your daughters, and whatsoever you have in this city, take them out of this place;

13 For we will destroy this place, because the cry of the oppressed has come before the LORD; and the LORD has sent us to destroy it.

14 Then Lot went out and spoke to his sons-in-law who married his daughters, and said, Arise, get out of this place; for the LORD will destroy it. But his sons-in-law thought he was joking.

15 ¶And when the morning dawned, the angels urged Lot, saying, Arise, take your wife and your two daughters who are not given in marriage, lest you be engulfed in the sins of the city.

16 But Lot lingered; then the angels held his hand, the hand of his wife, and the hands of his two daughters, because the LORD pitied him; and they took him out and set him outside the city.

17 ¶And it came to pass when they had brought them out of the city, they said to Lot: Now escape for your life; do not look back nor stop anywhere in the plain, but flee to the mountain lest you be consumed.

18 And Lot said to them, I beseech you, my lords,

19 Behold now, your servant has found mercy in your sight, and great is the favor which you have shown to me in saving my life; but I cannot escape to the mountain, lest evil overtake me and I die;

20 Behold now, this town is near to flee to, and it is a little one. Oh, let me escape there, and behold, because it is a little one my life will be spared.

21 And he said to him, See, I have granted you this thing also that I will not overthrow the city of which you have spoken.

22 Make haste and escape there; for I cannot do anything till you enter into it. Therefore the name of the city was called Zoar.

23 ¶The sun was risen upon the earth when Lot entered into Zoar.

24 Then the LORD rained upon Sodom and upon Gomorrah brimstone and fire from the presence of the LORD out of heaven;

25 And he overthrew those cities and all the plain and all the inhabi-

tants of the region and that which grew on the ground.

26 ¶But his wife looked back from behind him and she became a pillar of salt. [1]

27 ¶And Abraham rose up early in the morning and went to the place where he had stood before the LORD;

28 And he looked toward Sodom and Gomorrah and toward all the region of the plain, and beheld, lo, the smoke of the country went up like the smoke of a furnace.

29 ¶And it came to pass when God destroyed the cities of the plain that God remembered Abraham and sent Lot out of the midst of the devastated region, when he overthrew the cities wherein Lot dwelt.

30 ¶And Lot went up out of Zoar and dwelt in the mountain, and his two daughters were with him; for he was afraid to live in Zoar; and he dwelt in a cave, both he and his two daughters.

31 And the first-born said to the younger, Behold our father is old and there is not a man in the land to take us for wives after the manner of all the earth:

32 Come, let us make our father drink wine and we will lie with him so that we may raise an offspring from our father.

33 And they made their father drink wine that night; and the first-born went in and lay with her father; and he did not know when she lay down, nor when she arose.

34 And it came to pass on the next day, the first-born said to the younger, Behold, I lay last night with my father; let us make him drink wine tonight also; and then you go in and lie with him so that we may raise offspring from our father.

35 So they made their father drink wine that night also; and the younger went in and lay with him; and he did not know when she lay down, nor when she arose.

36 Thus were both the daughters of Lot with child by their father.

37 And the first-born bore a son and called his name Moab; he is the father of the Moabites to this day.

38 And the younger also bore a son and called his name Bar-ammi; he is the father of the Ammonites to this day.

CHAPTER 20

AND Abraham journeyed from thence toward the south country, and settled between Rakim and Gadar, and Abraham sojourned in Gadar.

2 And Abraham said of Sarah his wife, She is my sister; and Abimeleck king of Gadar sent and took Sarah.

3 But God came to Abimeleck in a dream by night and said to him, Behold, you will die on account of the woman whom you have taken; for she is another man's wife.

4 But Abimeleck had not touched her; and he said, O LORD, wilt thou slay an innocent people?

5 Behold, he said, She is my sister; and she herself also said, He is my brother; in the innocence of my heart and purity of my hands have I done this.

6 And God said to him in a dream, Yea, I know that you have done this in the innocence of your heart; for I also restrained you from sinning against me; therefore I did not permit you to touch her.

7 Now therefore restore the man's wife, for he is a prophet, and he shall pray for you, and you shall live; but if you do not restore her, then know that you will surely die, you, and all your family.

8 Therefore Abimeleck rose early in the morning and called all of his servants and told them all these words; and the men were exceedingly afraid.

9 Then Abimeleck called Abraham and said to him, What have I done to you? and what crime have I committed against you, that you have brought on me and on my kingdom such a great sin? You have done to me things that ought not to be done.

10 And Abimeleck said to Abra-

---

[1] Aramaic: *Pillar of salt* means that she became petrified with fear and died.

ham, What induced you to do this thing?

11 And Abraham said, Because I thought, perhaps there is no fear of God in this country; and they will slay me for my wife's sake.

12 And yet truly she is my sister; she is the daughter of my father, but not the daughter of my mother; and she became my wife.

13 And it came to pass when God brought me forth out of my father's house, I said to her, This is the favor which you shall do to me; at every place whither we shall go, say of me, He is my brother.

14 And Abimeleck took sheep and oxen and male and female servants and gave them to Abraham and restored to him Sarah his wife.

15 Then Abimeleck said to Abraham, Behold, my land is before you; dwell wherever you please.

16 And to Sarah he said, Behold, I have given a thousand pieces of silver to your brother; behold, it is given for you, because you have been humbled in the eyes of my people, and because of the other things for which I have reproved you.

17 ¶So Abraham prayed to God and God healed Abimeleck and his wife and his maidservants, and they bore children.

18 For the LORD had fast closed up the wombs of all women in the household of Abimeleck because of Sarah, Abraham's wife.

CHAPTER 21

AND the LORD remembered Sarah, as he had said, and the LORD did to Sarah as he had spoken.

2 For Sarah conceived and bore Abraham a son in his old age, at the set time of which God had spoken to him.

3 And Abraham called the name of his son that was born to him, whom Sarah bore to him, Isaac.

4 And Abraham circumcised his son Isaac when he was eight days old, as God had commanded him.

5 And Abraham was a hundred years old when his son Isaac was born to him.

6 ¶And Sarah said, God has made me to rejoice today exceedingly; everyone that hears the news will rejoice with me.

7 And she said, Who would have said to Abraham that Sarah would give suck to children? For I have borne him a son in his old age.

8 And the child grew and was weaned; and Abraham made a great feast on the day that Isaac was weaned.

9 ¶And Sarah saw the son of Hagar, the Egyptian, whom she had borne to Abraham, mocking.

10 Therefore she said to Abraham, Expel this maidservant and her son; for the son of this maidservant shall not be heir with my son Isaac.

11 And the thing was very grievous in Abraham's sight because of his son.

12 ¶And God said to Abraham, Let it not be grievous in your sight because of the boy and because of your maidservant; whatever Sarah tells you, hearken to her voice; for your descendants shall come through Isaac.

13 And also of the son of the maidservant will I make a great nation because he is your offspring.

14 And Abraham rose up early in the morning and took bread and a skin containing water and gave them to Hagar, putting them on her shoulder, and the boy; and sent her away. And she departed, and lost her way in the wilderness of Beer-sheba.

15 And the water in the skin was spent, and she cast the boy under one of the shrubs.

16 And she went and sat down opposite him about the distance of a bowshot; for she said, Let me not see the death of the boy. And she sat down opposite him and lifted up her voice and wept.

17 And the LORD heard the voice of the boy; and the angel of God called to Hagar from heaven, and said to her, What troubles you, Hagar? Fear not; for God has heard the voice of the boy where he is.

18 Arise, take up the boy, and hold him fast in your arms; for I will make him a great nation.

19 Then God opened her eyes and

she saw a well of water; and she went and filled the skin with water and gave the boy a drink.

20 And God was with the boy; and he grew up and dwelt in the wilderness of Paran and learned to become an archer in the wilderness of Paran.

21 And his mother took him a wife out of the land of Egypt.

22 ¶And it came to pass at that time that Abimeleck and Phichol, the general of his army, said to Abraham, God is with you in all that you do;

23 Now therefore swear to me by God in this place that you will never deal falsely with me, nor with my family, nor with my descendants; but according to the kindness that I have done to you, you shall do to me and to the land wherein you have sojourned.

24 And Abraham said, I will swear.

25 And Abraham reproved Abimeleck because of a well which Abraham's servants had dug and which Abimeleck's servants had seized.

26 And Abimeleck said, I do not know who has done this thing; neither did you tell me, nor have I heard of it until today.

27 And Abraham took sheep and oxen and gave them to Abimeleck; and both of them made a covenant.

28 And Abraham set seven ewe lambs of the flock by themselves.

29 And Abimeleck said to Abraham, What is the meaning of these seven ewe lambs of the flock which you have set by themselves?

30 And he said, For these seven ewe lambs you shall take of my hands that they may be a witness for me that I have digged this well.

31 Therefore he called that place Beer-sheba, because there they swore both of them.

32 Thus they made a covenant at Beer-sheba; then Abimeleck and Phichol, the general of the army, rose up and returned to the land of the Philistines.

33 ¶And Abraham planted a grove in Beer-sheba and called there on the name of the LORD Everlasting.

34 And Abraham sojourned in the land of the Philistines for a long time.

CHAPTER 22

AND it came to pass after these things that God tested Abraham and said to him, Abraham. And he said, Behold, here I am.

2 And he said, Take now your son, your only son Isaac, whom you love, and go to the land of the Amorites; and offer him there for a burnt offering upon one of the mountains of which I will tell you.

3 ¶And Abraham rose up early in the morning and saddled his ass and took two of his young men with him and Isaac his son, and cut wood for the burnt offering and rose up and went to the place of which God had told him.

4 And on the third day Abraham lifted up his eyes and saw the place afar off.

5 And he said to his young men, You stay here with the ass, and I and the boy will go yonder to worship and return to you.

6 And Abraham took the wood for the burnt offering and laid it upon Isaac his son, and he took the fire in a container and a knife in his hand, and they went both of them together.

7 And Isaac spoke to Abraham his father and said, My father. And he answered, Here I am, my son. And Isaac said, Behold the fire and the wood: but where is the lamb for a burnt offering?

8 And Abraham said, God will provide himself the lamb for a burnt offering, my son. So they went both of them together.

9 And they came to the place of which God had told him; and Abraham built an altar there and laid the wood in order and bound Isaac his son and laid him on the altar upon the wood.

10 Then Abraham stretched forth his hand and took the knife to slay his son.

11 And the angel of the LORD called to him from heaven and said, Abraham! Abraham! And he said, Here am I.

12 And he said to him, Do not lay your hand on the boy, neither shall

you harm him; for now I know that you are a man who reveres God, seeing that you have not withheld your son, your only son, from me.

13 And Abraham lifted up his eyes and looked, and behold a ram caught in a thicket by his horns; and Abraham went and took the ram and offered it up for a burnt offering instead of his son.

14 And Abraham called the name of that place Mariah-nekhzey, that is, the LORD will provide, as it is said to this day on this mountain, The LORD shall provide.

15 ¶And the angel of the LORD called to Abraham from heaven a second time

16 And said, I have sworn by myself, says the LORD, for because you have done this thing and have not withheld your son, your only son, from me,

17 I will surely bless you, and I will surely multiply your descendants as the stars of the heaven, and as the sand which is on the sea shore; and your descendants shall inherit the lands of their enemies;

18 And by your seed [1] shall all the nations of the earth be blessed because you have obeyed my voice.

19 So Abraham returned to his young men and they rose up and went together to Beer-sheba, and Abraham dwelt in Beer-sheba.

20 ¶And it came to pass after these things that it was told Abraham, saying, Behold, Milcah has also borne children to your brother Nahor:

21 Uz his first-born, Buz his brother, and Kemuel the father of Aram,

22 And Khasar, Hazo, Pilrash, Jarlaph, and Bethuel.

23 And Bethuel begot Rebekah; these eight Milcah did bear to Nahor, Abraham's brother.

24 And his concubine, whose name was Romah, also bore Tebah, Gaham, Thahash, and Maachah.

CHAPTER 23

AND Sarah was a hundred and twenty-seven years old; these were the years of the life of Sarah.

[1] *Seed* in Aramaic also means teaching.

2 And Sarah died at Koriath Gabarey (the Town of the Giants); that is Hebron in the land of Canaan; and Abraham came to mourn for Sarah and to weep for her.

3 ¶And Abraham rose up from before the bier of his dead and spoke to the sons of Heth, saying,

4 I am a stranger and a sojourner with you; give me the possession of a burial ground with you that I may bury my dead out of my sight.

5 And the sons of Heth answered and said to Abraham,

6 Hear us, our lord; you are a prince of God among us; bury your dead in the choicest of our sepulchres; none of us will withhold from you his sepulchre for the burial of your dead.

7 And Abraham stood up and bowed himself to the people of the land, that is, to the Hittites.

8 And he discussed the matter with them and said to them, If you consent that I may bury my dead out of my sight, hear me and entreat for me to Ephron the son of Zohar,

9 That he may give me the double cave which belongs to him, which is by the side of his field; let him give it to me for a full price as a possession for a burial ground among you.

10 And Ephron dwelt among the Hittites; and Ephron the Hittite answered Abraham in the presence of the Hittites and in the presence of all that went in at the gate of his city, saying,

11 No, my lord, listen to me; I will give you the field and the cave which is in it, I will give it to you; in the presence of my people I give it to you; bury your dead.

12 And Abraham bowed down before the people of the land.

13 Then he said to Ephron in the presence of the people of the land, If you are willing, then hearken to me; I will give you money for the price of the field; take it from me, and I will bury my dead there.

14 And Ephron answered Abraham and said,

15 My lord, hearken to me; the land is worth four hundred shekels of sil-

ver; what is that between me and you? You may bury your dead.

16 And Abraham hearkened to Ephron; and Abraham weighed to Ephron the sum of money which he had named in the presence of the Hittites, four hundred shekels of silver, legal tender with the merchants.

17 ¶Thus the field of Ephron, which was by the side of the double cave which was before Mamre, that is, the Field of the Cave and the cave which was in it and all the trees that were in the field that were on its borders round about were made sure

18 And sold to Abraham in the presence of the Hittites and in the presence of all that went in at the gate of his city.

19 And after this, Abraham buried Sarah his wife in the double cave which is in the field before Mamre; the same is Hebron in the land of Canaan.

20 Thus the field and the cave that is in it were deeded to Abraham for a possession of a burial ground by the Hittites.

CHAPTER 24

NOW Abraham was old and well advanced in years; and the LORD had blessed him in all things.

2 And Abraham called his eldest servant, the steward of his house, who was in charge of everything that he had; and he said to him, Put your hand under my thigh;

3 And I will make you swear by the LORD, the God of heaven and the God of the earth, that you shall not take to my son a wife of the daughters of the Canaanites, among whom I dwell;

4 But that you will go to my country and to my kindred, and take a wife for my son Isaac.

5 And the servant said to him, Suppose the woman will not be willing to follow me to this land; must I then take your son back to the land from whence you came?

6 And Abraham said to him, Beware that you do not take my son thither again.

7 ¶The LORD God of heaven, who took me from thence, from my father's household and from the land of my kindred, and who spoke to me, and who made a covenant with me, saying, To your descendants will I give this land; he shall send his angel before you, and you shall take a wife to my son from there.

8 And if the woman will not be willing to follow you, then you shall be clear from this my oath; only you must not take my son there again.

9 So the servant put his hand under the thigh of Abraham his master, and swore to him concerning this matter.

10 ¶And the servant took ten camels of the camels of his master, and departed, carrying with him all kinds of choice things of his master; and he arose, and went to Aram-nahrin (Mesopotamia), to the city of Nahor.

11 And he made his camels to kneel down outside the city by a well of water in the evening, the very time when women go out to draw water.

12 And he prayed, saying, O LORD God of my master Abraham, prosper my journey, and show kindness to my master Abraham.

13 Behold, I stand here by the well of water; and the daughters of the men of the city are coming out to draw water.

14 Let it come to pass that the damsel to whom I shall say, Let down your pitcher, that I may drink; and she shall say to me, Drink, and I will water your camels also; let the same be she that thou hast selected for thy servant Isaac; and by this token shall I know that thou hast shown kindness and faithfulness to my master.

15 ¶And it came to pass, before he had finished speaking, that, behold, Rebekah came out, who was born to Bethuel, son of Milcah, the wife of Nahor, Abraham's brother, with her pitcher on her shoulder.

16 And the damsel was very beautiful to look upon, a virgin whom no man had known; and she went down to the well and filled her pitcher and came up.

17 And the servant ran to meet her and said, Let me drink a little water from your pitcher.

18 And she said, Drink, my lord; and she hastened and let down the pitcher upon her hands and gave him a drink.

19 And when she had finished giving him a drink, she said, I will draw water for your camels also, until they are all watered.

20 So she hastened and emptied her pitcher into the trough and ran again to the well to draw water, and she drew water for all his camels.

21 And as the man watered his camels he scrutinized her, and waited to know whether the LORD had made his journey prosperous or not.

22 And it came to pass, when the camels were through drinking, the man took golden earrings weighing a shekel and two bracelets for her wrists weighing ten shekels of gold,

23 And said to her, Whose daughter are you? tell me, is there room in your father's house for us to lodge?

24 And she said to him, I am the daughter of Bethuel the son of Milcah, whom she bore to Nahor.

25 And she said moreover to him, We have plenty of straw and hay, and room to lodge in.

26 And the man knelt on the ground and worshipped the LORD.

27 And he said, Blessed be the LORD God of my master Abraham, who has not withheld his grace and his truth from my master; while I was on the road, the LORD led me to the house of my master's brother, to take his brother's daughter to his son.

28 Then the damsel ran, and related these things to her father's household.

29 ¶And Rebekah had a brother, and his name was Laban; so Laban ran out to the man, to the well.

30 And it came to pass, when he saw the earrings and the bracelets on his sister's hands and when he heard the words of Rebekah his sister, saying, Thus spoke the man to me, he came to the man; and, behold, he was standing by the camels at the well.

31 And he said to him, Come in, you blessed of the LORD; why do you stand in the street? For I have prepared the house and a place for the camels.

32 ¶So the man came into the house and ungirded the camels and gave straw and hay for the camels, and was given water to wash his feet and the feet of the men who were with him.

33 And there was set food before them to eat; but Abraham's steward said, I will not eat until I have told my errand. And they said, Speak on.

34 And he said, I am Abraham's servant.

35 And the LORD has blessed my master greatly, so that he has become great; and he has given him flocks and herds, silver and gold, menservants and maidservants, and camels and asses.

36 And Sarah my master's wife bore a son to my master when she was old; and to him he has given all that he has.

37 And my master made me swear, saying, You must not take a wife to my son of the daughters of the Canaanites, in whose land I dwell;

38 But you shall go to my father's house and to my kindred, and take a wife to my son.

39 And I said to my master, Suppose the woman will be unwilling to follow me?

40 And he said to me, The LORD before whom I worship will send his angel with you, and prosper your way; and you shall take a wife for my son of my kindred and of my father's house;

41 Then you shall be clear from my oath, when you go to my kindred; and if they do not give you a bride, you shall be clear from my oath.

42 And I came today to the well, and said, O LORD God of my master Abraham, if now thou do prosper my mission for which I came,

43 Behold, I am standing by the well of water, and it shall come to pass that when the damsel comes forth to draw water, and I say to her, Let me drink a little water from your pitcher,

44 And she say to me, Drink, and

I will also draw for your camels, let the same be the woman whom the LORD has appointed for my master's son.

45 And before I was through speaking in my heart, behold, Rebekah came forth with her pitcher on her shoulder; and she went down to the fountain, and drew water; and I said to her, Let me drink a little water from your pitcher.

46 And she hastened, and let down her pitcher from her shoulder, and said, Drink, and I will water your camels also; so I drank, and she watered my camels also.

47 Then I asked her, and said, Whose daughter are you? And she said, The daughter of Bethuel, the son of Nahor, whom Milcah bore to him; and I put the earrings on her ears and the bracelets on her hands.

48 And I knelt and worshipped the LORD, and blessed the LORD God of my master Abraham, who had led me in the right way to the house of my master's brother to take my master's brother's daughter to his son.

49 And now if you will deal kindly and truly with my master, tell me; and if not, tell me; so that I may know what to do.

50 Then Laban and Bethuel answered and said, The thing proceeded from the LORD; we cannot say anything to you good or bad.

51 Behold, Rebekah is before you; take her and go, and let her become the wife of your master's son, as the LORD has spoken.

52 And it came to pass that, when Abraham's servant heard their words, he worshipped the LORD, bowing himself to the earth.

53 And the servant brought forth jewels of gold and jewels of silver and raiment, and gave them to Rebekah; he also gave gifts to her brother and to her mother.

54 And he and the men who were with him ate and drank, and spent the night there; and the servant rose up in the morning, and said to them, Send me away to my master.

55 And her brother and her mother said to him, Let the damsel stay with us a month, or at least a few days; and then she shall go.

56 And he said to them, Do not delay me, seeing the LORD has prospered my errand; send me away that I may go to my master.

57 And they said, We will call the damsel, and ask her.

58 So they called Rebekah, and said to her, Will you go with this man? And she said, I will go.

59 And they sent away Rebekah their sister and her nurse and Abraham's servant and his men.

60 And they blessed Rebekah their sister, and said to her, You are our sister, be the mother of thousands and of millions, and let your descendants inherit the lands of their enemies.

61 ¶Then Rebekah arose with her maids, and they rode upon the camels, and followed the man; and the servant took Rebekah and went his way.

62 And Isaac had returned from the well of Khaya-khezan; for he dwelt in the south country.

63 Now Isaac strolled in the field in the evening; and he lifted up his eyes and saw, and behold, the camels were coming.

64 And Rebekah lifted up her eyes, and when she saw Isaac, she leaned over the camel,

65 And she said to the servant, Who is this man who is walking in the field to meet us? And the servant said, It is my master; therefore she took a veil and covered herself.

66 And the servant told Isaac all the things that she had done.

67 And Isaac brought her into his mother Sarah's tent, and took Rebekah, and she became his wife; and he loved her; and Isaac was comforted after his mother's death.

CHAPTER 25

THEN again Abraham took another wife, and her name was Kenturah.

2 And she bore him Zimran, Jokshan, Medan, Midian, Ishbak, and Shuah.

3 And Jokshan begot Sheba and

Daran. And the sons of Daran were Asshurim, Letushim, and Ammim.

4 And the sons of Midian were Ephah, Haphar, Hanoch, Abidah, and Eldaah. All these were the children of Kenturah.

5 ¶And Abraham gave everything that he had to Isaac.

6 But to the sons of his concubine, Abraham gave gifts, and sent them away from Isaac, his son, eastward to the east country, while he was still alive.

7 And these are the days of the years of Abraham's life which he lived, a hundred and seventy-five years.

8 Then Abraham became sick, and died in a good old age, an old man satisfied with his days; and was gathered to his people.

9 And his sons Isaac and Ishmael buried him in the double cave, (Machpelah) which is in the field of Ephron the son of Zohar the Hittite, which is before Mamre;

10 The field which Abraham purchased from the sons of Heth, as a possession for a burial ground. There was Abraham buried, and Sarah his wife.

11 ¶And it came to pass after the death of Abraham that God blessed his son Isaac; and Isaac dwelt by the well of Khaya-khezan (The Well of The Living One who saw me).

12 ¶Now these are the generations of Ishmael, Abraham's son, whom Hagar the Egyptian, Sarah's maid, bore to Abraham;

13 And these are the names of the sons of Ishmael, by their names, according to their generations: the firstborn of Ishmael, Nebioth, and Kedar, Arbal, and Mibsam,

14 Mishma, Romah, Massa,

15 Hadar, Tema, Nator, Naphish, and Kedem.

16 These are the sons of Ishmael, and these are their names by their villages and by their sheepfolds, twelve princes according to their nations.

17 And these are the years of the life of Ishmael, a hundred and thirty-seven years; and he became sick and died; and was gathered to his people.

18 And they dwelt from Havilah as far as Shud, which extends from the border of Egypt to the gateway of Assyria; he dwelt adjacent to the lands of all his brethren.

19 ¶These are the generations of Isaac, Abraham's son: Abraham begot Isaac;

20 And Isaac was forty years old when he took Rebekah to wife, the daughter of Bethuel the Aramean of Padan-aram, the sister of Laban, the Aramean (Syrian).

21 And Isaac prayed before the LORD for his wife, because she was barren; and the LORD answered him, and Rebekah his wife conceived.

22 And the children struggled together within her womb; and she said, If it is to be like this, why do I live? So she went to enquire of the LORD.

23 And the LORD said to her, Two peoples are in your womb, and two nations shall be separated from your body; and the one nation shall be stronger than the other nation; and the elder shall serve the younger.

24 ¶And when her days to be delivered were fulfilled, behold, there were twins in her womb.

25 And the first came out red, all covered with ringlets of hair; and they called his name Esau.

26 And after him his brother came forth, and his hand held Esau's heel; and his name was called Jacob; [1] and Isaac was sixty years old when Rebekah bore them.

27 And the boys grew up; and Esau became an expert hunter, a man of outdoor life; but Jacob was a simple man, living in a tent.

28 And Isaac was fond of Esau, because he ate of Esau's game; but Rebekah was fond of Jacob.

29 ¶And Jacob cooked pottage,[2] and behold, his brother Esau came in from the field, and he was very hungry;

30 And Esau said to Jacob, Give me some of that pottage, for I am

---

[1] Heel holder.   [2] Lentil stew.

famished; that is why he was called Edom.

31 And Jacob said, Sell me this day your birthright.

32 And Esau said, Behold, I am at the point of death; and what profit shall a birthright be to me?

33 And Jacob said to him, Swear to me this day; and he swore to him; and he sold his birthright to Jacob.

34 Then Jacob gave Esau bread and pottage; and he ate, and drank, and rose up and went his way; thus Esau despised his birthright.

CHAPTER 26

AND there was a famine in the land, besides the first famine that was in the days of Abraham. And Isaac went to Gadar, to Abimeleck king of the Philistines.

2 And the LORD appeared to him, and said, Do not go down to Egypt; dwell in the land of which I shall tell you;

3 Sojourn in this land, and I will be with you and will bless you; for to you and to your descendants I will give all these kingdoms, and I will perform the oath which I swore to Abraham your father;

4 And I will make your descendants to multiply as the stars of heaven, and will give to your descendants all these lands; and by your descendants shall all the nations of the earth be blessed;

5 Because that Abraham obeyed my voice, and kept my charge, my commandments, my statutes, and my laws.

6 ¶And Isaac dwelt in Gadar;

7 And the men of the place asked him concerning his wife; and he said, She is my sister; for he was afraid to say, She is my wife; lest the men of the place should kill him on account of Rebekah, because she was fair to look upon.

8 And it came to pass when he had been there a long time that Abimeleck king of the Philistines looked out of a window and saw Isaac fondling Rebekah his wife.

9 So Abimeleck called Isaac, and said, Behold, she is your wife; how then did you say, She is my sister? And Isaac said to him, Because I said, Lest I may die on account of her.

10 And Abimeleck said to him, What is this thing that you have done to us? One of the people might easily have lain with your wife, and you would have brought sin upon us.

11 And Abimeleck charged all the people, saying, Whoever harms this man or his wife shall surely be put to death.

12 Then Isaac sowed in that land, and received in the same year a hundredfold; and the LORD blessed him.

13 And the man became great, and went forward and grew until he became very great;

14 And he had possessions of flocks and possessions of herds and much wealth, so that the Philistines envied him.

15 For all the wells which his father's servants had dug in the days of Abraham his father, the Philistines had polluted them and filled them with earth.

16 And Abimeleck said to Isaac, Go away from among us; for you are much mightier than we.

17 ¶So Isaac departed from thence, and encamped in the valley of Gadar, and dwelt there.

18 And Isaac digged again the wells of water which had been dug by the servants of his father in the days of Abraham his father; for the Philistines had polluted them after the death of Abraham; and he called their names after the names by which his father had called them.

19 And Isaac's servants dug in the valley, and found there a well of living water.

20 And the herdsmen of Gadar quarreled with Isaac's herdsmen, saying, The water is ours; and he called the name of the well Aska (difficulty); because they disputed with him.

21 And they dug another well, and they quarreled over that also; and he called the name of it Satana (the adversary).

22 Then he moved from there, and

dug another well; but over that they did not quarrel; and he called the name of it Rehoboth (to enlarge); and he said, For now the LORD has made room for us, and we shall multiply in the land.

23 And he went up from thence to Beer-sheba.

24 And the LORD appeared to him the same night, and said, 1 am the God of Abraham your father; fear not, for I am with you, and I will bless you, and multiply your descendants for my servant Abraham's sake.

25 And he built an altar there, and called upon the name of the LORD, and pitched his tent there; and there Isaac's servants dug a well.

26 ¶Then Abimeleck went to him from Gadar, and Ahuzzath one of his friends, and Phichol the general of his army.

27 And Isaac said to them, Why have you come to me, seeing that you hate me, and have sent me away from you?

28 And they said, We saw certainly that the LORD is with you; so we said, Let there be now an oath between us and you, and let us make a covenant with you,

29 That you will do us no evil, just as we have not hurt you, and as we have done nothing but good to you, and have sent you away in peace; you are now the blessed of the LORD.

30 And he made them a feast, and they did eat and drink.

31 And they rose up in the early morning, and took oaths one with another; and Isaac sent them away, and they departed from him in peace.

32 And it came to pass the same day that Isaac's servants came, and spoke to him concerning the well which they had dug, and said to him, We have found water.

33 And he called it Sheba; therefore the name of the town is called Beer-sheba to this day.

34 ¶And Esau was forty years old when he took to wife Judith the daughter of Beeri the Hittite, and Bismath the daughter of Elon the Hivite;

35 And they made life miserable for Isaac and Rebekah.

CHAPTER 27

AND it came to pass, when Isaac was old and his eyes were dim so that he could not see, he called Esau his eldest son, and said to him, My son; and he said to him, Behold, here I am.

2 And Isaac said to him, Behold now, I am old, and I do not know the day of my death;

3 Now therefore take your weapons, your sword and your bow, and go out into the field and hunt game;

4 And make me stewed meat, such as I like, and bring it to me, that I may eat, that my soul may bless you before I die.

5 And Rebekah heard when Isaac spoke to Esau his son. So Esau went to the field to hunt game and to bring it.

6 ¶Then Rebekah said to Jacob her son, Behold, I heard your father say to Esau your brother,

7 Bring me game, and make me stewed meat, that I may eat and bless you in the presence of the LORD before 1 die.

8 Now therefore, my son, listen to me according to that which I command you.

9 Go now to the flock, and bring me from there two kids of the goats; and I will make from them stew for your father, such as he likes;

10 And you shall bring it to your father, that he may eat, and that he may bless you in the presence of the LORD before his death.

11 And Jacob said to Rebekah his mother, Behold, Esau my brother is a hairy man and I am a smooth man;

12 Perhaps my father will feel me, and I shall seem to him as a mocker; and I shall bring a curse upon myself, and not a blessing.

13 And his mother said to him, Let your curses be upon me, my son; only listen to me, and go and fetch them to me.

14 So he went and picked them up, and brought them to his mother; and his mother made a stew, such as his father liked.

15 And Rebekah took the best

clothes of her elder son Esau, which were with her in the house, and put them upon Jacob her younger son;

16 And she put the skins of the kids of the goats upon his hands, and upon the back of his neck;

17 And she gave the stew and the bread which she had prepared into the hand of her son Jacob.

18 ¶And he brought them in to his father, and said, My father; and he said, Here am I. Then he said, Who are you, my son?

19 And Jacob said to his father, I am Esau, your first-born; I have done as you told me; now arise and sit up and eat of my game, that your soul may bless me.

20 And Isaac said to his son, How is it that you have found it so quickly, my son? And he said, Because the LORD your God brought it my way.

21 Then Isaac said to Jacob his son, Come near me, that I may feel you, my son, to know whether you are my son Esau or not.

22 And Jacob drew near to Isaac his father; and he felt him, and said, The voice is Jacob's voice, but the hands are Esau's.

23 But he did not recognize him, because his hands were hairy, like his brother Esau's hands; so he blessed him.

24 And he said, Are you my very son Esau? And Jacob said, I am.

25 And he said, Bring the stew near to me, and I will eat of my son's game, that my soul may bless you. And he brought it near to him, and he did eat; and he brought him wine, and he drank.

26 And his father Isaac said to him, Come near now, and kiss me, my son; so he drew near and kissed him;

27 And he came near, and kissed him; and he smelled the smell of his garments, and blessed him, and said, See, the smell of my son is like the smell of a field which the LORD has blessed;

28 Therefore may God give you of the dew of heaven and the richness of the earth, and the abundance of wheat and wine;

29 Let people serve you, and na-tions bow down to you; be a prince over your brethren, and let your mother's sons bow down to you; cursed be they who curse you, and blessed be they who bless you.

30 ¶And it came to pass when Isaac had finished blessing Jacob and Jacob had gone out from the presence of Isaac his father, behold, Esau his brother came in from his hunting.

31 And he also made stew, and brought it to his father, and said to his father, Let my father arise, and eat of his son's game, that your soul may bless me.

32 And Isaac his father said to him, Who are you? And he said, I am your son, your first-born, Esau.

33 And Isaac was greatly alarmed, and said, Who was it then that hunted game and brought it to me? I have eaten of everything before you came, and I have blessed him, yea, and he shall be blessed.

34 And when Esau heard the words of his father, he cried out bitterly, and said to his father, Bless me, even me also, O my father.

35 But his father said, Your brother came with deceit, and has already received your blessing.

36 And Esau said, Is he not rightly named Jacob? For he has acted treacherously toward me twice: he took away my birthright; and, behold, now he has taken away my blessing. And Esau said to his father, Have you not reserved a blessing for me?

37 And Isaac answered and said to Esau, Behold, I have made him a prince over you, and all his brethren have I given to him for servants; and with wheat and wine have I sustained him; and what shall I do now for you, my son?

38 And Esau said to his father, Have you only one blessing, my father? Bless me, even me also, O my father. And Esau lifted up his voice and wept.

39 And Isaac his father answered and said to him, Behold, your dwell-ing shall be in the fertile places of the earth, and the dew of heaven shall fall upon you from above;

40 And by your sword you shall

live, and you shall serve your brother; but if you shall repent, his yoke shall pass away from off your neck.

41 ¶And Esau hated Jacob because of the blessings with which his father had blessed him; and Esau said in his heart, After the days of mourning for my father are over, then I will slay my brother Jacob.

42 And the words of Esau her elder son were told to Rebekah; so she sent and called her younger son Jacob, and said to him, Behold, your brother Esau is threatening to kill you.

43 Now therefore, my son, hearken to me; and arise, and go to Laban my brother, to Haran;

44 And stay there a few days, until your brother's fury is spent;

45 Until your brother's anger turns away from you, and he forgets what you have done to him; then I will send messengers, and bring you back from there; lest I be deprived also of both of you in one day.

46 Then Rebekah said to Isaac, I am weary of my life because of the daughters of Heth; if Jacob takes a wife of the daughters of Heth, such as these which are of the daughters of the land, what good will my life be to me?

CHAPTER 28

THEN Isaac called Jacob, and blessed him, and charged him, and said to him, You shall not take a wife of the daughters of Canaan.

2 Arise, go to Padan-aram, to the house of Bethuel your mother's father; and take for yourself a wife from there of the daughters of Laban your mother's brother.

3 May God Almighty bless you and make you fruitful and multiply you, that you may become a multitude of peoples;

4 And give the blessings of Abraham to you and to your descendants with you, that you may inherit the land in which you dwell, which God gave to Abraham.

5 And Isaac sent away Jacob; and he went to Padan-aram, to Laban, the son of Bethuel, the Aramean, the brother of Rebekah, Jacob's and Esau's mother.

6 ¶When Esau saw that Isaac had blessed his brother Jacob and sent him away to Padan-aram to take for himself a wife from there, and that as he blessed him, he charged him, saying, You shall not take a wife of the daughters of Canaan;

7 And Jacob obeyed his father and his mother, and went to Padan-aram;

8 And Esau saw that Isaac his father despised the daughters of Canaan;

9 Then Esau went to Ishmael, Abraham's son, and took Bismath, the daughter of Ishmael, Abraham's son, the sister of Nebioth, to be his wife, in addition to his other wives.

10 ¶And Jacob went out from Beersheba, on his way to Haran.

11 And he arrived at a certain place, and spent the night there, because the sun was set; and he took of the stones of the place, and put them for his pillows, and lay down in that place to sleep.

12 And he dreamed, and behold a ladder was set upon the earth, and the top of it reached to heaven; and behold the angels of God were ascending and descending on it.

13 And, behold, the LORD stood above it and said, I am the LORD God of Abraham your father, and the God of Isaac; the land whereon you are lying, I will give to you and to your descendants;

14 And your descendants shall be as numerous as the dust of the earth, and you shall spread abroad to the east and to the west and to the north and to the south; and in you and through your descendants shall all the families of the earth be blessed.

15 And, behold, I am with you, and will keep you wherever you go, and will bring you back to this land; for I will not leave you until I have done the thing of which I have spoken to you.

16 ¶And Jacob awoke from his sleep, and he said, Surely the LORD is in this place; and I did not know it.

17 And Jacob was exceedingly fearful, and he said, How sacred is this place today! This is none other but

the house of God, and this is the gate of heaven.

18 And Jacob rose up early in the morning, and took the stone which he had put for his pillow, and set it up for a pillar, and poured oil on the top of it.

19 Then Jacob called the name of that place Beth-el (the house of God); but at the first the name of that place was called Luz.

20 And Jacob vowed a vow, saying, If God will be with me and will protect me in this way that I go, and will give me food to eat and clothing to wear

21 So that I may return to my father's house in peace, then the LORD shall be my God;

22 And this stone which I have set up for a pillar shall be God's house; and of all that thou shalt give me I will give the tenth to thee.

CHAPTER 29

THEN Jacob hastened on his journey, and came to the land of the people of the east.

2 And he looked, and beheld a well in the field, and, lo, there were three flocks of sheep lying by it; for out of that well they watered the flocks; and a large stone was upon the well's mouth.

3 And all the flocks were gathered there; and the shepherds rolled the stone from the well's mouth, and watered the sheep, and then put the stone back in its place upon the well's mouth.

4 And Jacob said to them, My brethren, where do you come from? And they said, We are from Haran.

5 And he said to them, Do you know Laban the son of Nahor? And they said, We do know him.

6 And he said to them, Is he well? And they said, He is well; and, behold, Rachel his daughter is coming with the sheep.

7 And Jacob said, Lo, the sun is still high, it is not yet time that the cattle should be gathered together; water the sheep, and go and feed them.

8 And they said, We cannot until all the flocks are gathered together and the shepherds roll the stone from the well's mouth; then we water the sheep.

9 ¶And while he was still conversing with them, Rachel came with her father's sheep; for she was a shepherdess.

10 And it came to pass, when Jacob saw Rachel the daughter of Laban his mother's brother and the sheep of Laban his mother's brother, that Jacob drew near and rolled the stone from the well's mouth and watered the sheep of Laban his mother's brother.

11 And Jacob kissed Rachel, and lifted up his voice, and wept.

12 And Jacob told Rachel that he was her father's kinsman and that he was Rebekah's son; and she ran and told her father.

13 And it came to pass when Laban heard the tidings of Jacob his sister's son, he ran to meet him and embraced him and kissed him and brought him to his house. And Jacob related to Laban all these things.

14 And Laban said to him, Surely you are my bone and my flesh. And he stayed with him for a month.

15 ¶And Laban said to Jacob, Because you are my kinsman, should you therefore work for me for nothing? Tell me, what shall your wages be?

16 And Laban had two daughters: the name of the older was Leah, and the name of the younger Rachel.

17 And Leah had attractive eyes; but Rachel was beautiful and well favored.

18 And Jacob loved Rachel; and he said, I will serve you seven years for Rachel, your younger daughter.

19 And Laban said to him, It is better that I give her to you than that I should give her to another man; abide with me.

20 Thus Jacob served seven years for Rachel; and they seemed to him but a few days because he was in love with her.

21 ¶And Jacob said to Laban, Give me my wife, for my days are fulfilled, that I may go in unto her.

22 And so Laban gathered together all the men of the place and made a feast.

23 And it came to pass in the evening, he took Leah his daughter, and brought her to him; and Jacob went in unto her.

24 And Laban gave Zilpah his maid to his daughter Leah for a servant.

25 And it came to pass in the morning, behold, it was Leah; and Jacob said to Laban, What is this thing that you have done to me? Did not I serve with you for Rachel? Why then have you deceived me?

26 Then Laban said to Jacob, It is not so done in our country, to give the younger in marriage before the elder.

27 Finish the wedding feast [1] for this one, and then I will give you the other also for the service which you shall serve with me yet another seven years.

28 And Jacob did so, and finished her wedding feast; and Laban gave him his daughter Rachel to wife.

29 And Laban gave Bilhah his maid to Rachel his daughter to be her maid.

30 And he went in unto Rachel also, and he loved Rachel also more than Leah, and served with Laban another seven years.

31 ¶And when the LORD saw that Leah was hated, he opened her womb; but Rachel was barren.

32 And Leah conceived, and bore a son, and she called his name Reuben; for she said, Because the LORD has seen my affliction, now therefore my husband will love me.

33 And she conceived again, and bore a son; and said, Because the LORD has heard that I am hated, he has therefore given me this son also; so she called his name Simeon.

34 And she conceived again, and bore a son; and said, Now this time my husband will surely love me, because I have born him three sons; therefore she called his name Levi.

35 And she conceived again, and bore a son; and she said, This time I will praise the LORD; therefore she called his name Judah; and then she ceased bearing.

CHAPTER 30

AND when Rachel saw that she was not bearing children to Jacob, she envied her sister; and said to Jacob, Give me children, or else I die.

2 And Jacob's anger was kindled against Rachel; and he said to her, Am I in the place of God, that I have prevented you from having a child?

3 Then she said to him, Behold my maid Bilhah, go in unto her; and she shall bear upon my knees, that I may also be comforted by her.

4 And she gave him her maid Bilhah to wife; and Jacob went in unto her.

5 And Bilhah conceived, and bore Jacob a son.

6 And Rachel said, God has judged me, and has also heard my voice, and has given me a son; therefore she called his name Dan.

7 And Bilhah, Rachel's maid, conceived again, and bore Jacob a second son.

8 And Rachel said, I have besought the LORD, and pleaded with my sister, and I have attained my desire; and she called his name Naphtali.

9 When Leah saw that she had ceased bearing children, she took her maid Zilpah, and gave her to Jacob to wife.

10 And Zilpah, Leah's maid, bore Jacob a son.

11 And Leah said, My fortune has come; so she called his name Gad.

12 And Zilpah, Leah's maid, bore Jacob a second son.

13 And Leah said, The girls will sing my praise, so she called his name Asher.

14 ¶And Reuben went at the time of the wheat harvest and found mandrakes in the field and brought them to his mother Leah. Then Rachel said to Leah, Give me some of your son's mandrakes.

15 But Leah said to her, Is it not enough for you that you have taken

[1] Three days or seven days according to social standing.

away my husband? And would you take away my son's mandrakes also? And Rachel said, He may lie with you tonight for your son's mandrakes.

16 And when Jacob came home from the field in the evening, Leah went out to meet him, and said, You must come in unto me; for surely I have hired you with my son's mandrakes. And he lay with her that night.

17 And God hearkened to Leah, and she conceived, and bore Jacob the fifth son.

18 And Leah said, God has rewarded me, because I have given my maid to my husband; so she called his name Issachar.

19 And Leah conceived again, and bore Jacob the sixth son.

20 And Leah said, God has enriched me exceedingly; now my husband will surely have more affection for me, because I have borne him six sons; so she called his name Zebulun.

21 And afterwards she bore a daughter, and called her name Dinah.

22 ¶And God remembered Rachel, and God hearkened to her and opened her womb.

23 And she conceived, and bore a son; and said, God has taken away my reproach;

24 And she called his name Joseph; and said, The LORD shall add to me another son.

25 ¶And it came to pass, when Rachel had borne Joseph, that Jacob said to Laban, Send me away, that I may go to my own place, and to my land.

26 Give me my wives and my children, for whom I have served you, and let me go; for you know the service which I have rendered you.

27 And Laban said to Jacob, If I have found favor in your eyes, I have proven by experience that the LORD has blessed me for your sake.

28 Then he said, Specify your wages, and I will give them.

29 And Jacob said to him, You yourself know the service which I have given you, and how your cattle have prospered with me.

30 For it was little which you had before I came, and now it has increased abundantly; and the LORD has blessed you for my sake; and now what shall I do in order to provide for my own household also?

31 And Laban said, What shall I give you? And Jacob said, You shall not give me anything; if you will do for me the thing which I will tell you, I will go back to feed and keep your flock.

32 I will pass through all your flock today, and select for myself from it every speckled and spotted lamb, and every brown lamb, and the spotted and speckled among the goats; and of such shall be my wages.

33 Just as my innocence is evident today, so it will be in the future when my wages are brought before your presence; every one that is not speckled and spotted among the goats and brown among the white sheep, that shall be counted stolen by me.

34 Laban said to him, Yes, let it be according to your word.

35 And he removed that day the he goats that were speckled and spotted, and all the she goats that were speckled and spotted, and every one that had some white on it, and all the brown among the white sheep, and entrusted them to his sons.

36 And he set three days journey between himself and Jacob; and Jacob fed the rest of Laban's flocks.

37 ¶And Jacob took some fresh white rods of almond and poplar trees; and peeled white streaks in them, and made the white appear which was in the rods.

38 And he set the rods which he had peeled before the flocks in the running water, in the watering troughs where the flocks came to drink; and they conceived when they came to drink.

39 And the flocks conceived before the rods, and brought forth lambs that were speckled and spotted.

40 And Jacob separated the lambs, and set the faces of the flocks toward the speckled and spotted, and all the brown in the flock of Laban; and he put his own flocks by themselves, and

did not mix them with Laban's flock.

41 And it came to pass, whenever the stronger of the flock did conceive, Jacob laid the rods in front of the sheep in the troughs, that they might conceive by the means of the rods.

42 But when the sheep were feeble, he did not put the rods in; so the feebler were Laban's and the stronger Jacob's.

43 And the man grew exceedingly rich, and had large flocks, menservants, maidservants, and she asses, camels, and he asses.

CHAPTER 31

AND Jacob heard the words of Laban's sons, saying, Jacob has taken away all that was our father's; and of that which was our father's has he acquired all of this wealth.

2 And Jacob saw that Laban's countenance toward him was not as it had been yesterday and the day before.

3 And the LORD said to Jacob, Return to the land of your fathers, and to your kindred; and I will be with you.

4 So Jacob sent and called Rachel and Leah to the field to his flock,

5 And said to them, I see that your father's countenance toward me is not as it has been yesterday and the day before; but the God of my father has been with me.

6 And you know that I have worked for your father with all my strength.

7 And yet your father has deceived me, and changed my wages ten times; but God has not permitted him to hurt me.

8 If he said thus, The speckled shall be your wages, then all the flock bore speckled; and if he said thus, The spotted shall be your wages; then all the flock bore spotted.

9 Thus God has selected some of your father's cattle, and given them to me.

10 And it came to pass at the time when the sheep conceive, I lifted up my eyes and saw in a dream, and, behold, the rams that leaped upon the sheep were speckled, spotted, and striped.

11 And the angel of God said to me in a dream, Jacob; and I said, Here am I.

12 Then he said, Lift up now your eyes, and see; all the rams that leap upon the sheep are speckled, spotted, and ringstreaked; for I have seen all that Laban has done to you.

13 I am the God of Beth-el, the place where you anointed a pillar to me, and where you vowed a vow to me; now arise, get out from this land, and return to the land of your kindred.

14 And Rachel and Leah answered and said to him, We have no portion or inheritance in our father's house.

15 Behold, we are counted by him as strangers, for he has sold us, and has squandered also our money.

16 For all the riches which God has selected from our father belong to us and our children; now then, whatever God has said to you, do it.

17 ¶Then Jacob rose up and set his sons and his wives on camels;

18 And he carried away all his cattle and all his wealth which he had gained in Padan-aram, to go to Isaac his father in the land of Canaan.

19 Now Laban went to shear his sheep; and Rachel stole the images that belonged to her father.

20 And Jacob deceived Laban, the Aramean, in that he did not tell him that he was going.

21 So he fled with all that he had; and he rose up, and crossed the river, and set his face toward mount Gilead.

22 And it was told Laban on the third day that Jacob had fled.

23 And he took his brethren with him, and pursued after him seven days journey; and they overtook him on mount Gilead.

24 And God came to Laban, the Aramean, in a dream by night, and said to him, Take heed that you speak not to Jacob either good or bad.

25 ¶Then Laban overtook Jacob. Now Jacob had pitched his tent on the mount; and Laban with his brethren encamped on mount Gilead.

26 And Laban said to Jacob, What have I done to you, that you have deceived me and carried away my

daughters as though they were captives taken with the sword?

27 Why did you flee secretly, and deceive me; and did not tell me, for I would have sent you away with joy and songs, and with harp and tambourine?

28 And you did not permit me to give a farewell kiss to my sons and my daughters? Now you have done foolishly in so doing.

29 I could have done you harm, but the God of your fathers said to me last evening, Take heed that you speak not to Jacob either good or bad.

30 And now you are on your way, because you longed for your father's house; yet why did you steal my gods?

31 And Jacob answered and said to Laban, Because I was afraid; for I said, Perhaps you would take your daughters from me by force.

32 With whomsoever you find your gods, he shall not live; moreover, in the presence of our brethren point out whatever I have that belongs to you, and take it for yourself. For Jacob did not know that Rachel had stolen them.

33 And Laban went into Jacob's tent and into Leah's tent and into the tent of the two maidservants; but he did not find the gods. So he went out of Leah's tent into Rachel's tent.

34 Now Rachel had taken the images, and put them in the camel's saddle bag, and sat upon them. And Laban had searched all the tent, but did not find them.

35 And Rachel said to her father, Let it not displease my lord that I cannot rise up before you; for I am with child. Nevertheless he searched, but did not find the images.

36 And Jacob was displeased, and argued with Laban; and Jacob answered and said to Laban, What is my trespass? and what is my fault, that you have hotly pursued after me?

37 Behold you have searched all my baggage, and what have you found of all your household articles? Put it here before my brethren and your brethren, that they may judge between us both.

38 Behold, I have been with you for the past twenty years; your ewes and your she goats have not cast their young, and I have not eaten of the rams of your flock.

39 That which was torn by wild beasts I never brought to you; I bore the loss of it; of my hand you did require it; likewise that which was stolen by the day or by the night.

40 Thus by day I was scorched by the heat, and at night suffered from cold; and my sleep departed from my eyes.

41 Behold, I have been twenty years in your house; I served you fourteen years for your two daughters, and six years for your flock; and you have changed my wages ten times.

42 And if it had not been for the God of my father, the God of Abraham, and your regard for Isaac, which have been on my side, surely you would have sent me away now empty. God saw my toil and the labor of my hands, and rebuked you last evening.

43 ¶Then Laban answered and said to Jacob, These daughters are my daughters, and these children are my children, and the flocks are my flocks, and all that you see is mine; and what can I do this day for these my daughters, or for their children whom they have borne?

44 Now therefore come then, let us make a covenant, I and you; and let it be for a witness between me and you.

45 So Jacob took a stone and set it up for a pillar.

46 And Jacob said to his brethren, Gather stones; and they took stones, and made a heap; and they did eat there upon the heap.

47 And Laban called it Jegar-sahadutha (the Pillar of Witness); but Jacob called it Galead (Gilead).

48 And Laban said, This heap is a witness between me and you this day. Therefore he called its name Galead.

49 And a watchtower; for he said, Let the LORD watch between me and you, because we are parting one from another.

50 If you despise my daughters, or

if you shall take other wives besides my daughters, now no man is with us; see, God only is witness between me and you.

51 And Laban said to Jacob, Behold this heap, and behold this pillar, which I have set between me and you;

52 This heap is a witness, and this pillar is a witness, that I will not pass over this pillar against you, and that you also shall not pass over this pillar against me or this heap for harm.

53 The God of Abraham and the God of Nahor and the God of our forefathers judge between us. And Jacob swore by the reverence of his father Isaac.

54 Then Jacob offered a sacrifice on the mountain, and invited his brethren to eat bread; and they did eat food, and spent the night on the mountain.

55 And early in the morning Laban rose up and kissed his grandsons and his daughters, and blessed them; then Laban returned and went to his country.

CHAPTER 32

AND Jacob also went on his journey, and the angels of God met him.

2 And when Jacob saw them, he said, This is God's host; so he called the name of that place Mahanaim.

3 And Jacob sent messengers before him to Esau his brother to the land of Seir, the country of Edom.

4 And he commanded them, saying, Thus shall you speak to my lord Esau; Thus says your servant Jacob, I have sojourned with Laban, and stayed there until now;

5 I have oxen, asses, flocks, menservants, and maidservants; and I have sent to tell my lord, that I may find mercy in your sight.

6 ¶And the messengers returned to Jacob, saying, We came to your brother Esau, and behold he also is coming to meet you, and four hundred men with him.

7 Then Jacob was afraid and greatly distressed; and he divided the people that were with him, and the flocks and herds and camels, into two groups;

8 And Jacob said, If my brother Esau should come against one group and destroy it, then the group which is left shall escape.

9 ¶And Jacob prayed, and said, O God of my father Abraham, and God of my father Isaac, the LORD who didst say to me, Return to the land of your fathers and to your kindred, and I will deal well with you;

10 I am not worthy of the least of all thy favors, and of all the truth that thou hast shown to thy servant; for alone with my staff I crossed over this Jordan; and now I have become two companies.

11 Deliver me, I pray thee, from the hands of my brother Esau; for I am afraid of him, lest he will come to smite me, and the mothers with their children.

12 And thou didst say, I will surely do you good, and make your descendants numerous as the sand of the sea which cannot be numbered for multitude.

13 ¶And he spent that night there; and took of that which he had with him as a present for his brother Esau;

14 Two hundred she goats, and twenty he goats, two hundred ewes, and twenty rams,

15 Thirty milch camels with their colts, forty cows, and ten bulls, twenty she asses, and ten foals.

16 And he entrusted them to his servants, every drove by itself; and said to his servants, Pass over before me, and keep a distance between drove and drove.

17 And he commanded the leader of the first drove, and said to him, When Esau my brother meets you, and asks you, saying, Who are you? and where are you going? and whose are these that are before you?

18 Then you shall say to him, They belong to your servant Jacob; they are a present which he has sent to my lord Esau; and, behold, also he is coming behind us.

19 And so he commanded the second and the third and all who followed with the droves, saying, In this

manner you shall speak to Esau, when you find him.

20 And you shall say to him, moreover, Behold, your servant Jacob also is behind us. For he said, I may appease him with the present that goes before me, and afterward I will see his face; and perhaps he will accept me.

21 So the present went over before him; and he himself lodged that night in the encampment.

22 And he rose up in the night, and took his two wives and his two maidservants and his eleven sons, and led them to the desert of Jabbok.

23 And he took them, and brought them over the brook, and then he brought across everything that he had.

24 ¶And Jacob was left alone; and there a man wrestled with him until daybreak.

25 And when the man saw that he did not prevail against him, he touched the hollow of his thigh; and the hollow of Jacob's thigh was out of joint, as he wrestled with him.

26 And the man said to him, Let me go, for day is breaking. And he said, I will not let you go unless you bless me.

27 And he said to him, What is your name? And he said, Jacob.

28 And he said to him, Your name shall no more be called Jacob, but Israel (the Prince of God); for you have proved your strength wrestling with an angel and with man, and have prevailed.

29 And Jacob asked him, and said, Tell me your name. And he said, Why is it that you ask my name? And the angel blessed him there.

30 And Jacob called the name of that place Peniel; for he said, I have seen an angel face to face, and my life is preserved.

31 The sun rose upon him just as he left Peniel, and he limped because of his thigh.

32 That is why the children of Israel do not eat of the sinew of the hip, which is on the hollow of the thigh, to this day; because the angel touched the hollow of Jacob's thigh on the sinew of the thigh.

CHAPTER 33

AND Jacob raised his eyes, and looked, and, behold, Esau was coming, and with him four hundred men. And he divided the children among Leah, Rachel, and the two maids.

2 Then he brought the maids and their children to the front, and Leah and her children next, and kept Rachel and Joseph in the rear.

3 And he himself went on before them, and bowed himself to the ground seven times, until he came near to his brother.

4 And Esau ran to meet him, and embraced him, and fell on his neck and kissed him; and they wept.

5 Then Esau raised his eyes and saw the women and the children, and said, Where did you get these? And Jacob said to him, They are the children whom God has graciously given your servant.

6 Then the maids drew near, they and their children, and they bowed themselves.

7 And Leah also with her children drew near, and bowed themselves; and afterwards came Rachel and Joseph who also drew near, and bowed themselves.

8 And Esau said to Jacob, Where did you get all this company which I met? And Jacob said to him, Because I have found favor in the sight of my lord.

9 Then Esau said to him, I have plenty, my brother; keep what you have to yourself.

10 But Jacob said to him, If now I have found mercy in your sight, then receive my present from my hands; because now I have seen your face, as I saw the face of an angel, and you were pleased with me.

11 Now accept my blessings that I have brought to you; because God has dealt graciously with me, and because I have enough. And Jacob urged him, and he did accept them.

12 Then Esau said to him, Let us depart, and go, and I will go before you.

13 But Jacob said, My lord knows

that the children are too young, and that the flocks and herds with young are with me; and if I should overdrive them one day, all the flock will die.

14 Let my lord pass before his servant, and I will travel slowly, according to the pace of the cattle which are before me and according to the pace of the children, until I come to my lord to Seir.

15 And Esau said to him, Let me leave with you some of the men that are with me. But Jacob said, What need have I for them? Let me find mercy in the sight of my lord.

16 ¶So Esau returned that day on his way to Seir.

17 And Jacob journeyed to Succoth, and built himself a house, and made sheepfolds for his cattle; therefore he called the name of the place Succoth.

18 ¶And Jacob came to Shalem, a city of Shechem, which is in the land of Canaan, when he came forth from Padan-aram; and encamped before the city.

19 And he bought a parcel of a field from the children of Hamor, father of Shechem, for a hundred ewes.

20 And he pitched his tent there, and erected an altar, and called it El-Alaha di Israel (God, the God of Israel).

CHAPTER 34

AND Dinah the daughter of Leah, whom she had borne to Jacob, went out to see the native girls.

2 And when Shechem the son of Hamor the Hivite, prince of the country, saw her, he took her and lay with her, and defiled her.

3 And his soul longed for Dinah the daughter of Jacob, and he loved the girl, and spoke kindly to the girl, and won her heart.

4 And Shechem spoke to his father Hamor, saying, Get me this girl to wife.

5 And Jacob heard that Dinah his daughter had been defiled; now his sons were with the cattle in the field; so Jacob held his peace until they came.

6 ¶And Hamor the father of Shechem went out to Jacob to speak with him.

7 And the sons of Jacob came from the field, and when they heard the news, they were grieved; and they were very indignant, because they had wrought folly in Israel in the disgracing of Jacob's daughter, which thing ought not to be done.

8 And Hamor spoke with them, saying, The soul of my son Shechem longs for your daughter; give her to him in marriage.

9 Intermarry with us, and give your daughters to us in marriage, and take our daughters to you,

10 And dwell with us; behold, the land is before you; dwell and trade in it and inherit in it.

11 And Shechem said to her father and to her brothers, Let me find mercy in your presence, and whatever you shall ask of me I will give.

12 Ask me as much as you wish, both dowry and gifts, and I will give you according as you shall say to me; but give me this girl to wife.

13 And the sons of Jacob answered Shechem and Hamor his father deceitfully, because they had defiled Dinah their sister,

14 And they said to them, We cannot do this thing, to give our sister to a man who is uncircumcised; for that would be a reproach to us;

15 But on this condition will we consent to you: that you will become like us, and circumcise every male as we are circumcised;

16 Then we will give our daughters to you in marriage, and take your daughters to us in marriage, and we will dwell with you, and we will become one people.

17 But if you will not hearken to us, to be circumcised, then we will take our daughter and we will be gone.

18 And their words pleased Hamor, and Shechem, Hamor's son.

19 And the young man did not delay to do the thing, because he was delighted with Jacob's daughter and he was honored above all the household of his father.

20 ¶Then Hamor and Shechem his son came to the gate of their town and spoke to the men of their town, saying,

21 These men are peaceable with us; therefore let them dwell in the land, and trade in it, for the land is large enough before them; let us take their daughters to us for wives, and let us give them our daughters.

22 But only on this condition will the men consent to dwell with us, to become one people, when every male among us is circumcised, as they are circumcised.

23 Behold, their wealth, their possessions, and all their cattle will eventually be ours; only let us consent to their proposals, and they will dwell with us.

24 And when all the adults of the town had heard from Shechem and from his father Hamor, they circumcised every male, those that went out of the gate [1] of his town.

25 ¶And it came to pass on the third day, when the men were sore, two sons of Jacob, Simeon and Levi, Dinah's brothers, took each man his sword, and came against the town quietly, and slew every male.

26 And they slew Hamor and Shechem his son with the edge of the sword, and took Dinah out of Shechem's house, and went out.

27 Then the sons of Jacob came back to the slain, and plundered the town, because they had defiled their sister.

28 They took their sheep and their oxen and their asses and whatever was in the town and in the field.

29 And all their wealth and all their little ones; and their wives they carried captive, and plundered everything that was in the town.

30 Then Jacob said to Simeon and Levi, You have done me a great harm, for you have hurt my reputation among the inhabitants of the land, among the Canaanites and the Perizzites; and I being few in numbers, they may gather themselves together against me, and attack me;

I shall be destroyed, both I and my household.

31 But they said, Our sister has been treated like a harlot.

CHAPTER 35

AND God said to Jacob, Arise, go up to Beth-el, and dwell there; and build there an altar to God, who appeared to you when you fled from the presence of your brother Esau.

2 Then Jacob said to his household and to all who were with him, Put away the strange gods that are among you, and cleanse yourselves, and change your garments;

3 And let us arise and go up to Beth-el; and I will build there an altar to God, who answered me in the day of my distress, and was with me in the journey that I took.

4 So they gave to Jacob all the strange gods that were in their possession, and the earrings that were in their ears; and Jacob buried them under the oak which was by Shechem.

5 And they journeyed; and the fear of God fell upon the towns that were round about them, and they did not pursue after Jacob and his sons.

6 ¶So Jacob came to Luz, that is Beth-el, which is in the land of Canaan, he and all the people that were with him.

7 And he built there an altar, and called the place Beth-el (the house of God), because there God appeared to him when he fled from the presence of his brother Esau.

8 Then Deborah Rebekah's nurse died, and she was buried below Beth-el under an oak; so the name of the oak was called Betemtha dabkhatha (the oak of weeping).

9 ¶And God appeared to Jacob again, when he came from Padan-aram, and blessed him.

10 And God said to him, Your name shall no longer be called Jacob, but Israel shall be your name; so he called his name Israel.

11 And God said to him, I am God Almighty; be fruitful and multiply; a people and a multitude of peoples

[1] *went out of the gate* is an idiom which means *grown up*

5

shall come from you, and kings shall come out of your loins;

12 And the land which I gave to Abraham and Isaac, I will give to you, and to your descendants after you will I give the land.

13 And God went up from him in the place where he talked with him.

14 And Jacob set up a pillar in the place where he had talked with him, a pillar of stone, and he poured out a drink offering on it, and he poured oil on it.

15 And Jacob called the name of the place where God spoke with him, Beth-el.

16 ¶And they journeyed from Beth-el, and continued until they came within the distance of a mile from the entrance to Ephrath; and Rachel travailed, and she had hard labor while she was being delivered.

17 And it came to pass, when she was in hard labor, the midwife said to her, Fear not; for this one also is a son for you.

18 And it came to pass, as her soul was departing and she was dying, she called the child's name Bar-kebai (the Son of My Sorrow); but his father called him Benjamin (the Son of My Right Hand).

19 And Rachel died, and was buried on the way to Ephrath, which is Beth-lehem.

20 And Jacob set up a pillar upon the grave of Rachel; that is the pillar of Rachel's grave to this day.

21 ¶And Israel journeyed, and pitched his tent beyond the tower of Gadar.

22 And it came to pass, when Israel dwelt in that land, that Reuben went and lay with Bilhah, his father's concubine; and Israel heard of it. Now the sons of Jacob were twelve:

23 The sons of Leah: Reuben, Jacob's first-born, Simeon, Levi, Judah, Issachar, and Zebulun.

24 And the sons of Rachel: Joseph, and Benjamin.

25 And the sons of Bilhah, Rachel's maid: Dan, and Naphtali.

26 And the sons of Zilpah, Leah's maid: Gad, and Asher. These are the sons of Jacob that were born to him in Padan-aram.

27 ¶And Jacob came to his father Isaac to Mamre, to Koriath Gabarey, which is Hebron, where Abraham and Isaac had sojourned.

28 And the days of Isaac were a hundred and eighty years.

29 Then Isaac grew weak and died; and he was gathered to his people, being very old and full of days; and his sons Esau and Jacob buried him in the burial ground which his father Abraham had purchased.

CHAPTER 36

NOW these are the generations of Esau, who is Edom.

2 Esau took his wives from among the daughters of Canaan: Adah the daughter of Elon the Hittite, Aholibamah the daughter of Anah, the son of Zibeon the Hivite;

3 And Bismath, Ishmael's daughter, sister of Nebioth.

4 And Adah bore to Esau Eliphaz; and Bismath bore Reuel;

5 And Aholibamah bore Jeush, Jaalan, and Korah; these are the sons of Esau that were born to him in the land of Canaan.

6 And Esau took his wives, his sons, his daughters, and all the persons of his household, and all his cattle, and all the wealth which he had acquired in the land of Canaan; and went to the land of Seir from the presence of his brother Jacob.

7 For their wealth was too great for them to dwell together; and the land in which they sojourned could not sustain them because of their cattle.

8 Thus Esau dwelt in mount Seir; Esau is Edom.

9 ¶And these are the generations of Esau the father of the Edomites in mount Seir;

10 These are the names of Esau's sons: Eliphaz the son of Adah the wife of Esau, Reuel the son of Bismath the wife of Esau.

11 And the sons of Eliphaz were Teman, Omar, Zepho, Gatham, and Kenaz.

12 And Timna was a concubine of

Eliphaz, Esau's son; and she bore to Eliphaz Amalek. These were the sons of Adah, Esau's wife.

13 And these are the sons of Reuel: Nahath, Zerah, Shammah, and Mizzah; these were the sons of Bismath, Esau's wife.

14 ¶These are the sons of Aholibamah, the daughter of Anah the son of Zibeon, Esau's wife; and she bore to Esau Jeush, Jaalan, and Korah.

15 ¶These are the chiefs of the sons of Esau, the sons of Eliphaz the firstborn of Esau: chief Teman, chief Omar, chief Zepho, chief Kenaz,

16 Chief Gatham, chief Korah, and chief Amalek; these are the chiefs that came of Eliphaz in the land of Edom; these were the sons of Adah.

17 ¶And these are the sons of Reuel, Esau's son: chief Nahath, chief Zerah, chief Shammah, and chief Mizzah; these are the chiefs that came of Reuel in the land of Edom; these are the sons of Bismath, Esau's wife.

18 ¶These are the sons of Aholibamah, Esau's wife: chief Jeush, chief Jaalan, and chief Korah; these were the sons of Aholibamah, the daughter of Anah, Esau's wife.

19 These are the sons of Esau, who is Edom, and these are their chiefs.

20 ¶These are the sons of Seir the Horite, the inhabitants of the land: Lotan, Shobal, Zibeon, Anah,

21 Dishon, Ezer, and Dishan; these are the chiefs of the Horites, the children of Seir in the land of Edom.

22 And the sons of Lotan were Hori and Heman; and Lotan's sister was Timna.

23 These are the sons of Shobal: Alvan, Manahath, Ebal, Shapar, and Oiam.

24 And these are the sons of Zibeon: Ana and Anah; he is the Anah who discovered water in the desert while he was feeding the asses of Zibeon his father.

25 These are the children of Anah: Dishon and Aholibamah, the daughter of Anah.

26 These are the sons of Dishon: Hemran, Eshban, Ithran, and Cheran.

27 These are the sons of Ezer: Bilhan, Zaavan, and Akan.

28 These are the sons of Dishan: Uz and Aran.

29 These are the chiefs of the Horites: chief Lotan, chief Shobal, chief Zibeon, chief Anah,

30 Chief Dishon, chief Ezer, and chief Dishan; these are the chiefs of the Horites, according to their chiefs in the land of Seir.

31 ¶And these are the kings who reigned in the land of Edom, before there reigned any king over the children of Israel:

32 Bela, the son of Beor, reigned in Edom; and the name of his city was Dihab.

33 And Bela died, and Jobab the son of Zerah of Bozrah. reigned in his stead.

34 And Jobab died, and Husham of the land of Teman reigned in his stead.

35 And Husham died, and Hadad, the son of Bedad, who smote the Midianites in the fields of Moab, reigned in his stead; and the name of his city was Gevith.

36 And Hadad died, and Samlah of Masrekah reigned in his stead.

37 And Samlah died, and Saul of Rehoboth by the river reigned in his stead.

38 And Saul died, and Baal-hanan, the son of Abcor, reigned in his stead.

39 And Baal-hanan, the son of Abcor died, and Hadad reigned in his stead; and the name of his city was Pau; and his wife's name was Mehetabel, the daughter of Matred, the daughter of Mezahab.

40 And these are the names of the chiefs of Esau, according to their families, and according to their generations, by their names: chief Timnah, chief Anvah, chief Jetheth,

41 Chief Aholibamah, chief Elah, chief Pinon,

42 Chief Kenaz, chief Teman, chief Mibzar,

43 Chief Magdiel, chief Giram; these are the chiefs of the Edomites, according to their habitations in the land of their possession; Edom is Esau the father of the Edomites.

CHAPTER 37

AND Jacob dwelt in the land where-in his father was a sojourner, in the land of Canaan.

2 These are the generations of Jacob. Joseph, being seventeen years old, was feeding the flock with his brothers; and the lad was reared with the sons of Zilpah, and with the sons of Bilhah, his father's wives; and Joseph brought an evil report of them to their father.

3 Now Israel loved Joseph more than all his other sons, because he was the son of his old age; and he had made him a rich robe with long sleeves.

4 And when his brothers saw that their father loved him more than all his brothers, they hated him, and could not speak peaceably to him.

5 ¶And Joseph dreamed a dream, and he told it to his brothers; and they hated him yet the more.

6 And he said to them, Listen to this dream which I have dreamed:

7 Behold, we were binding sheaves in the field, and, lo, my sheaf arose and stood upright; and, behold, your sheaves stood round about and bowed down to my sheaf.

8 And his brothers said to him, Are you indeed going to reign over us? Or are you going to have dominion over us? And they hated him yet the more for his dreams, and for his words.

9 ¶And he dreamed another dream, and told it to his brothers, and said, Behold, I have dreamed another dream; and, behold, the sun and the moon and the eleven stars bowed down to me.

10 And when he told it to his father and to his brothers, his father rebuked him, and said to him, What is this dream that you have dreamed? Shall I and your mother and your brothers indeed come to bow down ourselves to the ground to you?

11 And his brothers envied him; but his father observed the sayings.

12 ¶And Joseph's brothers went to feed their father's flock in Shechem.

13 And Israel said to Joseph, Be-hold, your brothers are feeding the flocks in Shechem; come, I will send you to them. And he said to him, Here am I.

14 Then his father said to him, Go, see whether it is well with your brothers and well with the flocks; and bring me word again. So Jacob sent him from the valley of Hebron, and he came to Shechem.

15 And a certain man found him while he was wandering in the field; and the man asked him, and said to him, What are you seeking?

16 And he said, I am seeking my brothers; do tell me where they are feeding their flocks.

17 And the man said, They have departed from here; for I heard them say, Let us go to Dothan. So Joseph went after his brothers, and found them in Dothan.

18 And they saw him from afar, and before he came near to them, they conspired against him to kill him.

19 And they said to one another, Behold, here comes the dreamer.

20 Come now therefore, and let us slay him, and throw him into one of the pits; and then we will say that a wild beast has devoured him, and we shall see what will become of his dreams.

21 And Reuben heard it, and he delivered him out of their hands; and he said to them, Let us not kill him.

22 And Reuben said to them, Shed no blood; throw him into this pit that is in the wilderness, but do not harm him; that he might deliver him from their hands, and bring him back to his father.

23 ¶And it came to pass, when Joseph was come to his brothers, they stripped him of the rich robe that he was wearing;

24 And they took him, and threw him into a pit; and the pit was empty, there was no water in it.

25 And they sat down to eat bread; and they lifted up their eyes and looked, and, and, behold, a caravan of Arabians coming from Gilead, with their camels bearing gum, balm and myrrh, and they were on their way to carry it down to Egypt.

26 And Judah said to his brothers, What profit is it if we slay our brother, and conceal his blood?

27 Come, let us sell him to the Arabians, and let us not harm him; for he is our brother and our flesh. And his brothers listened to him.

28 Then some Midianite merchants passed by; and they drew and lifted up Joseph out of the pit, and sold Joseph to the Arabians for twenty pieces of silver; and they brought him into Egypt.

29 ¶And then Reuben returned to the pit, and, behold, Joseph was not in the pit; and he tore his clothes.

30 And he returned to his brothers, and said to them, Where is the boy; and as for me, where shall I go?

31 And they took Joseph's robe, and killed a kid of the goats, and dipped the robe in the blood;

32 And they sent the robe with long sleeves, and they brought it to their father; and said, This we have found: know now whether it be your son's coat or not.

33 And he recognized it, and said, It is my son's coat; a wild beast has devoured him; my son Joseph is surely torn to pieces.

34 Then Jacob tore his clothes, and put sackcloth upon his loins, and mourned for his son many days.

35 And all his sons and all his daughters made an effort to comfort him; but he refused to be comforted; and he said, I will go down to Sheol to my son mourning. Thus his father wept for him.

36 And the Midianites sold Joseph in Egypt to Potiphar, one of Pharaoh's officers, the commander of the guard.

CHAPTER 38

AND it came to pass at that time that Judah went down from his brothers, and turned in to a certain Arlemite, whose name was Hirah.

2 And Judah saw there the daughter of a certain Canaanite, whose name was Shuah; and he took her, and went in unto her.

3 And she conceived, and bore a son; and he called his name Er.

4 And she conceived again, and bore a son; and he called his name Onan.

5 And she conceived again, and bore a son; and he called his name Shelah; and after she bore him she stopped bearing.

6 And Judah took a wife for Er, his first-born, whose name was Tamar.

7 And Er, Judah's first-born, was wicked in the sight of the LORD; and the LORD slew him.

8 And Judah said to Onan, Go in to your brother's wife, and perform the duty of a brother-in-law to her, and raise up an offspring to your brother.

9 And Onan knew that the offspring would not be his; and it came to pass when he went in unto his brother's wife that he spilled the semen on the ground, lest that he should raise an offspring to his brother.

10 And the thing which he did was displeasing in the sight of the LORD; wherefore he slew him also.

11 Then said Judah to Tamar, his daughter-in-law, Remain a widow in your father's house, until my son Shelah grows up; for he said, Lest he die also, as his brothers did. And Tamar went and dwelt in her father's house.

12 ¶And in the course of time Shuah's daughter, the wife of Judah, died; and Judah was comforted, and went up to his sheepshearers to Timnath, he and his friend Hirah the Arlemite.

13 And it was told Tamar, saying, Behold your father-in-law is going up to Timnath to shear his sheep.

14 And she put off her widow's dress, and adorned herself, and covered her face with a veil, and sat down at the parting of the road to Timnath; for she saw that Shelah was grown up, and she was not given to him to wife.

15 When Judah saw her, he thought her to be a harlot; because she had covered her face.

16 And he turned to her by the way and said to her, Come, let me come in unto you (for he did not know

that she was his daughter-in-law). And she said, What will you give me that you may come in unto me?

17 And he said, I will send you a kid from the flock. And she said, Will you give me a pledge until you send it?

18 And he said, What kind of a pledge shall I give you? And she said, Your ring and your robe and the staff that is in your hand. So he gave them to her, and then went in unto her, and she conceived by him.

19 And she arose and went away and took off her veil from her and put on the garments of her widowhood.

20 And Judah sent the kid by the hand of his friend the Arlemite, to receive the pledge from the woman's hand; but he could not find her.

21 Then he asked the men of the place, saying, Where is the harlot who sat at the parting of the road? And they said, There is no harlot here.

22 And he returned to Judah, and said, I cannot find her; and also the men of the place said, No harlot has been here.

23 And Judah said, Let her keep the pledge, lest I be laughed at; behold, I sent this kid, but you could not find her.

24 ¶And it came to pass, about three months later, that it was told Judah, saying, Tamar, your daughter-in-law, has played the harlot; and moreover, she is with child because of her harlotry. And Judah said, Bring her out, and let her be burned.

25 When they brought her out, she sent to her father-in-law, saying, By the man to whom these articles belong, I am with child; and she said, Determine whose they are, the ring, the robe, and the staff.

26 And Judah recognized them, and said, She is more righteous than I; because I did not give her in marriage to Shelah my son. And he knew her again no more.

27 ¶And it came to pass in the time of her travail that, behold, there were twins in her womb.

28 And it came to pass, when she travailed, that one of the babes put out his hand; and the midwife took and bound upon his hand a scarlet thread, saying, This came out first.

29 And it came to pass, as he drew back his hand, behold, his brother came out; and she said, What a breach has been made for you! Therefore his name was called Pharez.

30 And afterward came out his brother, who had the scarlet thread on his hand; and she called his name Zarah.

CHAPTER 39

AND Joseph was brought down to Egypt; and Potiphar, an officer of Pharaoh, commander of the guard, an Egyptian, bought him from the Arabians who had brought him down there.

2 And the LORD was with Joseph, and he became a prosperous man in the house of his master, the Egyptian.

3 And his master saw that the LORD was with him, and that the LORD made all that he did to prosper under his hands.

4 And Joseph found favor in his sight, and served him; and he made him steward of his house, and all that he had he put in his charge.

5 And it came to pass from the time that he had made him steward of his house, and over all that he had, that the LORD blessed the Egyptian's house for Joseph's sake; and the blessing of the LORD was upon all that he had both in the house and in the field.

6 And he left all that he had in Joseph's charge; and he did not know what he had, except the food that he ate. And Joseph was very handsome and pleasant to look at.

7 ¶And it came to pass after these things that his master's wife cast her eyes upon Joseph; and she said to him, Lie with me.

8 But he refused, and said to his master's wife, Behold, my master does not know what he has in the house, and he has put everything that he has in my charge;

9 There is no one greater in this house than I; neither has he kept back

anything from me except yourself, because you are his wife; how then can I do this great wickedness, and sin against God?

10 And it came to pass, as she spoke to him daily, he did not listen to her, to lie with her, or to be with her.

11 And it came to pass one day that Joseph went in to the house to do his work; and none of the men of the household were there in the house.

12 And she caught him by his garment, and said to him, Lie with me; but he left the garment in her hands, and fled, and got out to the street.

13 And it came to pass, when she saw that he had left his garment in her hands, and had fled out to the street,

14 She called to the men of her household, and said to them, See, he has brought in a Hebrew servant to us to disgrace us; he came in to me to lie with me, and I cried out with a loud voice;

15 And when he heard that I lifted up my voice and cried aloud, he left his garment in my hands, and fled, and got out to the street.

16 And she laid up his garment by her, until his master came home.

17 And she spoke to him according to these words, saying, The Hebrew servant whom you brought to us, came in to disgrace me;

18 But as I lifted up my voice and cried aloud, he left his garment in my hands, and fled, and got out to the street.

19 And when the master heard the words of his wife, which she spoke to him, saying, After this manner did your servant to me; his wrath was kindled.

20 And Joseph's master took him, and put him into the prison, a place where the king's prisoners were confined; and he remained there in the prison.

21 ¶But the LORD was with Joseph, and showed him mercy, and gave him favor in the sight of the keeper of the prison.

22 And the keeper of the prison intrusted to Joseph's care all the prisoners who were in the prison; and he was in charge of whatever they did there.

23 The keeper of the prison did not look to anything that was in Joseph's charge, because the LORD was with him, and whatever he did, the LORD made it to prosper.

CHAPTER 40

AND it came to pass after these things that the chief butler of the king of Egypt and the chief baker had offended their lord the king of Egypt.

2 And Pharaoh was wroth against two of his officers, against the chief of the butlers, and against the chief of the bakers.

3 And he put them into the prison in the house of the commander of the guard, in the ward where Joseph was bound.

4 And the commander of the guard charged Joseph with them, and he served them; and they remained for some time in the prison.

5 ¶And they both dreamed, each man his own dream in the same night, each man according to the interpretation of his dream, the butler and the baker of the king of Egypt, who were bound in the prison.

6 And Joseph came in to them in the morning, and saw them, and behold, they were sad.

7 So he asked Pharaoh's officers who were with him in the prison of his master's house, saying, Why do you look so sad today?

8 And they said to him, We have dreamed a dream, and there is no one to interpret it. And Joseph said to them, Behold, the interpretations belong to God; tell them to me.

9 Then the chief butler told his dream to Joseph, and said to him, In my dream, behold, a vine was before me;

10 And in the vine were three branches; and when it budded, its blossoms shot forth; and the clusters thereof brought forth ripe grapes;

11 And Pharaoh's cup was in my hand; and I took the grapes, and pressed them into Pharaoh's cup, and I gave the cup into Pharaoh's hands.

12 And Joseph said to him, This is the interpretation of your dream: The three branches are three days;

13 After three days Pharaoh shall remember you and restore you to your position; and you shall give Pharaoh's cup into his hand, as you did before when you were his butler.

14 But remember me when it shall be well with you, and do me a favor and justice, and make mention of me in the presence of Pharaoh, and bring me out of this prison house;

15 For indeed I was stolen away out of the land of the Hebrews; and here also I have done nothing that they should put me into the prison.

16 When the chief baker saw that the interpretation was good, he said to Joseph, I also saw in my dream, and, behold, I had three baskets containing white bread on my head;

17 And in the uppermost basket there was of every kind of food for Pharaoh, prepared by a baker; and the birds of prey were eating it out of the basket on my head.

18 And Joseph answered and said to him, This is the interpretation of your dream: The three baskets are three days;

19 After three days Pharaoh shall have you beheaded, and then shall crucify you on a tree, and the birds of prey shall eat your flesh from off you.

20 ¶And it came to pass on the third day, which was Pharaoh's birthday, that he made a banquet for all his servants; and he remembered the chief butler and the chief baker among his servants.

21 And he restored the chief butler to his position; and he gave the cup into Pharaoh's hands:

22 But he crucified the chief baker, as Joseph had interpreted to them.

23 Yet the chief butler did not remember Joseph, but forgot him.

CHAPTER 41

AND it came to pass, two years later, Pharaoh dreamed; and he was standing by the river.

2 And, behold, there came up out of the river seven beautiful and fat cows; and they fed in a meadow.

3 And, behold, seven other cows came up after them out of the river, ill-favored and lean; and stood beside the other cows on the bank of the river.

4 And the ill-favored and lean cows ate up the seven beautiful and fat cows. So Pharaoh awoke.

5 And he slept and dreamed a second time; and, behold, seven ears of grain were growing on a single stalk, rank and good.

6 And, behold, seven thin ears blasted by the east wind, sprang up after them.

7 And the seven thin ears devoured the seven rank and full ears. And Pharaoh awoke, and, behold, it was a dream.

8 And it came to pass in the morning that his spirit was troubled; so he sent and called for all the magicians and all the wise men of Egypt; and Pharaoh told them his dreams; but there was no man who could interpret them to Pharaoh.

9 ¶Then the chief butler spoke in the presence of Pharaoh, and said, I will mention my offense today;

10 Pharaoh was angry with his servants, and put me in the prison in the commander of the guard's house, both me and the chief baker;

11 And we dreamed dreams in the same night, I and he; we dreamed each man according to the interpretation of his dream.

12 And there was with us a young man, a Hebrew, a servant of the commander of the guard; and we told him our dreams, and he interpreted to us our dreams; to each man according to his dream he did interpret.

13 And it came to pass, as he interpreted to us, so it was; I was restored to my position, and he was crucified.

14 ¶Then Pharaoh sent and called Joseph, and they brought him hastily out of the dungeon; and he shaved himself, and changed his clothes, and came in before Pharaoh.

15 And Pharaoh said to Joseph, I have dreamed a dream, and there is

none that can interpret it; and I have heard concerning you, that when you hear a dream you can interpret it.

16 And Joseph answered and said to Pharaoh, Do you think, perhaps, that without God I am able to give Pharaoh an answer that everything will be well?

17 Then Pharaoh said to Joseph, In my dream I was standing on the bank of the river;

18 And, behold, there came up out of the river seven fat and beautiful cows; and they fed in a meadow;

19 And, behold, seven other cows came up after them, poor and ill-favored and lean. I had never seen such ill-favored cows in all the land of Egypt.

20 And the lean and ill-favored cows ate up the first seven fat cows;

21 And when they had eaten them up, it could not be known that they had eaten them; for they were still ill-favored, as at the beginning. Then I awoke.

22 And again, I saw in my dream, and, behold, seven ears of grain growing on one stalk, full and good;

23 And, behold, seven other ears, thin and blasted by the east wind, sprang up after them;

24 And the thin ears devoured the seven good ears; and I told this to the magicians; but there was no one who could interpret these dreams to me.

25 ¶And Joseph said to Pharaoh, The dream of Pharaoh is one; God has shown Pharaoh what he is about to do.

26 The seven good cows are seven years; and the seven good ears are seven years; the dream is one.

27 And the seven lean and ill-favored cows that came up after them are seven years; and the seven thin ears blasted by the east wind shall be seven years of famine.

28 It is the thing which I told Pharaoh; what God is about to do he has shown to Pharaoh.

29 Behold, there are coming seven years of great plenty throughout all the land of Egypt;

30 And there shall arise after them seven years of famine; and all the plenty shall be forgotten in the land of Egypt; and the famine shall consume the land;

31 And the plenty shall not be remembered in the land because of the famine which shall follow; for it shall be very severe.

32 And as for that the dream was repeated to Pharaoh twice; it is because the thing is already prepared by God, and God will hasten to bring it to pass.

33 Now therefore let Pharaoh find a discreet and wise man, and appoint him an overseer over the land of Egypt.

34 Let Pharaoh do this, and let him appoint officers over the land of Egypt to take the fifth part of the produce of the land of Egypt during the seven plenteous years.

35 And let them gather all the wheat of these good years that are coming, and store up the grain under the authority of Pharaoh, and let them keep the grain in the towns.

36 And let the grain be kept for the land against the seven years of famine which shall come in the land of Egypt; so that the land may not perish through the famine.

37 ¶And the thing was good in the eyes of Pharaoh, and in the eyes of all his servants.

38 And Pharaoh said to his servants, Can we find such a man as this, in whom the Spirit of God is?

39 Then Pharaoh said to Joseph, Forasmuch as God has shown you all this, there is none so wise and discreet as you are;

40 You shall be over my household, and according to your word shall all my people be ruled; only on the throne will I be greater than you.

41 And Pharaoh said to Joseph, See, I have made you governor over all the land of Egypt.

42 Then Pharaoh took off his ring from his hand, and put it on Joseph's hand, and arrayed him in robes of fine linen, and put a gold chain about his neck;

43 And he made him to ride in another chariot which belonged to him;

and they cried before him, Father and governor! Thus he made him governor over all the land of Egypt.

44 And Pharaoh said to Joseph, I Pharaoh have commanded that without your orders no man shall undertake anything in all the land of Egypt.

45 Then Pharaoh called Joseph's name Zaphnath-paaneah (because the hidden things were revealed to him); and he gave him to wife Asiath the daughter of Potipherah priest of On. And Joseph went throughout all the land of Egypt.

46 ¶And Joseph was thirty years old when he stood before Pharaoh king of Egypt. And Joseph went out from the presence of Pharaoh, and went throughout all the land of Egypt.

47 And in the seven plenteous years the land brought forth abundantly.

48 And he gathered up all the grain of the seven plenteous years which were in the land of Egypt, and stored up the grain in towns; the grain of the fields which was round about every town he stored in the same.

49 And Joseph stored up grain as the sand of the sea, very much, until he was tired of numbering it; for it was without number.

50 And to Joseph were born two sons before the years of famine came, whom Asiath the daughter of Potipherah priest of On bore to him.

51 And Joseph called the name of his first-born Manasseh; For God, said he, has made me forget all my troubles, and all my father's house.

52 And the name of the second he called Ephraim; For God has made me to be fruitful in the land of my affliction.

53 ¶And the seven years of plenty that were in the land of Egypt came to an end.

54 And the seven years of famine began to come, according as Joseph had said; and there was famine in all lands; and in all the land of Egypt there was no bread.

55 And when all the land of Egypt was famished, the people complained against Pharaoh because of the lack of bread; and Pharaoh said to all the Egyptians, Go to Joseph; and what he says to you, do.

56 And the famine was over all the face of the land, and Joseph opened all the storehouses, and sold to the Egyptians;

57 And the famine was severe in the land of Egypt. And the people from all lands came to Egypt to Joseph to buy grain; because the famine was severe in all lands.

CHAPTER 42

NOW when Jacob saw that there was grain in Egypt, Jacob said to his sons, Fear not.

2 Behold, I have heard that there is grain in Egypt; go down there, and buy for us from there; that we may live, and not die.

3 ¶And so Joseph's ten brothers went down to buy grain in Egypt.

4 But Benjamin, Joseph's brother, Jacob did not send with his brothers; for he said, Lest some misfortune might befall him.

5 And the sons of Israel came to buy grain with those that came; for the famine was severe in the land of Canaan.

6 Now Joseph was the governor over the land, and he it was who sold the grain to all the people of the land; and Joseph's brothers came, and bowed down themselves before him with their faces to the ground.

7 And Joseph saw his brothers and recognized them, but he deceived them and spoke harshly to them; and he said to them, Where have you come from? And they said, We came from the land of Canaan to buy grain.

8 And Joseph recognized his brothers, but they did not recognize him.

9 Then Joseph remembered the dreams which he had dreamed about them, and said to them, You are spies; you have come to get a report about the land.

10 And they said to him, No, our lord, but to buy grain your servants have come.

11 We are all one man's sons; we are pious men; your servants are not spies.

12 And Joseph said to them, It is not so, but to get a report about the land you have come.

13 And they said to him, Your servants are twelve brothers, the sons of one man in the land of Canaan; and, behold, the youngest is this day with our father, and one is dead.

14 And Joseph said to them, It is just as I said to you, you are spies:

15 By this you shall be proved; by the life of Pharaoh you shall not go forth from this place, except your younger brother comes here.

16 Send one of you, and let him bring your brother, and you shall be bound in prison, so that your words may be proved, to see if your statements are true; and if they are not true, by the life of Pharaoh, surely you are spies.

17 And he put them all together in prison for three days.

18 And on the third day Joseph said to them, Do this, and live; for I worship God;

19 If you are pious men, let one of your brothers be bound in your prison; and the rest of you, go and carry grain for the famished who are in your household;

20 But bring your youngest brother to me; so shall your words be verified, and you shall not die. And they did so.

21 ¶And they said one to another, Truly we are guilty concerning our brother, for we saw the anguish of his soul when he pleaded with us, and we would not listen to him; therefore is this distress come upon us.

22 And Reuben answered and said to them, Did I not tell you, Do not sin against the boy; but you did not listen? So now his blood is required.

23 And they did not know that Joseph understood them; for he spoke to them by an interpreter.

24 And he turned aside from them and wept; and he returned to them again, and conversed with them, and took Simeon from them, and bound him before their eyes.

25 ¶Then Joseph commanded the servants to fill their sacks with wheat, and to restore every man's money into his sack, and to give them provisions for the journey; and they did so for them.

26 And they loaded their asses with their wheat, and departed thence.

27 And as one of them opened his sack to give his ass provender in the inn, he saw his money in the mouth of his sack.

28 And he said to his brothers, My money has been returned; and, lo, it is in the mouth of my sack; and their hearts failed them, and they were amazed, staring at one another, saying, What is this that God has done to us?

29 ¶And they came to Jacob their father to the land of Canaan, and told him all that had befallen them, saying,

30 The man who is the lord of the land spoke roughly to us, and took us for spies of the land.

31 But we said to him, We are pious men; we are not spies;

32 We are twelve brothers, sons of our father; and one is dead, and the youngest is this day with our father in the land of Canaan.

33 And the man, the lord of the land, said to us, By this shall I know that you are pious men; leave one of your brothers here with me, and take wheat for the famished who are in your households, and go your way;

34 And bring your youngest brother to me; then shall I know that you are not spies, but that you are pious men; so I will deliver your brother to you, and you shall trade in the land.

35 ¶And it came to pass as they emptied their sacks, behold, every man's bag of money was in his sack; and when both they and their father saw the bags of money, they were afraid.

36 And Jacob their father said to them, You have bereaved me of my children: Joseph is dead, and Simeon is missing, and now you will take Benjamin away; all these things are against me.

37 Then Reuben said to his father, Put to death my two sons if I do not bring him back to you; intrust him to me, and I will bring him back to you.

38 And he said, My son shall not go down with you; for his brother is dead, and he alone is left to his mother: if misfortune should befall him by the way in which you go, then you shall bring down my gray hairs with sorrow to Sheol.

CHAPTER 43

THE famine was very severe in the land.
2 And when they had finished eating the wheat which they had brought from Egypt, their father Jacob said to them, Go down to Egypt, and buy us a little grain.
3 And Judah said to him, The man did solemnly charge us, saying, You shall not see my face except your brother is with you.
4 If you will send our brother with us, we will go down and buy grain for ourselves;
5 But if you will not send him, we will not go down; for the man said to us, You shall not see my face except your brother is with you.
6 Then their father Israel said to them, Why did you cause me this displeasure, as to tell the man whether you had another brother?
7 And they said, The man asked us straitly about ourselves and our kindred, saying, Is your father still alive? Have you another brother? And we told him simply because of these words; could we have known in advance that he would say to us that we should bring our brother down?
8 And Judah said to Israel his father, Send the lad with us, and we will arise and go; that we may live, and not die, both we, and you, and also our little ones.
9 And I will be surety for him; of my hands shall you require him; if I do not bring him back to you, and set him before you, then I shall be guilty before my father forever;
10 For if we had not delayed, perhaps we would have now returned a second time.
11 And their father Israel said to them, If it must be so now, then do this: take some of the best fruits of the land in your sacks, and carry down the man a present, a little balm, and a little honey, gum, and myrrh, pistachio nuts, and almonds;
12 And take double money with you; and the money that was brought back in the mouth of your sacks, take it again with you; perhaps it was an oversight;
13 Take also your brother, and arise, and go again to the man;
14 And may God Almighty give you mercy before the man, that he may send away your other brother, and Benjamin with you. And as for me, if I am bereaved of my children, I am bereaved.
15 ¶So the men took the present, and they took double money with them, and Benjamin; and rose up and went down to Egypt and stood before Joseph.
16 And when Joseph saw Benjamin with them, he said to the steward of his house, Bring these men into the house, and kill a sheep, and make ready; for these men shall dine with me at noon.
17 And the servant did as Joseph had told him; and brought the men into Joseph's house.
18 And they were afraid, when they brought them into Joseph's house; and they said, It is because of the money that was returned in our sacks at the first time that we are brought in; so that he may seek occasion against us, and conspire against us, that they may make us slaves, and take away our asses.
19 So they came near to the steward of Joseph's house and spoke with him at the door of the house,
20 And said, We beseech you, O our lord, we truly came down at the first time to buy grain;
21 And it came to pass when we came to the inn that we opened our sacks, and, behold, every man's money was in the mouth of his sack, our money in full weight; and we have brought it back again with us.
22 And we have brought other money down with us to buy grain; we did not know who put our money in our sacks.
23 He said to them, Peace be to

you, fear not; your God, and the God of your father, has put a treasure in your sacks; I had your money. And he brought Simeon out to them.

24 Then the servant brought the men into Joseph's house and gave them water, and they washed their feet; and he put fodder before their asses.

25 And the men made ready the present before Joseph came at noon; for they heard that they should eat bread there.

26 ¶And when Joseph came home, they brought him the present which they had in their hands into the house, and bowed themselves to him to the ground.

27 And he asked them of their welfare, and said to them, Is your father well, the old man of whom you spoke to me? Is he still alive?

28 And they answered, Your servant our father is well, he is still alive. And they bowed down their heads and made obeisance.

29 And he raised up his eyes and saw his brother Benjamin, his mother's son, and said to them, Is this your youngest brother, of whom you spoke to me? And he said, May God be gracious to you, my son.

30 And Joseph made haste; for his heart did yearn for his brother; and he sought where to weep; and he entered into his chamber and wept there.

31 Then he washed his face and went out and controlled his emotions and said, Let us eat.

32 And they served Joseph by himself, and them by themselves, and the Egyptians, who did eat with him, by themselves; because the Egyptians could not eat bread with the Hebrews; for that is an abomination to the Egyptians.

33 And they sat before him, the firstborn according to his birthright, and the youngest according to his youth; and the men looked at one another and marveled.

34 And the servants took portions to them from before Joseph; but Benjamin's portion was five times as much as any of theirs. And they drank and were merry with him.

CHAPTER 44

AND he commanded the steward of his house, saying, Fill the men's sacks with wheat, as much as they can carry, and put every man's money in his sack's mouth.

2 And take my cup, the silver cup, and put it in the sack's mouth of the youngest, with his money for the wheat. And the servant did according to the word that Joseph had spoken.

3 As soon as the morning was light, the men started on their way, together with their asses.

4 And when they were gone out of the city, but not yet far off, Joseph said to the steward, Arise, pursue the men; and when you overtake them, say to them, Why have you returned evil for good?

5 This is the cup from which my lord drinks, and by which indeed he divines. You have done evil in so doing.

6 ¶And he overtook them, and he spoke to them these same words.

7 They said to him, Let not our lord speak such words. Far be it from your servants that they should do such a thing;

8 Behold, the money which we found in our sacks' mouths we brought back to you from the land of Canaan; how then should we steal from your master's house gold or silver?

9 With whomsoever of your servants it be found, both let him die, and we also will be to our lord servants.

10 And he said to them, Now also let it be according to your words; he with whom it is found shall be my servant; and the rest of you shall be blameless.

11 Then they speedily took down every man his sack to the ground, and opened every man his sack.

12 And they searched, beginning with the eldest and ending with the youngest; and the cup was found in Benjamin's sack.

13 And they tore their clothes, and loaded every man his ass, and returned to the town.

14 ¶And Judah and his brothers came to Joseph's house; for he was still there; and they fell before him on the ground.

15 And Joseph said to them, What deed is this that you have done? Did you not know that such a man as I can certainly divine?

16 And Judah said, What shall we say to my lord? What shall we speak? Or how shall we clear ourselves? God has found out the iniquity of your servants; behold, we are my lord's servants, both we, and he also with whom the cup is found.

17 And he said to them, Far be it from me that I should do such a thing; only the man with whom the cup has been found, he shall be my servant; and as for you, go up in peace to your father.

18 ¶Then Judah came near to him and said, I beg you, O my lord, let your servant speak a few words in my lord's presence, and let not your anger burn against your servant; for you are even like Pharaoh.

19 My lord asked his servants, saying, Have you a father, or a brother?

20 And we said to my lord, We have a father, an old man, and he has a young son, the child of his old age; and his brother is dead, and he alone is left of his mother, and his father loves him.

21 Then you said to your servants, Bring him down to me, that I may set my eyes upon him.

22 And we said to my lord, The lad cannot leave his father; for if he should leave his father, his father would die.

23 And you said to your servants, Unless your youngest brother comes down with you, you shall see my face no more.

24 And when we came up to your servant our father, we told him the words of my lord.

25 And your servant our father said to us, Go back again and buy us a little grain.

26 And we said to our father, We cannot go down; if our youngest brother goes down with us, then we will go down; for we cannot see the man's face unless our youngest brother is with us.

27 Then your servant our father said to us, You know that my wife bore me two sons;

28 And the one of them left me, and I said, Surely he has been killed; and I have never seen him since;

29 And now you want to take this one also from me, and if misfortune should befall him, you will bring down my gray hairs with sorrow to Sheol.

30 Now therefore when we come to your servant our father, and the lad is not with us; seeing that his life is dear to him like his own life;

31 It shall come to pass when he sees that the lad is not with us, he will die; and your servants shall bring down the gray hairs of your servant our father with sorrow to Sheol.

32 For your servant became surety for the lad to our father, saying, If I do not bring him back to you, then I shall be guilty before my father forever.

33 Now therefore, let your servant stay here instead of the lad as a servant to my lord; and let the lad go up with his brothers.

34 For how can I go up to my father, if the lad is not with me? Lest I see the misfortune which will come on my father.

CHAPTER 45

THEN Joseph could no longer control his emotions before all those who stood in his presence; and he said, Cause everyone to go out from me. And there remained no one with him when Joseph made himself known to his brothers.

2 And he wept aloud; and the Egyptians and the household of Pharaoh heard it.

3 And Joseph said to his brothers, I am Joseph your brother; is my father still alive? But his brothers could not answer him because they were afraid at his presence.

4 And Joseph said to his brothers, Come near to me; and they came near. And he said to them, I am

Joseph your brother, whom you sold to the Egyptians.

5 Now do not be grieved, nor displeased with yourselves, that you sold me here; for it was to provide for you that God sent me before you.

6 For behold the famine has been in the land for two years; and yet there are five years, in which there will be no one that sows or that reaps.

7 And God sent me before you to preserve you a remnant on the earth, and to save your lives by a great deliverance.

8 So now it was not you who sent me here, but God; and he has made me a father to Pharaoh, and lord over all his house, and a ruler throughout all the land of Egypt.

9 Hasten, and go up to my father, and say to him, Thus says your son Joseph, God has made me lord over all Egypt; come down to me, do not delay;

10 And you shall dwell in the land of Goshen, and you shall be near me, you and your children and your children's children and your flocks and your herds and all that you have;

11 And there I will provide for you; for the famine will yet last five years more; lest you, your household, and all that you have perish.

12 And, behold, your eyes see, and the eyes of my brother Benjamin, that it is my mouth that speaks to you.

13 And you must tell my father of all my glory in Egypt and of all that you have seen; and you shall hasten and bring down my father here.

14 Then he fell upon his brother Benjamin's neck and wept; and Benjamin wept upon his neck.

15 Moreover he kissed all his brothers and wept upon them; and after that, his brothers talked with him.

16 ¶And the news of their meeting was reported in Pharaoh's house, saying, Joseph's brothers are come; and the news pleased Pharaoh well, and his servants.

17 And Pharaoh said to Joseph, Say to your brothers, Do this: load your beasts with wheat, and go, and carry it to the land of Canaan;

18 And take your father and your households, and come to me; and I will give you the best of the land of Egypt, and you shall eat of the fat of the land.

19 Behold, you are the governor; say to your brothers, Do this: take wagons from the land of Egypt for your wives and for your little ones, and bring your father, and come.

20 And do not regard your stuff which you leave behind; for the choicest of all the land of Egypt is yours.

21 And the sons of Israel did so; and Joseph gave them wagons, according to the command of Pharaoh, and gave them provisions for the journey.

22 To all of them he gave each man two pairs of garments; but to Benjamin he gave three hundred pieces of silver and five pairs of garments.

23 And to his father he sent after this manner: ten asses laden with the good things of Egypt, and ten she-asses laden with wheat, wine, and provisions for his father's journey.

24 So he sent his brothers away, and they departed; and he said to them, Quarrel not on the journey.

25 ¶And they went up out of Egypt, and came to the land of Canaan to their father Jacob.

26 And they told him, saying, Joseph is still alive, and he is governor over all the land of Egypt. But Jacob disregarded their story, for he did not believe them.

27 And they told him all the words which Joseph had said to them; and when he saw the wagons which Joseph had sent to carry him, their father Jacob was content.

28 And he said, This is great news for me, for my son Joseph is still alive; I will go and see him before I die.

CHAPTER 46

AND Israel journeyed with all that he had, and came to Beer-sheba, and offered sacrifices to the God of his father Isaac.

2 And God spoke to Israel in a vision of the night, and said, Jacob, Jacob. And he said, Here am I.

3 Then he said to him, I am El, the God of your father; fear not to go down to Egypt; for I will there make of you a great people;

4 I will go down with you into Egypt; and I will also surely bring you up again; and Joseph shall close your eyes when you die.

5 And Jacob rose up from Beersheba; and the sons of Israel carried Jacob their father, their little ones, and their wives in the wagons which Pharaoh had sent to carry him.

6 And they took their cattle and their goods which they had gotten in the land of Canaan, and came into Egypt, Jacob and all his offspring with him;

7 His sons and his grandsons, his daughters and his sons' daughters, and all his offspring he brought with him into Egypt.

8 ¶And these are the names of the children of Israel, who came into Egypt, Jacob and his sons: Reuben, Jacob's first-born.

9 And the sons of Reuben: Hanoch, Pallu, Hezron, and Carmi.

10 ¶The sons of Simeon: Jemuel, Jamin, Ohar, Jachin, Zohar, and Shaul the son of a Canaanitish woman.

11 ¶The sons of Levi: Gershon, Kohath, and Merari.

12 ¶The sons of Judah: Er, Onan, Shelah, Pharez, and Zarah; but Er and Onan died in the land of Canaan. And the sons of Pharez were Hezron and Hamul.

13 ¶The sons of Issachar: Tola, Phuvah, Job, and Shimron.

14 ¶The sons of Zebulun: Seder, Elon, and Nahlael.

15 These are the sons of Leah, whom she bore to Jacob in Padanaram, together with his daughter Dinah; the number of persons, his sons and his daughters being thirty-three in all.

16 ¶The sons of Gad: Ziphion, Haggi, Shuni, Ezbon, Adi, Arod, and Adri.

17 ¶And the sons of Asher: Jimnah, Ishuah, Isui, and Beriah, and Serah their sister; and the sons of Beriah: Heber, and Malchiel.

18 These are the sons of Zilpah, whom Laban gave to Leah his daughter, and these she bore to Jacob, sixteen persons.

19 The sons of Rachel Jacob's wife: Joseph, and Benjamin.

20 ¶And to Joseph in the land of Egypt were born Manasseh and Ephraim, whom Asiath the daughter of Potipherah priest of On bore to him.

21 ¶The sons of Benjamin: Belah, Akbar, Ashkel, Gera, Naaman, Ehi, Arosh, Muppim, Huppim, and Ard.

22 These are the sons of Rachel, whom she bore to Jacob, fourteen persons in all.

23 ¶The son of Dan: Hushim.

24 ¶And the sons of Naphtali: Nahzael, Guni, Jezer, and Shillem.

25 These are the sons of Bilhah, whom Laban gave to Rachel, his daughter, and she bore these to Jacob, seven persons in all.

26 All the persons that came with Jacob into Egypt, who came out of his loins, besides Jacob's sons' wives, were sixty-six persons in all;

27 And the sons of Joseph who were born to him in Egypt were two persons; thus all the persons of the house of Jacob who came into Egypt were seventy.

28 ¶And he sent Judah before him to Joseph to present himself before him in Goshen; and they came into the land of Goshen.

29 And Joseph made ready his chariots, and went up to meet Israel his father in Goshen, and he presented himself to him, and fell on his neck, and wept on his neck for a while.

30 And Israel said to Joseph, Now let me die, since I have seen your face, my son, because you are still alive.

31 And Joseph said to his brothers and to his father's household, I will go up and inform Pharaoh, and say to him, My brothers and my father's household, who were in the land of Canaan, have come to me;

32 And the men are shepherds, for they are cattle raisers; and they have brought their flocks and their herds and all that they have.

33 And it shall come to pass, when Pharaoh shall call you and shall say to you, What is your occupation?

34 You shall say to him, Your servants are cattle raisers from their youth even until now, both we and also our fathers; that you may dwell in the land of Goshen; for the Egyptians despise all those who feed sheep.

CHAPTER 47

THEN Joseph came and informed Pharaoh, and said to him, My father and my brothers and their flocks and their herds and all that they have, are come from the land of Canaan; and, behold, they are now settled in the land of Goshen.

2 And he took from among his brothers five men and presented them to Pharaoh.

3 And Pharaoh said to Joseph's brothers, What is your occupation? And they said to Pharaoh, Your servants are shepherds, both we and also our fathers, from our youth.

4 They said moreover to Pharaoh, We have come to sojourn in the land; for there is no pasture for your servants' flocks; for the famine is severe in the land of Canaan; now, therefore, let your servants dwell in the land of Goshen.

5 And Pharaoh said to Joseph, Your father and your brothers have come to you;

6 The land of Egypt is before you; settle your father and your brothers in the best of the land; let them dwell in the land of Goshen; and if you know of any able men among them, make them overseers over all my cattle.

7 And Joseph brought in Jacob his father and presented him to Pharaoh; and Jacob blessed Pharaoh.

8 And Pharaoh said to Jacob, How old are you?

9 And Jacob said to Pharaoh, The days of the years of my pilgrimage are a hundred and thirty years; few and difficult have been the years of my life, and I have not attained to the days of the years of the life of my fathers in the days of their pilgrimage.

10 And Jacob blessed Pharaoh and went out from before Pharaoh.

11 ¶Then Joseph settled his father and his brothers, and gave them a possession in the land of Egypt in the best of the land, in the land of Rameses, as Pharaoh had commanded.

12 And Joseph supplied his father and his brothers and all his father's household with wheat according to their families.

13 ¶And there was no grain in all the land; for the famine was very severe, so that the land of Egypt and the land of Canaan were desolate by reason of the famine.

14 And Joseph gathered up all the money that was to be found in the land of Egypt and in the land of Canaan for the grain which they bought; and Joseph brought the money into Pharaoh's house.

15 And when the money was spent from the land of Egypt and from the land of Canaan, all the Egyptians came to Joseph and said to him, Give us wheat that we may live, and not die in your presence; for the money is spent.

16 And Joseph said to them, Give me your cattle, and I will give you grain for your cattle, if your money is spent.

17 So they brought their cattle to Joseph; and Joseph gave them grain in exchange for horses and for flocks and for herds and for asses; and he supplied them with food in exchange for all their herds that year.

18 When that year was ended, they came to him the second year, and said to him, We will not hide it from our lord, for the money is spent; and our lord also has all the herds and cattle; there is nothing left in the sight of our lord but our persons and our lands;

19 Why should we die before your eyes, both we and our lands? Buy us and our lands for bread, and we and our lands will be servants to Pharaoh; and give us seed, that we may live, and not die and that the land be not desolate.

20 And Joseph bought all the land

of Egypt for Pharaoh; for the Egyptians sold every man his field, because the famine prevailed over them; so the land became Pharaoh's.

21 And as for the people, he removed them from town to town from one end of the borders of Egypt to the other end thereof.

22 Only the land of the priests he did not buy; for the priests had a grant from Pharaoh, and did eat their portion which Pharaoh gave them; therefore they did not sell their lands.

23 Then Joseph said to the people, Behold, I have bought you this day and your lands for Pharaoh; lo, here is seed for you, and you shall sow the land.

24 And it shall come to pass when the crops are gathered in, you shall give the fifth part to Pharaoh, and four parts shall be your own, for seed of the field and for your food and for food for your household and for food for your little ones.

25 And they said, You have saved our lives; let us find mercy in the sight of our lord, and we will be Pharaoh's servants.

26 And Joseph made it a law over the land of Egypt to this day that Pharaoh should have the fifth part, except the land of the priests only, for it did not belong to Pharaoh.

27 ¶And Israel dwelt in the land of Egypt in the region of Goshen; and they became powerful in it, and grew, and multiplied exceedingly.

28 And Jacob lived in the land of Egypt seventeen years; so the whole age of Jacob was a hundred and forty-seven years.

29 And when the time drew near that Israel must die, he called his son Joseph, and said to him, If now I have found grace in your sight, put your hand under my thigh, and I will make you to swear by the LORD that you will deal graciously and truly with me; do not bury me in Egypt;

30 But when I sleep with my fathers, you shall carry me out of Egypt and bury me in their burial place. And Joseph said, I will do as you have said.

31 And he said, Swear to me. And he swore to him. And Israel bowed himself upon the head of his staff.

CHAPTER 48

AND it came to pass after these things that Joseph was told, Behold, your father is sick; and he took with him his two sons, Manasseh and Ephraim.

2 And they informed Jacob, and said to him, Behold, your son Joseph has come to you; and Israel strengthened himself, and sat up on the bed.

3 And Jacob said to Joseph, God Almighty appeared to me at Luz in the land of Canaan and blessed me,

4 And he said to me, Behold, I will bless you, and multiply you, and I will make of you a multitude of peoples; and I will give this land to your descendants after you for an everlasting possession.

5 ¶And now your two sons, Ephraim and Manasseh, who were born to you in the land of Egypt before I came to you into the land of Egypt, are mine; as Reuben and Simeon, they shall be mine.

6 But the children that you begot after them shall be yours, and shall be called after the name of their brothers when they come into their inheritance.

7 And as for me, when I was coming from Padan-aram, Rachel died at my side in the land of Canaan on the way, within the distance of three or four miles from the entrance to Ephrath; and I buried her there on the road to Ephrath; the same is Bethlehem.

8 And when Israel saw Joseph's sons, he said to him, Who are these?

9 And Joseph said to his father, They are my sons whom God has given me in this place. And he said, Bring them near me, and I will bless them.

10 Now the eyes of Israel were dim because of age, so that he could not see well. And Joseph brought them near to him; and he kissed them and embraced them.

11 And Israel said to Joseph, I had not thought to see your face; and, lo, God has shown me your children also.

12 And Joseph removed them from before his knees, and they bowed themselves before him with their faces to the ground.

13 Then Joseph took both of his sons, Ephraim in his right hand toward Israel's left hand, and Manasseh in his left hand toward Israel's right hand, and brought them near to him.

14 And Israel stretched out his right hand, and laid it upon Ephraim's head, who was the younger, and his left hand upon Manasseh's head; he changed the position of his hands [1] wittingly, even though Manasseh was the first-born.

15 ¶And Jacob blessed Joseph his son, saying, The God before whom my fathers Abraham and Isaac walked righteously, the God who has supplied my needs from my youth to this day,

16 The angel who has delivered me from all evil, bless the lads; and let them bear my name and the names of my fathers, Abraham and Isaac; and let them grow and multiply in the midst of the earth.

17 And when Joseph saw that his father laid his right hand upon the head of Ephraim, it displeased him; and he held up his father's hand, to remove it from Ephraim's head to Manasseh's head.

18 And Joseph said to his father, Not so, my father; for this is the first-born; put your right hand upon his head.

19 But his father refused, and said, I know it, my son, I know it; he also shall become a people, and he also shall be great: but his younger brother shall be greater than he, and his descendants shall become a multitude of peoples.

20 And he blessed them that day, saying, By you shall Israel bless, and they shall say, May God make you as Ephraim and as Manasseh; and thus he set Ephraim before Manasseh.

21 Then Israel said to Joseph, Behold, I am dying, but God shall be with you, and bring you again to the land of your fathers.

22 Moreover I have given to you one portion of the land more than your brothers, which I took from the hand of the Amorites with my sword and with my bow.

CHAPTER 49

THEN Jacob called his sons and said to them, Gather yourselves together that I may tell you that which shall befall you in the last days.

2 Gather yourselves together and listen, O sons of Jacob; and hearken to Israel your father.

3 ¶Reuben, you are my first-born, my might, and the beginning of my strength, and the excellency of dignity, and the excellency of power:

4 You went astray like water, you shall not excel; because you went up to your father's bed; truly, you have defiled my bed by going up into it.

5 ¶Simeon and Levi are brothers; instruments of anger are in their nature.

6 I never agreed to their counsels; nor did I lower myself to sit in their assembly; for in their anger they slew men and in their rage they destroyed a town wall.

7 Cursed be their anger, for it is raging; and their wrath, for it is fierce; I will divide them in Jacob, and scatter them in Israel.

8 ¶Judah, your brothers shall praise you; your hand shall be on the neck of your enemies; your father's sons shall bow down before you.

9 Judah is a lion's whelp; from the prey, my son, you are gone up; he stooped down, he crouched as a lion, and as a young lion; who shall rouse him up?

10 The sceptre shall not depart from Judah, nor a lawgiver from between his feet, until the coming of the One to whom the sceptre belongs,[2] to whom the Gentiles shall look forward.

11 He shall tie up his foal to the vine, and his ass's colt to a branch; he shall bleach his garments with wine, and his robe with the juices of the grape;

12 His eyes shall be radiant with

[1] Departed from custom.   [2] Messiah.

wine, and his teeth white with milk.[1]

13 ¶Zebulun shall dwell at the shore of the seas; and he shall be a haven for ships; and his border shall extend as far as Zidon.

14 ¶Issachar is a mighty man couching by the highways;

15 And he saw that his dwelling place was good, and his land fertile; and he bowed his shoulder to servitude, and became a servant to tribute.

16 ¶Dan shall judge his people as if the tribes of Israel were one.

17 Dan shall be a serpent by the way, an adder in the paths, that bites the horse's heel and causes its rider to fall backward.

18 I have waited for thy salvation, O Lord.

19 ¶Gad shall go out to raid, and shall pursue at the heels of his enemies.

20 ¶As for Asher, his land is good, and he shall supply kings with food.

21 ¶Naphtali is a swift messenger; he gives goodly words.

22 ¶Joseph is a disciplined son, an educated son; a fruitful bough by a spring, whose branches run over the wall.

23 A company of men quarreled with him, and being great in numbers, envied him;

24 But in strength he bent his bow, and his arms were made strong by the hands of the mighty One of Jacob; (by the name of the Shepherd, the Strength of Israel:)

25 May the God of your father help you and the Almighty bless you with the blessings of heaven above, blessings of the deep beneath, blessings of the breasts, and of the womb;

26 The blessings of your father have prevailed above the blessings of my forbears to the utmost bound of the everlasting hills; they shall be on the head of Joseph, on the crown of the head of him who is the prince of his brothers.

27 ¶Benjamin is a plundering wolf; in the morning he shall devour the prey, and in the evening he shall divide the spoil.

28 ¶All these are the twelve tribes of Israel; and this is what their father Jacob said to them; he addressed them, then he blessed them, according to his blessing, he blessed every one of them.

29 Then their father blessed them, and charged them, and said to them, I am to be gathered to my people; bury me with my fathers in the cave that is in the field of Ephron the Hittite,

30 In the cave which is in the field of Ephron the Hittite, in the double cave which is in the field, before Mamre, in the land of Canaan, the field which Abraham bought from Ephron the Hittite as a possession for a burial ground.

31 There they buried Abraham and Sarah his wife; there they buried Isaac and Rebekah his wife; and there I buried Leah.

32 The field and the cave which is in it were purchased from the children of Heth.

33 And when Jacob had finished charging his sons, he stretched his feet on his bed, and grew weak, and died, and was gathered to his people.

CHAPTER 50

AND Joseph fell upon his father's face, and wept over him, and kissed him.

2 Then Joseph commanded his servants the physicians to embalm his father; and the physicians embalmed Israel.

3 And forty days were fulfilled for him; for so are fulfilled the days of those who are embalmed; and the Egyptians mourned for him seventy days.

4 And when the days of his mourning were past, Joseph spoke to the household of Pharaoh, saying, If now I have found mercy in your eyes, speak in the presence of Pharaoh, saying,

5 My father made me swear, saying, Behold I am dying; in my grave which I bought for myself in the land of Canaan, there you shall bury me. Now therefore let me go up and

---

[1] An Aramaic idiom meaning *abundance of wine and milk.*

bury my father, and I will come back again.

6 And Pharaoh said, Go up and bury your father, according as he made you swear.

7 ¶So Joseph went up to bury his father; and with him went up all the servants of Pharaoh, the elders of his household, and all the elders of the land of Egypt,

8 And all the household of Joseph, his brothers, and his father's household; only their little ones, their flocks, and their herds, they left in the land of Goshen.

9 And there went up with him both chariots and horsemen; and it was a very great company.

10 And they came to the threshing floor of Atar, which is beyond the Jordan, and there they mourned with a great and very sore lamentation; and Joseph made a mourning for his father seven days.

11 And when the inhabitants of the land, the Canaanites, saw the mourning in the threshing floor of Atar, they said, This is a grievous mourning to the Egyptians; therefore the name of it was called Abel-mizrin, which is beyond Jordan.

12 And his sons did to Jacob just as he had commanded them;

13 For they carried him into the land of Canaan, and buried him in the double cave, which is in the field, which Abraham purchased with the field for a possession for a burial ground from Ephron, the Hittite, before Mamre.

14 ¶And Joseph returned to Egypt, he and his brothers, and all who went up with him to bury his father, after he had buried his father.

15 ¶And when Joseph's brothers saw that their father was dead, they were afraid, saying, It may be Joseph will harm us, and perhaps he will requite us all the evil which we did to him.

16 So they came to Joseph and said to him, Your father did command before he died, saying,

17 Thus shall you say to Joseph, Forgive, we pray you now, the trespass of your brothers and their sins; for they did evil to you; and now forgive the trespass of the servants of the God of your father. And Joseph wept when they spoke to him.

18 And his brothers also went and fell down before him; and they said, Behold, we are your servants.

19 But Joseph said to them, Fear not; for I am a servant of God.

20 But as for you, you thought evil against me; but God meant it for good, to do as he has done this day, to save many lives.

21 Now therefore do not be afraid; I will provide for you and your little ones. And he comforted them, and spoke kindly to them.

22 ¶And Joseph dwelt in Egypt, he, and all his father's house; and Joseph lived a hundred and ten years.

23 And Joseph saw Ephraim's children of the third generation; the children also of Machir the son of Manasseh were brought up upon Joseph's knees.

24 And Joseph said to his brothers, I am dying; and God will surely remember you, and bring you up out of this land to the land which he swore to Abraham, to Isaac, and to Jacob.

25 And Joseph took an oath of the children of Israel, saying, God will surely remember you, and you shall carry up my bones from here with you.

26 So Joseph died, being a hundred and ten years old; and they embalmed him and put him in a coffin in Egypt.

THE SECOND BOOK OF MOSES, CALLED

EXODUS

CHAPTER 1

THESE are the names of the children of Israel, who came into Egypt; every man and his household came with Jacob:

2 Reuben, Simeon, Levi, and Judah,

3 Issachar, Zebulun, and Benjamin,

4 Dan, and Naphtali, Gad, and Asher.

5 And all the persons that came out of the loins of Jacob were seventy persons; for Joseph was in Egypt already.

6 And Joseph died, and all his brothers, and all that generation.

7 ¶And the children of Israel were fruitful and increased abundantly, and multiplied and grew exceedingly strong; and the land was filled with them.

8 Now there rose up a new king over Egypt who knew not Joseph.

9 And he said to his people, Behold, the people of the children of Israel are more numerous and stronger than we;

10 Come, let us deal wisely with them, before they multiply, lest when we chance to be at war, they will be added also to our enemies, and fight against us, and so drive us out of the land.

11 Therefore they appointed over them cruel taskmasters to afflict them with their burdens. And they built for Pharaoh cities with storehouses, Pithom and Raamses.

12 But the more they oppressed them, the more they multiplied and became strong. And the Egyptians were grieved because of the children of Israel.

13 So the Egyptians oppressed the children of Israel severely;

14 And they made their lives bitter with hard labor, in mortar and in bricks and in all manner of work in the field; all their service wherein they made them serve was with rigor.

15 ¶And the king of Egypt spoke to the Hebrew midwives, of whom the name of the one was Puah and the name of the other Shoprah;

16 And he said to them, When you do perform your duties as midwives to the Hebrew women, look out when they kneel to deliver; if it is a male, then you must kill him; but if it is a female, then let her live.

17 But the midwives feared God, and did not do as the king of Egypt commanded them, but let the boys live.

18 So the king of Egypt called for the midwives and said to them, Why have you done this thing, and let the boys live?

19 And the midwives said to Pharaoh, The Hebrew women are not like the Egyptian women; for they themselves are midwives, and are delivered before a midwife comes in to them.

20 Therefore God dealt well with the midwives, because they spared the males; and the people multiplied, and grew exceedingly strong.

21 And it came to pass, because the midwives feared God, he blessed them with families.

22 And Pharaoh charged all the people, saying, Every son that is born you shall cast into the river, and every daughter you shall save alive.

CHAPTER 2

AND there went a man from the house of Levi, and took to wife a daughter of the house of Levi.

66

2 And the woman conceived and bore a son; and when she saw that he was a handsome boy, she hid him for three months

3 And when she could no longer hide him, she took for herself an ark made of acacia wood, and daubed it with slime and with pitch, and put the child into it; and laid it among the reeds by the river's bank.

4 And his sister stood afar off, to know what would be done to him.

5 ¶And the daughter of Pharaoh came down to bathe in the river; and her maidens walked along by the river's side; and when she saw the ark among the reeds, she sent her maidens to fetch it.

6 And when she had opened it, she saw the child; and, behold, the babe was weeping. And she had compassion on him, and said, This is one of the Hebrews' children.

7 Then his sister said to Pharaoh's daughter, Shall I go and call for you a nurse of the Hebrew women, that she may nurse this child for you?

8 And Pharaoh's daughter said to her, Go. And the girl went and called the child's mother.

9 And Pharaoh's daughter said to her, Take this child away and nurse him for me, and I will give you your wages. So the woman took the child and nursed him.

10 And the child grew, and she brought him to Pharaoh's daughter, and he became her son. And she called his name Moses; for she said, I drew him out of the water.

11 ¶And it came to pass in those days, when Moses was grown up, that he went out among his brethren, and saw their oppression; and he saw an Egyptian beating a Hebrew, one of his brethren of the children of Israel.

12 And he looked this way and that way, and when he saw that there was no man watching, he slew the Egyptian and hid him in the sand.

13 And when he went out the second day, he looked, and behold, two Hebrew men were quarreling together; and he said to him that did the wrong, Why do you beat your fellow?

14 And he replied, Who made you a prince and a judge over us? Do you intend to kill me, as you killed the Egyptian yesterday? And Moses was afraid, and said, Surely this thing is known.

15 Now when Pharaoh heard this thing, he sought to slay Moses. But Moses fled from the presence of Pharaoh, and went to the land of Midian; and he sat down by a well.

16 Now the priest of Midian had seven daughters; and they came and drew water, and filled the troughs to water their father's flock.

17 And the shepherds came and drove them away; but Moses rose up and rescued them, and watered their flock.

18 And when they came to Reuel their father, he said to them, How is it that you have watered the flock so soon today?

19 And they said to him, An Egyptian delivered us out of the hands of the shepherds and also drew water for us and watered our flock.

20 And he said to his daughters, And where is he? Why is it that you have left the man? Go, invite him, that he may eat bread.

21 And Moses was content to dwell with the man; and he gave Moses Zipporah his daughter.

22 And she bore a son, and he called his name Gershon; for Moses said, I have been a stranger in a strange land. And she bore again, the second son to Moses, and he called his name Eleazar, saying, For the God of my fathers has helped me and has delivered me from the sword of Pharaoh.

23 ¶And it came to pass after a long time that the king of Egypt died; and the children of Israel groaned because of severe oppression, and they prayed, and their cry came up to God because of severe oppression.

24 And God heard their groaning, and God remembered his covenant with Abraham, with Isaac, and with Jacob.

25 And God looked upon the children of Israel, and God noticed their oppression.

CHAPTER 3

NOW Moses was feeding the flock of Jethro [1] his father-in-law, the priest of Midian; and he led the flock to the desert and came to the mountain of God, even to Horeb.

2 And the angel of the LORD appeared to him in a flame of fire out of the midst of a bush; and he looked, and, behold, the bush was on fire, and the bush was not consumed.

3 And Moses said, I will now turn aside and see this great sight, why the bush is not burned.

4 And when the LORD saw that he turned aside to see, God called to him out of the midst of the bush, and said, Moses, Moses. And he said, Here am I.

5 And he said, Do not draw near; take your shoes from off your feet, for the place whereon you are standing is holy ground.

6 Moreover he said, I am the God of your father, the God of Abraham, the God of Isaac, and the God of Jacob. And Moses hid his face; for he was afraid to look at God.

7 ¶And the LORD said, I have surely seen the affliction of my people who are in Egypt, and I have heard their cry because of their taskmasters; for I know their sorrows;

8 And I have come down to deliver them out of the hand of the Egyptians, and to bring them up out of that land to a good and large land, to a land flowing with milk and honey; to the land of the Canaanites, the Hittites, the Amorites, the Perizzites, the Hivites, and the Jebusites.

9 Now therefore, behold, the cry of the children of Israel is come to me; and I have also seen the oppression wherewith the Egyptians oppress them.

10 Come now, therefore, and I will send you to Pharaoh, that you may bring forth my people, the children of Israel, out of Egypt.

11 ¶And Moses said to God, Who am I that I should go to Pharaoh, and that I should bring the children of Israel out of Egypt?

12 And God said to him, I will be with you; and this shall be a sign to you that I have sent you: when you have brought forth the people out of Egypt, you shall worship God upon this mountain.

13 And Moses said to God, Behold, when I go to the children of Israel and say to them, The God of your fathers has sent me to you; and they shall say to me, What is his name? what shall I say to them?

14 And God said to Moses, I am AHIAH ASHAR HIGH (that is, THE LIVING GOD); and he said, Thus you shall say to the children of Israel: AHIAH has sent me to you.

15 And God said moreover to Moses, Thus shall you say to the children of Israel: The LORD God of your fathers, the God of Abraham, the God of Isaac, and the God of Jacob, has sent me to you; this is my name for ever, and this is my memorial to all generations.

16 Go and gather the elders of Israel together, and say to them, The LORD God of your fathers, the God of Abraham, of Isaac, and of Jacob, appeared to me, saying, I have surely remembered you and seen that which is done to you in Egypt;

17 And I have said, I will bring you up out of the affliction of the Egyptians to the land of the Canaanites, the Hittites, the Amorites, the Perizzites, the Hivites, and the Jebusites, to a land flowing with milk and honey.

18 And they shall hearken to your voice; and you and the elders of Israel shall go to the king of Egypt, and you shall say to him, The LORD God of the Hebrews has appeared to us; and now let us go three days' journey into the wilderness that we may sacrifice to the LORD our God.

19 ¶And I know that the king of Egypt will not let you go, except by force.

20 And I will stretch out my hand and smite the Egyptians with all kinds of wonders which I will do among them; and after that Pharaoh will let you go.

[1] A priestly title, meaning *His Excellency*, or *Reverend*, applied to Reuel.

21 And I will give this people favor in the sight of the Egyptians; and it shall come to pass that, when you go, you shall not go empty-handed;

22 But every woman shall borrow of her neighbor and of her that sojourns in her house, jewels of silver and jewels of gold and clothes; and you shall put them on your sons, and on your daughters; and you shall despoil the Egyptians.

CHAPTER 4

AND Moses answered and said, But, behold, they will not believe me, nor listen to my voice; for they will say, The LORD has not appeared to you.

2 And the LORD said to him, What is that in your hand? He said, A staff.

3 And the LORD said, Cast it on the ground. And he cast it on the ground, and it became a serpent; and Moses fled from before it.

4 And the LORD said to Moses, Put forth your hand and take it by the tail. And he put forth his hand and caught it, and it became a staff in his hand;

5 This is done that they may believe that the LORD God of their fathers, the God of Abraham, the God of Isaac, and the God of Jacob, has appeared to you.

6 ¶And the LORD said furthermore to him, again, Put now your hand into your bosom. And he put his hand into his bosom; and when he took it out, behold, his hand was leprous, as white as snow.

7 Then the LORD said to him, Put your hand back into your bosom again. And he put his hand back into his bosom; and when he took it out of his bosom, behold, it was clean like his other flesh.

8 And if they will not believe you, neither hearken to the voice of the first sign, they will believe the voice of the latter sign.

9 And if they will not believe also these two signs, neither listen to your voice, you shall take some of the water of the river and pour it upon the dry land; and the water which you take from the river shall become blood upon the dry land.

10 ¶And Moses said to the LORD, I beseech thee, O my LORD, I am not eloquent, neither heretofore nor since thou has spoken to thy servant; for I am a stutterer and slow of speech.

11 The LORD said to him, Who has made man's mouth? or who makes the dumb, or the deaf, or the seeing, or the blind? Is it not I the LORD?

12 Now therefore go, and I will be with your mouth and teach you what you shall speak.

13 And Moses said to him, O my LORD, send I beseech thee, by the hand of whomsoever thou wilt send.

14 And the anger of the LORD kindled against Moses, and he said to him, Behold, Aaron, your brother, the Levite. I know that he is a good speaker, and also, behold, he will come forth to meet you, and when he sees you, he will be glad in his heart.

15 And you shall speak to him and put my words in his mouth; and I will be with your mouth and with his mouth, and will teach you what you shall do.

16 And he shall be your spokesman to the people; and he shall be an interpreter for you, and you shall be to him instead of God.

17 And you shall take this staff in your hand, with which you shall do signs.

18 ¶And Moses returned, and went to Jethro his father-in-law, and said to him, Let me go and return to my brethren who are in Egypt and see whether they are still alive. And Jethro said to Moses, Go in peace.

19 And the LORD said to Moses in Midian, Go, return to Egypt; for all the men who sought your life are dead.

20 And Moses took his wife and his sons, and set them upon an ass, and started on his way back to Egypt; and he took the staff of God in his hand.

21 And the LORD said to Moses, When you return to Egypt, see that you perform all the wonders before Pharaoh which I have performed by your hand, but I will harden his heart

so that he will not let the people go.

22 And you shall say to Pharaoh, Thus says the LORD, Israel is my first-born son;

23 And I say to you, Let my son go, that he may serve me; and if you refuse to let him go, behold, I will slay your first-born son.

24 ¶And it came to pass when Moses was on his way to the inn that the LORD met him and sought to kill him.

25 Then Zipporah took a flint and cut off the foreskin of her son, and she fell down at the feet of the LORD and said, I have a bloody husband.

26 So the LORD let him go. Then she said, You are a bloody husband, because of the circumcision.

27 ¶And the LORD said to Aaron, Go into the wilderness to meet Moses. And he went and met him in the mountain of God, Horeb, and kissed him.

28 And Moses told Aaron all the words of the LORD, who had sent him, and all the signs which he had commanded him to perform.

29 ¶Then Moses and Aaron went and gathered together all the elders of the children of Israel;

30 And Aaron spoke all the words which the LORD had said to Moses, and performed the signs in the presence of the people.

31 And the people believed; and when they heard that the LORD had remembered the children of Israel, and that he had seen their affliction, then they knelt down and worshipped before the LORD.

CHAPTER 5

AND afterward Moses and Aaron went into the palace and told Pharaoh, Thus says the LORD God of Israel, Let my people go that they may hold a feast to me in the wilderness.

2 And Pharaoh said, Who is the LORD, that I should obey his voice to let Israel go? I do not know the LORD, neither will I let Israel go.

3 And they said, The LORD God of the Hebrews has appeared to us; now let us go three days' journey into the wilderness that we may sacrifice to the LORD our God; lest he fall upon us with the sword or with pestilence.

4 And the king of Egypt said to them, Wherefore do you, Moses and Aaron, cause the people to stop from their work? Go back to your tasks.

5 And Pharaoh said to them, Behold, the people of the land now are many, and you cause them to stop from their work.

6 And Pharaoh commanded the same day the taskmasters of the people and their scribes, saying,

7 You shall no more give the people straw to make bricks, as heretofore; let them go and gather straw for themselves.

8 But the number of bricks which they did make heretofore, you shall lay upon them; you shall not reduce the number thereof; for they are idle; that is why they cry, saying, Let us go and sacrifice to our God.

9 Let more work be assigned to the men, that they may be occupied, so that they may not think to engage in vain conversations.

10 ¶And the taskmasters of the people and their scribes went out and said to the people, Thus says Pharaoh, I will not give you straw.

11 Go, get straw for yourselves wherever you can find it; but your work shall not be reduced.

12 So the people were scattered throughout all the land of Egypt to gather the stubble.

13 And the taskmasters pressed them, saying, Complete your work as you have always done, as when straw was given to you.

14 And the scribes of the children of Israel, whom Pharaoh's taskmasters had appointed over them, were beaten, and demanded, Why have you not completed your quota of bricks both yesterday and today, as heretofore?

15 ¶Then the scribes of the children of Israel came and complained to Pharaoh, saying, Why are your servants treated in this manner?

16 There is no straw given to your servants, and yet they say to us, Make bricks: and, behold, your servants are

beaten; and you sin against your people.

17 But Pharaoh said to them, You are surely idle; therefore you say, Let us go and sacrifice to the LORD.

18 Go therefore now and work; and straw shall not be given you, yet you shall deliver the number of bricks.

19 And the scribes of the children of Israel saw that they were in a bad situation, for it was said to them, You must not reduce the number of your bricks, of your daily task.

20 ¶And they met Moses and Aaron standing opposite them, as they came out from the presence of Pharaoh;

21 And they said to them, May the LORD look upon you and judge; because you have made us to be in disfavor in the eyes of Pharaoh and in the eyes of his servants, to put a sword in their hands to kill us.

22 And Moses returned to the LORD and said, O my LORD, Why hast thou caused this people to be ill-treated? And why didst thou send me here?

23 For since the hour I came to Pharaoh to speak in thy name, he has ill-treated this people; and thou hast not delivered thy people at all.

CHAPTER 6

THEN the LORD said to Moses, Now you shall see what I will do to Pharaoh; for with a strong hand shall he let them go, and by a mighty arm shall he drive them out of his land.

2 And God spoke to Moses and said to him, I am the LORD,

3 Who appeared to Abraham, to Isaac, and to Jacob, by the name of God Almighty; but my name the LORD I did not make known to them.

4 And I have also established my covenant with them, to give them the land of Canaan, the land of their pilgrimage, wherein they dwelt.

5 And I have also heard the groaning of the children of Israel, whom the Egyptians keep in bondage; and I have remembered my covenant.

6 Therefore say to the children of Israel, I am the LORD your God, and I will bring you out from under the burdens of the Egyptians, and I will deliver you from their bondage, and I will save you by a strong hand and by a mighty arm and with great judgments;

7 And I will take you to me for a people, and I will be to you a God; and you shall know that I am the LORD your God, who brings you out from under the burdens of the Egyptians.

8 And I will bring you into the land concerning which I swore to give it to Abraham, to Isaac, and to Jacob; and I will give it to you for an inheritance; I am the LORD.

9 ¶And Moses spoke so to the children of Israel; but they did not listen to him, because of their misery and because of bondage.

10 And the LORD spoke to Moses, saying,

11 Go in, and speak to Pharaoh king of Egypt that he let the children of Israel go out of his land.

12 But Moses said to the LORD, Behold, the children of Israel have not hearkened to me; how then shall Pharaoh listen to me, for I am a stutterer?

13 And the LORD spoke to Moses and to Aaron and gave them a charge to the children of Israel and to Pharaoh king of Egypt to bring the children of Israel out of the land of Egypt.

14 ¶These are the heads of their fathers' houses: the sons of Reuben the first-born of Israel; Hanoch, and Pallu, Hezron, and Carmi; these are the families of Reuben.

15 And the sons of Simeon: Jemuel, Jamin, Ohar, Jachin, Zohar, and Shaul, the son of a Canaanitish woman; these are the families of Simeon.

16 ¶And these are the names of the sons of Levi according to their generations: Gershon, Kohath, and Merari; and the years of the life of Levi were a hundred and thirty-seven years.

17 The sons of Gershon: Libni, and Shimi, according to their families.

18 And the sons of Kohath: Amram, Izhar, Hebron, and Uzziel; and

the years of the life of Kohath were a hundred and thirty-three years.

19 The sons of Merari: Mahali and Mushi; these are the families of the Levites according to their generations.

20 And Amram took his uncle's daughter Jokhaber, and she bore him Aaron, Moses, and Miriam; and the years of the life of Amram were a hundred and thirty-seven years.

21 ¶And the sons of Izhar: Korah, Nepheg, and Zichri.

22 And the sons of Uzziel: Minshael, Elizphan, and Zithri.

23 And Aaron took to wife Elisabeth, the daughter of Amminadab, sister of Nehshon, and she bore him Nadab, Abihu, Eleazar, and Ithamar.

24 And the sons of Korah: Assir, Hilkanah, and Akensap; these are the families of the Korhites.

25 And Eleazar, Aaron's son, took him one of the daughters of Puntiel to wife; and she bore him Phinehas; these are the heads of the families of the Levites according to their tribes.

26 These are Moses and Aaron, to whom the LORD said, Bring out the children of Israel from the land of Egypt with all of their armies.

27 It was they who spoke to Pharaoh king of Egypt, to bring out the children of Israel from the land of Egypt: Moses and Aaron.

28 ¶And it came to pass on the day when the LORD spoke to Moses in the land of Egypt,

29 That the LORD spoke to Moses, and said to him, I am the LORD; speak to Pharaoh king of Egypt all that I say to you.

30 And Moses said to the LORD, My tongue stutters; how shall Pharaoh hearken to me?

CHAPTER 7

AND the LORD said to Moses, See, I have made you a god to Pharaoh; [1] and Aaron your brother shall be your prophet.

2 You shall speak all that I command you; and Aaron your brother shall speak to Pharaoh that he send the children of Israel out of his land.

[1] Given you power over Pharaoh.

3 And I will harden Pharaoh's heart, and multiply my signs and my wonders in the land of Egypt.

4 But Pharaoh will not hearken to you, that I may smite Egypt, and bring forth my hosts and my people the children of Israel out of the land of Egypt by great judgments.

5 And the Egyptians shall know that I am the LORD, when I lift up my hand against Egypt and bring out the children of Israel from among them.

6 And Moses and Aaron did as the LORD commanded them, so did they.

7 And Moses was eighty years old and Aaron eighty-three when they spoke to Pharaoh.

8 ¶And the LORD spoke to Moses and to Aaron, saying,

9 If Pharaoh should say to you, Show me a sign; then you shall say to Aaron, Take your staff and cast it down before Pharaoh, and it shall become a serpent.

10 ¶So Moses and Aaron went to Pharaoh, and they did as the LORD had commanded; and Aaron cast down his staff before Pharaoh and before his noblemen, and it became a serpent.

11 Then Pharaoh called the wise men and the magicians; now the magicians of Egypt, they also did the same with their magic.

12 For they cast down every man his staff and they became serpents; but Aaron's staff swallowed up their staffs.

13 However Pharaoh's heart was hardened, and would not let them go, as the LORD had said.

14 ¶Then the LORD said to Moses, Pharaoh's heart is hardened, he refuses to let the people go.

15 Go to Pharaoh in the morning; behold, he goes out to his daily duty; and you stand toward him by the river's brink and wait; and take in your hand the staff which was turned into a serpent.

16 And you shall say to him, The LORD God of the Hebrews has sent me to you, saying, Let my people go that they may serve me in the wilder-

ness; and, behold, hitherto you have not listened.

17 Thus says the LORD, By this you shall know that I am the LORD: behold, with the staff that is in my hand I will strike upon the waters of the river, and they shall be turned to blood.

18 And the fish that are in the river shall die, and the river shall stink; and the Egyptians shall loathe to drink of the water of the river.

19 ¶And the LORD said to Moses, Say to Aaron, Take your staff and lift up your hand upon the waters of Egypt, upon their rivers, upon their ponds, and upon all their pools of water, and upon the streams, and they shall become blood; and there shall be blood throughout all the land of Egypt, in both vessels of wood and vessels of stone.

20 And Moses and Aaron did as the LORD had commanded them; and Aaron lifted up the staff which was in his hand and smote the waters of the river, in the sight of Pharaoh and in the sight of his servants; and all the waters that were in the river were turned into blood.

21 And the fish that were in the river died; and the river stank, and the Egyptians could not drink the water of the river; and there was blood throughout all the land of Egypt.

22 And the magicians of Egypt did the same by their enchantments; but Pharaoh's heart was hardened and he did not listen to them, as the LORD had said.

23 And Pharaoh turned and went into his house, and he did not take to heart even this sign.

24 And all the Egyptians dug round about the river for water to drink; for they could not drink of the water of the river.

25 And seven days passed after the LORD had smitten the river.

CHAPTER 8

THEN the LORD said to Moses, Go to Pharaoh and say to him, Thus says the LORD, Let my people go that they may serve me.

2 And if you refuse to let them go, behold, I will smite all your borders with frogs;

3 And the river shall swarm with frogs, which shall come up and enter into your house and into your bedchamber and into your bed and into the houses of your servants and of your people and into your inner chambers and into your kneading troughs;

4 And the frogs shall come up both on you and on all your people.

5 ¶And the LORD said to Moses, Say to Aaron your brother, Lift up your hand with your staff over the rivers and over the streams and over the ponds, and cause frogs to come up upon the land of Egypt.

6 So Aaron lifted up his hand over the waters of Egypt; and the frogs came up and covered the land of Egypt.

7 And the magicians did the same with their enchantments, and brought up frogs upon the land of Egypt.

8 ¶Then Pharaoh called for Moses and Aaron and said to them, Pray to the LORD, that he may take away the frogs from me and from my people; and I will let the people go that they may sacrifice to the LORD.

9 And Moses said to Pharaoh, Appoint a time; when shall I pray for you and for your servants and for your people, to destroy the frogs from you and your house?

10 And he said to him, Tomorrow. And Moses said, Be it according to your word, that you may know that there is none like the LORD our God.

11 And the frogs shall depart from you and from your house and from your servants and from your people; they shall remain in the river only.

12 And Moses and Aaron went out from the presence of Pharaoh; and Moses prayed before the LORD because of the frogs which he had brought against Pharaoh.

13 And the LORD did according to the word of Moses; and the frogs died that were in the houses and in the courtyards and in the fields.

14 And they gathered them together in heaps; and the land stank.

15 And when Pharaoh saw that there was respite, he hardened his heart and would not listen to them, as the LORD had said to Moses.

16 ¶And the LORD said to Moses, Say to Aaron, Lift up your staff and smite the dust of the earth, that it may become lice throughout all the land of Egypt.

17 And he did so; and Aaron lifted up his hand with his staff and smote the dust of the earth, and it became lice on men and on cattle; all the dust of the land became lice throughout all the land of Egypt.

18 And the magicians did the same by means of their magic to bring forth lice, but they could not get rid of the lice; so there were lice on men and on cattle.

19 Then the magicians said to Pharaoh, This is the finger of God; and Pharaoh's heart was hardened, and he did not listen to them, as the LORD had said.

20 ¶And the LORD said to Moses, Rise up early in the morning and stand before Pharaoh; lo, he goes out again to his daily duty; and say to him, Thus says the LORD, Let my people go that they may serve me.

21 Else, if you will not let my people go, behold, I will send swarms of flies upon you and upon your people and upon your house; and the houses of the Egyptians shall be filled with swarms of flies, like a field when it is covered with them.

22 And I will set apart on that day the land of Goshen, in which my people dwell, that no swarms of flies shall be there, to the end that you may know that I am the LORD in the midst of the earth.

23 And I will put a division between my people and your people; tomorrow shall this sign be.

24 And the LORD did so; and he brought great swarms of flies into the house of Pharaoh and into his servants' houses and into all the land of Egypt; and the land was ruined by reason of the swarms of flies.

25 ¶Then Pharaoh called for Moses and for Aaron, and said to them, Go, sacrifice to your God within the land.

26 And Moses said, It is not proper to do so; for we shall sacrifice to the LORD our God some of the animals that are an abomination to the Egyptians. And if we should sacrifice animals that are idols before Egyptian eyes, they would stone us.

27 We will go three days' journey into the wilderness and sacrifice to the LORD our God, as he has commanded us.

28 And Pharaoh said, I will let you go that you may sacrifice to the LORD your God in the wilderness; only you shall not go very far away, and you must pray for me also.

29 And Moses said, Behold, I go out from your presence and I will pray before the LORD and he will cause the swarms of flies to depart from Pharaoh, from his servants, and from his people, tomorrow; but let not Pharaoh deal deceitfully any more by refusing to allow the people to go to sacrifice to the LORD.

30 So Moses went out from the presence of Pharaoh and prayed before the LORD.

31 And the LORD did according to the word of Moses; and he removed the swarms of flies from Pharaoh and from his servants and from his people; there remained not one.

32 And Pharaoh hardened his heart at this time also and did not let the people go.

CHAPTER 9

THEN the LORD said to Moses, Go to Pharaoh and say to him, Thus says the LORD God of the Hebrews, Let my people go that they may serve me.

2 For if you refuse to let them go (and until now you have withheld them),

3 Behold, the LORD will smite your cattle which are in the desert, the horses, the asses, the camels, the oxen, and the sheep; there shall be a very severe plague.

4 And the LORD will discriminate between the cattle of Israel and the cattle of the Egyptians, so that none of the cattle that belong to the children of Israel shall die, not even one.

5 And the LORD appointed a set time, saying, Tomorrow the LORD shall do this thing in the land.

6 And the LORD did that thing the next day, and all the cattle of the Egyptians died; but of the cattle of the children of Israel not one died.

7 And Pharaoh sent, and, behold, there was not one of the cattle of the Israelites dead. And the heart of Pharaoh was hardened and he did not let the people go.

8 ¶And the LORD said to Moses and to Aaron, Take two handfuls of the ashes of the furnace and let Moses scatter it toward the heaven in the sight of Pharaoh.

9 And it shall become fine dust in all the land of Egypt, and there shall be boils breaking forth with sores upon men, and upon cattle, throughout all the land of Egypt.

10 So they took ashes of the furnace and stood before Pharaoh; and Moses scattered it toward the heaven in the sight of Pharaoh; and it became blistering boils, breaking out with sores upon men, and upon cattle.

11 And the magicians could not stand before Moses because of the boils; for the boils had spread among the magicians and throughout all the land of Egypt.

12 And the LORD hardened the heart of Pharaoh and he did not listen to them, as the LORD had said to Moses.

13 ¶And the LORD said to Moses, Arise early in the morning, and stand before Pharaoh, and say to him, Thus says the LORD God of the Hebrews, Let my people go that they may serve me.

14 For this time I will send my plague on your heart and on your servants and on your people, that you may know that there is none like me in all the earth.

15 For now I will stretch out my hand that I may strike you and your people with pestilence; and you shall perish from the earth.

16 But for this cause have I raised you to the throne, to show you my power, and that my name may be declared throughout all the earth.

17 As yet you are continuing to detain this people and refusing to let them go.

18 Behold, tomorrow about this time I will cause a severe storm of hail, such as there has not been in Egypt from the day that it was founded even until now.

19 Send therefore now, and gather your cattle, and all that you have in the field; for upon every man and the cattle which be found in the field, and shall not be brought home, the hail shall come down upon them, and they shall die.

20 He who feared the word of the LORD among the servants of Pharaoh brought his servants and his cattle into the house.

21 But he who regarded not the word of the LORD left his servants and his cattle in the field.

22 ¶And the LORD said to Moses, Lift up your hand toward heaven that there may be hail in all the land of Egypt, upon men and upon cattle and upon all the grass in the field, throughout the land of Egypt.

23 And Moses lifted up his staff toward heaven; and the LORD sent thunder and hail, and lightning ran along on the ground; and the LORD showered hail upon the land of Egypt.

24 So there was hail, and flaming fire mingled with the hail, very grievous, such as had never been in all the land of Egypt since it became a nation.

25 And the hail smote throughout all the land of Egypt all that was in the field, both man and cattle; and the hail destroyed all the herbs of the field and broke every tree of the field.

26 Only in the land of Goshen where the children of Israel dwelt, was there no hail.

27 ¶Then Pharaoh sent and called for Moses and Aaron, and said to them, I have sinned this time; the LORD is righteous, and I and my people are wicked.

28 Pray before the LORD, for there is yet a chance for forgiveness in his presence that there be no more mighty thunderings and hail; and I will let you go, and you shall stay no longer.

29 And Moses said to him, As soon as I am gone out of the city, I will stretch forth my hands to the LORD; and the thunder shall cease and there shall be no more hail, that you may know that the earth belongs to the LORD.

30 But as for you and your servants, I know that you have not yet feared the LORD God.

31 And the flax and the barley were lost; for the barley was in the ear and the flax was bolled.

32 But the wheat and the rye were not lost; for they were sown late.

33 And Moses went out of the city from the presence of Pharaoh, and spread out his hands to the LORD; and the thunders and hail ceased, and the rain was not poured upon the earth.

34 And when Pharaoh saw that the rain and the hail and the thunders had ceased, he sinned yet more, and his heart was hardened, and the heart of his servants.

35 And the heart of Pharaoh was hardened and he did not let the children of Israel go, as the LORD had sent word to him by Moses.

CHAPTER 10

AND the LORD said to Moses, Go in to Pharaoh; for I have hardened his heart and the hearts of his servants, that I may perform these signs among them,

2 That you may relate in the presence of your son and of your son's son the things which I have done to the Egyptians and the signs which I have performed among them, that you may know that I am the LORD.

3 And Moses and Aaron came to Pharaoh, and said to him, Thus says the LORD God of the Hebrews, How long will you refuse to fear me? Let my people go that they may serve me.

4 Else, if you refuse to let my people go, behold, tomorrow I will bring locusts upon all your domain;

5 And they shall cover the face of the land so that men cannot see the ground; and they shall eat the residue of that which is left to you from the hail and shall eat all the trees which have budded for you in the field;

6 And they shall fill your houses and the houses of your servants and the houses of all the Egyptians such as neither your fathers nor your grandfathers have seen, from the day that they were upon the earth even to this day. And they turned, and went out from the presence of Pharaoh.

7 And Pharaoh's servants said to him, How long shall we suffer this disaster? Let the men go that they may serve the LORD their God; do you not yet know that Egypt is destroyed?

8 So Moses and Aaron were brought again to Pharaoh; and he said to them, Go, serve before the LORD your God; but who are they that are going?

9 And Moses said to him, We will go with our young and with our old, with our sons and with our daughters; with our flocks and with our herds will we go, for it is a festival of the LORD for all of us.

10 And Pharaoh said to them, Let the LORD be with you, but when I let you and your little ones go, look to it; perhaps you have evil intent.

11 Let it not be so; go now, the older men, and serve before the LORD; for it is the rest that you desire. And they were driven out from Pharaoh's presence.

12 ¶And the LORD said to Moses, Lift up your hand over the land of Egypt for the locusts, that they may come up upon the land of Egypt and eat the herbs of the land, even all that the hail has left.

13 And Moses lifted up his staff over the land of Egypt, and the LORD brought an east wind upon the land all that day and all that night; and when it was morning, the east wind brought the locusts.

14 And the locusts went up over all the land of Egypt and rested in all the domain of the Egyptians; it was a great swarm; before them there were no such swarms of locusts as they, neither after them shall be such.

15 For they covered the face of the whole earth so that the land was darkened; and they did eat all the herbs of the land and all the fruit of

the trees which the hail had left; and there remained no leaf on the trees, neither grass in the field, through all the land of Egypt.

16 ¶Then Pharaoh called for Moses and Aaron in haste; and he said to them, I have sinned against the LORD your God and against you.

17 Now therefore, forgive me my fault this time also, and pray before the LORD your God that he may remove from me this death.

18 And Moses went out from the presence of Pharaoh and prayed before the LORD.

19 And the LORD turned a mighty strong west wind, which took away the locusts and cast them into the Red Sea; there remained not one locust in all the domain of Egypt.

20 But the LORD hardened Pharaoh's heart so that he would not let the children of Israel go.

21 ¶Then the LORD said to Moses, Lift up your hand toward the heaven that there may be darkness over the land of Egypt, even thick darkness.

22 And Moses lifted up his hand toward heaven; and there was a thick darkness in all the land of Egypt three days;

23 They did not see one another, nor rose any from his place for three days; but all the children of Israel had light in their dwellings.

24 ¶And Pharaoh called to Moses and said to him, Go, serve before the LORD your God; only let your flocks and herds remain here; let your little ones also go with you.

25 Then Moses said to Pharaoh, You must give us also sacrifices and burnt offerings that we may sacrifice to the LORD our God.

26 Our cattle also shall go with us; there shall not an hoof be left behind; for thereof must we take to serve before the LORD our God; and we do not know what else we must offer to the LORD until we come there.

27 ¶But the LORD hardened Pharaoh's heart and he would not let them go.

28 And Pharaoh said to Moses, Get away from here, take heed to yourself, do not try to see my face again,

for in the day that you see my face you shall die.

29 And Moses said, You have spoken well, I will not try to see your face any more.

CHAPTER 11

AND the LORD said to Moses, Yet will I bring one plague more upon Pharaoh, and upon the Egyptians; then I will let you go from here; when he shall let you go, then you must get out altogether.

2 Speak now in the presence of the people that they ask every man of his neighbor, and every woman of her neighbor, jewels of silver and jewels of gold.

3 And the LORD gave the people favor in the sight of the Egyptians. Moreover the man Moses was well honored in the land of Egypt in the sight of Pharaoh's servants and in the sight of the people.

4 And Moses said, Thus says the LORD, About midnight I will go forth into the midst of Egypt;

5 And all the first-born in the land of Egypt shall die, from the first-born of Pharaoh who sits on his throne even to the first-born of the maidservant who sits behind the mill; and all the first-born of the animals.

6 And there shall be a great wailing throughout all the land of Egypt, such as there was none like it, nor shall there be any like it any more.

7 But of the children of Israel no one shall be harmed, not even a dog shall bark against man or animals; that you may know that the LORD distinguishes between the Egyptians and Israel.

8 And all these your servants shall come down to me and bow down themselves to me, saying, Get out, both you and all the people that are with you; and after that I will go out. And Moses departed from the presence of Pharaoh in a great anger.

9 And the LORD said to Moses, Pharaoh shall not listen to you; that my wonders may be multiplied in the land of Egypt.

10 And Moses and Aaron did all

these wonders before Pharaoh; but the LORD hardened Pharaoh's heart so that he would not let the children of Israel go out of his land.

CHAPTER 12

THEN the LORD spoke to Moses and Aaron in the land of Egypt, saying,

2 This month shall be to you the beginning of months; it shall be the first month of the year to you.

3 ¶Speak to all the congregation of Israel, saying, On the tenth day of this month they shall take to themselves every man a lamb for his own household, and a lamb for his father's household;

4 And if the household is too little for the lamb, let him and his neighbor next to his house take it according to the number of the persons; every man according to the portion of his eating shall make your count for the lamb.

5 The lamb shall be without blemish, a male of the first year; you shall take it from the lambs or from the kids:

6 And you shall keep it until the fourteenth day of this same month; and the whole assembly of the congregation of Israel shall kill it at sunset.

7 And they shall take some of the blood thereof and sprinkle it on the two door posts and on the lintel and on the houses wherein they shall eat it.

8 And they shall eat the meat in that night, roasted with fire, with unleavened bread; and with bitter herbs they shall eat it.

9 You shall not eat any of it raw, nor cooked with water, but roasted with fire; its head with its legs, and the entrails thereof.

10 And you shall leave none of it remaining until morning; and that which remains of it until the morning you shall burn with fire.

11 ¶And thus you shall eat it; with your loins girded, your shoes on your feet, and your staff in your hand; and you shall eat it in haste; for it is the LORD's passover.

12 For I will pass through the land of Egypt this night, and all the firstborn of the land of Egypt shall die, both man and beast; and against all the idols of Egypt I will execute judgment; I am the LORD.

13 And the blood shall be to you for a sign upon the houses where you are; and when I see the blood, I will make you glad, and the plague shall not be among you to destroy you when I smite the land of Egypt.

14 And this day shall be to you for a memorial; and you shall keep it a feast to the LORD, a festival throughout your generations; you shall keep it a feast by an ordinance for ever.

15 Seven days you shall eat unleavened bread; and from the first day you shall put away leaven out of your houses; for whosoever eats leavened bread from your houses from the first day until the seventh day, that person shall perish from Israel.

16 On the first day there shall be a holy convocation and on the seventh day there shall be a holy convocation to you; no manner of work shall be done in them; except that which every man must eat, that only may be prepared by you.

17 And you shall observe the feast of unleavened bread; for on this very day have I brought your hosts out of the land of Egypt; therefore you shall observe this day throughout your generations by an ordinance for ever.

18 ¶In the first month, on the fourteenth day of the month at evening, you shall eat unleavened bread until the twenty-first day of the month at evening.

19 Seven days there shall be no leaven found in your houses; for whoever eats that which is leavened, that person shall perish from the congregation of Israel, whether he is a stranger or a native of the land.

20 You shall eat nothing leavened; in all your habitations you shall eat unleavened bread.

21 ¶Then Moses called all the elders of the children of Israel and said to them, Hasten, take lambs for your-

selves according to your families and kill the passover lamb.

22 And you shall take a bunch of hyssop and dip it in the blood of the lamb and sprinkle the lintel and the two side posts with the blood that is in the basin; and none of you shall go out of the door of his house until the morning.

23 For the LORD will pass through to smite the Egyptians; and when he sees the blood upon the lintel and on the two side posts, the LORD will bring joy to the doors and will not suffer the destroyer to come into your houses to smite you.

24 And you shall observe this rite and this ordinance for yourselves and your sons for ever.

25 And it shall come to pass, when you come to the land which the LORD will give you, as he has promised, you shall observe this service.

26 And it shall come to pass when your children shall say to you, What is the meaning of this service?

27 You shall say, It is the sacrifice of the LORD's passover, who brought joy to the house of the children of Israel in Egypt when he smote the Egyptians and delivered our houses. Then the people bowed their heads and worshipped the LORD.

28 And the children of Israel went away and did as the LORD had commanded Moses and Aaron; so did they.

29 ¶And it came to pass that at midnight the LORD slew all the first-born in the land of Egypt, from the first-born of Pharaoh who sits on his throne to the first-born of the captive who was in the prison; and all the first-born of cattle.

30 And Pharaoh rose up in the night, he and all his servants and all the Egyptians; and there was a great wailing in the land of Egypt; for there was not a house where there was not one dead.

31 ¶And Pharaoh called Moses and Aaron that night, and said to them, Rise up and get out from among my people, both you and the children of Israel; and go, serve the LORD, as you have said.

32 Also take your flocks and your herds, as you have said, and be gone; and bless me also.

33 And the Egyptians urged the people, that they might get them out of the land of Egypt in haste; for they said, We shall all die.

34 And the people took their kneading dough before it was leavened and their cold kneading dough wrapped up in their mantles upon their shoulders.

35 And the children of Israel did according to the word of Moses; and they borrowed of the Egyptians jewels of silver and jewels of gold and clothing;

36 And the LORD gave the people favor in the sight of the Egyptians, so that they lent to them whatever they asked. And thus they stripped the Egyptians.

37 ¶Then the children of Israel journeyed from Rameses to Succoth, about six hundred thousand men on foot, besides the little ones.

38 And a mixed multitude went up also with them; and their flocks, and herds, and many cattle.

39 And they baked on a griddle unleavened bread of the dough which they had brought forth out of the land of Egypt, for it was not leavened; because the Egyptians drove them out, and they could not make it into flat loaves, neither had they prepared for themselves any provisions for the journey.

40 ¶Now the sojourning of the children of Israel, who dwelt in Egypt, was four hundred and thirty years.

41 And it came to pass at the end of the four hundred and thirty years, on this very day that all the hosts of the LORD went out from the land of Egypt.

42 It was a night to be observed to the LORD for bringing them out of the land of Egypt; therefore, this very night is to be observed to the LORD by all the children of Israel throughout their generations.

43 ¶Then the LORD said to Moses and Aaron, This is the ordinance of the passover; no foreigner shall eat of it;

44 But every man's servant who is bought for money, when you have circumcised him, then shall he eat of it.

45 An alien and a hired servant shall not eat thereof.

46 In one house shall it be eaten; you shall not take any of the meat outside of the house; neither shall you break a bone thereof.

47 All the congregation of Israel shall keep the feast.

48 And when a stranger shall sojourn with you who would keep the passover to the LORD, when he has circumcised every male in his household, then he may draw near to take part in it; and he shall be considered as a native of the land; for no uncircumcised person shall eat thereof.

49 There shall be one law for the natives and for the strangers who sojourn among you.

50 Thus did all the children of Israel; as the LORD had commanded Moses and Aaron, so did they.

51 And it came to pass on that very day that the LORD brought the children of Israel out of the land of Egypt with all their hosts.

CHAPTER 13

AND the LORD spoke to Moses, saying,

2 Sanctify to me every first-born that opens the womb among the children of Israel, both of men and of animals; for they are mine.

3 ¶And Moses said to the people, Remember this day in which you came out from Egypt, out of the house of bondage; for by a strong hand the LORD brought you out from this place; there shall no leavened bread be eaten on this day.

4 In this day you are going forth in the month of Abib.

5 ¶And it shall be when the LORD shall bring you into the land of the Canaanites, the Hittites, the Amorites, the Hivites, the Jebusites, and the Perizzites, which he swore to your fathers to give you, a land flowing with milk and honey, therefore you shall keep this service in this month.

6 Seven days you shall eat unleavened bread, and on the seventh day there shall be a festival to the LORD.

7 Unleavened bread shall you eat for seven days; and there shall no leavened bread be seen with you throughout all your territory.

8 ¶And you shall tell your son on that day, This is done because of what my God did for me when I came forth out of Egypt.

9 And it shall be to you for a sign, a token of remembrance upon your hand, and for a memorial between your eyes, so that the law of the LORD may be in your mouth; for with a strong hand has the LORD brought you out of Egypt.

10 You must therefore keep this ordinance and this law at its appointed time from year to year.

11 ¶And it shall be when the LORD brings you into the land of the Canaanites, as he swore to you and to your fathers, and shall give it to you,

12 You shall set apart to the LORD every first-born that opens the womb and every firstling that comes of the animals that you have; the males shall be the LORD's.

13 And every firstling male of the cattle you shall redeem with a lamb; but if you do not wish to redeem it, then you must kill it: and every first-born of men among your sons you shall redeem.

14 ¶And it shall be when your son asks you in time to come, saying, What is this? You shall say to him, By a strong hand the LORD brought us out of Egypt from the house of bondage;

15 And it came to pass, when Pharaoh was stubborn, and would not let us go, the LORD slew all the first-born in the land of Egypt, from the first-born of man to the first-born of animals; that is why I sacrifice to the LORD all that open the womb, being males; but all the first-born of my sons I redeem.

16 And it shall be as a token on your hand and as a memorial between your eyes; for by a strong hand the LORD brought you out of Egypt.

17 ¶And it came to pass when Pharaoh had let the people go, God did

not lead them by the way of the land of the Philistines, although that was near; for God said, Lest the people be afraid when they see war, and return to Egypt:

18 But God led the people by the way of the wilderness by the Red Sea; and the children of Israel went up armed out of the land of Egypt.

19 And Moses took the bones of Joseph with him; for he had solemnly made the children of Israel to swear, saying, God will surely remember you; and you must carry up my bones from here with you.

20 ¶And they journeyed from Succoth and encamped at Etham, on the edge of the wilderness.

21 And the LORD went before them by day in a pillar of cloud, to lead them on the way; and by night in a pillar of fire, to give them light; so that they might travel by day and by night;

22 The pillar of cloud by day and the pillar of fire by night never failed to go before the people.

CHAPTER 14

THEN the LORD spoke to Moses, saying,

2 Speak to the children of Israel that they turn back and encamp by the inlet of Kheritha,[1] between Migdol and the sea, in front of Baal-zephon; opposite it shall you encamp by the sea.

3 For Pharaoh will say of the children of Israel, They are strangers in the land, the wilderness has shut them in.

4 And the LORD said to Moses, I will harden Pharaoh's heart, and he will pursue them; and I will triumph over Pharaoh, and over all his army; and the Egyptians shall know that I am the LORD. And they did so.

5 ¶And it was told the king of Egypt that the people had gone away; and the heart of Pharaoh and of his servants changed against the people, and they said, What have we done that we have let Israel go from serving us?

1 Dry at low tide.

6 And he made ready his chariots and took his people with him:

7 And he took six hundred chosen chariots and all chariots of the Egyptians and warriors over every one of them.

8 And the LORD hardened the heart of Pharaoh, king of Egypt and he pursued the children of Israel; but the children of Israel had gone out victoriously.

9 And the Egyptians pursued after them, all the horses and chariots of Pharaoh, and his horsemen and his army, and overtook them encamping by the inlet of Kheritha, before Baal-zephon.

10 ¶And when Pharaoh drew near, the children of Israel lifted up their eyes and saw the Egyptians marching after them; and they were terribly afraid; and the children of Israel prayed before the LORD.

11 And they said to Moses, Is it because there were no graves in Egypt that you have taken us away to die in the wilderness? Why have you dealt thus with us, and brought us out of Egypt?

12 Is not this the word that we told you in Egypt, saying, Let us alone that we may serve the Egyptians? For it would have been better for us to serve the Egyptians than to die in this wilderness.

13 ¶And Moses said to the people, Fear not, wait, and see the salvation of the LORD, which he will perform for you today; for the Egyptians whom you have seen today, you shall see them again no more for ever.

14 The LORD will fight for you, and you shall hold your peace.

15 ¶And the LORD said to Moses, Why do you pray before me? Tell the children of Israel to go forward;

16 And as for you, lift up your staff and stretch out your hand over the sea and divide it; and the children of Israel shall go on dry ground through the sea.

17 And, behold, I will harden the hearts of the Egyptians, so that they shall follow them; and I will triumph

over Pharaoh and over all his army, his chariots, and his horsemen.

18 And the Egyptians shall know that I am the LORD, when I have been triumphant over Pharaoh, over all his army, his chariots, and his horsemen.

19 ¶And the angel of God, who went before the camp of Israel, moved and went behind them; and the pillar of the cloud moved from before them and stood behind them:

20 And it came between the army of the Egyptians and the camp of Israel; and it was cloudy and dark all the night, but it gave light all the night to the children of Israel, so that they could not draw near one to another all the night.

21 And Moses lifted up his hand over the sea; and the LORD caused the sea to go back by a strong east wind all that night and made the sea dry land, and the waters were divided.

22 And the children of Israel went into the midst of the sea on the dry ground; and the waters were like a wall to them on their right hand and on their left.

23 ¶And the Egyptians pursued and went into the sea after them, all of Pharaoh's horses, his chariots, and his horsemen.

24 And it came to pass that in the morning watch the LORD appeared to the Egyptian army in a pillar of fire and of cloud, and threw the Egyptian army into confusion.

25 Thus clogging their chariot wheels that they drew heavily, so that the Egyptians said, Let us flee from before the house of Israel; for the LORD fights for them against Egypt.

26 ¶And the LORD said to Moses, Stretch out your hand over the sea that the waters may come back upon the Egyptians, upon their chariots and upon their horsemen.

27 And Moses lifted up his hand over the sea, and the sea returned to its place when the morning appeared; and the Egyptians fled against it; and the LORD overthrew the Egyptians in the midst of the sea.

28 And the waters returned, and covered the chariots and the horse-

men and all the host of Pharaoh that came into the sea after them; there remained not a single one of them.

29 But the children of Israel walked through the sea as if they were walking on the dry land; and the waters were like a wall to them on their right hand and on their left.

30 Thus the LORD saved Israel that day out of the hand of the Egyptians; and Israel saw the Egyptians lying dead upon the seashore.

31 And Israel saw that great work which the LORD did against the Egyptians; and the people feared the LORD, and believed the LORD and his servant Moses.

CHAPTER 15

THEN Moses and the children of Israel sang this song to the LORD, saying, I will sing to the LORD, for he has triumphed gloriously; the horse and his rider he has thrown into the sea.

2 He is mighty and glorious, The LORD JEHOVAH has become our Saviour; he is our God, and we will praise him; our father's God, and we will exalt him.

3 The LORD is a mighty warrior: the LORD is his name.

4 Pharaoh's chariots and his host he cast into the sea; his valiant men also are drowned in the Red Sea.

5 The depths have covered them; they sank to the bottom like stones.

6 Thy right hand, O LORD, has become glorious in power; thy right hand, O LORD, has defeated thy enemies.

7 And in the greatness of thy might thou hast overthrown them that hate thee; thou sentest thy wrath, and it consumed them like stubble.

8 And with the blast of thy nostrils the waters piled up, the floods stood up as if it were in sheepskins; the waves gathered in heaps in the heart of the sea.

9 The enemy said, I will pursue, I will overtake, I will divide the spoil; my soul will devour them; I will draw my sword, my hand shall destroy them.

10 Thou didst blow with thy wind,

the sea covered them; they sank as lead in the mighty waters.

11 Who is like unto thee, O LORD? Who is like unto thee, glorious in his holiness, revered and praised, doing wonders?

12 Thou didst lift up thy right hand, the earth swallowed them.

13 Thou in thy mercy hast led forth this people whom thou hast saved; thou hast guided them in thy strength to thy holy habitation.

14 The people heard and they trembled; fear took hold on the inhabitants of Philistia.

15 Then the princes of Edom were afraid; the mighty men of Moab, trembling seized them; all the inhabitants of Canaan were heartbroken.

16 Fear and dread shall fall upon them; by the greatness of thine arm they shall sink as stones, till thy people, O LORD, pass over; till this people whom thou hast saved pass over.

17 Thou shalt bring them in and plant them on the mountain of thine inheritance, in the place, O LORD, which thou hast made for thee to dwell in; even thy sanctuary, O LORD; establish it by thy hands.

18 The LORD shall reign for ever and ever.

19 For the horses of Pharaoh, with his chariots and his horsemen, went through the sea, and the LORD brought back the waters of the sea upon them; but the children of Israel walked on the dry land in the midst of the sea.

20 ¶Then Miriam the prophetess, the sister of Aaron, took a timbrel in her hand; and all the women went out after her with tambourines and with timbrels.

21 And Miriam answered them, Sing to the LORD, for he has triumphed gloriously; the horse and his rider he has thrown into the sea.

22 So Moses brought Israel from the Red Sea, and they went out into the wilderness of Shud; and they went three days in the wilderness, and found no water.

23 ¶And when they came to Morath,[1] they could not drink the waters of Morath, for they were bit-

ter; therefore the name of the place was called Morath.

24 And the people murmured against Moses, saying, What shall we drink?

25 And Moses prayed before the LORD; and the LORD showed him a tree, and when he cast it into the water, the water became sweet; there the LORD taught him laws and ordinances, and there he tested him,

26 And said to him, If you will diligently hearken to the voice of the LORD your God and will do that which is right in his sight and will obey his commandments and keep all his statutes, I will bring none of these plagues upon you which I have brought upon the Egyptians; for I am the LORD your Healer.

27 ¶And they came to Elim, where there were twelve springs of water and seventy palm trees; and they encamped there by the water.

CHAPTER 16

AND they journeyed from Elim, and the whole congregation of the children of Israel came to the wilderness of Seen, which is between Elim and Sinai, on the fifteenth day of the second month after their departure from the land of Egypt.

2 And the whole congregation of the children of Israel murmured against Moses and Aaron in the wilderness;

3 And the children of Israel said to them, Would that we had died by the hand of the LORD in the land of Egypt, when we sat by the pots of meat, and when we did eat bread to the full; for you have brought us forth into this wilderness to destroy the whole assembly of Israel with hunger.

4 ¶Then the LORD said to Moses, Behold, I will rain bread from heaven for you; and the people shall go out and gather sufficient food, day by day, for I will prove them, whether they will keep my laws or not.

5 And it shall come to pass that on the sixth day they shall prepare that which they bring in; and it shall be twice as much as they gather daily.

6 And Moses and Aaron said to all

---

[1] Bitter.

the children of Israel, At evening, then you shall know that the LORD has brought you out from the land of Egypt;

7 And in the morning, then you shall see the glory of the LORD; for your murmuring has been heard before the LORD; but as for us, what are we that you should murmur against us?

8 And Moses said, When the LORD shall give you in the evening meat to eat and in the morning bread to the full, then the LORD has heard your murmuring which you murmured against him; but as for us, what are we? Your murmurings are not against us but against the LORD.

9 ¶And Moses said to Aaron, Say to all the congregation of the children of Israel, Come near before the LORD; for he has heard your murmurings.

10 And it came to pass, as Aaron spoke to the whole congregation of the children of Israel, they turned their faces toward the wilderness, and, behold, the glory of the LORD appeared in the cloud.

11 ¶Then the LORD spoke to Moses, saying,

12 I have heard the murmurings of the children of Israel; say to them, At evening you shall eat meat, and in the morning you shall be filled with bread; and you shall know that I am the LORD your God.

13 And it came to pass that at evening the quails came up and covered the camp; and in the morning the dew lay round about the camp.

14 And when the dew that lay was gone up, behold, upon the face of the wilderness there lay a thin round crust, like the hoar frost on the ground.

15 And when the children of Israel saw it, they said one to another, Manna-ho? (What is it?) For they did not know what it was. And Moses said to them, This is the bread which the LORD has given you to eat.

16 ¶This is the thing which the LORD has commanded, Gather of it every man according to his eating, an omer for every man, according to the number of your persons; each

man shall take it for those in his tent.

17 And the children of Israel did so, and gathered, some more, some less.

18 And when they measured it with an omer, he that gathered much had nothing over, and he that gathered little had no lack; they gathered every man according to his eating.

19 And Moses said to them, Let no man leave of it till the morning.

20 Notwithstanding they listened not to Moses; but some of them left of it until the morning, and it bred worms and stank; and Moses was angry with them.

21 And they gathered it every morning, every man according to his eating; and when the sun grew hot, it melted.

22 ¶And it came to pass that on the sixth day they gathered twice as much bread, two omers for one person; and all the elders of the congregation came and told Moses.

23 Moses said to them, This is what the LORD has said, Tomorrow is a day of holy rest, a sabbath to the LORD; bake that which you will bake today, and cook what you will cook; and that which is left over, keep it cold for yourselves until the morning.

24 So they left over some of it till the morning, as Moses had commanded them; and it did not stink, neither was there any worm in it.

25 And Moses said to them, Eat it today; for today is a sabbath to the LORD; today you shall not find it in the field.

26 Six days you shall gather it; but on the seventh day, which is the sabbath, in it there shall be none.

27 ¶And it came to pass that there went out some of the people on the seventh day to gather, and they found none.

28 And the LORD said to Moses, How long will you refuse to keep my commandments and my laws?

29 See, for the LORD has given you the sabbath, therefore he gives you on the sixth day bread for two days; abide every man in his place; let no man go out of his house on the seventh day.

30 So the people rested on the seventh day.

31 And the children of Israel called the name thereof manna; and it was like coriander seed, white; and the taste of it was like honeycomb.

32 ¶And Moses said, This is the thing which the LORD has commanded, Fill an omer to be kept for your generations, that they may see the bread with which I have fed you in the wilderness when I brought you forth from the land of Egypt.

33 And Moses said to Aaron, Take a pot, and put an omer full of manna therein, and lay it before the LORD, to be kept for your generations.

34 As the LORD commanded Moses, so Aaron laid it up as a testimony, to be kept.

35 And the children of Israel did eat manna for forty years until they came to an inhabited land; they did eat manna until they reached the border of the land of Canaan.

36 Now an omer is the tenth of an ephah.

CHAPTER 17

AND the whole congregation of the children of Israel journeyed from the wilderness of Seen, after their journeys, according to the command of the LORD, and camped at Rephidim; and there was no water for the people to drink.

2 Wherefore the people quarreled with Moses, and said to him, Give us water that we may drink. And Moses said to them, Why do you quarrel with me? Why do you tempt the LORD?

3 And the people thirsted there for water; and they murmured against Moses, and said to him, Why did you bring us up out of Egypt, to kill us and our children and our cattle with thirst?

4 And Moses prayed to the LORD, saying, What shall I do with this people? They were almost ready to stone me.

5 And the LORD said to Moses, Go on before the people and take with you some of the elders of Israel; and

your staff with which you smote the river, take it in your hand and go.

6 Behold, I will stand before you there on the flinty rock at Horeb, and you shall strike the flinty rock, and there shall gush water out of it, that the people may drink. And Moses did so in the sight of the elders of Israel.

7 And he called the name of the place Nassah and Meribah, because of the quarreling of the children of Israel, and because they tested the LORD, saying, Let us see if the LORD is among us or not?

8 ¶Then came Amalek to fight with Israel at Rephidim.

9 And Moses said to Joshua, Choose for yourself men, and go out, fight with Amalek tomorrow; and I will stand on the top of the hill with the staff of God in my hand.

10 So Joshua did as Moses had said to him, and he went to fight with Amalek; and Moses, Aaron, and Hur went up to the top of the hill.

11 And it came to pass, when Moses lifted up his hand, Israel prevailed; and when he let down his hands, Amalek prevailed.

12 But Moses' hands became tired; so they took a stone and put it under him, and he sat upon it; and Aaron and Hur supported his hands, the one on one side, and the other on the other side; and his hands were steady until the going down of the sun.

13 And Joshua defeated Amalek with the edge of the sword.

14 Then the LORD said to Moses, Write this for a memorial in a book and place it before Joshua; for I will utterly blot out the remembrance of Amalek from under heaven.

15 And Moses built an altar, and called the name of it Jehovah-nasi:

16 For he said, Behold, as the LORD has sworn, the LORD will fight with Amalek from generation to generation.

CHAPTER 18

AND Jethro, the priest of Midian, Moses' father-in-law, heard of all that God had done for Moses and for

Israel his people, and that the Lord had brought the children of Israel out of Egypt;

2 Then Jethro, Moses' father-in-law, took his daughter Zipporah, Moses' wife, after he had sent her back,

3 And her two sons; of whom the name of the one was Gershon; for he said, I have been an alien in a foreign land;

4 And the name of the other was Eliezer; For the God of my fathers, said he, was my help, and delivered me from the sword of Pharaoh;

5 And Jethro, Moses' father-in-law, came with his sons and his wife to Moses in the wilderness, where he encamped at the mountain of God;

6 And Moses was told, Behold, your father-in-law Jethro has come to you with your wife and your two sons accompanying him,

7 ¶And Moses went out to meet his father-in-law, and did obeisance and kissed him, and they asked each other of their welfare; and they went into the tent.

8 And Moses told his father-in-law all that the Lord had done to Pharaoh and the Egyptians for Israel's sake, and all the travail that they had suffered on the journey, and how the Lord had delivered them.

9 And Jethro rejoiced for all the goodness which the Lord had done to Israel, because he had delivered them out of the hand of the Egyptians and out of the hand of Pharaoh.

10 And Jethro said, Blessed be the Lord, who has delivered you out of the hand of the Egyptians and out of the hand of Pharaoh, for he has delivered his people from under the rule of the Egyptians.

11 Now I know that the Lord is greater than all gods; for despite the counsel which the Egyptians had devised against them, he triumphed over them.

12 And Jethro, Moses' father-in-law, offered burnt offerings and sacrifices to the Lord; and Aaron came, and all the elders of Israel, to eat bread with Moses' father-in-law before God.

13 ¶And it came to pass the next day that Moses sat to judge the people; and the people stood by Moses from morning to evening.

14 And when Moses' father-in-law saw all that he did for the people, he said to him, What is this thing that you are doing for the people? Why do you sit in judgment all alone, and all the people stand by you from morning to evening?

15 And Moses said to his father-in-law, Because the people come to me to inquire of God;

16 And when they have a controversy, they come to me; and I judge between one and another, and I make them know the statutes of God and his laws.

17 And Moses' father-in-law said to him, The thing that you are doing is not good.

18 You will surely wear yourself out, both you, and all this people that is with you; for this thing is too heavy for you; you are not able to do it alone.

19 Listen now to my voice, I will give you counsel, and God shall be with you; you must become a teacher from God to the people, to bring their disputes before God;

20 And you shall warn them to keep the ordinances and laws that you may show them how to conduct themselves and the works that they must do.

21 Moreover you shall provide out of all the people able men who fear God, truthful men who hate bribes and deceit; and appoint such over them to be officers of thousands, of hundreds, of fifties, and of tens.

22 Let them judge the people at all times; and when they have an important matter, let them come to you; but every small matter they shall judge for themselves; so it shall be easier for you, and they shall bear the burden with you.

23 If you shall do this thing, and God commands you so, then you shall be able to endure, and all this people shall also go each one to his own house in peace.

24 So Moses listened to the voice of his father-in-law, and did all that he had told him.

25 And Moses chose able men out of all Israel, and appointed them officers over the people, officers of thousands, of hundreds, of fifties, and of tens.

26 And they judged the people at all times; the hard cases they brought to Moses, but every small matter they judged themselves.

27 ¶Then Moses let his father-in-law depart, and he went to his own land.

CHAPTER 19

IN the third month after the departure of the children of Israel out of the land of Egypt, on the same day they came to the wilderness of Seen.

2 Then they journeyed from Rephidim and came to the wilderness of Sinai, and they encamped in the wilderness; and there Israel camped before the mountain.

3 And Moses went up to God, and God called to him out of the mountain and said to him, Thus shall you say to the house of Jacob, and tell the children of Israel,

4 You have seen what I did to the Egyptians, and how I bore you as though you were on eagles' wings and brought you to myself.

5 Now therefore, if you will obey my voice indeed and keep my covenant, then you shall be my beloved ones above all peoples, for all the earth is mine;

6 And you shall be to me a kingdom and priests and an holy people. These are the words which you shall speak to the children of Israel.

7 ¶And Moses came and called for the elders of the people, and said in their presence all these words which the LORD commanded him.

8 And all the people answered together and said, All that the LORD has spoken we will do. And Moses returned the words of the people to the LORD.

9 And the LORD said to Moses, Lo, I am coming to you in a thick cloud, that the people may hear when I speak with you and also believe you for ever. And Moses told the words of the people before the LORD.

10 ¶And the LORD said to Moses, Go to the people and sanctify them today and tomorrow, and let them wash their clothes,

11 And be ready by the third day; for on the third day the LORD will come down in the sight of all the people upon mount Sinai.

12 And you shall publish a warning among the people, saying, Take heed to yourselves, neither go up into the mountain, nor draw near to the border of it; whoever draws near to the mountain shall be put to death:

13 No hand shall touch it, but he shall surely be stoned and hurled down; whether it be beast or man, it shall not live; when the trumpet is silent, then you are permitted to ascend the mountain.

14 ¶And Moses went down from the mountain to the people and sanctified the people; and they washed their clothes.

15 And he said to the people, Be ready on the third day; do not touch your wives.

16 ¶And it came to pass on the third day in the morning that there were thunders and lightnings and a thick cloud appeared upon the mountain and the sound of the trumpet exceedingly loud; so that all the people that were in the camp trembled.

17 Then Moses brought forth the people out of the camp to meet God; and they stood at the base of the mountain.

18 And the whole mountain of Sinai was smoking because the LORD descended upon it in fire; and the smoke thereof ascended like the smoke of a furnace, and the whole mountain quaked greatly.

19 And when the blast of the trumpet sounded long and grew louder and louder, Moses spoke, and God answered him by a voice.

20 And the LORD came down upon mount Sinai, to the very top of the mountain; and the LORD called Moses up to the top of the mountain; and Moses went up.

21 And the LORD said to Moses, Go

down, warn the people, lest they break through to the LORD to gaze, and many of them perish.

22 And let the priests also who come near to the LORD sanctify themselves, lest the LORD break forth upon them.

23 And Moses said to the LORD, The people cannot come up to mount Sinai; for thou didst warn us, saying, Set bounds about the mountain and sanctify it.

24 And the LORD said to him, Hasten, go down, and then come up, you, and Aaron your brother with you; but let not the priests and the people break through to come up before the LORD, lest he kill them.

25 So Moses went down to the people and told them.

CHAPTER 20

AND God spoke all these words, saying,

2 I am the LORD your God, who brought you out of the land of Egypt, out of the house of bondage.

3 You shall have no other gods except me.

4 You shall not make for yourself any graven image, or any likeness of anything that is in heaven above or that is in the earth beneath or that is in the water under the earth;

5 You shall not worship them nor serve them; for I the LORD your God am a zealous God, visiting the offenses of the fathers upon their children to the third and fourth generations of those who hate me;

6 And showing mercy to thousands of generations of those who love me and keep my commandments.

7 You shall not take a false oath in the name of the LORD your God; for the LORD will not declare him innocent who takes an oath in his name falsely.

8 Remember the sabbath day to keep it holy.

9 Six days shall you labor and do all your work;

10 But the seventh day is a sabbath to the LORD your God; in it you shall not do any work, you, nor your son, nor your daughter, nor your man-

servant, nor your maidservant, nor your cattle, nor the sojourner who dwells in your towns;

11 For in six days the LORD made heaven and earth, the seas, and all things that are in them, and rested on the seventh day; therefore the LORD blessed the sabbath day and sanctified it.

12 ¶Honor your father and your mother, that your days may be long upon the land which the LORD your God gives you.

13 You shall not kill.

14 You shall not commit adultery.

15 You shall not steal.

16 You shall not bear false witness against your neighbor.

17 You shall not covet your neighbor's house, you shall not covet your neighbor's wife, nor his manservant, nor his maidservant, nor his ox, nor his ass, nor anything that is your neighbor's.

18 ¶And all the people observed the thunderings and the lightning flashes and the sound of the trumpet and the mountain smoking; and when the people saw all of this, they were afraid and they stood afar off.

19 And they said to Moses, You speak to us, and we will listen; but let not God speak with us, lest we die.

20 And Moses said to the people, Fear not; for God is come to prove you, that his worship may be before your faces, and that you may not sin.

21 And the people stood afar off, and Moses drew near to the thick darkness where God was.

22 ¶And the LORD said to Moses, Thus you shall say to the children of Israel, You have seen that I have talked with you from heaven.

23 You shall not make for yourselves gods of gold to be worshipped along with me, neither shall you make for yourselves gods of silver.

24 ¶An altar of earth shall you make to me, and you shall sacrifice on it your burnt offerings and your peace offerings, your sheep and your oxen; in every place where I shall make a memorial to my name I will come to you and I will bless you.

25 And if you make me a stone altar, you shall not build it of hewn stones; for if you lift a tool of iron upon it, you will have polluted it.

26 Neither shall you go up by steps to my altar, that your nakedness be not exposed [1] on it.

CHAPTER 21

NOW these are the judgments which you shall set before them.

2 When you buy a Hebrew servant, six years he shall serve you; and in the seventh year he shall go out free from your house without price.

3 If he came in single, he shall go out single; if he were married, then his wife shall go out with him.

4 If his master has given him a wife and she has borne him sons or daughters, the wife and her children shall be his master's and he shall go out alone.

5 And if the servant shall say, I love my master, my wife, and my children; I will not go out free;

6 Then his master shall bring him to the judges; he shall also bring him to the door, or to the door post; and his master shall bore his ear through with an awl; and he shall serve him for ever.

7 ¶And when a man sells his daughter to be a maidservant, she shall not go out free as the menservants do.

8 If her master hates her, so that he will not take her to himself as a wife, then he shall let her be redeemed; he shall have no authority to sell her to a foreign people, because he has dealt deceitfully with her.

9 And if he takes her for wife to his son, then he shall deal with her after the manner of daughters.

10 If he takes to himself another wife, he shall not diminish her food, her clothes, and her conjugal rights.

11 And if he does not these three things to her, then she shall go out free without price.

12 ¶He who strikes a man so that he dies shall surely be put to death.

13 But if he did not lie in wait for him, but God delivered him into his hand, then I will appoint for you a place to which he may flee.

14 But if a man ventures to attack his neighbor and slay him treacherously, you shall take him even from my altar to put him to death.

15 ¶He who strikes his father or his mother shall surely be put to death.

16 ¶He who steals a person and sells him, or he is found in his possession, he shall surely be put to death.

17 ¶He who curses his father or his mother shall surely be put to death.

18 ¶And if two men quarrel, and one strikes another with a stone or with his fist, and he does not die but is put to bed from the injury:

19 If he rises again and walks in the street with his staff, then the one who struck him shall be acquitted, except that he shall pay for the loss of his time and the physician's fee.

20 ¶And if a man strikes his servant, or his maid with a staff, and he dies under his hand, he shall surely be punished.

21 But if the victim is well after a day or two, he shall not be punished; for he is his property.

22 ¶If two men quarrel, and strike a woman with child so that she miscarries, and yet no mischief follow; he shall surely pay a fine such as the woman's husband will lay upon him; and he shall pay as the judges determine.

23 But if any mischief follow, then you shall give life for life,

24 Eye for eye, tooth for tooth, hand for hand, foot for foot,

25 Burning for burning, wound for wound, slap for slap.

26 ¶And if a man strike the eye of his servant or the eye of his maid, and injure it, he shall let him go free for his eye's sake.

27 And if he knocks out the tooth of his manservant or the tooth of his maidservant, he must let him go free for his tooth's sake.

28 ¶If an ox gores a man or a woman that he or she die; then the ox shall be surely stoned and its meat shall not be eaten; but the owner of the ox shall be blameless.

[1] Undergarments, such as we have today, were not worn then.

29 But if the ox were known to be in the habit of goring in the past, and its owner has been warned, and he has not kept it in, and it kills a man or a woman; the ox shall be stoned, and its owner also shall be put to death.

30 But if a sum of money is imposed on him, then he shall give for the ransom of his life whatever they ask from him.

31 Whether the ox has gored a son or a daughter, according to this judgment it shall be done to him.

32 If the ox gores a manservant or a maidservant, the owner shall give to their master thirty shekels of silver and the ox shall be stoned.

33 ¶And if a man shall open a wheat pit or a man shall dig a well, and not cover them, and an ox or an ass fall into it;

34 The owner of the pit shall pay money to the owner of the animal, and the dead animal shall be his.

35 ¶And if one man's ox gores another man's ox so that it dies; then they shall sell the live ox and divide the money; and the dead ox also they shall divide.

36 But if it be known that the ox has been in the habit of goring, and his owner has not kept it in; he shall surely pay ox for ox; and the dead animal shall belong to him.

CHAPTER 22

IF a man shall steal an ox or a ewe, and kill it, or sell it; he shall restore five oxen for an ox and four ewes for a ewe.

2 ¶If a thief is found breaking into a house and is wounded so that he dies, there is no penalty for bloodshed.

3 But if the sun be risen upon him, there shall be blood penalty for him; and he should make full restitution; if he has nothing, then he shall be sold for his theft.

4 If the animal is found in his possession alive, whether it is an ox or an ass, or a ewe, he shall restore double.

5 ¶If a man shall cause a field or a vineyard to be eaten, and shall let his cattle loose to feed in another man's field, of the best of his own field and of the best of his own vineyard, he shall make restitution.

6 ¶If fire breaks out and catches in the thorns so that the shocks of grain or the standing wheat or the field is consumed, he who kindled the fire shall surely make restitution.

7 ¶If a man shall deliver to his neighbor money or stuff to keep and it is stolen out of the man's house, if the thief is found, let him pay double.

8 If the thief is not found, then the master of the house shall be brought to the judges to see whether he had a hand in the theft of his neighbor's goods.

9 For all manner of trespass, whether it be for an ox for an ass for a lamb for clothing or for any manner of lost thing which another man claims to be his, the case of both parties shall come before the judges; and whomever the judges shall convict, he shall make two-fold restitution to his neighbor.

10 If a man delivers to his neighbor an ass or an ox or a lamb or any kind of animal to keep; and it dies or is hurt or taken away in plunder and no man saw it;

11 Then there shall be an oath of the LORD between them both, that he had no hand in the theft of his neighbor's property; and the owner of it shall accept the oaths and he shall not make restitution.

12 But if it is stolen from him, he shall make restitution to the owner thereof.

13 If it is torn in pieces, then let him bring it as evidence, and he shall not make good that which was torn.

14 ¶And if a man borrow of his neighbor an animal, and it dies or it is injured, the owner thereof not being with it, he shall surely make restitution.

15 But if the owner thereof is with it, he shall not make restitution; and if it was hired, it came for its hire.

16 ¶And if a man entices a virgin who is not betrothed, and lies with her, he shall surely marry her.

17 If her father refuses to give her to him, he shall pay money according to the dowry of a virgin.

18 ¶You shall not suffer a witch to live.

19 ¶Whoever lies with an animal shall surely be put to death.

20 ¶He who sacrifices to idols shall be utterly destroyed; but to the LORD alone shall he sacrifice.

21 ¶You shall neither harm a stranger nor oppress him; for you were strangers in the land of Egypt.

22 ¶You shall not harm any widow or orphan.

23 If you harm them, and they pray before me, I will surely hear their prayer;

24 And my wrath shall kindle, and I will kill you with the sword; and your wives shall become widows and your children fatherless.

25 ¶If you lend money to any of my people who are the poor among you, you shall not be to him as an usurer, neither shall you take any usury from him.

26 If you at all take your neighbor's clothes as a pledge, you must give them back to him by sunset;

27 For they are his only covering, it is his raiment for his body; with what shall he sleep? And if he prays before me, I will hear him; for I am compassionate.

28 ¶You shall not revile the judge nor curse the ruler of your people.

29 ¶You shall not delay to offer the first fruits of the harvest of your threshing floor, and of your wine press; the first-born of your sons you shall give to me.

30 Likewise you shall do with your oxen and with your sheep: seven days it shall be with its dam; on the eighth day you shall give it to me.

31 ¶And you shall be holy men to me; neither shall you eat any flesh that has been torn by beasts in the field; you shall throw it to the dogs.

CHAPTER 23

YOU shall not confirm a false report; do not stretch out your hand taking oaths with the guilty to become a false witness for him.

2 ¶You shall not follow a multitude to do evil; neither shall you testify in a lawsuit so as to pervert justice, in order to side with a multitude which deviates from justice.

3 ¶Neither shall you be partial to a poor man in his lawsuit.

4 ¶If you meet your enemy's ox or his ass going astray, you shall surely bring it back to him again.

5 If you should see the ass of your enemy lying under its burden, and you are unwilling to help him lift it up, you should surely help him to lift it up nevertheless.

6 You shall not pervert the justice due to a poor man in his lawsuit.

7 Keep far from a false matter; and the innocent and righteous you shall not slay; for I will not justify the wicked.

8 ¶And you shall take no bribe; for a bribe blinds the eyes of the wise in judgment and perverts the words of the righteous.

9 ¶You shall not oppress strangers; for you know the life of a stranger; you were strangers in the land of Egypt.

10 For six years you shall sow your land and shall gather in the crops thereof:

11 But the seventh year you shall leave it fallow, so that the poor of your people may eat of the fruits of it; and what is left the wild beasts may eat. You shall do in like manner with your vineyard and with your olive yard.

12 Six days you shall do your work, and on the seventh day you shall rest, that your ox and your ass may rest and the son of your handmaid; and that the stranger in your towns may be refreshed.

13 Take heed of all things that I have said to you; and make no mention of the name of false idols, neither think of them.

14 ¶Three times in the year you shall celebrate a festival for me.

15 You shall keep the festival of the unleavened bread (you shall eat unleavened bread for seven days, as I commanded you, at the time appointed of the month of Abib; for in

the month of Abib you came out of the land of Egypt; you shall not appear before me without a gift offering:)

16 And the festival of the harvest, the first fruits of your grain which you sow in the field; and the festival of the ingathering, which is at the end of the year, when you have gathered your crop from the field.

17 Three times in the year all your gift offerings shall appear before the LORD your God.

18 You shall not offer the blood of a sacrifice with leavened bread; neither shall the fat of the festival sacrifices remain until morning.

19 The best of the first fruits of your land you shall bring into the house of the LORD your God. You shall not cook the meat of a kid in its mother's milk.

20 ¶Behold, I send an angel before you to guard you on the way and to bring you into the land which I have prepared.

21 Heed him and obey his voice; do not strive against him; perhaps he will not pardon your transgressions; for my name is upon him.

22 But if you shall indeed obey his voice and do all that he says to you, then I will hate those who hate you and oppress your enemies.

23 For my angel shall go before you and bring you against the Amorites and the Hittites and the Perizzites and the Canaanites and the Hivites and the Jebusites; and I will destroy them.

24 You shall not worship their gods nor serve them nor do after their works; but you shall utterly overthrow them and break down their statues.

25 And you shall serve the LORD your God, and he shall bless your bread and your water; and I will take sickness away from your houses.

26 ¶There shall nothing cast their young nor be barren in your land; the number of your days I will fulfil.

27 I will send my fear before you and will destroy all the peoples against whom you shall go to war, and I will make all your enemies flee from you.

28 And I will send fierce armies before you, and will destroy the Canaanites and the Hittites from before you.

29 I will not destroy them from before you in one year, lest the land become desolate and the wild beasts multiply against you.

30 Little by little I will destroy them before you, till you become strong and inherit the land.

31 And I will set your boundaries from the Red Sea as far as the sea of the Philistines, and from the desert to the river Euphrates; for I will deliver the inhabitants of the land into your hands; and you shall destroy them.

32 You shall make no covenant with them, nor with their idols.

33 They shall not dwell in your land, lest they make you sin before me; you shall not serve their gods, lest they be a stumbling block to you.

CHAPTER 24

AND he said to Moses, Come up to the LORD, you and Aaron, Nadab and Abihu, and seventy of the elders of Israel; and you shall worship afar off.

2 And Moses alone shall come near the LORD; but they shall not draw near; neither shall the people come up with him.

3 ¶And Moses came and told the people all the words of the LORD and all the ordinances; and all the people answered with one voice, and said, Everything which the LORD has said we will do.

4 And Moses wrote all the words of the LORD, and rose up early in the morning and built an altar at the foot of the mountain, and twelve pillars, according to the twelve tribes of Israel.

5 And he sent young men of the children of Israel, who offered burnt offerings and sacrificed peace offerings of oxen to the LORD.

6 And Moses took half of the blood, and put it into basins; and half of the blood he sprinkled on the altar.

7 And he took the book of the covenant and read it in the presence of the people; and they said, All that

the LORD has said we will obey and do.

8 And Moses took the blood and sprinkled it on the people and said, This is the blood of the covenant which the LORD has made with you concerning all these words.

9 ¶Then Moses and Aaron, Nadab and Abihu, and seventy of the elders of Israel went up;

10 And they saw the God of Israel; and there was under his feet as it were a paved work of sapphire stone, clear as the color of the sky.

11 And he did not harm the elders of the children of Israel; and they saw God, and ate and drank.

12 ¶And the LORD said to Moses, Come up to me to the mountain, and present yourself there; and 1 will give you tablets of stone, and the laws and commandments which I have written; that you may teach them.

13 And Moses rose up and his minister Joshua; and Moses went up to the mountain of God.

14 And he said to the elders, You wait here for us until we return to you; and, behold, Aaron and Hur are with you; whoever has a problem, let him come to them.

15 And Moses went up to the mountain, and a cloud covered the mountain.

16 And the glory of the LORD rested upon mount Sinai, and the cloud covered it for six days; and on the seventh day the LORD called to Moses out of the midst of the cloud.

17 And in the sight of all the children of Israel he saw the glory of the LORD like a burning fire on the top of the mountain.

18 And Moses went into the midst of the cloud and went up to the mountain; and Moses was in the mountain forty days and forty nights.

CHAPTER 25

AND the LORD spoke to Moses, saying,

2 Speak to the Israelites to set aside an offering for me; of every man that gives it willingly with his heart you shall take an offering.

3 And this is the offering which you shall take of them: gold, silver, and brass,

4 Blue, purple, and scarlet, fine linen, and goats' hair,

5 And rams' skins dyed red, skins dyed with vermilion, and shittim wood,

6 Oil for the lamps, spices for anointing oil, and for sweet incense.

7 Onyx stones, and precious stones to be set in the ephod and in the breastplate.

8 And let them make me a sanctuary, that I may dwell among them.

9 According to all that I show you, after the pattern of the tabernacle and the pattern of all the vessels thereof, even so shall you make it.

10 ¶And they shall make an ark of shittim wood, two and a half cubits long, and a cubit and a half broad, and a cubit and a half high.

11 And you shall overlay it with pure gold, without and within shall you overlay it, and shall make upon it a crown of gold round about.

12 And you shall cast four rings of gold for it, and put them in the four corners thereof; and two rings on the one side of it, and two rings on the other side of it.

13 And you shall make poles of shittim wood, and overlay them with gold.

14 And you shall put the poles into the rings by the sides of the ark, that the ark may be borne with them.

15 The poles shall remain in the rings of the ark; they shall never be taken out of them.

16 And you shall put into the ark the testimony which I shall give you.

17 And you shall make a mercy seat of pure gold, two and a half cubits long, and a cubit and a half broad.

18 And you shall make two cherubim of gold, of cast work shall you make them, on the two sides of the mercy seat.

19 And make one cherub on the one side, and the other cherub on the other side of the mercy seat; thus you shall make two cherubim on the two sides thereof.

20 And the cherubim shall spread

forth their wings on high, covering the mercy seat with their wings, and their faces shall look one to another; toward the mercy seat shall the faces of the cherubim be.

21 And you shall put the mercy seat on top of the ark; and in the ark you shall put the testimony that I shall give you.

22 And there I will meet you, and I will commune with you from above the mercy seat, from between the two cherubim which are upon the ark of the testimony, of all things which I will command you concerning the children of Israel.

23 ¶You shall also make a table of shittim wood, two cubits long, a cubit broad, and a cubit and a half high.

24 And you shall overlay it with pure gold, and make for it a crown of gold round about.

25 And you shall make for it a border of a handbreadth round about, and you shall make a golden crown for the border thereof round about.

26 And you shall make for it four rings of gold, and put the rings in the four corners that are on the four feet thereof.

27 The rings shall be put toward the border to be places for the poles to carry the table.

28 You shall make the poles of shittim wood, and overlay them with gold, that the table may be borne with them.

29 You shall make dishes, spoons, jars, and bowls to pour out wine with them; of pure gold you shall make them.

30 And you shall set shewbread on the table before me always.

31 ¶And you shall make a candlestick of pure gold; of cast work shall the candlestick be made; its shaft, its branches, its bowls, its buds, and its flowers shall be of one piece.

32 And six branches shall come out of the sides of it; three branches of the candlestick out of the one side, and three branches of the candlestick out of the other side;

33 Three bowls shall be fastened on one shaft, with buds and flowers on one branch; and three bowls shall be fastened on another shaft, with buds and flowers on the other branch; so on all the six branches that come out of the candlestick.

34 And on the candlestick shall be four bowls made like almonds, with their buds and flowers.

35 And there shall be a bud under two branches of the same, and a bud under two branches of the same, and a bud under two branches of the same, likewise for the six branches that come out of the candlestick.

36 Their buds and their branches shall be of one piece; all of it shall be of one piece cast of pure gold.

37 And you shall make the seven lamps thereof; and they shall light the lamps thereof, that they may give light over against it.

38 And you shall make snuffers thereof, and snuff dishes thereof of pure gold.

39 Of a talent of pure gold shall you make it, with all these vessels.

40 And see that you make them after the same pattern which I have shown you on the mountain.

CHAPTER 26

MOREOVER you shall make the tabernacle with ten curtains of fine twined linen, and blue and purple and scarlet material; with cherubim, the workmanship of a craftsman shall you make them.

2 The length of each curtain shall be twenty-eight cubits, and the breadth of each curtain four cubits; all the curtains shall be of the same measure.

3 Five curtains shall be coupled one to another; and the other five curtains shall be coupled one to another.

4 And you shall make loops of blue on the edge of the one curtain from the selvedge in the coupling; and likewise shall you make loops on the edge of the other curtain from the selvedge in the coupling of the second.

5 Fifty loops shall you make on the edge of one curtain, and fifty loops shall you make on the edge of the other curtain that is in the coupling of the second; and the loops shall be directly opposite one another.

6 And you shall make fifty taches of gold, and couple the curtains together with the taches; and it shall be one tabernacle.

7 ¶And you shall make curtains of goats' hair for a covering of the tabernacle; eleven curtains shall you make.

8 The length of each curtain shall be thirty cubits, and the breadth of each curtain four cubits; all the eleven curtains shall be of the same measure.

9 And you shall couple five curtains by themselves, and six curtains by themselves, and shall double the sixth curtain in the forefront of the tabernacle.

10 And you shall make fifty loops on the edge of the curtain that is outermost in the coupling, and fifty loops on the edge of the curtain which couples the second.

11 And you shall make fifty taches of brass, and put the taches into the loops, and couple the tent together that it may be one.

12 And what is left over of the curtains of the tent, the half curtain that remains, shall hang over the back of the tabernacle.

13 And a cubit on the one side and a cubit on the other side of that which is left over in the length of the curtains of the tent shall hang over the sides of the tabernacle on this side and on that side to cover it.

14 And you shall make a covering for the tent of rams' skins dyed red and a covering of rams' skins dyed with vermilion.

15 ¶You shall make boards for the tabernacle of shittim wood standing up.

16 Ten cubits shall be the length of each board; and a cubit and a half, the breadth of each board.

17 There shall be two tenons to each board, set in order, one opposite the other; thus shall you make all the boards of the tabernacle.

18 And you shall make the boards for the tabernacle, twenty boards on the south side.

19 And you shall make forty sockets of silver under the twenty boards; two sockets under one board for its two tenons, and two sockets under another board for its two tenons.

20 And for the other side of the tabernacle on the north side there shall be twenty boards;

21 And their forty sockets of silver; two sockets under one board and two sockets under another board.

22 And for the sides of the tabernacle westward you shall make six boards.

23 And two boards shall you make for the corners of the tabernacle on the two sides.

24 And they shall be even at the bottom, and shall be coupled together above the head of it to one ring; thus it shall be for both sockets; they shall be for the two corners.

25 And there shall be eight boards, and their sockets of silver, sixteen sockets; two sockets under one board and two sockets under another board.

26 ¶And you shall make bars of shittim wood; five for the boards of the one side of the tabernacle,

27 And five bars for the boards of the other side of the tabernacle, and five bars for the boards at the westward side of the tabernacle.

28 And the middle bar in the midst of the boards shall reach from end to end.

29 And you shall overlay the boards with gold, and make their rings of gold for places for the bars; and you shall overlay the bars with gold.

30 And you shall erect the tabernacle according to the right pattern thereof which I have shown you on the mountain.

31 ¶And you shall make a veil of blue, purple, and scarlet material, and fine twined linen, the work of a craftsman; with cherubim shall it be made;

32 And you shall hang it upon four pillars of shittim wood overlaid with gold; with their hooks of gold, upon the four sockets of silver.

33 ¶And you shall hang up the veil under the taches, and then bring in thither within the veil the ark of the testimony; and you shall spread the veil between the holy place and the most holy.

34 And you shall put the mercy seat upon the ark of the testimony in the most holy place.

35 And you shall set the table outside the veil, and the candlestick opposite the table on the side of the tabernacle toward the south; and you shall put the table on the north side.

36 And you shall make a curtain for the door of the tent, of blue, and purple, and scarlet material and fine twined linen made of embroidered work.

37 And you shall make for the curtain five pillars of shittim wood, and overlay them with gold, and their hooks shall be of gold; and you shall make five sockets of brass for them.

CHAPTER 27

AND you shall make an altar of shittim wood, five cubits long and five cubits broad; the altar shall be foursquare; and the height thereof three cubits.

2 And you shall make the horns of it on the four corners thereof; its horns shall be of the same; and you shall overlay it with brass.

3 And you shall make pots for the use thereof; and its cauldrons and its shovels and its fleshhooks and censers, all the vessels thereof you shall make of brass.

4 You shall make for it a grating of network of brass; and upon the grating you shall make four rings of brass at its four corners.

5 And you shall put it under the ledge of the altar, that the grate may reach to the midst of the altar.

6 And you shall make poles for the altar, poles of shittim wood, and overlay them with brass.

7 And the poles shall be put into the rings, and they shall be on both sides of the altar, when they carry it.

8 Hollow with boards shall you make it; as I have shown you on the mountain, so shall they make it.

9 ¶And you shall make the court of the tabernacle; on the south side, there shall be hangings for the court of fine twined linen a hundred cubits long for one side;

10 And the twenty pillars thereof and their twenty sockets shall be of brass; the hooks of the pillars and their fillets shall be of silver.

11 And likewise for the north side there shall be hangings a hundred cubits long, and its twenty pillars and their twenty sockets shall be of brass; the hooks of the pillars and their fillets of silver.

12 ¶And for the breadth of the court on the west side there shall be hangings of fifty cubits, their pillars ten and their sockets ten.

13 And the breadth of the court on the east side shall be fifty cubits.

14 The hangings for one side of the gate shall be fifteen cubits, their pillars three and their sockets three.

15 And on the other side shall be fifteen hangings, their pillars three and their sockets three.

16 ¶And for the gate of the court there shall be a hanging of twenty cubits of blue and purple and scarlet material and fine twined linen made of embroidered work; and their pillars shall be four and their sockets four.

17 All the pillars round about the court shall be filleted with silver; their hooks shall be of silver and their sockets of brass.

18 ¶The length of the court shall be a hundred cubits, the breadth fifty everywhere, and the height five cubits of fine twined linen and their sockets of brass.

19 All the vessels of the tabernacle in all the service thereof and all the pins thereof and all the tent-pins of the court shall be of brass.

20 ¶And you shall command the children of Israel that they bring you pure olive oil from beaten olives for the light, so that the lamps may burn always.

21 In the tabernacle of the congregation outside the veil which is before the testimony, Aaron and his sons shall set them in order burning from evening to morning before the LORD; it shall be a statute for ever to your generations from the children of Israel.

CHAPTER 28

AND bring to you Aaron your brother, and his sons with him, from among the children of Israel, that they may minister to me in the priest's office, even Aaron, Nadab, and Abihu, Eleazar and Ithamar, Aaron's sons.

2 And you shall make holy vestments for Aaron your brother for glory and for beauty.

3 And you shall speak to all who are wise hearted, whom I have filled with the spirit of wisdom, that they may make holy vestments for Aaron to consecrate him that he may minister to me in the priest's office.

4 And these are the vestments which they shall make for them: a breastplate and an ephod and a robe and an embroidered coat and a mitre and a girdle; and they shall make holy vestments for Aaron your brother and his sons that they may minister to me in the priest's office.

5 And they shall take gold and blue and purple and scarlet material and fine twined linen.

6 ¶And they shall make the ephod of gold, of blue and purple and scarlet material and fine twined linen, work of a craftsman.

7 It shall have the two shoulderpieces thereof joined at the two edges; so it shall be joined together,

8 And the embroidered girdle of the ephod which is upon it shall be of the same, according to the work thereof; of gold, of blue and purple and scarlet material and fine twined linen.

9 And you shall take two onyx stones, and engrave on them the names of the sons of Israel;

10 Six of their names on one stone, and the other remaining six on the other stone, according to their birth;

11 With the work of an engraver in stones, like the engravings of a signet, you shall engrave the two stones with the names of the sons of Israel; and you shall mount them on the settings of gold.

12 And you shall put the two stones upon the shoulders of the ephod for stones of memorial to the children of Israel; and Aaron shall bear their names before the LORD upon his two shoulders for a memorial.

13 ¶And you shall make settings of gold;

14 And two chains of pure gold, of braided work you shall make; twine, and fasten the two chains of braided work to the settings.

15 ¶And you shall make the breastplate of judgment with the work of a craftsman; like the work of the ephod you shall make it; of gold, of blue and of purple and of scarlet material and fine twined linen.

16 It shall be foursquare being doubled; a span is its length and a span its width.

17 And you shall set in it settings of stones, four rows of stones; the first row shall be a sardius, a topaz, and an emerald:

18 And the second row a carbuncle, a sapphire, and a jasper.

19 And the third row a jacinth (zircon), carnelian, and an amethyst.

20 And the fourth row a beryl, an onyx, and a jasper; they shall be set in gold in their enclosings.

21 And the stones shall be engraved with the names of the sons of Israel, twelve, according to their names, like the engravings of a signet; every one shall be engraved with his name according to the number of the twelve tribes.

22 ¶And you shall make upon the breastplate twin chains, braided work of pure gold.

23 And you shall make upon the breastplate two rings of pure gold, and shall put the two rings on the two ends of the breastplate.

24 And you shall fasten the two braided chains of gold on the two rings which are on the ends of the breastplate.

25 And the other two ends of the braided chains you shall fasten in the two settings, and put them on the shoulder-pieces of the ephod in front of it.

26 ¶And you shall make two rings of gold, and you shall put them upon the two ends of the breastplate on the

border thereof which is in the side of the ephod from within.

27 And you shall make two rings of gold, and shall put them on the two shoulder-pieces of the ephod underneath, toward the forepart thereof, over against the joining thereof, above the embroidered girdle of the ephod.

28 And they shall bind the breastplate by its rings to the rings of the ephod with a lace of blue that it may rest upon the embroidered girdle of the ephod, so that the breastplate may not come loose from the ephod.

29 And Aaron shall bear the names of the sons of Israel in the breastplate of judgment upon his heart, when he enters the holy place, for a continual memorial before the LORD.

30 ¶And you shall put in the breastplate of judgment the Urim and the Thummim; and they shall be upon Aaron's heart when he enters before the LORD; and Aaron shall bear the judgments of the children of Israel upon his heart before the LORD continually.

31 ¶And you shall make the robe of the ephod all of blue.

32 And there shall be an opening in the top of it, in the midst thereof; and it shall have a binding of woven work round about the opening of it, hemmed on the edge so that it may not be torn.

33 ¶And on the hem of it you shall make pomegranates of blue and of purple and of scarlet round about the hem thereof; and bells of gold shall be between them round about:

34 A golden bell and a pomegranate, a golden bell and a pomegranate, on the hem of the robe round about.

35 And it shall be upon Aaron when he ministers; and its sound shall be heard when he enters the holy place before the LORD and when he comes out, that he may not die.

36 ¶And you shall make a crown of pure gold, and engrave upon it, like the engravings of a signet, HOLINESS TO THE LORD.

37 And you shall put it on blue lace, that it may be upon the mitre;

upon the forefront of the mitre it shall be.

38 And it shall be upon Aaron's forehead, and Aaron shall bear the sins of the children of Israel when they shall offer holy sacrifices and all their holy gifts; and the mitre shall be always upon his forehead, that they may be accepted before the LORD.

39 ¶And you shall make the coat of fine linen, and you shall also make the mitre of fine linen and a girdle of embroidered work.

40 ¶And for Aaron's sons you shall make coats, and you shall make for them girdles, and bonnets you shall make for them, for glory and for beauty.

41 And you shall put them upon Aaron your brother, and upon his sons with him; and shall anoint them and consecrate them and sanctify them, that they may minister to me in the priest's office.

42 And you shall make them breeches of fine linen to cover their nakedness; from their loins to their thighs they shall reach;

43 And they shall be upon Aaron and upon his sons when they enter the tabernacle of the congregation or when they come near to the altar to minister in the holy place; that they may not bear iniquity and die; it shall be a statute for ever to Aaron and to his descendants after him.

CHAPTER 29

AND this is the thing that you shall do to them to consecrate them, to minister to me in the priest's office: take one young bullock and two rams without blemish

2 And unleavened bread and unleavened cakes mixed with oil and unleavened wafers mixed with oil; of fine wheat flour shall you make them.

3 And you shall put them in one basket and bring them in the basket with the bullock and the two rams.

4 And Aaron and his sons you shall bring to the door of the tabernacle of the congregation, and you shall wash them with water.

5 And you shall take the vestments and put upon Aaron the coat and the robe of the mitre, the ephod, and the breastplate, and gird him with the embroidered girdle of the ephod;

6 And you shall put the mitre on his head, and put the holy crown upon the mitre.

7 Then you shall take the anointing oil, and pour it upon his head, and anoint him.

8 And you shall bring his sons and put coats upon them.

9 And you shall gird them with girdles, Aaron and his sons, and put the bonnets on them; and the priest's office shall be theirs for a perpetual statute; and thus you shall consecrate Aaron and his sons.

10 And you shall bring a bullock before the tabernacle of the congregation; and Aaron and his sons shall put their hands on the head of the bullock.

11 And you shall slaughter the bullock before the LORD at the door of the tabernacle of the congregation.

12 And you shall take some of the blood of the bullock and sprinkle it upon the horns of the altar with your finger and pour all the rest of the blood at the bottom of the altar.

13 And you shall take all the fat that covers the entrails, and the caul that is above the liver, and the two kidneys and the fat that is on them and burn them upon the altar.

14 But the flesh of the bullock and its skin and its dung you shall burn with fire outside the camp; it is a sin offering.

15 ¶You shall also take one ram; and Aaron and his sons shall put their hands on the head of the ram.

16 And you shall slaughter the ram; and you must take some of its blood and sprinkle it round about upon the altar.

17 And then you shall cut the ram into pieces, and wash its entrails and its legs, and put them over its pieces and over its head.

18 And you shall burn the whole ram upon the altar; it is a burnt offering to the LORD; it is a sweet savour,

an offering made by fire to the LORD.

19 ¶And you shall take the other ram; and Aaron and his sons shall put their hands upon the head of the ram.

20 Then you shall slaughter the ram, and take some of its blood, and sprinkle it upon the tip of the right ear of Aaron and upon the tips of the right ears of his sons and upon the thumbs of their right hands and upon the great toes of their right feet, and sprinkle the blood upon the altar round about.

21 And you shall take some of the blood that is on the altar and some of the anointing oil, and sprinkle it upon Aaron and upon his vestments and upon his sons and upon the vestments of his sons with him; and he shall be consecrated and his vestments and his sons and his sons' vestments with him.

22 And you shall take of the fat and the rump, and the fat that covers the entrails, the caul of the liver, the two kidneys, and the fat that is on them and the right shoulder; for it is a ram of consecration;

23 And you shall take one loaf of bread and one loaf of bread baked with oil and a cake baked with flour and oil out of the basket of the unleavened bread that is before the LORD;

24 And you shall put all of these in the hands of Aaron and in the hands of his sons; and you shall wave them for a wave offering before the LORD.

25 And you shall receive them from their hands, and burn the breast of the ram upon the altar for a burnt offering, for a sweet savour before the LORD; it is an offering made by fire to the LORD.

26 And you shall take the breast of the ram of Aaron's consecration and wave it for a wave offering before the LORD; and it shall become your share.

27 And you shall sanctify the breast of the wave offering and the thigh of the heave offering which is waved and which is placed upon the altar from the ram of the consecration,

even of that which is for Aaron, and of that which is for his sons;

28 And it shall belong to Aaron and his sons by a statute for ever from the children of Israel; for it is a heave offering; and it shall be a heave offering from the children of Israel from their peace offerings, an oblation to the LORD.

29 ¶And the holy vestments of Aaron shall belong to his sons after him, to be anointed in them and to be consecrated in them.

30 And one of his sons who is to become priest in his stead shall put them on seven days, when he enters into the tabernacle of the congregation to minister in the holy place.

31 ¶And you shall take the ram of the consecration and cook its meat in the holy place.

32 And Aaron and his sons shall eat the meat of the ram and the bread that is in the basket at the door of the tabernacle of the congregation.

33 And they shall eat of those things with which the atonement was made, to consecrate and to sanctify them; but a stranger shall not eat of them because they are holy.

34 And if any of the meat of the consecration, or of the bread, remain unto the morning, then you shall burn what is left over with fire; it shall not be eaten because it is holy.

35 And thus shall you do to Aaron and to his sons, just as I have commanded you; seven days shall you consecrate them.

36 And you shall offer every day a bullock for a sin offering for atonement; and you shall sprinkle blood on the altar, when you make an atonement for it, and you shall anoint it to sanctify it.

37 Seven days you shall make an atonement for the altar and sanctify it; and the altar shall be most holy; whatever touches the altar shall be holy.

38 ¶Now this is what you shall offer upon the altar: two lambs of the first year day by day continually.

39 One lamb you shall offer in the morning and the other lamb you shall offer in the evening;

40 And with the one lamb you shall offer a tenth part of an ephah of fine flour mixed with a fourth part of a hin of beaten oil, and a fourth part of a hin of wine for a drink offering.

41 And the other lamb you shall offer in the evening, and shall do to it according to the meat offering of the morning and according to the drink offering thereof for a sweet savour, an offering made by fire to the LORD.

42 It shall be a continual burnt offering throughout your generations at the door of the tabernacle of the congregation before the LORD, where I will meet you, to speak there to you.

43 And there I will meet with the children of Israel, and the people shall be sanctified by my glory.

44 And I will sanctify the tabernacle of the congregation and the altar; I will also sanctify both Aaron and his sons to minister to me in the priest's office.

45 ¶And I will dwell among the children of Israel and will be their God.

46 And they shall know that I am the LORD their God who brought them forth out of the land of Egypt that I may dwell among them; I am the LORD their God.

CHAPTER 30

YOU shall make an altar to burn incense upon; of shittim wood shall you make it.

2 A cubit long, and a cubit wide; foursquare shall it be; and its height shall be two cubits; the horns thereof shall be of one piece of the same material.

3 And you shall overlay it with pure gold, the top thereof, and the sides thereof round about, and the horns thereof; and you shall make for it a crown of gold round about.

4 And two golden rings you shall make for it under the crown of it, on the two corners thereof, upon the two sides of it shall you make it; and they shall be for places for the poles to carry it with them.

5 And you shall make the poles of shittim wood and overlay them with gold.

6 And you shall put it before the veil that is by the ark of the testimony, before the mercy seat that is over the testimony, where I will meet with you.

7 And Aaron shall burn upon it sweet incense every morning; when he prepares the lamps, he shall burn incense upon it.

8 And when Aaron lights the lamps in the evening, he shall burn incense upon it, a perpetual incense before the LORD throughout your generations.

9 You shall not offer strange incense thereon, nor burnt offering, nor meat offering; neither shall you pour drink offering thereon.

10 And Aaron shall make an atonement upon the horns of it once in a year with the blood of the sin offering of atonement; once in a year shall he make atonement upon it throughout your generations; it is most holy to the LORD.

11 ¶And the LORD spoke to Moses, saying,

12 When you receive the sum of the children of Israel after their number, then every man shall give a ransom for himself to the LORD, when you have numbered the people; that there be no plague among them, when you number them.

13 This is what everyone who is included in the number shall give, half a shekel according to the shekel of the sanctuary (a shekel is twenty gerahs); half a shekel shall be the offering to the LORD.

14 Every one among them who is included in the number from twenty years old and upward shall give an offering to the LORD.

15 The rich shall not give more, and the poor shall not give less than half a shekel, when they give an offering to the LORD to make an atonement for your souls.

16 And you shall take the atonement money from the children of Israel, and shall give it for the work of the tabernacle of the congregation; that it may be a memorial to the children of Israel before the LORD, to make an atonement for your souls.

17 ¶And the LORD spoke to Moses, saying,

18 You shall also make a laver of brass, and its base of brass, for washing; and you shall put it between the tabernacle of the congregation and the altar, and you shall put water into it.

19 And Aaron and his sons shall wash their hands and their feet thereat;

20 When they enter into the tabernacle of the congregation, they shall wash with water, that they die not; or when they draw near to the altar to minister, and to burn incense, and to offer an offering to the LORD.

21 So they shall wash their hands and their feet, that they die not; and it shall be a statute for ever to them, even to him and to his descendants throughout their generations.

22 ¶Moreover the LORD spoke to Moses, saying,

23 Take the choicest spices, of pure myrrh five hundred shekels and of sweet cinnamon half so much, that is, two hundred and fifty shekels, and of sweet calamus two hundred and fifty shekels,

24 And of cassia five hundred shekels, by the weight of the sanctuary, and of olive oil a hin:

25 And you shall make it an oil of holy ointment, an ointment compounded after the art of the perfumer; it shall be a holy anointing oil.

26 And you shall anoint the tabernacle of the congregation with it, and the ark of the testimony,

27 And the table and all its vessels, and the candlestick and its vessels, and the altar of incense,

28 And the altar of the burnt offering with all its vessels, and the laver and its base.

29 And you shall sanctify them, and they shall become most holy; whatsoever touches them shall be holy.

30 And you shall anoint Aaron and his sons, and consecrate them that they may minister to me in the priest's office.

31 And you shall speak to the children of Israel, saying, This shall be

a holy anointing oil to me throughout your generations.

32 Upon men's bodies shall it not be rubbed, neither shall you make any other oil like it, after the composition of it; because it is holy, and it shall be holy to you.

33 Whosoever compounds any like it or whosoever shall give any of it to a stranger shall be cut off from his people.

34 ¶And the LORD said to Moses, Take sweet spices, stacte and onycha and galbanum; sweet spices, with pure frankincense; of each shall there be equal weight;

35 And you shall make it a perfume, a compound made by the work of the perfumer, tempered together, pure and holy;

36 And you shall beat some of it very fine, and put of it before the testimony in the tabernacle of the congregation, where I will meet with you; it shall be to you most holy.

37 And as for the perfume which you shall make, you shall not make to yourselves according to its composition; it shall be to you holy for the LORD.

38 Whosoever shall make any like it, to anoint with it, shall be cut off from his people.

CHAPTER 31

THE LORD spoke to Moses, saying, 2 See, I have called by name Bezaliel the son of Uri, the son of Hur, of the tribe of Judah;

3 And I have filled him with the Spirit of God, in wisdom and in understanding, and in knowledge and in all manner of workmanship,

4 To teach cunning works, to do work in gold and in silver and in brass

5 And in the art of cutting of stones to be set and in the carving of timber and in all manner of workmanship.

6 And I, behold, have appointed with him Elihab, the son of Ahisamakh, of the tribe of Dan; and I have put wisdom in the heart of every skillful man that he may make all things which I have commanded you:

7 The tabernacle of the congregation, and the ark of the testimony, and the mercy seat that is thereupon, and all the vessels of the tabernacle,

8 And the table and all its vessels, and the pure candlestick with all its instruments, and the altar of incense,

9 And the altar of burnt offering with all its vessels, and the laver and its base,

10 And the vestments for the service, and the holy vestments for Aaron the priest, and the vestments for his sons, to minister to me in the priest's office,

11 And the anointing oil, and the sweet incense for the holy place; according to all that I have commanded you, shall they do.

12 ¶And the LORD spoke to Moses, saying,

13 Speak to the children of Israel saying, My sabbaths you must keep; for it is a sign between me and you throughout your generations; that you may know that I am the LORD your God who sanctifies you.

14 You shall keep the sabbath; for it is holy to you; every one who defiles it shall surely be put to death; and whoever shall do any work on it, that soul shall surely be cut off from among his people.

15 Six days you shall do work; but the seventh day is the sabbath of rest, holy to the LORD; whosoever does any work on the sabbath day shall surely be put to death.

16 Wherefore the children of Israel shall keep the sabbath to the LORD to observe the sabbath throughout all their generations for a perpetual covenant.

17 It is a sign between me and the children of Israel for ever; for in six days the LORD made heaven and earth and the seas and all that are therein, and on the seventh day he ceased from work and rested.

18 ¶And he gave to Moses, when he had made an end of talking with him on mount Sinai, two tablets of testimony, the stone tablets written by the finger of God.

CHAPTER 32

WHEN the people saw that Moses delayed to come down from the mountain, they gathered themselves together unto Aaron and said to him, Arise, make us gods that they may go before us; as for this man Moses who brought us up out of the land of Egypt, we do not know what has become of him.

2 And Aaron said to them, Remove the golden earrings which are in the ears of your wives, of your sons, and of your daughters, and bring them to me.

3 So all the people removed the golden earrings which were in their ears, and brought them to Aaron.

4 And he received them, and drew a design, and made it a molten calf; and they said, This is your god, O Israel, who brought you up out of the land of Egypt.

5 And Aaron was afraid, and he built an altar before it; then Aaron made a proclamation, and said, To-morrow is a feast to the LORD.

6 And they rose up early on the morrow and offered burnt offerings and brought peace offerings; and the people sat down to eat and to drink, and rose up to play and to quarrel.

7 ¶And the LORD said to Moses, Go down, get away from here; for your people whom you have brought out of the land of Egypt have corrupted themselves;

8 They have turned aside quickly from the way which I commanded them; they have made for themselves a molten calf, and have worshipped it, and have sacrificed to it, and said, This is your god, O Israel, who has brought you out of the land of Egypt.

9 And the LORD said to Moses, I have seen this people, and, behold it is a stiff-necked people;

10 Now therefore let me alone, that my wrath may be kindled against them and that I may destroy them; and I will make of you a great nation.

11 But Moses prayed before the LORD his God and said, Not so, O LORD, let not thy wrath kindle against

thy people whom thou hast brought forth out of the land of Egypt with great power and with a mighty hand.

12 Why should the Egyptians say, It was for their injury he did bring them out to slay them in the mountains and to consume them from the face of the earth? Rest from thy fierce anger and be reconciled concerning the evil deed of thy people.

13 Remember Abraham, Isaac, and Israel, thy servants, to whom thou didst swear by thine own self and didst say to them, I will multiply your descendants as the stars in heaven, and all the land that I have spoken of I will give to thy descendants, and they shall inherit it for ever.

14 And the LORD was reconciled concerning the evil which he had purposed to do to his people.

15 ¶And Moses turned and went down from the mountain, and the two stone tablets of the testimony were in his hand, the tablets that were written on both sides; on the one side and on the other were they written.

16 The tablets were the work of God, and the writing was the writing of God, engraved upon the tablets.

17 And when Joshua heard the noise of the people fighting, he said to Moses, There is a noise of war in the camp.

18 Moses said to him, It is not the sound of the cry of mighty men, neither is it the sound of the cry of weak men; but it is the sound of sin that I hear.

19 ¶And it came to pass as soon as they came near to the camp, he saw the calf and the cymbals; and Moses' anger raged, and he threw the tablets out of his hand and broke them at the foot of the mountain.

20 And he took the calf which they had made, and burned it in the fire, and filed it with a file until it was ground into dust, and he scattered it upon the water, and made the children of Israel drink of it.

21 And Moses said to Aaron, What has this people done to you that you have brought so great a sin upon them?

22 And Aaron said, Let not the anger of my lord rage; you yourself know this people, that they are bad.

23 For they said to me, Make us gods that they shall go before us; as for this Moses who brought us up out of the land of Egypt, we do not know what has become of him.

24 And I said to them, Whosoever has any gold bring it to me. So they brought it to me; then I cast it into the fire, and it became this calf.

25 ¶And when Moses saw that the people had sinned; (for Aaron had caused them to sin, and to leave a bad name behind them);

26 Then Moses stood in the gate of the camp and said, Who is on the LORD's side? Let him come to me. And all the Levites gathered themselves together to him.

27 And Moses said to them, Thus says the LORD God of Israel: Put every man his sword by his side, and go in and out from door to door throughout the camp, and slay every man his brother, his friend, and his neighbor.

28 And the Levites did according to the word of Moses; and there fell of the people that day about three thousand men.

29 And Moses said to them, Strengthen yourselves today before the LORD, every man with his son and with his brother; for a blessing shall come upon you today.

30 ¶And it came to pass on the next day, Moses said to the people, You have sinned this great sin; and now I will go up to the LORD; perhaps he may forgive your transgressions.

31 So Moses returned to the LORD and said, I beseech thee, O LORD God, truly this people have sinned a great sin and have made for themselves gods of gold.

32 But now, if thou wilt, forgive their sins; and if not, blot me, I pray thee, out of thy book which thou hast written.

33 And the LORD said to Moses, Whosoever has sinned against me, him will I blot out of my book.

34 Therefore now go, lead the people to the place where I tell you; behold, my angel shall go before you; nevertheless in the day when I punish I will visit their sins upon them.

35 And the LORD smote the people because they worshipped the calf which Aaron made.

CHAPTER 33

AND the LORD said to Moses, Depart, and go up hence, you and the people whom you have brought up out of the land of Egypt, to the land which I swore to Abraham, Isaac, and Jacob, saying, To your descendants will I give it;

2 And I will send an angel before you; and he will destroy the Canaanites, the Amorites, the Hittites, the Perizzites, the Hivites, and the Jebusites;

3 Go to a land flowing with milk and honey; for I will not go up among you; for you are a stiff-necked people; lest I consume you on the way.

4 ¶And when the people heard this bad news, they mourned; and no man did put on him his armor.

5 Then the LORD said to Moses, Say to the children of Israel, You are a stiff-necked people; I will come up among you in a moment, and consume you; therefore now put off your armor from you, that I may know what to do to you.

6 And the children of Israel stripped themselves of their armor by mount Horeb.

7 And Moses took his tent and pitched it outside the camp, afar off from the camp, and called it the tabernacle of the congregation. And it came to pass that every one who sought to inquire of the LORD went out to the tabernacle of the congregation, which was outside the camp.

8 And it came to pass when Moses went out to the tabernacle that all the people rose up and stood every man at his tent door and looked after Moses until he entered the tabernacle.

9 And it came to pass as Moses entered into the tabernacle the pillar of cloud descended and stood at the door of the tabernacle and the LORD talked with Moses.

10 And all the people saw the pillar

of cloud standing at the door of the tabernacle; and all the people rose up and worshipped, every man in his tent door.

11 And the LORD spoke to Moses face to face, as a man speaks to his friend. And he returned to the camp; but his servant Joshua, the son of Nun, a young man, departed not from the tabernacle.

12 ¶And Moses said to the LORD, See, thou sayest to me, Bring up this people; and thou hast not let me know whom thou wilt send with me. Yet thou hast said, I know you by name, and thou hast also found favor in my sight.

13 Now therefore, if I have found favor in thy sight, show me now the way that I may know thee, that I may find favor in thy sight; and consider that this thy people is a great nation.

14 And the LORD said to Moses, Go ahead of me, and I will give you rest.

15 And he said to him, If thou thyself will not go with us, let us not leave this place.

16 For wherein shall it be known here that I and thy people have found mercy in thy sight? Is it not in that thou goest with us? So that we be distinguished, I and thy people, from all the people that are upon the face of the earth.

17 And the LORD said to Moses, I will do this thing also that you have spoken; for you have found grace in my sight, and I know you by your name.

18 And Moses said, Show me thy glory.

19 And he said, I will make all my goodness pass before you, and I will proclaim the name of the LORD before you; and I will be gracious to whom I will be gracious, and will show mercy on whom I will show mercy.

20 And he said, You cannot see my face; for no man can see me and live.

21 And the LORD said to Moses, Behold, there is a place in front of me, and you shall stand upon the rock;

22 And it shall come to pass when my glory passes by that I will put you in a cave of the rock and will rest my hand upon you till I pass by;

23 And I will take away my hand, and you shall see my back; but my face shall not be seen.

CHAPTER 34

AND the LORD said to Moses, Hew two tablets of stone like the first ones; and write upon the tablets the words that were on the first tablets, which you broke.

2 And be ready in the morning, and come up in the morning to mount Sinai, and present yourself there to me on the top of the mountain.

3 And no man shall come up with you, neither shall any man be seen throughout all the mountain; neither let the flocks nor herds feed opposite that mountain.

4 ¶And Moses hewed two tablets of stone like the first ones; and he arose early in the morning and went up to the top of mount Sinai, as the LORD had commanded him, and took in his hand the two stone tablets.

5 And the LORD descended in the cloud and stood with him there and announced the name of the LORD.

6 And the LORD passed by before him, and proclaimed, The LORD, The LORD, The God merciful and compassionate, longsuffering, and abundant in goodness and truth,

7 Keeping mercy for thousands of generations, forgiving sins and transgressions, who by no means justifies the guilty; visiting the iniquity of the fathers upon the children, and upon the children's children, to the third and fourth generation.

8 And Moses made haste and fell on the ground and worshipped.

9 And he said, If now I have found mercy in thy sight, O my LORD, let now my LORD go with us; for it is a stiff-necked people; and pardon our offenses and our sins and our guilty conscience.

10 ¶And the LORD said, Behold, I will make a covenant before all your people; I will do marvels such as have not been done in all the earth, nor in any of the nations; and all this people

among whom you are shall see the work of the LORD; for it is a terrible thing that I will do with you.

11 Observe the things which I command you this day; behold, I will destroy from before you the Canaanites, the Amorites, the Hittites, the Perizzites, the Hivites, and the Jebusites.

12 Take heed to yourself lest you make a covenant with the inhabitants of the land whither you go, lest they become a stumbling block to you.

13 But you must destroy their altars, break their images, and cut down their idols.

14 For you shall worship no other god; for the LORD whose name is zealous,[1] is a zealous God.

15 You shall not make a covenant with the inhabitants of the land, so that the people may not go astray after their idols and sacrifice to their gods, and they shall invite you, and you shall eat of their sacrifices;

16 And you shall take of their daughters to your sons, and give your daughters to their sons; and your daughters shall go astray after their gods, and their daughters cause your sons to go astray after their gods.

17 You shall make to yourself no molten gods.

18 ¶The feast of unleavened bread you shall keep. Seven days you shall eat unleavened bread, as I commanded you, in the time of the month of Abib; for in the month of Abib you came out from Egypt.

19 All that opens the womb is mine; and every firstling among your cattle, both of the oxen and of the lambs.

20 And all the firstlings of the cattle you shall redeem with a lamb; but if you shall not redeem it, then you shall kill it. All the first-born of your sons you shall redeem. And none shall appear before me empty-handed.

21 ¶Six days you shall work, but on the seventh day you shall rest; in the time of ploughing and during harvest you shall rest.

22 ¶And you shall observe the feast of weeks, the feast of the firstfruits of wheat harvest, and the feast of ingathering at the year's end.

23 ¶Three times a year shall all your memorial offerings be brought before the LORD, the God of Israel.

24 For I will destroy the nations from before you, and enlarge your borders; neither shall any man covet your land when you shall go up to appear before the LORD your God three times in a year.

25 You shall not offer the blood of a sacrifice with leavened bread; neither shall the sacrifice of the feast of the passover be left over to the morning.

26 The first of the firstfruits of your land you shall bring to the house of the LORD your God. You shall not cook a kid in its mother's milk.

27 And the LORD said to Moses, Write these words; for by these words I have made a covenant with you and with all Israel.

28 And he was there with the LORD forty days and forty nights; he neither ate bread nor drank water. And he wrote upon the tablets the words of the covenant, the ten commandments.

29 ¶And it came to pass, when Moses came down from mount Sinai with the two tablets of testimony in his hand, when he came down from the mountain, Moses knew not that the skin of his face shone while the LORD talked with him.

30 And when Aaron and all the children of Israel saw Moses' face, behold, the skin of Moses' face shone; and they were afraid to come near to him.

31 So Moses called to them; and Aaron and all the leaders of the congregation returned to him; and Moses talked with them.

32 And afterward all the children of Israel came near to him; and he gave them in commandment all that the LORD had spoken with him in mount Sinai.

33 And when Moses had finished speaking with them, he put a veil on his face.

34 But when Moses went in before

---

[1] In Aramaic the same word may mean either zealous or jealous. God was not jealous of idols, but was zealous to keep his people from worshipping idols.

the LORD to speak with him, he took the veil off until he came out. And he came out and spoke to the children of Israel that which he was commanded.

35 And the children of Israel saw the face of Moses, that the skin of Moses' face shone; and Moses took off the veil from his face when he went in to speak with the LORD.

CHAPTER 35

AND Moses gathered all the congregation of the children of Israel together and said to them, These are the things which the LORD has commanded to be done.

2 Six days shall work be done, but the seventh day shall be holy to you, a sabbath of rest to the LORD; whosoever does any work on it shall be put to death.

3 You shall kindle no fire throughout your habitations on the sabbath day.

4 ¶And Moses spoke to all the congregation of the children of Israel, saying, This is the thing which the LORD has commanded to be done:

5 Take from among you an offering for the LORD; whosoever is of a willing heart, let him bring an offering to the LORD, gold, silver, and brass,

6 Blue, purple, and scarlet material, and fine linen, and goats' hair,

7 And rams' skins dyed red, and dark blue skins, and shittim wood,

8 And oil for the light, and spices for anointing oil and for the sweet incense,

9 And onyx stones, and precious stones for the ephod, and for the breastplate.

10 And every wisehearted one among you shall come, and make all that the LORD has commanded;

11 The tabernacle, its tent, and its covering, its taches, and its boards, its bars, its pillars, and its sockets,

12 The ark, and its poles, the mercy seat, and the veil of the covering,

13 The table, and its poles, and all its vessels, and the shewbread,

14 The candlestick for the light, and its instruments and its lamps, and the oil for the light,

15 And the incense altar, and its poles, and the anointing oil, and the sweet incense, and the hanging for the door at the entrance of the tabernacle,

16 The altar of burnt offering, with its bronze grate, its poles, and all its vessels, the laver, and its base,

17 The hangings of the court, its pillars, and their sockets, and the hanging for the door of the court,

18 The pins of the tabernacle, and the pins of the court, and their cords,

19 The vestments of service, to minister in the holy place, the holy vestments for Aaron the priest, and the vestments for his sons, to minister in the priest's office.

20 ¶And the whole congregation of the children of Israel departed from the presence of Moses.

21 And they came, every one who was willing in his heart and every one whose spirit made him willing, and they brought offerings for the LORD, to the work of the tabernacle of the congregation, and for all its service, and for the holy vestments.

22 And they came, both men and women, as many as were willinghearted, and brought bracelets and earrings and rings and necklaces and all sorts of jewels of gold; and every man that had set aside an offering of gold brought it to the LORD.

23 And every man with whom was found blue, and purple, and scarlet material, and fine linen, and goats' hair, and red skins of rams, and dark blue skins, brought them.

24 Every one who had set aside an offering of silver and brass brought it as an offering for the LORD; and every man with whom was found shittim wood for any work of the service brought it.

25 And all the women who were skillful did spin with their hands, and brought that which they had spun, both of blue, and of purple, and of scarlet material, and of fine linen.

26 And all the women who were willing skillfully spun goats' hair.

27 And the princes brought onyx stones and precious stones for the ephod and for the breastplate,

28 And spices, and oil for the light,

and for the anointing oil, and for the sweet incense.

29 The children of Israel brought a willing offering to the LORD, every man and woman who were willing-hearted to bring material for all manner of work which the LORD had commanded to be done by Moses.

30 ¶Then Moses said to the children of Israel, See, the LORD has called by name Bezaliel the son of Uri, the son of Hur, of the tribe of Judah;

31 And he has filled him with the Spirit of God, with wisdom and with understanding, and with knowledge, and with all manner of workmanship,

32 To devise artistic works, to work in gold, and in silver, and in brass,

33 And in the cutting of stones to be set, and in the carving of wood to make any manner of art work.

34 And he has inspired him to teach, both he and Elihab, the son of Ahisamakh, of the tribe of Dan.

35 Both of them he has filled with wisdom and inspiration to do all manner of work of the carpenter and of the workman of art and of the embroiderer in blue, and in purple, in fine linen, and in scarlet material, and in weaving, and of those who do any kind of work, and of those who devise skillful work.

CHAPTER 36

THEN Bezaliel and Elihab and every wise man to whom the LORD gave wisdom and understanding to know how to work all manner of work for the service of the sanctuary did everything, according to all that the LORD had commanded.

2 And Moses called Bezaliel and Elihab and every skillful man in whose heart the LORD had put wisdom, every one whose heart stirred him up to come to do the work.

3 And they received of Moses all the offering which the children of Israel had brought for the service of the tabernacle of the congregation, with which to make it. And they brought yet to him free offerings every morning.

4 And all the skillful men who did the work of the sanctuary brought in every man some of his work which he made;

5 ¶And they said to Moses, The people bring much more than is necessary for the service of the work which the LORD commanded to make.

6 And Moses gave command, which the heralds proclaimed throughout the camp, saying, Let neither man nor woman make any more work for the offering of the sanctuary. So the people were restrained.

7 For the stuff they had was sufficient for all the things they had to make, and some was left over.

8 ¶And all the skillful men among those who did the work of the tabernacle made ten curtains of fine twined linen and blue and purple and scarlet material; with cherubim artistically wrought they made them.

9 The length of each curtain was twenty-eight cubits, and the breadth of each curtain four cubits; the curtains were all of one size.

10 And they coupled the five curtains one to another; and the other five curtains they coupled one to another.

11 And they made loops of blue on the edge of each curtain from the selvedge in the coupling; likewise they wrought on the other edge of the curtain, on the coupling of the second.

12 They made fifty loops on the one curtain and fifty loops on the edge of the curtain which was in the coupling of the second; the loops were opposite each other.

13 And they made fifty clasps of gold, and coupled the curtains one to another with the clasps so that it became one tabernacle.

14 ¶And they made curtains of goats' hair for the tent over the tabernacle; they made eleven curtains.

15 The length of each curtain was thirty cubits, and the breadth of each curtain four cubits; the eleven curtains were of one size.

16 And they coupled five curtains by themselves, and six curtains by themselves.

17 And they made fifty loops on the edge of the curtain in the coupling,

and fifty loops on the edge of the curtain which coupled the second.

18 And they made fifty clasps of brass to couple the tent together, that it might be one.

19 And they made a covering for the tent of rams' skins dyed red and a covering of badgers' skins above that.

20 ¶And they made boards for the tabernacle of shittim wood, standing up.

21 The length of each board was ten cubits, and the breadth of each board one cubit and a half.

22 Each board had two sockets, one exactly opposite the other; thus did they make all the boards of the tabernacle.

23 And they made boards for the tabernacle; twenty boards for the south side:

24 And forty sockets of silver they made under the twenty boards; two sockets under one board for its two tenons, and two sockets under another board for its two tenons.

25 And for the other side of the tabernacle, which is toward the north side, they made twenty boards,

26 And their forty sockets of silver; two sockets under one board, and two sockets under another board.

27 And for the side of the tabernacle westward they made six boards.

28 And two boards made they for the corners of the tabernacle on the two sides.

29 And they were coupled beneath, and coupled together at the top thereof, to one ring; thus they made both of them in both the corners.

30 And there were eight boards; and their sockets were sixteen sockets of silver, under every board two sockets.

31 ¶And they made bars of shittim wood; five bars for the boards of the one side of the tabernacle,

32 And five bars for the boards of the other side of the tabernacle, and five bars for the boards of the tabernacle for the side westward.

33 And they made the middle bar to pass through the boards from the one end to the other.

34 And they overlaid the boards with gold, and made their rings of gold to be places for the bars, and overlaid the bars with gold.

35 ¶And they made a veil of blue and purple and scarlet material and fine twined linen; with cherubim made they it of the work of an artist.

36 And they made for it four pillars of shittim wood, and overlaid them with gold; their hooks were of gold; and they cast for them four sockets of silver.

37 ¶And they made a hanging for the door of the tabernacle, of blue and purple and scarlet material and fine twined linen of needlework;

38 And they made the five pillars of it with their hooks; and they overlaid their capitals and their fillets with gold; but their five sockets were of brass.

CHAPTER 37

THEN Bezaliel made the ark of shittim wood; two cubits and a half was the length of it, and a cubit and a half the breadth of it, and a cubit and a half the height of it:

2 And he overlaid it with pure gold within and without, and made a crown of gold for it round about.

3 And he cast for it four rings of gold to be set on its four corners; two rings on one side of it and two rings on the other side of it.

4 And he made poles of shittim wood, and overlaid them with gold.

5 And he put the poles into the rings by the sides of the ark to carry the ark.

6 ¶And he made the mercy seat of pure gold; two cubits and a half was its length and one cubit and a half its breadth.

7 And he made two cherubim of gold; of casting work he made them, on the two ends of the mercy seat;

8 One cherub on one side and the other cherub on the other side; above the mercy seat made he the cherubim on its two ends.

9 And the cherubim spread out their wings on high, covering the mercy seat with their wings, with their faces

9

one to another; over the mercy seat were the faces of the cherubim.

10 ¶And he made the table of shittim wood; two cubits was its length and a cubit its breadth and a cubit and a half its height;

11 And he overlaid it with pure gold, and made for it a crown of gold round about.

12 Also he made for it a border of a handbreadth round about; and made a crown of gold for the border thereof round about.

13 And he cast for it four rings of gold, and fastened the rings on the four corners that were in the four feet thereof.

14 Over against the border were the rings, the places for the poles to carry the table.

15 And he made the poles of shittim wood, and overlaid them with gold to carry the table with them.

16 And he made the vessels which were upon the table, its flagons, its spoons, its cups, and its bowls, wherein the drink offering is poured out, of pure gold.

17 ¶And he made the candlestick of pure gold; of cast work made he the candlestick; its shaft, its branches, its bowls, its buds, and its flowers were of the same;

18 And six branches went out of its sides; three branches of the candlestick went out of the one side of it and three branches of the candlestick out of the other side of it;

19 Three bowls were fastened on one shaft with their buds and flowers; and three bowls were fastened on another shaft with their buds and flowers; so, throughout the six branches going out of the candlestick.

20 And in the candlestick were four bowls fastened to it with their buds and flowers;

21 And a bud under two branches of the same, and a bud under two branches of the same, and a bud under two branches of the same; likewise for the six branches going out of the candlestick.

22 Their buds and branches were of the same; all of it was one piece of molten work of pure gold.

23 And he made its seven lamps and its snuffers and its snuff dishes of pure gold.

24 Of a talent of pure gold he made it, and all its vessels.

25 ¶And he made the incense altar of shittim wood; the length of it was a cubit and the breadth of it a cubit; it was foursquare; and two cubits was the height of it; and its horns were of the same.

26 And he overlaid it with pure gold, both the top of it and its sides round about, and the horns of it; and he made for it a crown of gold round about.

27 And he made two rings of gold for it under its crown, by the two corners of it, upon the two sides thereof, as places for the poles to carry it with them.

28 And he made the poles of shittim wood, and overlaid them with gold.

29 ¶And he made the holy anointing oil and the pure incense of sweet spices, according to the work of a perfumer.

CHAPTER 38

AND he made the altar of burnt offering of shittim wood; five cubits was its length and five cubits its breadth; it was foursquare; and three cubits were the height thereof.

2 And he made its horns on the four corners of it; its horns were of the same; and he overlaid it with brass.

3 And he made all the vessels of the altar, the pots, the cauldrons, the hanging pots, the fleshhooks, the shovels, the censers; all its vessels he made of brass.

4 And he made for the altar a bronze grate of network halfway under the base of it.

5 And he cast four rings for the four corners of the grate of brass to be places for the poles.

6 And he made the poles of shittim wood, and overlaid them with brass.

7 And put the poles into the rings on the sides of the altar to carry it with them; he made the altar hollow with boards.

8 ¶And he placed the laver of brass

and its base of brass at the assembly house, for the women who came to pray at the door of the tabernacle of the congregation.

9 ¶And he made the court: for the south side southward the hangings of the court were of fine twined linen, a hundred cubits;

10 Their pillars were twenty, and their bronze sockets twenty; the hooks of the pillars and their fillets were of silver.

11 And for the north side the hangings were a hundred cubits, their pillars were twenty, and their sockets of brass twenty; the hooks of the pillars and their fillets were of silver.

12 And for the west side were hangings of fifty cubits, their pillars ten, and their sockets ten; the hooks of the pillars and their fillets were of silver.

13 And for the east side eastward fifty cubits.

14 The hangings of the one side of the gate were fifteen cubits; their pillars three, and their sockets three.

15 And for the other side, on this hand and that of the gate of the court, were hangings of fifteen cubits for each side; their pillars three, and their sockets three.

16 All the hangings of the court round about were of fine twined linen.

17 And the sockets of the pillars were of brass; the hooks of the pillars and their fillets were of silver; and the overlaying of their capitals of silver; and all the pillars of the court were overlaid with silver.

18 And the hanging for the gate of the court was needlework, of blue, and purple, and scarlet material, and fine twined linen; and twenty cubits long, and the height and the width were five cubits, opposite the hangings of the court.

19 And their pillars were four, and their sockets of brass four; their hooks of silver, and the overlaying of their capitals and their fillets of silver.

20 And all the pins of the tabernacle, and of the court round about, were of brass.

21 ¶This is the sum of the taber-nacle, even of the tabernacle of the testimony, as it was counted, ac-cording to the commandment of Moses, and the work of the Levites, under the supervision of Ithamar, the son of Aaron, the priest.

22 And Bezaliel the son of Uri, the son of Hur, of the tribe of Judah, made all that the LORD commanded Moses.

23 And with him was Elihab, the son of Ahisamakh, of the tribe of Dan, a carpenter, and a craftsman, and an embroiderer in blue, and in purple, and in scarlet material, and in fine linen.

24 All the gold that was used for the work in all the work of the holy place, even the gold of the offering, was twenty-nine talents, and four hun-dred and thirty shekels, by the weight of the sanctuary.

25 And the silver of those who were numbered of the congregation was a hundred talents, and a thousand seven hundred and seventy-five shekels, by the shekel of the sanctuary:

26 A shekel for every head, that is half a shekel, by the weight of the sanctuary, for every one who was in-cluded in the number, from twenty years old and upward, for six hun-dred thousand and three thousand and five hundred and fifty men.

27 And the total sum was one hun-dred talents of silver, for the casting of the sockets of the sanctuary, and the sockets of the veil; a hundred sockets were made from a hundred talents, a talent for a socket.

28 And of the thousand seven hun-dred and seventy-five shekels he made hooks for the pillars, and overlaid their capitals, and overlaid the hooks with silver.

29 And the total sum of the brass of the offering was seventy talents, and two thousand and four hundred shekels.

30 And with it he made the sockets of the door of the tabernacle of the congregation, and the bronze altar, and the bronze grate for it, and all the vessels of the altar,

31 And the sockets of the court round about, and the sockets of the

court gate, and all the pins of the tabernacle, and all the pins of the court round about.

CHAPTER 39

AND of the blue and purple and scarlet material, they made vestments for the service, to minister in the sanctuary, and made the holy vestments for Aaron, as the LORD commanded Moses.

2 And they made the ephod of gold, blue, and purple, and scarlet, and fine twined linen.

3 And they did beat the gold into thin plates, and cut it into wires, to be worked in the blue, and in the purple, and in the scarlet material, and in the fine linen, with artistic workmanship.

4 They made shoulder-pieces for it, to join it together; by the two edges was it joined together.

5 And the embroidered girdle of the ephod that was upon it was of the same material, according to the work thereof; of gold, blue, and purple, and scarlet material, and fine twined linen; as the LORD commanded Moses.

6 ¶And they made the onyx stones inclosed and set in work of gold, engraved, as signets are engraved, with the names of the sons of Israel.

7 And they put them on the shoulder-pieces of the ephod, that they should be stones for a memorial for the sons of Israel; as the LORD commanded Moses.

8 ¶And they made the breastplate, the work of an artist, like the work of the ephod; of gold, blue, and purple, and scarlet material, and fine twined linen.

9 It was foursquare; they made the breastplate double; a span was its length and a span its breadth, being doubled.

10 And they set it in four rows of stones; the first row was a sardius, a topaz, and an emerald; this was the first row.

11 And the second row, a carbuncle, a sapphire, and a jasper.

12 And the third row, a jacinth, a carnelian, and an amethyst.

13 And the fourth row, a beryl, an onyx, and a jasper; they were inclosed and set in the work of gold in their inclosings.

14 And the stones were according to the names of the sons of Israel, twelve, according to their names, engraved like the engravings of signets, everyone with his name, according to the twelve tribes.

15 And they made upon the breastplate chains at the two ends, of braided work of pure gold.

16 And they made two settings of gold and two gold rings; and put the two rings on the two ends of the breastplate.

17 And they fastened the two braided chains of gold to the two rings on the ends of the breastplate.

18 And the two ends of the two braided chains they fastened to the two settings, and put them on the shoulder-pieces of the ephod, in the front of it.

19 And they made two rings of gold, and put them on the two ends of the breastplate, on the border of it, which was on the side of the ephod from within.

20 And they made two other golden rings, and put them on the two shoulder-pieces of the ephod from within, toward the front of it, over against the other coupling thereof, above the embroidered girdle of the ephod.

21 And they did bind the breastplate by its rings to the rings of the ephod with a cord of blue, that it might be above the embroidered girdle of the ephod and that the breastplate might not be loosed from the ephod; as the LORD commanded Moses.

22 ¶And they made the robe of the ephod of fine woven work, all of blue.

23 And the opening of the robe was within it, as the hole of a coat of mail, with a binding round about the opening, that it might not be torn.

24 And they made on the hems of the robe pomegranates of blue and purple and scarlet material and fine twined linen.

25 And they made bells of pure gold, and fastened the bells between the pomegranates on the hem of the

robe, round about between the pomegranates;

26 A bell of gold and a pomegranate, and a bell of gold and a pomegranate, round about the hem of the robe to minister in; as the LORD commanded Moses.

27 ¶And they made coats of fine linen of woven work for Aaron and for his sons,

28 And a mitre of fine linen, and goodly bonnets of fine linen, and breeches of fine linen,

29 And a girdle of fine twined linen, and blue and purple and scarlet needlework; as the LORD commanded Moses,

30 ¶And they made the plate of the holy crown of pure gold, and wrote upon it an inscription like to the engraving of a signet, HOLINESS TO THE LORD.

31 And they tied to it a cord of blue to fasten it over the mitre; as the LORD commanded Moses.

32 ¶Thus all the work of the tabernacle of the congregation was finished; and the children of Israel did according to all that the LORD commanded Moses, so did they.

33 ¶And they brought the tabernacle to Moses, the tent and all its vessels, its rings, its clasps, its boards, its pins, its bars, its pillars, and its sockets,

34 And the covering of rams' skins dyed red, and the covering of badgers' skins, and the veil for the covering of the door,

35 The ark of the testimony, and its poles, and the mercy seat,

36 The table, and all its vessels, and the shewbread,

37 The pure candlestick, with its lamps, and with the lamps to be set in order, and all its vessels, and the oil for light,

38 And the golden altar, and the anointing oil, and the sweet incense, and the hanging for the tabernacle door,

39 The altar of brass, and its grate of brass, its poles, and all its vessels, the laver and its base,

40 The hangings of the court, its pillars, its sockets, and the hanging for the court gate, its cords, its pins, and all the vessels of the service of the tabernacle of the congregation,

41 The vestments of the service to minister in the holy place, and the holy vestments for Aaron the priest, and vestments for his sons, to minister in the priest's office.

42 According to all that the LORD commanded Moses, so the children of Israel made all the work.

43 And Moses looked upon all the work, and, behold, they had done it as the LORD had commanded Moses, even so had they done it; and Moses blessed them.

CHAPTER 40

AND the LORD said to Moses, 2 On the first day of the first month you shall set up the tabernacle of the congregation.

3 And you shall put in it the ark of the testimony, and cover the ark with the veil.

4 And you shall bring in the table, and set in order the things that are to be placed upon it; and you shall bring in the candlestick and light the lamps thereof.

5 And you shall set the altar of gold for the incense before the ark of the testimony, and fasten the hanging to the entry of the tabernacle.

6 And you shall set the altar of the burnt offering in front of the door of the tabernacle of the congregation.

7 And you shall set the laver between the tent of the congregation and the altar, and shall put water in it.

8 And you shall set up the court round about, and hang up the hanging at the court gate.

9 And you shall take the anointing oil, and anoint the tabernacle and all that is in it, and shall sanctify it and all its vessels; and it shall be holy.

10 And you shall anoint the altar of the burnt offering and all its vessels, and sanctify the altar; and it shall be an altar most holy.

11 And you shall anoint the laver and its base, and sanctify it.

12 Then you shall bring Aaron and his sons to the door of the tabernacle

of the congregation, and wash them with water.

13 And you shall put upon Aaron the holy vestments and anoint him and sanctify him; that he may minister to me in the priest's office.

14 Then you shall bring his sons and clothe them with coats;

15 And you shall anoint them, as you did anoint Aaron your brother, that they may minister to me in the priest's office; for their anointing shall surely be an everlasting priesthood throughout their generations.

16 Thus did Moses according to all that the LORD commanded him; so did he.

17 ¶And it came to pass in the first month in the second year, on the first day of the week, that the tabernacle was set up.

18 And Moses set up the tabernacle and fastened its pegs and set up its boards and put in its bars and raised up its pillars.

19 And he spread the covering over the tabernacle and put the covering of skins over it; as the LORD commanded Moses.

20 ¶And he took the testimony and put it into the ark and set the poles on the ark and put the mercy seat above upon the ark:

21 And he brought the ark into the tabernacle and set up the veil of the covering of the door and covered the ark of the testimony; as the LORD commanded Moses.

22 ¶And he put the table in the tent of the congregation on the side of the tabernacle northward, outside the veil.

23 And he set the bread in order upon it before the LORD; as the LORD had commanded Moses.

24 ¶And he put the candlestick in the tabernacle of the congregation, over against the table on the side of the tabernacle southward.

25 And he lighted the lamps before the LORD; as the LORD commanded Moses.

26 ¶And he put the golden altar in the tabernacle of the congregation in front of the veil;

27 And he burnt sweet incense upon it; as the LORD commanded Moses.

28 ¶And he set up the hanging at the door of the tabernacle.

29 And he put the altar of burnt offering at the door of the tabernacle of the congregation, and offered upon it the burnt offering and the meal offering; as the LORD commanded Moses.

30 ¶And he set the laver between the tent of the congregation and the altar, and put water there to wash with it.

31 And Moses and Aaron and his sons washed their hands and their feet at it;

32 When they went into the tent of the congregation, and when they came near to the altar, they washed; as the LORD commanded Moses.

33 And he set up the court round about the tabernacle and the altar, and set up the hanging of the court gate. So Moses finished the work.

34 ¶Then a cloud covered the tent of the congregation, and the glory of the LORD filled the tabernacle.

35 And Moses was not able to enter into the tent of the congregation, because the cloud abode upon it, and the glory of the LORD filled the tabernacle.

36 And when the cloud was lifted up from over the tabernacle, the children of Israel started onward in all their journeys;

37 But if the cloud was not lifted up, then they did not journey till the day that it was lifted up.

38 For the cloud of the LORD was upon the tabernacle by day, and fire was on it by night in the sight of all the house of Israel throughout all their journeys.

THE THIRD BOOK OF MOSES, CALLED

LEVITICUS

CHAPTER 1

AND the Lord called to Moses and spoke to him from the tabernacle of the congregation, saying,

2 Speak to the children of Israel and say to them, When any man of you brings an offering to the Lord, you shall bring your offerings of the cattle, even of the herd and of the flock.

3 If his offering be a burnt sacrifice of the herd, let him offer a male without blemish; he shall offer it at the door of the tabernacle of the congregation to make reconciliation for himself before the Lord.

4 And he shall put his hand upon the head of his burnt offering; and it shall be accepted for him to make atonement for him.

5 And he shall kill the bullock before the Lord; and the priests, Aaron's sons, shall bring the blood and sprinkle the blood round about upon the altar that is by the door of the tabernacle of the congregation.

6 And he shall flay the burnt offering and cut it into pieces.

7 And the priests, Aaron's sons, shall put fire upon the altar and lay the wood in order upon the fire;

8 And the priests, Aaron's sons, shall lay the parts, the head and the fat, in order upon the wood that is on the fire which is upon the altar;

9 But its entrails and its legs he shall wash with water; and the priest shall burn all on the altar; it is a burnt offering, an offering of a sweet savour made by fire to the Lord.

10 ¶And if his offering be of the flocks, of the sheep or of the goats, for a burnt sacrifice, he shall offer a male without blemish.

11 And he shall kill it on the north side of the altar before the Lord; and the priests, Aaron's sons, shall sprinkle its blood round about upon the altar.

12 And he shall cut it into pieces, with its head and its fat; and the priest shall lay them in order on the wood, that is on the fire, which is upon the altar;

13 But he shall wash the entrails and the legs with water; and the priest shall offer it all and burn it upon the altar; it is a burnt sacrifice, an offering made by fire, a sweet savour to the Lord.

14 ¶And if the burnt sacrifice for his offering to the Lord be of fowls, then he shall bring his offering of turtledoves or of young pigeons.

15 And the priest shall bring it to the altar, and wring off its head and burn it on the altar; and its blood shall be wrung out at the side of the altar round about;

16 And he shall pluck away its crop with its feathers, and cast it beside the altar on the east side in the place of the ashes;

17 And he shall cleave it between its wings, but shall not divide it asunder; and the priest shall burn it upon the altar, upon the wood that is upon the fire; it is a burnt sacrifice, an offering made by fire, a sweet savour to the Lord.

CHAPTER 2

WHEN any person shall offer a meal offering to the Lord, his offering shall be of fine flour; and he shall pour oil upon it and put frankincense thereon;

2 And he shall bring it to Aaron's sons, the priests; and he shall take from it his handful of the fine flour,

and from the oil, with all the frankincense thereof; and the priest shall burn his memorial offering upon the altar to be an offering made by fire, a sweet savour to the LORD.

3 And the remnant of the meal offering shall be for Aaron and his sons; it is a thing most holy of the offerings of the LORD made by fire.

4 ¶And when you offer a meal offering baked in the oven, it shall be unleavened cakes of fine flour mixed with oil or unleavened wafers mixed with oil.

5 ¶And if your offering be a meal offering baked on a griddle, it shall be of fine unleavened flour mixed with oil.

6 You shall part it in pieces and pour oil upon the meal offering.

7 ¶And if your offering is a meal offering baked in a pan, it shall be made of fine flour with oil.

8 And you shall bring the meal offering that is made of these things to the LORD; and you shall present it to the priest and he shall place it upon the altar to the LORD.

9 And the priest shall take from the meal offering a memorial thereof and shall burn it upon the altar; it is an offering made by fire, a sweet savour to the LORD.

10 And what is left of the meal offering shall be for Aaron and his sons; it is a thing most holy of the offerings of the LORD made by fire.

11 Every meal offering which you shall offer to the LORD shall be made without leaven, for you shall burn no leaven nor any honey in any offering of the LORD made by fire.

12 ¶As for the offerings of the first-fruits, you shall offer them to the LORD; but they shall not be burnt on the altar for a sweet savour.

13 And every offering of your meal offering you shall season with salt; neither shall you let the salt of the covenant of your God to be lacking from your meal offering; with all your offerings you shall offer salt.

14 And if you offer a meal offering of the first-fruits to the LORD, you shall offer for the meal offering a handful of pure ears of wheat parched by fire; wheat beaten out of full ears, pure, you shall offer of your first-fruits.

15 And you shall put oil upon it and lay frankincense thereon; for it is a meal offering.

16 And the priest shall burn the memorial offering of it, part of the beaten wheat and part of the oil with all the frankincense thereof; it is an offering made by fire to the LORD.

CHAPTER 3

IF his offering is a sacrifice of peace offering, if he offer it of the herd, whether it be a male or a female, he shall offer it without blemish before the LORD.

2 And he shall lay his hand upon the head of his offering and kill it at the door of the tabernacle of the congregation and Aaron's sons, the priests, shall sprinkle the blood upon the altar round about.

3 And he shall offer of the sacrifice of the peace offering an offering made by fire to the LORD, the fat that covers the entrails, and all the fat that is on the entrails

4 And the two kidneys, and the fat that is on them which is by the flanks, and the caul above the liver, with the kidneys, he shall take away.

5 And Aaron's sons shall burn it on the altar upon the burnt sacrifice which is upon the wood that is on the fire; it is an offering made by fire, a sweet savour to the LORD.

6 ¶And if his offering for a sacrifice of peace offering to the LORD be of the flock, male or female, he shall offer it without blemish.

7 If he offer a lamb for his offering, then shall he offer it before the LORD.

8 And he shall lay his hand upon the head of his offering and kill it before the LORD at the door of the tabernacle of the congregation and Aaron's sons shall sprinkle its blood round about upon the altar.

9 And he shall offer of the sacrifice of the peace offering an offering made by fire to the LORD; its fat and the whole rump shall he remove close to the backbone, and the fat that

covers the entrails, and all the fat that is upon the entrails,

10 And the two kidneys, and the fat that is upon them which is by the flanks, and the caul above the liver, with the kidneys, shall he remove.

11 And the priest shall burn it upon the altar; it is a food offering made by fire to the LORD.

12 ¶And if his offering be of the goats, then he shall offer it before the LORD.

13 And he shall lay his hand upon the head of it and kill it before the tabernacle of the congregation; and the sons of Aaron shall sprinkle its blood upon the altar round about.

14 And he shall offer part of it as his offering made by fire to the LORD; the fat that covers the entrails, and all the fat that is upon the entrails

15 And the two kidneys, and the fat that is upon them which is by the flanks, and the caul above the liver, with the kidneys, shall he remove.

16 And the priest shall burn them upon the altar; it is a food offering made by fire for a sweet savour; all the fat is the LORD's.

17 It shall be a perpetual statute for your generations throughout all your dwellings that you eat neither fat nor blood.

CHAPTER 4

AND the LORD spoke unto Moses, saying,

2 Speak to the children of Israel, saying, If a person shall sin through ignorance against any of the commandments of the LORD concerning things which ought not to be done, and shall do any one of them;

3 If the priest that is anointed do sin according to the sins of the people; then let him offer for the sin which he has committed a young bullock without blemish to the LORD for his sin offering.

4 And he shall bring the bullock to the door of the tabernacle of the congregation before the LORD; and he shall lay his hand upon the bullock's head and kill the bullock before the LORD.

5 And the anointed priest shall take of the blood of the bullock and bring it to the tabernacle of the congregation;

6 And the priest shall dip his finger in the blood and sprinkle of the blood seven times before the LORD before the veil of the sanctuary.

7 And the priest shall put some of the blood upon the horns of the altar of sweet incense before the LORD, which is in the tabernacle of the congregation; and he shall pour all the rest of the blood of the bullock at the bottom of the altar of the burnt offering, which is at the door of the tabernacle of the congregation.

8 And he shall take off from it all the fat of the bullock for the sin offering, the fat that covers the entrails, and all the fat that is on the entrails,

9 And the two kidneys, and the fat that is on them which is by the flanks, and the caul above the liver, with the kidneys, it he shall take away,

10 Just as it was taken off from the bullock of the sacrifice of peace offering; and the priest shall burn them upon the altar of the burnt offering.

11 And the skin of the bullock and all its flesh, with its dung, its head, its legs, and its entrails,

12 The whole bullock he shall carry forth outside the camp to a clean place where the ashes are poured out and shall burn it on the wood which is upon the fire; where the ashes are poured out it shall be burnt.

13 ¶And if the whole congregation of Israel go wrong, and the thing is hidden from the eyes of the assembly, and they have done somewhat against any of the commandments of the LORD concerning things which should not be done and are guilty;

14 When the sin which they have committed against it is known, then the whole congregation shall offer a young bullock for the sin and bring it before the tabernacle of the congregation.

15 And the elders of the congregation shall lay their hands upon the head of the bullock before the LORD

and the bullock shall be killed before the LORD.

16 And the priest that is anointed shall bring of the blood of the bullock to the tabernacle of the congregation;

17 And the priest shall dip his finger in the blood and sprinkle it seven times before the LORD in front of the veil.

18 And he shall put some of the blood upon the horns of the altar which is before the LORD, in the tabernacle of the congregation, and shall pour out all the blood at the bottom of the altar of the burnt offering, which is at the door of the tabernacle of the congregation.

19 And he shall take all its fat from it and burn it upon the altar.

20 And he shall do with the bullock just as he did with the bullock for a sin offering, so shall he do with this; and the priest shall make an atonement for them and it shall be forgiven them.

21 And they shall carry forth the bullock outside the camp and burn it as he burned the first bullock; it is a sin offering for the congregation.

22 ¶When a ruler shall sin and shall do something through ignorance against any of the commandments of the LORD his God concerning things which should not be done, and is guilty;

23 Or if his sin which he has committed is made known to him, he shall bring as his offering a kid of the goats, a male without blemish;

24 And he shall lay his hand upon the head of the goat and kill it in the place where they kill the burnt offering before the LORD; it is a sin offering.

25 And the priest shall take some of the blood of the sin offering with his finger and put it upon the horns of the altar of burnt offering and pour out the rest of the blood at the bottom of the altar of burnt offering.

26 And he shall burn all its fat upon the altar as the fat of the sacrifice of peace offerings; and the priest shall make an atonement for him for his sin and it shall be forgiven him.

27 ¶And if any one of the common people of the land sin through ignorance, while he does something against any of the commandments of the LORD concerning things which ought not to be done, and be guilty;

28 Or if his sin which he has committed is made known to him; then he shall bring as his offering a kid of the goats, a female without blemish, for his sin which he has committed.

29 And he shall lay his hand upon the head of the sin offering and slay the sin offering in the place where burnt offering is killed.

30 And the priest shall take some of the blood with his finger and sprinkle it upon the horns of the altar of burnt offering and the rest of the blood he shall pour out at the bottom of the altar.

31 And he shall take away all the fat thereof, as the fat is taken away from the sacrifice of peace offerings; and the priest shall burn it upon the altar for a sweet savour to the LORD; and the priest shall make an atonement for him and it shall be forgiven him.

32 And if he bring of the lambs for his sin offering, then he shall bring a female without blemish.

33 And he shall lay his hand upon the head of the sin offering and slay it for a sin offering at the place where burnt offering victims are killed.

34 And the priest shall take some of the blood of the sin offering with his finger and sprinkle it upon the horns of the altar of burnt offering and the rest of the blood he shall pour out at the bottom of the altar;

35 And he shall take away all its fat, as the fat of the lamb is taken away from the sacrifice of the peace offerings; and the priest shall burn them upon the altar according to the offerings made by fire to the LORD; and the priest shall make an atonement for his sin that he has committed and it shall be forgiven him.

CHAPTER 5

WHEN a person sins and hears the voice of swearing and is a witness, whether he has seen or known of it, if he do not tell it, then he shall suffer for his iniquity.

2 Or if any person touches any unclean thing, whether it be a carcass of an unclean beast or a carcass of unclean cattle or the carcass of unclean creeping things, and disregards it, he also is unclean and guilty.

3 Or if he touches the uncleanness of man, whatever uncleanness it be that a man shall be defiled with, and disregards it, and he knows that he has sinned;

4 Or if any person swears with his lips to do evil or to do good, in whatever decision a man has sworn by an oath, and he disregards it, and yet he knows that he has sinned in one of these things,

5 And it shall be when he shall be guilty in one of these things that he shall confess that he has sinned in that thing;

6 And he shall bring as his trespass offering to the LORD for his sin that he has committed, a female from the flock, a lamb or a female kid of the goats, for a sin offering; and the priest shall make an atonement for him concerning his sin;

7 And if he cannot afford to bring a she lamb, then he shall bring for his sin offering two turtledoves or two young pigeons, one for a sin offering and the other for a burnt offering.

8 And he shall bring them to the priest, who shall offer that which is for the sin offering first, and he shall wring off its head from its neck, but shall not sever it;

9 And he shall sprinkle some of the blood of the sin offering upon the side of the altar; and the rest of the blood shall be wrung out at the bottom of the altar; it is a sin offering.

10 And he shall offer the second for a burnt offering, according to the ritual; and the priest shall make an atonement for him for his sin which he has committed and it shall be forgiven him.

11 ¶But if he cannot afford two turtledoves or two young pigeons, then he shall bring for his offering for the sin which he has committed the tenth part of an ephah of fine flour for a sin offering; he shall put no oil upon it, neither shall he put any frankincense thereon; for it is a sin offering.

12 Then he shall bring it to the priest, and the priest shall take his handful of it as a memorial thereof and burn it on the altar according to the offerings made by fire to the LORD; it is a sin offering.

13 And the priest shall make an atonement for him for the sin which he has committed in any one of these things, and it shall be forgiven him; and the rest shall be the priest's as a meal offering.

14 ¶And the LORD spoke to Moses, saying,

15 If any person commits a trespass and sins through ignorance in the holy things of the LORD; then he shall bring for his trespass offering to the LORD a ram without blemish out of the flocks, valued in money at two shekels of silver, according to the shekel of the sanctuary, for a trespass offering;

16 And the sinner shall make amends for the harm that he has done in the holy thing, and shall add a fifth part to it and give it to the priest; and the priest shall make an atonement for him with the ram of the trespass offering and it shall be forgiven him.

17 ¶And if any person sins and commits any of these things which are forbidden to be done by the commandments of the LORD; though he does not know that he has sinned, yet he is guilty and shall suffer for his iniquity.

18 And he shall bring to the priest a ram of value without blemish out of the flocks for a trespass offering; and the priest shall make an atonement for him for his ignorance in erring, even though he knew it not, and it shall be forgiven him.

19 It is a trespass offering; he certainly shall bring an offering to the LORD.

CHAPTER 6

AND the LORD spoke to Moses, saying,

2 If any person sins and commits an

iniquity against the LORD or lies to his neighbor over a pledge or partnership or takes away a thing by violence or has defrauded his neighbor

3 Or has found that which was lost, and lies about it, and swears falsely; in any of these things that a man does, sinning therein;

4 Then it shall be, because he has sinned and is guilty, he shall restore what he took violently or what he got deceitfully or the pledge which was delivered to him to keep or the lost thing which he found

5 Or anything about which he has sworn falsely; he shall restore it in the principal and shall add a fifth part more to it and give it to him to whom it belongs on the day of his trespass offering.

6 And he shall bring his trespass offering to the LORD, a ram of value without blemish out of the flocks for a trespass offering to the priest;

7 And the priest shall make an atonement for him before the LORD; and it shall be forgiven him for any of the things that he has done in trespassing therein.

8 ¶And the LORD spoke to Moses, saying,

9 Command Aaron and his sons, saying, This is the law of the burnt offering: It is the burnt offering because of the burning upon the altar all night unto the morning, and the fire of the altar shall be kept burning in it.

10 And the priest shall put on his linen garment, and his linen breeches shall be put upon his body, and he shall remove the ashes which the fire has consumed with the burnt offering on the altar, and he shall put them beside the altar.

11 Then he shall put off his garments and put on other garments and carry forth the ashes outside the camp to a clean place.

12 And the fire upon the altar shall be kept burning on it; it shall not be put out; and the priest shall pile up wood on it from morning to morning and lay the burnt offering in order upon it; and he shall burn on it the fat of the peace offerings.

13 The fire shall be kept burning upon the altar continually; it shall never go out.

14 ¶This is the law of the meal offering: the sons of Aaron shall offer it before the LORD, before the altar.

15 And the priest shall take of it his handful of the fine flour of the meal offering and of the oil thereof and all the frankincense which is upon the meal offering, and shall burn it upon the altar for a sweet savour, as a memorial to the LORD.

16 And the remainder of it shall Aaron and his sons eat; with unleavened bread shall it be eaten in a holy place; in the court of the tabernacle of the congregation shall they eat it.

17 It shall not be baked with leaven. I have given it to them for their portion of my offerings made by fire; it is most holy, as is the sin offering and as is the trespass offering.

18 All the males among the children of Aaron shall eat of it. It shall be a statute for ever throughout your generations out of the offerings of the LORD made by fire; every one that touches them shall be holy.

19 ¶And the LORD spoke to Moses, saying,

20 This is the offering of Aaron and of his sons which they shall offer to the LORD on the day when he is anointed: a tenth part of an ephah of fine flour for a perpetual meal offering, half of it in the morning and half of it in the evening, continually.

21 On a griddle it shall be made with oil; he shall bake it soft, and the baked pieces of the meal offering you shall offer for a sweet savour to the LORD.

22 And the priest of his sons who is anointed in his stead shall offer it; it is a statute for ever to the LORD; it shall be wholly burned.

23 For every meal offering for the priest shall be wholly burned; it shall not be eaten.

24 ¶And the LORD spoke to Moses, saying,

25 Speak to Aaron and to his sons, saying, This is the law of the sin offering: In the place where the burnt offering is killed shall the sin offering

be killed before the LORD; it is most holy.

26 The priest who offers it for sin shall eat it; in a holy place shall it be eaten, in the court of the tabernacle of the congregation.

27 Whosoever shall touch the meat thereof shall be holy; and when there is sprinkled of its blood upon any garment, you shall wash that whereon it was sprinkled in a holy place.

28 But the earthen vessel in which it was cooked shall be broken; and if it is cooked in a bronze vessel, it shall be both scoured, and rinsed in water.

29 All the priests among Aaron's sons shall eat of it; it is most holy.

30 And no sin offering whereof any of the blood is brought into the tabernacle of the congregation to make atonement in the holy place shall be eaten; it shall be burned in the fire.

CHAPTER 7

THIS is the law of the trespass offering; it is most holy.

2 In the place where they kill the burnt offering they shall kill the trespass offering; and its blood shall they sprinkle round about upon the altar.

3 Then he shall offer of it all its fat; the rump, and the fat that covers the entrails,

4 And the two kidneys, and the fat that is on them which is by the flanks, and the caul above the liver, with the kidneys, it he shall take away;

5 And the priest shall burn them upon the altar for an offering made by fire to the LORD; it is a trespass offering.

6 Every male among the children of Aaron shall eat of it; it shall be eaten in the holy place; it is most holy.

7 As the sin offering is, so is the trespass offering; there is one law for them: the priest who makes atonement with it shall have it.

8 And the priest who offers any man's burnt offering, even the priest shall have to himself the skin of the burnt offering which he has offered.

9 And all the meal offering that is baked in the oven and all that is baked on the griddle and in the pan

shall belong to the priest who offers it.

10 And every meal offering, mixed with oil or dry, shall belong to all the sons of Aaron, every one according to his portion.

11 And this is the law of the sacrifice of peace offering, which is offered to the LORD.

12 If he offers it for a thanksgiving, then he shall offer with the sacrifice of thanksgiving unleavened cakes mixed with oil and unleavened wafers anointed with oil and soft baked cakes of fine flour mixed with oil.

13 Besides the cakes, he shall offer for his offering leavened bread with the sacrifice of thanksgiving of his peace offerings.

14 And of it he shall offer one cake out of the whole offering as an offering to the LORD, and it shall be the portion of the priest who sprinkles the blood of the peace offering.

15 And the meat of the sacrifice of his peace offerings for his thanksgiving shall be eaten the same day that it is offered; nothing of it shall be left over until the morning.

16 But if the sacrifice of his offering is a vow or a gift offering, it shall be eaten on the same day that he offers his sacrifice; and on the morrow also the remainder of it shall be eaten;

17 But what is left over of the meat of the sacrifice on the third day shall be burned with fire.

18 And if any of the meat of the sacrifice of the peace offering be eaten at all on the third day, it shall not be accepted, neither shall it be imputed to him that offers it; it shall be an abomination, and the person who eats of it shall suffer for his iniquity.

19 And the meat that touches any unclean thing shall not be eaten; it shall be burned with fire; and as for the meat, all who are clean shall eat of it.

20 But the person who eats of the meat of the sacrifice of the peace offering that pertains to the LORD, having his uncleanness upon him, that person shall be cut off from his people.

21 Moreover the person that shall

touch any unclean thing, such as the uncleanness of man or any unclean beast or any unclean creeping thing, and eat of the meat of the sacrifice of peace offerings which pertain to the LORD, that person shall be cut off from his people.

22 ¶And the LORD spoke to Moses, saying,

23 Speak to the children of Israel, saying, You shall eat no manner of fat, of oxen or of lambs or of goats.

24 And the fat of the beast that dies of itself, and the fat of that which is torn by wild beasts, may be used in any other use; but you shall in no wise eat of it.

25 For whosoever eats the fat of the animal of which men offer an offering made by fire to the LORD, the person that eats it shall be cut off from his people.

26 Moreover you shall eat no manner of blood, whether it be of fowl or of beast, in any of your dwellings.

27 Whosoever eats any manner of blood, that person shall be cut off from his people.

28 ¶And the LORD spoke to Moses, saying,

29 Speak to the children of Israel, saying, He that offers the sacrifice of his peace offerings to the LORD shall bring his offering to the LORD from the sacrifice of his burnt offering.

30 His own hands shall bring his offering for the LORD made by fire; he shall bring the fat which is upon the breast, that the breast may be waved for a wave offering before the LORD.

31 And the priest shall burn the fat upon the altar; but the breast shall be for Aaron and his sons.

32 And the right shoulder shall you give to the LORD for an offering of the sacrifices of your peace offerings.

33 He among the sons of Aaron who offers the blood and the fat of the peace offering shall have the right shoulder for his part.

34 For the wave breast and the shoulder offering have I taken from the children of Israel from off the sacrifices of their peace offerings, and have given them to Aaron the priest

and to his sons by a statute for ever from among the children of Israel.

35 ¶This is the portion of the anointing of Aaron and of the anointing of his sons from the offerings of the LORD made by fire, on the day when they are presented to minister to the LORD in the priest's office;

36 That which the LORD commanded to be given them of the children of Israel, on the day that he anointed them, by a statute for ever throughout their generations.

37 This is the law of the burnt offering, of the meal offering, of the sin offering, of the trespass offering, of the consecration, and of the sacrifice of the peace offerings,

38 Which the LORD commanded Moses on mount Sinai on the day that he commanded him concerning the children of Israel to offer their offerings to the LORD in the wilderness of Sinai.

CHAPTER 8

AND the LORD spoke to Moses, saying,

2 Take Aaron and his sons with him, and take the vestments and the anointing oil and a bullock for the sin offering and two rams and a basket of unleavened bread,

3 And gather all the congregation together at the door of the tabernacle of the congregation.

4 And Moses did as the LORD commanded him; and the assembly was gathered together at the door of the tabernacle of the congregation.

5 And Moses said to the congregation, This is the commandment which the LORD has commanded to be done.

6 And Moses brought Aaron and his sons, and washed them with water;

7 And put upon him the coat and girded him with the girdle and clothed him with the robe and bound the loin cloth on his loins and put the ephod upon him and girded him with the embroidered girdle of the ephod.

8 And he put the breastplate upon him; and he put on the breastplate the Urim and the Thummin.

9 And he put the mitre upon his

head; and upon the mitre upon his forefront, he put the golden plate, the holy crown; as the LORD commanded Moses.

10 Then Moses took the anointing oil and anointed the tabernacle and all that was in it and sanctified them.

11 And he sprinkled of it upon the altar seven times and anointed the altar and all its vessels and the laver and its base and sanctified them.

12 And he poured some of the anointing oil upon Aaron's head and anointed him and sanctified him.

13 And Moses brought Aaron's sons and put linen vestments upon them and girded them with girdles and put mitres upon them; as the LORD commanded Moses.

14 And he brought the bullock for the sin offering, and Aaron and his sons laid their hands upon the head of the bullock for the sin offering.

15 And he killed it; and Moses took some of the blood with his finger and sprinkled it upon the horns of the altar round about and purified the altar, and the rest of the blood he poured at the base of the altar and sanctified it to make atonement for it.

16 And he took all the fat that was upon the entrails, and the caul above the liver, and the two kidneys, and their fat, and Moses burned it upon the altar.

17 But the bullock and its hide and its meat and its dung he burned with fire outside the camp; as the LORD commanded Moses.

18 ¶And he brought the ram for the burnt offering; and Aaron and his sons laid their hands upon the head of the ram.

19 And he killed it; and Moses sprinkled the blood upon the altar round about.

20 And he cut the ram into pieces; and Moses burned the head and the pieces and the fat.

21 And he washed the entrails and the legs in water; and Moses burned the whole ram upon the altar; it was a burnt sacrifice for a sweet savour, an offering to the LORD; as the LORD commanded Moses.

22 ¶And he brought the other ram, the ram of consecration; and Aaron and his sons laid their hands upon the head of the ram.

23 And Moses killed it; and he took some of the blood of it, and sprinkled it on the tip of Aaron's right ear and upon the thumb of his right hand and upon the great toe of his right foot.

24 And he brought Aaron's sons, and Moses sprinkled some of the blood on the tips of their right ears and on the thumbs of their right hands and on the great toes of their right feet; and Moses sprinkled the blood upon the altar round about.

25 And he took the fat and the rump and all the fat that was upon the entrails and the caul above the liver and the two kidneys, and their fat, and the right shoulder;

26 And out of the basket of unleavened bread that was before the LORD, he took one unleavened cake and a cake of bread with oil and one wafer, and put them on the fat and upon the right shoulder;

27 And he put all upon Aaron's hands, and upon his sons' hands, and waved them for a wave offering before the LORD.

28 And Moses took them from off their hands, and burned them on the altar as a burnt offering; they were consecration offerings for a sweet savour, an offering made by fire to the LORD.

29 And Moses took the breast and waved it for a wave offering before the LORD; for of the ram of consecration it was Moses' portion; as the LORD commanded Moses.

30 And Moses took some of the anointing oil and of the blood which was upon the altar, and sprinkled it upon Aaron and upon his garments and upon his sons and upon his sons' garments with him, and sanctified Aaron and his garments and his sons and his sons' garments with him.

31 ¶And Moses said to Aaron and to his sons, Cook the meat at the door of the tabernacle of the congregation, and there eat it with the bread that is in the basket of consecration, as I

commanded, saying, Aaron and his sons shall eat it.

32 And that which remains of the meat and of the bread you shall burn with fire.

33 And you shall not go out of the door of the tabernacle of the congregation for seven days, until the days of your consecration are at an end; for your consecration will be completed in seven days.

34 Just as I have done this day, so the Lord has commanded to do to make an atonement for you.

35 Therefore you shall remain at the door of the tabernacle of the congregation day and night for seven days and keep the charge of the Lord's observance, that you die not; for so I am commanded.

36 So Aaron and his sons did all things which the Lord commanded by the hand of Moses.

CHAPTER 9

AND it came to pass on the eighth day, Moses called Aaron and his sons and the elders of Israel;

2 And he said to Aaron, Take for yourself a young calf for a sin offering and a ram for a burnt offering, both without blemish, and offer them before the Lord.

3 And he said to the children of Israel, Take for yourselves a kid of the goats for a sin offering, and a calf and a lamb, both of the first year, without blemish, for a burnt offering;

4 Also a bullock and a ram for a peace offering, to sacrifice before the Lord; and a meal offering mixed with oil; for today the Lord will appear to you.

5 ¶And they brought everything that Moses had commanded before the tabernacle of the congregation; and all the congregation drew near and stood before the Lord.

6 And Moses said, This is the thing which the Lord commanded that you should do, and the glory of the Lord shall appear to you.

7 And Moses said to Aaron, Draw near to the altar, and offer your sin offering and your burnt offering, and make an atonement for yourself and for the people; and offer the offering of the people, and make an atonement for them; as the Lord commanded.

8 ¶Aaron therefore drew near to the altar, and killed the calf of the sin offering, which was for himself.

9 And the sons of Aaron brought the blood to him; and he dipped his finger in the blood and sprinkled it upon the horns of the altar, and poured out the blood at the bottom of the altar;

10 But the fat and the kidneys and the caul above the liver of the sin offering he burned upon the altar; as the Lord commanded Moses.

11 And the meat and the hide he burned with fire outside the camp.

12 And he slew the burnt offering; and Aaron's sons presented to him the blood, and he sprinkled it round about upon the altar.

13 And they presented the burnt offering to him, and he cut it into pieces and burned the head upon the altar.

14 And he washed the entrails and the legs, and burned them for a burnt offering upon the altar.

15 ¶And he brought the people's offering, and took the goat which was for the sin offering for the people, and killed it and washed it and offered it for sin, as the first.

16 And he brought the burnt offering, and offered it according to the ritual.

17 And he brought the meal offering and filled his hand from it and burned it upon the altar beside the burnt sacrifice of the morning.

18 Then he killed the bullock also and the ram for a sacrifice of peace offering which was for the people; and Aaron's sons presented to him the blood, which he sprinkled upon the altar round about,

19 And the fat of the bullock and of the ram, the rump, the fat that covers the entrails, and the kidneys, and the caul above the liver;

20 And they put the fat upon the breasts, and he burned the fat upon the altar;

21 And the breasts and the right

shoulder Aaron waved for a wave offering before the LORD; as Moses commanded.

22 And Aaron lifted up his hand toward the people and blessed them, and came down from offering of the sin offering and the burnt offering and the peace offering.

23 And Moses and Aaron went into the tabernacle of the congregation, and came out and blessed the people; and the glory of the LORD appeared in the presence of all the people.

24 And there came a fire out from before the LORD and consumed the burnt offering and the fat upon the altar, which all the people saw; they gave praise and fell on their faces.

CHAPTER 10

AND Nadab and Abihu, the sons of Aaron, each took his censer and put fire therein and laid incense on it and offered strange fire before the LORD, not at its appointed time, and not as he had commanded them.

2 And there went out fire from before the LORD and devoured them, and they died before the LORD.

3 Then Moses said to Aaron, This is what the LORD has spoken, saying, I will be sanctified by those that come near me, and before all the people I will be glorified. And Aaron held his peace.

4 And Moses called Manshael and Elizphan, the sons of Uzziel the uncle of Aaron, and said to them, Come near, carry your brethren from before the sanctuary out of the camp.

5 So they drew near and carried them in their vestments out of the camp; as Moses had said.

6 Then Moses said to Aaron, and to Eleazar and to Ithamar, his sons who were left to him, Do not shave your heads, neither rend your clothes, lest you die, and lest wrath come upon all the people; but let all your brethren, the whole house of Israel, bewail over the victims, whom the LORD burned.

7 And you shall not go out from the door of the tabernacle of the congregation, lest you die; for the anointing oil of the LORD is upon you. And

they did according to the word of Moses.

8 ¶And the LORD spoke to Aaron, saying,

9 Do not drink wine nor strong drink, you, nor your sons with you, when you go into the tabernacle of the congregation, lest you die; it shall be a statute for ever throughout your generations;

10 That you may make a distinction between holy and unholy, and between clean and unclean;

11 And that you may teach the children of Israel all the statutes which the LORD has spoken to them by the hand of Moses.

12 ¶And Moses spoke to Aaron, and to Eleazar and to Ithamar, his sons that were left, Take the meal offering that remains of the offerings of the LORD made by fire, and eat it without leaven beside the altar; for it is most holy:

13 And you shall eat it in the holy place because it is your due and your sons' due from the offerings of the LORD made by fire; for so was I commanded.

14 And the wave breast and shoulder offering you shall eat in a clean place; you and your sons and your daughters with you; for they are your due and your sons' due which are given out of the sacrifices of peace offerings of the children of Israel.

15 The shoulder offering and the wave breast they shall bring with the offerings of the fat, made by fire, to wave it as a wave offering before the LORD; and it shall be yours and your sons with you by a statute for ever; as the LORD has commanded, that Aaron and his sons shall eat it.

16 ¶And Moses diligently sought the goat of the sin offering, and, behold, it was burned; and he was angry with Eleazar and Ithamar, the sons of Aaron that were left, and he said to them,

17 Why have you not eaten the sin offering in the holy place, seeing it is most holy, and I have given it to you to bear the iniquity of the congregation, to make atonement for them before the LORD?

18 Behold, the blood of it was not brought in within the sanctuary; you should indeed have eaten it in the holy place, as I was commanded, that Aaron and his sons shall eat it.

19 And Aaron said to Moses, Behold, this day they have offered their sin offerings and their burnt offerings before the LORD; and such things have befallen me; and if I had eaten the sin offering today, should it have been better accepted in the presence of the LORD?

20 And when Moses heard that, he was content.

CHAPTER 11

AND the LORD spoke to Moses and Aaron, and said to them,

2 Speak to the children of Israel and say to them, These are the beasts which you shall eat among all the beasts that are on the earth:

3 Whatever parts the hoof and is cloven-footed and chews the cud among the beasts, that you may eat.

4 Nevertheless these you shall not eat of: those that chew the cud, or those that divide the hoof, as the camel, because it chews the cud but does not divide the hoof; it is unclean to you.

5 And the coney, because it chews the cud but does not divide the hoof; it is unclean to you.

6 And the hare, because it chews the cud but it does not divide the hoof; it is unclean to you.

7 And the swine, though it divide the hoof and is cloven-footed, yet it does not chew the cud; it is unclean to you.

8 Of their flesh you shall not eat, and their carcass you shall not touch; they are unclean to you.

9 ¶These shall you eat of all that are in the waters; whatever has fins and scales in the waters, in the seas, and in the rivers, you shall eat.

10 But all that have not fins and scales in the seas and in the rivers, of all that move in the waters, and of any living thing that is in the waters, they are unclean to you;

11 You shall not eat of their flesh, and their carcasses you shall declare unclean.

12 Whatever has no fins nor scales in the waters is unclean to you.

13 ¶And these you shall abhor among the birds; they shall not be eaten, because they are unclean: the eagle and the vulture

14 And the raven after its kind;

15 And the ostrich and the night hawk after its kind;

16 And the little owl and the pelican, the great owl, the cuckoo, and the hawk after its kind;

17 And the stork, the bee eater,

18 And the swan and the hoopoe after their kind,

19 And the heron and the peacock.

20 All species that creep, going upon all fours, are unclean to you.

21 Yet these things you may eat of every flying insect that goes upon all fours, which have legs above their feet with which to leap on the earth;

22 Of these you may eat: the locust after its kind and the large winged locust after its kind,

23 But all other flying insects which have four feet are unclean to you.

24 And by these you shall be unclean; whosoever touches their carcasses shall be unclean until the evening.

25 And whosoever carries of their carcasses shall wash his clothes and be unclean until the evening.

26 The carcasses of every beast which divides the hoof and is not cloven-footed, nor chews the cud, are unclean to you; every one who touches them shall be unclean until the evening.

27 And whatever goes upon his paws, among all manner of beasts that go on all fours, are unclean to you; whosoever touches their carcasses shall be unclean until the evening.

28 And he who carries their carcasses shall wash his clothes and be unclean until the evening, because they are unclean to you.

29 ¶These also are unclean to you among all the creeping things that creep upon the earth: the weasel, and the mouse, the lizard after its kind,

30 And the ferret, and the mole, the

yellow lizard, and the chameleon, and the snail.

31 These are unclean to you among all that creep; whosoever touches them, when they are dead, shall be unclean until the evening.

32 And upon whatever thing any of them falls when they are dead, that thing shall be unclean; whether it be any vessel of wood or a garment or a skin or a sack or whatever vessel it be wherein any work is done, it must be put into water and it shall be unclean until the evening; so it shall be cleansed.

33 And every earthen vessel into which any of them falls, whatever is in it shall be unclean; and you shall break it.

34 Of all food which may be eaten, that on which such water falls shall be unclean; and all drink that may be drunk in every such vessel shall be unclean.

35 And everything upon which any part of their carcasses falls shall be unclean; whether it be oven or bake-house, they shall be broken down: for they are unclean, and shall be unclean to you.

36 Nevertheless a fountain or a cistern and the pools of water shall be clean; but whosoever touches their carcasses shall be unclean.

37 And if any part of their carcasses falls upon any sowing seed which is to be sown, it shall be clean.

38 But if any water be put upon the seed and any part of their carcasses falls on it, it shall be unclean to you.

39 And if any animal of which you may eat dies, he who touches the carcass thereof shall be unclean until the evening.

40 And he who eats of its carcass shall wash his clothes and shall be unclean until the evening; he also that carries the carcass of it shall wash his clothes and be unclean until the evening.

41 And every creeping thing that creeps upon the earth is unclean to you; it shall not be eaten.

42 Whatever goes upon its belly and whatever goes upon all fours or whatever has many feet among all creeping things that creep upon the earth, you shall not eat of them; for they are unclean.

43 You shall not make yourselves unclean with any creeping thing that creeps upon the earth, lest you become unclean with them; defile not yourselves with them.

44 For I am the LORD your God; you shall therefore sanctify yourselves, and you shall be holy; for I am holy; neither shall you defile yourselves with any manner of creeping thing that creeps upon the earth.

45 For I am the LORD your God who brought you up out of the land of Egypt to be your God; you shall therefore be holy, for I am holy.

46 This is the law of beast and of fowl and of every living creature that moves in the water and of every creature that creeps upon the earth;

47 To make a distinction between the unclean and the clean and between the beast that may be eaten and the beast that may not be eaten.

CHAPTER 12

AND the LORD spoke to Moses and said to him,

2 Speak to the children of Israel, saying, If a woman have conceived and bear a male child, then she shall be unclean seven days; according to the days of her menstruation she shall be unclean.

3 And on the eighth day the flesh of his foreskin shall be circumcised.

4 And she shall continue for thirty-three days in the blood of her purifying; she shall touch no hallowed thing, nor come into the sanctuary, until the days of her purifying be fulfilled.

5 But if she bears a female child, then she shall be unclean two weeks, as in her menstruation; and she shall continue in the blood of her purifying for sixty-six days.

6 And when the days of her purifying are fulfilled for a son or for a daughter, she shall bring a lamb of the first year for a burnt offering and a young pigeon or a turtledove for a sin offering to the door of the taber-

nacle of the congregation, to the priest;

7 And he shall offer it before the LORD and make an atonement for her; and she shall be cleansed from the issue of her blood. This is the law for her who has borne a male child or a female.

8 And if she cannot afford a lamb, then she shall bring two pigeons or two young turtledoves; the one for the sin offering and the other for the burnt offering; and the priest shall make an atonement for her and she shall be clean.

CHAPTER 13

AND the LORD spoke to Moses and Aaron, saying,

2 When a man shall have a sore on the skin of his body, or a scab or a shiny spot, and it be on the skin of his body like the plague of leprosy, then he shall be brought to Aaron the priest or to one of his sons the priests;

3 And the priest shall look on the disease on the skin of his body; and if the hair in the sore is turned white and the appearance of the plague is deeper than the skin of his body, it is a plague of leprosy; and the priest shall look on it and pronounce him unclean.

4 And if the shiny spot be white on the skin of his body, but does not appear to be deeper than the skin, and the hair in it has not turned white; then the priest shall observe the disease for seven days;

5 And the priest shall look on him on the seventh day, and if the disease has remained in its place and has not spread in the skin, then the priest shall observe it seven days more.

6 And the priest shall look on him after seven days, and if the disease has been checked and has not spread in the skin, the priest shall pronounce him clean; because it is only a scab, and he shall wash his clothes and be clean.

7 But if the scab spreads much in the skin after that the priest has seen it and cleaned it, he shall show it to the priest again;

8 And if the priest shall see that the scab has spread in the skin, then the priest shall pronounce him unclean because it is leprosy.

9 ¶When the plague of leprosy is in a man, then he shall be brought to the priest;

10 And the priest shall see him, and if there is a white swelling in the skin and it has turned the hair white and the indication of the flesh is raw in the swelling,

11 It is an old leprosy in the skin of his body, and the priest shall pronounce him unclean and shall not shut him up; for he is unclean.

12 And if the leprosy breaks out all over his skin, so that the leprosy covers all of the skin of him who has the plague from his head to his feet, wherever the priest looks,

13 Then the priest shall consider; and, behold, if the leprosy has covered all his body, he shall pronounce him clean of the plague; for it has all turned white; he is clean.

14 But on the day when raw flesh appears on him, he shall become unclean.

15 And the priest shall see the raw flesh, and pronounce the raw flesh unclean; for it is unclean; it is leprosy.

16 Or if the raw flesh turns again, and is changed to white, then he shall be brought to the priest;

17 And the priest shall see him; and if the plague has turned white, then the priest shall pronounce him clean that has the plague; he is clean.

18 ¶The flesh also, if there is in the skin thereof a boil and it is healed,

19 And in the place of the boil there be a white swelling or a shiny spot, white or reddish, it shall be shown to the priest;

20 And when the priest sees it, if it appears deeper than the skin and its hair has turned white, then the priest shall pronounce him unclean; for it is a plague of leprosy broken out of the boil.

21 But if the priest look on it, and, behold, there is no white hair in it and if it is not deeper than the skin but is even with the skin, then the priest shall observe it seven days;

22 And if it spreads much in the

skin, then the priest shall pronounce him unclean; because it is the plague of leprosy.

23 But if the shiny spot stays in its place and spreads not, it is a scar of the boil, and the priest shall pronounce him clean.

24 ¶Or if a person's body has a burn on its skin, and the quick flesh of the burn has a shiny spot, somewhat white or reddish,

25 Then the priest shall look on it, and if the hair in the shiny spot has turned white, and it appears to be deeper than the skin, it is a leprosy broken out in the burn; wherefore the priest shall pronounce him unclean; because it is the plague of leprosy.

26 But if the priest look on it, and there is no white hair in the shiny spot and it is no deeper than the skin, but is even; then the priest shall observe it seven days;

27 And the priest shall look upon him the seventh day; and if it has spread in the skin, then the priest shall pronounce him unclean; because it is the plague of leprosy.

28 And if the shiny spot stays in its place and does not spread in the skin and is somewhat even, it is a scab of the burn, and the priest shall pronounce him clean; because it is the scab of the burn.

29 ¶If a man or woman has a disease on the head or the beard;

30 Then the priest shall see the disease; and, if it appears deeper than the skin, and there be in it yellow thin hair, then the priest shall pronounce him unclean; because it is the disease of leprosy of the head or beard.

31 And if the priest look on the disease, and it does not appear deeper than the skin and there is no black hair in it; then the priest shall observe it seven days;

32 And on the seventh day the priest shall look on the disease; and if the disease has not spread, and if there is no yellow hair in it and the appearance of the disease is not deeper than the skin,

33 Then he shall shave the sides of the sore, but the sore he shall not shave; and the priest shall observe the disease seven days more;

34 And on the seventh day the priest shall look on the disease; and if the disease has not spread in the skin and does not appear deeper than the skin, then the priest shall pronounce him clean, and he shall wash his clothes and be clean.

35 But if the disease spreads much in the skin after his cleansing,

36 Then the priest shall look on him; and if the disease has spread in the skin, the priest shall not look for yellow hair; he is unclean.

37 But if the disease remains in its place and there is black hair grown up in it; the disease is healed, he is clean; and the priest shall pronounce him clean.

38 ¶If a man or a woman have in the skin of the body shiny spots, bright or white spots,

39 Then the priest shall look; and if the shiny spots in the skin of the body are darkish white or reddish, it is a scab that has grown on the skin; he is clean.

40 And the man whose hair is fallen off his head, he is bald; yet he is clean.

41 And he whose hair has fallen off from the part of his head toward his face, he is forehead bald; yet he is clean.

42 And if there is on his bald head or bald forehead a white or reddish sore, it is leprosy breaking out on his bald head or his bald forehead.

43 Then the priest shall look on the swelling of the sore; and if the sore is white or reddish on his bald head or on his bald forehead like the appearance of leprosy in the skin of the body,

44 He is a leprous man, he is unclean; the priest shall pronounce him utterly unclean; for the disease is on his head.

45 And he who has the plague, his clothes shall be rent and his head shaved, and he shall cover his lips and call himself unclean.

46 All the days wherein the plague is on him he shall be defiled; for he is unclean; he shall dwell alone; out-

side the camp shall his habitation be.

47 ¶If a garment has leprous disease in it, whether it be a woolen garment or a linen garment,

48 Whether it be in the warp or woof, of linen or of woolen, in a skin or in anything made of skin,

49 And if the plague is greenish or reddish in the garment or in the skin, either in the warp or in the woof or in anything of skin, it is a plague of leprosy and shall be shown to the priest;

50 And the priest shall look upon the plague and observe it seven days;

51 And the priest shall look on the plague on the seventh day; if the disease has spread in the garment, either in the warp or in the woof or in a skin or in any article that is made of skin, the plague is a malignant leprosy; it is unclean.

52 He shall therefore burn the garment, whether warp or woof, in woolen or in linen, or anything of skin in which is the plague; for it is a malignant leprosy; it shall be burned in the fire.

53 And if the priest shall look, and the plague has not spread in the garment, either in the warp or in the woof or in anything of skin,

54 Then the priest shall command that they wash the thing in which is the plague and he shall observe it seven days more;

55 And the priest shall look on the plague after it is washed; and if the plague has not changed its appearance and the disease has not changed its color and the plague has not spread, it is unclean; you shall burn it in the fire; it has been diseased when it was new or when old.

56 And if the priest sees that the disease has diminished after being washed, then he shall rend it out of the garment or out of the skin or out of the warp or out of the woof;

57 And if it appears still in the garment, either in the warp or in the woof or in anything of skin, they shall burn it with fire, for the plague has spread in it.

58 And the garment, either warp or woof or anything of skin which has been washed, if the disease departs from them, then it shall be washed the second time and shall be clean.

59 This is the law of the plague of leprosy in a garment of woolen or linen, either in the warp or woof or anything of skin, to pronounce it clean or to pronounce it unclean.

CHAPTER 14

AND the Lord spoke to Moses, saying,

2 This shall be the law for the leper in the day of his cleansing: He shall be brought to the priest;

3 And the priest shall go forth out of the camp; and the priest shall look, and if the plague of leprosy is healed in the leper,

4 Then the priest shall command to take for him who is to be cleansed two birds alive and clean and cedar wood and scarlet material and hyssop;

5 And the priest shall command that one of the birds be killed in an earthen vessel over running water;

6 Then he shall take the living bird and the cedar wood and the scarlet dye and the hyssop, and shall dip them and the living bird in the blood of the bird that was killed over the running water;

7 And he shall sprinkle upon him who is to be cleansed from the leprosy seven times, and shall pronounce him clean, and shall let the living bird fly into the open field.

8 And he who is to be cleansed shall wash his clothes and shave off all his hair and bathe himself in water, that he may be clean; and after that he shall come into the camp but shall tarry outside his tent seven days.

9 And on the seventh day he shall shave all the hair off his head and his beard and his eyebrows, even all his hair he shall shave off; and he shall wash his clothes and bathe his body in water, and he shall be clean.

10 And on the eighth day he shall take two male lambs without blemish and one ewe lamb of the first year without blemish and three tenth deals of fine flour, for a meal offering mixed with oil, and one half pint of oil.

11 And the priest who does the cleansing shall present the man who is to be cleansed and those things before the LORD at the door of the tabernacle of the congregation;

12 And the priest shall take one male lamb and offer it for a trespass offering, and the half pint of oil, and wave them for a wave offering before the LORD;

13 And he shall kill the male lamb in the place where he kills the sin offering and the burnt offering, in the holy place; for as the sin offering belongs to the priest, so does the trespass offering; it is most holy;

14 And the priest shall take some of the blood of the trespass offering, and the priest shall sprinkle it on the tip of the right ear of him who is to be cleansed and on the thumb of his right hand and on the great toe of his right foot;

15 And the priest shall take some of the oil, and pour it into the palm of his own left hand;

16 Then the priest shall dip his right finger in the oil that is in his left hand and shall sprinkle some of the oil with his finger seven times before the LORD;

17 And of the rest of the oil that is in his hand the priest shall sprinkle it upon the tip of the right ear of him who is to be cleansed and upon the thumb of his right hand and upon the great toe of his right foot, upon the place of the blood of the trespass offering;

18 And the rest of the oil that is in the priest's hand he shall pour upon the head of him who is to be cleansed; and the priest shall make an atonement for him before the LORD.

19 And the priest shall offer the sin offering and make an atonement for the man who is to be cleansed from his uncleanness; and afterward he shall kill the burnt offering;

20 And the priest shall offer the burnt offering and the meal offering upon the altar; and the priest shall make an atonement for him and he shall be clean.

21 And if he is poor and cannot afford so much, then he shall take one lamb for a trespass offering to be waved, to make an atonement for him, and one tenth of an ephah of fine flour mixed with oil for a meal offering, and a half pint of oil;

22 And two turtledoves or two young pigeons such as he can afford; and the one shall be a sin offering and the other a burnt offering.

23 And he shall bring them on the eighth day for his cleansing to the priest, to the door of the tabernacle of the congregation, before the LORD.

24 And the priest shall take one lamb and the half pint of oil, and the priest shall wave them for a wave offering before the LORD;

25 Then he shall kill the lamb of the trespass offering, and the priest shall take some of the blood of the trespass offering, and sprinkle it upon the tip of the right ear of him who is to be cleansed and upon the thumb of his right hand and upon the great toe of his right foot;

26 And the priest shall pour some of the oil into the palm of his own left hand;

27 And the priest shall sprinkle with his right finger some of the oil that is in his left hand seven times before the LORD;

28 And the priest shall sprinkle some of the oil that is in his hand upon the tip of the right ear of him who is to be cleansed and upon the thumb of his right hand and upon the great toe of his right foot, in the place of the blood of the trespass offering;

29 And the rest of the oil that is in the priest's hand he shall sprinkle upon the head of him who is to be cleansed, to make an atonement for him before the LORD.

30 And he shall offer one of the turtledoves or of the young pigeons such as he can afford;

31 One shall be for a sin offering and the other for a burnt offering, with the meal offering; and the priest shall make an atonement for him who is to be cleansed before the LORD.

32 This is the law of him in whom is the plague of leprosy who cannot

afford the regular offerings for his cleansing.

33 ¶And the LORD spoke to Moses and Aaron, saying,

34 Speak to the children of Israel and say to them, When you come into the land of Canaan which I give to you for a possession, and I put the plague of leprosy in a house of the land of your possession,

35 The owner of the house shall come and tell the priest, saying, It seems to me that there is a plague of leprosy in the house.

36 Then the priest shall command that they empty the house before the priest shall go into it to see the plague, that all that is in the house may not be made unclean; and afterward the priest shall go in to see the house;

37 And he shall look on the plague, and, behold, if the plague be in the walls of the house with greenish or reddish scales, and appear to be deeper than the wall;

38 Then the priest shall go out of the house and stand at the door and observe the house seven days;

39 And the priest shall come back again on the seventh day and shall see if the plague has spread in the walls of the house;

40 Then the priest shall command that they take away the stones in which the plague of leprosy is, and they shall cast them into an unclean place outside the city;

41 And they shall scrape the house within round about, and they shall throw out the dust that they scrape off outside the city into an unclean place;

42 And they shall take other stones and put them in the place of those stones; and they shall take other mortar and plaster the house.

43 And if the plague spreads and breaks out in the house after the stones have been taken away and after the house has been scraped and plastered,

44 Then the priest shall go in and look, and if the plague has spread in the house, it is a malignant leprosy in the house; it is unclean.

45 And they shall demolish the house, its stones and its timber and all the mortar of the house; and they shall carry them forth out of the town into an unclean place and burn it with fire.

46 Moreover, he who enters the house while it is shut up shall be unclean until the evening.

47 And he who lies in the house shall wash his clothes; and he who eats in the house shall wash his clothes.

48 And if the priest shall come in and look upon it, and, and, behold, the plague has not spread in the house after the house was plastered, then the priest shall pronounce the house clean, because the plague has been healed.

49 And he shall take to cleanse the house two birds alive and clean and cedar wood and hyssop and scarlet material;

50 And the priest shall command and they shall kill one of the birds in an earthen vessel over running water;

51 And he shall take the other living bird, the cedar wood, and the hyssop, and the scarlet material and dip them in the blood of the bird that was killed and in the running water, and sprinkle the house seven times;

52 And he shall cleanse the house with the blood of the bird and with the running water and with the live bird and with the cedar wood and with hyssop and with the scarlet material;

53 But he shall let the live bird fly out of the town into the open field and make an atonement for the house; and it shall be clean.

54 This law shall be for all manner of plagues of leprosy

55 And for the plague of leprosy in a garment and of a house

56 And for a swelling and for a scab and for a shiny spot;

57 To distinguish between clean, and unclean; this is the law of leprosy.

CHAPTER 15

THE LORD spoke to Moses and to Aaron, saying,

2 Speak to the children of Israel

and say to them, When any man has a seminal discharge from his body, his discharge is unclean,

3 And this shall be his uncleanness in his discharge: whether his body runs with its discharge or his body has stopped from its discharge, it is his uncleanness.

4 Every bed on which he who has the discharge lies shall be unclean, and everything on which he sits shall be unclean.

5 And any man who touches his bed shall wash his clothes and bathe himself in water and be unclean until the evening.

6 And he who sits on anything on which sat he who has the discharge shall wash his clothes and bathe himself in water and be unclean until the evening.

7 And he who touches the body of him who has the discharge shall wash his clothes and bathe himself in water and be unclean until the evening.

8 And if he who has the discharge spits on him who is clean, then he shall wash his clothes and bathe himself in water and be unclean until the evening.

9 And anything on which he rides who has the discharge shall be unclean,

10 And whosoever touches anything that has been under him shall be unclean until the evening; and he who carries any of those things shall wash his clothes and bathe himself in water and be unclean until the evening.

11 And any one who touches him who has the discharge, and has not washed his hands in water, he shall wash his clothes and bathe himself in water and be unclean until the evening.

12 And the earthen vessel which he touched who has the discharge shall be broken; and every vessel of wood or of brass shall be washed in water.

13 And when he who has a discharge is cleansed of his discharge, then he shall number to himself seven days for his cleansing, and wash his clothes and bathe his body in running water and shall be clean.

14 And on the eighth day he shall take two turtledoves or two young pigeons and bring them before the LORD at the door of the tabernacle of the congregation and give them to the priest,

15 And the priest shall offer them, the one for a sin offering and the other for a burnt offering; and the priest shall make an atonement for him before the LORD for his discharge.

16 And if any man has an emission of semen, then he shall bathe all his body in water and be unclean until the evening.

17 And every garment or bed on which the semen has fallen shall be washed with water and be unclean until the evening.

18 If a woman also lie with a man having an emission of semen, they shall both bathe themselves in water and be unclean until the evening.

19 ¶And if a woman has a discharge of blood, and her discharge is in her body, she shall be put apart for seven days in her menstruation, and whosoever touches her shall be unclean until the evening.

20 And everything upon which she lies during her menstruous discharge shall be unclean; and everything also that she sits upon shall be unclean.

21 And whosoever touches her bed shall wash his clothes and bathe himself in water and be unclean until the evening.

22 And whosoever touches anything that she sits upon shall wash his clothes and bathe himself in water and be unclean until the evening.

23 And if it be on the bed or on anything on which she sits, when he touches it, he shall be unclean until the evening.

24 And if any man lies with her and some of her menstruous discharge falls on him, he shall be unclean for seven days; and every bed on which he lies shall be unclean.

25 And if a woman has a menstruous discharge of blood for many days, not at the time of her menstruation, or if she has a menstruous discharge beyond the time of her menstruation,

all the days of the discharge of her uncleanness shall be as the days of her menstruation; she shall be unclean.

26 Every bed on which she lies all the days of her discharge shall be to her as the bed of her menstruation; and everything upon which she sits shall be unclean, as the uncleanness of her menstruation.

27 And whosoever touches those things shall be unclean and shall wash his clothes and bathe himself in water and be unclean until the evening.

28 But if she is cleansed of her discharge, then she shall number for herself seven days, and after that she shall be clean.

29 And on the eighth day she shall take to herself two turtledoves or two young pigeons and bring them to the priest, to the door of the tabernacle of the congregation.

30 And the priest shall offer them, the one for a sin offering and the other for a burnt offering; and the priest shall make an atonement for her before the LORD for the discharge of her uncleanness.

31 Thus shall you admonish the children of Israel concerning their uncleanness, that they may not die in their uncleanness and that they may not defile my tabernacle that is among them.

32 This law shall be for him who has a discharge and for him who has an emission of semen and is defiled therewith;

33 And for her who has monthly course and for him who has a discharge, male or female, and for the man who lies with a woman who is unclean.

CHAPTER 16

AND the LORD spoke to Moses after the death of the two sons of Aaron, when they offered strange fire before the LORD and died;

2 And the LORD said to Moses, Speak to Aaron your brother that he come not at all times into the holy place within the veil before the mercy seat which is upon the ark, that he die not; for I will appear in the cloud upon the mercy seat.

3 Thus shall Aaron come into the holy place: with a young bullock for a sin offering and a ram for a burnt offering.

4 He shall put on the holy linen coat and he shall have linen breeches upon his body and shall be girded with a linen girdle and shall put a linen mitre upon his head; because these are the vestments of the sanctuary; therefore he shall bathe his body in water, and then put them on.

5 And he shall take from the congregation of the children of Israel two kids of the goats for a sin offering and one ram for a burnt offering.

6 And Aaron shall offer the bullock of the sin offering, which is for himself, and make an atonement for himself and for his house.

7 And he shall take the two goats and present them alive before the LORD at the door of the tabernacle of the congregation.

8 And Aaron shall cast lots upon the two goats, one lot for the LORD and the other lot for Azazael.

9 And Aaron shall bring the goat upon which the LORD's lot fell and offer it for a sin offering.

10 But the goat on which the lot of Azazael fell shall be presented alive before the LORD to make an atonement with it and to send it away to Azazael into the wilderness.

11 And Aaron shall bring the bullock of the sin offering which is for himself, and shall make an atonement for himself and for his house; and shall kill the bullock of the sin offering;

12 And he shall take a censer full of burning coals of fire from the altar before the LORD and his hands full of sweet incense beaten small, and enter within the veil;

13 And he shall put the incense on the fire before the LORD, that the cloud of the incense may cover the mercy seat that is upon the testimony, that he die not;

14 And he shall take some of the blood of the bullock and sprinkle it with his finger upon the mercy seat

eastward; before the mercy seat shall he sprinkle of the blood with his finger seven times.

15 ¶Then he shall kill the goat of the sin offering which is for the people and bring its blood within the veil, and do with its blood as he did with the blood of the bullock, and sprinkle it upon the mercy seat and before the mercy seat;

16 And he shall make an atonement for the holy place, because of the uncleanness of the children of Israel and because of their transgressions in all their sins; and so shall he do for the tabernacle of the congregation which remains among them in the midst of their uncleanness.

17 And there shall be no man in the tabernacle of the congregation when he goes in to make an atonement in the holy place, until he comes out and has made an atonement for himself and for his household and for all the congregation of Israel.

18 And he shall go out to the altar that is before the LORD and make an atonement for it; and shall take some of the blood of the bullock and some of the blood of the goat, and sprinkle it upon the horns of the altar round about.

19 And he shall sprinkle some of the blood upon it with his finger seven times, and cleanse it and hallow it from the uncleanness of the children of Israel.

20 ¶And when he has made an end of atoning for the holy place and the tabernacle of the congregation and the altar, he shall bring the live goat;

21 And Aaron shall lay both his hands upon the head of the live goat and confess over it all the iniquities of the children of Israel and all their transgressions and all their sins, putting them upon the head of the goat, and shall send it away by the hand of a fit man into the wilderness;

22 And the goat shall bear upon him all their iniquities to a barren land; and he shall leave the goat in the wilderness.

23 And Aaron shall come into the tabernacle of the congregation, and shall put off the linen vestments which he put on when he went into the holy place, and shall leave them there;

24 And he shall bathe his body in water in the holy place and put on his garments, and come forth and offer his burnt offering and the burnt offering of the people, and make an atonement for himself and for the people.

25 And the fat of the sin offering he shall burn upon the altar.

26 And he who let go the goat for Azazael shall wash his clothes and bathe his body in water and afterward shall come into the camp.

27 And the bullock for the sin offering and the goat for the sin offering, some of whose blood was brought in to make atonement in the holy place, they shall carry forth outside the camp; and they shall burn in the fire their skins and their meat and their dung.

28 And he who burns them shall wash his clothes and bathe his body in water and afterward he shall come into the camp.

29 ¶And this shall be a statute for ever to you: that in the seventh month, on the tenth day of the month, you shall humble yourselves and do no work at all, both you and the proselytes who sojourn among you;

30 For on this day shall the priest make an atonement for you, that you may be clean from all your sins and that you may be clean before the LORD.

31 It shall be a sabbath and a rest to you, and you shall humble yourselves; it is a statute for ever.

32 And the priest who shall be anointed and who is consecrated to minister in the priest's office in his father's stead shall make the atonement and shall put on the linen clothes, even the holy garments;

33 And he shall make an atonement for the holy sanctuary, and he shall make an atonement for the tabernacle of the congregation and for the altar, and he shall make an atonement for the priests and for all the people of the congregation.

34 And this shall be an everlasting statute for you, to make an atonement

for the children of Israel for all their sins once a year. And he did as the LORD commanded Moses.

CHAPTER 17

AND the LORD spoke to Moses, saying,

2 Speak to Aaron and to his sons and to all the children of Israel, and say to them, This is the thing which the LORD has commanded, saying,

3 Any man whosoever be of the house of Israel, who kills an ox or a lamb or a goat in the camp, or who kills it outside the camp,

4 And does not bring it to the door of the tabernacle of the congregation to offer it as an offering to the LORD before the tabernacle of the LORD, blood shall be imputed to that man because he has shed blood; and that man shall be cut off from among his people,

5 To the end that the children of Israel may bring their sacrifices which they offer in the open field, that they may bring them before the LORD to the door of the tabernacle of the congregation, to the priest, and offer them for peace offerings to the LORD.

6 And the priest shall sprinkle the blood upon the altar of the LORD at the door of the tabernacle of the congregation and burn the fat for a sweet savour to the LORD.

7 And they shall no more offer their sacrifices to the demons after whom they have gone astray. This shall be a statute for ever to them throughout their generations.

8 ¶And you shall say to them, Any man of the house of Israel or of the proselytes who sojourn among you who offers a burnt offering or a sacrifice

9 And does not bring it to the door of the tabernacle of the congregation to offer it to the LORD, that man shall be cut off from among his people.

10 ¶And if any man of the children of Israel or of the proselytes who sojourn among you eats any manner of blood, I will pour out my anger against that person who eats blood, and will cut him off from among his people.

11 For the life of the flesh is in the blood; and I have given it to you upon the altar to make an atonement for yourselves; for it is the blood that makes an atonement for the soul.

12 Therefore I have said to the children of Israel, No person among you shall eat blood, neither shall the proselytes who sojourn among you eat blood.

13 And any man of the children of Israel or of the proselytes who sojourn among you who hunts and catches any beast or fowl that may be eaten, he shall pour out its blood and cover it with dust.

14 For the life of all flesh is the blood thereof; therefore I said to the children of Israel, You shall not eat the blood of any flesh, for the life of all flesh is the blood thereof; whosoever eats it shall be cut off.

15 And every person who eats that which died of itself or that which was torn by wild beasts, whether it be one of you or one of the proselytes who sojourn among you, he shall both wash his clothes and bathe himself in water and be unclean until the evening; then shall he be clean.

16 But if he does not wash them nor bathe his body, then he shall suffer for his iniquity.

CHAPTER 18

AND the LORD spoke to Moses, saying,

2 Speak to the children of Israel and say to them, I am the LORD your God.

3 You shall not do according to the doings of the land of Egypt wherein you dwelt, neither shall you do according to the doings of the land of Canaan whither I bring you; neither shall you walk in their ordinances.

4 But you shall do my judgments and keep my commandments and walk in them; I am the LORD your God.

5 You shall therefore keep my commandments and my judgments, which if a man do, he shall live in them; I am the LORD.

6 ¶None of you shall be intimate with any that is near of kin to him

to uncover her nakedness; I am the LORD.

7 You shall not shame your father by approaching your mother; she is your mother, you shall not uncover her nakedness.

8 You shall not approach your father's wife; it is your father's nakedness.

9 You shall not approach your sister, the daughter of your father or the daughter of your mother, whether she is begotten of your father or of another man.

10 You shall not approach your son's daughter or your daughter's daughter, because they are your own kin.

11 You shall not approach your father's wife's daughter, begotten of your father, she is your sister; you shall not uncover her nakedness.

12 You shall not approach your father's sister, she is your father's near kinswoman.

13 You shall not approach your mother's sister, for she is your mother's near kinswoman.

14 You shall not put to shame your father's brother; you shall not approach his wife: for she is your aunt, you shall not uncover her nakedness.

15 You shall not approach your daughter-in-law; for she is your son's wife; you shall not uncover her nakedness.

16 You shall not approach your brother's wife; it is your brother's nakedness.

17 You shall not approach a woman and her daughter; neither shall you take her son's daughter or her daughter's daughter to uncover nakedness; for they are her near kinswomen; it is wickedness.

18 And you shall not take to wife a sister of your wife, to distress her, to uncover her nakedness, beside the other in her life time.

19 You shall not be intimate with a woman while she is unclean during her menstruation.

20 Moreover you shall not lie carnally with your neighbor's wife to defile yourself with her.

21 You shall not let any of your semen be cast into a strange woman to cause her to be pregnant; neither shall you profane the name of your God; I am the LORD.

22 You shall not lie with a male as with a woman; because it is an abomination.

23 Neither shall you lie with any beast to defile yourself with it; neither shall any woman stand before a beast to lie with it; because it is an abomination.

24 Do not defile yourselves in any of these things; for it was in all these that the nations are defiled which I am casting out before you;

25 And the land is defiled; therefore I do visit the iniquity thereof upon it so that the land is bereaved of its inhabitants.

26 You shall therefore keep my statutes and my judgments, and shall not commit any of these abominations; neither you nor any proselytes who sojourn among you

27 (For all these sins have the men of the land done who were before you, and the land is defiled);

28 Do not defile the land, lest it cast you out as it cast out the nations that were before you.

29 For whosoever shall commit any of these abominations, even the persons who commit them shall be cut off from among their people.

30 Therefore you shall keep my ordinance, and you shall not commit any of these abominable customs which were committed before you, and you shall not defile yourselves by them; I am the LORD your God.

CHAPTER 19

AND the LORD spoke to Moses, saying,

2 Speak to all the congregation of the children of Israel and say to them, You shall be holy; for I the LORD your God am holy.

3 ¶You must revere every man his father and his mother, and keep my commandments; for I am the LORD your God.

4 ¶You shall not turn to idols nor make to yourselves molten gods; I am the LORD your God.

5 ¶And if you offer a sacrifice of peace offering to the LORD, you shall offer the ones which are acceptable.

6 It shall be eaten the same day you offer it and on the morrow; and what is left over until the third day, it shall be burned in the fire and shall not be eaten.

7 And if it is eaten at all on the third day, it is abominable; and it shall not be accepted.

8 Therefore every one who eats of it shall suffer for his iniquity, because he has profaned the hallowed thing of the LORD; and that person shall be cut off from among his people.

9 ¶And when you reap the harvest of your land, you shall not reap your field to the very corners, neither shall you gather the gleanings of your harvest.

10 And you shall not glean your vineyards, neither shall you gather that which is fallen from your olive trees, but you shall leave them for the poor and the proselytes; for I am the LORD your God.

11 ¶You shall not steal; you shall not deal falsely; neither shall you lie to one another.

12 ¶You shall not swear by my name falsely and so profane the name of your God; I am the LORD.

13 ¶You shall not oppress your neighbor, neither carry him away by force; the wages of him who is hired shall not remain with you all night until the morning.

14 ¶You shall not curse the deaf, nor put a stumbling block before the blind, but you shall revere your God; I am the LORD.

15 ¶You shall do no injustice in judgment; you shall not be partial to the poor, nor respect the person of the mighty; but in righteousness shall you judge your neighbor.

16 ¶You shall not accuse your own people neither shall you stand against the blood of your neighbor; I am the LORD.

17 ¶You shall not hate your brother in your heart; but you shall in any wise rebuke your neighbor, lest you incur sin because of him.

18 ¶You shall not bear any enmity against the children of your own people, but you shall love your neighbor as yourself; I am the LORD.

19 ¶You shall keep my statutes. You shall not let your cattle breed with a diverse kind; you shall not sow your field with mixed seed; neither shall you wear a mantle made of mixed materials.

20 ¶And whosoever lies carnally with a woman who is his bondmaid betrothed to a husband, and not yet redeemed nor given her freedom, an inquiry shall be made into their case; and they shall not be put to death, because she was not free.

21 And he shall bring his trespass offering to the LORD, to the door of the tabernacle of the congregation, a ram for a trespass offering.

22 And the priest shall make an atonement for him with the ram of the trespass offering before the LORD for his sin which he has committed; and the sin which he has committed shall be forgiven him.

23 ¶And when you shall come into the land and shall have planted all kinds of trees for food, then you shall leave them for three years, and you shall not eat of their fruit.

24 And in the fourth year all their fruit shall be holy to praise the LORD withal.

25 And in the fifth year you shall eat of the fruit thereof, that it may yield to you the increase thereof; I am the LORD your God.

26 ¶You shall not eat blood; you shall not practice divination with birds, nor shall you consult an oracle.

27 You shall not let the hair of your heads grow, neither shall you trim the corners of your beard.

28 You shall not make any cuttings in your flesh for the dead, nor inscribe any marks upon you; I am the LORD.

29 ¶You shall not permit your daughter to become a whore, lest the land fall to whoredom and the land become full of wickedness.

30 ¶You shall keep my commandments and reverence my sanctuary; I am the LORD.

31 ¶You shall not go after diviners,

neither after the soothsayers, nor shall you consult them to be defiled by them; I am the LORD your God.

32 ¶You shall rise up before an elder and honor the person who is older than you and revere your God; I am the LORD your God.

33 ¶And when a proselyte sojourns with you in your land, you shall not wrong him;

34 But let him be among you as one of you; and the proselytes who sojourn among you, you must love them as yourselves; for you also were sojourners in the land of Egypt; I am the LORD your God.

35 ¶You shall do no injustices in judgment, in balances, in weight, or in measure.

36 You shall have just balances, just weights, a just ephah, and a just hin; I am the LORD your God who brought you out of the land of Egypt.

37 Therefore you shall keep all my commandments and all my judgments, and do them; I am the LORD.

CHAPTER 20

AND the LORD spoke to Moses, saying,

2 Say to the children of Israel, Any man of the children of Israel or of the proselytes who sojourn in Israel who shall cast any of his semen into an alien woman, he shall surely be put to death; the people of the land shall stone him with stones.

3 And I will pour out my anger against that man and will cut him off from among his people; because he has cast his semen into an alien woman to defile my sanctuary and to profane my holy name.

4 And if the people of the land do in any way ignore the offense of the man who has cast of his semen into an alien woman, that they may not kill him,

5 Then I will set my anger against that man and against his family, and will cut him off and all who go astray after him, because they go astray after alien women from among their people.

6 ¶And the person that goes after diviners and soothsayers to go astray after them, I will pour out my anger against that person and will cut him off from among his people.

7 ¶Sanctify yourselves, therefore, and be holy; for I am the LORD your God.

8 You shall keep my commandments and do them; I am the LORD who sanctifies you.

9 ¶And he who curses his father or his mother shall be surely put to death; he has cursed his father or his mother; his blood shall be upon him.

10 ¶And the man who commits adultery with another man's wife, even he who commits adultery with his neighbor's wife, both the adulterer and the adulteress shall surely be put to death.

11 And the man who lies with his father's wife has uncovered his father's nakedness; both of them shall surely be put to death; their blood shall be upon them.

12 And if a man lies with his daughter-in-law, both of them shall surely be put to death, because they have committed a sin; their blood shall be upon them.

13 If a man lies with a male as he lies with a woman, both of them have committed an abomination; they shall surely be put to death; their blood shall be upon them.

14 And if a man takes a wife and her mother, it is wickedness; they shall be burned with fire, both he and they, that there may be no wickedness among you.

15 And if a man lies with a beast, he shall surely be put to death and the beast shall be stoned.

16 And if a woman approaches any beast and lies with it, you shall kill the woman and the beast; they shall surely be put to death; their blood shall be upon them.

17 And if a man shall take his sister, his father's daughter or his mother's daughter, and be intimate with her and she be intimate with him, it is a shameful thing; and they shall be cut off in the sight of their people; he has uncovered his sister's

nakedness; they shall suffer for their iniquity.

18 And if a man shall lie with a woman having her menstruation and shall be intimate with her, he has uncovered her fountain and she has uncovered the fountain of her blood; and both of them shall be cut off from among their people.

19 And you shall not be intimate with your mother's sister nor your father's sister; for he uncovers the nakedness of his near kin; they shall suffer for their iniquity.

20 And if a man shall lie with his uncle's wife, he has uncovered his uncle's nakedness; they shall suffer for their sin; they shall die childless.

21 And if a man shall take his brother's wife, it is an iniquity, for he has uncovered his brother's nakedness; they shall be childless.

22 ¶You shall therefore keep all my commandments and all my judgments and do them, that the land whither I bring you to dwell therein may not be bereaved of you.

23 And you shall not walk in the manners of the nations which I am casting out before you; for they committed all these things, and therefore I was grieved by them.

24 But I have said to you, You shall inherit their land and I will give it to you to possess it, a land flowing with milk and honey; I am the LORD your God who have separated you from other peoples.

25 You shall therefore make a distinction between clean beasts and unclean, and between clean fowls and unclean; and you shall not make yourselves abominable by beast or by fowl or by any manner of living thing that creeps on the ground, which I have separated from you as unclean.

26 And you shall be holy to me; for I the LORD am holy and have separated you from other peoples, that you should be mine.

27 ¶A man or a woman who is a diviner, or soothsayer shall surely be put to death; they shall stone them with stones; their blood shall be upon them.

CHAPTER 21

THE LORD said to Moses, Speak to the priests the sons of Aaron and say to them, There shall none of you defile himself by mourning for the dead among his people,[1]

2 Except for his kin who is near to him, that is, for his father and for his mother and for his son and for his daughter and for his brother,

3 And for his virgin sister, who is near to him, who had no husband; for her he may defile himself.

4 But he shall not defile himself for the prince of his people, lest he profane himself.

5 They shall not make baldness upon their head, neither shall they shave off the corner of their beard, nor make any cuttings in their flesh.

6 But they shall be holy to their God, and not profane the name of their God; for the offerings of the LORD made by fire and the bread of their God they do offer; therefore they shall be holy.

7 They shall not marry a harlot or an unclean woman; neither shall they marry a woman who has been put away from her husband; for he is holy to his God.

8 You shall sanctify him therefore; for he offers the bread of your God; he shall be holy to you; for he is holy, because I am the LORD who sanctifies you.

9 ¶And the daughter of any priest, when she starts playing the whore, she profanes her father; she shall be burned with fire.

10 And the priest who is the high priest among his brethren, upon whose head the anointing oil was poured, and who is consecrated to put on the vestments, shall not shave his head nor rend his clothes;

11 Neither shall he go near any dead body, nor defile himself by mourning for his father or for his mother;

12 Neither shall he go out of the sanctuary nor profane the sanctuary of his God; for the crown of the

---

[1] The dead were considered unclean.

anointing oil of his God is upon him; I am the LORD.

13 And he shall take a wife in her virginity.

14 A widow or a woman who is put away or one who is defiled by whoredom, these he shall not take; but he shall take a virgin of his own people to wife.

15 Neither shall he profane his descendants among his people; for I am the LORD who sanctifies him.

16 ¶And the LORD spoke to Moses, saying,

17 Speak to Aaron and say to him, Whosoever he be of your descendants throughout their generations who has any blemish, let him not approach to offer the bread of his God.

18 For any man who has a blemish, he shall not approach: a lame man or a blind man or one whose nose is cut off or one who is deprived of ears

19 Or a man who has a broken foot or broken hand

20 Or crooked back or is a dwarf or whose eyebrows have fallen or whose eyes are dimmed or has cataract in his eyes or has leprosy or a hunchback or has one testicle;

21 No man of the descendants of Aaron the priest who has a blemish shall come near to offer the offerings of the LORD made by fire; for he has a blemish; he shall not come near to offer the bread of his God.

22 He shall eat the bread of his God, both of the most holy and of the holy.

23 But he shall not go in to the veil nor come near to the altar, because he has a blemish, that he may not profane my sanctuary; for I am the LORD who sanctifies them.

24 So Moses told it to Aaron and to his sons and to all the children of Israel.

CHAPTER 22

AND the LORD spoke to Moses, saying,

2 Say to Aaron and to his sons, that they may keep themselves separate from the holy things of the children

of Israel and that they may not profane my holy name in those things which they hallow to me; I am the LORD.

3 Say to them, Whosoever he be of all your descendants throughout your generations who approaches to the holy things which the children of Israel hallow to the LORD while he is unclean, that person shall be cut off from my presence; I am the LORD.

4 Any man of the descendants of Aaron who is a leper or has a discharge, he shall not eat of the holy things until he is clean. And whosoever touches anything that is unclean through contact with the dead or a man who has an emission of semen,

5 Or whoever touches any creeping thing whereby he may be made unclean, or a man of whom he may take uncleanness, whatever uncleanness he has,

6 Any person who touches him shall be unclean until evening and shall not eat of the holy things unless he has bathed his body in water.

7 And when the sun is down, he shall be clean and shall afterward eat of the holy things, because it is his food.

8 That which has been torn by wild beasts, he shall not eat that he may not defile himself by it; I am the LORD.

9 They shall therefore keep my ordinances, lest they bear sins for it and die because of them, if they had profaned themselves; I am the LORD who sanctifies them.

10 There shall no alien eat of the holy things; a sojourner of the priest, or a hired servant, shall not eat of the holy thing.

11 But if a priest buys any person with his money, he shall eat of his food, and those that are born in his house shall eat of his food.

12 If a priest's daughter is married to a stranger,[1] she also may not eat of an offering of the holy things.

13 But if a priest's daughter has become a widow or is divorced, and has no children, and shall return to her father's house as in her youth, she

_____
[1] Not of the priestly tribe.

11

shall eat of her father's food; but no stranger shall ever eat of it.

14 ¶And if a man eats of the holy thing unwittingly, then he shall add a fifth part thereof to it and shall give it to the priest with the holy thing.

15 And the children of Israel shall not profane the holy things which they offer to the LORD;

16 And thus shall suffer for the iniquity and sins, when they eat of their holy things; for I am the LORD who sanctifies them.

17 ¶And the LORD spoke to Moses, saying,

18 Speak to Aaron and to his sons and to all the children of Israel, and say to them, Any one of the house of Israel and of the proselytes who dwell in Israel that will offer his offering for all their vows and for all their freewill offerings which they offer to the LORD for a burnt offering,

19 You shall offer acceptable ones, a male without blemish, of the herds or of the lambs or of the goats.

20 But whatsoever has a blemish, that you shall not offer; for it shall not be acceptable for you.

21 And whosoever offers a sacrifice of peace offering to the LORD to fulfill his vow or a freewill offering from oxen or from goats, it shall be perfect to be accepted; there shall be no blemish in it.

22 Any blind animal or broken or scabbed or maimed or scurvy, you shall not offer to the LORD nor make an offering by fire of them upon the altar to the LORD.

23 A bullock or a lamb which has the ear or the tail cut off you may offer for a freewill offering; but for a vow it shall not be accepted.

24 You shall not offer to the LORD that which is bruised, cut off, or broken; neither shall you make such offerings in your land.

25 Neither from a stranger's hand shall you offer the bread of your God of any of these; because they are corrupt and there is blemish in them; they shall not be accepted from you.

26 ¶And the LORD spoke to Moses, saying,

27 When a bullock or a lamb or a goat is born, it shall remain seven days with its dam; and from the eighth day on it shall be accepted for an offering made by fire to the LORD.

28 And whether it be a cow or a sheep, you shall not slaughter it and its young both in one day.

29 And when you will offer a sacrifice of thanksgiving to the LORD, you shall offer it in an acceptable manner.

30 On the same day it shall be eaten up; you shall leave none of it until morning; I am the LORD.

31 Therefore you shall keep my commandments and do them; I am the LORD.

32 Neither shall you profane my holy name, which is holy among the children of Israel; I am the LORD who sanctifies you,

33 Who brought you out of the land of Egypt to be your God; I am the LORD.

CHAPTER 23

AND the LORD spoke to Moses, saying,

2 Speak to the children of Israel and say to them, Concerning the feasts of the LORD which you shall proclaim to be holy convocations, these are my feasts.

3 Six days you shall do work; but the seventh day is the sabbath of rest, it shall be holy to the LORD; you shall do no work thereon; it is the sabbath to the LORD in all your dwellings.

4 ¶These are the feasts of the LORD, even the holy convocations which you shall proclaim in their seasons:

5 On the fourteenth day of the first month at evening is the LORD's passover.

6 And on the fifteenth day of the same month is the feast of the unleavened bread to the LORD; for seven days you must eat unleavened bread.

7 On the first day you shall have a holy convocation; you shall do no manner of work thereon.

8 But you shall offer an offering made by fire to the LORD seven days; on the seventh day is a holy convocation; you shall do no manner of work thereon.

9 ¶And the LORD spoke to Moses, saying,

10 Speak to the children of Israel and say to them, When you come into the land which I give to you and shall reap the harvest thereof, then you shall bring a sheaf of the first fruits of your harvest to the priest;

11 And he shall wave the sheaf before the LORD to be accepted for you; on the morrow the priest shall wave it.

12 You shall offer that day when you wave the sheaf a male lamb of the first year without blemish for a burnt offering to the LORD.

13 And its meal offering shall be two tenths of an ephah of fine flour mixed with oil, an offering made by fire to the LORD for a sweet savour; and the drink offering thereof shall be of wine, a fourth part of a hin.

14 And you shall eat neither bread nor parched wheat nor green ears until that same day, until the day when you have brought an offering to your God; it shall be a statute for ever throughout your generations in all your dwellings.

15 ¶And you shall count to you from the morrow, that is, from the day that you brought the sheaf of the wave offering; seven sabbaths shall be complete;

16 Even to the morrow after the seventh sabbath you shall count fifty days; and you shall offer a meal offering of new wheat to the LORD.

17 You shall bring out of your dwellings two wave loaves of two tenths of an ephah; they shall be of fine flour; they shall be baked with leaven; they are the firstfruits to the LORD.

18 And you shall offer with the bread seven lambs without blemish of the first year and one young bullock and two rams; they shall be for a burnt offering to the LORD, with their meal offering and their drink offering made by fire, an offering for a sweet savour to the LORD.

19 Then you shall sacrifice one kid of the goats for a sin offering and two lambs of the first year for a sacrifice of peace offering.

20 And the priest shall wave them with the bread of the firstfruits for a wave offering before the LORD, with the two lambs; they shall be holy before the LORD for the priest.

21 And you shall proclaim on the same day, that it may be a holy convocation to you; you shall do no manner of work thereon; it shall be a statute for ever in all your dwellings throughout your generations.

22 ¶And when you reap the harvest of your land, you shall not reap your fields to their very corners, neither shall you gather any gleaning of your harvest; but you shall leave them to the poor and to the proselytes; I am the LORD your God.

23 ¶And the LORD spoke to Moses, saying,

24 Speak to the children of Israel and say to them, The seventh month on the first day of the month shall be to you a day of rest, and a memorial of blowing of trumpets, a holy convocation.

25 You shall do no manner of work thereon; but you shall offer an offering by fire to the LORD.

26 ¶And the LORD spoke to Moses, saying,

27 Speak to the children of Israel and say to them, Also the tenth day of this seventh month is the day of atonement; it shall be a holy convocation to you; and you shall humble yourselves and offer an offering made by fire to the LORD.

28 And you shall do no work on this same day; for it is a day of atonement, to make an atonement for you before the LORD your God.

29 For whatever person it be who does not humble himself on this same day, he shall be cut off from among his people.

30 And whatever person it be who does any work on this same day, the same person will I destroy from among his people.

31 You shall do no manner of work; it shall be a statute for ever throughout your generations in all your dwellings.

32 It is the sabbath of sabbaths to you, and you shall humble yourselves;

on the ninth day of the month at evening, from evening to evening, shall you keep your sabbaths.

33 ¶And the Lord spoke to Moses, saying,

34 Speak to the children of Israel and say to them, On the fifteenth day of this seventh month you shall keep the feast of tabernacles for seven days to the Lord.

35 The first day shall be a holy convocation to you; you shall do no manner of work thereon.

36 Seven days you shall offer an offering made by fire to the Lord; the eighth day shall be a holy convocation to you; and you shall offer an offering made by fire to the Lord; and you shall be assembled together; and you shall do no manner of work thereon.

37 These are the feasts of the Lord, which you shall proclaim to be holy convocations, to offer on them offerings made by fire to the Lord, burnt offerings and a meal offering and drink offerings and sacrifices, as it is due on each day;

38 Besides the sabbaths of the Lord, and besides your offerings, and besides your gifts, and besides all your vows, and besides all your freewill offerings, which you give to the Lord.

39 But on the fifteenth day of the seventh month, when you have gathered in the produce of the land, you shall celebrate a feast to the Lord for seven days; on the first day shall be suspension of labor, and on the eighth day shall be a solemn rest.

40 And you shall take for yourselves on the first day the fruits of goodly trees, citron, branches of palm trees, myrtle, and willows of the brook; and you shall rejoice before the Lord your God seven days, all the people of the house of Israel.

41 And you shall keep this feast to the Lord seven days in the year. It is a statute for ever throughout your generations; you shall celebrate it in the seventh month.

42 You shall dwell in huts seven days; all the house of Israel shall dwell in huts,

43 That your generations may know that I made the children of Israel to dwell in huts when I brought them out of the land of Egypt; I am the Lord your God.

44 And Moses declared to the children of Israel the feasts of the Lord.

CHAPTER 24

AND the Lord spoke to Moses, saying,

2 Command the children of Israel to bring to you pure olive oil, beaten, to cause the lamps to burn continually.

3 Outside the veil of the testimony, in the tabernacle of the congregation, shall Aaron set them in order from the evening to the morning before the Lord continually; it is a statute for ever throughout your generations.

4 He shall set the lamps in order upon the large candlestick before the Lord continually.

5 ¶And you shall take fine flour, and bake twelve cakes of it; two tenths of an ephah shall be in each cake.

6 And you shall set them in order in two rows, six in a row, upon the pure table before the Lord.

7 And you shall put pure frankincense upon each row before the Lord, that it may be on the bread for a memorial, even an offering made by fire to the Lord.

8 On the sabbath day Aaron shall set them in order before the Lord continually, as a gift from the children of Israel for an everlasting covenant.

9 And it shall be Aaron's and his sons'; and they shall eat it in a holy place; for it is a most holy to him of the offerings of the Lord made by fire by a perpetual statute.

10 ¶And the son of an Israelite woman, whose father was an Egyptian, went out among the children of Israel; and this son of the Israelite woman and a man of Israel quarreled in the camp;

11 And the Israelite woman's son blasphemed the name of the Lord and cursed it. And they brought him to Moses (and his mother's name was Shelomith, the daughter of Dibri, of the tribe of Dan),

12 And they put him in prison, till the LORD's decision might be made known to them.

13 And the LORD spoke to Moses and said to him,

14 Bring outside the camp him who has cursed; and let all who heard him lay their hands upon his head, and let all the congregation stone him.

15 And you shall speak to the children of Israel, saying, Whosoever curses his God shall suffer for his sin.

16 And he who blasphemes the name of the LORD shall surely be put to death, and all the congregation shall surely stone him; the proselyte as well as the Israelite, when he blasphemes my name, shall be put to death.

17 ¶And he who kills any man shall surely be put to death.

18 And he who kills a beast shall make it good; beast for beast.

19 And if a man causes a blemish in his neighbor, as he has done, so shall it be done to him;

20 Wound for wound, eye for eye, tooth for tooth; as he has caused a blemish in his neighbor, so shall it be done to him.

21 And he who kills a beast shall restore it; and he who kills a man shall be put to death.

22 You shall have one manner of justice; as for a proselyte, so for an Israelite; for I am the LORD your God.

23 ¶And Moses spoke to the children of Israel, and they brought forth him who had cursed outside the camp, and stoned him with stones and he died. And the children of Israel did as the LORD commanded Moses.

CHAPTER 25

AND the LORD spoke to Moses on mount Sinai, saying,

2 Speak to the children of Israel and say to them, When you come into the land which I give you for an inheritance, then shall the land keep a sabbath to the LORD.

3 Six years you shall sow your fields and six years you shall prune your vineyards and six years you shall gather in your produce;

4 But the seventh year shall be a sabbath of rest to the land, and it shall be to you a sabbath for the LORD; you shall neither sow your fields nor prune your vineyards.

5 That which grows of itself of your harvest you shall not reap, neither gather the grapes of your undressed vine; for it is the year of rest to the land.

6 And the sabbath of the land shall be food for you, for yourself and for your servants and for your maids and for your hired laborers and for the stranger that sojourns with you

7 And for your cattle and for the beasts that are in your land shall all its increase be for food to you.

8 ¶And you shall count seven sabbaths of years to you, seven times seven years; and the space of the seven sabbaths of years shall be to you forty-nine years.

9 Then you shall cause the trumpet of the jubilee to sound on the tenth day of the seventh month; on the day of atonement shall you sound the trumpet throughout all your land.

10 And you shall hallow the fiftieth year and proclaim liberty throughout all the land to all the inhabitants thereof; it shall be a jubilee to you; and you shall return every man to his own possession, and you shall return every man to his family.

11 A jubilee shall that fiftieth year be to you; you shall not sow, neither reap that which grows of itself in it, nor gather the grapes from the undressed vine.

12 For it is the jubilee; it shall be holy to you; you shall eat the produce out of the field.

13 In this year of jubilee you shall return every man to his own possession.

14 And if you sell to your neighbor or buy from your neighbor, you shall not defraud one another:

15 According to the number of years after the jubilee you shall buy from your neighbor, and according to the number of years of the produce he shall sell to you;

16 In proportion to the multitude

of years you shall increase the price thereof, and in proportion to the fewness of years you shall decrease the price of it; for according to the number of the years of produce does he sell to you.

17 You shall not therefore defraud one another; but you shall fear your God; for I am the LORD your God.

18 ¶Wherefore you shall do my commandments and keep my judgments and do them; and you shall dwell in the land in safety.

19 And the land shall yield its fruit, and you shall eat your fill and dwell therein in safety.

20 And if you shall say, What shall we eat in the seventh year? For we shall not sow, nor gather in the produce thereof;

21 Then I will send my blessings upon you in the sixth year, and it shall bring forth fruit for three years.

22 And you shall sow in the eighth year, and eat yet of old produce until the ninth year; until the new produce comes in, you shall eat of the old produce.

23 ¶Surely the land shall not be sold outright; for the land is mine; you are strangers and sojourners with me.

24 And in all the land of your possession you shall grant a redemption for the land.

25 ¶If your brother becomes poor and sells some of his possession, then his nearest kin shall come and redeem that which his brother has sold.

26 And if the man has no one to redeem it, and himself has sufficient means and is able to redeem it,

27 Then let him count the years of the sale thereof and refund the overplus to the man to whom he sold it, that he may return to his possession.

28 But if he cannot afford to pay him back, then that which he sold shall remain secure in the hand of him who has bought it until the year of jubilee; and in the jubilee it shall be released, and he shall return to his possession.

29 If a man sells a dwelling house in a walled city, then he may redeem it within a whole year after it is sold;

within a full year he may redeem it.

30 And if it is not redeemed within a full year, then the house that is in the walled city shall be confirmed for ever to him who bought it throughout his generations; it shall not be released in the jubilee.

31 But the houses of the villages which have no walls round about them shall be counted as the fields of the country; they may be redeemed, and they shall be released in the jubilee.

32 Notwithstanding the cities of the Levites, and the houses which are in the cities of their possession, the Levites shall have the right to redeem for ever.

33 And if a man purchases of the Levites, then the house that was sold, and the city of his possession, shall be released in the year of jubilee; for the houses in the cities of the Levites are their possessions among the children of Israel.

34 But the field of the suburbs of their cities may not be sold; for it is their perpetual possession.

35 ¶And if your brother becomes poor and stretches out his hand for help, you shall not look upon him as a stranger or a sojourner; he shall live with you.

36 You shall not take a discount of him or usury; but fear your God, that your brother may live with you.

37 You shall not lend him your money with a discount nor give him your food with usury.

38 I am the LORD your God, who brought you forth out of the land of Egypt to give you the land of Canaan and to be your God.

39 ¶And if your brother becomes poor and be sold to you, you shall not compel him to serve as a bondservant;

40 But as a hired laborer, and as a sojourner, he shall be with you, and shall serve you until the year of jubilee;

41 And then he shall depart from you, both he and his children with him, and shall return to his own family, and to the possession of his fathers shall he return.

42 For they are my servants whom I brought forth out of the land of

Egypt; they shall not be sold as bondmen.

43 You shall not compel them to do hard work; but shall fear your God.

44 But as for your male servants and your female servants whom you may have from among the people that are round about you, of them shall you buy bondmen and bondwomen.

45 Moreover of the children of the strangers who have sojourned among you, of them shall you buy, and of their families that are with you, who have been born in your land; and they shall be your possession.

46 And you shall bequeath them to your children after you, to inherit them as a possession; you may make slaves of them for ever; but as for your brethren the children of Israel, you shall not compel them to do hard work.

47 ¶And if a sojourner or stranger who dwells with you becomes rich, and your brother who dwells with him becomes poor and is sold to the stranger or sojourner who dwells with you or to a native born of the stranger's family who dwells with you,

48 After that he is sold he may be redeemed again; one of his brethren may redeem him;

49 Either his uncle or his uncle's son may redeem him, or any of his near kin belonging to his family may redeem him; or if he can afford it, he may redeem himself.

50 He shall reckon with him who bought him from the year that he was sold him to the year of jubilee; and the price of his sale shall be according to the number of years, according to the time of a hired servant shall it be with him.

51 If there are still many years remaining, according to them he shall give again the price of his redemption out of the money that he was bought for.

52 And if there remain but a few years to the year of jubilee, then he shall count with him, and according to his years shall he give him again the price of his redemption.

53 As a yearly hired servant shall he be with him; and he shall not subject him to hard labor in your sight.

54 And if he is not redeemed in any of these ways, then he shall go out in the year of jubilee, both he and his children with him.

55 For to me the children of Israel are servants; they are my servants whom I brought forth out of the land of Egypt; I am the LORD your God.

CHAPTER 26

YOU shall make for yourselves no idols nor graven images, neither shall you erect obelisks for yourselves, nor shall you set up any image of stones in your land to bow down to them or worship them; for I am the LORD your God.

2 ¶You shall keep my commandments and reverence my sanctuary; I am the LORD.

3 ¶If you walk in my statutes and keep my commandments and do them,

4 Then I will give you rain in due season, and the land shall yield its increase, and the trees of the field shall yield their fruit.

5 And your threshing shall last to the time of vintage, and the vintage shall last to the sowing time; and you shall eat your bread to the full and dwell in your land safely.

6 And I will give peace in your land, and you shall lie down and none shall make you afraid; and I will rid vicious beasts out of the land, neither shall the sword go through your land.

7 And you shall chase your enemies, and they shall fall before you by the sword.

8 And five of you shall chase a hundred, and a hundred of you shall pursue ten thousand; and your enemies shall fall before you by the sword.

9 For I will return to you and make you great and multiply you and establish my covenant with you.

10 And you shall eat grain which has been stored, and bring forth the old grain before the new.

11 And I will set my tabernacle among you; and my soul shall not abhor you.

12 And I will walk among you and

will be your God, and you shall be my people.

13 I am the LORD your God, who brought you forth out of the land of Egypt that you should not be their bondmen; and I have broken the bands of your yoke and made you walk upright.

14 ¶But if you will not hearken to me and will not do all these commandments,

15 And if you despise my laws, or if your soul abhor my judgments so that you will not do all my commandments, and make my covenant of no effect;

16 I also will do this to you: I will visit you with terror, leprosy, scab, and the burning ague, that shall consume the eyes and cause life to waste away; and you shall sow your seed in vain, for your enemies shall eat it.

17 And I will pour out my anger against you, and you shall be defeated before your enemies; they that hate you shall reign over you; and you shall flee when none pursue you.

18 And if you will not yet for all these things hearken to me, then I will punish you seven times more for your sins.

19 And I will break the pride of your power; and I will make your heaven like iron and your earth like brass;

20 And your strength shall be spent in vain; for your land shall not yield its increase, neither shall the trees of the land yield their fruits.

21 ¶And if you walk contrary to me and will not hearken to me, I will bring seven times more plagues upon you according to your sins.

22 I will also send wild beasts against you, which shall bereave you of your children and destroy your cattle and make you few in number; and your highways shall be desolate.

23 And if by these things you shall not be disciplined, but continue to walk contrary to me;

24 Then I also will walk contrary to you and will punish you yet seven times for your sins.

25 And I will bring a sword upon you, which shall avenge the breaking of the covenant; and you shall flee to your cities; I will send pestilence among you; and you shall be delivered into the hand of the enemy.

26 And when I have broken the staff of your grain, ten women shall bake your bread in one oven, and they shall deliver your bread by weight; and you shall eat and not be satisfied.

27 And if you will not for all these things hearken to me, but walk contrary to me;

28 Then I will also walk contrary to you in fury; and I, even I, will chastise you seven times for your sins.

29 And you shall eat the flesh of your sons, and the flesh of your daughters shall you eat.

30 And I will destroy your high places and break your idols and cast your carcasses upon the carcasses of your idols, and my soul shall abhor you.

31 And I will make your cities waste and reduce your sanctuaries to desolation, and I will not smell the savour of your sweet odors.

32 And I will bring the land into desolation; and your enemies who dwell therein shall be astonished at it.

33 I will scatter you among the Gentiles, and will draw out a sword against you; and your land shall be desolate, and your cities waste.

34 Then shall the land enjoy its sabbaths as long as it lies desolate, while you are in your enemies' land; even then shall the land rest and enjoy its sabbaths.

35 As long as it lies desolate it shall rest; because it did not rest in your sabbaths when you dwelt upon it.

36 And as for those who are left among you, I will send a faintness into their hearts in the lands of their enemies; and the sound of a shaken leaf shall chase them; and they shall flee as fleeing from the sword; and they shall fall when none pursues them.

37 And they shall stumble one after another, as it were from the sword, when none pursues them; and they shall have no power to stand before their enemies.

38 And you shall perish among the Gentiles, and the land of your enemies shall devour you.

39 And those of you who are left shall pine away in their iniquity in their enemies' lands; and also in the iniquity of their fathers shall they pine away with them.

40 If they shall confess their iniquity and the iniquity of their fathers, with their wickedness with which they transgressed against me, and also that they have walked contrary to me;

41 And that I also walked contrary to them, and brought them into the land of their enemies; and if then their uncircumcised heart shall be humbled, and they then shall accept the punishment of their iniquity;

42 Then I will remember my covenant with Jacob, and also my covenant with Isaac, and my covenant with Abraham will I remember; and I will remember the land.

43 The land also shall be left by them, and shall enjoy its sabbaths while it lies desolate without them; and they shall accept the punishment of their iniquity because they have despised my judgments and because their soul abhorred my statutes.

44 And yet for all that, when they are in the land of their enemies I will not abhor them, neither will I cast them away to destroy them utterly, nor have I nullified my covenant with them; for I am the LORD their God.

45 But I will for their sakes remember the covenant of their ancestors whom I brought forth out of the land of Egypt in the sight of the nations, and I became their God; I am the LORD.

46 These are the commandments and laws and judgments which the LORD made between him and the children of Israel in mount Sinai by the hand of Moses.

CHAPTER 27

AND the LORD spoke to Moses, saying,

2 Speak to the children of Israel and say to them, When a man makes a special vow with the price of persons to the LORD,

3 Then the valuation of a male from twenty years old up to sixty years old shall be fifty shekels of silver, after the shekel of the sanctuary.

4 And if it is a female, then her valuation shall be thirty shekels.

5 And if it is from five years old up to twenty years old, then the valuation of the male shall be twenty shekels, and for the female ten shekels.

6 And if it is from a month old up to five years old, then the valuation of males shall be for the male five shekels of silver, and for the female three shekels of silver.

7 And if it is from sixty years old and up, if it is a male, his valuation shall be fifteen shekels, and for the female ten shekels.

8 But if he is poorer than the valuation, then he shall present himself before the priest, and the priest shall value him; according to the ability of the person who vowed shall the priest value him.

9 And if it is an animal whereof men bring an offering to the LORD, all that any man gives of such to the LORD shall be holy.

10 He shall not exchange it, a good for a bad, or a bad for a good; and if he shall at all exchange an animal for an animal, then both it and the one exchanged for it shall be holy to the LORD.

11 And if it is an unclean animal of which they do not offer a sacrifice to the LORD, then he shall present the animal before the priest;

12 And the priest shall value it, whether it be good or bad; and as the priest values it, so shall it be.

13 But if he wishes to redeem it, then he shall add a fifth part to its valuation.

14 ¶And when a man shall sanctify his house to be holy to the LORD, then the priest shall value it, whether it be good or bad, and as the priest shall estimate it, so shall it stand.

15 And if he who sanctified it will redeem his house, then he shall add a fifth of the money of its estimation to it, and it shall be his.

16 And if a man shall sanctify to

the Lord some part of a field of his possession, then its valuation shall be according to the seed thereof; about ten ephahs of barley seed shall be valued at fifty shekels of silver.

17 If he sanctifies his field from the year of jubilee, according to its estimation so it shall stand.

18 But if he sanctify his field after the jubilee, then the priest shall reckon to him the money according to the years that remain until the year of jubilee, and he shall deduct from its valuation.

19 And if the man who sanctifies the field wishes to redeem it, then he shall add a fifth of the money of the valuation to it, and it shall be his.

20 And if he will not redeem the field, or if he sell it to another man, it shall not be redeemed any more.

21 But the field, when it is released in the jubilee, shall be holy to the Lord, as a field devoted; its possession shall be the priest's.

22 And if a man sanctifies to the Lord a field which he has bought, which was not a field of his inheritance,

23 Then the priest shall reckon the valuation thereof until the year of jubilee; and he shall give the price of the valuation thereof in that day as a holy thing to the Lord.

24 In the year of the jubilee the field shall return to him from whom it was bought, even to him to whom the inheritance of the land did belong.

25 And all the valuations thereof shall be according to the shekel of the sanctuary; twenty gerahs shall be the shekel.

26 ¶But the firstling of an animal, which should be the Lord's firstling, no man shall sanctify it; whether it be ox or sheep, it is the Lord's.

27 And if it is of an unclean beast, then he shall redeem it according to its valuation, and shall add a fifth part to it; or if it is not redeemed, then it shall be sold according to its valuation.

28 But every devoted thing that a man shall devote to the Lord of all that he has, both of man and beast and of the field of his inheritance, shall not be sold or redeemed; every devoted thing is most holy to the Lord.

29 Every devoted thing which shall be devoted by men shall not be redeemed, but shall surely be put to death.

30 And all the tithe of the land, whether of the seed of the land or of the fruit of the trees, is the Lord's; it is holy to the Lord.

31 And if a man wishes to redeem some of his tithes, he shall add to it a fifth part thereof.

32 And all the tithe of the herd or of the flock, even of whatever passes under the shepherd's staff, the tenth shall be holy to the Lord.

33 He shall not inquire whether it is good or bad, neither shall he exchange it; and if he exchanges it at all, then both it and the exchange thereof shall be holy; it shall not be redeemed.

34 These are the commandments which the Lord commanded Moses for the children of Israel in mount Sinai.

THE FOURTH BOOK OF MOSES, CALLED

NUMBERS

CHAPTER 1

AND the LORD spoke to Moses in the wilderness of Sinai, in the tabernacle of the congregation, on the first day of the second month, in the second year after the children of Israel were come out of the land of Egypt, saying,

2 Take the census of all the congregation of the children of Israel, by their families, by the house of their fathers, with the number of their names, every male by their polls;

3 From twenty years old and upward, all who are able to go forth to war in Israel; you and Aaron your brother shall number them by their armies.

4 And with you there shall be a man of every tribe; every one the head of the house of his fathers.

5 ¶And these are the names of the men who shall help you: of the tribe of Reuben, Elizur the son of Shedeur.

6 Of Simeon, Shelmuiel the son of Zurishaddai.

7 Of Judah, Nahshon the son of Amminadab.

8 Of Issachar, Nethanael the son of Zuar.

9 Of Zebulun, Eliab the son of Helon.

10 Of the sons of Joseph, of Ephraim, Elishama the son of Ammihud; of Manasseh, Gamaliel the son of Perzur.

11 Of Benjamin, Abidan the son of Gideoni.

12 Of Dan, Ahiezer the son of Ammishaddai.

13 Of Asher, Pagiel the son of Ocran.

14 Of Gad, Eliasaph the son of Reuel.

15 Of Naphtali, Ahida the son of Enan.

16 These were the renowned of the congregation, princes of the tribes of their fathers, heads of thousands of the army of Israel.

17 ¶And Moses and Aaron took these men who were chosen by their names;

18 And they assembled all the congregation together on the first day of the second month, and they were numbered after their families, by the house of their fathers, according to the number of their names from twenty years old and upward, by their polls.

19 As the LORD commanded Moses, so he numbered them in the wilderness of Sinai.

20 And the children of Reuben, Israel's first-born, by their generations, after their families, by the house of their fathers, according to the number of the names, by their polls, every male from twenty years old and upward, all who were able to go forth to war in Israel;

21 The number of the tribe of Reuben was forty-six thousand and five hundred.

22 ¶Of the children of Simeon, by their generations, after their families, by the house of their fathers, those that were numbered of them, according to the number of the names, by their polls, every male from twenty years old and upward, all who were able to go forth to war in Israel;

23 The number of the tribe of Simeon was fifty-nine thousand and three hundred.

24 ¶Of the children of Gad, by their generations, after their families, by the house of their fathers, according

to the number of the names, by their polls, every male from twenty years old and upward, all who were able to go forth to war in Israel;

25 The number of the tribe of Gad was forty-five thousand and six hundred and fifty.

26 ¶Of the children of Judah, by their generations, after their families, according to the number of the names, from twenty years old and upward, all who were able to go forth to war in Israel;

27 The number of the tribe of Judah was seventy-four thousand and six hundred.

28 ¶Of the children of Issachar, by their generations, after their families, by the house of their fathers, according to the number of the names, from twenty years old and upward, all who were able to go forth to war in Israel;

29 The number of the tribe of Issachar was fifty-four thousand and four hundred.

30 ¶Of the children of Zebulun, by their generations, after their families, by the house of their fathers, according to the number of the names, from twenty years old and upward, all who were able to go forth to war in Israel;

31 The number of the tribe of Zebulun was fifty-seven thousand and four hundred.

32 ¶Of the children of Joseph, namely, of the children of Ephraim, by their generations, after their families, by the house of their fathers, according to the number of the names, from twenty years old and upward, all who were able to go forth to war in Israel;

33 The number of the tribe of Ephraim was forty thousand and five hundred.

34 ¶Of the children of Manasseh, by their generations, after their families, by the house of their fathers, according to the number of the names, from twenty years old and upward, all who were able to go forth to war in Israel;

35 The number of the tribe of Manasseh was thirty-two thousand and two hundred.

36 ¶Of the children of Benjamin, by their generations, after their families, by the house of their fathers, according to the number of the names, from twenty years old and upward, all who were able to go forth to war in Israel;

37 The number of the tribe of Benjamin was thirty-five thousand and four hundred.

38 ¶Of the children of Dan, by their generations, after their families, by the house of their fathers, according to the number of the names, from twenty years old and upward, all who were able to go forth to war in Israel;

39 The number of the tribe of Dan was sixty-two thousand and seven hundred.

40 ¶Of the children of Asher, by their generations, after their families, by the house of their fathers, according to the number of the names, from twenty years old and upward, all who were able to go forth to war in Israel;

41 The number of the tribe of Asher was forty-one thousand and five hundred.

42 ¶Of the children of Naphtali, by their generations, after their families, by the house of their fathers, according to the number of the names, from twenty years old and upward, all who were able to go forth to war in Israel;

43 The number of the tribe of Naphtali was fifty-three thousand and four hundred.

44 These are those who were numbered, whom Moses and Aaron numbered, and the princes of Israel, being twelve men; each one was from the house of his fathers.

45 So were all those that were numbered of the children of Israel, by the house of their fathers, from twenty years old and upward, all who were able to go forth to war in Israel;

46 The total number of the children of Israel was six hundred and three thousand and five hundred and fifty.

47 ¶But the Levites and the tribe of their fathers were not numbered among them.

48 Because the LORD had spoken to Moses, saying,

49 You shall not number the tribe

of Levi, neither take the sum of them among the children of Israel;

50 But you shall appoint the Levites over the tabernacle of the testimony and over all its vessels and over all that belongs to it; they shall carry the tabernacle and all its vessels; and they shall minister to it, and shall encamp round about the tabernacle.

51 And when the tabernacle shall set forward, the Levites shall take it down; and when the tabernacle is to be pitched, the Levites shall set it up; and the stranger who comes near shall be put to death.

52 And the children of Israel shall pitch their tents, every man by his own camp and every man by his own standard, throughout their hosts.

53 But the Levites shall pitch round about the tabernacle of the testimony, that there be no wrath against the congregation of the children of Israel; and the Levites shall keep the charge of the tabernacle of the testimony.

54 And the children of Israel did according to all that the LORD commanded Moses, so did they.

CHAPTER 2

AND the LORD spoke to Moses and to Aaron, saying,

2 Every man of the children of Israel shall encamp by his own standard, at the places of their father's house; far off round about the tabernacle of the congregation shall they encamp.

3 Those who encamp first toward the east shall be of the standard of the camp of Judah throughout their armies; and Nahshon the son of Amminadab shall be chief of the children of Judah.

4 And the number of his host was seventy-four thousand and six hundred.

5 And those who encamp next to him shall be the tribe of Issachar; and Nethanael the son of Zuar shall be chief of the children of Issachar.

6 And the number of his host was fifty-four thousand and four hundred.

7 Then shall encamp the tribe of Zebulun; and Eliab the son of Helon shall be chief of the children of Zebulun.

8 And the number of his host was fifty-seven thousand and four hundred.

9 The total number of the camp of Judah was one hundred and eighty-six thousand and four hundred, throughout their armies. They shall march first.

10 ¶On the south side shall be the standard of the camp of Reuben according to their armies; and the chief of the children of Reuben shall be Elizur the son of Shedeur.

11 And the number of his host was forty-six thousand and five hundred.

12 And those who encamp by him shall be the tribe of Simeon; and the chief of the children of Simeon shall be Shelmuiel the son of Zurishaddai.

13 And the number of his host was fifty-nine thousand and three hundred.

14 Then shall encamp the tribe of Gad; and the chief of the sons of Gad shall be Eliasaph the son of Reuel.

15 And the number of his host was forty-five thousand six hundred and fifty.

16 The total number of the camp of Reuben was one hundred and fifty-one thousand four hundred and fifty, throughout their armies. They shall march in the second place.

17 ¶Then the tabernacle of the congregation shall march with the camp of the Levites in the midst of the camps; as they encamped so shall they march, every man by his standard throughout their armies.

18 ¶On the west side shall be the standard of the camp of Ephraim according to their armies; and the chief of the children of Ephraim shall be Elishama the son of Ammihud.

19 And the number of his host was forty thousand and five hundred.

20 And those who encamp by him shall be the tribe of Manasseh; and the chief of the children of Manasseh shall be Gamaliel the son of Perzur.

21 And the number of his host was thirty-two thousand and two hundred.

22 Then shall encamp the tribe of Benjamin; and the chief of the sons of Benjamin shall be Abidan the son of Gideoni.

23 And the number of his host was

thirty-five thousand and four hundred.

24 The total number of the camp of Ephraim was an hundred and eight thousand and one hundred, throughout their armies. They shall march in the third place.

25 ¶The standard of the camp of Dan shall be on the north side by their armies; and the chief of the children of Dan shall be Ahiezer the son of Ammishaddai.

26 And the number of his host was sixty-two thousand and seven hundred.

27 And those that encamp by him shall be the tribe of Asher; and the chief of the children of Asher shall be Pagiel the son of Ocran.

28 And the number of his host was forty-one thousand and five hundred.

29 ¶Then shall encamp the tribe of Naphtali; and the chief of the children of Naphtali shall be Ahida the son of Enan.

30 And the number of his host was fifty-three thousand and four hundred.

31 The total number of the camp of Dan was a hundred and fifty-seven thousand and six hundred. They shall march last with their standards.

32 ¶These are the numbers of the children of Israel by the house of their fathers; all those who were numbered of the camps throughout their hosts were six hundred and three thousand and five hundred and fifty.

33 But the Levites and the tribe of their fathers were not numbered among the children of Israel; as the LORD commanded Moses.

34 And the children of Israel did according to all that the LORD commanded Moses; so they marched by their standards, and so they encamped, every man in his camp, according to the house of his fathers.

CHAPTER 3

THESE are the generations of Aaron and Moses in the day that the LORD spoke with Moses on mount Sinai.

2 And these are the names of the sons of Aaron: Nadab, his first-born, and Abihu, Eleazar, and Ithamar.

3 These are the names of the sons of Aaron the priest, who were anointed and consecrated to minister in the priest's office.

4 But Nadab and Abihu died before the LORD when they offered strange fire before the LORD in the wilderness of Sinai, and they had no children; and Eleazar and Ithamar ministered in the priest's office during the lifetime of Aaron their father.

5 ¶And the LORD spoke to Moses, saying,

6 Bring the tribe of Levi near, and present them before Aaron the priest, that they may minister to him.

7 And they shall keep his charge and the charge of the whole congregation in the presence of the LORD before the tabernacle of the congregation, to do the service of the tabernacle.

8 And they shall keep all the instruments of the tabernacle of the congregation and the charge of the children of Israel, to do the service of the tabernacle.

9 And you shall give the Levites to Aaron and to his sons; they are wholly given to him as a gift out of the children of Israel.

10 And you shall appoint Aaron and his sons, and they shall wait on their priest's office; and the stranger that comes near shall be put to death.

11 And the LORD spoke to Moses, saying,

12 Behold I have taken the Levites from among the children of Israel instead of all the first-born that open the womb among the children of Israel; therefore the Levites shall be mine;

13 Because all the first-born are mine; for on the day that I smote all the first-born in the land of Egypt, I consecrated to me all the first-born in Israel, both man and beast; they shall be mine; I am the LORD.

14 ¶And the LORD spoke to Moses in the wilderness of Sinai, saying,

15 Number the children of Levi after the house of their fathers, by their families; every male from a

month old and upward, you shall number them.

16 So Moses numbered them according to the word of the LORD, as he was commanded.

17 These were the sons of Levi by their names: Gershon and Kohath and Merari.

18 And these are the names of the sons of Gershon by their families: Libni and Shimei.

19 And the sons of Kohath by their families: Amram and Izhar, Hebron and Uzziel.

20 And the sons of Merari by their families: Mahali and Mushi. These are the families of the Levites according to the house of their fathers.

21 Of Gershon was the family of the Libnites and the family of the Shimites; these are the families of the Gershonites.

22 Their number, according to the number of all the males from a month old and upward was seven thousand and five hundred.

23 The families of the Gershonites shall encamp behind the tabernacle westward.

24 And the chief of the house of the fathers of the Gershonites shall be Eliasaph the son of Eliab.

25 And the charge of the sons of Gershon in the tabernacle of the congregation shall be the tabernacle and the tent, its covering and the curtains for the door of the tabernacle of the congregation

26 And the curtains of the court and the covering for the door of the court which is by the tabernacle and by the altar round about, and the cords of it, and all the instruments thereof.

27 ¶And of Kohath was the family of the Amramites and the family of the Izeharites and the family of the Hebronites and the family of the Uzzielites; these are the families of the Kohathites.

28 Their number according to the number of all the males, from a month old and upward, was eight thousand and six hundred, looking after the sanctuary.

29 The families of the sons of Ko-hath shall encamp on the side of the tabernacle southward.

30 And the chief of the house of the fathers of the families of the Kohathites shall be Elizphan the son of Uzziel.

31 And their charge shall be the ark and the table and the candlestick and the altars and the vessels of the sanctuary with which they minister and the curtain of the door and all the service thereof.

32 And Eleazar the son of Aaron the priest shall be the chief over the chiefs of the Levites and have the oversight over those who have charge of the sanctuary.

33 ¶Of Merari was the family of the Mahlites and the family of the Mushites; these are the families of Merari.

34 Their number according to the number of all the males, from a month old and upward, was six thousand and two hundred.

35 And the chief of the house of the fathers of the families of Merari was Zuriel the son of Abihail; they shall encamp on the side of the tabernacle northward.

36 And under the custody and charge of the sons of Merari shall be the boards of the tabernacle and its bars and its pillars and its sockets and all the vessels thereof and all that pertains to it

37 And the pillars of the court round about and their sockets and their pins and their cords.

38 ¶But those that encamp before the tabernacle toward the east, even before the tabernacle of the congregation eastward, shall be Moses and Aaron and his sons, keeping the charge of the sanctuary in addition to the charge of the children of Israel; and the stranger who comes near shall be put to death.

39 All who were numbered of the Levites, whom Moses numbered at the commandment of the LORD, by their families, all the males from a month old and upward, were twenty and two thousand.

40 ¶And the LORD said to Moses, Number all the first-born of the

males of the children of Israel from a month old and upward, and take the number of their names.

41 And you shall present the Levites for me (I am the LORD) instead of all the first-born among the children of Israel; and the cattle of the Levites instead of all the firstlings among the cattle of the children of Israel.

42 And Moses numbered, as the LORD commanded him, all the first-born among the children of Israel,

43 And all the first-born males by the number of names, from a month old and upward, and their number was twenty-two thousand two hundred and seventy-three.

44 ¶And the LORD spoke to Moses, saying,

45 Present the Levites instead of all the first-born among the children of Israel, and the cattle of the Levites instead of their cattle; and the Levites shall be mine; I am the LORD.

46 And for the redemption of the two hundred and seventy-three of the first-born of the children of Israel, that are above the number of the Levites,

47 You shall take five shekels apiece by the poll, by the shekel of the sanctuary shall you take them (the shekel is twenty gerahs).

48 And you shall give the money wherewith the excess number of them is to be redeemed to Aaron and to his sons.

49 So Moses took the redemption money from those who were over and above them that were redeemed by the Levites;

50 From the first-born of the children of Israel he took the money, one thousand three hundred and sixty-five shekels, by the shekel of the sanctuary:

51 And Moses gave the redemption money to Aaron and to his sons, according to the word of the LORD, as the LORD commanded Moses.

CHAPTER 4

AND the LORD spoke to Moses and to Aaron, saying,

2 Take the sum of the sons of Kohath from among the sons of Levi,

after their families, by the house of their fathers,

3 From thirty years old and upward to fifty years old, all who can enter into the host to do the work in the tabernacle of the congregation.

4 This is the service of the sons of Kohath in the tabernacle of the congregation concerning the most holy things;

5 ¶And when the camp marches forward, Aaron and his sons shall come in, and they shall take down the covering veil and cover the ark of testimony with it,

6 And shall put on it the covering of badgers' skins, and shall spread over it a cloth all of blue, and shall put in the poles thereof.

7 And upon the table of shewbread they shall spread a cloth of blue, and put upon it the dishes, the spoons, the bowls, the flagons for drink offering; and the continual shewbread shall be on it;

8 And they shall spread thereon a cloth of scarlet, and cover the same with a covering of badgers' skins, and shall put in the poles thereof.

9 And they shall take a cloth of blue, and cover the candlestick of the light and its lamps and its tongs and its snuffdishes and all the oil vessels thereof with which they minister to it;

10 And they shall put it and all its vessels within a covering of badgers' skins, and shall put it upon its poles.

11 And upon the golden altar they shall spread a cloth of blue, and cover it with a covering of badgers' skins, and shall put it upon its poles;

12 And they shall take all the vessels of the ministry wherewith they minister in the sanctuary, and put them in a cloth of blue, and cover them with a covering of badgers' skins, and shall put them on poles;

13 And they shall take apart the altar, and spread a purple cloth over it;

14 And they shall put with it all the vessels thereof, with which they minister upon it, the censers, the meathooks and the shovels and the basins and all the vessels of the altar;

and they shall spread upon it a covering of badgers' skins, and put in its poles.

15 And when Aaron and his sons have finished covering the sanctuary and all the vessels of the sanctuary, as the camp is to march after that, the sons of Kohath shall come in to bear it, that they may not touch any holy thing, lest they die. These things are to be borne by the sons of Kohath in the service of the tabernacle of the congregation.

16 ¶And to the office of Eleazar the son of Aaron the priest pertains the charge of the oil for the light and the sweet incense and the daily meal offering and the anointing oil and the oversight of all the tabernacle and of all the things that are in it and of the sanctuary and its vessels.

17 ¶And the LORD spoke to Moses and to Aaron, saying,

18 You shall not destroy the tribe of the families of the Kohathites from among the Levites;

19 But do this to them, that they may live, and not die, when they enter into the most holy place; Aaron and his sons shall go in and appoint them every one to his service and to his burden;

20 But they shall not go in to observe when the holy things are covered, lest they die.

21 ¶And the LORD spoke to Moses, saying,

22 Take also the sum of the sons of Gershon, throughout the houses of their fathers, by their families:

23 From thirty years old and up until fifty years old you shall number them; all who are able-bodied to perform the service, to do the work in the tabernacle of the congregation.

24 This is the service of the families of the Gershonites, to serve, and to bear burdens;

25 They shall carry the curtains of the tabernacle, and the tabernacle of the congregation itself, the veil of the door thereof, and the covering of the badgers' skins that is upon it, and the hangings of the door of the tabernacle of the congregation,

26 And the hangings of the court, and the hanging for the entrance of the door of the court which is by the tabernacle and by the altar round about, and the cords thereof, and all the instruments of their service, and all that they do and serve.

27 At the command of Aaron and his sons shall be all the service of the sons of Gershon, in all their burdens and in all their service; and you shall appoint unto them in charge all their burdens.

28 This is the service of the families of the sons of Gershon in the tabernacle of the congregation; and their charge shall be under the hand of Ithamar the son of Aaron the priest.

29 ¶As for the sons of Merari, you shall number them after their families, by the house of their fathers;

30 From thirty years old and upward to fifty years old you shall number them, every able man, to do the work of the tabernacle of the congregation.

31 And this is the charge of their burden, and of all their service in the tabernacle of the congregation; the boards of the tabernacle, its bars and its pillars and its sockets,

32 And the pillars of the court round about and their sockets, their pins and their cords, with all their instruments and with all their service; and by name you shall count the instruments included in their burden.

33 This is the service of the families of the sons of Merari, and all their service in the tabernacle of the congregation, under the hand of Ithamar the son of Aaron the priest.

34 ¶And Moses and Aaron and the chiefs of the congregation numbered the sons of the Kohathites after their families, by the house of their fathers,

35 From thirty years old and upward to fifty years old, every able man, for the work of the tabernacle of the congregation;

36 And their number by their families was two thousand and seven hundred and fifty.

37 These were the numbers of the

families of Kohath, all that might do service in the tabernacle of the congregation, whom Moses and Aaron numbered according to the commandment of the LORD by Moses.

38 And the number of the sons of Gershon by their families, and by the house of their fathers,

39 From thirty years old and upward to fifty years old, every able man, for the work in the tabernacle of the congregation,

40 And their number by their families and by the house of their fathers was two thousand and six hundred and thirty.

41 These were the numbers of the family of the sons of Gershon, all who served in the tabernacle of the congregation, whom Moses and Aaron numbered according to the commandment of the LORD.

42 ¶And the number of the families of the sons of Merari by their families, by the house of their fathers,

43 From thirty years old and upward to fifty years old, every able man, for the work in the tabernacle of the congregation,

44 And their number by their families was three thousand and two hundred.

45 These are the numbers of the sons of Merari, whom Moses and Aaron numbered according to the commandment of the LORD by the hand of Moses.

46 All those who were numbered of the Levites, whom Moses and Aaron and the chiefs of Israel numbered, after their families and by the house of their fathers,

47 From thirty years old and upward to fifty years old, all able men, to do the service of the ministry and the work of the burden in the tabernacle of the congregation,

48 Their number was eight thousand and five hundred and eighty.

49 According to the commandment of the LORD they were numbered by the hand of Moses, every one according to his service and according to his burden; thus they were numbered as the LORD commanded Moses.

CHAPTER 5

THE LORD spoke to Moses, saying,

2 Command the children of Israel that they put out of the camp every leper and every one who has a discharge and whosoever has defiled himself;

3 Both male and female shall you put outside the camp, that they may not defile your camps, for I dwell among you.

4 And the children of Israel did so, and put them outside the camp; as the LORD had said to Moses, so did the children of Israel.

5 ¶And the LORD spoke to Moses, saying,

6 Say to the children of Israel, When a man or a woman shall commit any sin that men commit, to do wrong in the sight of the LORD, and that person shall be guilty,

7 Then he shall confess his sins which he has committed; and his guilt shall return upon his own head; and he shall add a fifth part thereof, and give it to him whom he had wronged.

8 And if the person has no kinsman to whom to recompense the trespass, let the trespass offering which they bring on his behalf before the LORD be given to the priest in addition to the ram of the atonement with which an atonement is made for him.

9 And every offering of all the holy things of the children of Israel which they bring to the priest shall be his.

10 And every man's hallowed things shall be his; and whatever any man gives to the priest, shall be his.

11 ¶And the LORD spoke to Moses, saying,

12 Speak to the children of Israel and say to them, If any man's wife does wrong, and commits a trespass against him,

13 And a man lies with her carnally and it is hidden from the eyes of her husband and the act is kept secret and she is defiled and there is no witness against her, neither is she caught in the act,

14 And the temper of jealousy

comes upon him and he be jealous of his wife and she is defiled; or if the temper of jealousy comes upon him and he becomes jealous of his wife and she is not defiled,

15 Then the man shall bring his wife to the priest, and he shall bring as his offering a tenth part of an ephah of barley flour; and he shall pour no oil upon it, nor put frankincense upon it; for it is a meal offering of jealousy, a meal offering for a memorial, bringing iniquity to remembrance.

16 And the priest shall bring her near, and she shall stand before the LORD;

17 And the priest shall take holy water in an earthen vessel; and some of the dust that is in the base of the altar of the tabernacle the priest shall take and put it into the water;

18 And the priest shall set the woman before the LORD and shave the woman's head and put the offering of memorial in her hands, which is the jealousy offering; and the priest shall have in his hand the bitter water of testing;

19 And the priest shall charge the woman by an oath, and say to her, If no man has lain with you besides your husband, and if you have not done wrong and become unclean, be absolved from these charges by this bitter water of testing;

20 But if you have done wrong by having lain with another man besides your husband, and if you have defiled yourself, and some other man has lain with you besides your husband;

21 Then the priest shall adjure the woman with the oaths of cursing, and the priest shall say to the woman, The LORD make you a curse and an oath among your people, when the LORD makes your thigh to rot and your belly to swell;

22 And this water of testing shall go into your belly and make your belly to swell and your thighs to rot; and the woman shall say, Amen, amen.

23 And the priest shall write these curses in a book, and he shall blot out the writing in the water of testing;

24 And he shall make the woman drink the bitter water of testing; and the water of testing shall enter into her, to try her.

25 Then the priest shall take the jealousy meal offering out of the woman's hand, and shall wave the meal offering before the LORD, and offer it upon the altar;

26 And the priest shall take some of the meal offering as the memorial thereof, and burn it upon the altar, and afterward shall make the woman drink the water.

27 And when he has made her drink the water, if she has defiled herself and has committed iniquity against her husband, the water of testing shall enter into her, and shall try her, and if her belly shall swell and her thighs shall rot, then that woman shall be a curse among her people.

28 But if the woman has not defiled herself, but is pure, then she shall be absolved, and shall bear a male child.

29 This is the law of jealousy when a woman does wrong by having lain with another man besides her husband and defiles herself,

30 Or when the temper of jealousy comes upon a man and he is jealous over his wife and shall set the woman before the LORD, and the priest shall execute upon her all this law;

31 Then the man shall be blameless from guilt, but the woman shall bear her iniquity.

CHAPTER 6

THE LORD spoke to Moses, saying, 2 Speak to the children of Israel and say to them, When a man or woman shall separate himself to vow a vow of a Nazarite, to separate himself to the LORD,

3 He shall abstain from wine and strong drink, and shall drink no vinegar of wine or vinegar of strong drink, neither shall he drink any juice of grapes, or eat grapes or raisins;

4 All the days of his separation he shall eat nothing that is made of the grapevine, from the skins even to the stones of raisins.

5 All the days of the vow of his

separation there shall no razor come upon his head; until the days are fulfilled for which he separated himself to the LORD, he shall be holy and shall let the locks of the hair of his head grow.

6 All the days that he separates himself to the LORD he shall not come near a dead body.

7 He shall not defile himself for his father or for his mother, for his brother or for his sister when they die; because the crown of consecration of his God is upon his head.

8 All the days of his separation he is holy unto the LORD.

9 And if any man dies very suddenly by him, he has defiled the crown of his separation; then he shall shave his head on the day of his cleansing, on the seventh day shall he shave it.

10 And on the eighth day he shall bring two turtledoves or two young pigeons to the priest, to the door of the tabernacle of the congregation;

11 And the priest shall offer the one for a sin offering and the other for a burnt offering, and make an atonement for him, for the sin that he sinned by the dead body; and shall sanctify his head that same day.

12 And he shall consecrate to the LORD the days of his separation, and he shall bring a lamb of the first year for a trespass offering; but the previous days of his separation shall be void, because his separation was defiled.

13 ¶This is the law of the Nazarite when the days of his separation are fulfilled: he shall be brought to the door of the tabernacle of the congregation,

14 And he shall offer his offering to the LORD, one male lamb of the first year without blemish for a burnt offering and one ewe lamb without blemish for a sin offering and one ram without blemish for a peace offering

15 And a basket of unleavened bread, cakes of fine flour mixed with oil and wafers of unleavened bread mixed with oil and their meal offering and their drink offering.

16 And the priest shall bring them before the LORD, and shall offer his sin offering and his burnt offering:

17 And he shall offer the ram for a sacrifice of peace offering to the LORD, with the basket of unleavened bread; the priest shall offer also his meal offering and his drink offering.

18 And the Nazarite shall shave his head as a sign of his separation at the door of the tabernacle of the congregation, and shall take the hair of his head of his separation and put it in the fire which is under the sacrifice of the peace offering.

19 And the priest shall take the cooked shoulder of the ram and one unleavened cake from the basket and one unleavened wafer, and shall put them in the hands of the Nazarite after he has shaved his hair as a sign of his separation;

20 And the priest shall wave them for a wave offering before the LORD: this is holy for the priest, with the wave breast and the shoulder; and after that the Nazarite may drink wine.

21 This is the law of the Nazarite who has made a vow, and of his offering to the LORD for his separation, excepting what he can afford in addition; according to the vow which he has vowed, so shall he do after the law of his separation.

22 ¶And the LORD spoke to Moses, saying,

23 Speak to Aaron and to his sons and say to them, Thus you shall bless the children of Israel, saying to them,

24 The LORD bless you and keep you;

25 The LORD make his face shine upon you and give you life;

26 The LORD lift up his countenance upon you and give you peace.

27 And they shall put my name upon the children of Israel, and I will bless them.

CHAPTER 7

AND it came to pass on the day that Moses had finished setting up the tabernacle and had anointed it and sanctified it and all the instruments thereof, both the altar and all its vessels, and had anointed them and sanctified them;

2 That the princes of Israel, heads of the house of their fathers who were the princes of the tribes and were over those who were numbered,

3 Brought their offerings before the LORD, six excellently constructed wagons and twelve oxen, a wagon for two of the princes, and for each one an ox; and they brought them before the tabernacle.

4 And the LORD said to Moses,

5 Take the offerings from them, that they may be used to do the service of the tabernacle of the congregation, and give them to the Levites, to every man according to his service.

6 And Moses took the oxen and the wagons, and gave them to the Levites.

7 Two wagons and four oxen he gave to the sons of Gershon, according to their service;

8 And four wagons and eight oxen he gave to the sons of Merari, according to their service, under the hand of Ithamar, the son of Aaron the priest.

9 But to the sons of Kohath he gave none, because the service of the sanctuary assigned to them was that they should carry upon their shoulders.

10 ¶And the princes offered offerings for the dedication of the altar on the day that it was anointed; and the princes offered their offerings before the LORD.

11 And the LORD said to Moses, They shall offer each their offerings, each prince on his day, for the dedication of the altar.

12 ¶And he who offered his offering on the first day was Nahshon the son of Amminadab, the prince of the tribe of Judah;

13 And his offering was one silver plate, weighing a hundred and thirty shekels, one silver bowl of seventy shekels, according to the shekel of the sanctuary; both of them were full of fine flour mixed with oil for a meal offering;

14 One spoon of gold of ten shekels, full of incense;

15 One young bullock, one ram, one lamb of the first year, for a burnt offering;

16 One kid of the goats for a sin offering;

17 And for a sacrifice of peace offering, two oxen, five rams, five kids of the goats, five lambs of the first year; this was the offering of Nahshon the son of Amminadab.

18 ¶On the second day, Nethanael the son of Zuar, prince of Issachar, did offer.

19 He offered for his offering one silver plate, weighing a hundred and thirty shekels, one silver bowl of seventy shekels, according to the shekel of the sanctuary; both of them were full of fine flour mixed with oil for a meal offering;

20 One spoon of gold of ten shekels, full of incense;

21 One young bullock, one ram, one lamb of the first year, for a burnt offering;

22 One kid of the goats for a sin offering;

23 And for a sacrifice of peace offering, two oxen, five rams, five kids of the goats, and five lambs of the first year; this was the offering of Nethanael the son of Zuar.

24 ¶On the third day Eliab the son of Helon, prince of the tribe of Zebulun, did offer.

25 His offering was one silver plate, weighing a hundred and thirty shekels, one silver bowl of seventy shekels, according to the shekel of the sanctuary; both of them were full of fine flour mixed with oil for a meal offering;

26 One golden spoon of ten shekels, full of incense;

27 One young bullock, one ram, one lamb of the first year, for a burnt offering;

28 One kid of the goats for a sin offering;

29 And for a sacrifice of peace offering, two oxen, five rams, five kids of the goats, five lambs of the first year; this was the offering of Eliab the son of Helon.

30 ¶On the fourth day Elizur the son of Shedeur, the prince of the tribe of Reuben, did offer.

31 His offering was one silver plate, weighing a hundred and thirty shekels, one silver bowl of seventy shekels, according to the shekel of the sanctuary; both of them were full of fine flour mixed with oil for a meal offering;

32 One golden spoon of ten shekels, full of incense;

33 One young bullock, one ram, one lamb of the first year, for a burnt offering;

34 One kid of the goats for a sin offering;

35 And for a sacrifice of peace offering, two oxen, five rams, five kids of the goats, five lambs of the first year; this was the offering of Elizur the son of Shedeur.

36 ¶On the fifth day Shelmuiel the son of Zurishaddai, prince of the tribe of Simeon, did offer.

37 His offering was one silver plate, weighing a hundred and thirty shekels, one silver bowl of seventy shekels, according to the shekel of the sanctuary; both of them were full of fine flour mixed with oil for a meal offering;

38 One golden spoon of ten shekels, full of incense;

39 One young bullock, one ram, one lamb of the first year, for a burnt offering;

40 One kid of the goats for a sin offering;

41 And for the sacrifice of peace offering, two oxen, five rams, five kids of the goats, and five lambs of the first year; this was the offering of Shelmuiel the son of Zurishaddai.

42 ¶On the sixth day Eliasaph the son of Reuel, prince of the tribe of Gad, did offer.

43 His offering was one silver plate, weighing a hundred and thirty shekels, one silver bowl of seventy shekels, according to the shekel of the sanctuary; both of them were full of fine flour mixed with oil for a meal offering;

44 One golden spoon of ten shekels, full of incense;

45 One young bullock, one ram, one lamb of the first year, for a burnt offering;

46 One kid of the goats for a sin offering:

47 And for a sacrifice of peace offering, two oxen, five rams, five kids of the goats, five lambs of the first year; this was the offering of Eliasaph the son of Reuel.

48 ¶On the seventh day Elishama the son of Ammihud, prince of the tribe of Ephraim, offered.

49 His offering was one silver plate, weighing a hundred and thirty shekels, one silver bowl of seventy shekels, according to the shekel of the sanctuary; both of them were full of fine flour mixed with oil for a meal offering;

50 One golden spoon of ten shekels, full of incense;

51 One young bullock, one ram, one lamb of the first year, for a burnt offering;

52 One kid of the goats for a sin offering;

53 And for a sacrifice of peace offering, two oxen, five rams, five kids of the goats, five lambs of the first year; this was the offering of Elishama the son of Ammihud.

54 ¶On the eighth day Gamaliel the son of Perzur, prince of the tribe of Manasseh, offered.

55 His offering was one silver plate, weighing a hundred and thirty shekels, one silver bowl of seventy shekels, according to the shekel of the sanctuary; both of them were full of fine flour mixed with oil for a meal offering;

56 One golden spoon of ten shekels, full of incense;

57 One young bullock, one ram, one lamb of the first year, for a burnt offering;

58 One kid of the goats for a sin offering;

59 And for a sacrifice of peace offering, two oxen, five rams, five kids of the goats, five lambs of the first year; this was the offering of Gamaliel the son of Perzur.

60 ¶On the ninth day Abidan the son of Gideoni, prince of the tribe of Benjamin, offered.

61 His offering was one silver plate, weighing a hundred and thirty shekels, one silver bowl of seventy shekels, according to the shekel of the sanctuary; both of them were full of fine

flour mixed with oil for a meal offering;

62 One golden spoon of ten shekels, full of incense;

63 One young bullock, one ram, one lamb of the first year, for a burnt offering;

64 One kid of the goats for a sin offering;

65 And for a sacrifice of peace offering, two oxen, five rams, five kids of the goats, and five lambs of the first year; this was the offering of Abidan the son of Gideoni.

66 ¶On the tenth day Ahiezer the son of Ammishaddai, prince of the tribe of Dan, offered.

67 His offering was one silver plate, weighing a hundred and thirty shekels, one silver bowl of seventy shekels, according to the shekel of the sanctuary; both of them were full of fine flour mixed with oil for a meal offering;

68 One golden spoon of ten shekels, full of incense;

69 One young bullock, one ram, one lamb of the first year, for a burnt offering;

70 One kid of the goats for a sin offering;

71 And for a sacrifice of peace offering, two oxen, five rams, five kids of the goats, five lambs of the first year; this was the offering of Ahiezer the son of Ammishaddai.

72 ¶On the eleventh day Pagiel the son of Ocran, prince of the tribe of Asher, offered.

73 His offering was one silver plate, weighing a hundred and thirty shekels, one silver bowl of seventy shekels, according to the shekel of the sanctuary; both of them were full of fine flour mixed with oil for a meal offering;

74 One golden spoon of ten shekels, full of incense;

75 One young bullock, one ram, one lamb of the first year, for a burnt offering;

76 One kid of the goats for a sin offering;

77 And for a sacrifice of peace offering, two oxen, five rams, five kids of the goats, five lambs of the first

year; this was the offering of Pagiel the son of Ocran.

78 ¶On the twelfth day Ahida the son of Enan, prince of the tribe of Naphtali, offered.

79 His offering was one silver plate, weighing a hundred and thirty shekels, one silver bowl of seventy shekels, according to the shekel of the sanctuary; both of them were full of fine flour mixed with oil for a meal offering;

80 One golden spoon of ten shekels, full of incense;

81 One young bullock, one ram, one lamb of the first year, for a burnt offering;

82 One kid of the goats for a sin offering;

83 And for a sacrifice of peace offering, two oxen, five rams, five kids of the goats, and five lambs of the first year; this was the offering of Ahida the son of Enan.

84 This was the dedication offering from the princes of Israel for the altar, on the day that it was anointed: twelve plates of silver, twelve silver bowls, twelve spoons of gold,

85 Each plate of silver weighing a hundred and thirty shekels, and each bowl seventy. All the silver of the vessels weighed two thousand and four hundred shekels, according to the shekel of the sanctuary.

86 The golden spoons were twelve, full of incense, weighing ten shekels apiece, according to the shekel of the sanctuary; all the gold of the spoons was a hundred and twenty shekels.

87 All the oxen for the burnt offering were twelve bullocks, the rams twelve, the lambs of the first year twelve, with their meal offering; and the kids of the goats for sin offering twelve;

88 And all the oxen for the sacrifice of the peace offering twenty and four bullocks, the rams sixty, the kids of the goats sixty, the lambs of the first year sixty; this was the dedication offering for the altar, after it was anointed.

89 And when Moses entered into the tabernacle of the congregation, he heard a voice speaking to him from

off the mercy seat that was upon the ark of the testimony, from between the two cherubim; and he spoke to him.

CHAPTER 8

THE LORD spoke to Moses, saying, 2 Speak to Aaron and say to him, When you light the lamps, the seven lamps shall give light in front of the candlestick.

3 And Aaron did so; he lighted the seven lamps thereof in front of the candlestick, as the LORD commanded Moses.

4 And the work of the candlestick was of molten gold; from its base to its flower was of cast work; according to the pattern which the LORD had shown to Moses, so he made the candlestick.

5 ¶And the LORD spoke to Moses, saying,

6 Take the Levites from among the children of Israel, and cleanse them.

7 And thus you shall do to them to cleanse them: Sprinkle purifying water upon them, and let them shave all the body, and let them wash their clothes, and so make themselves clean.

8 Then let them take a young bullock with its meal offering, a dish full of fine flour mixed with oil, and another young bullock shall you offer for a sin offering.

9 And you shall bring the Levites before the tabernacle of the congregation; and you shall gather the whole assembly of the children of Israel together;

10 Then you shall bring the Levites before the LORD; and the children of Israel shall put their hands upon the Levites;

11 And Aaron shall offer the Levites before the LORD for an offering from the children of Israel, that they may perform the service of the LORD.

12 And the Levites shall lay their hands upon the heads of the bullocks, and you shall offer the one for a sin offering and the other for a burnt offering to the LORD, to make an atonement for the Levites.

13 And you shall make the Levites stand before Aaron and before his sons, and offer them for an offering to the LORD.

14 Thus shall you separate the Levites from among the children of Israel; and the Levites shall be mine.

15 And after that the Levites shall go in to do the service of the tabernacle of the congregation; and you shall cleanse them, and offer them for an offering before the LORD.

16 For they are wholly given to me as a gift from among the children of Israel; instead of all that open the womb, even instead of the first-born of all the children of Israel, have I taken them to me.

17 For all the first-born of the children of Israel are mine, both man and beast; on the day that I smote every first-born in the land of Egypt I sanctified them for myself.

18 And I have taken the Levites for all the first-born of the children of Israel.

19 And I have given the Levites as a gift to Aaron and to his sons from among the children of Israel, to do the service of the children of Israel in the tabernacle of the congregation and to make an atonement for the children of Israel, that there be no plague among the children of Israel when they come near to the sanctuary.

20 And Moses and Aaron and all the congregation of the children of Israel did to the Levites according to all that the LORD had commanded Moses concerning the Levites; so did the children of Israel to them.

21 And the Levites were purified, and they washed their clothes; and Aaron offered them as an offering before the LORD; and Aaron made an atonement for them and cleansed them.

22 And after that the Levites went in to do their service in the tabernacle of the congregation before Aaron and before his sons; as the LORD had commanded Moses concerning the Levites, so did unto them the children of Israel.

23 ¶And the LORD spoke to Moses, saying,

24 This shall be the law for the Levites: from twenty-five years old

and upward they shall go in to do the work of the tabernacle of the congregation;

25 And from the age of fifty years they shall cease from the service and shall serve no more,

26 But shall minister with their brethren in the tabernacle of the congregation to keep guard, and shall do no service. Thus shall you do to the Levites concerning their charge.

CHAPTER 9

THE LORD spoke to Moses in the wilderness of Sinai in the first month of the second year after the children of Israel had come out of the land of Egypt, saying,

2 Let the children of Israel keep the passover at its appointed time.

3 On the fourteenth day of this month, in the evening, you shall keep it at its appointed time; according to all its rites, and according to all its ceremonies, shall you keep it.

4 And Moses told the children of Israel that they should keep the passover.

5 And they kept the passover on the fourteenth day of the first month, at evening, in the wilderness of Sinai; according to all that the LORD commanded Moses, so did the children of Israel.

6 ¶And there were certain men who were defiled by touching the dead body of a man so that they could not keep the passover on that day; and they came before Moses and before Aaron on that day.

7 And those men said unto them, We are defiled by touching the dead body of a man; why are we kept back from offering the offering of the LORD at the appointed time among the children of Israel?

8 And Moses said to them, Stay where you are, and I will hear what the LORD will command concerning you.

9 ¶And the LORD spoke to Moses, saying,

10 Speak to the children of Israel and say to them, If any man of you or of your posterity shall be unclean by touching a dead body, or is on a jour-

ney afar off, yet he shall keep the passover to the LORD.

11 On the fourteenth day of the second month at the evening they shall keep it, and shall eat it with unleavened bread and bitter herbs.

12 They shall leave none of it to the morning, nor break any bone of it; according to all the ordinances of the passover they shall keep it.

13 But the man who is clean, and is not on a journey, and yet fails to keep the passover, at its appointed time, that person shall be cut off from among his people; because he brought not the offering of the LORD at its appointed time, that man shall suffer for his sin.

14 And if a proselyte shall sojourn among you and will keep the passover to the LORD, according to the ordinance of the passover and according to its statutes, so shall he do; you shall have one ordinance, both for the proselyte and for the native of the land.

15 ¶And on the day that the tabernacle was set up, the cloud covered the tabernacle of the congregation; in front of the door of the tent of the testimony at evening there was upon the tabernacle as it were the appearance of fire, until the morning.

16 So it was always: the cloud covered it by day, and the appearance of fire by night;

17 And when the cloud was taken up from the tabernacle, after that the children of Israel journeyed and at the place where the cloud abode, there the children of Israel encamped.

18 At the commandment of the LORD the children of Israel journeyed, and at the commandment of the LORD they encamped; all the days that the cloud abode upon the tabernacle they remained in their tents.

19 And when the cloud tarried long upon the tabernacle many days, then the children of Israel kept the charge of the LORD and journeyed not.

20 Sometimes the cloud was a few days upon the tabernacle; then according to the commandment of the LORD they remained in their tents, and according to the commandment of the LORD they journeyed.

21 And sometimes the cloud was upon the tabernacle from evening to morning; and when the cloud was taken up in the morning, then they journeyed; whether it was by day or by night that the cloud was taken up, they journeyed.

22 And whether it was a few days or months or a year, as long as the cloud tarried upon the tabernacle, resting thereon, the children of Israel remained in their tents and journeyed not; but when the cloud was taken up, they journeyed.

23 At the commandment of the LORD they encamped, and at the commandment of the LORD they journeyed; they kept the ordinances of the LORD, at the commandment of the LORD by the hand of Moses.

CHAPTER 10

THE LORD spoke to Moses, saying, 2 Make two trumpets of silver; of casting work shall you make them, that you may use them for the calling of the assembly and for the journeying of the camps.

3 And when they shall blow with them, all the people shall assemble themselves to you at the door of the tabernacle of the congregation.

4 And if they blow but with one trumpet, the princes and the heads of the thousands of Israel shall gather themselves to you.

5 When they blow the trumpet, the camps that lie on the east side shall take their journey.

6 And when they blow with the second trumpet, the camps that lie on the south side shall take their journey; they shall blow a trumpet for their journeys.

7 But when the congregation is to be gathered together, you shall blow, but you shall not make a joyful noise.

8 And the sons of Aaron the priest shall blow with the trumpets; and they shall be to you for an ordinance for ever throughout your generations.

9 And if you go to war in your land against the enemies that oppress you, you shall blow with the trumpets; and you shall be remembered before the LORD your God, and you shall be delivered from your enemies.

10 Also in the day of your gladness and in your solemn days and in the beginning of your months you shall blow with the trumpets over your burnt offerings and over the sacrifices of your peace offerings, that they may be to you for a memorial before your God; I am the LORD your God.

11 ¶And it came to pass on the twentieth day of the second month, in the second year, the cloud was taken up from over the tabernacle of the testimony.

12 And the children of Israel took their journeys from the wilderness of Sinai; and the cloud rested in the wilderness of Paran.

13 And they took their journey for the first time according to the commandment of the LORD by the hand of Moses.

14 ¶In the first place went the standard of the camp of the children of Judah according to their armies; and over their host was Nahshon the son of Amminadab.

15 And over the host of the tribe of the children of Issachar was Nethanael the son of Zuar.

16 And over the host of the tribe of the children of Zebulun was Eliab the son of Helon.

17 And the tabernacle was taken down; and the sons of Gershon and the sons of Merari set forward, carrying the tabernacle.

18 ¶And then the standard of the camp of Reuben set forward according to their armies; and over their host was Elizur the son of Shedeur.

19 And over the host of the tribe of the children of Simeon was Shelumiel the son of Zurishaddai.

20 And over the tribe of the children of Gad was Eliasaph the son of Reuel.

21 Then the Kohathites set forward, carrying the sanctuary; and they set up the tabernacle before the people came.

22 ¶And the standard of the camp of the children of Ephraim set forward according to their armies; and

over their host was Elishama the son of Ammihud.

23 And over the host of the tribe of the children of Manasseh was Gamaliel the son of Perzur.

24 And over the host of the tribe of the children of Benjamin was Abidan the son of Gideoni.

25 ¶And the standard of the children of Dan set forward, which was at the end of all the camps throughout their hosts; and over the host of the tribe of the children of Dan was Ahiezer the son of Ammishaddai.

26 And over the host of the tribe of the children of Asher was Pagiel the son of Ocran.

27 And over the host of the tribe of Naphtali was Ahida the son of Enan.

28 Thus was the order of the journeyings of the children of Israel according to their hosts.

29 ¶And Moses said to Hobab, the son of Reuel the Midianite, Moses' father-in-law, We are journeying to the place of which the LORD said, I will give it to you. Come with us, and we will do you good; for the LORD has spoken good concerning Israel.

30 But he said to him, I will not go; but I will depart to my own land, where I was born.

31 And Moses said to him, Do not leave us, for you know how we are to encamp in the wilderness, and you will serve as a guide for us.

32 And if you shall go with us, it shall be that whatever goodness the LORD shall do to us, the same will we do to you.

33 ¶And they departed from the mount of God three days' journey; and the ark of the covenant of the LORD went before them a day's journey to prepare a resting place for them.

34 And the cloud of the LORD was upon them by day, when they went out of the camp.

35 And it came to pass, when the ark set forward, Moses said, Arise, O LORD, and let them that hate thee be scattered; and let thy enemies flee before thee.

36 And when it rested, he said, Return, O LORD, to the many thousands of Israel.

CHAPTER 11

AND when the people complained, it displeased the LORD; and the LORD heard it, and his anger was kindled; and the fire of the LORD burned among them and consumed in the uttermost parts of the camp.

2 And the people cried to Moses; and Moses prayed to the LORD, and the fire was quenched.

3 And he called the name of that place Yakdana (a burning), because the fire of the LORD burned among them.

4 ¶And the mixed multitude that was among them had a strong craving; and they went about and caused the children of Israel to weep, saying, Who shall give us meat to eat?

5 We remember the fish that we used to eat in Egypt freely, the cucumbers, the melons, the leeks, the onions, and the garlic;

6 But now our soul is dried up; there is nothing at all, besides this manna, before our eyes.

7 And the manna was like coriander seed, and its color as the color of beryllium.

8 And the people went about and gathered it and ground it in a mill or beat it in a mortar and baked it in pans and made cakes of it; and the taste of it was as the taste of bread kneaded with oil.

9 And when the dew came down upon the camp in the night, the manna fell upon it.

10 ¶Then Moses heard the people weeping throughout their families, every man in the door of his tent; and the anger of the LORD was kindled greatly; Moses also was displeased.

11 And Moses said to the LORD, My LORD, why hast thou caused displeasure to thy servant? And why have I not found favor in thy sight, that thou layest the burden of all this people upon me?

12 Have I conceived all this people? Or have I begotten them, that thou

shouldest say to me, Carry them in your bosom, as a nursing father carries the suckling child, to the land which thou swearest to their fathers?

13 Where can I find meat to give to all this people? For they weep protesting to me, saying, Give us meat, that we may eat.

14 I am not able to bear all this people alone, because the burden is too heavy for me.

15 And if thou deal thus with me, kill me right away, if I have found favor in thy sight; and let me not see my wretchedness.

16 ¶And the LORD said to Moses, Gather to me seventy men of the elders of Israel, whom you know to be chiefs of the people and its scribes; and bring them to the tabernacle of the congregation, that they may be ready there with you.

17 And I will come down and talk with you there; and I will take some of the spirit which is upon you, and will put it upon them; and they shall bear the burden of the people with you, that you may not bear it yourself alone.

18 And Moses said to the people, Sanctify yourselves for tomorrow and you shall eat meat: for you have wept before the LORD, saying, Who shall give us meat to eat? For it was well with us in Egypt; therefore the LORD will give you meat, and you shall eat.

19 You shall not eat one day, nor two days, nor five days, neither ten days, nor twenty days;

20 But you shall eat it for a whole month, till it comes out of your nostrils and it become loathsome to you, because you have despised the LORD who is among you and have wept before him, saying, Why did we come forth out of Egypt?

21 Then Moses said before the LORD, The people, among whom I am, are six hundred thousand footmen, and thou hast said, I will give them meat, that they may eat a whole month.

22 Shall the flocks and the herds be slaughtered for them, to suffice them? Or shall all the fish of the sea be caught for them, to suffice them?

23 And the LORD said to Moses, The LORD'S hand is full; now you shall see whether my word shall come true to you or not.

24 ¶And Moses went out and told the people the words of the LORD, and gathered the seventy men of the elders of the people, and made them stand round about the tabernacle.

25 And the LORD came down in a cloud and spoke to him, and took of the spirit that was upon him and gave it to the seventy elders; and it came to pass that, when the spirit rested upon them, they prophesied, and then they ceased to complain.

26 But there remained two men in the camp, the name of the one was Eldad, and the name of the other Medad; and the spirit rested upon them; and they were among those who were registered, but they went not out to the tabernacle; and they prophesied in the camp.

27 And there ran a young man, and told Moses, and said, Eldad and Medad are prophesying in the camp.

28 And Joshua the son of Nun, who had ministered to Moses from his youth, answered and said, My lord Moses, forbid them.

29 But Moses said to him, Are you jealous for my sake? Would God that all the LORD'S people were prophets, and that the LORD would put his spirit upon them!

30 Then Moses came into the camp, he and the elders of Israel.

31 ¶And there went forth a wind from before the LORD, and brought quails from the sea, and let them fall by the camp, about a day's journey on this side and about a day's journey on the other side, round about the camp, and about two cubits high upon the face of the earth.

32 And the people rose all that day and all that night and all the next day, and they gathered the quails; he that gathered least gathered ten homers; and they spread them out in the sun for themselves round about the camp.

33 And while the meat was yet between their teeth, before it was chewed, the wrath of the LORD was kindled against the people, and the

LORD smote the people with a very great plague.

34 And he called the name of that place Kabrey di Rigta (the graves of craving); because it was there that they buried the people who craved meat.

35 And the people journeyed from Kabrey di Rigta to Hazeroth, and abode at Hazeroth.

CHAPTER 12

AND Miriam and Aaron spoke against Moses because of the Ethiopian woman whom he had married; for he had married an Ethiopian woman.

2 And they said, Has the LORD indeed spoken only by Moses? Has he not spoken by us also? And the LORD heard it.

3 (Now the man Moses was very meek, above all the men that were upon the face of the earth.)

4 And the LORD spoke suddenly to Moses and to Aaron and to Miriam, Come out, you three, to the tabernacle of the congregation. And the three of them came out.

5 And the LORD came down in a pillar of cloud and stood in the door of the tabernacle and called Aaron and Miriam; and they both came forth.

6 And the LORD said to them, Hear now my words: If you are prophets, I the LORD will reveal myself to you in a vision and will speak to you in a dream.

7 Not so with my servant Moses, who is faithful in all my house.

8 With him I will speak mouth to mouth, in a vision, and not in similes; and the glory of the LORD has he seen: why then were you not afraid to speak against my servant Moses?

9 And the anger of the LORD was kindled against them; and he departed.

10 And the cloud departed from off the tabernacle; and, behold, Miriam became leprous, white as snow; and when Aaron turned toward Miriam, behold, she was leprous;

11 Then Aaron said to Moses, Oh, my lord, I beseech you, do not lay the sin upon us, wherein we have done foolishly and wherein we have sinned.

12 Let her not be as one dead, of whom the flesh is half consumed when he comes out of his mother's womb.

13 And Moses cried to the LORD, saying, Heal her now, O God, I beseech thee.

14 ¶And the LORD said to Moses, If her father had but spit in her face, should she not be ashamed seven days? Let her be shut out from the camp seven days, and after that let her come in again.

15 And Miriam was shut out from the camp seven days; and the people did not journey till Miriam came in again.

16 And after that the people journeyed from Hazeroth, and encamped in the wilderness of Paran.

CHAPTER 13

THE LORD spoke to Moses, saying, 2 Send men that they may spy out the land of Canaan, which I give to the children of Israel; of every tribe of their fathers shall you send a man, every one a chief among them.

3 And Moses sent them from the wilderness of Paran by the commandment of the LORD; all of those men were chieftains of the children of Israel.

4 And these were their names: from the tribe of Reuben, Shammua the son of Zaccur.

5 From the tribe of Simeon, Shaphat the son of Hadi.

6 From the tribe of Judah, Caleb the son of Jophaniah.

7 From the tribe of Issachar, Negail the son of Joseph.

8 From the tribe of Ephraim, Hosea the son of Nun.

9 From the tribe of Benjamin, Palti the son of Daphu.

10 From the tribe of Zebulun, Gaddi the son of Sori.

11 From the tribe of Joseph, namely, of the tribe of Manasseh, Gaddi the son of Susi.

12 From the tribe of Dan, Gamaliel the son of Gamli.

13 From the tribe of Asher, Sethur the son of Michael.

14 From the tribe of Naphtali, Nahbi the son of Vophsi.

15 From the tribe of Gad, Geuel the son of Machir.

16 These are the names of the men whom Moses sent to spy out the land. And Moses called Hosea, the son of Nun, Joshua.

17 ¶And Moses sent them to spy out the land of Canaan, and said to them, Go up this way into the south,[1] and go up on the mountain

18 And see what the land is, and the people who dwell in it, whether they are strong or weak, few or many;

19 And what the land is, in which they dwell, whether it is fertile, or poor, or whether it has trees in it or not.

20 Be of good courage, and bring some of the fruit of the land. Now the time was the season of the first ripe grapes.

21 ¶So they went up and spied out the land from the wilderness of Zin to Rehob, which is at the entrance of Hamath.

22 And they went up into the south, and came as far as Hebron, where Ahiman, Sheshai, and Tolmai, the sons of giants were. (Now Hebron was built seven years before Zoan in Egypt.)

23 And they came as far as the valley of Segola,[2] and cut down from there a branch with one bunch of grapes, and they carried it between two of them on a pole; and they brought some pomegranates and some figs.

24 That place was called the valley of Segola, because of the bunch of grapes which the children of Israel cut down from there.

25 And they returned from spying out the land after forty days.

26 ¶And they came to Moses and Aaron and to all the congregation of the children of Israel, to the wilderness of Paran, to Rakim; and they brought back word to them and to all the congregation, and showed them the fruit of the land.

27 And they related to Moses, and said, We went to the land to which you sent us, and surely it flows with milk and honey; and this is the fruit of it.

28 Nevertheless the people who dwell in the land are strong, and the cities are fortified and very great: and moreover we saw the sons of giants there.

29 The Amalekites dwell in the land of the south; and the Hittites and the Jebusites and the Amorites dwell in the mountains; and the Canaanites dwell by the sea and by the banks of Jordan.

30 Then Caleb stilled the people before Moses and said, Let us go up at once, and possess it; for we are well able to overcome it.

31 But the men who went up with him said, We are not able to go up against the people; for they are stronger than we.

32 And they brought up to the children of Israel an evil report of the land which they had spied out, saying, The land through which we have gone to spy out is a land that devours its inhabitants; and all the people that we saw in it are men of a great stature.

33 There we saw giants, the sons of giants, the descendants of giants; and we were in their sight like grasshoppers, and so we were in their eyes.

CHAPTER 14

THEN all the congregation was in commotion, and lifted up their voices and cried; and the people wept that night.

2 And all the children of Israel murmured against Moses and against Aaron; and the whole congregation said to them, Would God we had died in the land of Egypt! Or would God that we had died in this wilderness!

3 Why has the LORD brought us into this land, to fall by the sword, that our wives and children should

---

1 Negeb.   2 A bunch of grapes.

be a prey? We were better off when we dwelt in Egypt.

4 And they said one to another, Let us appoint a leader, and let us return to Egypt.

5 Then Moses and Aaron fell on their faces before all the assembly of the congregation of the children of Israel.

6 ¶And Joshua the son of Nun, and Caleb the son of Jophaniah, who were of those who had spied out the land, rent their clothes;

7 And they said to all the congregation of the children of Israel, The land through which we passed to spy it out is an exceedingly good land.

8 If the LORD delights in us, he will bring us into this land and give it to us, a land which flows indeed with milk and honey.

9 Only do not rebel against the LORD, neither be afraid of the people of the land; for their conquest will be as easy as eating bread;[1] their strength has left them, and the LORD is with us; fear them not.

10 But the whole congregation said to stone them with stones. And the glory of the LORD appeared in the cloud in the tabernacle of the congregation before all the children of Israel.

11 ¶And the LORD said to Moses, How long will this people provoke me? And how long will they not believe me, for all the signs which I have done among them?

12 I will smite them with pestilence, and destroy them, and I will make of you a nation which is greater and mightier than they.

13 ¶And Moses said to the LORD, Then the Egyptians shall hear it (for thou didst bring up this people in thy might from among them),

14 And they will tell it to the inhabitants of this land; for they have heard that thou LORD art in the midst of this people, that thou LORD art seen face to face, and that thy cloud stands over them, and that thou goest before them in a pillar of cloud by day and in a pillar of fire by night.

15 ¶And if thou shalt kill all this people as one man, then the nations who have heard the fame of thee will say,

16 Because the LORD was not able to bring this people into the land which he swore to them, therefore he has slain them in the wilderness.

17 And now, let thy power, O LORD, be great according as thou hast spoken, saying,

18 The LORD is longsuffering and of great mercy, and thou forgivest iniquity and transgression, by no means clearing the guilty, but visiting the iniquity of the fathers upon the children and upon their children's children to the third and fourth generation.

19 Pardon the iniquity of this people according to the greatness of thy mercy, and as thou hast forgiven them from Egypt even until now.

20 And the LORD said to Moses, I have forgiven them according to your word;

21 But as truly as I live, the whole earth shall be filled with the glory of the LORD.

22 And yet all the men who have seen my glory and the signs which I did in Egypt and in the wilderness have tempted me, behold now, these ten times, and have not hearkened to my voice;

23 Surely they shall not see the land which I swore to their fathers, neither shall any one of those who provoked me see it;

24 But my servant Caleb, because he has my spirit with him and has followed me fully, I will bring into the land into which he went; and his descendants shall possess it.

25 (Now the Amalekites and the Canaanites dwelt in the mountains.) Tomorrow turn and set out for the wilderness by the way of the Red Sea.

26 ¶And the LORD spoke to Moses and to Aaron, saying,

27 How long shall this wicked congregation murmur in my presence? I have heard the complaints of the children of Israel which they murmur in my presence.

[1] In Aramaic when a task is simple or easy, it is said, *It is like eating bread.*

28 Say to them, As I live, says the LORD, as you have spoken in my presence, so will I do to you;

29 Your corpses shall fall in this wilderness; and all that were numbered of you, according to your whole number, from twenty years old and upward, because you have murmured against me.

30 You shall not come into the land concerning which I swore to make you dwell therein, except Caleb the son of Jophaniah, and Joshua the son of Nun.

31 But your little ones, who you said would become the prey, and your sons who today do not know good and evil, they shall enter into the land, and I will bring them there, and they shall know the land which you have despised.

32 But as for you, your corpses shall fall in this wilderness.

33 And your sons shall be shepherds forty years in this wilderness, and shall suffer for your whoredom until your corpses are consumed in this wilderness.

34 According to the number of the days in which you spied out the land, even forty days, a year for each day, shall you suffer for your iniquities, forty years; then you shall know that it is because you have murmured before me.

35 I the LORD have said, I will surely do it to all this evil congregation that are gathered together before me; in this wilderness they shall be consumed, and there they shall die.

36 And the men whom Moses sent to spy out the land, who returned and made all the congregation murmur against him by publishing an evil report concerning the land,

37 These men who published an evil report of the land died by a sudden plague before the LORD.

38 But Joshua the son of Nun, and Caleb the son of Jophaniah, who were of the men who went to spy out the land, still lived.

39 And Moses told these sayings to all the children of Israel; and the people mourned greatly.

40 ¶And they rose up early in the morning and went up to the top of the mountain, saying, Behold, we will go up to the place which the LORD has promised us; for we have sinned.

41 And Moses said to them, Why now do you transgress the commandment of the LORD? Therefore you shall not succeed.

42 Do not go up, for the LORD is not with you; lest you be defeated before your enemies.

43 For the Canaanites and the Amalekites are there before you, and you shall fall by the sword; because you are turned away from following the LORD, therefore the LORD will not be with you.

44 Yet they started to go up to the top of the mountain; but neither the ark of the covenant of the LORD nor Moses departed out of the camp.

45 Then the Amalekites and the Canaanites who dwelt in that mountain came down and smote them and pursued them as far as Hirmah.

CHAPTER 15

AND the LORD spoke to Moses, saying,

2 Speak to the children of Israel and say to them, When you come into the land of your habitation, which I give to you for an inheritance,

3 You shall offer an offering to the LORD, a burnt offering or a sacrifice in performing a vow, or in a freewill offering, or in your solemn feasts, to make a sweet savour to the LORD, of the herd, or of the flock;

4 Then shall he who offers his offering to the LORD bring a meal offering of a tenth part of an ephah of fine flour mixed with a fourth part of a hin of oil.

5 And a fourth part of a hin of wine for a drink offering shall you offer with the burnt offering or sacrifice, for one lamb.

6 Or for a ram, you shall prepare for a meal offering two tenths of an ephah of fine flour mixed with a third part of a hin of oil.

7 And for a drink offering you shall offer a third part of a hin of wine, for a sweet savour to the LORD.

8 And when you offer a bullock for

a burnt offering, or for a sacrifice in performing a vow, or as a peace offering to the LORD;

9 Then you shall offer with the bullock a meal offering of three tenths of an ephah of fine flour mixed with half a hin of oil.

10 And you shall bring for a drink offering half a hin of wine, for an offering made by fire, of a sweet savour to the LORD.

11 Thus shall you do for one bullock, or for one ram, or for a lamb, or a kid of the goats.

12 According to the number that you shall prepare, so shall you do to every one according to their number.

13 All the house of Israel shall do these things after this manner, and shall offer an offering made by fire, of a sweet savour to the LORD.

14 And if a proselyte sojourn with you, or whoever is among you throughout your generations, and will offer an offering made by fire, of a sweet savour to the LORD; as you do, so shall he do.

15 One ordinance shall be both for you and for the proselyte who sojourns with you, an ordinance for ever throughout your generations; the proselyte shall be like you before the LORD.

16 One law and one ordinance shall be for you and for the proselyte who sojourns with you.

17 ¶The LORD spoke to Moses, saying,

18 Speak to the children of Israel and say to them, When you come into the land whither I will bring you,

19 Then it shall be that when you eat of the bread of the land, you shall offer up a heave offering to the LORD.

20 You shall offer up a cake of the first of your dough as an offering to the LORD; as you make the offering of the threshing floor, so shall you offer it.

21 Of the first of your dough you shall give to the LORD a heave offering throughout your generations.

22 ¶And if you err, and do not observe all these commandments which the LORD has spoken to Moses,

23 Even all that the LORD has commanded you by the hand of Moses from the day that the LORD commanded Moses and henceforward throughout your generations;

24 Then it shall be, if the error was committed in the presence of the congregation, all the congregation shall offer one young bullock for a burnt offering, for a sweet savour to the LORD, with its meal offering and its drink offering, according to the ordinance thereof, and one kid of the goats for a sin offering.

25 And the priest shall make atonement for the whole congregation of the children of Israel, and it shall be forgiven them; for it was an error; and they shall bring their offering, a sacrifice made by fire to the LORD, and their sin offering to the LORD for their folly;

26 And it shall be forgiven all the congregation of the children of Israel and the proselyte who sojourns among them, because all the people had erred.

27 ¶And if any person sins through an error, then he shall offer a she-goat of the first year for a sin offering.

28 And the priest shall make atonement for the person who sins, when he sins by an error before the LORD, to make an atonement for him; and it shall be forgiven him.

29 You shall have one law for him who does anything through ignorance, both for the children of Israel and for the proselytes who sojourn among you.

30 ¶But the person who commits sin wittingly, whether he be of you or of the proselytes, the same blasphemes before the LORD; and that person shall be cut off from among his people.

31 Because he has despised the word of the LORD and has broken his commandments, that person shall utterly be cut off; his iniquity shall be upon him.

32 ¶And while the children of Israel were in the wilderness, they found a man gathering sticks on the sabbath day.

33 And those who found him gathering sticks brought him to Moses.

13

and Aaron, and to all the congregation.

34 And they put him in prison, because it had not been declared what should be done to him.

35 And the LORD said to Moses, The man shall be surely put to death; all the congregation shall stone him with stones outside the camp.

36 And all the congregation brought him outside the camp, and stoned him with stones, and he died; as the LORD commanded Moses.

37 ¶And the LORD spoke to Moses, saying,

38 Speak to the children of Israel and bid them that they make fringes on the borders of their mantles throughout their generations, and that they put upon the fringes of the borders a ribbon of blue;

39 And it shall be to you for a fringe, that you may look upon it and remember all the commandments of the LORD your God and do them; and that you may not go astray, seeking after your own hearts and your own mind, after which you used to go astray;

40 That you may remember, and do all my commandments, and be holy to your God.

41 I am the LORD your God, who brought you out of the land of Egypt, to be your God; I am the LORD your God.

CHAPTER 16

NOW Korah, the son of Izhar, the son of Kohath, the son of Levi, and Dathan and Abiram, the sons of Eliab, and On, the son of Peleth, sons of Reuben, started a faction;

2 And they rose up before Moses with certain of the children of Israel, two hundred and fifty chiefs of the assembly, who at that time were men of renown;

3 And they gathered themselves together against Moses and against Aaron and said to them, Is it not enough for you, seeing all the congregation are holy, every one of them, and the LORD is among them; wherefore then do you lift up yourselves above the whole congregation of the LORD?

4 And when Moses heard it, he fell upon his face;

5 And he spoke to Korah and to all his company and said to them, In the morning the LORD will show who are his, and who are holy; and he will cause them to come near to him; and those whom he has chosen will he cause to come near to him.

6 This do: Take for yourselves censers, you Korah, and all your company;

7 And put fire into them, and put incense into them before the LORD tomorrow; and it shall be that the man whom the LORD chooses, he shall be holy; this is enough for you, O you sons of Levi.

8 And Moses said to Korah, Hear again, O you sons of Levi;

9 Is it not enough for you that the God of Israel has separated you from the whole congregation of Israel and brought you near to himself to do the service of the tabernacle of the LORD and to stand before the congregation to minister to them?

10 And he has brought you near to him, and all your brethren the sons of Levi with you; and do you seek the priesthood also?

11 Therefore both you and all your company gather yourselves together before the LORD tomorrow; and what is Aaron, that you should murmur against him?

12 ¶And Moses sent to call Dathan and Abiram, the sons of Eliab; but they said, We will not come up;

13 Is it not enough for you that you have brought us out of a land that flows with milk and honey, to kill us in the wilderness, but that you should also make yourselves princes over us?

14 Moreover you have not brought us into a land that flows with milk and honey, nor given us inheritance of fields and vineyards; even if you should put out our eyes, we will not come up.

15 And Moses was greatly displeased, and said to the LORD, Respect not thou their offerings, because I have not taken an ass from one of

them, neither have I hurt one of them.

16 And Moses said to Korah, Present yourselves, you and all your company before the LORD, you and they and Aaron, tomorrow;

17 And take every man his censer, and put fire into it, and put incense into it, and bring before the LORD every man his censer, two hundred and fifty censers; you also and Aaron, each of you his censer.

18 So they took every man his censer, and put fire into it, and laid incense upon it, and stood in the door of the tabernacle of the congregation with Moses and Aaron.

19 And Korah gathered all the congregation against them at the door of the tabernacle of the congregation; and the glory of the LORD appeared to all the congregation.

20 And the LORD spoke to Moses and to Aaron, saying,

21 Separate yourselves from the midst of this congregation, that I may destroy them in a moment.

22 And they fell upon their faces and said, O God, the God of the spirits of all flesh, shall one man sin, and shall the wrath come upon all the congregation?

23 ¶And the LORD spoke to Moses, saying,

24 Speak to all the congregation, saying, Keep away from about the tents of Korah, Dathan, and Abiram.

25 And Moses rose up and went to Dathan and Abiram; and the elders of Israel followed him.

26 And he spoke to all the congregation and said to them, Depart from the tents of these sinful men and touch nothing of theirs, lest you be consumed in their sins.

27 So they withdrew from the tents of Korah, Dathan, and Abiram; and Dathan and Abiram came out, and stood in the door of their tents with their wives and their sons and their little ones.

28 And Moses said, Hereby you shall know that the LORD has sent me to do all these works; for I have not done them of my own mind.

29 If these men die the common death of all men or if they be visited after the visitation of all men, then the LORD has not sent me.

30 But if the LORD make a new thing, and the earth opens its mouth and swallows them up with all things that belong to them, and they go down alive with all that belongs to them into Sheol, then you shall know that these men have provoked the LORD.

31 ¶And when Moses had finished speaking these words, the ground split asunder under them;

32 And the earth opened its mouth and swallowed them up with their households and all the men who were with Korah and all their goods.

33 They, and all that belonged to them went down alive into Sheol, and the earth closed upon them, and they perished from among the congregation.

34 And all Israel that were round about them fled at the cry of them, saying, Lest the earth swallow us up also.

35 And there came out a fire from before the LORD and consumed the two hundred and fifty men that offered incense.

36 ¶And the LORD spoke to Moses, saying,

37 Speak to Eleazar the son of Aaron the priest, to take up the censers from among the burned men and scatter the fire yonder; for they are sanctified.

38 The censers of these who sinned against their own souls, make them thin plates for a covering of the altar; for they offered them before the LORD, therefore they are holy; and they shall be a sign to the children of Israel.

39 So Eleazar the priest took the bronze censers, with which they who were burned had offered incense, and they were made thin plates for a covering of the altar,

40 To be a memorial to the children of Israel, so that no stranger, who is not of the descendants of Aaron, come near to offer incense before the LORD; that he be not as Korah and all his company, whom the earth opened its mouth and swallowed, just as the LORD had spoken by the hand of Moses.

41 ¶But on the morrow all the con-

gregation of the children of Israel murmured against Moses and Aaron, saying, You have killed the people of the LORD.

42 And when all the congregation was gathered against Moses and against Aaron, they turned toward the tabernacle of the congregation; and, behold, the cloud covered it, and the glory of the LORD appeared.

43 And Moses and Aaron came before the tabernacle of the congregation.

44 ¶And the LORD spoke to Moses and to Aaron, saying,

45 Get you away from the midst of this congregation, that I may destroy them in a moment. And they fell upon their faces.

46 ¶And Moses said to Aaron, Take a censer, and put fire therein from off the altar, and put on incense, and carry it quickly to the congregation, and make an atonement for them; for wrath has gone out from before the LORD; the plague has already begun among the people.

47 And Aaron took it as Moses commanded, and ran into the midst of the congregation; and, behold, the plague had already begun among the people; and he put on incense, and made atonement for the people.

48 And he stood between the dead and the living; and the plague ceased.

49 Now those who died in the plague were fourteen thousand and seven hundred, besides those who died in the sedition of Korah.

50 And Aaron returned to Moses at the door of the tabernacle of the congregation; and the plague had ceased.

CHAPTER 17

AND the LORD spoke to Moses, saying,

2 Speak to the children of Israel, and take from every one of them a rod according to the house of their fathers, from all their princes according to the house of their fathers, twelve rods; write each man's name upon his rod.

3 And you shall write Aaron's name upon the rod of Levi; for one rod shall be for the head of the tribe of their fathers.

4 And you shall put them in the tabernacle of the congregation before the testimony, where I will meet with you.

5 And it shall come to pass, that the rod of the man with whom I am pleased shall bud; thus I will make to cease from me the murmurings of the children of Israel, whereby they murmur against you.

6 ¶And Moses spoke to the children of Israel, and every one of their princes gave him a rod apiece, for each prince one, according to their fathers' houses, twelve rods; and the rod of Aaron was in the midst of their rods.

7 And Moses placed the rods before the LORD in the tabernacle of the testimony.

8 And on the morrow Moses went into the tabernacle of the testimony; and, behold, the rod of Aaron for the house of Levi was budded, and blossomed, and yielded ripe almonds.

9 And Moses brought out all the rods from before the LORD to all the children of Israel; and they looked, and took every man his rod.

10 ¶And the LORD said to Moses, Bring Aaron's rod back before the testimony, to be kept as a token for the rebellious children; so that their murmurings may cease from me, that they die not.

11 And Moses did so; as the LORD commanded him, so did he.

12 And the children of Israel said to Moses, Behold, we perish and are lost, we all perish.

13 Whosoever comes near to the tabernacle of the LORD shall die; and, behold, we also are near to perish.

CHAPTER 18

AND the LORD said to Aaron, You and your sons and your father's house with you shall bear any guilt in connection with the sanctuary; and you and your sons with you shall bear any guilt in connection with your priesthood.

2 And your brethren also of the

tribe of Levi, the tribe of your father, you shall bring with you, that they may accompany you and minister to you; but you and your sons with you shall minister before the tabernacle of the testimony.

3 And they shall keep your charge and the charge of all the tabernacle; but they shall not come near the vessels of the sanctuary and the vessels of the altar, that neither they, nor you also, die.

4 And they shall accompany you, and keep the charge of the tabernacle of the congregation for all the service of the tabernacle; and a stranger shall not come near you.

5 And you shall have charge of the sanctuary, and charge of the altar, that there be no wrath any more upon the children of Israel.

6 And I, behold, I have taken your brethren the Levites from among the children of Israel; they are given as a gift for the LORD, to do the service of the tabernacle of the congregation.

7 Therefore you and your sons with you shall keep your priest's office for everything of the altar and within the veil; and you shall serve; I have given your priest's office as a gift; and the stranger who comes near shall be put to death.

8 ¶And the LORD said to Aaron, Behold, I also have given you the charge of my gift offerings and all the hallowed things of the children of Israel; I have given them to you by reason of the anointing, and to your sons by an ordinance for ever.

9 This shall be yours of the most holy things from offerings made by fire: every offering of theirs, every meal offering of theirs, and every sin offering of theirs, and all the offerings of theirs which they shall offer to me shall be most holy for you and for your sons.

10 In the most holy place shall you eat it; every male shall eat it; it shall be holy to you.

11 And this is the offering of your gifts, with all the wave offerings of the children of Israel; I have given them to you and to your sons and to your daughters with you, by a statute for ever; every one who is clean in your household shall eat of it.

12 All the best of the oil and all the best of the wheat and of the wine, the firstfruits of them that they shall give to the LORD, I have given them to you.

13 The first ripe fruits of all that is in their land which they shall bring to the LORD shall be yours; every one who is clean in your household shall eat of it.

14 Everything dedicated in Israel shall be yours.

15 Everything that opens the womb of all flesh which they offer to the LORD, whether it be of man or beasts, shall be yours; nevertheless the firstborn of man shall you surely redeem, and the firstling of unclean beasts shall you redeem.

16 And those that are to be redeemed from a month old and upward shall you redeem, for a price of money of fifty shekels, after the shekel of the sanctuary, which is twenty gerahs.

17 But the firstlings of the cattle or the firstlings of the sheep or the firstlings of the goats, you shall not redeem, because they are holy; you shall sprinkle their blood upon the altar and shall burn their fat for an offering made by fire, for a sweet savour to the LORD.

18 But their meat shall be yours, as the wave breast and as the right shoulder are yours.

19 All the gift offerings of the holy things which the children of Israel offer to the LORD have I given to you and to your sons and your daughters with you, by a statute for ever; it is a covenant of salt [1] for ever before the LORD to you and to your descendants with you.

20 ¶And the LORD said to Aaron, You shall have no inheritance in their land, neither shall you have any portion among them; but your portion and your inheritance among the chil-

---

[1] Salt is considered sacred, and is a token of loyalty and true friendship. When people make covenants they break bread and eat salt together.

dren of Israel shall be the gift offerings and the holy things of the LORD.

21 And, behold, I have given to the children of Levi all the tithes of the children of Israel for an inheritance, for their service which they serve, even the service of the tabernacle of the congregation.

22 Neither shall the children of Israel henceforth come near the tabernacle of the congregation, lest they bear sin and die.

23 But the Levites shall do the service of the tabernacle of the congregation, and they shall bear their iniquity; it shall be a statute for ever throughout their generations, that among the children of Israel they have no inheritance.

24 For the tithes of the children of Israel which they offer to the LORD I have given to the Levites for an inheritance; therefore I have said to them, Among the children of Israel they shall have no inheritance.

25 ¶The LORD spoke to Moses, saying,

26 Speak to the Levites and say to them, When you take from the children of Israel the tithes which I have given you from them for your inheritance, then you shall offer some of them as a gift offering to the LORD, a tenth part of the tithe.

27 And this your gift offering shall be reckoned to you, as though it were the grain from the threshing floor, and as the gift offering of the wine press.

28 Thus you also shall offer a gift offering to the LORD of all your tithes which you receive from the children of Israel; and you shall give from it the LORD's gift offering to Aaron the priest and to his sons.

29 Out of all your gifts you shall offer every gift offering to the LORD, of all the best of them and the hallowed of them.

30 Therefore you shall say to them, When you have set apart the best thereof from it, then it shall be counted to the Levites as the produce of the threshing floor, and as the produce of the wine press.

31 And you shall eat it in any place,

you and your households; for it is your wages for your service in the tabernacle of the congregation.

32 And you shall bear no sin by reason of it, when you have offered the best of it; neither shall you pollute the holy things of the children of Israel, lest you die.

CHAPTER 19

AND the LORD spoke to Moses and to Aaron, saying,

2 This is the ordinance of the law which the LORD has commanded, saying, Speak to the children of Israel, that they bring you a red heifer, perfect, in which there is no blemish, and upon which never came yoke;

3 And you shall give her to Eleazar the priest, that he may bring her forth outside the camp, and one shall slaughter her in his sight;

4 And Eleazar the priest shall take some of her blood with his finger, and sprinkle of her blood towards the front of the tabernacle of the congregation seven times;

5 And one shall burn the heifer in his sight; her skin and her blood and her flesh, with her dung, shall he burn;

6 And the priest shall take cedar wood and hyssop and scarlet material, and cast them into the midst of the burning of the heifer.

7 Then the priest shall wash his clothes, and he shall bathe his body in water, and afterward he shall come into the camp; and the priest shall be unclean until the evening.

8 And he who burns the heifer shall wash his clothes and bathe his body in water; and he shall be unclean until the evening.

9 And a man who is clean shall gather up the ashes of the heifer and lay them outside the camp in a clean place, and it shall be kept for all the congregation of the children of Israel for the water of sprinkling, because it is a purification for sin.

10 And he who gathers the ashes of the heifer shall wash his clothes and be unclean until the evening; and it shall be to the children of Israel

and to the proselytes who sojourn among them for a statute for ever.

11 ¶He who touches the dead body of any man shall be unclean seven days.

12 He shall purify himself by sprinkling with the water on the third day, and on the seventh day he shall be clean; but if he does not purify himself by sprinkling on the third day, then on the seventh day he shall not be clean.

13 Whosoever touches the body of any man who is dead, and does not purify himself by sprinkling, defiles the tabernacle of the LORD; and that person shall be cut off from Israel, because the water of purification was not sprinkled upon him, he shall be unclean; his uncleanness is yet with him.

14 This is the law when a man dies in a tent: all who come into the tent and every one who is in the tent shall be unclean for seven days.

15 And every open vessel which is not covered is unclean.

16 And whosoever in the open field touches one who is slain with a sword, or a dead body or a bone of a man or a grave shall be unclean seven days.

17 And for an unclean person they shall take some of the ashes of the burnt sin offering and shall pour running water into it in a vessel;

18 And a clean person shall take hyssop and dip it in the water and sprinkle it upon the tent and upon all the vessels and upon the persons who were there and upon him who touched a bone or a slain person or one dead or a grave;

19 And the clean person shall sprinkle upon the unclean on the third day and on the seventh day; and on the seventh day he shall wash his clothes and bathe himself in water, and shall be clean in the evening.

20 But the man who shall be unclean and shall not purify himself, that soul shall be cut off from among the congregation, because he has defiled the sanctuary of the LORD; the water of sprinkling has not been sprinkled upon him; he is unclean.

21 And it shall be a perpetual statute to you that he who sprinkles the water of purification shall wash his clothes; and he who touches the water of sprinkling shall be unclean until evening.

22 And whatever the unclean person touches shall be unclean; and the person who touches it shall be unclean until evening.

CHAPTER 20

THEN came the children of Israel, the whole congregation, into the wilderness of Zin in the first month; and the people abode in Rakim; and Miriam died there, and was buried there.

2 And there was no water for the people to drink; and they gathered themselves together against Moses and against Aaron.

3 And the people quarreled with Moses and with Aaron, saying, Would God that we had died with the death with which our brethren died before the LORD!

4 Why have you brought the congregation of the LORD into this wilderness, that we and our cattle should die here?

5 And why have you made us to come up out of Egypt, and have brought us to this evil place? It is no place for grain, or for wine or figs or pomegranates; neither is there any water to drink.

6 Then Moses and Aaron went from the presence of the assembly to the door of the tabernacle of the congregation, and they fell upon their faces; and the glory of the LORD appeared to them.

7 ¶And the LORD spoke to Moses, saying,

8 Take the rod, and gather the assembly together, you and Aaron your brother, and speak over the rock before their eyes; and it shall give forth its water, and you shall bring forth to them water out of the rock, so that you shall give the congregation and their cattle drink.

9 And Moses took the rod from be-

fore the LORD, as he commanded him.

10 And Moses and Aaron gathered the congregation together before the rock, and he said to them, Hear now, you rebels; out of this rock we will bring forth water for you.

11 And Moses lifted up his hand and struck the rock with his rod twice; and the water came out abundantly, and the people drank and all their cattle also.

12 ¶And the LORD said to Moses and Aaron, Because you did not believe in me, to sanctify me in the presence of the children of Israel, therefore you shall not bring this congregation into the land which I have given them.

13 These are the waters of Mesotha (contention); because the children of Israel strove before the LORD, and he was sanctified among them.

14 ¶And Moses sent messengers from Rakim to the king of Edom, saying, Thus says your brother Israel: You know all the trouble that has befallen us,

15 How our fathers went down into Egypt, and we have dwelt in Egypt a long time; and the Egyptians oppressed us and our fathers;

16 And when we prayed before the LORD, he heard our voice and sent an angel, and has brought us forth out of Egypt; and, behold, we are in Rakim, a town in the uttermost of your border;

17 Now let us pass through your land; we will not pass through the fields, nor through the vineyards, neither will we drink the water of the wells; but we will go by the king's highway, we will not turn to the right hand nor to the left until we have passed your borders.

18 But Edom said to him, You shall not pass through my border, lest I come out against you with the sword.

19 And the children of Israel said to him, We will go up by the highway; and if we and our cattle drink of your water, then we will pay for it; we will only pass through it on foot.

20 But Edom said, You shall not pass through. And Edom came out against them with a strong force, and with a strong hand.

21 Thus Edom refused to give Israel passage through his border; wherefore Israel turned away from him.

22 ¶And the children of Israel, the whole congregation, journeyed from Rakim, and came to mount Hor.

23 And the LORD said to Moses and Aaron at mount Hor by the border of the land of Edom,

24 Aaron shall be gathered to his people for he shall not enter into the land which I have given to the children of Israel, because you rebelled against my word at the water of Mesotha, and did not sanctify me at the water in their presence.

25 Take Aaron and Eleazar his son, and bring them up to mount Hor;

26 And strip Aaron of his garments, and put them upon Eleazar his son; and Aaron shall be gathered unto his people and shall die there.

27 And Moses did as the LORD commanded him; and they went up into mount Hor in the sight of all the congregation.

28 And Moses stripped Aaron of his garments, and put them upon Eleazar his son; and Aaron died there on mount Hor; and Moses and Eleazar came down from the mountain.

29 And when all the congregation saw that Aaron was dead, they mourned for Aaron thirty days, all the house of Israel.

CHAPTER 21

WHEN the Canaanite, the king of Gadar who dwelled in the south, heard that Israel came by the way of the spies, then he fought against Israel and took some of them prisoners.

2 And Israel vowed a vow to the LORD and said, If thou wilt surely deliver this people into our hands, then we will utterly destroy their cities.

3 And the LORD hearkened to the voice of Israel, and delivered up the Canaanites into their hands; and they utterly destroyed them and their cities;

and they called the name of that place Hirmah.

4 ¶And they journeyed from mount Hor by the way of the Red Sea, to go around the land of Edom; and the people were much distressed because of the way.

5 And the people murmured against God and against Moses, saying, Why have you brought us up out of Egypt to die in the wilderness? For neither is there bread, nor water; and our soul is wearied with this inferior bread (manna).

6 And the LORD sent fiery serpents against the people, and they bit the people, so that many people of Israel died.

7 ¶Therefore the people came to Moses and said to him, We have sinned, for we have murmured against the LORD and against you; pray before the LORD, that he take the serpents away from us. And Moses prayed for the people.

8 And the LORD said to Moses, Make a fiery serpent of brass, and set it upon a pole; and it shall come to pass that every one who is bitten by a serpent, when he looks upon it, shall live.

9 So Moses made a serpent of brass, and put it upon a pole, and it came to pass that if a serpent had bitten any man, when he beheld the serpent of brass, he lived.

10 ¶And the children of Israel journeyed, and encamped in Aboth.

11 And they journeyed from Aboth, and encamped at the Een di Ebraye (the spring of the Hebrews), in the wilderness which is before Moab, to the east toward the sunrise.

12 ¶From thence they journeyed, and encamped in the valley of Zared.

13 From thence they journeyed, and encamped on the other side of Arnon, which is in the wilderness that extends from the border of the Amorites; for Arnon is the border of Moab, between Moab and the Amorites.

14 Wherefore it is said in the book of the wars of the LORD, A flame of fire is in the whirlwind and in the river of Arnon,

15 And he made straight the slope of the valleys which extended to the site of Ad, which lies over the border of Moab.

16 And there is the Bera; that is, the well of which the LORD said to Moses, Gather the people together and I will give them water.

17 ¶Then Israel sang this song, Spring up, O well; sing ye to it:

18 The well which the princes dug, which the nobles of the people uncovered and searched out with their staves. And from the wilderness they went to Mattanah;

19 And from Mattanah to Nahaliel; and from Nahaliel to Bamoth;

20 And from Bamoth in the valley, which is in the country of Moab, to the top of the hill which looks toward Ashimon (the desert).

21 ¶And Israel sent messengers to Sihon, king of the Amorites, saying,

22 Let us pass through your land; we will not turn aside into the fields or into the vineyards; we will not drink water from the wells; but we will go along by the king's highway until we have passed through your borders.

23 And Sihon would not let Israel pass through his borders; but Sihon gathered all his army together, and went out against Israel into the wilderness; and he came to Jahaz and fought against Israel.

24 And Israel smote him with the edge of the sword, and possessed his land from Arnon to Jabbok, and as far as the border of the children of Ammon; for the border of the children of Ammon was fortified.

25 And Israel took all those cities; and Israel settled in all the cities of the Amorites, in Heshbon and in all the villages thereof.

26 For Heshbon was the capital city of Sihon the king of the Amorites, who had fought against the former king of Moab and taken all his land out of his hand as far as Arnon.

27 Wherefore they say in the proverbs, Come into Heshbon, let the city of Sihon be built and prepared;

28 For a fire has gone out of Heshbon, a flame from the city of Sihon. It has consumed Ad of Moab, and

the worshippers of the high places of Arnon.

29 Woe to you, O Arnon! Woe to you, O Moab! You are destroyed, O people of Chemosh; he has given his sons hostages, and his daughters into captivity to Sihon king of the Amorites.

30 The fields of Heshbon have perished as far as Ribon, and have been laid waste as far as Lanhakh, which is in the wilderness.

31 ¶Thus Israel dwelt in the land of the Amorites.

32 And Moses sent to spy out Jaazer, and they captured its villages, and destroyed the Amorites that were there.

33 ¶And they turned and went up to the land of Mathnin; and Og the king of Mathnin went out against them, he and all his people, to the battle at Ardai.

34 And the LORD said to Moses, Fear him not; for I will deliver him into your hands, and all his people and his country; and you shall do to him as you did to Sihon king of the Amorites, who dwelt in Heshbon.

35 So they smote him and his sons and all his people until there was not a survivor left to him; and they possessed his land.

CHAPTER 22

AND the children of Israel journeyed, and encamped in the plains of Moab on this side of Jordan by Jericho.

2 ¶And Balak the son of Zippor saw all that Israel had done to the Amorites.

3 And the Moabites were in great fear of the people because they were many; and Moab was distressed at the presence of the children of Israel.

4 And Moab said to the elders of Midian, Now this multitude is licking up all that are around about us, as the ox licks up the grass of the field. And Balak the son of Zippor was king of the Moabites at that time.

5 So he sent messengers to Balaam the son of Beor, an interpreter of dreams, who dwelt by the river of the land of the children of Ammon, to call him, saying, Behold, there is a people come out from Egypt; they cover the face of the land, and they are settled over against me.

6 Come now therefore and curse this people for me, for they are too mighty for me; perhaps I shall be able to defeat some of them and destroy them out of the land; for I know that he whom you bless is blessed and he whom you curse is cursed.

7 And the elders of Moab and the elders of Midian departed with gifts for divination in their hands; and they came to Balaam and told him the words of Balak.

8 And he said to them, Lodge here this night and I will give you an answer as the LORD shall speak to me; and the princes of Moab stayed with Balaam.

9 And God came to Balaam and said to him, Who are these men that are with you?

10 And Balaam said to God, Balak the son of Zippor, king of Moab, has sent to me, saying,

11 Behold, there is a people come out of Egypt who cover the face of the earth; come now, and curse them for me; perhaps I shall be able to fight against them and destroy them.

12 And God said to Balaam, You shall not go with them; and you shall not curse the people; for they are blessed.

13 And Balaam rose up in the morning and said to the princes of Balak, Go to your land; for the LORD refuses to permit me to go with you.

14 So the princes of Moab rose up and went to Balak, and said to him, Balaam refused to come with us.

15 ¶And again Balak sent messengers who were greater and more honorable than they.

16 And they came to Balaam and said to him, Thus says Balak the son of Zippor, Let nothing hinder you from coming to me;

17 For I will surely honor you exceedingly, and I will do for you whatever you say to me; come therefore, curse this people for me.

18 And Balaam answered and said

to the servants of Balak, If Balak would give me his house full of silver and gold, I could not transgress against the word of the LORD my God, neither concerning a small matter nor concerning a great matter.

19 Now, therefore, tarry you also here this night, that I may know what more the LORD will say to me.

20 And God came to Balaam at night and said to him, If these men have come to call you, rise up and go with them; but only the word which I shall say to you, that shall you do.

21 So Balaam rose up in the morning and saddled his ass and went with the princes of Balak.

22 ¶And God's anger was kindled against him because he went; and the angel of the LORD stood in the way for an adversary against him. Now as he was riding on his she-ass, and his two servants with him,

23 The she-ass saw the angel of the LORD standing in the way, and his sword drawn and held in his hand; and the she-ass turned aside out of the way and went into the field; and Balaam struck the she-ass to turn her into the way.

24 But the angel of the LORD stood in a path of the vineyard, a wall being on this side and a wall on that side.

25 And when the she-ass saw the angel of the LORD, she thrust herself against the wall and pressed Balaam's foot against the wall; and he struck her again.

26 And the angel of the LORD went further, and stood in a narrow place where there was no way to turn either to the right or to the left.

27 And when the she-ass saw the angel of the LORD, she lay down under Balaam; and Balaam's anger was kindled, and he struck the she-ass with a staff.

28 And the LORD opened the mouth of the she-ass and she said to Balaam, What have I done to you that you have struck me these three times?

29 And Balaam said to the she-ass, Because you have mocked me; I would there were a sword in my hands, for now would I kill you.

30 And the she-ass said to Balaam, Am I not your she-ass upon which you have ridden from your youth even to this day? Have I ever behaved in this manner toward you? And he said to her, No.

31 Then the LORD opened the eyes of Balaam and he saw the angel of the LORD standing in the way with his sword drawn and held in his hand; and he bowed down his head and worshipped on his face.

32 And the angel of the LORD said to him, Why have you struck your she-ass these three times? Behold, I went out to be an adversary against you, because you have directed your course contrary to me;

33 And the she-ass saw me and turned aside from me these three times; and if she had not turned aside from me, surely now I would have slain you, and saved her alive.

34 And Balaam said to the angel of the LORD, I have sinned; for I did not know that thou didst stand in the way against me; now therefore, if my mission is evil in thy eyes, I will turn back again.

35 And the angel of the LORD said to Balaam, Go with the men; but only the command that I shall speak to you, that shall you do. So Balaam went with the princes of Balak.

36 ¶And when Balak heard that Balaam was come, he went out to meet him in a town of Moab, which is in the border of Arnon at the utter-most end of the border.

37 And Balak said to Balaam, Did I not earnestly send messengers to you to call you? Why did you not come to me? Perhaps you were saying that I am not able to honor you?

38 And Balaam said to Balak, Lo, I have come to you; have I now any power at all to say anything? The word that God puts in my mouth, that shall I speak.

39 And Balaam went with Balak, and they came to Koriath-Hizroth.

40 And Balak slaughtered oxen and sheep, and sent to Balaam and to the princes who were with him.

41 And in the morning Balak took Balaam and brought him to a high place of Baal, and from there he saw

the uttermost part of the people of Israel.

CHAPTER 23

AND Balaam said to Balak, Build me here seven altars, and prepare me here seven oxen and seven rams.

2 And Balak did as Balaam had told him; and Balak and Balaam offered on every altar a bullock and a ram.

3 And Balaam said to Balak, Stand here by your burnt offerings, and I will go. Perhaps the LORD will come to meet me; and whatever he shows me I will tell you. So he went away quietly.

4 And God appeared to Balaam and said to him, You have prepared seven altars, and have offered upon every altar a bullock and a ram.

5 Then the LORD put a word in Balaam's mouth and said to him, Return to Balak, and thus you shall speak.

6 And he returned to him, and, lo, he stood by his burnt offerings, he and all the princes of Moab.

7 And he took up his parable and said, Balak the king of the Moabites has brought me from Aram,[1] from the mountains of the east, saying, Come, curse Jacob for me, and come, destroy Israel for me.

8 How can I curse whom God has not cursed? How can I destroy whom the LORD has not destroyed?

9 For from the top of the mountains I see him, and from the hills I behold him; lo, the people are dwelling alone and are not reckoned among the nations.

10 Who can count the multitude of the descendants of Jacob, and the number of the fourth part of Israel? Let me die the death of the righteous, and let my end be like theirs!

11 And Balak said to Balaam, What have you done to me? I called you to curse my enemies, and, behold, you have surely blessed them.

12 And Balaam answered and said, Behold, whatever the LORD puts in my mouth that thing will I speak.

13 And Balak said to him, Come

[1] Mesopotamia.

with me to another place, from which you may see them; but you shall see the utmost part of them, and shall not see them all; and curse them for me from thence.

14 ¶And he brought him to the field of watchmen, to the top of the hill, and built seven altars, and offered a bullock and a ram on every altar.

15 And Balaam said to Balak, Stand here by your burnt offerings while I go yonder.

16 And the LORD appeared to Balaam and put a word in his mouth and said to him, Go again to Balak and say thus.

17 And when he came to him, he was standing by his burnt offerings, and the princes of Moab with him. And Balak said to him, What has the LORD spoken?

18 And he took up his parable and said, Rise up, Balak, and hear; and give ear to my testimony, O son of Zippor;

19 God is not a man that he should lie; neither the son of man that he should be given counsel; he speaks and he shall do it, and his word abides for ever.

20 Behold, I was brought here to bless; and I cannot reverse the blessing.

21 I do not behold iniquity in Jacob, neither have I seen malice in Israel; the LORD his God is with him, and the glory of his King is among them.

22 God brought them out of Egypt with his might and excellency.

23 For there is no augury in Jacob, neither is there any divination in Israel; according to this time it shall be said of Jacob and of Israel, What has God wrought!

24 Behold, the people shall rise up as a lion and march like a lion; he shall not lie down until he eats the prey and drinks the blood of the slain.

25 ¶Then Balak said to Balaam, Neither curse them at all, nor bless them at all.

26 But Balaam answered and said to Balak, Did I not tell you, All that

the LORD speaks to me, that very thing I must do?

27 ¶And Balak said to Balaam, Come, I will take you to another place; perhaps it will please God that you may curse them for me from there.

28 Then Balak took Balaam to the top of Peor, that looks toward Ashimon.

29 And Balaam said to Balak, Build me here seven altars and prepare me seven bullocks and seven rams.

30 And Balak did as Balaam had said, and offered a bullock and a ram on every altar.

CHAPTER 24

AND when Balaam saw that it pleased the LORD to bless Israel, he did not go, as at other times, to seek divination; but set his face toward the wilderness.

2 And Balaam lifted up his eyes, and he saw Israel encamping, tribe by tribe; and the spirit of God came upon him.

3 And he took up his parable, and said, Balaam the son of Beor has said, and the man whose eyes are open has said;

4 He has said, who heard the word of God, who saw the vision of God, falling into a trance but having his eyes open:

5 How beautiful are your tents, O Jacob, and your tabernacles, O Israel!

6 Like the valleys that flow, like gardens by the river's side, like the tabernacle which the LORD has pitched, and like cedar trees beside the waters.

7 A man shall rise up from among his sons, and his offspring shall dwell by many waters; he shall be greater than Agag, and his kingdom shall be exalted.

8 The God who brought them forth out of Egypt with his might and excellency, he shall devour the nations that are their enemies, and shall break their bones in pieces, and cut off their loins.

9 He couched, he lay down as a lion, and as a young lion; who shall rouse him up? Blessed are they who bless you, and cursed are they who curse you.

10 ¶And Balak's anger was kindled against Balaam, and he struck his hands together; and Balak said to Balaam, I called you to curse my enemies, and, behold, you have surely blessed them these three times.

11 Therefore, now get you out and go to your own country; for I had said, I will surely honor you but, lo, the LORD has deprived you of my honors.

12 And Balaam answered and said to Balak, Did I not say to your messengers whom you sent to me,

13 If Balak would give me his house full of silver and gold, I would not transgress the commandment of the LORD to do either good or bad of my own mind; but what the LORD says, that will I speak.

14 And now, behold, I am going to my land; come, therefore, and I will give you counsel what this people shall do to your people in the latter days.

15 ¶And he took up his parable and said, Balaam the son of Beor has said, and the man whose eyes are open has said;

16 He has said, who heard the words of God and knew the knowledge of the Most High, who saw the vision of God, falling into a trance but having his eyes open;

17 I have seen him, but not clearly enough; I beheld him, but he was not nigh; there shall come a Star out of Jacob, and a Prince shall rise out of Israel, and shall destroy the mighty men of Moab and subdue all the children of Sheth.

18 And Edom shall be his possession; Seir, also the possession of his enemies, shall be his; and Israel shall gain strength.

19 Out of Jacob shall come he that shall have dominion, and shall destroy him who has survived out of the city.

20 ¶And when he looked on Amalek, he took up his parable and said, Amalek is the chief of the nations; but in the end he shall perish for ever.

21 And he looked on the Kenites and took up his parable and said,

Strong is your dwelling place, and your nest is set in a rock.

22 Nevertheless the Kenite shall be wasted until Assyria shall carry you away captive.

23 And he took up his parable and said, Alas, who shall live when God does this!

24 And legions shall come from the **land of China,**[1] **and shall** conquer Assyria, and shall subdue the Hebrews, and they also shall perish for ever.

25 Then Balaam rose up and returned to his country; and Balak also went his way.

CHAPTER 25

AND Israel abode in Shittim, and the people began to commit whoredom with the daughters of Moab.

2 And they invited the people to the sacrifices offered to their gods; and the people did eat, and worshipped their gods.

3 And Israel joined himself to Baal-peor; and the anger of the LORD was kindled against the children of Israel.

4 And the LORD said to Moses, Take all the chiefs of the people and expose them before the LORD in the daylight that the fierce anger of the LORD may be turned away from the children of Israel.

5 And Moses said to the judges of Israel, Slay every one of you his men who have joined themselves to Baal-peor.

6 ¶And, behold, one of the men of the children of Israel came to his brethren, and then he went in to a Midianite woman in the sight of Moses and in the sight of all the congregation of the children of Israel while they were weeping at the door of the tabernacle of the congregation.

7 And when Phinehas, the son of Eleazar, the son of Aaron the priest, saw it, he rose up from the midst of the congregation and took a spear in his hand;

8 And he went in after the man of Israel into the private chamber and thrust both of them through, the man of Israel and the woman through

1 Cathay.

her belly. So the plague was stayed from the children of Israel.

9 And those that died in the plague were twenty-four thousand.

10 ¶Then the LORD spoke to Moses and said to him.

11 Phinehas, the son of Eleazar, the son of Aaron the priest, has turned my wrath away from the children of Israel because he was moved with my zeal among them that I did not consume the children of Israel in my anger.

12 Therefore I said, Behold, I will give to him my covenant of peace;

13 And he shall have it and his sons after him, the covenant of an everlasting priesthood, because he was zealous for his God and made atonement for the children of Israel.

14 Now the name of the Israelite who was slain with the Midianite woman was Zimri, the son of Salu, a chief of a father's house of the tribe of Simeon.

15 And the name of the Midianite woman was Cozbi, the daughter of Zur; he was the chief of the people of his father's house in Midian.

16 ¶And the LORD spoke to Moses, saying,

17 Harass the Midianites and destroy them;

18 For they have distressed you with their treachery, wherewith they have plotted against you in the matter of Peor and in the matter of Cozbi, the daughter of a prince of Midian, their sister, who was slain in the day of the plague in the matter of Peor.

CHAPTER 26

AND it came to pass after the plague that the LORD said to Moses and to Eleazar the son of Aaron the priest,

2 Take a census of all the congregation of the children of Israel, from twenty years old and upward, throughout their fathers' houses, all that are able to go to war in Israel.

3 And Moses and Eleazar the priest talked with the people in the plains of Moab by the Jordan at Jericho.

4 And Moses numbered them from

twenty years old and upward, as the LORD commanded Moses and the children of Israel who went forth out of the land of Egypt.

5 ¶Reuben, the first-born of Israel; the sons of Reuben, Hanoch, the family of the Hanochites; of Pallu, the family of the Palluites;

6 Of Hezron, the family of the Hezronites; of Carmi, the family of the Carmites.

7 These are the families of the Reubenites; and their number was forty-three thousand and seven hundred and thirty.

8 And the son of Pallu, Eliab.

9 And the sons of Eliab, Nebuel, and Dathan, and Abiram, the prominent men of the congregation who strove against Moses and against Aaron in the company of Korah when they strove against the LORD;

10 And the earth opened its mouth and swallowed them up together with Korah when that company died, when the fire devoured two hundred and fifty men; and they became an example.

11 Notwithstanding, the children of Korah did not die.

12 ¶The sons of Simeon after their families: of Jemuel, the family of the Jemuelites; of Jamin, the family of the Jaminites; of Jachin, the family of the Jachinites;

13 Of Zerah, the family of the Zarhites; of Shaul, the family of the Shaulites.

14 These are the families of the Simeonites, twenty-two thousand and two hundred.

15 ¶The sons of Gad after their families: of Zephon, the family of the Zephonites; of Haggi, the family of the Haggites; of Shuni, the family of the Shunites;

16 Of Ozni, the family of the Oznites; of Edi, the family of the Edites;

17 Of Arod, the family of the Arodites; of Adel, the family of the Adelites;

18 These are the families of the sons of Gad according to those that were numbered of them, forty thousand and five hundred.

19 ¶The sons of Judah were Er and Onan; and Er and Onan died in the land of Canaan.

20 And the sons of Judah after their families were: of Shelah, the family of the Shelanites; of Pharez, the family of the Pharzites; of Zerah, the family of the Zarhites.

21 And the sons of Pharez were: of Hezron, the family of the Hezronites; of Hamul, the family of the Hamulites.

22 These are the families of Judah according to those that were numbered of them, seventy-six thousand and five hundred.

23 ¶The sons of Issachar after their families: of Tola, the family of the Tolaites; of Pua, the family of the Puaites;

24 Of Jashub, the family of the Jashubites; of Shimron, the family of the Shimronites.

25 These are the families of Issachar according to those that were numbered of them, sixty-four thousand and three hundred.

26 ¶The sons of Zebulun after their families: of Seder, the family of the Sadrites; of Elon, the family of the Elonites; of Nahlael, the family of the Nahlaites.

27 These are the families of the Zebulunites according to those that were numbered of them, sixty thousand and five hundred.

28 ¶The sons of Joseph after their families were Manasseh and Ephraim:

29 Of the sons of Manasseh: of Machir, the family of the Machirites; and Machir begat Gilead; of Gilead comes the family of the Gileadites.

30 These are the sons of Gilead: of Jeezer, the family of the Jeezerites; of Helek, the family of the Helekites;

31 And of Ashdael, the family of the Ashdaelites; and of Shechem, the family of the Shechemites;

32 And of Shemida, the family of the Shemidaites; and of Hepher, the family of the Hepherites.

33 ¶And Zelophehad the son of Hepher had no sons, but daughters; and the names of the daughters of Zelophehad were Mahlah, Joah, Hoglah, Milcah, and Tirzah.

34 These are the families of Manas-

seh and those that were numbered of them, fifty-two thousand and seven hundred.

35 ¶These are the sons of Ephraim after their families: of Shuthelah, the family of the Shuthalhites; of Becher, the family of the Bachrites; of Tahan, the family of the Tahanites.

36 And these are the sons of Shuthelah: of Edan, the family of the Edanites.

37 These are the families of the sons of Ephraim according to those that were numbered of them, thirty-two thousand and five hundred. These are the sons of Joseph after their families.

38 ¶The sons of Benjamin after their families: of Bela, the family of the Belaites; of Ashbel, the family of the Ashbelites; of Ahiram, the family of the Ahiramites;

39 Of Shupham, the family of the Shuphamites; of Hupham, the family of the Huphamites.

40 And the sons of Bela were Ard and Naaman: of Ard, the family of the Ardites; and of Naaman, the family of the Naamites.

41 These are the sons of Benjamin after their families; and those that were numbered of them were forty-five thousand and six hundred.

42 ¶These are the sons of Dan after their families: of Shuham, the family of the Shuhamites. These are the families of Dan after their families.

43 All the families of the Shuhamites, according to those that were numbered of them, were sixty-four thousand and four hundred.

44 ¶The sons of Asher by their families: of Jimna, the family of the Jimnites; of Jesui, the family of the Jesuites; of Beriah, the family of the Berites.

45 The sons of Beriah: of Heber, the family of the Heberites; of Malchiel, the family of the Malchielites.

46 And the name of the daughter of Asher was Sarah.

47 These are the families of the sons of Asher according to those that were numbered of them; fifty-three thousand and four hundred.

48 ¶The sons of Naphtali after their families: Nahzeel, the family of the Nahzeelites; of Guni, the family of the Gunites;

49 Of Jezer, the family of the Jezerites; of Shillem, the family of the Shillemites.

50 These are the families of Naphtali according to their families; and they that were numbered of them were forty-five thousand and four hundred.

51 These were the numbers of the children of Israel, six hundred and one thousand, seven hundred and thirty.

52 ¶And the LORD spoke to Moses, saying,

53 To these the land shall be divided for an inheritance according to the number of names.

54 To a large family you shall give a large inheritance and to a small family you shall give a small inheritance; every one shall receive his inheritance according to those that were numbered of him.

55 Notwithstanding the land shall be divided by lots; according to the names of the tribes of their fathers they shall inherit.

56 According to the lots shall their inheritance be divided between the larger families and the smaller families.

57 ¶These are they that were numbered of the Levites after their families: of Gershon, the family of the Gershonites; of Kohath, the family of the Kohathites; of Merari, the family of the Merarites.

58 These are the families of the Levites: the family of the Libnites, the family of the Hebronites, the family of the Mahlites, the family of the Mushites, the family of the Korathites. And Kohath begat Amram.

59 And the name of Amram's wife was Jochaber, the daughter of Levi, who was born to Levi in Egypt; and she bore to Amram, Aaron and Moses and their sister Miriam.

60 And to Aaron were born Nadab, Abihu, Eleazar, and Ithamar.

61 But Nadab and Abihu died when they offered strange fire before the LORD.

62 And those that were numbered of them were twenty-three thousand, all males from a month old and upward; for they were not numbered among the children of Israel, because there was no inheritance given them among the children of Israel.

63 ¶These are those that were numbered by Moses and Eleazar the priest, who numbered the children of Israel in the plains of Moab by the Jordan near Jericho.

64 But among these there was not a man of those whom Moses and Aaron the priest numbered, when they numbered the children of Israel in the wilderness of Sinai.

65 For the LORD had said of them, They shall surely die in the wilderness. And there was not left a man of them except Caleb the son of Jophaniah and Joshua the son of Nun.

CHAPTER 27

THEN came the daughters of Zelophehad, the son of Hepher, the son of Gilead, the son of Machir, the son of Manasseh, of the families of Manasseh the son of Joseph; and these are the names of his daughters: Mahlah, Joah, and Hogla, and Milcah, and Tirzah.

2 And they stood before Moses and before Eleazar the priest and before the princes and all the congregation at the door of the tabernacle of the congregation, saying,

3 Our father died in the wilderness, and he was not in the company of those who revolted before the LORD in the company of Korah; but he died in his own sins and had no sons.

4 Why should the name of our father be lost from among his family because he had no son? Give to us therefore a possession among the brothers of our father.

5 And Moses brought their cause before the LORD.

6 ¶And the LORD said to Moses,

7 The daughters of Zelophehad speak right, you shall surely give them a possession of an inheritance among their father's brothers; and you shall cause the inheritance of their father to pass to them.

8 And you shall say to the children of Israel, If a man dies and has no son, then you shall cause his inheritance to pass to his daughter.

9 And if he has no daughter, then you shall give his inheritance to his brothers.

10 And if he has no brothers, then you shall give his inheritance to his father's brothers.

11 And if his father has no brothers, then you shall give his inheritance to his kinsman that is next to him of his family, and he shall possess it; and it shall be to the children of Israel a statute of judgment, as the LORD commanded Moses.

12 ¶And the LORD said to Moses, Go up into this mountain of the Hebrews and see the land which I have given to the children of Israel.

13 And when you have seen it, you also shall be gathered to your people, as Aaron your brother was gathered.

14 Because you rebelled against my commandment in the wilderness of Zin, in the strife of the congregation, and you did not sanctify me before their eyes; that is, the waters of Mesotha, at Rakim in the wilderness of Zin.

15 ¶And Moses spoke to the LORD, saying,

16 Let the LORD, the God of the spirits of all flesh, appoint a man over the congregation

17 Who may go out before them and who may come in before them, and who may lead them out and bring them in; that the congregation of the LORD may not be as sheep which have no shepherd.

18 And the LORD said to Moses, Take Joshua the son of Nun, a man in whom is the spirit, and lay your hand upon him;

19 And make him to stand before Eleazar the priest and before all the congregation; and put him in charge in their sight.

20 And you shall put some of your honor upon him that all the congregation of the children of Israel may obey him.

21 And he shall stand before Eleazar the priest, who shall ask for him after the ordinance of the law before the LORD; at his word they shall go out and at his word they shall come in, both he and all the children of Israel with him, the whole congregation.

22 And Moses did as the LORD commanded him; and he took Joshua and made him stand before Eleazar the priest and before all the congregation;

23 And he laid his hands upon him, and gave him authority, as the LORD commanded by the hand of Moses.

CHAPTER 28

AND the LORD spoke to Moses and said to him,

2 Command the children of Israel and say to them, My offerings and the bread of my offerings made by fire for a sweet savour to me they shall observe, to offer to me in their due season.

3 And you shall say to them, This is the offering made by fire which you shall offer to the LORD: two lambs of the first year without blemish day by day for a continual burnt offering.

4 The one lamb you shall offer in the morning and the other lamb you shall offer at evening;

5 And a tenth part of an ephah of fine flour for a meal offering, mixed with a fourth part of a hin of beaten oil.

6 It is a continual burnt offering which was ordained in mount Sinai for a sweet savour, a sacrifice made by fire to the LORD.

7 And the drink offering thereof shall be a fourth of a hin for the one lamb; in the holy place you shall pour out the old wine before the LORD for a drink offering.

8 And the other lamb you shall offer at evening; as the meat offering of the morning and as its drink offering you shall offer it, a sacrifice made by fire for a sweet savour to the LORD.

9 ¶And on the sabbath day two lambs of the first year without blemish and two tenths of an ephah of fine flour mixed with oil for a meal offering with its drink offering;

10 This is the burnt offering of every sabbath, besides the continual burnt offering and its drink offering.

11 ¶And in the beginning of your months you shall offer burnt offerings to the LORD: two young bullocks, and one ram, seven lambs of the first year without blemish;

12 And three tenths of an ephah of fine flour mixed with oil for a meal offering, for one bullock; and two tenths of an ephah of fine flour mixed with oil, for a meal offering, for one ram;

13 And a tenth of an ephah of fine flour mixed with oil for a meal offering for one lamb; for a burnt offering of a sweet savour, a sacrifice made by fire to the LORD.

14 And their drink offerings shall be half a hin of wine to a bullock and a third part of a hin to a ram and a fourth part of a hin to a lamb; this is the burnt offering of the beginning of every month throughout the months of the year.

15 And one kid of the goats for a sin offering to the LORD shall be offered, besides the continual burnt offering and its drink offering.

16 And on the fourteenth day of the first month is the passover of the LORD.

17 And on the fifteenth day of this month is the feast; seven days shall unleavened bread be eaten.

18 On the first day shall be a holy convocation; you shall do no manner of hard work;

19 But you shall offer sacrifices made by fire for burnt offerings to the LORD; two young bullocks and one ram and seven lambs of the first year: they shall be to you without blemish:

20 And their meal offering shall be of fine flour mixed with oil; three tenths of an ephah shall you offer for a bullock, and two tenths of an ephah for a ram;

21 And a tenth of an ephah you shall offer for every lamb; thus you shall do for every one of the seven lambs.

22 And one yearling goat for a sin offering to make atonement for you.

23 You shall offer these besides the burnt offering of the morning, which is for a continual burnt offering.

24 After this manner you shall offer daily for seven days the bread of the sacrifice made by fire for a sweet savour to the LORD; it shall be offered besides the continual burnt offering and its drink offering.

25 And on the seventh day you shall have a holy convocation; you shall do no manner of work.

26 ¶Also on the day of first fruits, when you offer a meal offering of new wheat to the LORD at your feast of weeks, you shall have a holy convocation; you shall do no manner of hard work;

27 But you shall offer the burnt offerings for a sweet savour to the LORD; two young bullocks, one ram, seven lambs of the first year;

28 And their meal offering of fine flour mixed with oil, three tenths of an ephah for each bullock, two tenths of an ephah for one ram,

29 And a tenth of an ephah for each lamb, likewise for each of the seven lambs;

30 And one kid of the goats to make atonement for you.

31 You shall offer them besides the continual burnt offering and its meal offering; you shall offer them without blemish, and their drink offerings.

CHAPTER 29

AND on the first day of the seventh month you shall have a holy convocation; you shall do no manner of hard work; it is a day of blowing trumpets to you.

2 And you shall offer burnt offerings for a sweet savour to the LORD; one young bullock, one ram, and seven lambs of the first year without blemish;

3 And their meal offering shall be of fine flour mixed with oil, three tenths of an ephah for a bullock and two tenths of an ephah for a ram,

4 And one tenth of an ephah for each lamb, likewise for each of the seven lambs;

5 And one kid of the goats for a sin offering, to make atonement for you;

6 Besides the burnt offering of the beginning of the month and its meal offering and the daily burnt offering and their meal offering and their drink offering, according to their manner, for a sweet savour, a sacrifice made by fire to the LORD.

7 ¶And you shall have on the tenth day of this seventh month a holy convocation; and you shall do no manner of hard work;

8 But you shall offer burnt offerings to the LORD for a sweet savour: one young bullock, one ram, and seven lambs of the first year without blemish;

9 And their meal offering shall be of fine flour mixed with oil, three tenths of an ephah for the bullock and two tenths of an ephah for the one ram,

10 And a tenth of an ephah for one lamb, likewise for each of the seven lambs;

11 One kid of the goats for a sin offering; besides the sin offering of atonement and the continual burnt offering and the meal offering of it and their drink offerings.

12 ¶And on the fifteenth day of this seventh month you shall have a holy convocation; you shall do no manner of hard work, and you shall keep a feast to the LORD for seven days;

13 And you shall offer burnt offerings, a sacrifice made by fire, a sweet savour to the LORD; thirteen young bullocks, two rams, and fourteen lambs of the first year; they shall be without blemish:

14 And their meal offering shall be of fine flour mixed with oil, three tenths of an ephah for every bullock of the thirteen bullocks, two tenths of an ephah for each of the two rams,

15 And a tenth of an ephah for each lamb of the fourteen lambs,

16 And one kid of the goats for a sin offering; besides the continual burnt offering, its meal offering, and its drink offering.

17 ¶And on the second day you shall offer twelve young bullocks,

two rams, and fourteen lambs of the first year without blemish;

18 And their meal offering and their drink offerings for the bullocks, for the rams, and for the lambs, shall be according to their number, after the ritual;

19 And one kid of the goats for a sin offering; besides the continual burnt offering, and its meal offering, and their drink offering.

20 ¶And on the third day eleven bullocks, two rams, and fourteen lambs of the first year without blemish;

21 And their meal offering and their drink offering for the bullocks, for the rams, and for the lambs, according to their number, according to the ritual;

22 And one kid of the goats for a sin offering; besides the continual burnt offering and its meal offering and its drink offering.

23 ¶And on the fourth day ten bullocks, two rams, and fourteen lambs of the first year without blemish;

24 Their meal offering and their drink offering for the bullocks, for the rams, and for the lambs, according to their number, according to the ritual;

25 And one kid of the goats for a sin offering; besides the continual burnt offering, its meal offering, and its drink offering.

26 ¶And on the fifth day nine bullocks, two rams, and fourteen lambs of the first year without blemish;

27 And their meal offering and their drink offering for the bullocks, for the rams, and for the lambs, according to their number, according to the ritual;

28 And one goat of the first year for a sin offering; besides the continual burnt offering and its meal offering and its drink offering.

29 ¶And on the sixth day eight bullocks, two rams, and fourteen lambs of the first year without blemish;

30 And their meal offering and their drink offering for the bullocks, for the rams, and for the lambs, according to their number, according to the ritual;

31 And one goat of the first year for a sin offering; besides the continual burnt offering, its meal offering, and its drink offering.

32 ¶And on the seventh day seven bullocks, two rams, and fourteen lambs of the first year without blemish;

33 And their meal offering and their drink offerings for the bullocks, for the rams and for the lambs, according to their number, according to the ritual;

34 And one he-goat of the first year for a sin offering; besides the continual burnt offering, its meal offering, and its drink offering.

35 ¶On the eighth day you shall have a solemn assembly; you shall do no manner of hard work;

36 But you shall offer burnt offerings, a sacrifice made by fire, of a sweet savour to the LORD: one bullock, one ram, and four lambs of the first year without blemish;

37 Their meal offering and their drink offering for the bullock, for the ram, and for the lambs, according to their number, according to the ritual;

38 And one goat of the first year for a sin offering; besides the continual burnt offering and its meal offering and its drink offering.

39 These things you shall do to the LORD at the time of your feasts, besides your vows and your freewill offerings and your burnt offerings and your meal offerings and your drink offerings.

40 And Moses told the children of Israel according to all that the LORD commanded Moses.

CHAPTER 30

AND Moses spoke to the chiefs of the tribes of the children of Israel and said to them, This is the thing which the LORD has commanded:

2 When a man vows a vow to the LORD and swears an oath to bind himself by a bond, he shall not break his word; he shall do according to all that proceeds out of his mouth.

3 If a woman also vows a vow to

the LORD and binds herself by a bond while she is in her father's house in her youth,

4 And her father hears of her vows and the bonds wherewith she has bound herself, and her father shall keep silent toward her; then all her vows shall stand and every bond wherewith she has bound herself shall stand.

5 But if her father shall make them void in the day that he hears of all the vows and all the bonds by which she has bound herself, then they shall not stand; and the LORD shall forgive her because her father had declared them void.

6 And if she is given in marriage to a husband, and her vows are upon her or she has uttered anything out of her lips by which she bound herself,

7 And her husband hears of it and keeps silent in the day that he hears it; then all her vows shall stand and her bonds by which she has bound herself shall stand.

8 But if her husband makes them void on the day that he hears of it, then shall her vows be void and that which she uttered with her lips, and the gifts which she promised, by which she bound herself, shall be of none effect; and the LORD shall forgive her.

9 But as to the vow of a widow or a deserted woman, everything by which she has bound herself shall stand against her.

10 And if she vowed in her husband's house or bound herself with an oath,

11 And her husband heard it but kept silent toward her and did not nullify it; then her vow shall stand, and the bond by which she has bound herself shall stand.

12 But if her husband has utterly made her vows void on the day when he heard them; then whatsoever proceeded out of her lips concerning her vows or concerning the bonds by which she bound herself shall not stand, because her husband has made them void; and the LORD shall forgive her.

13 Every vow and every binding oath to afflict the soul her husband may establish or her husband may make it void.

14 But if her husband should remain silent toward her from day to day; then he confirms all her vows and all her bonds which are upon her; he confirms them because he kept silent toward her on the day that he heard them.

15 But if he shall make them void after he has heard them, then he shall bear her iniquity.

16 These are the statutes, which the LORD commanded Moses, between a man and his wife, between a father and his daughter while she is still in her youth in her father's house.

CHAPTER 31

AND the LORD spoke to Moses, saying,

2 Avenge the children of Israel against the Midianites; afterward you shall be gathered to your people.

3 And Moses said to the people, Arm some of the men from among you for the host, and let them go against the Midianites to avenge the LORD against Midian.

4 Of every tribe, a thousand from each tribe, throughout all the tribes of Israel, you shall send into the army.

5 So there were selected out of the tribes of Israel a thousand men from each tribe, twelve thousand armed for war.

6 Then Moses sent them to war, a thousand from each tribe, twelve thousand armed men, them and Phinehas the son of Eleazar the priest, to the army, with the holy vessels of the sanctuary and with trumpets to blow in his hand.

7 And they warred against Midian, as the LORD commanded Moses; and they slew all the males.

8 And they slew the kings of Midian with the rest of those that were slain; namely, Evi, Rakim, Zur, Hur, and Reba, the five kings of Midian; Balaam also, the son of Beor, they slew with the sword.

9 And the children of Israel took all the women of Midian captives; and their little ones and all their

cattle and all their flocks and all their wealth they plundered.

10 And they burned all the cities wherein they dwelt and all their unwalled villages with fire.

11 And they carried away all the spoil and all the booty, both of men and of beasts.

12 And they brought the captives, the booty, and the spoil, to Moses and to Eleazar the priest and to the congregation of the children of Israel, to the camp at the plains of Moab which are by the Jordan near Jericho.

13 ¶And Moses and Eleazar the priest and all the princes of the congregation went forth to meet them outside the camp.

14 And Moses was wroth with the officers of the army, the commanders of thousands and captains over hundreds who had come from the battle.

15 And Moses said to them, Why have you let all the women live?

16 For it was they who caused the children of Israel, through the counsel of Balaam, to commit trespass against the LORD in the matter of Peor, and there was a plague in the congregation of the LORD.

17 Now therefore kill every male among the little ones and kill every woman who has known man by lying with him.

18 But all the female children, who have not known a man by lying with him, keep alive for yourselves.

19 And as for you, you shall abide outside the camp seven days; whosoever has killed any person and whosoever has touched any slain purify both yourselves and your captives on the third day and on the seventh day,

20 And purify all your garments and all that is made of skin and all the work of goats' hair and all things made of wood.

21 ¶And Eleazar the priest said to the men of war who had returned from the battle, This is the ordinance of the law which the LORD commanded Moses:

22 Only the gold, and the silver, the brass, the iron, the tin, and the lead,

23 Everything that may abide the fire, you shall make it to go through the fire and it shall be clean; nevertheless it shall be purified with the water which is used for cleansing; and all that cannot abide the fire, you shall make pass through the water.

24 And you must wash your clothes on the seventh day, and you shall be clean, and afterward you shall come into the camp.

25 ¶And the LORD spoke to Moses, saying,

26 Take the count of the prey that was taken and of the captives, both of man and of beast, you and Eleazar the priest and the chiefs of the fathers of the congregation;

27 And divide the booty into two parts; between the men of war who went out to battle and between all the congregation;

28 And levy a tribute for the LORD from the men of war who went out to battle; out of all the congregation, one person of every five hundred, both of the persons and of the oxen and of the asses and of the sheep;

29 Take it from their half and give it to Eleazar the priest as an offering to the LORD.

30 And from the children of Israel's half, you shall take one out of every fifty, of the persons, of the oxen, of the asses, and of the flocks, and of all the beasts, and give them to the Levites, who have charge of the tabernacle of the LORD.

31 And Moses and Eleazar the priest did as the LORD commanded Moses.

32 And the booty and the captives which the men of war had plundered was six hundred and seventy-five thousand sheep,

33 And seventy-two thousand oxen,

34 And sixty-one thousand asses,

35 And thirty-two thousand persons in all, of women who had not known man by lying with him.

36 And the half, which was the portion of those who went out to war was in number three hundred and thirty-seven thousand and five hundred sheep;

37 And the LORD's tribute of the sheep was six thousand and seven hundred and fifty.

38 And the oxen were thirty-six thousand; of which the LORD's tribute was seven hundred and twenty.

39 And the asses were thirty thousand and five hundred; of which the LORD's tribute was six hundred and ten.

40 And the persons were sixteen thousand; of which the LORD's tribute was three hundred and twenty persons.

41 And Moses gave the tribute, which was the LORD's gift offering, to Eleazar the priest, as the LORD commanded Moses.

42 And of the children of Israel's half, which Moses divided from the men who had gone out to war,

43 (Now the half that pertained to the congregation was three hundred and thirty-seven thousand and five hundred sheep,

44 And thirty-six thousand oxen,

45 And thirty thousand and five hundred asses,

46 And sixteen thousand persons),

47 Even of the children of Israel's half, Moses took one portion of every fifty, both of man and of beasts, and gave them to the Levites, who have charge of the tabernacle of the LORD; as the LORD commanded Moses.

48 ¶And the officers who were over thousands of the host, the commanders of thousands and the captains of hundreds came near to Moses;

49 And they said to Moses, Your servants have taken the sum of the men of war who are under our charge and there lacks not one man of us.

50 We have therefore brought as an offering for the LORD what every man has found, articles of gold, ankle chains, and bracelets, rings, earrings, and necklaces, to make atonement for our souls before the LORD.

51 And Moses and Eleazar the priest took the gold from them, all wrought jewels.

52 And all the gold of the gift offering that they offered to the LORD, from the commanders of thousands and from the captains of hundreds, was sixteen thousand seven hundred and fifty shekels.

53 (For the men of war had plundered every man for himself.)

54 And Moses and Eleazar the priest took the gold from commanders of thousands and from captains of hundreds and brought it into the tabernacle of the congregation for a memorial for the children of Israel before the LORD.

CHAPTER 32

NOW the children of Reuben and the children of Gad had a very great multitude of cattle; and when they saw the land of Jazer and the land of Gilead, behold, the place was a place for cattle;

2 The children of Reuben and the children of Gad came and said to Moses and to Eleazar the priest and to the princes of the congregation,

3 Ataroth, Ribon, Jazer, Nimrah, Heshbon, Elealeh, Sheba, Nebo, and Beon,

4 The land which the LORD smote before the children of Israel is a land for cattle, and your servants have cattle;

5 Wherefore, they said, if we have found mercy in your sight, let this land be given to your servants for a possession, and bring us not across the Jordan.

6 ¶And Moses said to the children of Reuben and to the children of Gad, Shall your brethren go to war, while you settle here?

7 Why do you discourage the heart of the children of Israel from going over into the land which the LORD has given them?

8 Thus did your fathers, when I sent them from Rakim-gia to spy out the land.

9 For when they went up as far as the valley of Segola, and spied out the land, they discouraged the heart of the children of Israel that they should not go into the land which the LORD had given them.

10 And the LORD's anger was kindled against them on that day, and he swore, saying,

11 Surely none of the men who came up out of the land of Egypt, from twenty years old and upward,

shall see the land which I swore to Abraham, to Isaac, and to Jacob; because they have not wholly followed me;

12 Except Caleb the son of Jophaniah the Kenezite and Joshua the son of Nun; for they have wholly followed the LORD.

13 And the LORD's anger was kindled against Israel, and he made them wander in the wilderness forty years until all the generation that had done evil in the sight of the LORD was consumed.

14 And, behold, you also are risen up in your father's stead, a generation of sinful men, to augment still the fierce anger of the LORD against Israel.

15 For if you turn away from after the LORD, he will again make you wander in the wilderness; and you shall destroy all this people.

16 ¶Then they came near to him and said, We will build sheepfolds here for our cattle and cities for our little ones;

17 But we ourselves will arm and go before the children of Israel, until we have brought them to their place; and our little ones shall dwell in fortified cities because of the inhabitants of the land.

18 We will not return to our houses until the children of Israel have inherited every man his inheritance;

19 For we will not inherit with them on the other side of the Jordan or beyond; because we have already received our inheritance on this side of the Jordan eastward.

20 ¶And Moses said to them, If you will do this thing and arm yourselves before the LORD for war,

21 And will go all of you armed across the Jordan before the LORD, to war, until he has destroyed his enemies from before his presence,

22 And the land is subdued before the LORD; then after that you shall return and be guiltless before the LORD and before Israel; and this land shall be your possession before the LORD.

23 But if you will not do so, behold, you will be sinning against the LORD;

and be sure your sins will overtake you.

24 Build cities for your little ones and folds for your sheep; and do that which you have promised.

25 And the children of Reuben and the children of Gad said to Moses, Your servants will do as our lord commands.

26 Our little ones, our wives, our flocks, and all our cattle shall remain there in the cities of Gilead;

27 But your servants will pass over, every man armed for war, before the LORD for battle, as our lord said.

28 So concerning all of them Moses commanded Eleazar the priest and Joshua the son of Nun and the chiefs of the fathers of the tribes of the children of Israel;

29 And Moses said to them, If the children of Reuben and the children of Gad will cross with you over the Jordan, every man armed for battle before the LORD, and the land shall be subdued before you, then you shall give them the land of Gilead for a possession;

30 But if they will not cross over with you armed, they shall have possessions among you in the land of Canaan.

31 And the children of Reuben and the children of Gad answered, saying, As the LORD has said to your servants, so will we do.

32 We will pass over armed before the LORD into the land of Canaan to war, that the possession of our inheritance on this side of the Jordan may be ours.

33 And Moses gave to them, to the children of Reuben and to the children of Gad and to half of the tribe of Manasseh the son of Joseph, the kingdom of Sihon king of the Amorites and the kingdom of Og king of Mathnin, all the land with its cities throughout its territories and the towns of the country round about it.

34 ¶And the children of Gad built Ribon and Ataroth and Adoer

35 And Atroth, Shopham and Jazer and Jogbehah,

36 Beth-nimrah and Beth-hauran, fenced cities and folds for sheep.

37 And the children of Reuben built Heshbon, Elealeh, Koriathaim,

38 Nebo, and Baal-meon (their names being changed), and Sibmah; and gave other names to the cities which they built.

39 And the children of Machir the son of Manasseh went to Gilead and took it, and destroyed the Amorites who were in it.

40 And Moses gave Gilead to Machir the son of Manasseh; and he dwelt therein.

41 And Jair the son of Manasseh went and took their villages, and called them Caproney Jair (hamlets of Jair, to this day).

42 And Nocah went and took Keeth and its villages, and called it Nocah, after his own name.

CHAPTER 33

THESE are the journeys of the children of Israel when they went forth out of the land of Egypt with their armies under the command of Moses and Aaron.

2 And Moses wrote down their goings out and their journeys by the commandment of the LORD; and these are their journeys according to their goings out.

3 They departed from Rameses in the first month, on the fifteenth day of the first month; on the morrow after the passover the children of Israel went out with a mighty hand in the sight of all the Egyptians,

4 While the Egyptians were burying all their first-born whom the LORD had slain among them; upon their gods also the LORD executed judgments.

5 And the children of Israel departed from Rameses and encamped in Succoth.

6 And they departed from Succoth and encamped in Etham, which is on the edge of the wilderness.

7 And they departed from Etham and encamped at the entrance of Heritha, the canal, which is before Baal-sephon; and they encamped before Migdol.

8 And they departed from the entrance of Heritha and passed through the midst of the sea into the wilderness, and went three days' journey in the wilderness of Etham and encamped in Morath.

9 And they departed from Morath and came to Elim; and in Elim were twelve fountains of water and seventy palm trees; and they encamped there by the water.

10 And they departed from Elim and encamped by the Red Sea.

11 And they departed from the Red Sea and encamped in the wilderness of Seen.

12 And they departed from the wilderness of Seen, and encamped at Raphka.

13 And they departed from Raphka and encamped in Alush.

14 And they departed from Alush and encamped at Rephidim, where there was no water for the people to drink.

15 And they departed from Rephidim and encamped in the wilderness of Sinai.

16 And they departed from the wilderness of Sinai, and encamped at Kabrey di ragrigtha.[1]

17 And they departed from Kabrey di ragrigtha, and encamped at Hazeroth.

18 And they departed from Hazeroth, and encamped at Rithmah.

19 And they departed from Rithmah, and encamped at Rimmon-parez.

20 And they departed from Rimmon-parez, and encamped at Libnah.

21 And they departed from Libnah, and encamped at Rissah.

22 And they departed from Rissah, and encamped at Kehlat.

23 And they departed from Kehlat, and encamped at mount Shapher.

24 And they departed from mount Shapher, and encamped at Haradah.

25 And they departed from Haradah, and encamped at Makheloth.

26 And they departed from Makheloth, and encamped at Tahath.

27 And they departed from Tahath, and encamped at Tarah.

28 And they departed from Tarah, and encamped at Mithcah.

1 Graves of lust.

29 And they departed from Mithcah, and encamped at Hashmonah.

30 And they departed from Hashmonah, and encamped at Moseroth.

31 And they departed from Moseroth, and encamped at Bene-jaakan.

32 And they departed from Bene-jaakan, and encamped at Had-gadgad.

33 And they departed from Had-gadgad, and encamped at Jotbath.

34 And they departed from Jotbath, and encamped at Acronah.

35 And they departed from Acronah, and encamped at Ezion-gaber.

36 And they departed from Ezion-gaber, and encamped in the wilderness of Zin, which is Kadesh.

37 And they departed from Kadesh, and encamped at mount Hor on the edge of the land of Edom.

38 And Aaron the priest went up on mount Hor at the commandment of the LORD, and died there, in the fortieth year after the children of Israel were come out of the land of Egypt, on the first day of the first month.

39 And Aaron was a hundred and twenty-three years old when he died on mount Hor.

40 And the king of Gadar the Canaanite, who dwelt in the south in the land of Canaan, heard of the coming of the children of Israel.

41 And they departed from mount Hor, and encamped at Zalmonah.

42 And they departed from Zalmonah, and encamped at Punon.

43 And they departed from Punon, and encamped in Aboth.

44 And they departed from Aboth, and encamped at Een-Ebraye, in the border of Moab.

45 And they departed from Een-Ebraye, and encamped at Ribon-gad.

46 And they journeyed from Ribon-gad, and encamped at Almon-diblathaim.

47 And they journeyed from Almon-diblathaim, and encamped at the mountain of Hebrews, which is before Nebo.

48 And they departed from the mountain of the Hebrews, and encamped in the plains of Moab by the Jordan near Jericho.

49 And they encamped by the Jordan from Beth-ashimon as far as Abel-shittim in the plains of Moab.

50 ¶And the LORD said to Moses in the plains of Moab by the Jordan near Jericho,

51 Speak to the children of Israel and say to them, When you cross the Jordan into the land of Canaan;

52 Then you shall destroy all the inhabitants of the land from before you and destroy all their idols and destroy all their molten images and demolish all their high places;

53 And you shall possess the land and dwell therein; for I have given you the land to possess it.

54 And you shall divide the land by lot for an inheritance among your families; and to the large families you shall give a large inheritance, and to the small families you shall give a small inheritance; every man's inheritance shall be in the place where his lot falls; according to the tribes of their fathers they shall inherit.

55 But if you will not destroy the inhabitants of the land from before you, then it shall come to pass, that those who are left of them shall be splinters in your eyes, and spears in your sides, and shall trouble you in the land wherein you dwell.

56 And as I thought to do to them, I shall do to you.

CHAPTER 34

AND the LORD spoke to Moses, saying,

2 Command the children of Israel and say to them, When you enter the land of Canaan (this is the land which shall be divided to you for an inheritance, even the land of Canaan with its territories),

3 Then your south boundary shall be from the wilderness of Zin along by the border of Edom, and your southern border shall be from the end of the salt sea eastward;

4 And your boundary shall turn from the south to the ascent of Sepharvim, and pass on to Zin; and the limits thereof shall be from the south of Rakim-gia, and shall go on to Hazar-addar, and pass on to Azmon;

5 And the boundary shall turn from Azmon to the river of Egypt, and the limits thereof shall be at the sea.

6 And as for the western border, you shall have the Great Sea and its coasts; this shall be your western border.

7 And this shall be your northern border: from the Great Sea you shall mark out for you a boundary to mount Hor;

8 From mount Hor you shall mark out the boundary to the entrance of Hamath; and the limits of the border shall be at Zedad;

9 ¶And the border shall go on to Ziphron, and its end shall be at Hazar-enan; these shall be your northern boundaries.

10 And you shall mark out your eastern boundary from Hazar-enan to Shepham;

11 And the boundary shall go down from Shepham to Diblath, on the east side of Ain; and the boundary shall descend and shall reach to the side of the sea of Chinnereth eastward;

12 And the border shall go down to the Jordan, and its limits shall be at the salt sea; this shall be your land with the borders thereof round about.

13 And Moses commanded the children of Israel, saying, This is the land which you shall divide by lots, which the LORD has commanded to give to the nine tribes, and to the half tribe;

14 For the tribe of the children of Reuben according to the house of their fathers, and the tribe of the children of Gad according to the house of their fathers, and the half tribe of Manasseh, have received their inheritance;

15 The two tribes and the half tribe have received their inheritance on this side of the Jordan near Jericho eastward, toward the sunrise.

16 And the LORD spoke to Moses, saying,

17 These are the names of the men who shall divide the land to you for an inheritance: Eleazar the priest and Joshua the son of Nun.

18 And you shall take one prince of every tribe to divide the land to you.

19 And these are the names of the chiefs: of the tribe of Judah, Caleb the son of Jophaniah.

20 Of the tribe of Simeon, Shelmuel the son of Ammihud.

21 Of the tribe of Benjamin, Eldad the son of Chislon.

22 Of the tribe of Dan, Bakki the son of Jogli.

23 Of the tribe of Joseph, of the tribe of Manasseh, Nahlael the son of Ephod.

24 Of the tribe of Ephraim, Kemuel the son of Shiptan.

25 Of the tribe of Zebulun, Elizaphan the son of Parnach.

26 Of the tribe of Issachar, Petael the son of Azzor.

27 Of the tribe of Asher, Ahihud the son of Shelomi.

28 Of the tribe of Naphtali, Pedahel the son of Ammihud.

29 These are they whom the LORD commanded to divide the inheritance to the children of Israel in the land of Canaan.

CHAPTER 35

THE LORD spoke to Moses in the plains of Moab by the Jordan near Jericho, saying,

2 Command the children of Israel that they give to the Levites of the inheritance of their possession cities to dwell in; and they shall give also to the Levites the suburbs of the cities round about them.

3 And the cities they shall have to dwell in; and their suburbs shall be for their cattle and for their herds and for all their beasts.

4 And the suburbs of the cities which you shall give to the Levites shall reach from the wall of the city and outward a thousand cubits round about.

5 And you shall measure from outside the city on the east side two thousand cubits, and on the south side two thousand cubits, and on the west side two thousand cubits, and on the north side two thousand cubits; and the city shall be in the midst; this shall be to them the suburbs of the cities.

6 And among the cities which you shall give to the Levites, six cities

shall be set aside for you for refuge, that the manslayer who had slain his neighbor without intent may flee thither; and to them you shall add forty-two other cities.

7 So all the cities which you shall give to the Levites shall be forty-eight cities in all, together with their suburbs.

8 And with regard to the cities which you shall give of the inheritance of the children of Israel: from those that have many you shall take many; but from those that have few you shall take few; every one shall give of his cities to the Levites in proportion to the inheritance which he inherits.

9 ¶And the LORD spoke to Moses, saying,

10 Speak to the children of Israel and say to them, When you cross the Jordan into the land of Canaan,

11 Then you shall select for yourselves cities to be cities of refuge for you; that the person who kills someone unawares may flee there.

12 And they shall be to you cities for refuge from the avenger, that the manslayer may not be killed until he stand before the congregation in judgment.

13 And of these cities which you shall give, six cities shall you have for refuge.

14 You shall give three cities on this side of the Jordan, and three cities you shall give in the land of Canaan, which shall be cities of refuge.

15 These six cities shall be for refuge, both for the children of Israel and for the proselytes and for the sojourner among them; that every one who kills any person unawares may flee there.

16 But if he struck him with an instrument of iron, so that he might die, and he did die, he is a murderer; the murderer shall surely be put to death.

17 And if he struck him with a stone in the hand, so that he might die, and he did die, he is a murderer; the murderer shall surely be put to death.

18 Or if he struck him with an instrument of wood by hand, so that he might die, and he did die, he is a murderer; the murderer shall surely be put to death.

19 The avenger of blood himself shall slay the murderer when he meets him.

20 But if he wound him because of hatred, or shoot an arrow at him by lying in wait, that he might die, he is a murderer;

21 Or in enmity smite him with his hand, that he might die, and he did die, the murderer shall surely be put to death; the avenger of the blood himself shall slay the murderer when he meets him.

22 But if he thrust him suddenly without enmity, or have cast upon him anything without lying in wait,

23 Or with any stone with which a man may die, without seeing him when he cast it upon him, and he died, and was not his enemy, neither sought his harm;

24 Then the congregation shall judge between the slayer and the avenger of the blood according to these judgments;

25 And the congregation shall deliver the slayer from the hand of the avenger of blood, and the congregation shall send him to the city of refuge, to which he had fled; and he shall dwell in it until the death of the high priest, who was anointed with the holy oil.

26 But if the slayer shall at any time go outside the bounds of the city of his refuge, to which he has fled;

27 And the avenger of the blood find him outside the bounds of the city of his refuge, and the avenger of the blood kill the slayer; he shall not be guilty of blood;

28 Because he should have remained in the city of his refuge until the death of the high priest; but after the death of the high priest the slayer shall return to the land of his possession.

29 So these things shall be for a statute of judgment to you throughout your generations in all of your dwellings.

30 Whosoever kills any person, the

murderer shall be put to death on the testimony of witnesses; but just one witness shall not testify against any person that he may be put to death.

31 Moreover you shall not accept a bribe for the life of a slayer, who is guilty of death; but he shall be surely put to death.

32 And you shall not take a bribe that he may flee to the city of refuge, that he should come again to dwell in the land, until the death of the high priest.

33 So you shall not pollute the land in which you live; for blood defiles the land; and the land in which blood is shed cannot be cleansed except by the shedding of the blood of him who shed it.

34 Defile not therefore the land in which you dwell, and wherein I dwell; for I the LORD dwell among the children of Israel.

CHAPTER 36

THEN the chief fathers of the families of the children of Gilead, the son of Machir, the son of Manasseh, the son of Joseph, came near, and spoke before Moses and before Eleazar the priest and before the princes of the congregation, the chief fathers of the children of Israel;

2 And they said, The LORD commanded our lord to give the land for an inheritance by lot to the children of Israel: and our lord was commanded by the LORD to give the inheritance of Zelophehad our brother to his daughters.

3 And if they be married to any of the sons of the other tribes of the children of Israel, then shall their inheritance be taken from the inheritance of their fathers, and shall be added to the inheritance of the tribe into which they married; so shall it be taken from the lot of our inheritance.

4 And when the jubilee year of the children of Israel shall come, then shall their inheritance be added to the inheritance of the tribes into which they married; so shall their inheritance be taken away from the inheritance of the tribe of their fathers.

5 And Moses commanded the children of Israel according to the word of the LORD, saying, The tribe of the sons of Joseph has said well.

6 This is the thing which the LORD has commanded concerning the daughters of Zelophehad, saying, Let them marry whom they think best; but only within the family of the tribe of their father shall they marry,

7 So that no inheritance of the children of Israel shall be transferred from one tribe to another tribe; for every one of the children of Israel shall cleave to the inheritance of the tribe of his father.

8 And every daughter who possesses an inheritance in any tribe of the children of Israel shall be wife to one of the family of the tribe of her father, that the children of Israel may inherit every man the inheritance of his fathers.

9 Neither shall the inheritance be transferred from one tribe to another; but every one of the tribes of the children of Israel shall cleave to his own inheritance.

10 Just as the LORD had commanded Moses, so did the daughters of Zelophehad;

11 For Mahlah, Tirzah, Hagla, Milcah, and Joah, the daughters of Zelophehad, were married to the sons of their father's brothers;

12 And they were married into the families of the sons of Manasseh the son of Joseph; and their inheritance remained in the tribe of the family of their father.

13 These are the commandments and the judgments which the LORD commanded by the hand of Moses concerning the children of Israel in the plains of Moab by the Jordan near Jericho.

THE FIFTH BOOK OF MOSES, CALLED

DEUTERONOMY

CHAPTER 1

THESE are the words which Moses spoke to all Israel beyond the Jordan in the wilderness, in the low desert plain opposite the Red Sea, between Paran and Tophel and Lebanon and Hazeroth and Dizahab.

2 (There are eleven days' journey from Horeb to mount Seir to Rakimgia.)

3 And it came to pass in the fortieth year, in the eleventh month, on the first day of the month, that Moses spoke to the children of Israel according to all that the LORD had given him in commandment concerning them;

4 After he had slain Sihon the king of the Amorites, who dwelt in Heshbon, and Og the king of Mathnin, who dwelt in Astaroth and in Erdei,

5 Beyond the Jordan, in the land of Moab; Moses began to explain this law, saying,

6 The LORD our God said to us in Horeb, You have dwelt long enough in this mountain;

7 Turn and set out on your journey, and go to the mountain of the Amorites, and to all the places round about it, in the low desert plain, in the mountain, in the lowland and in the south and by the sea side, to the land of the Canaanites, and to Lebanon, as far as the great river, the river Euphrates.

8 Behold, I have given you the land before you; go in and possess the land which the LORD swore to your fathers, Abraham, Isaac, and Jacob, to give to them and to their descendants after them.

9 ¶And I said to you at that time, I am not able to bear you myself alone;

10 The LORD your God has multiplied you, and behold, you are this day as the stars of heaven in multitude.

11 (May the LORD God of your fathers make you a thousand times as many more as you are, and bless you, as he has promised you!)

12 How can I myself bear alone your encumbrance and your burden and your strife?

13 Choose for yourselves wise men, who have understanding and are renowned among your tribes, and I will make them chiefs over you.

14 And you answered and said to me, The thing that you have spoken is good for us to do.

15 So I took the chiefs of your tribes, wise men and renowned, and made them chieftains over you, commanders over thousands and captains over hundreds and officers over fifty and officers over ten and scribes for your tribes.

16 And I charged your judges at that time, saying, Hear the causes between your brethren, and judge righteously between a man and his brother, and the stranger that is with him.

17 You shall not be partial to persons in judgment; but you shall hear the small as well as the great; you shall not be afraid of the face of man, for the judgment is God's; and the cause that is too hard for you, bring it to me, and I will hear it.

18 And I commanded you at that time all the things that you should do.

19 ¶And when we journeyed from Horeb, we went through all that great and terrible wilderness, which you saw by the way of the mountain of

202

the Amorites, as the LORD our God commanded us; and we came as far as Rakim-gia.

20 And I said to you, You have come to the mountain of the Amorites, which the LORD our God has given us.

21 Behold, the LORD your God has given the land before you; go up and possess it, as the LORD God of your fathers has said to you; fear not, neither be terrified.

22 ¶Then all of you came near to me and said, Let us send men before us, and they shall spy out the land for us, and bring us word again and show us the way by which we must go up and the cities into which we shall come.

23 And the saying pleased me well; and I took twelve men of you, one man of each tribe;

24 And they turned and went up into the mountain, and came as far as the valley of Segola, and spied out the land.

25 And they took some of the fruit of the land in their hands, and brought it down to us, and they brought us word again and said to us, It is a good land which the LORD our God does give to us.

26 But in spite of this, you would not go up, but rebelled against the commandment of the LORD your God;

27 And you murmured in your tents and said, It is because the LORD hated us that he has brought us forth out of the land of Egypt, to deliver us into the hand of the Amorites, to destroy us.

28 Whither shall we go up? Our brethren have discouraged our heart, saying, The people are greater and taller than we; the cities are great and walled up to heaven; and moreover we have seen the sons of giants there.

29 Then I said to you, Fear not, neither tremble of them.

30 The LORD your God, who goes before you, shall fight for you, just as he did for you in Egypt before your eyes;

31 And in the wilderness, where you saw how the LORD your God nourished you, just as a man nourishes

his son, in all the way that you went, until you came to this place.

32 Yet in this thing you did not believe the LORD your God,

33 Who went in the way before you to prepare a place for you to encamp in it, in fire by night to show you by what way you should go, and in a cloud by day.

34 And the LORD heard the voice of your complaining, and was angry, and swore, saying,

35 Surely there shall not one of these men of this evil generation see the good land which I swore to give to your fathers,

36 Except Caleb the son of Jophaniah; he shall see it, and to him will I give the land upon which he has trodden, and to his children, because he has wholly followed the LORD.

37 Also the LORD was angry with me on your account, saying, You also shall not go in thither.

38 But Joshua the son of Nun, who stands before you, he shall go in there; encourage him; for he shall cause Israel to inherit it.

39 Moreover your little ones, who you said would be a prey, and your children, who in that day had no knowledge between good and evil, shall go in there, and to them will I give it, and they shall possess it.

40 But as for you, turn you and take your journey into the wilderness by the way of the Red Sea.

41 Then you answered and said to me, We have sinned against the LORD our God, we will go up and fight, just as the LORD our God commanded us. And when you had girded on every man his weapons of war, you were stirred up to go up into the mountain.

42 And the LORD said to me, Say to them, You shall not go up, neither fight; for I am not among you; lest you be defeated before your enemies.

43 So I spoke to you; and you would not listen, and you rebelled against the commandment of the LORD, and went presumptuously up into the mountain.

44 And the Amorites, who dwelt in that mountain, came out against you

and chased you as smoked-out bees do, and drove you away from Seir, as far as Hirmah.

45 Then you sat down and wept before the LORD; but the LORD would not hearken to your voice nor give ear to you.

46 So you remained in Rakim many days, according to the days that you remained there.

CHAPTER 2

THEN we turned, and journeyed into the wilderness by the way of the Red Sea, as the LORD spoke to me; and we circled mount Seir for many days.

2 And the LORD spoke to me, saying,

3 You have circled this mountain long enough; turn northward.

4 And command the people, saying, You are going to pass through the territory of your brethren the children of Esau, who dwell in Seir; and they shall be afraid of you; take heed to yourselves therefore;

5 Do not provoke them; for I will not give you a possession of their land, no, not so much as the breadth of a foot to tread on, because I have given mount Seir to Esau for a possession.

6 You may buy grain from them for money, that you may eat; and you may also buy water from them for money, that you may drink.

7 For the LORD your God has blessed you in all the work of your hand; he knows how to lead you through this great wilderness; behold, these forty years the LORD your God has been with you; you have lacked nothing.

8 And when we passed by from our brethren the children of Esau, who dwelt in Seir, and from the way of the desert plain, from Elath and from Ezion-gaber we turned and passed by the way of the wilderness of Moab.

9 And the LORD said to me, Do not distress the Moabites, neither provoke them to battle; for I will not give you of their land for a possession; because I have given it to the children of Lot for an inheritance.

10 The Amney dwelt in it formerly, a people great and many and tall, like giants;

11 For they were giants, and also were accounted as giants; but the Moabites call them Amney.

12 The Horites also dwelt formerly in Seir; but the children of Esau possessed them and destroyed them from before them and settled in their land, as Israel did to the land of his possession, which the LORD gave to them.

13 Now rise up and go over the brook Zered. So we went over the brook Zered.

14 And the time in which we journeyed from Rakim-gia until we crossed the brook Zered was thirty-eight years; until all the generation of the men of war had perished from the midst of the camp, as the LORD had sworn to them.

15 For indeed the hand of the LORD was also against them, to destroy them from the midst of the camp until they were consumed.

16 ¶So it came to pass, when all the men of war were consumed and dead from among the people,

17 The LORD spoke to me, saying,

18 You are to pass over through the border of Moab and Ad this day;

19 And when you come near the territory of the children of Ammon, do not oppress them nor provoke them; for I will not give you of the land of the children of Ammon any possession, because I have given it to the children of Lot for a possession.

20 (That also was accounted a land of giants; giants dwelt in it formerly; and the Ammonites call them Zamzumins;

21 A people great and many and tall, like giants; but the LORD destroyed them from before them; and they succeeded them, and dwelt in their land,

22 As the children of Esau did, who dwelt in Seir when they destroyed the Horites from before them, and they succeeded them and settled in their land even to this day;

23 And the Avites who dwelt in Hazerim, as far as Azzah, the Caphedokian, who came out of Caphedoki,

destroyed them and dwelt in their land.)

24 ¶Rise up, take your journey, and cross over the river Arnon; behold, I have delivered into your hand Sihon the king of Heshbon, the Amorite, and his land; begin to destroy him, and provoke him to battle.

25 This day I will begin to put the dread of you and the fear of you upon the peoples that are under the whole heaven, who shall hear report of you, and shall tremble and be in anguish because of you.

26 ¶And I sent messengers from the wilderness of Kermoth to Sihon king of Heshbon with words of peace, saying,

27 Let me pass through your land; I will go along by the highway; I will neither turn to the right hand nor to the left.

28 You shall sell me grain for money, that I may eat; and sell me water for money, that I may drink; only let me pass through on foot;

29 Just as the children of Esau who dwell in Seir and the Moabites who dwell in Ad did for me; until I shall cross the Jordan into the land which the LORD our God gives us.

30 But Sihon king of Heshbon would not let us pass through his territory; for the LORD your God hardened his spirit and made his heart obstinate, that he might deliver him into your hands, as it is this day.

31 And the LORD said to me, Behold, I have begun to deliver Sihon and his land into your hands; begin to destroy him, and to possess his land.

32 Then Sihon came out against us, he and all his people, to fight at Jahaz.

33 And the LORD our God delivered him to us; and we smote him and his sons and all his people.

34 And we conquered all his cities at that time, and utterly destroyed all the towns; even the women and the little ones, we left none to remain;

35 Only the cattle we took for a prey to ourselves, and the spoil of the cities which we conquered.

36 From Adoer, which is by the brink of the river Arnon, and from the city that is in the valley, as far as Gilead, there was not one city too strong for us; the LORD our God delivered all to us;

37 Only to the land of the children of Ammon we did not draw near, nor to all that is by the river Jabbok, nor to the cities that are in the mountains, nor to whatever the LORD our God forbade us.

CHAPTER 3

THEN we turned and went up the way to Mathnin; and Og the king of Mathnin came out against us, he and all his people, to battle at Erdei.

2 And the LORD said to me, Do not fear him; for I have delivered him, and all his people and his land into your hand; and you shall do to him as you did to Sihon king of the Amorites, who dwelt in Heshbon.

3 So the LORD our God delivered into our hand Og also, the king of Mathnin, and all his people; and we smote him until none was left to him surviving.

4 And we captured all his cities at that time, and we left not a city which we did not take from them, sixty cities, all the region of Argob, the kingdom of Og in Mathnin.

5 All these cities were fenced with high walls, gates, and bars; besides the suburban towns a great many.

6 And we utterly destroyed them, as we did to Sihon the king of Heshbon, for we utterly destroyed all his cities, even the women and the little ones.

7 But all the cattle and the spoil of the cities, we took for a prey to ourselves.

8 And we took at that time out of the hand of the two kings of the Amorites the land that was on this side of the Jordan, from the river Arnon to mount Hermon

9 (The Sidonians call Hermon Sirion, and the Amorites call it Senir),

10 All the cities of the plain and all Gilead and all Mathnin as far as Salcah and Erdei, all the cities of the kingdom of Og in Mathnin.

11 For only Og the king of Mathnin

15

remained of the remnant of the giants; behold, his bedstead was a bedstead of iron; and behold, it is in Rabbath of the children of Ammon, nine cubits long and four cubits broad, according to the measure of the cubit of giants.

12 And this land we possessed at that time, from Adoer, which is by the river of Arnon; and half of mount Gilead, and its cities, I gave to the Reubenites and to the Gadites.

13 And the rest of Gilead, and all Mathnin, being the kingdom of Og, I gave to the half tribe of Manasseh; all the region of Argob, with all Mathnin, which is called the land of giants.

14 Jair the son of Manasseh took for himself all the region of Argob as far as the border of Geshur and Maachath; and called them after his own name, Mathnin and Caproney Jair, to this day.

15 To Machir I gave Gilead.

16 And to the Reubenites and to the Gadites I gave the region from Gilead as far as the valley of Arnon, and the inside of the valley, and its border as far as the river Jabbok, which is the border of the children of Ammon;

17 Along with the desert plain, and the Jordan, and the territory thereof, from Chinnereth as far as the sea of Arabah, the Salt Sea, which lies at the foot of Ashdod and Pisgah which is in the hilly country eastward.

18 ¶And I commanded you at that time, saying, The LORD your God has given you this land to possess it; you shall pass over armed before your brethren the children of Israel, all of you who are valiant men of war.

19 But your wives and your little ones and your cattle (for I know that you have much cattle) shall remain in your cities which I have given you

20 Until the LORD have given rest to your brethren, as he has given to you, and until they also possess the land which the LORD your God is giving them beyond the Jordan; and then shall you return every man to the possession which I have given you.

21 ¶And I commanded Joshua at that time, saying, Your eyes have seen all that the LORD your God has done to these two kings; so shall the LORD do to all these kingdoms through which you are going.

22 You shall not fear them; for it is the LORD your God who is fighting for you.

23 And I besought the LORD at that time, saying,

24 I beseech thee O LORD God, thou who hast begun to show thy servant thy greatness, and thy mighty hand, and thy outstretched arm (for what god is there in heaven or on earth who can do according to thy works and according to thy mighty deeds?),

25 I pray thee, let me now go over and see the good land that is beyond the Jordan, that goodly mountain, and Lebanon.

26 But the LORD was wroth with me on your account, and would not hearken to me; and the LORD said to me, Let it suffice for you; speak no more before me of this matter.

27 Go up to the top of the hill (Pisgah) and lift up your eyes eastward and westward and northward and southward, and behold it with your eyes; for you shall not cross this Jordan.

28 But charge Joshua, and encourage him, and strengthen him; for he shall go over before this people, and he shall cause them to inherit the land which you shall see.

29 So we dwelt in the valley opposite Beth-peor.

CHAPTER 4

NOW therefore hearken, O Israel, to the law and to the judgments which I teach you this day, to do them, that you may live and go in and possess the land which the LORD the God of your fathers gives you.

2 You shall not add to the commandment which I command you, neither shall you take from it, but you must keep the commandments of the LORD your God which I command you.

3 Your eyes have seen what the LORD did because of Baal-peor; for

every man who followed Baal-peor, the LORD your God has destroyed him from among you.

4 But you who did cleave to the LORD your God are all alive this day.

5 Behold, I have taught you statutes and judgments, as the LORD my God has commanded me, that you should do them in the land which you are entering, to possess it.

6 And you shall keep them, therefore, and do them; for this is your wisdom and your understanding in the sight of the nations which shall hear all these statutes, and will say, Surely this great nation is a wise and understanding people.

7 For what nation is there so great, whose god is so near to it as the LORD our God is in all things that we call upon him for?

8 And what nation is there so great, that has laws and judgments so righteous as all this law which I set before you this day?

9 Only take heed for yourselves, and keep your soul diligently, lest you forget the things which your eyes have seen, and lest they depart from your heart all the days of your life; but declare them to your children and your children's children.

10 The day that you stood before the LORD your God in Horeb, when the LORD said to me, Gather the people together before me, and I will make them hear my words, that they may learn to worship me all the days that they shall live upon the earth, and that they may teach their children.

11 And you came near and stood at the foot of the mountain; and the mountain burned with fire to the midst of heaven, with darkness, clouds, and thick darkness.

12 And the LORD spoke to you on the mountain out of the midst of the fire; you heard the sound of the words, but saw no form; there was only a voice.

13 And he declared to you his covenant, which he commanded you to perform, even ten commandments; and he wrote them upon two tablets of stone.

14 ¶And the LORD commanded me at that time to teach you statutes and judgments, that you might do them in the land into which you are going to possess it.

15 Take therefore good heed to yourselves; for you saw no manner of form on the day that the LORD spoke to you at Horeb out of the midst of the fire;

16 Lest you corrupt yourselves, and make for yourselves images and the forms of any figure, the likeness of male or female,

17 The likeness of any beast that is on the earth, the likeness of any winged fowl that flies in the air,

18 The likeness of anything that creeps on the ground, the likeness of any fish that is in the waters beneath the earth;

19 And lest you lift up your eyes to heaven, and when you see the sun and the moon, and the stars and all the host of heaven, should go astray and worship them and serve those things which the LORD your God has provided for all the peoples under heaven.

20 But the LORD has taken you, and brought you forth out of the iron furnace, even out of Egypt, to be to him a people and an inheritance, as you are this day.

21 Furthermore the LORD was angry with me on your account, and swore that I should not cross this Jordan, and that I should not enter the good land which the LORD your God gives you for an inheritance;

22 Because I must die in this land, I must not cross this Jordan; but you shall cross it and possess that good land.

23 Take heed to yourselves, lest you forget the covenant of the LORD your God, which he made with you, and corrupt yourselves, and make for yourselves images, or the likeness of anything, which the LORD your God has forbidden you.

24 For the LORD your God is a consuming fire, a zealous God.

25 ¶When you shall beget children and children's children, and you shall have remained long in the land, and

shall corrupt yourselves and make images or the likeness of any thing, and shall do evil in the sight of the LORD your God and provoke him to anger;

26 I call heaven and earth to witness against you this day, that you shall soon utterly perish from off the land which you are going across the Jordan to possess; you shall not live long upon it, but shall utterly be destroyed.

27 And the LORD shall scatter you among the nations, and you shall be left few in number among the nations where the LORD your God shall scatter you.

28 And there you shall serve gods, the work of men's hands, of wood and stone, which neither see nor hear nor eat nor smell.

29 But if from there you shall seek the LORD your God, you shall find him, if you search for him with all your heart and with all your soul.

30 When you are in tribulation, and all these things are come upon you in the latter days, if you return to the LORD your God and shall be obedient to his voice

31 (For the LORD your God is a merciful God), he will not destroy you, neither forsake you, nor forget the covenant which he swore to your fathers.

32 For ask now about the days that are past, which were before you, since the day that God created man upon the earth, and ask from one end of heaven to the other whether there has been any such thing as this great thing is, or has been heard like it.

33 Did any other people ever hear the voice of God speaking out of the midst of the fire, as you have heard, and live?

34 Or have they tried out the God who went forth and took for himself a nation from the midst of another nation, by trials, by signs and by wonders and by war and by a mighty hand and by a stretched out arm and by great visions, according to all that the LORD your God did to the Egyptians before your eyes?

35 You saw and knew that the LORD is God; there is none else besides him.

36 Out of heaven he made you to hear his voice, that he might teach you; and upon earth he showed you his great fire; he made you to hear his words out of the midst of the fire.

37 And because he loved your fathers, therefore he chose their descendants after them, and brought you out of Egypt with his own person, with a mighty power;

38 To destroy nations from before you, who are greater and mightier than you are, to bring you in, to give you their land for an inheritance, as it is this day.

39 Know therefore this day, and cause your heart to repent, for it is the LORD who is God in heaven above and upon the earth beneath; there is none else besides him.

40 You must keep therefore his statutes and his commandments, which I command you this day, that it may be well with you and with your children after you, and that you may prolong your days in the land which the LORD your God gives you for ever.

41 ¶Then Moses set apart three cities on this side of the Jordan toward the rising sun;

42 That the slayer might flee there, who might kill his neighbor unintentionally, and hated him not in time past; and that by fleeing to one of these cities he might live;

43 Namely, Bezer in the wilderness, in the plain country, of the Reubenites; and Ramath in Gilead, of the Gadites; and Golan in Mathnin, of the Manassites.

44 ¶This is the law which Moses set before the children of Israel;

45 These are the testimonies, the statutes, and the judgments which Moses spoke to the children of Israel after they came forth out of Egypt,

46 On this side of the Jordan, in the valley over against Beth-peor, in the land of Sihon king of the Amorites, who dwelt in Heshbon, whom Moses and the children of Israel slew when they came out of Egypt;

47 And they possessed his land, and the land of Og king of Mathnin, two

kings of the Amorites, who were on this side of Jordan toward the rising sun;

48 From Adoer, which is on the edge of the river Arnon, as far as mount Serion, which is Hermon,

49 And all the low desert on this side of Jordan eastward, as far as the sea of the plain which is at the foot of Ashdod and Pisgah.

CHAPTER 5

AND Moses called all Israel, and said to them, Hear, O Israel, the statutes and judgments which I speak in your presence this day, that you may learn them, and keep and do them.

2 The LORD our God made a covenant with us in Horeb.

3 It was not with our fathers that the LORD made this covenant, but with us, even us, who are all of us here alive this day.

4 The LORD talked with you face to face in the mountain out of the midst of the fire,

5 (I stood between the LORD and you at that time, to declare to you the words of the LORD your God; for you were afraid because of the fire, and did not go up into the mountain), saying,

6 ¶I am the LORD your God, who brought you out of the land of Egypt, from the house of bondage.

7 You shall have no other gods besides me.

8 You shall not make for yourself any graven image or any likeness of anything that is in heaven above, or that is on the earth beneath, or that is in the waters under the earth;

9 You shall not worship them, nor serve them; for I the LORD your God am a zealous God, visiting the iniquities of the fathers upon the children to the third and fourth generation of those who hate me,

10 But showing mercy to thousands of generations of those who love me and keep my commandments.

11 You shall not take an oath by the name of the LORD your God in vain; for the LORD will not hold him guiltless who takes an oath by his name in vain.

12 Keep the sabbath day and sanctify it, as the LORD your God has commanded you.

13 Six days you shall labor, and do all your work;

14 But the seventh day is the sabbath to the LORD your God; in it you shall not do any work, you, nor your son, nor your daughter, nor your manservant, nor your maidservant, nor your ox, nor your ass, nor any of your cattle, nor the sojourner that is in your towns; that your manservant and your maidservant may rest as well as you.

15 And remember that you were a servant in the land of Egypt, and that the LORD your God brought you out thence by a mighty hand and by a stretched out arm; therefore the LORD your God has commanded you to keep the sabbath day.

16 ¶Honor your father and your mother, as the LORD your God has commanded you; that your days may be prolonged, and that it may go well with you, in the land which the LORD your God gives you.

17 You shall not kill.

18 You shall not commit adultery.

19 You shall not steal.

20 You shall not bear false witness against your neighbor.

21 You shall not covet your neighbor's wife, neither shall you covet your neighbor's house, nor his field, nor his vineyard, nor his manservant, nor his maidservant, nor his ox, nor his ass, nor anything that is your neighbor's.

22 ¶These words the LORD spoke to all the assembly on the mountain out of the midst of the fire, in the cloud and in the thick darkness, with a loud voice which cannot be measured. And he wrote them upon two tablets of stone, and gave them to me.

23 And when you heard the voice out of the midst of the darkness and saw the mountain burning with fire, you came near to me, all the heads of your tribes and your elders;

24 And you said, Behold, the LORD our God has shown us his glory and

his greatness, and we have heard his voice out of the midst of the fire; we have seen this day that God does talk with man, and that he lives.

25 Now therefore why should we die? For this great fire will consume us; if we hear the voice of the LORD our God any more, then we shall die.

26 For who is there of all flesh, that has heard the voice of the living God speaking out of the midst of the fire, as we have, and lived?

27 Go near and hear all that the LORD our God shall say; and speak to us all that the LORD our God shall speak to you; and we will hear it and do it.

28 And the LORD heard the voice of your words, when you spoke to me; and the LORD said to me, I have heard the voice of the people and the words which they have spoken to you; they have well said all that they have spoken.

29 O that there were such a heart in them, to worship, and keep all my commandments always, that it might be well with them and with their children for ever!

30 Go and say to them, Return to your tents.

31 But as for you, stand here before me, and I will tell you all my commandments and my statutes and my judgments, which you shall teach them, that they may do them in the land which I give them to possess.

32 You must observe and do therefore as the LORD your God has commanded you; you shall not turn aside to the right hand or to the left.

33 You shall walk in all the ways which the LORD your God has commanded you, that you may live, and that it may be well with you, and that you may prolong your days in the land which you shall possess.

CHAPTER 6

NOW these are the commandments, the statutes, and the judgments which the LORD your God commanded me to teach you, that you shall do them in the land into which you are going to possess it;

2 That you may fear the LORD

your God, to keep all his commandments and his statutes and his judgments, which I commanded you, this day, you and your son and your son's son, all the days of your life; and that your days may be prolonged.

3 ¶Hear therefore, O Israel, and observe and do them; that it may be well with you, and that you may increase greatly; for the LORD God of your fathers has promised you that he will give you a land that flows with milk and honey.

4 Hear, O Israel: the LORD our God is one LORD;

5 And you shall love the LORD your God with all your heart and with all your soul and with all your might.

6 And these words which I command you this day shall be in your heart:

7 And you shall repeat them diligently to your children, and shall talk of them when you sit in your house and when you walk by the way and when you lie down and when you rise up.

8 And you shall bind them for a sign upon your hand, and they shall be as a token between your eyes.

9 And you shall write them upon the doorposts of your house and on your gates.

10 And it shall be, when the LORD your God shall have brought you into the land which he swore to your fathers, to Abraham, to Isaac, and to Jacob, to give you great and goodly cities, which you did not build,

11 And houses full of all good things, which you did not fill, and cisterns digged, which you did not dig, and vineyards and olive trees, which you did not plant; when you shall eat and be full;

12 Then take heed lest you forget the LORD your God, who brought you forth out of the land of Egypt, from the house of bondage.

13 You shall reverence the LORD your God, and serve him, and shall swear by his name.

14 You shall not go after other gods, the gods of the people who are round about you,

15 (For the LORD your God is a

zealous God among you) lest the anger of the LORD your God be kindled against you, and he destroy you from off the face of the earth.

16 ¶You shall not tempt the LORD your God, as you tempted him with temptations.

17 You shall diligently keep the commandments of the LORD your God and his testimonies and his statutes, which he has commanded you.

18 And you shall do that which is good and right in the sight of the LORD; that it may be well with you, and that you may go in and possess the good land which the LORD swore to your fathers,

19 And defeat all your enemies from before you, as the LORD has spoken.

20 And when your son asks you in time to come, saying, What mean the testimonies and the statutes and the judgments which the LORD our God has commanded you?

21 Then you shall say to your son, We were Pharaoh's slaves in Egypt; and the LORD brought us out of Egypt with a mighty hand;

22 And the LORD wrought signs and great wonders, and plagues in Egypt against Pharaoh and against all his army, before our eyes;

23 And the LORD brought us out from there, that he might bring us in and give us the land which he swore to our fathers.

24 And the LORD commanded us to do all these statutes, to revere the LORD our God, for our good always, that he might preserve us alive, as it is at this day.

25 And it shall be our righteousness, if we observe and do all these commandments before the LORD our God, as he has commanded us.

CHAPTER 7

WHEN the LORD your God shall bring you into the land which you are entering to possess, and has destroyed many nations before you, the Hittites, the Girgasites, the Amorites, the Canaanites, the Perizzites, the Hivites, and the Jebusites, seven nations greater and mightier than yourselves;

2 And when the LORD your God shall deliver them before you, and you shall defeat them; then you shall utterly destroy them; you shall make no covenant with them, nor show mercy to them;

3 Neither shall you make marriages with them; you shall not give your daughters to their sons, nor take their daughters for your sons,

4 That they may not turn away your sons from following me, and serve other gods; and then the anger of the LORD would kindle against you and destroy you quickly.

5 But thus shall you deal with them: you shall destroy their altars and break down their statues and cut down their ornaments and burn their graven images with fire.

6 For you are a holy people to the LORD your God; the LORD your God has chosen you to be a beloved people to himself, above all people that are upon the face of the earth.

7 It was not because you were more in number than any other peoples that the LORD was delighted in you and chose you, for you were the fewest of all peoples;

8 But it was because the LORD loved you, and because he would keep the oaths which he had sworn to your fathers, that the LORD brought you out with a mighty hand, and delivered you out of the house of bondage from the hand of Pharaoh king of Egypt,

9 That you may know therefore that the LORD your God, he is God, the faithful God, who keeps covenant and mercy with those that love him and keep his commandments to a thousand generations;

10 And repays those that hate him during their lifetime; he requites them that he may destroy them; he shall not be slack to those that hate him, but he repays them during their lifetime.

11 You shall therefore keep the commandments and the statutes and the judgments which I command you this day, and do them.

12 ¶Wherefore if you hearken to these judgments, and keep them and do them, the LORD your God shall keep with you the covenant and the mercy which he swore to your fathers;

13 And he will love you and bless you and multiply you; he will also bless the fruit of your womb and the fruit of your land, your grain and your wine and your oil, the increase of your cattle and the flocks of your sheep, in the land which he swore to your fathers to give you.

14 You shall be blessed above all peoples; there shall not be male or female barren among you or among your cattle.

15 And the LORD will take away from you all sickness; and all evil diseases of the Egyptians, which you know, he will not bring upon you; but will bring them upon your enemies.

16 And you shall consume all the peoples that the LORD your God shall deliver to you; your eye shall have no pity upon them; neither shall you serve their gods; for they are a snare to you.

17 If you shall say in your heart, These nations are greater than I; how will I be able to destroy them?

18 You shall not be afraid of them; but you shall remember what the LORD your God did to Pharaoh and to all Egypt;

19 The great trials which your eyes saw, the signs, the wonders, the mighty hand, and the outstretched arm, whereby the LORD your God brought you out; so shall the LORD your God do to all the peoples of whom you are afraid.

20 Moreover the LORD your God will send raiders among them, until they that are left and hide themselves from you, are destroyed.

21 You shall not be afraid of them, for the LORD your God is among you, a great and terrible God.

22 And the LORD your God will destroy those nations from before you little by little; you will not be able to destroy them quickly, lest the wild beasts increase upon you.

23 But the LORD your God shall deliver them to you, and shall smite them with a great destruction, until they are destroyed.

24 And he shall deliver their kings into your hands, and you shall destroy their name from under heaven; there shall no man be able to stand before you, until you have destroyed them.

25 The graven images of their gods you shall burn with fire; you shall not covet the silver or the gold that is on them, nor take it for yourselves, lest you become unclean with it; for it is an abomination before the LORD your God.

26 Neither shall you bring an abomination into your house, lest you be a cursed thing like it; but you shall utterly detest it, and you shall utterly abhor it; for it is a cursed thing.

CHAPTER 8

ALL the commandments which I command you this day you shall observe to do, that you may live and multiply, and go in and possess the land which the LORD swore to your fathers.

2 And you shall remember all the way which the LORD your God led you these forty years in the wilderness, that he might humble you, and prove you, to know what is in your heart, whether you would keep his commandments or not.

3 And he humbled you and suffered you to hunger and fed you with manna, which you did not know, neither did your fathers know; that he might make you to understand that man does not live by bread alone; but by everything that proceeds out of the mouth of the LORD does man live.

4 Your clothes did not wear out upon you, neither did your feet go bare during these forty years.

5 You must know in your heart that, as a man disciplines his son, so the LORD your God disciplines you.

6 Therefore you must keep the commandments of the LORD your God, to walk in his ways and fear him.

7 For the LORD your God brings you into a good land, a land of

brooks of water, of fountains and depths that spring out of valleys and mountains;

8 A land of wheat and barley, and of vines and fig trees and pomegranates; a land of olive trees, and of oil and honey;

9 A land wherein you shall eat bread without scarcity, you shall not lack anything in it; a land whose stones are iron, and out of whose mountains you may dig brass.

10 You shall eat and be full, and then you shall bless the LORD your God for the good land which he has given you.

11 Take heed, lest you forget the LORD your God, in not keeping his commandments and his judgments and his statutes, which I command you this day;

12 Lest when you have eaten and are full, and have built beautiful houses, and dwell in them;

13 And when your flocks and herds multiply, and your silver and gold are multiplied, and all that you have is multiplied;

14 Then your heart be lifted up, and you forget the LORD your God, who brought you forth out of the land of Egypt, from the house of bondage;

15 Who led you through the great and terrible wilderness, a place of fiery serpents and scorpions and droughts, a place where there was no water; who brought you forth water out of the flinty rock;

16 Who fed you in the wilderness with manna, which your fathers did not know, that he might humble you, and that he might prove you, to do you good at the end;

17 And you say in your heart, My power and the might of my hand have gotten me this wealth.

18 But you shall remember the LORD your God; for it is he who gives you power to get wealth, that he may establish his covenant which he swore to your fathers, as it is this day.

19 And if you do forget the LORD your God, and walk after other gods and serve them and worship them, I have testified against you this day that you shall surely perish.

20 As the nations which the LORD destroyed before you, so shall you perish if you are not obedient to the voice of the LORD your God.

CHAPTER 9

HEAR, O Israel: You are to cross the Jordan this day, to go in to destroy nations greater and mightier than yourselves, cities great and fenced up to heaven,

2 A people great and tall, the sons of giants, whom you know, and of whom you have heard it said, No man can stand up before the giants!

3 And that you may know therefore this day that the LORD your God is he who will go over before you; as a consuming fire he shall destroy them, and he shall defeat them before you; so that you shall rout them, and destroy them quickly, as the LORD has said to you.

4 Do not say in your heart, after the LORD your God has defeated them from before you, It is because of my righteousness that the LORD has brought me in to possess this land; but it is because of the wickedness of these nations that the LORD is destroying them from before you.

5 It is not because of your righteousness, or for the uprightness of your heart, that you are going in to possess their land; but it is because of the sins of these nations the LORD your God is destroying them from before you, and that he may perform the word which he swore to your fathers, Abraham, Isaac, and Jacob.

6 Know therefore, that it is not because of your righteousness that the LORD your God is giving you this good land to possess it; for you are a stiffnecked people.

7 ¶Remember, and forget not, how you provoked the LORD your God to wrath in the wilderness; from the day that you came out of Egypt until you came to this place, you have been rebellious against the LORD.

8 Also in Horeb you provoked the LORD to wrath, so the LORD was angry enough with you to have destroyed you.

9 When I went up on the mountain to receive the tablets of stone, the tablets of the covenant which the Lord made with you, and I abode on the mountain forty days and forty nights, I neither did eat bread nor drink water;

10 And the Lord gave me two tablets of stone, written with the finger of God; and on them were written all the words which the Lord had spoken with you in the mountain out of the midst of the fire on the day of the assembly.

11 And at the end of forty days and forty nights, the Lord gave me two tablets of stone, the tablets of the covenant.

12 And the Lord said to me, Arise and go down quickly from here; for your people whom you have brought forth out of Egypt have corrupted themselves; they have quickly turned aside out of the way which I commanded them; and they have made themselves a molten image.

13 Furthermore the Lord said to me, I have seen this people, and behold, it is a stiffnecked people:

14 Now let me alone, that I may destroy them, and blot out their name from under heaven; and I will make of you a nation mightier and greater than they.

15 So I turned and came down from the mountain, and the mountain was burning with fire and the two tablets of the covenant were in my two hands.

16 And I looked, and behold, you had sinned against the Lord your God, and had made to yourselves a molten calf; and you had turned aside quickly out of the way which the Lord your God had commanded you.

17 And I took the two tablets, and cast them out of my two hands, and broke them before your eyes.

18 Then I prayed before the Lord, as at the first, forty days and forty nights; I did neither eat bread nor drink water, because of all your sins which you sinned, in doing evil in the presence of the Lord, to provoke him to anger.

19 For I was afraid of the wrath and the anger wherewith the Lord was angry against you to destroy you. But the Lord hearkened to me at that time also.

20 And the Lord was angry enough with Aaron to have destroyed him; and I prayed for Aaron also the same time.

21 And I took the calf by which you sinned, which you had made, and burned it with fire, and ground it very small, until it was as fine as dust; and I threw the dust of it into the brook that flowed down out of the mountain.

22 And in heat, and in trials, and at the Kabrey di ragrigtha the people lusted for meat; you provoked the Lord to anger.

23 Likewise when the Lord sent you from Rakim-gia, and said to you, Go up and possess the land which I have given you; then you rebelled against the commandment of the Lord your God, and you did not believe him, nor hearken to his voice.

24 You have been rebellious against the Lord from the day that I knew you.

25 Thus I prayed before the Lord forty days and forty nights, because the Lord had said he would destroy you.

26 I prayed therefore before the Lord, and said, O Lord God, destroy not thy people and thy inheritance, whom thou hast saved through thy greatness, whom thou hast brought forth out of Egypt with a mighty hand.

27 But remember thy servants, Abraham, Isaac and Jacob; look not to the stubbornness of this people, nor to their wickedness, nor to their sins;

28 Lest the inhabitants of the land out of which thou didst bring them say, Because the Lord was not able to bring them into the land which he promised them, and because he hated them, he has brought them out to slay them in the wilderness.

29 Yet they are thy people and thy inheritance, whom thou broughtest out by thy mighty power and by thy outstretched arm.

CHAPTER 10

AT that time the LORD said to me, Hew two tablets of stone like the first, and come up to me on the mountain, and make yourself an ark of wood.

2 And I will write on the tablets the words that were on the first tablets which you broke, and you shall put them in the ark.

3 So I made an ark of shittim wood, and hewed two tablets of stone like the first, and went up on the mountain, having the two tablets in my hands.

4 And he wrote on the tablets, according to the first writing, the ten commandments, which the LORD spoke to you on the mountain out of the midst of the fire in the day of the assembly; and the LORD gave them to me.

5 And I turned and came down from the mountain, and put the tablets in the ark which I had made; and I left them in it, as the LORD commanded me.

6 ¶And the children of Israel took their journey from Beeroth of the children of Jaakan to Mosera; there Aaron died, and there he was buried, and Eleazar his son ministered in the priest's office in his stead.

7 From thence they journeyed to Gadgad; and from Gadgad to Jotbath, a land of brooks of waters.

8 ¶At that time the LORD set apart the tribe of Levi, to carry the ark of the covenant of the LORD, to stand before the LORD to minister to him, and to bless the name of the LORD, to this day.

9 Therefore Levi has no portion nor inheritance with his brethren; because the LORD is his inheritance, according as the LORD your God promised him.

10 And I stayed before the LORD on the mountain according to the first time, forty days and forty nights; and the LORD hearkened to me at that time also, and the LORD would not destroy you.

11 And the LORD said to me, Arise, take your journey before the people,

that they may go in and possess the land which I swore to their fathers to give to them.

12 ¶And now, Israel, what does the LORD your God require of you, but to revere the LORD your God, to walk in his ways, and to love him, and to serve the LORD your God with all your heart and with all your soul,

13 To keep the commandments of the LORD your God, and his statutes, which I command you this day for your good?

14 Behold, the heaven and the heaven of heavens belongs to the LORD your God, the earth also, with all that therein is.

15 Only the LORD had a delight in your fathers and he loved them, and he chose their descendants after them, even you above all peoples, as it is this day.

16 Circumcise therefore the foreskin of your heart,[1] and be no more stiff-necked.

17 For the LORD your God is he who is the God of gods, and the LORD of lords, a great God, a mighty and a terrible, who is never partial, nor takes bribes;

18 He does execute justice for the fatherless and the widows, and loves him who turns to him, and gives him food and clothing.

19 Love therefore those who turn to him; for you were sojourners in the land of Egypt.

20 You shall revere the LORD your God; him shall you serve, and to him shall you cleave, and swear by his name.

21 For he is your praise, and he is your God, who has done for you these great and wonderful things which your eyes have seen.

22 Your fathers went down to Egypt seventy persons; and now the LORD your God has made you as the stars of heaven in multitude.

CHAPTER 11

THEREFORE you shall love the LORD your God, and keep his precepts, his statutes, his judgments, and his commandments, always.

---

[1] Surrender your heart.

2 And know this day that I do not speak to your children who have not known and who have not seen the discipline of the LORD your God, his greatness, his mighty hand, and his outstretched arm,

3 And his signs, and his deeds, which he did in Egypt to Pharaoh the king of Egypt, and to all his land;

4 And what he did to the army of the Egyptians, to their horses and to their chariots and to their horsemen; how he made the water of the Red Sea to overflow them as they pursued after you, and how the LORD has destroyed them to this day;

5 And what he did to you in the wilderness, until you came into this place;

6 And what he did to Dathan and Abiram, the sons of Eliab, the son of Reuben; how the earth opened its mouth, and swallowed them up, and their children and their tents and everything which they had, as they stood on their feet in the midst of all Israel;

7 But it is your eyes that have seen all the great acts of the LORD which he did.

8 Therefore you shall keep all the commandments which I command you this day, that you may be strong and go in and possess the land which you are going over to possess;

9 And that you may prolong your days in the land which the LORD swore to your fathers to give to them and to their descendants, a land that flows with milk and honey.

10 ¶For the land into which you are entering to possess it is not like the land of Egypt, from which you came out, where you sowed your seed and watered it with your feet, like a vegetable garden;

11 But the land which you are going over to possess is a land of mountains and valleys, that drinks water of the rain from heaven;

12 A land which the LORD your God cares for always; the eyes of the LORD your God are upon it, from the beginning of the year to the end of the year.

13 ¶And if you shall hearken diligently to the commandments which I command you this day, to love the LORD your God, and to serve him with all your heart and with all your soul,

14 He will give you the rain of your land in its due season, the early rain and the latter rain, and you shall gather in your grain and your wine and your oil.

15 And he will make grass to grow in your fields for your cattle, that you shall eat and be full.

16 Take heed to yourselves, lest your heart be enticed, and you turn aside and serve other gods and worship them;

17 And then the LORD's anger be kindled against you, and he shut up the heaven, that there be no rain and that the land may not produce its fruit, and that you perish quickly from off the good land which the LORD your God gives you.

18 ¶Therefore you shall lay up these commandments in your heart and in your soul, and bind them for a sign upon your hands, that they may be a token between your eyes.

19 And you shall teach them to your children, that they may talk of them when you sit in your house, and when you walk by the way, when you lie down, and when you rise up.

20 And you shall write them on the doorposts of your houses, and upon your gates;

21 That your days and the days of your children, may be multiplied in the land which the LORD your God swore to your fathers to give them, as the days of heaven upon earth.

22 ¶For if you shall diligently keep all these commandments which I command you this day, and do them, and love the LORD your God, and walk in all his ways, and cleave to him;

23 Then the LORD will destroy all these nations from before you, and you shall possess nations greater and mightier than yourselves.

24 Every place whereon the sole of your foot treads shall be yours; from the wilderness and Lebanon, from the river, the great river Euphrates, to

the uttermost sea shall your territory be.

25 There shall no man be able to stand before you; for the LORD your God shall lay the fear of you and the dread of you upon all the land that you shall tread, as he has said to you.

26 ¶Behold, I set before you this day blessings and curses;

27 Blessings, if you obey the commandments of the LORD your God which I am commanding you this day:

28 And curses, if you will not obey the commandments of the LORD your God, and if you turn aside from the way which I command you this day, to go after other gods, which you have not known.

29 And it shall come to pass, when the LORD your God has brought you into the land whither you are entering to possess it, you shall put the blessings upon mount Gerizim, and the curses upon mount Gebel.

30 Behold, they are on the other side of the Jordan, behind the way, toward the setting of the sun, in the land of the Canaanites, who dwell in the low desert over against Gilgal, towards the house of the oak of Mamre.

31 For you are to cross the Jordan to go in to possess the land which the LORD your God gives you, and you shall possess it and dwell therein.

32 And you shall observe to do all the statutes and judgments which I set before you this day.

CHAPTER 12

THESE are the statutes and judgments which you shall observe to do in the land which the LORD God of your fathers gives you to possess all the days that you live upon the earth.

2 You must destroy all the places wherein the nations whom you are to possess worshipped, and all their gods upon high mountains and upon the hills and under every green tree;

3 And you shall tear down their altars and break their statues and burn their graven images with fire; and break the graven images of their gods, and destroy the names of them out of that place.

4 You shall not do so to the LORD your God.

5 But to the place which the LORD your God shall choose out of all your tribes to put his name there, his habitation shall you seek, and thither you shall go;

6 And thither you shall bring your burnt offerings and your sacrifices and your tithes and your gift offerings of your hands and your vows and your freewill offerings and the firstlings of your herds and of your flocks;

7 And there you shall eat before the LORD your God, and you shall rejoice in all that you put your hand to, you and your households, in which the LORD your God has blessed you.

8 You shall not do according to all the things that we are doing here this day, every man whatever is right in his own eyes.

9 For you are not as yet come to the dwelling place and to the inheritance which the LORD your God gives you.

10 But when you cross the Jordan and dwell in the land which the LORD your God gives you to inherit, and when he gives you rest from all your enemies round about you, so that you shall dwell in safety;

11 Then to the place which the LORD your God shall choose to cause his name to dwell there, thither you shall bring all the things that I command you, your burnt offerings and your sacrifices, your tithes and the gift offerings of your hands and all your choice things of your vows which you vow to the LORD.

12 And you shall rejoice before the LORD your God, you and your sons and your daughters and your menservants and your maidservants and the Levites that are living within your towns; because they have no portion nor inheritance with you.

13 Take heed to yourselves that you do not offer your burnt offerings in every place that you please;

14 But in the place which the LORD shall choose in one of your tribes, there you shall offer your burnt offer-

ings, and there you shall do all that I command you.

15 Notwithstanding you may slaughter and eat meat in all your towns, whatever your soul may desire, according to the blessing of the LORD your God which he has given you; the unclean and the clean may be eaten, such as of the gazelle, and as of the hart.

16 Only you shall not eat the blood; you shall pour it out upon the earth like water.

17 ¶It is unlawful to eat within your towns the tithes of your grain, or of your wine, or of your oil, or the firstlings of your herds, or of your flock, or any of things which you vow, nor your freewill offerings, nor gift offerings of your hands;

18 But you must eat them before the LORD your God yearly at the place which the LORD your God shall choose, you and your son and your daughter and your manservant and your maidservant and the Levite that is within your towns; and you shall rejoice before the LORD your God in all that you put your hand to.

19 Take heed to yourselves that you do not forsake the Levites as long as you live upon the earth.

20 ¶When the LORD your God shall enlarge your territory, as he has promised you, and you shall say, I will eat meat, because your soul longs to eat meat; you shall eat meat, whatever your soul may desire.

21 And if the place where the LORD your God shall choose to put his name is too far from you, then you may slaughter of your herds and of your flocks, which the LORD your God has given you, as I have commanded you, and you shall eat in your towns whatever your soul may desire.

22 But as the gazelle and the hart is eaten, so you shall eat of it, the clean and the unclean, you shall eat of it alike.

23 Only be sure that you do not eat the blood; for the blood is the life; and you shall not eat the life with the flesh.

24 You shall not eat it; but you must pour it out on the earth like water.

25 You shall not eat it; that it may go well with you, and with your children after you, when you shall do that which is right in the sight of the LORD your God.

26 Only the holy things which you have, and your votive offerings you shall take and go to the place which the LORD shall choose;

27 And you shall offer your burnt offerings, the flesh and the blood, upon the altar of the LORD your God; and the blood of your sacrifices shall be poured out upon the altar of the LORD your God, and you shall eat the meat.

28 Observe and hear all these commandments which I command you this day, that it may go well with you and with your children after you for ever, when you do that which is good and right in the sight of the LORD your God.

29 ¶When the LORD your God shall destroy the nations against whom you are going, and shall cut them off from before you, and you shall possess them and dwell in their land;

30 Take heed to yourselves that you may not go astray by following them, after the LORD has destroyed them from before you; and that you do not inquire after their gods, saying, How did these nations serve their gods? Even so I may do likewise.

31 You shall not do so to the LORD your God; for every thing abominable to the LORD, which he hates, they have done to their gods; even their sons and their daughters they have burnt in the fire to their gods.

32 Everything that I command you, that you must be careful to do; you shall not add nor take from it.

CHAPTER 13

IF there arise among you a prophet, or a dreamer of dreams, and give you a sign or a wonder,

2 And the sign or the wonder of which he speaks to you come to pass, and then he shall say to you, Come, let us go after other gods, which you have not known, and let us serve them;

3 You shall not listen to the words of that prophet, or that dreamer of dreams; for the LORD your God is proving you, to know whether you love the LORD your God with all your heart and with all your soul.

4 You shall walk after the LORD your God, and reverence him and keep his commandments and obey him, and you shall serve him and cleave to him.

5 And that prophet, or that dreamer of dreams, shall be put to death; because he has spoken iniquity before the LORD your God, who brought you out of the land of Egypt and delivered you out of the house of bondage, to cause you to go astray from the way in which the LORD your God commanded you to walk. So you shall put the evil away from the midst of you.

6 ¶If your brother, the son of your mother, or your son, or your daughter, or your lawful wife, or your friend, who is as your own soul, entices you secretly, saying, Let us go and serve other gods, which you have not known, you nor your fathers;

7 Namely, of the gods of the peoples who are round about you, who are near you, or far off from you, from the one end of the earth to the other end of the earth;

8 You shall not consent to him, nor listen to him; neither shall your eye pity him, neither shall you have mercy upon him, neither shall you conceal him;

9 But you shall surely kill him; your own hand shall start first to put him to death, and afterwards the hand of all the people.

10 And you shall stone him with stones, that he die; because he has sought to cause you to go astray from the LORD your God, who brought you out of the land of Egypt, from the house of bondage.

11 And all Israel shall hear and be afraid, and shall do no more any such an evil thing as this among you.

12 ¶When you shall hear, in one of your cities which the LORD your God gives you to dwell in, one saying,

13 Certain wicked men have gone out from among you, and have led astray the inhabitants of their cities, saying, Let us go and serve other gods, whom you have not known;

14 Then you shall inquire, and make search, and ask diligently; and behold, if the thing be true, that such an abomination has been done among you;

15 You shall surely smite the inhabitants of that city with the edge of the sword, destroying it utterly, and all that is therein, and its cattle, with the edge of the sword.

16 And you shall gather all the spoil of it into the midst of an open space beyond the walls thereof, and burn the city with fire, and all its spoil every bit, before the LORD your God; and it shall be a heap for ever; it shall not be built again.

17 And there shall not cleave to your hand anything of the cursed spoil; that the LORD may turn from the fierceness of his anger and show you mercy and have compassion upon you and multiply you, as he has sworn to your fathers;

18 When you shall hearken to the voice of the LORD your God, and keep all his commandments which I command you this day, you shall do that which is right in the sight of the LORD your God.

CHAPTER 14

YOU are the children of the LORD your God; you shall not make tattooed patterns in the skin, nor any baldness between your eyes for the dead.

2 For you are a holy people to the LORD your God, and the LORD has chosen you to be a beloved people to himself, above all the peoples that are on the face of the earth.

3 ¶You shall not eat any abominable thing.

4 These are the beasts which you shall eat: the ox, the sheep, the goat,

5 The hart, the gazelle, the roebuck, the wild goat, the buffalo, the rockgoat, the mountain goat.

6 Every animal that parts the hoof and has the hoof divided into two

parts and chews the cud among the animals, that you shall eat.

7 Nevertheless you shall not eat of these that chew the cud, or of these that have the hoof divided, such as the camel, the hare, and the coney; for they chew the cud, but their hoofs are not divided; therefore they are unclean for you.

8 And the swine, because it divides the hoof, but does not chew the cud, is unclean for you; you shall not eat of their meat, nor touch their dead carcasses.

9 ¶These you shall eat of all that are in the waters: all that have fins and scales you shall eat:

10 And whatever does not have fins and scales, you shall not eat; it is unclean for you.

11 ¶Of all clean birds you shall eat.

12 But these are the ones of which you shall not eat: the eagle, the vulture, and the raven after its kind,

13 The ostrich, and the hawk after its kind,

14 The owl, the pelican, the crow,

15 The little owl, the night hawk, and the bee eater,

16 The stork, the hoopoe after its kind,

17 The desert cock, and the peacock,

18 And all the brood of these birds is unclean for you, you shall not eat them.

19 But of all clean birds you shall eat.

20 ¶You shall not eat of anything that is unclean, but you shall give it to the stranger who is in your towns, that he may eat it.

21 Or you may sell it to an alien; for you are a holy people to the LORD your God. You shall not cook a kid in its mother's milk.

22 You shall truly tithe all the increase of your seed that the field brings forth year by year.

23 And you shall eat before the LORD your God, in the place where he shall choose to set his name, the tithes of your grain, of your wine and of your oil and of the firstlings of your herds and of your flocks; that you may learn to revere the LORD your God always.

24 And if the way is too long for you, so that you are not able to carry it; because the place where the LORD your God chooses to set his name is too far from you, when the LORD your God has blessed you;

25 Then you shall turn them into money, and bind up the money in a cloth and keep it in your possession, and go to the place which the LORD your God chooses;

26 And you shall buy with that money whatever you desire, oxen or sheep or wine or strong drink or whatever you may desire; and you shall eat there before the LORD your God, and you shall rejoice, you and your household,

27 And the Levite who is within your towns; you shall not forsake him; for he has no portion nor inheritance with you.

28 ¶At the end of three years you shall bring forth all the tithes of your crops the same year, and you shall lay it up within your towns;

29 And the Levite, who has no portion nor inheritance with you, and the proselyte and the orphan and the widow who are within your towns shall come, and shall eat and be satisfied; that the LORD your God may bless you in all the work of your hand which you shall do.

CHAPTER 15

AT the end of every seven years you shall make a release.

2 And this is the manner of the release: every creditor shall release any debt which his neighbor owes him; he shall not exact it of his neighbor, or of his brother; because it is called the year of the LORD's release.

3 Of a foreigner you may exact it again; but that which you have with your brother (kindred) you shall release,

4 So that there will be no poor among you; for the LORD your God shall greatly bless you in the land which the LORD your God gives you for an inheritance to possess,

5 If you hearken to the voice of the LORD your God, to observe to do all

these commandments which I command you this day.

6 For the LORD your God shall bless you, as he promised you; and you shall lend to many nations, but you shall not borrow; and you shall rule over many nations, but they shall not rule over you.

7 ¶If there is among you a poor person of one of your brethren within any of your towns in the land which the LORD your God gives you, you shall not harden your heart, nor shut your hand from your poor brother:

8 But you shall open your hand wide to him, and shall surely lend him whatsoever he lacks.

9 Beware that there be not a wicked thought in your heart, and you say, The seventh year, the year of release, is near; and your eye be evil toward your poor brother, and you give him nothing; and he cry to the LORD against you, and it be sin to you.

10 You shall surely give to him, and your heart shall not be displeased when you give to him; because for this thing the LORD your God shall bless you in all your works and in all things that you undertake.

11 For the poor shall never cease out of the land; therefore I command you, saying, You shall open your hand wide to your poor brother and to the needy in your land.

12 ¶And if your brother, a Hebrew man or a Hebrew woman, is sold to you, and he shall serve you six years, then in the seventh year you shall let him go free from you.

13 And when you let him go free from you, you shall not let him go away empty-handed;

14 But you shall set aside and give to him out of your flocks and out of your oxen and out of your threshing floor and out of your wine press; out of everything which the LORD your God gives you, you shall give to him.

15 And you shall remember that you were a bondman in Egypt, and the LORD your God delivered you; therefore I command you this thing today.

16 But if he says to you, I will not go away from you, because I love

you and your household, and because it is better for me to be with you,

17 Then you must take an awl, and thrust it through his ear to the door, and he shall be your servant for ever. You shall do likewise to your maidservant.

18 You shall not show displeasure when you let him go free from you; for he has served you double according to the wages of a hired servant, in serving you six years; and the LORD your God shall bless you in all that you do.

19 ¶All the firstling males that are born of your herds and of your flock you shall sanctify to the LORD your God; you shall do no work with the firstlings of your oxen, nor shear the firstlings of your sheep.

20 You shall eat a firstling before the LORD your God year by year in the place which the LORD shall choose, you and your household;

21 And if there is any blemish in it, or it is lame or blind, or have any ill blemish, you shall not sacrifice it to the LORD your God.

22 But you shall eat it within your towns; the unclean and the clean shall eat of it alike, as a gazelle, and as the hart.

23 Only you shall not eat the blood; but you must pour it out on the ground like water.

CHAPTER 16

OBSERVE the month of Abib[1] and keep the passover to the LORD your God; because in the month of Abib the LORD your God brought you out of Egypt by night.

2 You shall therefore sacrifice the passover to the LORD, of the flock and the herd, at the place where the LORD your God shall choose to set his name.

3 You shall eat no leavened bread with it; but seven days you shall eat unleavened bread with it, even the bread of affliction; for you came forth out of Egypt in haste; that you may remember the day when you came forth out of Egypt all the days of your life.

4 And there shall no leavened bread

[1] Aramaic *Hababey* (blossoms, that is, April).

be seen with you in all your territory for seven days; neither shall there anything of the meat, which you sacrifice on the evening of the first day, remain all night until the morning.

5 It is unlawful for you to sacrifice the passover within any of your towns which the LORD your God gives you:

6 But at the place where the LORD your God shall choose to set his name, there you shall sacrifice the passover in the evening at the going down of the sun, at the time that you came out of Egypt.

7 And you shall cook it and eat it in the place which the LORD your God shall choose; and you shall turn in the morning and go to your tents.

8 For six days you shall eat unleavened bread; and on the seventh day there shall be a solemn assembly to the LORD your God; you shall do no work therein.

9 ¶You shall count seven weeks to yourselves; begin to count the seven weeks from the time you begin to put the sickle to the standing grain.

10 And then you shall keep the feast of weeks to the LORD your God with sufficient of freewill offering of your hand, which you shall set aside as the LORD your God has blessed you;

11 And you shall rejoice before the LORD your God, you and your son and your daughter and your manservant and your maidservant and the Levite who is within your towns and the sojourner and the fatherless and the widow who is among you, at the place where the LORD your God has chosen to place his name.

12 And you must remember that you were a bondman in Egypt; so you shall observe and do these statutes.

13 ¶You shall observe the feast of tabernacles seven days, after you have gathered in from your threshing floor and from your wine press;

14 And you shall rejoice in your feast, you and your son and your daughter and your manservant and your maidservant and the Levite, the sojourner, the orphan, and the widow who is within your towns.

15 For seven days you shall keep a solemn feast to the LORD your God in the place which the Lord chooses; because the LORD your God shall bless you in all your increase and in all the works of your hand, and you shall rejoice.

16 ¶Three times in a year shall all your memorial gifts be brought before the LORD your God in the place which he shall choose; in the feast of unleavened bread, and in the feast of weeks, and in the feast of the tabernacles; and you shall not appear before the LORD your God emptyhanded;

17 But every man shall give as he is able, according to the blessing of the LORD your God which he has given you.

18 ¶You shall appoint to yourselves judges and scribes in all your cities, which the LORD your God gives you, throughout your tribes; and they shall judge the people with just judgment.

19 You shall not pervert judgment; you shall not be partial, neither take a bribe; for a bribe blinds the eyes of the wise men in judgment, and perverts the cause of the innocent.

20 But you must judge your neighbor righteously, that you may live and go in and inherit the land which the LORD your God gives you.

21 ¶You shall not plant for yourselves a grove of any trees near the altar of the LORD your God, which you shall make for yourselves.

22 Neither shall you set up for yourselves any statue, which the LORD your God hates.

CHAPTER 17

YOU shall not sacrifice to the LORD your God an ox or a lamb wherein is blemish, or anything impious; for that is an abomination in the sight of the LORD your God.

2 ¶If there is found among you, within any of your towns which the LORD your God gives you, a man or a woman who shall do evil in the sight of the LORD your God and transgress his covenant,

3 And shall go and serve other gods and worship them, either the sun, or the moon, or any of the host of

heaven, which I have not commanded; 4 And it is told you, and you shall hear of it, you shall inquire diligently, and if it is true that such an abomination has been committed in Israel; 5 Then you shall bring forth that man or that woman who has committed that wicked thing within your towns, whether he is a man or a woman; and you shall stone him with stones, till he die.

6 On the testimony of two witnesses or three witnesses shall he that is worthy of death be put to death; but on the testimoney of one witness he shall not be put to death.

7 And the hand of the witnesses shall be the first against him to put him to death, and afterward the hands of all the people. So you shall destroy the evildoers from among you.

8 ¶If there arise a matter which is too difficult for you to judge, between murder and murder, between lawsuit and lawsuit, and between a sore of leprosy and a sore of leprosy, any matters of controversy within your towns; then you shall arise and go to the place which the LORD your God shall choose for himself;

9 And you shall come to the priest, or the Levite, or to the judge who shall be in those days, and inquire; and they shall show you the sentence of judgment;

10 And you shall do according to the decision which they of that place shall show you, as the LORD has commanded; and you shall observe to do according to all that they teach you;

11 According to the sentence of the law which they shall declare to you, and according to the judgment which they shall tell you, you shall do; you shall not swerve from the sentence which they shall show you, neither to the right hand nor to the left.

12 And the man who will do presumptuously, and will not hearken to the priest who stands to minister there before the LORD your God, or to the judge, that man shall be put to death; you shall destroy the evildoers from Israel.

13 And all the people shall hear, and fear, and do no more presumptuously.

14 ¶When you shall come to the land which the LORD your God gives you, and you shall possess it and dwell therein, and shall say, I will set a king over me, like as all the nations that are about me;

15 You shall in any wise set a king over you whom the LORD your God shall choose; one from among your brethren you shall set king over you; it is unlawful for you to set a foreigner over you, who is not from among your brethren.

16 But he shall not multiply horses to himself, that he may not cause the people to return to Egypt, when his horses have multiplied; since the LORD has said to you, You shall never return that way again.

17 Neither shall he multiply wives to himself, that they may not cause his heart to turn away; neither shall he greatly multiply to himself silver and gold.

18 And when he sits upon the throne of his kingdom, he shall write for himself a copy of this law in a book out of that which is before the priests and the Levites;

19 And it shall be with him, and he shall read therein all the days of his life; that he may learn to fear the LORD his God, to keep all the words of this law, and these commandments, to do them;

20 That his heart may not be lifted up above his brethren, and that he may not turn aside from the commandments, neither to the right hand nor to the left; so that he may prolong his days in his kingdom, he and his children, in the midst of Israel.

CHAPTER 18

THE priests and the Levites, shall have neither portion nor inheritance among the children of Israel; but they shall eat sacrifices offered to the LORD, and his inheritance.

2 Therefore they shall have no inheritance among their brethren; the LORD is their inheritance, as he has said to them.

3 ¶And this shall be the priest's due from the people: from those who offer

a sacrifice, whether it be an ox or a lamb, they shall give to the priest the shoulder and the two cheeks and the maw.

4 The first fruits also of your grain, of your wine, and of your oil, and the first of the fleece of your sheep, you shall give him.

5 For the LORD your God has chosen him out of all your tribes, to stand to minister in the name of the LORD your God, him and his sons for ever.

6 ¶And if a Levite come from any of the towns of your brethren out of all Israel, where he sojourned, and come with all the desire of his soul to the place which the LORD shall choose;

7 Then he shall minister in the name of the LORD his God, as do all his brethren the Levites, who stand there before the LORD.

8 They shall have equal portion to eat, besides that which comes of the sale of his patrimony.

9 ¶When you come into the land which the LORD your God gives you, you shall not learn to do after the abominations of those nations.

10 There shall not be found among you any one who makes his son or his daughter pass through the fire, or who practices divination or black magic, or is an enchanter or a witch

11 Or a charmer or a consulter with familiar spirits or a sorcerer or a necromancer.

12 For whoever does these things is an abomination in the sight of the LORD your God; and because of these abominations the LORD your God is destroying them from before you.

13 You shall be innocent before the LORD your God.

14 For these nations which you are to possess hearken to men with familiar spirits and diviners; but as for you, the LORD your God has not allowed you to do so.

15 ¶The LORD your God will raise up to you a prophet like me from the midst of you, of your brethren; to him you shall hearken.

16 Just as you asked of the LORD your God at Horeb on the day of the assembly, saying, Let me not hear any

more the voice of the LORD my God, neither let me see this great fire any more, that I die not.

17 And the LORD said to me, They have well spoken that which they have spoken.

18 I will raise up for them a prophet like you from among their brethren, and will put my words in his mouth; and he shall speak to them all that I shall command him.

19 Whosoever will not hearken to my words which he shall speak in my name, I will require it of him.

20 But the prophet who shall presume to speak a word in my name which I have not commanded him to speak, or who shall speak in the name of other gods, that prophet shall be put to death.

21 And if you say in your heart, How shall we know the word which the LORD has not spoken?

22 When a prophet speaks in the name of the LORD, and the thing does not come to pass, nor follow; that is the thing which the LORD has not spoken, but the prophet has spoken it presumptuously; you shall not be afraid of him.

CHAPTER 19

WHEN the LORD your God has destroyed the nations whose land the LORD your God gives you, and you shall possess them and dwell in their cities, and in their houses;

2 You shall set apart for you three cities in the midst of your land which the LORD your God gives you as an inheritance.

3 You shall prepare for you a highway, and divide into three parts the land which the LORD your God gives you to inherit, that any slayer may flee thither.

4 ¶And this is the law in the case of the slayer who kills his neighbor and flees there that he may live, whosoever kills his neighbor unintentionally, whom he hated not in time past;

5 And when a man goes into the forest with his neighbor to cut wood, and as he lifts up his hand with the axe to cut down a tree, the iron head slips from the helve and strikes his

neighbor so that he dies; he shall flee to one of these cities, and live;

6 Lest the avenger of the blood pursue the slayer, while his anger is hot, and overtake him, because the way is long, and slay him; though he was not worthy of death, because he hated him not in time past.

7 Therefore I command you, saying, You shall set apart three cities for you.

8 And when the LORD your God shall enlarge your territory, as he has sworn to your fathers, and gives you all the land which he promised to give to your fathers;

9 If you shall keep all these commandments to do them, which I command you this day, to love the LORD your God, and to walk in his ways always; then you shall add three cities more for you besides these three;

10 That innocent blood may not be shed in the land which the LORD your God gives you, and that the guilt of innocent blood not be upon you.

11 ¶But if any man hate his neighbor, and lie in wait for him, and attack him, and smite him mortally so that he dies, and he flees to one of these cities;

12 Then the elders of his city shall send and fetch him from there, and deliver him into the hand of the avenger of blood, and he shall slay him.

13 Your eyes shall not pity him, but you shall kill him, and thus purge the guilt of innocent blood from Israel, that it may go well with you.

14 ¶You shall not remove your neighbor's landmark, which they of old time have set in your inheritance, which you shall inherit in the land that the LORD your God gives you to possess.

15 ¶A single witness shall not rise up against a man for any offense, or for any crime, in whatever offense or crime he may commit; on the testimony of two witnesses, or on the testimony of three witnesses, shall a charge be established.

16 ¶If a false witness rise up against any man, and testify against him that which is wrong;

17 Then both the men between whom the controversy is, shall stand before the LORD, before the priests and the judges who shall be in those days;

18 And the judges shall investigate the case diligently; and, behold, if the witness has deliberately testified falsely against his brother;

19 Then you shall do to him as he had thought to do to his brother; so shall you put the evil away from among you.

20 And those who remain shall hear, and fear, and shall never again commit any such an evil thing among you.

21 And your eye shall not pity; but life shall be for life, eye for eye, tooth for tooth, hand for hand, foot for foot.

CHAPTER 20

WHEN you go out to battle against your enemies, and see horses and chariots and a people more than you, you shall not be afraid of them; for the LORD your God is with you, who brought you up out of the land of Egypt.

2 And when you come near to the battle, the priest shall appproach and speak to the people,

3 And shall say to them, Hear, O Israel, you approach this day to the battle with your enemies; let not your heart faint, fear not, and do not tremble, neither be terrified because of them;

4 For the LORD your God is he that goes with you, who brought you out of the land of Egypt, and it is he who shall fight for you with your enemies, and he shall save you.

5 ¶Then the scribes shall speak to the people, saying, What man is there who has built a new house, and has not dedicated it? Let him return and go to his house, lest he die in the battle, and another man dedicate it.

6 And what man is there who has planted a vineyard, and has not yet trod the grapes of it? Let him return and go to his house, lest he die in the battle, and another man tread its grapes.

7 And what man is there who has

betrothed a wife, and has not taken her? Let him return and go to his house, lest he die in the battle, and another man take her.

8 And the scribes shall speak further to the people, and they shall say, What man is there who is fearful and fainthearted? Let him return and go to his house, lest his brethren's heart faint as well as his heart.

9 And when the scribes have made an end of speaking to the people, the commanders of the army shall stand at the head of the people.

10 ¶When you come near to a city to fight against it, then proclaim peace to it.

11 And if the city give you answer of peace, and it open to you, then all the people who are found in it shall be servants and tributaries to you, and they shall serve you.

12 But if it will not surrender to you, but will make war with you, then you shall besiege it;

13 And when the LORD your God has delivered it into your hands, you shall slay all its males with the edge of the sword;

14 But the women and the little ones and the cattle and all that is in the city, even all its spoil, you shall plunder for yourselves; and you shall eat of the spoil of your enemies, which the LORD your God gives you.

15 Thus shall you do to all the cities which are very far off from you, which are not of the cities of these nations.

16 But of the cities of these people which the LORD your God gives you for an inheritance, you shall save alive nothing that breathes;

17 But you shall utterly destroy them; namely, the Hittites, and the Amorites, the Canaanites, and the Perizzites, the Hivites, and the Jebusites; as the LORD your God has commanded you;

18 That they may not teach you to do after all their abominations, which they have done in worshipping their gods; so you should sin in the sight of the LORD your God.

19 ¶When you shall besiege a city a long time, in making war against it to capture it, you shall not destroy its trees, nor wield an axe against them; because you may eat of them, and you shall not cut them down (for the trees of the field are not like men to flee from before you at the time of the siege).

20 Only the trees which you know are not trees for food you may destroy and cut down that you may build bulwarks against the city that makes war with you, until it is captured.

CHAPTER 21

IF a person is found slain in the land which the LORD your God gives you to possess, lying in the field, and it is not known who has slain him;

2 Then your elders and your judges shall come forth, and they shall measure the distance to the cities which are round about him that is slain;

3 And the elders of the city which is nearest to the slain man shall take a heifer which has never been used for work nor has pulled in the yoke,

4 And the elders of that city shall bring down the heifer to a barren valley which has never been ploughed nor sown, and shall slaughter the heifer there in the valley;

5 And the priests the sons of Levi shall come near, for them the LORD your God has chosen to minister to him, and to bless in the name of the LORD; and by their word shall every lawsuit and every attack be tried;

6 And all the elders of that city which is nearest to the slain man shall wash their hands over the heifer which is slaughtered in the valley;

7 And they shall answer and say, Our hands have not shed this blood, neither have our eyes seen the victim.

8 Pardon, O LORD, thy people Israel, whom thou hast saved, and lay not innocent blood upon thy people Israel. And the guilt of blood shall be forgiven them.

9 So shall you put away the guilt of innocent blood from among you, when you shall do that which is right in the sight of the LORD.

10 ¶When you go forth to war against your enemies, and the LORD

your God delivers them into your hands, and you take them captive.

11 And see among the captives a beautiful woman, and you desire her, and would have her for yourself as a wife;

12 Then you shall bring her home to your house; and she shall shave her head and pare her nails;

13 And she shall put off the clothes of her captivity and shall remain in your house, and mourn for her father and her mother a full month; and after that you shall go in unto her, and be her husband, and she shall be your wife.

14 And it shall be, if you have no delight in her, then you shall let her go where she will; but you shall not sell her at all for money; you shall not make a harlot of her, for sake of a gain, because you have humbled her.

15 ¶If a man has two wives, one beloved and the other hated, and they have borne him children, both the beloved and the hated; and if the first-born son be hers that is hated;

16 Then it shall be, when he makes his sons to inherit his property, it is unlawful for him to make the son of the beloved wife first-born before the son of the hated;

17 But the first-born, the son of the hated, he must receive double portion of all that he has; for he is the first of his children; and the right of the first-born is his.

18 ¶If a man has a stubborn and rebellious son, who will not obey the voice of his father or the voice of his mother, and who, when they have chastised him, will not hearken to them;

19 Then his father and his mother shall lay hold on him, and bring him out to the elders of the city, at the gate of his place;

20 And they shall say to the elders of his city, This our son is stubborn and rebellious, he does not obey our voice; he is a glutton and a drunkard.

21 Then all the men of his city shall stone him with stones, that he die; so shall you put evil away fom among you; and all Israel shall hear, and fear.

22 ¶And if any man has committed a sin worthy of death, and he is crucified on a tree, and thus put to death;

23 His body shall not remain all night upon the tree, but you shall bury him the same day (for he who shall revile God shall be crucified), and you shall not defile your land, which the LORD your God gives you for an inheritance.

CHAPTER 22

YOU shall not see your brother's ox or his sheep go astray, and disregard them; but you shall surely bring them back to your brother.

2 And if your brother is not near you, or if you do not know him, then you shall bring it to your own house, and it shall be with you until your brother seeks after it, and you shall restore it to him again.

3 In like manner shall you do with his ox and with his ass, and so with his garment; and so shall you do with anything which your brother has lost, and you have found; it is unlawful for you to delay in restoring it.

4 ¶You shall not see your enemy's ass or his ox fallen down by the way, and turn away your eyes from them; but you shall surely help him to lift them up again.

5 ¶A woman shall not wear any garment that pertains to a man, neither shall a man put on a woman's garments; for whosoever does these things is an abomination in the sight of the LORD your God.

6 ¶When you chance to find a bird's nest before you in the way in any tree, or on the ground, with young ones or eggs and the mother sitting upon the young or upon the eggs, you shall not take the mother with her young;

7 But you shall surely let the mother go, and take the young for yourself; that it may be well with you, and that you may live long.

8 ¶When you build a new house, you must make a parapet for your roof, that no man may fall from it, and bring blood upon your house.

9 ¶You shall not sow your furrow

with mixed seeds, lest the produce of the seed which you have sown and the produce of your vineyard be seized for the sanctuary.

10 ¶You shall not plow with an ox and an ass together.

11 ¶You shall not wear a garment woven of different sorts of wool and cotton together.

12 ¶You shall make for yourself fringes on the four corners of your cloak, with which you cover yourself.

13 ¶If any man take a wife, and go in unto her, and then hate her,

14 And give an occasion of speech against her, charging her with adultery, and bring an evil name upon her, and say, I took this woman, and when I lay with her, I found her not a virgin;

15 Then shall the father of the damsel, and her mother, take and bring forth the tokens of the damsel's virginity to the elders of the city at the gate;

16 And the damsel's father shall say to the elders, I gave my daughter to this man to wife, and he hates her;

17 And, lo, he has given occasion of speech against her, charging her with whoredom, saying, I found not your daughter a virgin; and yet these are the tokens of my daughter's virginity. And they shall spread the cloth before the elders of the city.

18 And the elders of that city shall take that man and chastise him;

19 And they shall fine him a hundred shekels of silver, and give it to the father of the damsel, because he has brought an evil name upon a virgin daughter of Israel; and she shall be his wife; he has no right to put her away all his days.

20 But if this thing is true, and the tokens of virginity are not found for the damsel;

21 Then they shall bring out the damsel to the door of her father's house, and the men of the city shall stone her with stones that she die; because she has committed a shameful act in Israel, to play the whore in her father's house; so you shall put away evil from among you.

22 ¶If a man is found lying with another man's wife, then both of them shall surely die, the man who lay with the woman, and the woman; so shall you put away evil from Israel.

23 ¶If there is a damsel who is a virgin and who is betrothed to a man, and another man find her in the city and lie with her;

24 Then you shall bring them both out to the gate of that city, and you shall stone them with stones, that they die; the damsel, because she did not cry for help, being in the city; and the man, because he has treated shamefully his neighbor's wife; so shall you put away evil from among you.

25 ¶But if a man find a betrothed damsel in the field, and seize her by force, and lie with her; then the man only who lay with her shall die:

26 But to the damsel you shall do nothing; because there is in the damsel no sin worthy of death; for as when a man rises against his neighbor and slays him, even so is this case.

27 For he found her in the field, and the betrothed damsel cried for help, and there was no one to save her.

28 ¶If a man finds a damsel who is a virgin who is not betrothed, and seizes her, and lies with her, and they are found;

29 Then the man who lay with her shall give to the damsel's father fifty shekels of silver, and she shall be his wife; because he has humbled her, he has no right to put her away all his days.

30 ¶A man shall not take his father's wife, nor uncover the skirt of his father's wife.

CHAPTER 23

NO adulterer shall enter into the assembly of the LORD.

2 Neither shall a bastard enter into the assembly of the LORD; even to the tenth generation, his descendants shall not enter into the assembly of the LORD.

3 An Ammonite or Moabite shall not enter into the congregation of the LORD; even to the tenth generation, his descendants shall not enter into

the assembly of the LORD for ever;
4 Because they did not meet you
with bread and with water on the
way, when you came forth out of
Egypt; and because they hired against
you Balaam the son of Beor from
Pethor of Aram-nahrin (Mesopotamia) to curse you.

5 Nevertheless the LORD your God
would not hearken to Balaam; but the
LORD your God turned his curses into blessings to you, because the LORD
your God loved you.

6 You shall not seek their peace
nor their prosperity all the days of
your life for ever.

7 ¶You shall not drive away an
Edomite, for he is your brother; you
shall not drive away an Egyptian, because you were a sojourner in his
land.

8 The children that are born to
them shall enter into the assembly of
the LORD in their third generation.

9 ¶When you go forth into the
camp against your enemies, you shall
beware of every wicked thing.

10 ¶If there is among you any man
who is not clean by reason of an
emission at night, then he shall go
outside the camp, he shall not come
within the camp;

11 But when the evening comes on,
he shall bathe himself with water;
and when the sun is down, he shall
come into the camp again.

12 ¶You shall have a latrine outside
the camp, to which you shall go to
relieve yourself.

13 And you shall have a peg upon
your weapon; and it shall be, when
you relieve yourself, you shall dig
with it, and then you shall cover your
dung;

14 For the LORD your God walks
in the midst of your camp, to deliver
you and to subdue your enemies before you; therefore shall your camp
be holy, that he may not see anything unclean in your camp, and turn
away from you.

15 ¶You shall not deliver to his
master a servant who has escaped
from his master to you;

16 But he shall dwell with you in
the place which he shall choose in

one of your towns, where it pleases
him best; you shall not oppress him.

17 ¶There shall be no whore of the
daughters of Israel, also there shall
be no sodomite of the sons of Israel.

18 You shall not bring the hire of
a whore or the price of a dog into
the house of the LORD your God for
any vow; for both of these are an
abomination before the LORD your
God.

19 ¶You shall not lend with interest
to your brother: interest of money,
interest of grain, and the interest of
anything that is lent with interest;

20 To a foreigner you may lend
with interest; but to your brother you
shall not lend with interest, that the
LORD your God may bless you in all
that you set your hand to in the land
which you shall go in to possess.

21 ¶When you shall vow a vow to
the LORD your God, you shall not be
slack to pay it; for the LORD your
God will surely require it of you;
and it would be a sin in you.

22 But if you are unwilling to make
a vow, then it shall be no sin in you.

23 That which is gone out of your
lips you shall keep and perform; just
as you have vowed a freewill offering
to the LORD your God, which you
have promised with your mouth.

24 ¶When you come into your
neighbor's vineyard, then you may
eat grapes, your fill at your own pleasure; but you shall not put any into
your vessel.

25 When you come into the standing wheat of your neighbor, you may
pluck the ears with your hand; but
you shall not put a sickle to your
neighbor's standing grain.

CHAPTER 24

IF a man takes a wife, and lies with
her, and if she finds no favor in
his eyes, because he has found some
evidence of open prostitution in her;
then let him write her a bill of divorcement, and give it to her, and
send her out of his house.

2 And when she has left his house,
and if she goes and becomes another
man's wife,

3 And if that husband hates her,

and writes her a bill of divorcement, and gives it to her, and sends her out of his house, or if that husband who took her to be his wife dies;

4 Then her former husband, who sent her away, has no right to take her again to be his wife, after she has been defiled; for that is an abomination before the LORD; and you shall not cause the land to sin, which the LORD your God gives you for an inheritance.

5 ¶When a man takes a new wife, he shall not go out with the army, neither shall he be charged with any business; but he shall be free at his home for one year, and shall rejoice with his wife whom he has taken.

6 ¶No man shall take the nether or the upper millstone as a pledge; for he takes a man's life to pledge.

7 ¶If a man of the children of Israel is found stealing any of his brethren of the children of Israel, to make merchandise of him, or sell him; then that thief shall surely die; and you shall put evil away from among you.

8 ¶Take heed in the plague of leprosy, and be exceedingly careful, and do according to all that the priests and the Levites shall teach you; as I commanded them, so you shall be careful to do.

9 Remember what the LORD your God did to Miriam on the way, after you came forth out of Egypt.

10 If your neighbor owes you a debt, you shall not go into his house to fetch his pledge.

11 But you shall wait in the street, and the man who is your debtor shall bring out the pledge to you.

12 And if the man is poor, you shall not sleep with his mantle.[1]

13 But you shall return to him his mantle again when the sun goes down, that he may sleep in his own mantle, and bless you; and it shall be righteousness to you before the LORD your God.

14 ¶You shall not cheat the wages of a hired laborer who is poor and needy, whether he is of your brethren or of the strangers who are in your cities;

15 But you shall pay him his wages on the same day, neither shall the sun go down upon it; for he is poor, and it is because of his wages that he places himself at your disposal; lest he cry against you to the LORD, and it be sin against you.

16 The fathers shall not be put to death for their children, neither shall the children be put to death for their fathers; but every man shall be put to death for his own sin.

17 ¶You shall not pervert the justice due to the stranger, nor to the orphan; nor take a widow's garment as a pledge;

18 But you shall remember that you were a bondman in Egypt, and the LORD your God delivered you from there; therefore I command you to do this thing:

19 ¶When you reap the harvest in your field, and have forgotten a sheaf in the field, you shall not return to fetch it; it shall be for the stranger, for the fatherless, and for the widow, that the LORD your God may bless you in all the works of your hands.

20 When you beat your olive trees, you shall not go over the boughs again; it shall be for the stranger, for the orphan, and for the widow.

21 When you gather the grapes of your vineyard, you shall not glean it afterward; it shall be for the stranger, for the fatherless, and for the widow.

22 And you shall remember that you were a bondman in Egypt; therefore I command you to do this thing.

CHAPTER 25

IF there is a lawsuit between a man and his neighbor, they shall come before the judges, and the judges shall judge them; and they shall acquit the innocent, and condemn the guilty.

2 And it shall be, if the guilty man deserves punishment, the judge shall cause him to lie down, and have him flogged in his presence, according to

---

[1] In the East clothing and other garments are taken as a pledge, especially in places where poverty prevails and money is scarce.

his offense, with a certain number of stripes.

3 Forty stripes he may give him, but not more; lest, if he should exceed, and scourge him above this number of stripes, then your brother would be hurt severely before your eyes.

4 ¶You shall not muzzle an ox when it treads out the grain.

5 ¶When brothers dwell together, and one of them dies, and has no son, the wife of the dead shall not marry to a stranger; but her husband's brother shall take her, and she shall become his wife, and he shall perform the duty of a brother-in-law to her.

6 And it shall be, that the first-born which she bears shall be named after the name of his brother who is dead, that his name may not be forgotten in Israel.

7 And if the man refuses to take his brother's wife, then let his brother's wife go up to the gate to the elders, and say, My brother-in-law refuses to raise up to his brother a name in Israel, and is unwilling to take me as a wife.

8 Then the elders of his city shall call him, and speak to him; and if he should rise up and say, I will not take her;

9 Then his sister-in-law shall come to him in the presence of the elders, and loose his shoe from off his foot, and spit in his face, and say, So shall it be done to the man who will not raise a family to his brother.

10 And his name shall be called in Israel, the house of him that has his shoe loosed.

11 ¶When two brothers are fighting, and the wife of one draws near to deliver her husband out of the hands of his adversary, and puts forth her hand, and seizes him by the private parts;

12 Then you shall cut off her hand; your eye shall not pity her.

13 ¶You shall not have in your bag different weights, a large and a small.

14 You shall not have in your house different measures, a large and a small.

15 But you shall have a perfect and just weight; a perfect and a just measure shall you have, that your days may be prolonged in the land which the LORD your God gives you.

16 For all who do such things and all who act wickedly are an abomination before the LORD your God.

17 ¶Remember all that Amalek did to you by the way, when you came forth out of Egypt;

18 How he met you with the sword, and smote all of those who were left behind you, when you were faint and weary, and he feared not the LORD your God.

19 Therefore when the LORD your God has given you rest from all your enemies round about, in the land which the LORD your God gives you as an inheritance, you shall blot out the remembrance of Amalek from under heaven; you shall not forget it.

CHAPTER 26

AND when you come into the land which the LORD your God gives you as an inheritance, and possess it, and dwell in it;

2 You shall take some of the first of all the fruit of the land, which you shall bring in from the land which the LORD your God gives you, and shall put it in a basket, and you shall arise and go to the place where the LORD your God chooses to place his name.

3 And you shall go to the priest who shall be in those days, and say to him, I profess this day to the LORD your God that I have come into the land which the LORD swore to our fathers to give us.

4 And the priest shall take the basket from your hand, and set it down before the LORD your God.

5 And you shall speak and say before the LORD your God, My father was led to Aram and he went down into Egypt, and sojourned there for a short time, and there he became a nation, great, mighty, and populous;

6 And the Egyptians mistreated us and afflicted us and laid upon us hard work;

7 And when we cried to the LORD

God of our fathers, the LORD heard our voice and saw our affliction, our labor, and our oppression;

8 And the LORD brought us forth out of Egypt with a mighty hand and with an outstretched arm and with a great revelation and with signs and with wonders;

9 And we came to this place, and the LORD has given us this land, a land flowing with milk and honey.

10 And now, behold, I have brought the firstfruits of the land, which thou, O LORD, hast given me; and you shall set it down before the LORD your God, and worship there before the LORD your God;

11 And you shall rejoice in every good thing which the LORD your God has given to you and to your house, you and the Levite and the sojourner that is among you.

12 ¶When you have finished tithing all the tithes of your produce in the third year, which is the year of tithing, then you shall give to the Levite, the sojourner, the fatherless, and the widow, that they may eat within your towns and be filled;

13 Then you shall say before the LORD your God, I have brought all the hallowed things out of my house, and also have given them to the Levite, to the sojourner, to the fatherless, and to the widow, according to all thy commandments which thou hast commanded me; I have not transgressed thy commandments, neither have I forgotten them;

14 I have not eaten of them in my mourning, neither have I touched them while I was unclean, nor used any of them for funerals; [1] but I have hearkened to the voice of the LORD my God, and have done according to all that thou hast commanded me.

15 Look down from thy holy habitation, from heaven, and bless thy people Israel and the land which thou hast given us, as thou didst swear to our fathers, a land that flows with milk and honey.

16 ¶This day the LORD your God has commanded you to do these stat-utes and judgments; you shall therefore keep and do them with all your heart and with all your soul.

17 You have confessed the LORD this day to be your God, and promised to walk in his ways and to keep his statutes and his judgments and his commandments, and to hearken to his voice;

18 And the LORD has promised you again this day to be his beloved people, as he had promised you, that you shall keep and do all his commandments;

19 And that he shall exalt you above all nations which he has made, in praise, in name, and in honor; and that you may be a holy people to the LORD your God, as he has spoken.

CHAPTER 27

AND Moses and the elders of Israel commanded the people, saying, Keep all the commandments which I command you this day.

2 And it shall be on the day that you cross the Jordan into the land which the LORD your God gives you, you shall set up large stones, and cover them with plaster;

3 And you shall write upon them all the words of this law, when you have crossed the Jordan, that you may go into the land which the LORD your God gives you, a land flowing with milk and honey, as the LORD God of your fathers has promised you.

4 Therefore when you have crossed the Jordan, you shall set up these stones, which I command you this day, on mount Gebel,[2] and you shall cover them with plaster.

5 And there you shall build an altar to the LORD your God, an altar of stones; you shall not lift up any iron tool upon them.

6 You shall build the altar of the LORD your God of undressed stones, and you shall offer burnt offerings on it to the LORD your God:

7 And you shall offer peace offerings, and shall eat there and rejoice before the LORD your God.

[1] In the East the nearest relatives of the dead, after the burial, feed the mourners and the poor.
[2] Other versions, *Ebal.*

8 And you shall write upon the stones all the words of this law very plainly.

9 ¶And Moses and the priests and the Levites said to all Israel, Give ear and hearken, O Israel; this day you have become the people of the LORD your God.

10 You shall therefore obey the voice of the LORD your God, and do his commandments and his statutes which I command you this day.

11 ¶And Moses charged the people that same day, saying,

12 These tribes shall stand upon mount Gerizim to bless the people when you have crossed the Jordan: Simeon, Levi, Judah, Issachar, Joseph and Benjamin;

13 And these tribes shall stand upon Gebel to curse: Reuben, Gad, Asher, Zebulun, Dan, and Naphtali.

14 ¶And the Levites shall speak and say to all the people of Israel with a loud voice,

15 Cursed be the man who makes any graven or molten images, for they are an abomination before the LORD, the work of the hands of the craftsman, and puts them in a secret place. And all the people shall answer and say, Amen.

16 Cursed be he who reviles his father or his mother. And all the people shall say, Amen.

17 Cursed be he who removes his neighbor's landmark. And all the people shall say, Amen.

18 Cursed be he who causes a blind man to wander out of the way. And all the people shall say, Amen.

19 Cursed be he who perverts the judgment of the stranger, the fatherless, and the widow. And all the people shall say, Amen.

20 Cursed be he who lies with his father's wife; and thus uncovers his father's skirt. And all the people shall say, Amen.

21 Cursed be he who lies with any kind of beast. And all the people shall say, Amen.

22 Cursed be he who lies with his sister, the daughter of his father, or the daughter of his mother. And all the people shall say, Amen.

23 Cursed be he who lies with his mother-in-law. And all the people shall say, Amen.

24 Cursed be he who smites his neighbor secretly. And all the people shall say, Amen.

25 Cursed be he who takes a bribe to slay an innocent person. And all the people shall say, Amen.

26 Cursed be he who does not confirm all the words of this law to do them. And all the people shall say, Amen.

CHAPTER 28

AND if you shall hearken diligently to the voice of the LORD your God, to observe and to do all his commandments which I command you this day, the LORD your God will set you on high above all the nations of the earth;

2 And all these blessings shall come on you, and overtake you, if you shall hearken to the voice of the LORD your God.

3 Blessed shall you be in the city, and blessed shall you be in the field.

4 Blessed shall be the fruit of your body and the fruit of your ground, the bearing of your cattle, the increase of your herds, and the flocks of your sheep.

5 Blessed shall be your breadbasket and your dough.

6 Blessed shall you be when you come in, and blessed shall you be when you go out.

7 The LORD shall cause your enemies who rise up against you to surrender defeated before you; they shall come out against you by one way, and flee before you by seven ways.

8 The LORD shall command blessings upon you in your storehouses, and in all that you put your hand to; and he shall bless you in the land which the LORD your God gives you.

9 The LORD shall establish you a holy people to himself, as he has sworn to you, if you shall keep all the commandments of the LORD your God and walk in his ways.

10 And all the people of the earth shall see that you are called by the

name of the LORD, and they shall be afraid of you.

11 And the LORD shall enrich you in good things, in the fruit of your body and in the bearing of your cattle and in the fruit of your ground, in the land which the LORD swore to your fathers to give you.

12 The LORD shall open to you his good storehouse, the heaven, to give you rain to your land in its season; and he will bless all the works of your hands; and you shall lend to many nations, but you shall not borrow; and you shall rule over many nations, but they shall not rule over you.

13 And the LORD shall make you the head, and not the tail; [1] and you shall be on top only, and you shall not be beneath; if you will hearken to the commandments of the LORD your God which I command you this day, to observe and to do them.

14 And you shall not turn aside from any of the commandments which I command you this day, to the right hand, or to the left, and you shall not go after the Gentile gods, nor serve them.

15 ¶But if you will not hearken to the voice of the LORD your God, and do not observe and do all his commandments and his statutes which I command you this day, then all these curses shall come upon you and overtake you.

16 Cursed shall you be in the city, and cursed shall you be in the field.

17 Cursed shall be your breadbasket and your dough.

18 Cursed shall be the fruit of your body and the fruit of your land, the herds of your oxen and the flocks of your sheep.

19 Cursed shall you be when you come in, and cursed shall you be when you go out.

20 The LORD shall send upon you ruin, confusion, and rebuke in all that you set your hand to do, until you are destroyed, and until you perish quickly; because of your evil doings, because you have forsaken me.

21 The LORD shall send pestilence upon you, until he has consumed you from off the land which you are entering to possess.

22 The LORD shall afflict you with confusion and with skin disease and with an inflammation and with burning fever and with the sword and with blasting and with mildew; and they shall pursue you until you perish.

23 And the heaven that is over your head shall be brass, and the earth that is under you shall be iron.

24 The LORD shall make the rain of your land powder and dust; from heaven shall they come down upon you, until you are destroyed.

25 The LORD shall cause you to be routed before your enemies; you shall go out one way against them, but you shall flee seven ways before them; and you shall be a horror to all the kingdoms of the earth.

26 And your carcass shall be food for the fowls of the air and the beasts of the earth, and there shall be no one to drive them off.

27 The LORD will smite you with the boils of Egypt and with hemorrhoids and with leprosy and with the itch, and thereof you cannot be healed.

28 The LORD shall smite you with madness and blindness and dumbness of heart;

29 And you shall grope at noonday, as the blind grope in darkness, and you shall not prosper in your ways; and you shall be carried away violently, and oppressed and wronged all your days, and no man shall save you.

30 You shall betroth a wife, and another man shall take her; you shall build a house, and you shall not dwell in it; you shall plant a vineyard, and you shall not press grapes of it.

31 Your ox shall be slaughtered before your eyes, and you shall not eat of it; your ass shall be violently taken away from you, and shall not be restored to you; your sheep shall be given to your enemies, and you shall have none to rescue them.

32 Your sons and your daughters

---

[1] Idiom meaning *greatest, not least.*

shall be given to another people, and your eyes shall look on, and you shall grieve over them all the day long; and there shall be no might in your hand to do anything.

33 The fruit of your land and all your labors shall a nation which you know not eat up; and you shall be only wronged and oppressed always;

34 So that you shall be blinded of the sight with which your eyes shall see.

35 The LORD shall smite you in your knees and in your legs with malignant boils that cannot be healed, from the sole of your foot to the top of your head.

36 The LORD shall drive you away, and your king whom you have set over you, to a nation that neither you nor your fathers have known; and there you shall serve other gods, of wood and stone.

37 And you shall become a horror, a proverb, and a byword, among all nations where the LORD your God shall drive you.

38 You shall carry much seed into your field, and you shall gather but little in; for the locust shall consume it.

39 You shall plant a vineyard and dress it, but you shall neither drink of the wine nor gather the grapes, because the worms shall eat it.

40 You shall have olive trees throughout all your territory, but you shall not anoint yourself with the oil; for your olives shall drop off.

41 You shall beget sons and daughters, but they shall not remain yours; for they shall go into captivity.

42 All your trees and fruits of your land shall the locust consume.

43 The stranger who is in your midst shall rise up above you very high; and you shall come down very low.

44 He shall lend to you, and you shall not lend to him; he shall be the head, and you shall be the tail.

45 Moreover all these curses shall come upon you and shall pursue you and overtake you, until you are destroyed; because you did not hearken to the voice of the LORD your God,

and did not keep his commandments and his statutes which he commanded you;

46 And they shall be upon you for signs and wonders, and upon your descendants for ever.

47 Because you did not serve the LORD your God with joyfulness and with gladness of heart, for the abundance of all things;

48 Therefore you shall serve your enemies whom the LORD shall send against you, in hunger and in thirst and in nakedness and in want of all things; and he shall put a yoke of iron upon your neck, until he has destroyed you.

49 The LORD shall bring a nation against you from afar, from the ends of the earth, as swift as the eagle that flies; a nation whose language you do not understand;

50 A people of fierce countenance, who shall not regard the person of the old, nor show mercy to the young;

51 And they shall eat the young of your cattle and the fruit of your land, until they destroy you; they also shall not leave you either grain or wine or oil or herds of oxen or flocks of sheep, until they have destroyed you.

52 And they shall besiege you in all your cities, until your high and fortified walls in which you trust are taken throughout all your land; and they shall besiege you in all your cities throughout all your land, which the LORD your God has given you.

53 And you shall eat the fruit of your own body, the flesh of your sons and of your daughters, whom the LORD your God has given you; and you shall eat them in the siege and in the distress with which your enemies shall harass you;

54 So that the man who abounds in delights among you and lives a luxurious life, his eye shall be evil toward his brother and toward his lawful wife and toward the remnant of his children that are left;

55 So that he will not give to any of them of the flesh of his children whom he shall eat; because he has nothing left him in the siege and in the distress with which your enemies

shall harass you in all your cities.

56 The woman who abounds in delights, who lives a luxurious life among you, who would not venture to set the sole of her foot upon the ground because of her delicacy and tenderness, her eye shall be evil toward her husband and toward her son and toward her daughter

57 And toward the afterbirth that comes out from between her feet and toward her child whom she shall bear, when she eats them for want of all things in the siege and distress with which your enemy shall harass you in all your cities.

58 If you will not observe and do all the words of this law that are written in this book, that you may fear the glorious and wonderful name of the LORD your God;

59 Then the LORD will send your plagues and the plagues of your descendants, even great plagues of long duration, and sore sicknesses of long duration.

60 Moreover he will bring upon you all the diseases of Egypt, of which you were afraid; and they shall cleave to you.

61 Also all kinds of sickness and all plagues which are not written in this book of the law, then will the LORD bring upon you, until you are destroyed.

62 And you shall be left few in number, whereas you were as the stars of the heaven for multitude; because you would not obey the voice of the LORD your God.

63 And as the LORD rejoiced over you to do you good and to multiply you; so the LORD will rejoice over you to destroy you and exterminate you; and you shall be carried away from the land which you are entering to possess.

64 And the LORD shall scatter you among all peoples, from one end of the earth to the other; and there you shall serve other gods, of wood and stone, which neither you nor your fathers have known.

65 And among these nations you shall find no ease, neither shall the sole of your foot have rest; but the LORD shall give you there a trembling heart and failing of eyes and sorrow of the soul;

66 And your life shall be uncertain before you; and you shall fear day and night, and shall have no assurance of your life;

67 In the morning you shall say, Would God it were evening! and in the evening you shall say, Would God it were morning! because of the fear of your heart with which you shall fear, and because of the hardships which you shall see with your eyes.

68 And the LORD shall bring you back into Egypt with ships, by the way whereof he said to you, You shall see it no more again; and there you shall be sold to your enemies as bondmen and bondwomen, but there shall be no one to buy you.

CHAPTER 29

THESE are the words of the covenant which the LORD commanded Moses to make with the children of Israel in the land of Moab, besides the covenant which he made with them in Horeb.

2 ¶And Moses called to all Israel, and said to them, You have seen all that the LORD did to Pharaoh before your eyes in the land of Egypt and to all his servants and to all his army and to all his land;

3 The great trials which your eyes have seen, the signs, and those great marvels which you saw;

4 Yet to this day the LORD has not given you a heart to understand and eyes to see and ears to hear.

5 And I have led you forty years in the wilderness; your clothes are not worn out upon you and your shoes are not worn out upon your feet.

6 You have not eaten bread, neither have you drunk wine or strong drink, that you might know that I am the LORD your God.

7 And when you came to this place, Sihon the king of Heshbon and Og the king of Mathnin came out against us to battle, and we slew them;

8 And we took their land and gave it for an inheritance to the Reubenites

and to the Gadites and to the half tribe of Manasseh.

9 Keep therefore the words of this covenant and do them, that you may prosper in all that you do.

10 ¶You stand this day before the LORD your God, all the heads of your tribes, your elders and your scribes, all the men of Israel,

11 Your little ones, your wives, and the stranger who is in your camp, from the gatherer of your wood to the drawer of your water;

12 That you may not transgress the covenant of the LORD your God, and the oath of the LORD your God, which he made with you this day;

13 Because he will establish you this day a people to himself, and he will be to you the God, as he has promised you, and as he has sworn to your fathers, to Abraham, to Isaac, and to Jacob.

14 Neither is it with you only that I do make this covenant and this oath;

15 But with all who stand here with us this day before the LORD our God, and also with him who is not here with us this day

16 (For you know how we have sojourned in the land of Egypt; and how we came through the nations which you passed by;

17 And you have seen their abominations and their idols of wood and stone, overlaid with silver and gold).

18 Perhaps there is among you a man or woman or family or tribe whose heart turns away this day from the LORD our God, to go and serve the gods of these nations; or perhaps there is among you a root that springs up and bears poison and wormwood;

19 And when he hears the words of this oath, he shall reason in his heart, saying, I shall have peace, though I walk in the imagination of my heart, to add drunkenness to thirst;

20 The LORD would not forgive him, but then the anger of the LORD and his zealousness would be grievous against that man, and all the curses that are written in this book shall lie upon him, and the LORD shall blot out his name from under the heaven.

17

21 And the LORD shall single him out to misfortune from all the tribes of Israel, according to all the curses of the covenant that are written in this book of the law.

22 So that the generation to come, your children that shall rise up after you and the strangers that shall come from a far land, shall say, when they see the plagues of that land and the sicknesses which the LORD has brought upon it;

23 Laying it waste with brimstone and with scorched salt, that the whole land is not sown, nor any grass grows in it, like the overthrow of Sodom and Gomorrah, Admah and Zeboim, which the LORD overthrew in his anger and in his wrath;

24 And all the nations shall say, Why has the LORD done thus to this land? And why has his anger kindled so much?

25 Then men shall say, Because they have forsaken the covenant of the LORD God of their fathers, which he made with them when he brought them forth out of the land of Egypt;

26 And they went and served other gods, and worshipped them, gods whom they had not known, nor had they divided spoils among them;

27 Therefore the anger of the LORD was kindled against this land, to bring upon it all the curses that are written in this book;

28 And the LORD uprooted them from their land in anger and in wrath and in great indignation, and cast them into another land, as it is this day.

29 The secret things belong to the LORD our God; but those things that are revealed belong to us and to our children for ever, that we may keep and do all the words of this law.

CHAPTER 30

AND it shall come to pass, when all these are come upon you, the blessings and the curses which I have set before you, and you shall call them to mind among all the nations where the LORD your God has driven you,

2 And shall return to the LORD your

God and shall obey his voice according to all that I command you this day, you and your children, with all your heart and with all your soul;

3 Then the LORD your God will bring back again your captivity, and have compassion upon you, and will return and gather you from all the nations where the LORD your God has driven you.

4 If your scattered ones are in the outmost parts of heaven, O Israel, from thence will the LORD your God gather you, and from thence will he fetch you;

5 And the LORD your God will bring you into the land which your fathers possessed, and you shall possess it; and he will do you good, and multiply you more than your fathers.

6 And the LORD your God will circumcise your heart and the heart of your descendants, and then you will love the LORD your God with all your heart and with all your soul, because he will give you rest.

7 And the LORD your God will put all these curses upon your enemies, and on those who hate you, who persecuted you.

8 And you shall return and obey the voice of the LORD your God, and do all his commandments which I command you this day.

9 And the LORD your God will make you plenteous in every work of your hand, in the fruit of your body and in the bearing of your cattle and in the fruit of your land, for good; for the LORD will again rejoice over you for good, as he rejoiced over your fathers;

10 If you will obey the voice of the LORD your God, and keep his commandments and his statutes which are written in this book of the law, and if you turn to the LORD your God with all your heart and with all your soul.

11 ¶For this commandment which I command you this day is not hidden from you, neither is it far off.

12 It is not in heaven, that you should say, Who shall go up for us to heaven and bring it to us, that we may hear it and do it?

13 Neither is it beyond the sea, that you should say, Who shall go over the sea for us and bring it to us, that we may hear it and do it?

14 But the word is very near you, in your mouth and in your heart, that you may do it.

15 ¶See, I have set before you this day life and good, and death and misfortunes;

16 In that I command you this day to love the LORD your God, to walk in his ways, and to keep his commandments and his statutes and his judgments; then you shall live; and multiply exceedingly; and the LORD your God shall bless you in the land which you are entering to possess.

17 But if your heart turns away, so that you will not hear, but shall go astray, and worship other gods and serve them;

18 I declare to you this day that you shall surely perish, and that you shall not live long in the land which you are crossing over the Jordan to possess.

19 I call heaven and earth to bear witness against you this day, that I have set before you life and death, blessings and cursings; therefore choose life, that both you and your descendants may live;

20 That you may love the LORD your God, and that you may obey his voice, and that you may cleave to him; for he is your life and the length of your days; that you may dwell in the land which the LORD swore to your fathers, to Abraham, to Isaac, and to Jacob, to give to you.

CHAPTER 31

AND Moses went and spoke all these words to all Israel.

2 And he said to them, I am a hundred and twenty years old this day; I can no longer go out and come in; and the LORD has said to me, You shall not cross the Jordan.

3 The LORD your God, he will go over before you, and he will destroy these nations from before you, and you shall possess them; and Joshua shall go over before you, as the LORD has said.

4 And the LORD shall do to them as he did to Sihon and to Og, the kings of the Amorites, and to their lands, which he destroyed.

5 And the LORD shall deliver them also before you, and you shall do to them according to all the commandments which I have commanded you.

6 Be strong and of good courage, fear not, nor tremble before them; for it is the LORD your God who goes with you; he will not fail you, nor forsake you.

7 ¶Then Moses called Joshua, and said to him in the sight of all Israel, Be strong and of good courage; for you shall bring this people into the land which the LORD has sworn to their fathers to give them; and you shall cause them to inherit it.

8 And it is the LORD who goes before you; he will be with you, he will not fail you, nor forsake you; fear not, neither tremble, nor be dismayed.

9 ¶And Moses wrote this law, and gave it to the priests, the sons of Levi, who carried the ark of the covenant of the LORD, and to all the elders of Israel.

10 And Moses commanded them, saying, At the end of every seven years, at the time of the year of release, at the feast of tabernacles,

11 When all Israel comes to appear before the LORD your God in the place which he shall choose, you shall read this law before all Israel in their hearing.

12 Gather the people together, men and women and children and the stranger who is within your cities, that they may hear, and that they may learn and revere the LORD your God and observe and do all the words of this law;

13 And that their children, who have not known anything, may hear and learn to fear the LORD your God, as long as you live in the land which you are crossing the Jordan to possess.

14 ¶And the LORD said to Moses, Behold, the day is coming when you must die; call Joshua, and present yourselves in the tabernacle of the congregation, that I may give him a charge. And Moses and Joshua went, and presented themselves in the tabernacle of the congregation.

15 And the LORD appeared in the tabernacle in a pillar of cloud; and the pillar of cloud stood over the door of the tabernacle.

16 ¶And the LORD said to Moses, Behold, you shall sleep with your fathers; and this people will rise up and go astray after strange gods of the land where they go to dwell among them, and will forsake me and break my covenant which I have made with them.

17 Then my anger shall be kindled against them in that day, and I will forsake them, and I will turn away my face from them, and they shall be devoured, and many evils and troubles shall befall them; so that they will say in that day, Are not these evils come upon us because our God is not in our midst?

18 And I will surely turn away from them in that day for all the evils which they have done, in that they have gone astray after other gods.

19 Now therefore write this song for them, and teach it to the children of Israel; and put it into their mouths; this song will be a witness for me against the children of Israel.

20 For I will bring them into the land which I swore to their fathers, a land that flows with milk and honey; and when they have eaten and are full, and live in luxury, then they will go astray after other gods and serve them, and provoke me, and break my covenant.

21 And when many evils and troubles are befallen them, then this song shall be read before them as a witness; for it shall not be forgotten out of the mouths of their descendants; for I know their inclination and all that they do here this day, before I have brought them into the land which I swore to their fathers.

22 ¶Moses therefore wrote this song the same day, and taught it to the children of Israel.

23 And he gave Joshua the son of Nun a charge, and said to him, Be

strong and of good courage; for you shall bring the children of Israel into the land which I swore to their fathers; and I will be with you.

24 ¶And when Moses had made an end of writing the words of this law in a book, and they were finished,

25 He commanded the Levites who carried the ark of the covenant of the LORD, saying,

26 Take this book of the law, and put it in the side of the ark of the covenant of the LORD your God, that it may be there as a witness against you.

27 For I know how rebellious and stiffnecked you are; behold, while I am yet alive with you this day, you have been rebellious against the LORD; and how much more after my death?

28 ¶Gather to me all the elders of your tribes and your scribes, that I may speak these words to you, and call heaven and earth to witness against you.

29 For I know that after my death you will surely become corrupt and turn aside from the way which I have commanded you; and evil will befall you in the latter days; when you have done evil in the sight of the LORD and have provoked him to anger through the work of your hands.

30 And Moses spoke the words of this song before all the congregation of the children of Israel, until they were ended.

CHAPTER 32

GIVE ear, O heavens, and I will speak; and let the earth hear the words of my mouth.

2 My word shall drop as rain, my speech shall fall as dew, as the gentle wind upon the tender herbs, and as the showers upon the grass;

3 For I will call upon the name of the LORD; ascribe majesty to our God, the Mighty One.

4 For his works are perfect; and all his ways are just; he is a faithful God and without iniquity, just and upright is he.

5 They have corrupted themselves, and they are not his children because of blemish; they are a perverse and crooked generation.

6 Are these the things that you return unto the LORD, O foolish and unwise people? Is he not your father who has redeemed you? Has he not made you and established you?

7 ¶Remember the days of old, consider the years of many generations; ask your father, and he will show you; your elders, and they will tell you.

8 When the Most High divided the nations, when he separated mankind, he set the bounds of the people according to the number of the children of Israel.

9 For the LORD'S portion is his people; Jacob is the lot of his inheritance.

10 He found him in a desert land, and in the waste and howling wilderness; he made him to settle down, he loved him, he kept him as the apple of his eye.

11 As an eagle encircles his nest, fluttering over his young, spreading out its wings, taking them, bearing them on the strength of his wings;

12 So the LORD alone did lead Israel, and there was no strange god with him.

13 He made him to dwell in a fertile land, and fed him with the produce of the field; and he made him to suck honey out of the rock and oil out of the flinty rock;

14 And gave him butter of cows and milk of sheep, with fat of fatlings and rams of the breed of rock-goats and goats, with the fat and the best wheat; and he gave him wine to drink, and of the juices of grapes.

15 ¶And Israel grew fat and kicked; he became rich and mighty, he gained wealth; then he forsook God who made him, and reviled the Mighty One who had saved him.

16 They provoked him to zealousness with strange gods, they made him angry with idols.

17 They sacrificed to demons that were not gods; to gods whom they knew not, to new gods that were just made, whom your fathers had never worshipped.

18 But you forsook the Mighty One

who bore you, and you forgot the God who made you glorious.

19 And the LORD saw it, and was angry, because his sons and daughters provoked him.

20 And he said, I will turn away my face from them, I will see what their end will be; for they are a perverse generation, children in whom is no faith.

21 They have provoked me to zealousness with that which is not God; they have provoked me to anger with their idols; so I will move them to jealousy with those that are not my people; I will provoke them to anger with a foolish nation.

22 For a fire is kindled in my anger, and shall burn to the lowest parts of Sheol, and shall consume the earth and its increase, and set on fire the foundations of the mountains.

23 I will heap mischiefs upon them; I will spend my arrows upon them.

24 They shall be disabled with hunger, and I will deliver them to evil spirits, and I will deliver them to vultures; I will also stir up wild beasts upon them, with the poison of serpents which creep in the dust.

25 Outside the sword shall bereave, and terror in inner chambers shall destroy both the young men and the virgins, the suckling also with the men of gray hairs.

26 And I said, Where are they? I would blot out the memory of them from among men.

27 Had it not been for the wrath of the enemy, who had become strong, and had it not been for the boasting of the adversary, who would say, It is our hand that has prevailed, and the LORD has not done all this, I would have blotted them out.

28 For they are a nation void of counsel, neither is there any understanding in them.

29 O that they were wise, that they understood this, that they would consider their latter end!

30 How should one chase a thousand, and two put ten thousand to flight, except their Mighty One had delivered them to their enemies, and the LORD had hemmed them in?

31 For their strength is not as our strength, even our enemies themselves being judges.

32 For their vine is of the vine of Sodom, and of the fields of Gomorrah; their grapes are bitter grapes, the clusters are gall to them;

33 Their venom is the venom of dragons, and the cruel venom of asps.

34 Is not this laid up in store with me, and sealed up in my treasures?

35 To me belongs vengeance, and I will recompense them at the time when their foot shall slip; for the day of their destruction is at hand, and the misfortune that shall come upon them makes haste.

36 For the LORD shall judge his people, and be consoled for his servants, because he will see that their power is gone, and there is none to help or sustain.

37 And he shall say, Where are their mighty gods, those in whom they trusted,

38 Who ate the fat of their sacrifices, and drank the wine of their drink offerings? Let them now rise up and help you, let them be your protection.

39 See now that I, even I, am he, and there is no god besides me; I cause men to die, and I make alive; I wound, and I heal; and there is none that can escape out of my hands.

40 For I lift up my hand to heaven and say, I live for ever.

41 I will whet my glittering sword as the lightning, and my hand shall take hold of judgment; I will render vengeance on those that hate me, and cause my enemies to surrender.

42 I will make my arrows drunk with blood, and my sword shall devour flesh, with the blood of the slain and of the captives, from the crown of the head of the enemy.

43 Therefore praise his people, O you nations; for the blood of his servants shall be avenged, and he will take vengeance upon his adversaries, and will give absolution to his land and to his people.

44 ¶And Moses came and recited all the words of this song before the

people, he and Joshua the son of Nun.

45 And when Moses had finished reciting all these words to all Israel,

46 He said to them, Set your hearts to all the words which I testify among you this day, which you shall command your children to do, all the words of this law.

47 For it is not a vain thing for you, because it is your life; and through this thing you shall prolong your days in the land which you are crossing the Jordan to possess.

48 And the LORD spoke to Moses that same day, saying,

49 Go up into this mountain of the Abraye,[1] into mount Nebo, which is in the land of Moab, that is over toward Jericho; and view the land of Canaan, which I give to the children of Israel as a possession:

50 And die on the mountain which you ascend, and be gathered to your people; as Aaron your brother died on mount Hor, and was gathered to his people:

51 Because you transgressed against me among the children of Israel at the waters of Mesotha, which is at Rakim, in the wilderness of Zin; because you did not sanctify me in the midst of the children of Israel.

52 Yet you shall see the land before you, which I give to the children of Israel; but you shall not enter there.

CHAPTER 33

AND this is the blessing, wherewith Moses the servant of God blessed the children of Israel before his death.

2 And he said, The LORD came from Sinai, and shined upon us from Seir; he rose up from mount Paran; he came with ten thousands of saints at his right hand.

3 Yea, he supplied their needs; he also made them to be beloved by the nations; he blessed all his saints; and they followed closely after his feet, every one receiving one of his words.

4 Moses delivered to us a law, and he gave it as an inheritance to the congregation of Jacob.

5 And there shall be a king in Is-rael, when the heads of the people and the tribes of Israel are gathered together.

6 ¶Let Reuben live, and not die; and let his people be numerous.

7 ¶And this is the blessing of Judah: Hear, O LORD, the voice of Judah, and bring him close to his people; let his hands contend for him, and be thou a help to him from his oppressors.

8 ¶And of Levi he said, Let your consecration and your light be upon the just one whom thou didst prove in trials and whom thou didst test at the waters of Mesotha;

9 Who said of his father and of his mother, I have not seen them; neither did he recognize his brothers nor know his own children; for they have observed thy word and kept thy covenant.

10 They shall teach Jacob thy judgments, and Israel thy law; they shall put incense before thee when thou art angry, and whole burnt sacrifice upon thy altar.

11 Bless, O LORD, his substance, and accept the work of his hands; smite the loins of his adversaries, and of his enemies, that they rise not again.

12 ¶And of Benjamin he said, The beloved of the LORD shall dwell in safety; and the LORD shall have compassion on him all the day long, and he shall dwell in his bosom.

13 ¶And of Joseph he said, Blessed of the LORD be his land and its fruit, with the dew of heaven from above, with the deep that couches beneath,

14 With the fruit of the earth brought forth by the sun, with the products brought forth by the moon,

15 With the best fruits of the eastern mountains, with the fruit of the eternal hills,

16 With the precious things of the earth and the fulness thereof, and with the good will of him who dwelt in the bush; let blessing come upon the head of Joseph, and upon the crown of the head of his brothers.

17 His glory is like the firstlings of the bullocks, and his horns are like

---

[1] The Ammonites and the Moabites were known as Abraye, Hebrews, people who had crossed the river Euphrates. They were the descendants of Lot, the nephew of Abraham.

the horns of unicorns; with them he shall push the peoples together to the ends of the earth; and they are the ten thousands of Ephraim, and they are the thousands of Manasseh.

18 ¶And of Zebulun he said, Rejoice, O Zebulun, in your going out; and Issachar, in your tents.

19 They shall call the people to the mountain; there they shall offer sacrifices of righteousness; for they shall suck of the abundance of the sea, and of the treasures which lie hidden in ships on the beaches.

20 ¶And of Gad he said, Blessed be he who enlarges Gad; he dwells like a lion, and tears the arm together with the head.

21 And he provided the first part of the spoil for himself, out of which he set aside the portion of the lawgiver; he went out at the head of the people; he executed the justice of the LORD and his judgments with Israel.

22 ¶And of Dan he said, Dan is a lion's whelp, who sucks milk from Mathnin.

23 ¶And of Naphtali he said, O Naphtali, satisfied with abundance, and filled with the blessing of the LORD; he shall possess the west and the south.

24 ¶And of Asher he said, Let Asher be blessed with children; let him be acceptable to his brethren, and let him have abundance of oil.

25 Your shoes shall be iron and brass; and as to your days, so shall your strength be.

26 ¶There is none like the God of Israel, who rides through the heaven to your help, and in his excellency on the sky.

27 In the heaven of heavens is the dwelling of our God from everlasting, and below he creates men; and he shall destroy your enemies from before you; for he said, Destroy them.

28 Israel then shall dwell in safety alone; the fountain of Jacob shall be in a land of grain and wine and oil; also the heavens shall drop down dew.

29 Happy are you, O Israel; who is like you, a people whose salvation is sustained by the LORD, God is your

¹ Pisgah.

help, and your pride is not in the sword; your enemies shall deal treacherously with you; but you shall tread upon their necks.

CHAPTER 34

AND Moses went up from the plains of Moab to the mountain of Nebo, to the top of the hill ¹ which is opposite Jericho. And the LORD showed him all the land of Gilead as far as Dan,

2 And all Naphtali, and the land of Ephraim, and Manasseh, and all the land of Judah as far as the Mediterranean Sea,

3 And the south, and the plain of the valley of Jericho, the city of palm trees, as far as Zoar.

4 And the LORD said to him, This is the land which I swore to Abraham, to Isaac, and to Jacob, saying, I will give it to your descendants; I have permitted you to see it with your eyes, but you shall not go over to it.

5 ¶So Moses the servant of the LORD died there in the land of Moab, according to the word of the LORD.

6 And he buried him in a valley in the land of Moab, over against Beth-peor; but no man knows of his sepulchre to this day.

7 ¶And Moses was a hundred and twenty years old when he died; but his eye was not dim, nor the skin of his cheeks wrinkled.

8 ¶And the children of Israel wept for Moses in the plains of Moab thirty days; so the days of weeping and mourning for Moses were ended.

9 ¶And Joshua the son of Nun was full of the spirit of wisdom; for Moses had laid his hands upon him; and the children of Israel obeyed him, and did as the LORD commanded Moses.

10 ¶And there arose not a prophet since in Israel like Moses, whom the LORD knew face to face,

11 In all the signs and the wonders, which the LORD sent him to do in the land of Egypt to Pharaoh and to all his servants and to all his land,

12 And in all that mighty power, and in all the great signs which Moses wrought in the sight of all Israel.

THE BOOK OF

JOSHUA

CHAPTER 1

AFTER the death of Moses the servant of the LORD, the LORD said to Joshua the son of Nun, Moses' minister,

2 Moses my servant is dead; now therefore arise, cross this Jordan, you and all this people, into the land which I am giving to them, even to the children of Israel.

3 Every place that the sole of your foot shall tread upon, it shall be yours, as I promised Moses.

4 From the wilderness and this Lebanon even to the great river, the river Euphrates, all the land of the Hittites, as far as the Great Sea toward the going down of the sun shall be your boundaries.

5 No man shall be able to resist you all the days of your life; as I was with Moses, so I will be with you; I will not fail you, nor forsake you.

6 Be strong and of good courage; for you shall cause this people to inherit the land which I swore to their fathers to give them.

7 Only be strong and very courageous, that you may observe to do according to all the laws which Moses my servant has commanded you; turn not from it to the right hand or to the left, that you may succeed wherever you go.

8 This book of the law shall not depart out of your mouth; but you shall meditate thereon day and night, that you may observe to do according to all that is written therein; for then you shall succeed and prosper.

9 Behold, I have commanded you. Be strong and of good courage; fear not, neither be dismayed; for the LORD your God is with you wherever you go.

10 ¶Then Joshua commanded the officers of the people and their scribes, saying,

11 Pass through the camp, and command the people, saying, Prepare for yourselves provisions for a journey; for within three days you are to cross this Jordan, to go in to possess the land which the LORD your God gives you.

12 ¶And to the Reubenites and to the Gadites and to the half tribe of Manasseh, Joshua said,

13 Remember the word which Moses the servant of the LORD commanded you, saying, The LORD your God has given you rest, and has given you this land.

14 Your wives, your little ones, and your cattle shall remain in the land which Moses gave you on this side of the Jordan; but you shall cross armed before your brethren, all of you who are mighty men of valor, and help them;

15 Until the LORD gives rest to your brethren, as he has given you, and they also have possessed the land which the LORD your God gives them; then you shall return to the land of your possession, and shall inherit it, the land which Moses the servant of the LORD gave you on this side of the Jordan toward the sunrising.

16 ¶And the Reubenites, the Gadites, and the Manassites answered and said to Joshua, All that you have commanded us we will do, and wherever you send us, we will go.

17 Just as we obeyed Moses in all things, so will we obey you; only the LORD your God be with you, as he was with Moses.

244

18 Anyone who shall quarrel with you and will· not obey your word in all that you command him, he shall be put to death; only be strong and of good courage.

CHAPTER 2

AND Joshua the son of Nun sent out from Shittim two men who were familiar with the land, and said to them, Go view the land of Jericho. And they went, and came into the house of a woman who was a harlot, named Rahab, and lodged there.

2 And it was told the king of Jericho, saying, Behold, there came certain men here tonight from the children of Israel to spy in the country.

3 So the king of Jericho sent to Rahab, saying, Bring forth the men that have entered into your house at night; for they have come to spy in the country.

4 And the woman took the two men, and hid them, and said, Truly, the men came to me, but I did not know where they came from;

5 And it came to pass about the time of the shutting of the gate, when it was dark, they went out; and I did not know where they went. Pursue them quickly; for you will overtake them.

6 But she had brought them up to the roof of the house, and hid them beneath the stalks of flax which she had piled up on the roof.

7 And the men pursued after them by the way of the Jordan to the fords; and after the pursuers were gone out after the spies, they shut the gate.

8 ¶And before they lay down, she came up to them upon the roof;

9 And she said to the men, I know that the LORD has given you the land, and that your terror has fallen upon us, and that also all the inhabitants of the land are terrified because of you.

10 For we have heard how the LORD dried up the waters of the Red Sea before you, when you came out of Egypt; and what you did to the two kings of the Amorites, to Sihon and Og, whom you utterly destroyed.

11 And when we heard these things,

our hearts trembled, neither did there remain any more courage in any one of us, because of you; for the LORD your God, is he who is God in heaven above and on earth beneath.

12 Now therefore, swear to me by the LORD, because I have showed you kindness, that you also will show kindness to me and to my father's household, and give me a true sign;

13 And that you will save alive my father, my mother, my brothers, and my sisters, and all that belongs to us, and deliver our lives from death.

14 And the men said to her, We will give our lives to death instead of you, if you will not disclose this affair. And it shall be, when the LORD has given us this land, then we will deal kindly and truly with you.

15 Then she let them down by a rope through the window; for her house was joined to the city wall, and she dwelt upon the wall.

16 And she said to them, Go by way of the mountain, lest the pursuers meet you; and hide yourselves there three days, until the pursuers have returned, and then you shall go on your way.

17 And the men said to her, We will be blameless of this oath which you have made us swear.

18 Behold, when we come into the land, you must bind this cord of scarlet thread in the window through which you let us down; and you shall bring your father and your mother and your brothers and all your father's household home to you.

19 And it shall be, that whosoever shall go out of the door of your house into the street, his blood shall be on his head, and we will be guiltless; and whosoever shall be with you in the house, his blood shall be on our heads, and we are guilty if any man should harm him.

20 And if you disclose this affair, then we will be absolved from this oath which you have made us swear.

21 And she said, According to your words, so be it. And she sent them away, and they departed; and she bound the scarlet cord in the window.

22 And they went to the mountain,

and stayed there three days, until the pursuers were returned; and the pursuers sought them throughout all the way, and when they failed to find them, they returned.

23 ¶So the two spies came down from the mountain, and passed over and came to Joshua the son of Nun, and told him all that had befallen them.

24 And they said to Joshua, The LORD has delivered all the land into our hands; for the inhabitants of the land are afraid of us.

CHAPTER 3

AND Joshua rose early in the morning; and they journeyed from Shittim, and came to the Jordan, he and all the people of Israel, and lodged there and did not cross over.

2 And it came to pass after three days the officers went through the camp;

3 And they commanded the people, saying, When you see the ark of the covenant of the LORD your God, and the priests and the Levites carrying it, then you must proceed from your place, and go after it.

4 And there shall be a space between you and the ark, about two thousand cubits by measure; you shall not come near to it, that you may know the way by which you shall go; for you have not passed this way before.

5 And Joshua said to the people, Sanctify yourselves; for tomorrow the LORD will do wonders among you.

6 And Joshua said to the priests, Take up the ark of the covenant, and pass over before the people. And they took up the ark of the covenant, and went before the people.

7 ¶And the LORD said to Joshua, From this day I will begin to exalt you in the sight of all Israel, that they may know that as I was with Moses, so I will be with you.

8 And you shall command the priests who carry the ark of the covenant of the LORD, saying, When you are come to the brink of the waters of the Jordan, you shall stand still in the Jordan.

9 ¶And Joshua said to the children of Israel, Come hither, and hear the words of the LORD your God.

10 And Joshua said, Hereby you shall know that the living God is among you, and that he will destroy from before you the Hittites, the Canaanites, the Hivites, the Perizzites, the Girgashites, the Amorites, and the Jebusites.

11 Behold, the ark of the covenant of the LORD of all the earth is passing over before you in the Jordan.

12 Now therefore take twelve men from all the tribes of Israel, a man out of each tribe.

13 And when the soles of the feet of the priests who bear the ark of the covenant of the LORD, the LORD of all the earth, shall rest in the waters of the Jordan, the waters of the Jordan shall be divided, the waters that are flowing down from above shall pile up as though they were in sheepskins, one beside the other.

14 ¶And it came to pass, when the people set out from their tents to cross the Jordan and the priests who were bearing the ark of the covenant went before the people;

15 And as soon as those that bore the ark reached the Jordan, and the feet of the priests who were bearing the ark were dipped in the brim of the water (for the Jordan overflows its banks all the time of harvest);

16 That the waters that flowed down from above piled up as though they were in sheepskins, one beside the other; and extended for a long distance from the town of Aram, that is beside Zaretan; and those that flowed down toward the sea of the plain, the Salt Sea, failed to flow, and were divided; and the people passed over opposite Jericho.

17 And the priests who bore the ark of the covenant of the LORD stood on dry ground in the midst of the Jordan, and all the Israelites passed over on dry ground until all the people finished passing over the Jordan.

CHAPTER 4

AND when all the people had finished passing over the Jordan, the LORD said to Joshua,

2 Take twelve men from the people, a man out of every tribe,

3 And command them, saying, Take from here out of the midst of the Jordan, out of the place where the priests' feet stood, twelve stones, and you shall carry them over with you, and lay them in the lodging place where you lodge this night.

4 Then Joshua called the twelve men who were selected from the children of Israel, out of each tribe a man;

5 And Joshua said to them, Pass over before the ark of the LORD your God into the midst of the Jordan, and take up every man of you a stone upon his shoulder, according to the number of the tribes of the children of Israel;

6 That this may be a sign among you, that when your children ask you in time to come, saying, What is the meaning of these stones?

7 Then you shall tell them, The waters of the Jordan were divided before the ark of the covenant of the LORD; when we passed over the Jordan, the waters of the Jordan were divided; and these stones shall be for a memorial to the children of Israel for ever.

8 And the children of Israel did as Joshua commanded them, and took up twelve stones out of the midst of the Jordan, as the LORD had said to Joshua, according to the number of the tribes of the children of Israel, and carried them over with them to the place where they lodged, and laid them down there.

9 And they set up the twelve stones which they had taken out of the midst of the Jordan, where stood the feet of the priests who were bearing the ark of the covenant; and they are there to this day.

10 ¶And the priests who bore the ark stood in the midst of the Jordan until everything was finished that the LORD commanded Joshua to tell to the people, according to all that Moses had commanded Joshua; and the people made haste and passed over.

11 And when all the people had finished passing over, the ark of the LORD and the priests passed over before the people.

12 Then the Reubenites, the Gadites, and the half tribe of Manasseh, passed over armed before the children of Israel, as Moses had told them;

13 About forty thousand men armed for war passed over before the LORD to battle, to the plains of Jericho.

14 ¶On that very day the LORD exalted Joshua in the sight of all Israel; and they feared him, as they had feared Moses, all the days of his life.

15 And the LORD said to Joshua,

16 Command the priests who bear the ark of the testimony to come up out of the Jordan.

17 Joshua therefore commanded the priests, saying, Come up out of the Jordan.

18 And when the priests who bore the ark of the covenant of the LORD had come up out of the midst of Jordan, and the soles of the priests' feet rested firm on the dry land, the waters of the Jordan rushed to their place, and overflowed all its banks, as they did before.

19 ¶And the people came up out of the Jordan on the tenth day of the first month, and encamped in Gilgal, on the east border of Jericho.

20 And those twelve stones which they took out of the Jordan, Joshua set up at Gilgal.

21 And he said to the children of Israel, When your children shall ask you in time to come, saying, What is the meaning of these stones?

22 Then you shall explain them to your children, and say to them, The children of Israel crossed this Jordan on dry land.

23 For the LORD your God dried up the waters of the Jordan from before them, until they passed over, as the LORD your God did to the Red Sea, which he dried up from before us until we passed over;

24 So that all the peoples of the earth might know that the hand of the LORD is mighty, and that you may worship the LORD your God for ever.

CHAPTER 5

AND when all the kings of the Amorites, who were beyond the Jordan westward, and all the kings of the Canaanites, who were by the sea, heard that the LORD had dried up the waters of the Jordan from before the children of Israel, until they had passed over, their hearts trembled, and there was no strength left in them, because of the children of Israel.

2 ¶At that time the LORD said to Joshua, Make for yourself a flint knife, and circumcise again the children of Israel the second time.

3 So Joshua made a flint knife for himself, and circumcised the children of Israel the second time at the Hill of the Uncircumcised.

4 And these are the men whom Joshua did circumcise: every male child who had been born after they had come out of Egypt, because all the men of war had died in the wilderness on the journey, after they came out of Egypt.

5 Because all the people who came out had been circumcised; but all the people that were born in the wilderness during the journey after they came out of Egypt had not been circumcised.

6 For the children of Israel journeyed forty years in the wilderness, until all the people who were men of war and came out of Egypt had perished, because they did not obey the voice of their LORD; to whom the LORD had sworn that he would not show them the land which he had sworn to their fathers that he would give them, a land that flows with milk and honey.

7 And it was their children who came after them that Joshua circumcised; for they were uncircumcised, because they had not been circumcised on the journey.

8 And when all the people were circumcised, they remained in their places in the camp till they were healed.

9 And the LORD said to Joshua, This day I have taken away the reproach of the Egyptians from you. Where-fore the name of that place is called Gilgal to this day.

10 ¶And the children of Israel encamped in Gilgal, and kept the passover on the fourteenth day of the month at evening in the plain of Jericho.

11 And they ate from the grain of the land on the morrow after the passover, unleavened bread and parched wheat did they eat on that very day.

12 ¶And the manna ceased on the morrow after they had eaten of the grain of the land; neither had the children of Israel manna any more; but they did eat of the produce of the land of Canaan that year.

13 ¶And it came to pass, when Joshua was in the plain of Jericho, he lifted up his eyes and looked, and, behold, there stood a man opposite him with his sword drawn in his hand; and Joshua went to him, and said to him, Are you of us or of our enemies?

14 And he said to him, I am the commander of the host of the LORD, and now I have come here. And Joshua fell on his face to the earth, and worshipped, and said, What hath my LORD to say to his servant?

15 And the commander of the LORD's host said to Joshua, Take your shoes from off your feet; for the place whereon you stand is holy. And Joshua did so.

CHAPTER 6

NOW Jericho was shut up because of the presence of the children of Israel; none went out and none came in.

2 And the LORD said to Joshua, See, I have delivered Jericho into your hands, with its king and all its armed forces.

3 And you shall encircle the city, all the men of war, and you shall go round about the city once a day. Thus shall you do for six days.

4 And seven priests shall bear trumpets, and blow before the ark; and on the seventh day you shall go around the city seven times, and the priests shall blow with the trumpets.

5 And it shall come to pass that when they blow the trumpets and

when you hear the sound of the trumpet, then all the people shall shout with a great shout; and the wall of the city shall fall down flat, and the people shall go up every man straight before him.

6 ¶And Joshua the son of Nun called the priests, and said to them, Take up the ark of the covenant of the LORD, and let seven priests bear seven trumpets and blow them before the ark of the Lord.

7 And he said to the people, Pass on, and encircle the city, and let those who are armed march on before the ark of the LORD.

8 ¶And as Joshua had spoken to the people, the seven priests bearing seven trumpets passed on before the ark of the LORD, blowing on the trumpets; and the ark of the covenant of the LORD followed them.

9 ¶And the armed men went before the priests who blew on the trumpets, and the rest of the people who were gathered went after the ark, and they marched on blowing the trumpets.

10 But Joshua had commanded the people, saying, You shall not shout, nor let your voice be heard, neither shall any word come out of your mouth, until the day that I bid you to shout; then shall you shout.

11 So the ark of the LORD made a circuit of the city, going about it once; and they came into the camp, and lodged in the camp.

12 ¶And Joshua rose early in the morning, and the priests took up the ark of the LORD.

13 And seven priests bearing seven trumpets went before the ark of the LORD; they went on continually, and blew with the trumpets; and the armed men went before them; and the rest of the multitude went after the ark of the LORD, while the priests were blowing with trumpets.

14 And the second day they compassed the city once, and returned to the camp; so they did for six days.

15 And on the seventh day, they rose in the morning, and compassed the city after the same manner seven times; it was on that day only that they compassed the city seven times.

16 At the seventh time, when the priests blew the trumpets, Joshua said to the people, Shout; for the LORD has delivered the city to you.

17 ¶And this city and all that is therein, is to be devoted to the LORD; only Rahab the harlot you shall spare, she and all who are with her in the house, because she hid the spies that we sent.

18 And as for you, you are to be careful of the devoted things, lest you defile yourselves by taking some of the devoted things, and make the camp of Israel a curse, and trouble it.

19 But all the silver and gold and vessels of brass and iron are consecrated to the LORD; they shall come into the treasury of the LORD.

20 So the people shouted and the priests blew the trumpets; and it came to pass, when the people heard the sound of the trumpets, they shouted with a great shout, and the wall fell down flat, so that the people went up into the city, every man straight before him, and they took the city.

21 And they utterly destroyed all that were in the city, both men and women, young and old and oxen and sheep and asses, with the edge of the sword.

22 But Joshua said to the two men who had spied out the country, Go into the harlot's house, and bring out from there the woman and all that she has, as you swore to her.

23 And the spies went in, and brought out Rahab and her father and her mother and her brothers and all that she had; and they brought out all her kindred, and placed them outside the camp of Israel.

24 And they burned the city with fire, and all that was therein; only the silver and the gold and the vessels of brass and of iron, they brought into the treasury of the house of the LORD.

25 But Rahab the harlot and her father's household and all that she had, Joshua saved alive; and she dwelt among the children of Israel even to this day; because she hid the spies

whom Joshua sent to spy out Jericho.
26 ¶And Joshua swore at that time, saying, Cursed before the LORD be the man that rises up and rebuilds this city, Jericho; with the death of his first-born shall he build it, and with the death of his youngest son shall he set up its gates.
27 So the LORD was with Joshua; and his fame spread throughout all the land.

CHAPTER 7

BUT the children of Israel committed a trespass in the devoted things; for Achar, the son of Carmi, the son of Zabdi, the son of Zerah, of the tribe of Judah, took some of the devoted things, and hid them; and the anger of the LORD was kindled against the children of Israel.
2 And Joshua sent men from Jericho to Ai, which is beside Beth-aon, on the east side of Beth-el, and said to them, Go up and spy out the land. And the men went up and spied out Ai.
3 And they returned to Joshua, and said to him, Let not all the people go up; but let about two or three thousand men go up, and destroy Ai; and do not send all the people there, for the men of Ai are but few.
4 So there went up about three thousand men; and they fled before the men of Ai.
5 And the men of Ai smote thirty-six of the Israelites; and they chased them from before the gate until they were defeated, and they smote them with a great slaughter; wherefore the hearts of the people melted, and became as water.
6 ¶And Joshua rent his clothes, and fell to the earth upon his face before the ark of the LORD until the evening, he and the elders of Israel, and put dust upon their heads.
7 And Joshua said, Alas, O LORD God, why hast thou brought this people over the Jordan, to deliver us into the hands of the Amorites? Would to God we had been content, and dwelt on the other side of the Jordan!
8 Now, what shall I say, when Is-

rael has turned their backs before their enemies!
9 For the Canaanites and all the inhabitants of the land shall hear of it, and shall gather together against us, and cut off our name from the face of the earth; and what wilt thou do to thy great name?
10 ¶And the LORD said to Joshua, Get up; why do you lie upon your face on the earth?
11 Israel has sinned, and they have also transgressed the commandment which I commanded them; for they have even taken some of the devoted things, and have also stolen, and lied, and they have hidden them among their own stuff.
12 Therefore the children of Israel cannot stand again before their enemies, but they shall turn their backs before their enemies, because they are accursed; neither will I be with you any more, unless you remove the curse from among you.
13 Up, summon this people, and say, Be ready tomorrow; for thus says the LORD God of Israel, There is an accursed thing in the midst of you, O Israel; you cannot stand before your enemies any more until you remove the accursed thing from among you.
14 In the morning therefore you shall be brought near according to your tribes; and it shall be that the tribe which the LORD takes shall come by families; and the family which the LORD shall take shall come by households; and the household which the LORD shall take shall come man by man.
15 And it shall be that he who is taken with the devoted thing shall be burned with fire, he and all that he has; because he has transgressed the commandment of the LORD, and because he has done wickedness in Israel.
16 ¶So Joshua rose up early in the morning, and brought forward Israel by tribes; and the tribe of Judah was taken;
17 And he brought the tribe of Judah by families; and the family of the Zarhites was taken; and he

brought the family of the Zarhites man by man; and Zabdi was taken.

18 Then he brought his household man by man; and Achar, the son of Carmi, the son of Zabdi, the son of Zerah, of the tribe of Judah, was taken.

19 And Joshua said to Achar, Give glory to the LORD God of Israel, and give praise to him; and tell me now what you have done; and do not hide it from me.

20 Achar answered Joshua, and said, Truly I have sinned against the LORD God of Israel, and this is what I did:

21 When I saw among the spoils a beautiful Babylonian tapestry and two hundred shekels of silver and a wedge of gold weighing fifty shekels, then I coveted them and took them; and, behold, they are hidden in the earth inside of my tent, and the silver under it.

22 ¶So Joshua sent messengers, and they ran to his tent, and, behold, it was hidden in his tent, and the silver under it.

23 And they took them out of his tent, and brought them to Joshua and to all the people of Israel, and laid them out before the LORD.

24 And Joshua and all Israel with him took Achar the son of Zerah and the silver and the tapestry and the wedge of gold and his sons and his daughters and his oxen and his asses and his sheep and his tent and all that he had; and they brought them to the valley of Achar.

25 And Joshua said to him, Why have you troubled us? The LORD shall trouble you this day. And all Israel stoned him with stones, both him and all that he had, and burned them with fire.

26 And they raised over him a great heap of stones which remain to this day. So the LORD turned from his fierce anger. Therefore the name of that place is called the Valley of Achar, to this day.

CHAPTER 8

AND the LORD said to Joshua, Fear not, neither be dismayed; take all the men of war with you, and arise and go up to Ai; because I have delivered into your hands the king of Ai and his people, his city and his land;

2 And you shall do to Ai and its king as you did to Jericho and its king; only the spoil and the cattle shall you take as a prey for yourselves; lay an ambush against the city, from behind it.

3 ¶So Joshua arose, and all the men of war, to go up against Ai; and Joshua chose three thousand mighty men of valor, and sent them away by night.

4 And he commanded them, saying, Behold, when you shall lie in wait against the city, from behind it, do not go very far from the city, but all of you be ready;

5 And I and the men that are with me will approach the city; and it shall come to pass, when they first come out against us, we will flee before them;

6 For they will come out after us, and drive us away from the city, and they will say, They are fleeing before us, as at first; and behold, as we flee before them,

7 Then you shall rise up from your ambush, and seize upon the city; for the LORD your God will deliver it into your hands.

8 And it shall be, when you have taken the city, you shall set it on fire; according to the commandment of the LORD you shall do. See, I have commanded you.

9 ¶So Joshua sent them forth; and they went to the place of ambush, and lay between Beth-el and Ai, on the west side of Ai; but Joshua spent that night among the people.

10 And Joshua rose up early in the morning, and counted the people, and went up, he and the elders of Israel, before the people to Ai.

11 And all the men of war that were with him went up and drew near to the city, and encamped on the north side of Ai. Now there was a valley between them and Ai;

12 And Joshua took five thousand men, and set them in ambush between Beth-el and Ai, on the west side of the city;

13 And when he had set his men and all his host on the north side of the city, and the rear guard on the west of the city, Joshua went that night among the people.

14 ¶And when the king of Ai saw it, he hastened, and the men of the city rose up, and went out against Israel to battle; so all the people of Ai were in the plain; and they did not know that there was an ambush against them from behind the city.

15 And Joshua and all Israel scattered before them to flee by way of the wilderness.

16 And all the people of Ai shouted as they pursued them; and they followed Joshua, and were drawn out of the city.

17 And there was not a man left in Ai or Beth-el who did not go out after Israel; and they left the city open, and pursued Israel.

18 And the LORD said to Joshua, Stretch out the spear that is in your hand toward Ai; for I have delivered it into your hands. And Joshua stretched out the spear that was in his hand toward the city.

19 And the men in ambush arose quickly from their places, and they ran as soon as he had stretched out his hand; and they entered into the city and took it, and hasted and set the city on fire.

20 And when the men of Ai looked behind them, they saw the smoke of their city going up to heaven, and they had no power to flee this way or that way; and the people of Israel that fled to the wilderness turned back upon their pursuers.

21 And when Joshua and all Israel saw that the ambush had taken the city, and that the city was going up in smoke, then they turned back and slew the men of Ai.

22 And the others went out of the city to meet them; so the men of Ai were caught in the midst of Israel, some on this side and some on that side; and they smote them, so that they let none of them remain or escape.

23 And they took the king of Ai alive, and brought him to Joshua.

24 And when Israel had finished slaying all the inhabitants of Ai in the fields and in the wilderness where they pursued them, and when all of them had fallen by the edge of the sword until they were consumed, then all Israel returned to Ai and smote it with the edge of the sword.

25 And so it was, that twelve thousand men and women, all the inhabitants of Ai, fell that day.

26 For Joshua did not draw his hand back, wherewith he stretched out the spear until he had utterly destroyed all the inhabitants of Ai.

27 Only the cattle and the spoil of that city Israel took for a prey for themselves, according to the word of the LORD which he commanded Joshua.

28 And Joshua burned Ai, and made it a heap of ruins for ever to this day.

29 And the king of Ai he hanged on a tree until the evening; and when the sun was set, Joshua commanded, and they took his corpse down from the tree and cast it at the entrance of the gate of the city, and raised over it a heap of large stones that remains to this day.

30 ¶Then Joshua built an altar to the LORD God of Israel in mount Gebal,[1]

31 As Moses the servant of the LORD had commanded the children of Israel, as it is written in the book of the law of Moses, an altar of unhewn stones upon which no man has lifted up any iron instrument; and they offered thereon burnt offerings to the LORD, and sacrificed peace offerings.

32 ¶And he wrote there upon the stones of the altar a copy of the law of Moses, which he wrote in the presence of the children of Israel.

33 And all Israel and their elders and their scribes and their judges stood on this side of the ark, and on that side the priests and the Levites who carried the ark of the covenant of the LORD, the natives as well as the

---

[1] Ebal.

sojourners; half of them toward mount Gerizim, and half of them toward mount Gebal, as Moses the servant of the LORD had commanded, that they should bless the people of Israel as before.

34 And afterward Joshua read all the words of the law, the blessings and the cursings, according to all that is written in the book of the law.

35 There was not a word of all that Moses commanded which Joshua did not read before all the congregation of Israel and before the women and the little ones and sojourners who were among them.

CHAPTER 9

AND when all the kings who were on this side of the Jordan, in the mountains and in the valleys, and on all the coasts of the Great Sea toward Lebanon, the Hittites, the Amorites, the Canaanites, the Perizzites, the Hivites, and the Jebusites, heard of it;

2 And they gathered themselves together, with one accord, to fight with Joshua and with Israel.

3 ¶And when the inhabitants of Gibeon heard what Joshua had done to Jericho and to Ai,

4 They worked subtly, and prepared provisions, and laid old sacks upon their asses, and wine skins, old, torn, and patched;

5 They put on old shoes, or bound their feet with sandals, and dressed in old garments; and all the bread of their provision was dry and mouldy.

6 And they went to Joshua to the camp at Gilgal, and said to him and to the men of Israel, We have come from a far country; now therefore make a treaty with us.

7 And the men of Israel said to the Hivites, If you dwell among us, why then should you have a treaty?

8 And they said to Joshua, We are your servants. And Joshua said to them, Who are you? And where do you come from?

9 And they said to him, From a very far country your servants have come because of the name of the LORD your God; for we have heard the fame of him, and all that he did in Egypt,

10 And all that he did to the two kings of the Amorites, who were beyond the Jordan, to Sihon king of Heshbon, and to Og king of Mathnin, who lived at Astaroth.

11 Wherefore our elders and all the inhabitants of our country said to us, Take provisions with you for the journey, and go to meet them, and say to them, We are your servants; therefore now make a treaty with us.

12 Moreover, they also said to Joshua, This bread we took hot out of our houses for our provisions on the day we came forth to go to you; but now, behold, it is dry, and is mouldy.

13 And these wine skins, which we filled, were new; and, behold, they are worn out; and these our garments and our shoes were new when we put them on us, and, behold, now they are old because the journey was very long.

14 And the men took of their provisions and went away, and the Israelites did not ask counsel from the LORD.

15 And Joshua made peace with them, and he made a treaty with them to let them live; and the princes of the congregation swore to them.

16 ¶And at the end of three days after they had made the treaty with them, they heard that they were their neighbors, and that they dwelt among them.

17 And the children of Israel journeyed, and came to their cities on the third day. Now the names of their cities were Gibeon, Chephirah, Aeerooth and Koriath-naarin.

18 And the children of Israel did not kill them, because the princes of the congregation had sworn to them by the LORD God of Israel. And the whole congregation murmured and were in an uproar against the princes.

19 But the princes said to the congregation, We have sworn to them by the LORD God of Israel; now therefore we cannot harm them.

20 This we will do to them: we will let them live, lest wrath be upon us, because of the oaths which we swore to them.

21 And the princes said to the children of Israel, Let them live; but let them become gatherers of wood and drawers of water to all the congregation; so they became gatherers of wood and drawers of water to all the congregation of the land; as the princes had promised them.

22 ¶And Joshua called for them, and he said to them, Why have you deceived us, saying, We are very far from you, when you dwell among us?

23 Now therefore you are cursed, and there shall none of you be freed from being gatherers of wood and drawers of water for the house of God.

24 And they answered and said to Joshua, Because it was certainly told your servants that the LORD your God commanded Moses his servant to give you all the land and to destroy all the inhabitants of the land from before you, therefore we were exceedingly afraid for our lives because of you, and have done this thing.

25 And now, behold, we are in your hands; do to us as it seems good in your sight.

26 And so Joshua did unto them, and delivered them out of the hand of the Israelites, and they did not slay them.

27 And Joshua made them that day gatherers of wood and drawers of water for the congregation and for the altar of the LORD, even to this day, in the place which he should choose.

CHAPTER 10

WHEN Adoni-zedek king of Jerusalem heard how Joshua had captured Ai and had utterly destroyed it (as he had done to Jericho and its king, so he had done to Ai and its king) and how the inhabitants of Gibeon had made peace with Israel, and were among them;

2 He feared greatly, because Gibeon was a large city, like one of the royal cities, and it was larger than Ai, and all its men were mighty.

3 Wherefore Adoni-zedek king of Jerusalem sent to Hoham king of Hebron and to Baran king of Jarmuth and to Napia king of Lachish and to Debir king of Eglon, saying,

4 Come up to me and help me, and let us fight against Gibeon; for it has made peace with Joshua and with the children of Israel.

5 Therefore the five kings of the Amorites, the king of Jerusalem, the king of Hebron, the king of Jarmuth, the king of Lachish, and the king of Eglon, gathered themselves together, and came up, they and all their armies, and encamped before Gibeon and made war against it.

6 ¶And the men of Gibeon sent to Joshua in the camp at Gilgal, saying, Do not withhold your hands from your servants; because all the kings of the Amorites that dwell in the mountains are gathered together against us.

7 So Joshua went up from Gilgal, he, and all the men of war that were with him, and all the mighty men of valor.

8 ¶And the LORD said to Joshua, Fear them not; for I have delivered them into your hands; and there shall not a man of them stand before you.

9 Joshua therefore came to them suddenly, going up all night from Gilgal.

10 And the LORD discomfited them before Israel, and they smote them with great slaughter at Gibeon, and chased them along the way that goes up to Beth-hauran, and smote them as far as Akkar, and on to Makkar.

11 And as they fled from before Israel, and were going down in the descent of Beth-hauran, the LORD cast down great hailstones from heaven upon them as far as Akkar, and they died; and there were more that died from the hailstones than the children of Israel slew with the sword.

12 ¶Then spoke Joshua to the LORD on the day when the LORD delivered the Amorites to the children of Israel, and Joshua said in the sight of the children of Israel, Sun, stand thou still over Gibeon; and thou Moon, in the valley over Ajalon.

13 And the sun stood still, and the moon stayed, until the people had avenged themselves upon their en-

emies. And, behold, it is written in the Book of the Songs, So the sun stood still in the midst of heaven, and hasted not to go down, about a whole day.

14 And there was no day like that before it or after it, when the LORD hearkened to the voice of a man; for the LORD fought for Israel.

15 ¶Then Joshua returned, and all Israel with him, to the camp at Gilgal.

16 But these five kings fled, and hid themselves in the cave of Makkar.

17 And Joshua was told, The five kings have been found hidden in the cave of Makkar.

18 And Joshua said, Roll great stones, and put them upon the mouth of the cave, and leave men there to guard them.

19 Do not stay yourselves, but pursue your enemies and overtake them; and do not let them enter the city; for the LORD your God has delivered them into your hands.

20 When Joshua and the children of Israel had finished slaying them with a very great slaughter, till they were annihilated and no survivor was left of them; then they brought the men of Gibeon who had revolted against the kings into their walled cities.

21 And all the people returned in peace to the camp to Joshua at Makkar; and no man moved his tongue against any of the children of Israel.

22 Then said Joshua, Open the mouth of the cave, and bring out those five kings to me.

23 And they did as Joshua had commanded them, and they brought to him those five kings out of the cave, the king of Jerusalem, the king of Hebron, the king of Jarmuth, the king of Lachish, and the king of Eglon.

24 And when they brought out those kings to Joshua, Joshua called for all the commanders of the armed forces who went with him, and said to them, Come near, and put your feet upon the necks of these kings. And they came near, and put their feet upon the necks of the kings.

25 And Joshua said to them, Fear not, nor be dismayed; be strong and of good courage; for thus shall the LORD do to all your enemies against whom you fight.

26 And after that Joshua slew them, and hanged them on five trees; and they remained hung on the trees until the evening.

27 And at the time of the going down of the sun, Joshua commanded, and they took them down from the trees, and cast them into the cave where they had hidden themselves, and laid large stones at the mouth of the cave, which remain to this very day.

28 ¶And the same day Joshua captured Makkar, and smote it with the edge of the sword, and he slew the king thereof and all the persons that were in it; he left none remaining; and he did to the king of Makkar as he had done to the king of Jericho.

29 Then Joshua passed from Makkar, and all Israel with him, to Libnah, and they fought against Libnah;

30 And the LORD delivered it also into the hand of Israel, and they smote it and its king with the edge of the sword, and all the persons that were in it; he left none remaining in it; but Joshua did to its king as he had done to the king of Jericho.

31 ¶And Joshua passed from Libnah, and all Israel with him, to Lachish, and encamped against it, and fought against it;

32 And the LORD delivered Lachish into the hand of Israel, and he captured it on the second day, and smote it with the edge of the sword, and all the persons that were in it, as he had done to Libnah.

33 ¶Then Harmon the king of Gezer came up to help Lachish; and Joshua smote him and his people with the edge of the sword until he had left him none remaining.

34 ¶And Joshua passed from Lachish, and all Israel with him to Eglon, and they encamped against it and fought against it;

35 And they took it on that day, and smote it with the edge of the sword, and all the persons that were in it, as he had done to Lachish.

36 And Joshua went up from Eg-

lon and all Israel with him, to Hebron; and they fought against it;

37 And they captured it, and smote it with the edge of the sword, and its king and all its towns and all the persons that were in it; he left none remaining, as he had done to Eglon; but destroyed it utterly, and all the persons that were in it.

38 ¶Then Joshua returned, and all Israel with him, to Debir; and fought against it;

39 And he captured it and its king and all its towns; and they smote them with the edge of the sword and utterly destroyed all the persons that were in it; and he left none remaining; as he had done to Hebron, so he did to Debir and to its king; as he had done to Libnah and to its king.

40 ¶So Joshua smote all the land, the mountain region, the southern region, the plain, and Ashdod, and all their kings; he left none remaining, but utterly destroyed all their armies, as the LORD God of Israel had commanded him.

41 So Joshua smote them from Rakim-gia as far as Gaza, and all the country of Goshen as far as Gibeon.

42 And Joshua conquered all these kings and their countries at one time; because the LORD God of Israel was with him, and it was he who fought for Israel.

43 ¹And Joshua returned, and all Israel with him, to the camp at Gilgal.

CHAPTER 11

AND when Nabin king of Hazur heard of these things, he sent to Jobab king of Meron, and to the king of Shamrin, and to the king of Achshaph,

2 And to the kings that were north of him in the mountains, and to the south, and in the plain of Chinnereth, and in the valleys and in Napotdor on the west,

3 And to the Canaanites on the east and on the west, and to the Amorites and the Hittites and the Perizzites and the Jebusites in the mountains, and to the Hivites below mount Hermon in the land of Mizpeh.

4 And they came out with all their hosts, many people, as the sand that is upon the sea shore in multitude, with many horses and chariots.

5 And when all these kings were met together, they came and encamped together at the waters of Meron, and prepared to fight against Israel.

6 ¶And the LORD said to Joshua, Do not be afraid of them; for tomorrow about this time I will cause them to be routed before Israel; and I will annihilate their horses and burn their chariots with fire.

7 So Joshua came suddenly to the waters of Meron, he and all the people of war who were with him; and they fell upon them.

8 And the LORD delivered them into the hand of Israel, who smote them and pursued them as far as great Zidon, and to the lake, and as far as the valley of Mizpeh eastward; and they smote them, and they left none remaining.

9 And Joshua did to them as the LORD had told him: he utterly destroyed their horses and burned their chariots with fire.

10 ¶And Joshua at that time turned back and took Hazor, and slew its king with the sword; for Hazor before had been the head of all those kingdoms.

11 And they smote with the edge of the sword all the people that were in it, utterly destroying them; there was not a soul left among them; and he burned Hazor with fire.

12 And all the cities of those kings, and all their kings, Joshua took and smote them with the edge of the sword, and utterly destroyed them, as Moses the servant of the LORD had commanded him.

13 And all the towns that stood on the hills did Israel burn, and Joshua burned Hazor.

14 And all the spoil of these cities and the cattle, the children of Israel took for themselves; but every man they smote with the edge of the sword

---

¹ Verse 43 is not found in the Peshitta.

until they had annihilated them, and they did not leave a soul among them. 15 ¶Just as the LORD had commanded Moses his servant, so did Moses command Joshua, and so did Joshua; he left nothing undone of all that the LORD had commanded Moses.

16 So Joshua took all that land, the mountain country and all the south country and all the land of the plain and all the mountains and their lowlands;

17 From mount Paleg that goes up to Seir, as far as Gadgad in the valley of Lebanon below mount Hermon; and all their kings Joshua took and slew.

18 Joshua made war for a long time with all those kings.

19 There was not a city that was not delivered up to the children of Israel, and they destroyed it, except the Hivites who dwell in Gibeon, whom Joshua allowed to live, and work for Israel. Now all these kingdoms are seven in number, and Joshua destroyed them all.

20 For it was of the LORD to encourage their hearts, that they should come against Israel in battle, that they might destroy them utterly, and that they might not have compassion upon them, but that they might destroy them, as the LORD had commanded Moses.

21 ¶And at that time came Joshua and smote the giants who were in the mountains, from Hebron, from Debir, from Gebal and from all the mountains of Judah and from all the mountains of Israel; Joshua destroyed them utterly with their cities.

22 There was none of the giants left remaining in the land of the children of Israel; only in Gaza, in Gath, and in Ashdod, did any remain.

23 So Joshua took the whole land, according to all that the LORD had spoken to Moses; and Joshua gave it as an inheritance to Israel according to their divisions by their tribes. And the land rested from war.

CHAPTER 12

NOW these are the kings of the land whom the children of Israel smote, and whose lands they possessed beyond the Jordan toward the rising of the sun, from the river Arnon as far as mount Hermon, and all the plain on the east:

2 Sihon king of the Amorites, who dwelt in Heshbon and ruled from Adoer, which is on the bank of the river Arnon, and ruled the middle of the valley, and half of Gilead, as far as the river of Jabbok, which is the border of the children of Ammon;

3 And ruled from the plain to the sea of Chinnereth on the east, and to the sea of the plain, the Salt Sea on the east, the way of Beth-Ashimon; and from Teman, which is below the hill of Ashdoth;

4 ¶And the territory of Og king of Bashan, who was of the family of giants, who dwelt at Ashtaroth and at Erdei,

5 And ruled in mount Ashimon, and in Salcah, and in all Bashan, to the border of En-dor and of Maacath, and half Gilead, the border of Sihon king of Heshbon,

6 Whom Moses the servant of the LORD slew, and gave his land for a possession to the Reubenites and the Gadites and the half tribe of Manasseh.

7 ¶And these are the kings of the land whom Joshua and the children of Israel slew on this side of Jordan on the west, and from Gilgal which is in the valley of Lebanon as far as the mount of Paleg, that goes up to Seir; whose lands Joshua gave to the tribes of Israel as a possession according to their divisions;

8 In the mountains and in the valleys, in the low plain, in Ashdod, in the desert, and in the south country; the Hittites, the Amorites, the Canaanites, the Perizzites, the Hivites, and the Jebusites;

9 ¶These are the kings of the land whom Joshua slew: The king of Jericho, one; the king of Ai, which is beside Beth-el, one;

10 The king of Jerusalem, one; the king of Hebron, one;

11 The king of Jarmuth, one; the king of Lachish, one;

12 The king of Eglon, one; the king of Gezer, one;

13 The king of Debir, one; the king of Hirmah, one;

14 The king of Gadar, one; the king of Arad, one;

15 The king of Libnah, one; the king of Arlam, one;

16 The king of Makkar, one; the king of Beth-el, one;

17 The king of Tappuah, one; the king of Hepher, one;

18 The king of Aphik, one; the king of Nishron, one;

19 The king of Madon, one; the king of Hazor, one;

20 The king of Shamrin and Meron, one; the king of Achshaph, one;

21 The king of Taanach, one; the king of Megiddo, one;

22 The king of Rakim, one; the king of Nokneam and Carmel, one;

23 The king of Dor and of Napodor, one; the king of the low country and of Gilgal, one;

24 The king of Tirzah, one; all the kings whom Joshua slew were thirty-one.

CHAPTER 13

NOW Joshua was old and advanced in years; and the LORD said to him, Behold, you are old and advanced in years, and there remains yet very much land to be possessed.

2 This is the land that yet remains in all regions of the Philistines and in all the country of En-dor,

3 From Sihor, which is before Egypt, as far as the border of Ekron northward, which is counted to the Canaanites; five lords of the Philistines; the Gazathites, the Ashdothites, the Eshkalonites, the Gittites, and the Ekronites; and also the Avites to the south;

4 And all the land of the Canaanites, and Maarthah which belongs to the Sidonians, as far as Aphik, to the border of the Amorites;

5 And the land of Gebal, and all Lebanon, toward the sunrising, from Gilead below mount Hermon to the entrance of Hamath.

6 All the inhabitants of the mountains from Lebanon to the place of hot waters, and all the Sidonians, will I the LORD drive out from before the children of Israel; only divide the land by lot to the Israelites as I have commanded you.

7 Now therefore divide this land as an inheritance to the nine tribes, and the half tribe of Manasseh along with them,

8 Because the Reubenites and the Gadites and the half of the tribe of Manasseh have received their inheritance which Moses gave them beyond the Jordan eastward, as my servant Moses gave them;

9 From Adoer, which is on the bank of the river Arnon, and the city which is in the middle of the valley, and all the plain which is westward as far as Ribon;

10 And all the towns of Sihon king of the Amorites, who reigned in Heshbon, to the border of the children of Ammon;

11 And Gilead, and the territory of En-dor and of Koros, and all mount Hermon, and all Mathnin to Salcah;

12 All the kingdom of Og in Mathnin, who reigned in Ashtaroth and in Erdei, who was left of the remnant of the giants, whom Moses slew, and Israel possessed their land.

13 Nevertheless the children of Israel did not destroy the people of En-dor and Koros; so the En-dorites and the Korosites dwell among the children of Israel until this day.

14 Only to the tribe of Levi he gave no inheritance, because the offerings of the LORD God of Israel are their inheritance, as Moses had said.

15 ¶And Moses gave an inheritance to the tribe of the Reubenites according to their families.

16 And their territory was from Adoer, which is on the bank of the river Arnon, and the town which is in the middle of the valley, and all the plain as far as Riba;

17 And Heshbon, and all the towns which are in the plain; Ribon and Math-Baal and Beth-beni-ammon

18 And Jahaz and Kermoth and Aenath

19 And Koriathaim and Shammah and Jazreth and Seir on the mount of the valley

20 And Beth-peor and Ashtaroth

and Pisgah and Beth-jeshimoth
21 And all the cities of the plain and all the kingdom of Sihon king of the Amorites, who reigned in Heshbon, whom Moses and the children of Israel slew in Midian, both him and his princes, Evi, Rakim, and Zur, and Hur, and Reba, the five princes of Sihon, who dwelt in the land.
22 ¶Balaam also, the son of Beor, the soothsayer, did the children of Israel slay with the sword along with the rest of them that were slain by them.
23 And the border of the Reubenites was the region of the Jordan. This is the inheritance of the Reubenites according to their families, the cities and the villages thereof.
24 And Moses gave an inheritance to the tribe of Gad, according to their families.
25 And their territory was Jazer and all the cities of Gilead and half the land of the children of Ammon to Adoer which is before Rabbath;
26 And from Heshbon to Ramathmizpah, and Betonin; and from Mahanaim to the border of Debir;
27 And in the valley, Beth-atim and Beth-nimrah and Succoth and the region northward and the rest of the kingdom of Sihon king of Heshbon, and their borders extended as far as the Jordan, and to the edge of the sea of Chinnereth beyond the Jordan eastward.
28 This is the inheritance of the Gadites by their families, the cities and their villages.
29 ¶And Moses gave an inheritance to the half tribe of Manasseh; and this was the possession of the half tribe of Manasshites by their families.
30 And their territory was from Mahanaim, all Mathnin, all the kingdom of Og king of Mathnin, and all the villages of Jair, which are in Mathnin, sixty towns;
31 And half Gilead, and Ashtaroth and Edrei, cities of the kingdom of Og in Mathnin. These cities and their villages Moses gave to the children of Machir the son of Manasseh, to the half of the children of Machir by their families.

32 These two tribes and the half of the tribe of Manasseh Moses gave an inheritance in the plains of Moab, beyond the Jordan, eastward.
33 But to the tribe of Levi Moses gave no inheritance; because, as he said to them, the LORD God of Israel was their inheritance.

CHAPTER 14

AND these are the countries which the children of Israel inherited in the land of Canaan, which Eleazar the priest and Joshua the son of Nun and the heads of the fathers of the tribes of the children of Israel distributed as inheritance to them.
2 By lot was their inheritance divided, as the LORD had commanded by the hand of Moses, to be given to the nine tribes and to the half tribe.
3 For Moses had given the inheritance of two tribes and a half tribe beyond the Jordan; but to the Levites he gave no inheritance.
4 For the children of Joseph were two tribes, Manasseh and Ephraim; therefore he gave no portion to the Levites in the land, save cities to dwell in, with their suburbs for their cattle and for their substance.
5 As the LORD commanded Moses, so did the children of Israel, and they divided the land.
6 ¶Then the children of Judah came to Joshua in Gilgal; and Caleb the son of Jophaniah the Kenezite said to Joshua, You know the thing that the LORD spoke to Moses his servant concerning me and you at Rakim-gia.
7 I was forty years old when Moses the servant of the LORD sent me from Rakim-gia to spy out the land; and I brought him word again as it was in my heart.
8 Nevertheless our brethren who went up with us made the heart of the people quake; but I wholly followed the LORD my God.
9 And Moses swore at that time, saying, Surely the land on which your foot has trodden shall be your inheritance, and your children's forever, because you have wholly followed the LORD God.
10 And now, behold, the LORD has

given us rest, as he said; behold, it is forty-five years since the LORD spoke this word to Moses, while Israel wandered in the wilderness; and now, lo, I am this day eighty-five years old,

11 And today I am as strong as the day when Moses sent me; as my strength was then, so is my strength now, for war, both to go out and to come in.

12 Now therefore give me this mountain, of which the LORD spoke on that day; for you have heard on that day how the giants were there, and that the cities were great and fortified; perhaps the LORD will be with me, and I shall destroy them, as the LORD said.

13 And Joshua blessed Caleb the son of Jophaniah, and gave him Hebron and its environs as an inheritance.

14 Hebron therefore and its environs became the inheritance of Caleb the son of Jophaniah the Kenezite to this day, because he wholly followed the LORD God of Israel.

15 And the name of Hebron and its environs before was Koriath-arba, which belonged to the giants. And the land rested from war.

CHAPTER 15

THIS then was the lot of the tribe of the children of Judah by their families; it extended to the border of Edom, to the wilderness of Zin, to the uttermost of the southern border.

2 And their south border was from the southern end of the Salt Sea, and from thence went up to the bay that faces southward;

3 And it went out toward the ascent of Akrakam, and passed along to Zin, then went up on the south side of Rakim-gia, and passed along to Hezroth, and went up to Adar, and circled Karka;

4 Then it passed along to Azmon, and went out to the river of Egypt; and the limits of the border were at the sea; this shall be your south boundary.

5 And the east boundary was from the farthest end of the Salt Sea, as far as the mouth of the Jordan. And the border on the north side was from the bay of the Sea at the mouth of the Jordan;

6 And the border went up to Leban, which belongs to the descendants of Reuben.

7 And then the border went up toward Debir from the valley of Achar and so northward, turning toward Galilee, which is opposite the slope of Ramin, which is on the south side of the river; and the border passed toward the En-shemesh, and the limits of the border were at En-dogel;

8 And the border went up to the valley of the son of Hinnom to the south side of the Jebusite city, which is Jerusalem; and the boundary went up to the top of the mountain that lies before the valley of the son of Hinnom westward, which is at the end of the valley of the Giants:

9 And the border ran from the top of the mountain to the fountain of the waters of Nephtoah, and thence to the tip of mount Ebron; then the border ran to Baalah, which is Koriath-narin;

10 And the border continued from Baalah westward to mount Seir, and passed along to the side of mount Narim, that is Chesalon, on the north side, and went down to Beth-shemesh, and passed along to the south;

11 And the border went out to the side of Ekron northward; and the border was drawn to Shicron, and passed along to mount Baalah, and went out to Jahbael; and the limits of the border were at the Great Sea.

12 And the west border was extended to the Great Sea, and the coast thereof. This is the boundary of the descendants of Judah according to their families.

13 ¶And to Caleb the son of Jophaniah Joshua gave a portion among the children of Judah, according to the commandment of the LORD. And Caleb said to Joshua, Give me this Koriath-arba which belongs to the father of giants; and Joshua gave to Caleb Koriath-arba, that is, Hebron.

14 And Caleb slew there the three descendants of giants, Sheshai and Ahiman and Tholmai, the descendants of the giants.

15 And he went up thence against the inhabitants of Debir; and the name of Debir before was Koriath-sepra.

16 ¶And Caleb said, Whoever takes Koriath-sepra and destroys it, to him will I give Achsah my daughter to wife.

17 And Othniel the son of Kenaz, the brother of Caleb, took it; and he gave him Achsah his daughter to wife.

18 And it came to pass, when she became his wife, she desired from her father a field as an inheritance; and she alighted from her ass; and Caleb said to her, What troubles you, my daughter?

19 She said to him, Give me a blessing; because you have given me a heritage in the south land; give me also this pool of water. And Caleb gave her the upper pool and the lower pool.

20 This is the inheritance of the tribe of the descendants of Judah by their families.

21 And the uttermost cities of the tribe of the descendants of Judah extended toward the border of Edom southward. These are the names of the cities of the descendants of Judah: Kabzeel, Eder, Jagur,

22 Kinah, Jarmonah, Gadgada,

23 Kedesh, Hazor, Nathnin,

24 Zib, Atlam, Bealoth,

25 Hazor, Hadattah, Koriath-hezron,

26 Amam, Ashma, Moladah,

27 Hazar-ada, Heshmon, Beth-palet,

28 Darath-taaley, Beer-sheba, Beer-jothanah,

29 Baalah, Alian, Azem,

30 Altlam, Achsin, Hirmah,

31 Zinklag, Marmanah, Samsalah,

32 Lebaoth, Shaloh, and Airmon, all the cities are thirty-six with their villages;

33 And in the valley, Eshtaol, Zedaa, Ashtnah,

34 Khokh, En-gahom, Patoh, Eliam,

35 Jarmuth, Arlam, Socoh, Azekah,

36 Shatin, Azilthaim, Gathar, Gethronin; fifteen cities with their villages;

37 Zalan, Harshah, Migdal-gad,

38 Dilban, Kaspa, Nakthael,

39 Lachish, Ezkat, Eglon,

40 Cebshon, Lahmish, Kithlish,

41 Gederoth, Beth-dagon, Naamah, Nakdah; sixteen cities with their villages;

42 Libnah, Ether, Naphtah,

43 Ashan, Ashia, Zinklag,

44 Keilah, Achzib, and Mareshah; nine cities with their villages;

45 Ekron, with its towns and its villages westward;

46 And all the land of Ashdod with its villages;

47 And Ashdod with its villages and farm lands, Gaza with its towns and farm lands, to the river of Egypt, and the Great Sea, with its coast;

48 ¶And in the mountains, Shamir, Jattir, and Socoh,

49 Rannah, Koriath-sepra, that is, Debir,

50 Ganab, Eshtemoa, Elian,

51 Eshian, Holon, and Giloh; eleven towns with their villages;

52 Jab, Romah,[1] Ashan,

53 Jalom, Beth-tappuah, Aphekah,

54 Humta, Koriath-arba, that is, Hebron, and Zebaon; nine cities with their villages;

55 Maon, Carmel, Zib, Atna,

56 Jezreel, Nekemaam, Zaloh,

57 Cain, Gibeah, and Timnah; ten cities with their villages;

58 Halhul, Beth-zur, Gedar,

59 Maarath, Beth-anoth, and Lathkin; six cities with their villages:

60 Rabbath, and Koriath-baal, that is, Koriath-narin; two cities with their villages;

61 In the wilderness, Beth-arabah, Midian, Secasah,

62 Jashan, Air-mehel, and En-gad; six cities with their villages.

63 ¶As for the Jebusites, the inhabitants of Jerusalem, the descendants of Judah could not destroy them; so the Jebusites dwell among the descendants of Judah at Jerusalem to this day.

CHAPTER 16

AND the lot of the descendants of Joseph fell from the Jordan by Jericho to the waters of Jericho on the

[1] Rome, hills.

east, into the wilderness that goes up from Jericho to mount Beth-el,

2 And goes out from Beth-el to Luz, and then passes along to the border of Ebra and Ataroth,

3 And goes down westward to the border of Palta, as far as the border of Beth-hauran, the lower, then to Gadar; and its limits extended to the sea.

4 So the descendants of Joseph, Manasseh and Ephraim, received their inheritance.

5 ¶And the border of the descendants of Ephraim according to their families was thus: the boundary of their inheritance was Ataroth and Addar, as far as Beth-hauran, the upper;

6 Then the border went westward to the northern portion; after which the border turned eastward below Shiloh, and passed by it on the east of Jaloh;

7 And it went down from Jaloh to Ataroth and Jagrath and Pagar, and came to Jericho, and went out of Tappuah to the Jordan;

8 And the border went out westward to the river Kabah; and the limits thereof were at the sea. This is the inheritance of the tribe of the descendants of Ephraim by their families.

9 And the cities which were set apart for the descendants of Ephraim were within the inheritance of the children of Manasseh, all the cities with their villages.

10 And they did not destroy the Canaanites that dwelt in Gadar; so the Canaanites dwell among the Ephraimites to this day, but they were brought into subjection, and they pay tribute.

CHAPTER 17

AND Gilead became the lot for the tribe of Manasseh; for he was the first-born of Joseph; to Machir the first-born of Manasseh, the father of Gilead; because he was the first-born and a man of war, therefore he had Gilead and Mathnin.

2 And became also the portion for the rest of the children of Manasseh by their families; for the descendants of Abiezer and for the descendants of He-lek and for the descendants of Neshrael and for the descendants of Shopam and for the descendants of Hepher and for the descendants of Shemida; these were the male children of Manasseh the son of Joseph by their families.

3 ¶But Zelophehad, the son of Hepher, the son of Gilead, the son of Machir, the son of Manasseh, had no sons, but daughters; and these are the names of his daughters, Mahlah, and Joah, Hoglah, Milcah and Tirzah.

4 And they came near before Eleazar the priest, and before Joshua the son of Nun, and before the princes of Israel, saying, The LORD commanded Moses to give us an inheritance among our brethren; so he gave us according to the command of the LORD, among the brothers of our father. Now therefore give us an inheritance among the brethren of our father. So Joshua gave them an inheritance among the brethren of their father.

5 And there fell ten portions to Manasseh, besides the land of Gilead and Mathnin, which were on the other side of the Jordan;

6 Because the daughters of Manasseh received an inheritance among his sons; and the land of Gilead fell to the lot of the rest of the sons of Manasseh.

7 ¶And the border of Manasseh was from the boundary of Maacath, which lies on the right hand of the inhabitants of En-tappuah.

8 Thus their land was in the region of Tappuah and Patah, which became the boundary to the descendants of Manasseh the son of Joseph, and to the Ephraimites;

9 And the boundary went down to the river of the Sea, to the south of the river of the cities which belong to Ephraim among the cities of Manasseh; and the border of Manasseh ran on the north side of the river, and the outgoings thereof reached to the sea;

10 The land to the south went to Ephraim, and that to the north to Manasseh, and the sea as their border;

and they met together in Asher on the north, and in Issachar on the east.
11 And Manasseh had opposite Issachar and Asher, Beth-shean and its towns, and Neb-leam and its towns, and En-dor and its towns, and Taanach and its towns, and Megiddo and its towns, three districts.
12 Yet the Israelites could not destroy these cities, because the Canaanites took refuge and dwelt in them.
13 But when the children of Israel became strong, they subdued the Canaanites and made them pay tribute; but did not utterly destroy them.
14 And the descendants of Joseph spoke to Joshua, saying, Why have you given us but one portion to inherit, seeing we are a numerous people, forasmuch as the LORD has blessed us hitherto?
15 Joshua said to them, If you are a numerous people, then go up on the side of the mountain, and choose for yourselves a portion in the land of the Perizzites and of the giants, if mount Ephraim is too narrow for you.
16 And the descendants of Joseph said, The mountain and the cities of the Perizzites are not enough for us; for the Canaanites still dwell in the land of the valley, and in Beth-shean and its towns, and in the valley of Jezreel.
17 Then Joshua spoke to the house of Joseph, even to Ephraim and Manasseh, saying, You are a numerous people, and have a great power; if one portion is not enough for you,
18 Then choose for yourselves the mountain, and it will be enough for you, and the slopes of the mountain and its limits shall be yours; and you shall destroy the Canaanites and the Perizzites, though they have great iron chariots, and though they are strong.

CHAPTER 18

THEN the whole congregation of the children of Israel assembled together at Shiloh, and set up the tabernacle of the congregation there. And the land was subdued before them.

2 And there remained among the children of Israel seven tribes which had not yet received their inheritance.
3 And Joshua said to the children of Israel, How long will you be backward about going in and possessing the land which the LORD God of your fathers has given you?
4 Choose for yourselves three men from each tribe; and I will send them, and they shall rise and go through the land, and survey and describe it according to their inheritance; and they shall come again to me.
5 And they shall divide the land into seven parts; Judah shall remain in their territory on the south, and the house of Joseph shall remain in their territory on the north.
6 And you shall therefore map out the land into seven parts, and then bring the map here, and I will cast lots for you here before the LORD our God.
7 But the Levites have no part among you; for the priesthood of the LORD is their inheritance; and Gad and Reuben and half the tribe of Manasseh have received their inheritance beyond the Jordan to the east, which Moses the servant of the LORD gave them.
8 ¶And the men arose and went away; and Joshua charged those who went to map the land, saying, Go and walk through the land, and map it, and come again here to me, that I may cast lots for you before the LORD in Shiloh.
9 And the men went and passed through the land, and mapped it by towns into seven parts on a scroll, and came again to Joshua at the city of Shiloh.
10 ¶And Joshua cast lots for them in Shiloh before the LORD; and there Joshua divided the land to the children of Israel into districts.
11 ¶And the lot of the tribe of Benjamin came up according to their families; and the territory of their inheritance came forth between the children of Judah and the children of Joseph.
12 And their border on the north side was from the Jordan; and the

border went up to the side of Jericho on the north side, and went up through the mountain westward; and the extreme limits thereof were at the wilderness of Beth-aon.

13 And the border went over from thence toward Luz, to the side of Luz, that is Beth-el, southward; then the border descended to Ataroth-adar, upon the mountain that lies south of lower Beth-hauran.

14 And the border extended to the side of the sea southward, from the mountain that lies before Beth-hauran southward; and the limits thereof were at Koriath-baal, which is Koriath-narin, a city of the children of Judah: this is the sea side.

15 And the southern boundary was from the end of Koriath-narin, and the border went out to the sea, and went out to the fountain of waters of Naphtali:

16 Then the border descended to the end of the mountain that lies before the valley of the son of Hinnom, which is in the valley of the Giants on the north, and went down to the valley of the son of Hinnom, to the side of the Jebusites on the south, then descended to En-dogel,

17 And was drawn from the north, and went to the En-shemesh, and thence towards Galilee, which is opposite the ascent of Ramin, then descended to Leban, and Bohan which belonged to the son of Reuben,

18 And passed along towards the side which is opposite the plain northward, and went down to the plain;

19 Then the border passed along to the side of Beth-hoglah northward; and the limits of the border were at the northern bay of the Salt Sea at the side of the Jordan southward; this was the south border.

20 And the Jordan was its border on the east side. This was the inheritance of the children of Benjamin, by the borders thereof round about, according to their families.

21 Now the cities of the tribe of the children of Benjamin according to their families were Jericho, Beth-hoglah, Amak, and Keziz,

22 Beth-arabah, Zemaraim, Beth-el,

23 Avin, Parah, Ophrah,

24 Chephar-aomka, Ophli, and Gaba; fourteen cities with their villages;

25 Gibeon, Ramtha, Beeroth,

26 Mizpah, Chepirah, Mozah,

27 Rakim, Repeel, Taralah,

28 Zelah, Geberah, and Jebusi, that is, Jerusalem, Gibeath, and Koriath-aim; fourteen cities with their villages. This is the inheritance of the children of Benjamin according to their families.

CHAPTER 19

AND the second lot came forth for the tribe of the children of Simeon according to their families; and their inheritance was within the inheritance of the children of Judah.

2 And they had in their inheritance Beer-sheba, Sheba, Moladah,

3 Darath-taley, Balah, and Azem,

4 Eltolad, Beth-el, Hirmah,

5 Zinklag, Beth-marcaboth, Hazar-susah,

6 Beth-lebaoth, and Sharwenan; fourteen cities and their villages;

7 Ain, Remmon, Gather, and Ashan; four cities and their villages;

8 And all the villages that were round about these cities as far as Labath, Beth-ramtha of the south. This is the inheritance of the tribe of the children of Simeon according to their families.

9 Out of the portion of the children of Judah was the inheritance of the children of Simeon; because the portion of the children of Judah was too much for them; therefore the children of Simeon inherited some of their inheritance.

10 ¶And the third lot came up for the children of Zebulun according to their families; and the border of their inheritance extended as far as Ashdod;

11 And their border went up westward, and to Ramath-taley, and reached to Debbashet, then reached to the river that is before Nekemaam;

12 Then turned from Ashdod eastward toward the sunrise to the border of Chisloth and Bethor, and then ex-

tended to Rabbath, and went up to Naphia,

13 And from thence passed along eastward to Gath, to Hepher, to Attah, and to Kazin, and then went out to Remmon, and Mathwa, and Awa;

14 And the border turned around the north side of Haditon; and the limits thereof ended at the Valley of Chiphtanael;

15 And Kattath, Jahallal, Shamrin, Aralah and Beth-lehem; twelve cities with their villages.

16 This is the inheritance of the children of Zebulun according to their families.

17 ¶And the fourth lot came out to the children of Issachar, according to their families.

18 And their border included Jezreel, Chesulloth, Shunem,

19 Haphraim, Shinan, Ahtar,

20 Deblath, Kishon, Apaz,

21 Ramath-en, Einjan, En-hadah, and Beth-pizian;

22 And the border reached to Tabor, Shahazimah, and Beth-shemesh; and the limits of their border were at the Jordan; thirteen cities with their villages.

23 This is the inheritance of the tribe of the children of Issachar according to their families, the cities and their villages.

24 ¶And the fifth lot came out for the tribe of the children of Asher according to their families.

25 And their border was Haklath, Hali, Batan, Achshaph,

26 Amlekh, Amcar and Amshael; and reached to Carmel westward, and to Shihor, and to Labeth;

27 And then it turned toward the sunrise to Beth-dagon, and reached to Zebulun, and to the valley of Niphtahael toward the north side, and to Beth-aomka, and Neil, and it went out northward to Cobel,

28 And Ebron, Rehob, Hammon, and Kaah, as far as great Zidon;

29 And then the border turned to Ramtha, as far as the strong city of Tyre; the border then turned to Has; and the limits thereof reached to the west of the valley of Achzib;

30 Umkah also Aphik, and Rehob; twenty-two cities with their villages.

31 This is the inheritance of the tribe of the children of Asher according to their families, these cities with their villages.

32 ¶And the sixth lot went to the children of Naphtali, according to their families.

33 And their border was from Halpa, from Allon, and from Zinaam, Adama, Nekeb, and Nakbael, to Lakum; and the limits thereof were at the Jordan;

34 And then the boundary turned westward to Aznoth-boz, and went out from there to Hakik, and reached to Zebulun on the south side, and reached to Asher on the west side, and to Judah at the Jordan toward the sunrise.

35 And the great cities were Tyre, Zidon, Hammath, Karath, Chinnereth,

36 Adamah, Damah, Hazor,

37 Kedesh, Edrei, En-zur,

38 Dion, Migdal-el, Hadon, Beth-anoth, and Beth-shemesh; nineteen cities with their villages.

39 This is the inheritance of the tribe of Naphtali according to their families, the cities and their villages.

40 ¶And the seventh lot went to the tribe of Dan according to their families.

41 And the border of their inheritance was Zidah, Eshtaol, Kerith-shem-ish,

42 Shaalabbin, Ajalon, Nethlah,

43 Elon, Timmnah, Ekron,

44 Elkath, Gibbethon, Baalath,

45 Jehudith, Beldabak, Gath-rim-mon,

46 Mehrikon, and Carkon, as far as the territory which is opposite Elath.

47 And the territory of the children of Dan was not sufficient for them; therefore the Danites went up and fought against Eino, and captured it, and smote it with the edge of the sword, and possessed it, and dwelt in it, and called Eino, Dan, after the name of Dan their father.

48 This is the inheritance of the tribe of Dan according to their families, these cities with their villages.

49 ¶When they had finished dividing the land as their inheritance and de-

lineating its boundaries, the children of Israel gave an inheritance to Joshua the son of Nun among them; 50 According to the word of the LORD they gave him the city which he asked, Timnath-serah on mount Ephraim; and he built the city and dwelt in it.

51 These are the inheritances which Eleazar the priest and Joshua the son of Nun and the heads of the fathers of the tribes of Israel divided by lot at Shiloh before the LORD, at the door of the tabernacle of the congregation. So they completed the division of the land.

CHAPTER 20

THEN the LORD said to Joshua, 2 Speak to the children of Israel, saying, Reserve for you cities of refuge, of which I spoke to you through my servant Moses;

3 That the slayer who kills any person suddenly and unwittingly may flee there; and they shall be your refuge from the avenger of blood.

4 And when he that shall flee to one of these cities shall stand at the entrance of the gate of the city, and shall speak to the elders of that city and explain his case, they shall take him into the city with them and give him a place, that he may dwell among them.

5 And when the avenger of blood pursues him, then they shall not deliver the slayer into his hand; because he slew his neighbor unwittingly, and did not hate him beforehand.

6 And he shall dwell in that city until he stand before the congregation for judgment, and until the death of the high priest that shall be in those days; then the slayer shall return, and come to his own city and to his own house, to the city from which he fled.

7 ¶So they set apart these cities for the places of refuge: Rakim in Galilee in mount Naphtali, and Shechem in mount Ephraim, and Koriath-arba, which is Hebron, in the mountain of Judah.

8 And on the other side of the Jordan, east of Jericho, they assigned Bozer in the wilderness, which is situated upon the plain, from the tribe of Reuben, and Ramoth in Gilead, from the tribe of Gad, and Golan in Math-nin, from the tribe of Manasseh.

9 These were the cities set apart for all the children of Israel and for the strangers that sojourned among them, that any one who killed a person unawares might flee there, and not be delivered into the hand of the avenger of blood, until he had stood before the congregation.

CHAPTER 21

THEN the chiefs of the priests and the Levites came near to Eleazar the priest and to Joshua the son of Nun and to the heads of the fathers of the tribes of Israel,

2 And they said to them at Shiloh in the land of Canaan, The LORD commanded by the hand of Moses to give us cities to dwell in, with their suburbs for our cattle.

3 And the children of Israel gave to the Levites out of their inheritance, at the commandment of the LORD, these cities and their suburbs.

4 And lots were drawn for the families of the Kohathites; and the children of Aaron the priest, who were of the Levites, had by lot from the tribe of Judah, from the tribe of Simeon, and from the tribe of Benjamin, thirteen cities.

5 And the rest of the Kohathites had by lot from the tribe of Ephraim, from the tribe of Dan, and from the half tribe of Manasseh, ten cities.

6 And the Gershonites had by lot from the tribe of Issachar, from the tribe of Asher, from the tribe of Naphtali, and from the half tribe of Manasseh in Mathnin, thirteen cities.

7 And the descendants of Merari by their families had from the tribe of Reuben, from the tribe of Gad, and from the tribe of Zebulun, twelve cities.

8 And the children of Israel gave by lot to the Levites these cities with their suburbs, as the LORD had commanded Moses.

9 ¶These are the names of the cities

which they gave out of the tribe of Judah, and out of the tribe of Simeon, each city mentioned by its name.

10 They became the property of the descendants of Aaron, being of the family of the Kohathites, who were the children of Levi, for theirs was the first lot.

11 And they gave them Koriath-arba, which belonged to the father of giants, that is, Hebron, on the mountain of Judah, with its suburbs round about it.

12 But the fields of the city, with its villages, they gave to Caleb the son of Jophaniah for his possession.

13 ¶Thus they gave to the children of Aaron the priest, Hebron, the city of refuge for the slayers, with its suburbs, and Libnah with its suburbs,

14 And Jarath with its suburbs, and Eshtemoa with its suburbs,

15 Halol with its suburbs, Debir with its suburbs,

16 Ain with its suburbs, Aata with its suburbs, and Beth-shemesh with its suburbs; nine cities out of the tribes of Judah and Simeon.

17 And out of the tribe of Benjamin, Gibeon with its suburbs, Geba with its suburbs,

18 Anathoth with its suburbs, and Almon with its suburbs; four cities.

19 All the cities of the children of Aaron, the priest, were thirteen cities with their suburbs.

20 ¶And for the families of the Kohathites, the Levites, that remained of the children of Kohath, they had the cities of their lot out of the tribe of Ephraim.

21 For they gave them Shechem, the city of refuge for the slayers, with its suburbs, on mount Ephraim, Gedar with its suburbs,

22 Kibzaim with its suburbs, and Beth-hauran with its suburbs; four cities.

23 And out of the tribe of Dan, Ethleka with its suburbs, Gibethon with its suburbs,

24 Aijalon with its suburbs, and Gath-rimmon with its suburbs; four cities with their suburbs.

25 And out of the half tribe of Ma-

nasseh, Tanach with its suburbs, and Gath-rimmon with its suburbs; two cities with their suburbs.

26 All the towns and the cities were ten with their suburbs which went for the remaining families of the Kohathites.

27 ¶And the Gershonites, of the families of the Levites, had their cities out of the half tribe of Manasseh, Golan in Mathnin, the city of refuge for the slayer, with its suburbs, and Ashteroth with its suburbs; two cities with their suburbs.

28 And out of the tribe of Issachar, Kishian with its suburbs, Rabbath with its suburbs,

29 Jarmuth with its suburbs, En-gad with its suburbs; four cities with their suburbs.

30 And out of the tribe of Asher, Mishal with its suburbs, Acron with its suburbs,

31 Helkath with its suburbs, and Rehob with its suburbs; four cities with their suburbs.

32 And out of the tribe of Naphtali, Rakim in Galilee [1] with its suburbs, the city of refuge for the slayer, Hammoth-dor with its suburbs, and Kartan with its suburbs; three cities with their suburbs.

33 All the cities of the families of the Gershonites were thirteen cities with their suburbs.

34 ¶And the children of Merari, the rest of the Levites, received their cities out of the tribe of Reuben, Jahaz with its suburbs, Kermoth with its suburbs, Kiriathim with its suburbs,

35 And Ahshemoth with its suburbs, four cities with their suburbs.

36 And out of the tribe of Zebulun, Nacah with its suburbs, Karthan with its suburbs,

37 Ramin with its suburbs, and Jahlah with its suburbs, four cities with their suburbs.

38 And out of the tribe of Gad, Ramoth in Gilead with its suburbs, the city of refuge for the slayer, and Mahanaim with its suburbs,

39 Heshbon with its suburbs, and Jazer with its suburbs; four cities with their suburbs.

[1] Later called Kedesh.

40 So all the cities for the children of Merari by their families, who were remaining of the families of the Levites, were by their lot twelve cities with their suburbs.

41 All the cities of the Levites within the possession of the children of Israel were forty-eight cities with their suburbs.

42 These cities with their towns were situated thus, each town with its suburbs round about it; thus were all these towns with their cities.

43 ¶And the LORD gave to Israel all the land which he had sworn to give to their fathers; and they possessed it, and dwelt therein.

44 And the LORD gave them rest round about, according to all that he swore to their fathers; and there stood not a man of their enemies before them, but the LORD delivered all their enemies into their hands.

45 There failed not one of the good things which the LORD has spoken to the house of Israel; all came to pass.

CHAPTER 22

THEN Joshua called the Reubenites and the Gadites and the half tribe of Manasseh,

2 And said to them, You have kept all that Moses the servant of the LORD commanded you, and have obeyed my voice in all that I have commanded you;

3 You have not deserted your brethren these many days even to this time, but have kept the commandments of the LORD your God.

4 And now the LORD your God has given rest to your brethren, as he promised them; therefore now return, and go to your towns and to the land of your possession, which Moses the servant of the LORD gave you on the other side of the Jordan to the east.

5 But only take diligent heed to observe the commandments and the laws which Moses the servant of the LORD charged you, to love the LORD your God, to keep his commandments, and to cleave to him, and to serve him with all your heart and with all your soul.

6 So Joshua blessed them and sent them away; and they went to their towns.

7 ¶Now to the half of the tribe of Manasseh Moses had given an inheritance in Mathnin; but to the other half thereof Joshua had given an inheritance among their brethren on this side of the Jordan to the west. And when Joshua sent them away to their towns, he blessed them;

8 And he spoke to them, saying, Return to your towns and to the land of your inheritance with much wealth and with very many cattle, with silver, with gold, with brass, with iron, and with very much clothing; divide the spoil of your enemies with your brethren.

9 ¶So the Reubenites and the Gadites and the half tribe of Manasseh returned, and departed from the children of Israel out of Shiloh, which is in the land of Canaan, to go to the land of Gilead, to the land of their possessions, in which they were given an inheritance, according to the word of the LORD by the hand of Moses.

10 ¶And when they came to Gilgal, which is by the side of the Jordan in the land of Canaan, the Reubenites, the Gadites, and the half tribe of Manasseh built there an altar by the Jordan, a large and remarkable altar.

11 ¶And the children of Israel heard it said, Behold, the Reubenites and the Gadites and the half tribe of Manasseh have built an altar at the border of the land of Canaan, in Gilgal which is by the side of the Jordan, in the land of the children of Israel.

12 Then the whole congregation of the children of Israel gathered themselves together at Shiloh to go to war against them.

13 And the children of Israel sent to the Reubenites and to the Gadites and to the half tribe of Manasseh, into the land of Gilead, Phinehas the son of Eleazar the priest,

14 And with him ten princes, one prince from every tribe of Israel; and these men were chiefs of the armies of Israel.

15 ¶And they came to the Reubenites and to the Gadites and to the half

tribe of Manasseh, in the land of Gilead, and they spoke with them, saying,

16 Thus says the whole congregation of the LORD, What treachery is this which you have committed against the God of Israel, in turning away from following the LORD, in that you have builded yourselves an altar, that you might abandon the worship of the LORD?

17 Is the iniquity of Peor not enough for us, from which we are not cleansed until this day, although there was a plague in the congregation of the LORD?

18 And as for you, when you turned away this day from the worship of the LORD, tomorrow the anger will be against the whole congregation of Israel.

19 If, however, the land of your possession is unclean, then pass over to the land of the possession of the LORD, where the LORD's tabernacle dwells, and inherit land among us; but do not disdain the worship of the LORD, nor rebel against us by building for yourselves an altar beside the altar of the LORD the God of Israel.

20 Did you not see that when Achar the son of Carmi coveted and took the devoted things, wrath fell upon the whole congregation of Israel? He was but one man, yet he devoured us all in his iniquity.

21 ¶Then the Reubenites the Gadites and the half tribe of Manasseh answered and said to Phinehas the son of Eleazar the priest and to the heads of the armies of Israel,

22 The LORD is the God of gods, the God of gods is the LORD, and he is our God, and he knows Israel and he knows us also; if we shall depart from him, or if we shall transgress against the worship of the LORD in doing this thing, then let him not save us this day.

23 And if we have built us an altar to turn from the worship of the LORD, or to offer upon it burnt offerings, or use it for any other service, let the LORD himself seek vengeance against us;

24 And if we have not rather done
19

this thing because of reverence to him, so that in time to come your children might not say to our children, What have you to do with the LORD God of Israel, O you Reubenites and Gadites?

25 For the LORD has made the Jordan a boundary between us and you; now therefore you have no part in the LORD; so in time to come shall your children make our children cease from worshipping the LORD.

26 Therefore we said, Let us now prepare to build us an altar, not for burnt offering, nor for sacrifice;

27 But that it may be a witness between us and you, and between our generations after us, and between ourselves and our generations after us, that we might do the service of the LORD before him with our burnt offerings and with our sacrifices and with our peace offerings, in the place where the LORD chooses to dwell; so that your children may not say to our children in time to come, You have no part in the LORD.

28 Therefore we said that it shall be, if they should ever speak to us or to our generations in time to come, then we may say to them, Behold the pattern of the altar of the LORD which our fathers made not for burnt offerings, nor for sacrifices; but to be a witness between us and you.

29 God forbid that we should reject the worship of the LORD, and turn away from revering him, and build for ourselves an altar for burnt offerings, for gift offerings, or for sacrifices, besides the altar of the LORD God of Israel that is before his tabernacle.

30 ¶And when Phinehas the son of Eleazar the priest and the princes of the congregation and the heads of the armies of Israel who were with him heard the words that the Reubenites and the Gadites and the half tribe of Manasseh spoke, it pleased them.

31 And Phinehas the son of Eleazar the priest said to the Reubenites and to the Gadites and to the half tribe of Manasseh, This day we know that the LORD is among us, because you have not committed this trespass against the LORD; now you have de-

livered the children of Israel, that the hand of the Lord might not be against them with wrath.

32 ¶Then Phinehas the son of Eleazar the priest, and the princes who were with him, returned from the Reubenites and from the Gadites and the Manashites, out of the land of Gilead, to the land of Canaan, to the children of Israel, and brought them an answer.

33 And the answer pleased the children of Israel; and the children of Israel blessed God, and decided not to go up against them to battle to destroy the land wherein the Reubenites and the Gadites and the Manashites dwelt.

34 And the Reubenites and the Gadites and the Manashites called the altar which they had made, The Altar of Testimony, for it is a witness between us that the Lord is the only God.

CHAPTER 23

AND it came to pass after a long time, when the Lord had given rest to Israel from all their enemies round about, that Joshua was old, and well advanced in years.

2 And Joshua summoned all Israel, their elders, their heads, their judges, and their scribes, and said to them, I am old and well advanced in years;

3 And you have seen all that the Lord your God has done to all these nations, which he destroyed from before you; for it is the Lord your God who has fought for you.

4 Behold, I have not divided to you the land of these nations that remain, in the inheritance of your tribes; but from the Jordan, all the nations that I have destroyed, even to the Great Sea westward, have I divided among you.

5 The Lord your God will defeat them, and destroy them from before you; and you shall possess their land, as the Lord your God has promised you.

6 Only be strong to keep and do all that is written in the book of the law of Moses, the servant of God, and not turn aside from it, neither to the right hand nor to the left;

7 And you shall not mix with these nations that remain among you; neither make mention of the names of their gods, nor swear by them, neither serve them, nor worship them;

8 But cleave to the Lord your God, as you have done even to this day.

9 For the Lord has destroyed from before you great and strong nations; and no man has been able to stand against you to this day.

10 One man of you shall chase a thousand; for the Lord your God is with you, he it is who fights for you, as he has promised you.

11 Take good heed therefore to yourselves, to revere the Lord your God.

12 For if you ever turn back and join the remnant of these nations that remain among you and make marriages with them and mix with them and they with you;

13 Then know for sure that the Lord your God will no more destroy these nations from before you; but they shall be snares and traps to you, and spears in your sides and fishhooks in your eyes, until you perish from off this good land which the Lord your God has given you.

14 And as for me, I am now going the way of all the earth; and you know in all your hearts and in all your souls that not one thing has failed of all the good promises which the Lord your God spoke concerning you; all have come to pass to you, and not one thing has failed.

15 Therefore, just as all the good things have come upon you which the Lord your God promised, so shall come upon you all the curses, until he have destroyed you from off this good land which the Lord your God has given you;

16 If you should transgress against the covenant of the Lord your God and against the commandments which he commanded you, and go and serve other gods and worship them; then shall the anger of the Lord be kindled against you, and you shall perish

quickly from off the good land which he has given you.

CHAPTER 24

AND Joshua gathered all the tribes of Israel to Shechem, and called for the elders of Israel, their heads, their judges, and their scribes; and they presented themselves before God in front of the tabernacle of the congregation.

2 And Joshua said to all the people, Thus says the Lord God of Israel, Your fathers dwelt on the other side of the river Euphrates in olden times, even Terah, the father of Abraham and of Nachor; and they served there other gods.

3 And I took your father Abraham from the other side of the river Euphrates, and led him throughout all the land of Canaan, and multiplied his offspring, and I gave him Isaac,

4 And I gave to Isaac, Jacob and Esau; and I gave to Esau mount Seir for a possession; but Jacob and his children went down to Egypt.

5 I sent Moses and Aaron, and I plagued Egypt, and performed wonders among them; and afterward I brought you out.

6 And I brought your fathers out of Egypt; and I brought them to the sea; and the Egyptians pursued your fathers with chariots and horsemen to the Red Sea.

7 And when your fathers cried to the Lord, he put darkness between you and the Egyptians, and then the Lord divided the Red Sea, and brought your fathers through the midst thereof; then he brought the sea upon the Egyptians, and covered them; and your eyes have seen what I did to the Egyptians; and I brought you to the wilderness, and you dwelt in the wilderness a long time.

8 And I brought you to the land of the Amorites, who dwelt on the other side of the Jordan; and they fought with you; and I delivered them into your hands, and I destroyed them from before you and you possessed their land.

9 Then Balak the son of Zippor,

king of Moabites, arose and fought against Israel, and sent and called Balaam the son of Beor to curse you;

10 But I would not hearken to Balaam; therefore he blessed you still; so I delivered you from his hands.

11 And you crossed the Jordan, and came to Jericho; and the men of Jericho fought against you, the Amorites, the Canaanites, the Perizzites, the Hittites, the Girgasites, the Hivites, and the Jebusites; and I delivered them into your hands.

12 And I sent raiders before you, and I destroyed from before you the two kings of the Amorites; but not with your swords, nor with your bows.

13 And I have given you a land for which you did not labor, and cities which you did not build, and you dwell in them; and behold, you eat of vineyards and olive yards which you did not plant.

14 ¶Now therefore fear the Lord, and serve him in sincerity and in truth; and put away out of your heart the strange gods which your fathers served on the other side of the river Euphrates, and in Egypt; and serve the Lord.

15 And if it seems evil to you to serve the Lord, choose you this day whom you will serve; whether the gods which your fathers served on the other side of the river Euphrates, or the gods of the Amorites in whose land you dwell; but as for me and my house, we will serve the Lord.

16 And the people answered and said, God forbid that we should forsake the Lord to serve other gods;

17 For it is the Lord our God who has brought us up out of the land of Egypt, from the house of bondage, and who performed those great signs in our sight, and preserved us in all the way wherein we went, and among all the peoples through whom we passed;

18 And the Lord destroyed from before us all these peoples, the Amorites in whose land we dwell; the Lord destroyed them from before us; therefore we will serve the Lord; for he is the only God, and he is our God.

19 And Joshua said to the people, Behold, but it may be you cannot serve the LORD faithfully; for he is a holy God and a zealous God; he may not forgive your transgressions nor your sins.

20 If you forsake the LORD and serve strange gods of the land, then the LORD will turn and do you harm, and consume you after having been good to you.

21 And the people said to Joshua, Nay, we will not serve any other, but we will serve the LORD God.

22 And Joshua said to the people, You are witnesses against yourselves that you have chosen the LORD, to serve him. And they said, We are witnesses.

23 Then Joshua said to them, Now therefore put away the strange gods which are among you, and incline your hearts to the LORD God of Israel.

24 And the people said to Joshua, The LORD our God will we serve, and his voice will we obey.

25 So Joshua made a covenant with the people that day, and taught them the commandments and the ordinances in Shechem.

26 ¶And Joshua wrote these words in the book of the law of God, and took a great stone, and set it up there under an oak that was by the sanctuary of the LORD.

27 And Joshua said to all the people, Behold, this stone shall be a witness against us; for it has heard all the words of the LORD which he spoke to us; it shall be therefore a witness against you, lest you deal treacherously with the LORD your God.

28 And after Joshua had charged the people, he sent them away, every man to his inheritance.

29 ¶And it came to pass after these things, Joshua the son of Nun, the servant of the LORD, died, being a hundred and ten years old.

30 And they buried him in the border of his inheritance in Timnath-serah, which is on mount Ephraim, on the north side of mount Gaash.

31 And Israel served the LORD all the days of Joshua and all the days of the elders that outlived Joshua, and who had known all the works of the LORD that he had done for Israel.

32 ¶And the bones of Joseph, which the children of Israel brought up from Egypt, they buried in Shechem in a parcel of ground which Jacob bought from the sons of Hamor the father of Shechem for a hundred ewes; and it became the inheritance of the descendants of Joseph.

33 And Eleazar the priest, the son of Aaron the priest, died; and they buried him at Gibaatha that belongs to Phinehas his son, which was given him on mount Ephraim.

THE BOOK OF

JUDGES

CHAPTER 1

NOW after the death of Joshua, the servant of the LORD, the children of Israel inquired of the LORD, saying, Who shall go up for us against the Canaanites first, to fight against them?

2 And the LORD said, Judah shall go up; behold, I have delivered the land into his hands.

3 And Judah said to Simeon his

brother, Come up with me into my inheritance, that we may fight against the Canaanites; and I likewise will go up with you into your inheritance. So Simeon went with him.

4 And Judah went up; and the LORD delivered the Canaanites and the Perizzites into their hands; and they slew ten thousand of them in Bezek.

5 And they found the lord of Bezek in Bezek; and they fought against him, and they slew the Canaanites and the Perizzites.

6 But the lord of Bezek fled; and they pursued him and caught him, and cut off his thumbs and his great toes.

7 And the lord of Bezek said, Seventy kings, with their thumbs and great toes cut off, used to pick up bread under my table; as I have done, so God has requited me. And they brought him to Jerusalem, and there he died.

8 And the children of Judah fought against Jerusalem, and took it and smote it with the edge of the sword and set the villages thereof on fire.

9 ¶And afterwards the children of Judah went down to fight against the Canaanites, who dwelt in the mountain and in the south and in the plain.

10 And Judah went against the Canaanites who dwelt in Hebron (now the name of Hebron before was Koriath-arba); and they slew Sheshai and Ahiman and Talmai, the sons of the giants.

11 And from thence they went against the inhabitants of Debir; and the name of Debir before was Koriath-sephra;

12 And Caleb said, He who takes Koriath-sephra, and destroys it, I will give him Achsah my daughter to wife.

13 And Othniel the son of Kenaz, Caleb's younger brother, took it; and he gave him Achsah his daughter to wife.

14 And it came to pass, when she entered the city, she desired to ask of her father a field; and she alighted from her ass; and Caleb said to her, What troubles you, my daughter?

15 And she said to him, Give me a blessing; for you have given me a south land; give me also pools of water; and Caleb gave her the upper pools and the lower pools.

16 ¶And the children of the Kenite, Moses' father-in-law, went up from the city of palm trees with the children of Judah into the wilderness of Judah, which lies in the south of Adar; and they went and dwelt among the people.

17 And Simeon went with Judah his brother, and they slew the Canaanites that inhabited Zephath, and utterly destroyed it. And they called the name of the city Khirma.

18 Judah also took Gaza with its territory, and Ashkelon with its territory, and Ekron with its territory.

19 And the LORD was with Judah; and they possessed the mountain; but they could not destroy the inhabitants of the valley, because they had chariots of iron.

20 And they gave Hebron to Caleb, as Moses had said; and he destroyed from thence the three sons of giants.

21 But the children of Benjamin did not destroy the Jebusites who inhabited Jerusalem; but the Jebusites dwell with the children of Benjamin in Jerusalem to this day.

22 ¶The house of Joseph also went out against Beth-el; and the LORD was with them.

23 And the house of Joseph spied on Beth-el. (Now the name of the city before was Luz.)

24 And the spies saw a man coming out of the city, and they said to him, Show us the entrance into the city, and we will have mercy on you.

25 And when he had shown them the entrance into the city, they smote the city with the edge of the sword; but they spared the man and all his family.

26 And the man went to the land of the Hittites, and built a village and called its name Luz, which is its name to this day.

27 ¶Neither did Manasseh destroy the inhabitants of Beth-shean and its villages, nor Taanach and its villages, nor the inhabitants of Dor and its villages, nor the inhabitants of Abinaam and its villages, nor the inhabit-

ants of Megiddo and its villages; but the Canaanites that inhabited the land could not be subdued.

28 And it came to pass, when Israel was strong, they made the Canaanites pay tribute but did not utterly destroy them.

29 ¶Neither did Ephraim destroy the Canaanites who dwelt in Gezer; but the Canaanites dwelt in Gezer among them.

30 ¶Neither did Zebulun destroy the inhabitants of Kitron, nor the inhabitants of Jahlel; but the Canaanites dwelt among them, and paid tribute.

31 ¶Neither did Asher destroy the inhabitants of Accho nor the inhabitants of Zidon nor of Lahbel nor of Jezebel nor of Helbah nor of Aphik nor of Rehob;

32 But the Asherites dwelt among the Canaanites, the inhabitants of the land; for they did not destroy them.

33 ¶Neither did Naphtali destroy the inhabitants of Beth-shemesh nor the inhabitants of Beth-anoth; but he dwelt among the Canaanites, the inhabitants of the land; nevertheless the inhabitants of Beth-shemesh and of Beth-anoth paid tribute to them.

34 And the Amorites forced the children of Dan into the mountain; for they would not let them come down to the valley;

35 The Amorites sought refuge in the land of Hedas in the mountain and in Aijalon and in Shaalbim; but the hand of the house of Joseph prevailed against them, and they paid tribute.

36 And the border of the Amorites was from the ascent of Ekron, from the rock and upward.

CHAPTER 2

AND the angel of the LORD came up from Gilgal to Bikhian, and said to the children of Israel, Thus says the LORD, I have brought you up from the land of Egypt, and have brought you into the land which I swore to your fathers; and I said, I will never break my covenant with you.

2 And you shall make no league with the inhabitants of this land; you shall destroy their altars; but you have not obeyed my voice. Why have you done this?

3 Wherefore I also said, I will not destroy them from before you; but they shall become vanity, and their gods shall be a stumbling block to you.

4 And when the angel of the LORD spoke these words to the children of Israel, all the people lifted up their voices and wept.

5 And the people called the name of that place Bikhian; and they sacrificed there to the LORD.

6 ¶And when Joshua had dismissed the people, the children of Israel went away every man to his inheritance to possess the land.

7 And the people served the LORD all the days of Joshua and all the days of the elders who outlived Joshua, who had seen all the works of the LORD and the great things which he had done for Israel.

8 And Joshua the son of Nun, the servant of the LORD, died at the age of one hundred and ten years.

9 And they buried him in the land of his inheritance at Timnath-serah on the mount of Ephraim, on the north side of mount Gaash.

10 And all that generation were gathered to their fathers; and there arose another generation after them, who did not know the LORD nor the works which he had done for Israel.

11 ¶And the children of Israel did evil in the sight of the LORD, and served Baal;

12 And they forsook the LORD God of their fathers, who had brought them up out of the land of Egypt, and followed other gods, gods of the peoples who were round about them, and they worshipped them, and provoked the LORD to anger.

13 So they forsook the LORD and served Baal and Ashtaroth.

14 ¶And the anger of the LORD was kindled against Israel, and he delivered them into the hands of spoilers, and they plundered them, and he delivered them into the hands of their enemies round about them, so that they could no longer stand before their enemies.

15 Wherever they went, the hand of the LORD was against them for evil, as the LORD had said, and as the LORD had sworn to them; and they were greatly distressed.

16 ¶Then the LORD raised up judges among the Israelites, and they delivered them out of the hand of those who plundered them.

17 And yet they would not hearken to their judges, because they had gone astray after other gods and worshipped them; they turned aside quickly from the way in which their fathers walked, who had listened to the commandments of the LORD, but they did not do so.

18 And when the LORD raised up judges for them, then the LORD was with the judges, and delivered them out of the hand of their enemies all the days of the judges; the LORD would hear their groaning because of their oppressors and those that drove them away.

19 And it came to pass, when the judges were dead, they returned and became more corrupt than their fathers, in following other gods to serve and to worship them; they did not cease from their wickedness, nor from their evil ways.

20 ¶And the anger of the LORD was kindled against Israel; and he said, Because this people have transgressed my covenant which I commanded their fathers, and have not hearkened to my voice;

21 I also will no longer destroy any man from before them of the nations which Joshua left when he died;

22 That through them I may prove Israel whether they will keep the way of the LORD, and whether they will walk in it, as their fathers did keep it, or not.

23 Therefore the LORD left these nations, and did not destroy them hastily; neither had he delivered them into the hand of Joshua.

CHAPTER 3

NOW these are the nations which the LORD left, to test Israel by them, even the Israelites who had not experienced all the wars of Canaan.

2 Only that the generations of the children of Irsael might learn warfare, at least such as had not experienced it before;

3 Namely, the five lords of the Philistines, and all the Canaanites, and the Sidonians, and the Hivites who dwelt on mount Lebanon, from the mount of the people of mount Hermon as far as the entrance to Hamath.

4 And they were to prove Israel by them, to know whether they would obey the commandments of the LORD, which he commanded their fathers by the hand of Moses.

5 ¶So the children of Israel dwelt among the Canaanites, Hivites, Amorites, Perizzites, Hittites, and Jebusites;

6 And they took their daughters to be their wives, and gave their daughters to their sons, and served their gods.

7 And the children of Israel did evil in the sight of the LORD, and forgot the LORD their God, and served Baal and Ashtaroth.

8 ¶Therefore the anger of the LORD kindled against Israel, and he delivered them into the hand of Cushan the Wicked, king of Aram-nahrin (Mesopotamia); and the children of Israel served Cushan the Wicked eight years.

9 And when the children of Israel cried to the LORD, the LORD raised up a deliverer for the children of Israel, and they were delivered by Othniel, the son of Kenaz, Caleb's younger brother.

10 And the hand of the LORD was with him, and he judged Israel, and went out to war; and the LORD delivered Cushan the Wicked, king of Aram-nahrin, into his hands; and his hand prevailed against Cushan the Wicked.

11 And the land had rest forty years. Then Othniel the son of Kenaz died.

12 ¶And the children of Israel again did evil in the sight of the LORD; and the LORD strengthened Eglon the king of Moab against Is-

rael, because they had done evil in the sight of the LORD.

13 And he mobilized the children of Ammon and Amalek against them, and went and smote Israel, and possessed the city of palm trees.

14 So the children of Israel served Eglon the king of Moab eighteen years.

15 But when the children of Israel cried to the LORD, the LORD raised up for them a deliverer, Ehur the son of Gera, of the tribe of Benjamin, a man whose right hand was crippled, and the children of Israel sent a present by him to Eglon the king of Moab.

16 So Ehur made for himself a two edged dagger, and he made it short; and he girded it under his garment on his right thigh.

17 And he brought the present to Eglon king of Moab; and King Eglon was a simple-minded man.

18 And when Ehur had finished offering the present, he sent away the people that bore the present.

19 But he himself turned back from the quarries that were by Gilgal, and said, I have a secret message to impart to you, O king; and the king said to those who were present, Get away from here. And all that stood by him went out.

20 And Ehur came to him; and he was sitting alone in the upper room which was made for him. And Ehur said to him, I have a message from God to impart to you. So Eglon arose from his seat.

21 And Ehur put forth his left hand, and took the sword from his right thigh, and thrust it into his belly;

22 And the haft also went in after the blade; and the fat closed upon the blade, because he did not draw the sword out of his belly; and he went out hastily.

23 Then Ehur went out into the porch, and shut the doors of the upper room upon him, locked them, and left.

24 When he had gone out, the king's servants came in; and when they saw that the doors of the upper chamber were locked, they said, Perhaps he has gone to the toilet in the closet of the upper chamber.

25 And they waited for a long time; and seeing that he did not open the doors of the upper chamber, they took keys and opened them; and, behold, their lord was fallen down dead on the floor.

26 And while they were in confusion, Ehur passed beyond the quarries, and escaped to Seirath.

27 And it came to pass, when he had returned, he sounded the trumpet on the mountain of Ephraim, and the children of Israel went down with him from the mountain, and he went before them.

28 And he said to them, Follow after me; for the LORD has delivered your enemies the Moabites into your hands. And they went down after him, and seized the fords of the Jordan on the side of Moab, and allowed not a man to pass over.

29 And they slew of the Moabites at that time about ten thousand men, all great and valiant men; and there escaped not a man.

30 So the Moabites were subdued at that time under the hand of Israel. And the land had rest for eighty years.

31 ¶And after him was Shamgar the son of Anath, who slew six hundred of the Philistines with an ox goad; and he also delivered Israel.

CHAPTER 4

AND the children of Israel again did evil in the sight of the LORD, after Ehur was dead.

2 And the LORD delivered them into the hand of Nabin king of Canaan, who reigned in Hazor; the general of whose army was Sisera, who dwelt in Harosheth of the Gentiles.

3 And the children of Israel cried to the LORD; for he had nine hundred chariots of iron, and oppressed the children of Israel for twenty years.

4 ¶And Deborah, a prophetess, the wife of Lapithor, judged Israel at that time.

5 And Deborah dwelt under the

palm tree between Ramtha and children of Israel came up to her for judgment.

6 And she sent and called Barak the son of Abinoam from Rakim of Naphtali, and said to him, Has not the LORD God of Israel commanded you, saying, Go and dwell on mount Tabor, and take with you ten thousand men from the children of Naphtali and from the children of Zebulun?

7 And let them come with you to the river Kishon against Sisera, the general of Nabin's army, and against his chariots, and against his forces; and I will deliver him into your hands.

8 And Barak said to her, If you will go with me, then I will go; but if you will not go with me, then I will not go.

9 And she said, I will surely go with you; nevertheless you shall not glory on account of the journey which you are taking; for the LORD shall deliver Sisera into the hands of a woman. And Deborah arose and went with Barak to Rakim.

10 ¶And Barak mobilized Zebulun and Naphtali to Rakim; and ten thousand men went up with him; and Deborah also went up with him.

11 Now Heber the Kenite had left the Kenites, the descendants of Hobab the father-in-law of Moses, and had pitched his tent as far as the oak which is in Zaanaim, which is by Rakim.

12 And they told Sisera that Barak the son of Abinoam had gone up to mount Tabor.

13 And Sisera gathered together all of his chariots, nine hundred chariots of iron, and all the people that were with him, from Harosheth of the Gentiles as far as the river of Kishon.

14 And Deborah said to Barak, Arise, for this is the day in which the LORD has delivered Sisera into your hands; behold, the LORD is going out before you. So Barak went down from mount Tabor, and ten thousand men with him.

15 And the LORD defeated Sisera and all his chariots and all his army, with the edge of the sword before Barak; so that Sisera alighted from his chariot and fled on foot.

16 But Barak pursued his chariots and his army as far as Harosheth of the Gentiles; and all the army of Sisera fell by the edge of the sword; and not a man escaped.

17 However, Sisera fled on foot, and entered the tent of Anael the wife of Heber the Kenite, because there was peace between Nabin the king of Hazor and the house of Heber the Kenite.

18 ¶And Anael went out to meet Sisera, and said to him, Turn in, my lord, turn in to me; fear not. And he went in to her into the tent, and she covered him with a rug.

19 And he said to her, Give me a little water to drink; for I am thirsty. And she untied the milkskin and gave him a drink and covered him.

20 Again he said to her, Stand at the door of the tent, and if any man does come and ask you, and say, Is there any man here? You shall say to him, No.

21 Then Anael, Heber's wife, got a tent peg, and took a hammer in her hand and went to him as he was sleeping, and drove the peg into his temples, and pounded it into the ground while he was fast asleep, and he shivered and died.

22 And, behold, as Barak pursued Sisera, Anael went out to meet him and said to him, Come, and I will show you the man whom you seek. And he went into her tent, and, behold, Sisera lay dead, and the peg was through his temples.

23 So on that day God defeated Nabin the king of Canaan before the children of Israel.

24 And the hand of the children of Israel prospered and prevailed against Nabin the king of Canaan until they slew Nabin king of Canaan.

CHAPTER 5

THEN sang Deborah and Barak the son of Abinoam on that day, saying,

2 With requital has Israel been

avenged; praise the Lord with a song for avenging Israel.

3 Hear, O kings; give ear, O princes; I will sing to the Lord; I will sing praise to the Lord God of Israel.

4 Lord, when thou wentest out of Seir, when thou marchedst in the fields of Edom, the earth trembled and the heavens dropped, the clouds also dropped water.

5 The mountains melted from before the Lord, even this Sinai from the presence of the Lord the Holy One of Israel.

6 In the days of Shamgar the son of Anath, in the days of Anael, the highways were cut off, and the travellers who once walked on main roads, had to go through the crooked byways.

7 The little villages ceased in Israel; they ceased, until I Deborah arose, I arose as a mother in Israel.

8 The Lord will choose new things; then the barley bread,[1] and a sword or a spear shall not be seen among forty thousand in Israel.

9 My heart said to the lawgiver of Israel, They that are chosen among the people bless the Lord.

10 O you who ride on white asses, you who dwell in houses, and you who travel on the highways,

11 Meditate on the words of the inquirers, who are among the teachers; they shall execute the righteousness of the Lord, even his righteousness which he has multiplied in Israel; then shall the people of the Lord march to the gates.

12 Awake, awake, Deborah; awake, utter a song; arise, Barak, and lead away your captives, O son of Abinoam.

13 Then the deliverer went down to sing praise before the Lord; thou hast given me victory by the hand of a man out of Ephraim.

14 And Barak's works are known in Amalek; after you marched Benjamin with affection for you; out of Machir came forth a seer, and out of Zebulun those who write with the pen of a scribe.

15 And the princes of Issachar were with Deborah; even Issachar is like Barak among the peoples; he was sent on foot to a portion of Reuben; great are those who give oracles to comfort the heart.

16 Why abodest thou on the highways to hear the bleatings of the wild asses? For the divisions of Reuben there were great searchings of heart.

17 Gad abode beyond the Jordan; and Dan brought ships to the harbor; Asher dwelt on the sea shore, and remained in its harbors.

18 Zebulun and Naphtali were peoples who jeopardized their lives on the high places of his field.

19 The kings came and fought; then fought the kings of Canaan; they fought in Taanach by the waters of Megiddo; they took no goods nor money.

20 The stars fought from their courses; they fought from heaven against Sisera by the river Kishon.

21 The river Kishon and the river Karmin swept them away. O my soul, you have defeated an army!

22 Then the hoofs of his horses fell down, were broken because of the prancing of his mighty ones.

23 Curse ye Meroz, said the angel of the Lord, curse it, and curse the inhabitants thereof, because they came not with men to the help of the Lord.

24 Blessed above women shall Anael the wife of Heber the Kenite be, blessed shall she be above women in the tent.

25 He asked water, and she gave him milk; she brought forth butter in a giant bowl.

26 She put her hand to the peg and her right hand to the carpenter's hammer, and with the hammer she struck Sisera and crushed his head, when she had struck and pierced his temples.

27 At her feet he bowed, he fell, he lay down; at the place where he bowed, there he fell down dead, the plunderer.

28 The mother of Sisera looked out of the window and cried through

---

[1] Barley bread is symbolical of poverty.

the lattice, Why are the chariots of my son so long in coming? Why tarries the clatter of his chariots?

29 Her wise ladies answered her, saying,

30 Perhaps he went and found great spoil, dividing the prey, giving to every man a mule and great booty, and to Sisera a prey of diverse colors of needlework and divers colors of embroidered work, meet for the necks of them that take the spoil.

31 So let all thine enemies perish, O LORD; but let them that love thee be like the sun when he goeth forth in his might. And the land had rest for forty years.

CHAPTER 6

AND the children of Israel did evil in the sight of the LORD; and the LORD delivered them into the hand of the Midianites seven years.

2 And the hand of the Midianites prevailed against Israel, in that they fled from before the Midianites; and the children of Israel made for themselves dens in the mountains, and caves, and sheepfolds.

3 And whenever Israel had sown, the Midianites and the Amalekites and the Rakimites came up and encamped against them;

4 And they destroyed the produce of the whole land as far as the entrance of Gaza, and left no food for Israel to raise either oxen or sheep or asses.

5 For they came up with their cattle and their tents, and they came like locusts in multitude; for both they and their camels were without number; and they entered into the land to destroy it.

6 And Israel trembled exceedingly from before the Midianites;

7 ¶And the children of Israel cried to the LORD because of the Midianites,

8 And the LORD sent a prophet to the children of Israel, and he said to them, Thus says the LORD God of Israel, I brought you up out of the land of Egypt, and brought you forth out of the house of bondage;

9 And I delivered you from the hand of the Egyptians and from the hand of all your oppressors, and destroyed them from before you and gave you their land;

10 And I said to you, I am the LORD your God; you shall not worship the gods of the Amorites in whose land you dwell; but you have not obeyed my voice.

11 ¶And there came an angel of the LORD, and sat under an oak which was at Ophrah, the town of Joash the father of Azri; and his son Gideon was beating out wheat by the winepress, to hide it from the Midianites.

12 And the angel of the LORD appeared and said to him, The LORD is with you, you mighty man of valor.

13 And Gideon said to him, I beseech you, O my lord, if the LORD be with us, why then have all these misfortunes befallen us? And where are all his wonders of which our fathers have told us, saying, Did not the LORD bring us up from Egypt? But now the LORD has forsaken us and delivered us into the hand of the Midianites.

14 And the LORD turned to him, and said, Go with this might of yours, and you shall save Israel from the hand of the Midianites; behold, I have sent you.

15 And he said to him, I beseech thee, O my LORD, with what shall I save Israel? Behold, my family is the least in Manasseh, and I am the youngest in my father's family.

16 And the LORD said to him, I will be with you, and you shall smite the Midianites as one man.

17 And he said to him, If now I have found mercy in thy sight, then show me a sign that I may know that thou speakest with me.

18 Do not depart from here until I come to thee and bring out my meal and set it before thee. And he said, I will tarry until you come again.

19 ¶So Gideon went in and prepared a kid and unleavened cakes of an ephah of flour; the meat he put in a basket, and he put the broth in a pot, and brought it out to him under the oak and presented it.

20 And the angel of the Lord said to him, Take the meat and the unleavened cakes, and lay them on the rock, and pour out the broth over it. And he did so.

21 ¶Then the angel of the Lord put forth the end of the staff that was in his hand, and touched the meat and the unleavened cakes; and there rose up fire out of the rock, and consumed the meat and the unleavened cakes. Then the angel of the Lord vanished from his sight.

22 And when Gideon perceived that he was an angel of the Lord, Gideon said, Alas, O Lord God! for I have seen the angel of the Lord face to face.

23 And the Lord said to him, Peace be unto you; fear not; you shall not die.

24 Then Gideon built an altar there to the Lord, and called it Mariahshalama; and to this day it still stands in Ophrah, the town of the father of Azri.

25 ¶And it came to pass on that day, the Lord said to him, Take your father's bullock, and the second bullock seven years old, and pull down the altar of Baal, the idol of your father, and cut down the grove that is by it;

26 And build an altar to the Lord your God upon the top of this rock, in an orderly manner, and take the second bullock, and offer it upon it as a burnt offering with the wood of the grove which you shall cut down.

27 Then Gideon took ten men of his servants, and did as the Lord had said to him; and because he was afraid of doing it by day, because of his father's household and the men of the town, he did it by night.

28 ¶And when the men of the town arose early in the morning, behold, the altar of Baal was pulled down and the grove which was beside it was destroyed and the second bullock was offered upon another altar which had been built.

29 And they said one to another, Who has done this thing? And when they had asked and enquired, they said, Gideon the son of Joash has done this thing.

30 Then the men of the town said to Joash, Bring out your son, that he may die; because he has pulled down the altar of Baal and has cut down the grove that was by it.

31 And Joash said to all who stood against him, Will you plead for Baal? Or will you try to save him? Whosoever pleads for him shall be put to death while it is yet morning; if he is a god, let him plead for himself, because his altar has been thrown down.

32 Therefore on that day he called Gideon Nedo-baal, saying, Let Baal judge him, because he has thrown down his altar.

33 ¶Then all the Midianites and the Amalekites and the Rakimites were gathered together, and went over and encamped in the valley of Jezreel.

34 But the Spirit of the Lord came upon Gideon, and he blew a trumpet; and Jezreel shouted his approval.

35 And he sent his messengers throughout all Manasseh; and they also blew trumpets and followed him; and he sent his messengers to Asher and to Zebulun and to Naphtali; and they came up to meet them.

36 ¶And Gideon said to God, If thou wilt save Israel by my hand, as thou hast said,

37 Behold, I will put a fleece of wool on the threshing floor; and if there is dew on the fleece only, and it is dry on all the ground, then I shall know that thou wilt save Israel by my hand, as thou hast said.

38 And it was so; and he rose early the next day and pressed the fleece and wrung the dew out of the fleece, a bowlful of water.

39 And Gideon said to God, Let not thy anger kindle against me, and I will speak but this once; let me prove thee again but this once with the fleece; let now only the fleece be dry, and upon all the ground let there be dew.

40 And God did so that night; for only the fleece was dry, and there was dew on all the ground.

CHAPTER 7

THEN Nedo-baal, who is Gideon, and all the people who were with him, rose up early, and encamped beside the spring of Hadar; and the camp of Midian was north of the hill of Gibath, in the valley.

2 And the LORD said to Gideon, The people that are with you are too many for me to deliver the Midianites into their hands, lest Israel should glory in themselves, saying, My own hand has made me victorious.

3 Now therefore proclaim in the ears of the people, saying, Whoever is fearful and trembling, let him stay behind and return from mount Gilead. And there returned of the people twenty-two thousand; and there remained ten thousand.

4 And the LORD said to Gideon, The people are still too many; bring them down to the water, and I will try them for you there; and it shall be that he of whom I say to you, This one shall go with you, the same shall go with you; and of whomsoever I say to you, This one shall not go with you, the same shall not go.

5 So he brought down the people to the water; and the LORD said to Gideon, All who lap of the water with their tongues, as a dog laps, you shall make them stand together; likewise all who kneel down upon their knees to drink, you shall make them stand together.

6 And the number of those that lapped, putting the hand to the mouth, was three hundred men; but all the rest of the people knelt down upon their knees to drink water.

7 And the LORD said to Gideon, By the three hundred men that lapped I will save you and deliver the Midianites into your hands; and let all the other people go, every man to his place.

8 So the people took their provisions in their hands and their trumpets; and he dismissed all the children of Israel every man to his possession and to his tent, and he relied upon those three hundred men; and the camp of Midian was beneath him in the valley.

9 ¶And it came to pass the same night, that the LORD said to him, Arise, go down to the camp, for I have delivered it into your hands.

10 But if you fear to go down, go down with Pera your servant to the army camp;

11 And you shall hear what they say; and afterwards your hands shall be strengthened. So he went down with Pera his servant to a detachment of the armed men that were in the army camp.

12 And the Midianites and the Amalekites and all the Rakimites lay along the valley like locusts in multitude; and their camels were without number, as the sand by the seashore in multitude.

13 And when Gideon was come, behold, a man was relating a dream to his fellow, and he said to him, Behold, I dreamed a dream, and, lo, a cake of barley bread tumbled into the camp of Midian, and came as far as a tent, and struck it on the top, and the tent fell down.

14 And his fellow answered and said, This is nothing else but the sword of Gideon the son of Joash, the mighty man of Israel; for into his hand has God delivered the camp of Midian.

15 ¶Now when Gideon heard the telling of the dream and its interpretation, he worshipped and returned to the camp of Israel, and said, Arise, for the LORD has delivered the camp of Midian into your hands.

16 And he divided the three hundred men into three companies, and he put a trumpet in every man's hand, with empty pitchers, and torches inside the pitchers.

17 And he said to them, Watch me and do as I do; and, behold, when I come to the outside of the camp, as I do, so shall you do.

18 When I blow a trumpet, I and all the people who are with me, then you blow with trumpets also on every side of the camp, and say, The sword of the LORD, and of Gideon.

19 ¶So Gideon and the hundred

men that were with him, came to the
outside of the camp at the beginning
of the middle watch; and they had
but newly set the watch; and they
blew the trumpets, and broke the
pitchers.

20 And the three companies blew
their trumpets, and broke the pitchers,
and held the torches in their left
hands, and the trumpets in their right
hands; and they cried, The sword of
the LORD, and of Gideon.

21 And they stood every man in
his place round about the camp; and
all the host ran, and they blew a
trumpet, and fled.

22 And when the three hundred
blew the trumpets, the LORD set every
man's sword against his fellow, even
throughout all the army; and the
whole army fled as far as Beth-shab-
tey and Zeddath, and as far as the
border of Abel-meholah, which is by
Jatbath.

23 And the men of Israel gathered
themselves together from Naphtali
and from Asher and from all Manasseh, and pursued the Midianites.

24 ¶And Gideon sent messengers
throughout all mount Ephraim, saying, Come down against the Midianites and seize the waters as far as
Beth-barah, which is by the Jordan.
Then all the men of Ephraim gathered
themselves together and seized the
waters as far as Beth-barah by the
Jordan.

25 And they captured two princes
of Midian, Oreb and Zeeb; and they
slew Oreb at Tyre, and Zeeb they
slew at Beth-kabrab; and they pursued Midian, and they brought the
heads of Oreb and Zeeb to Gideon
on the other side of the Jordan.

CHAPTER 8

THEN the men of Ephraim said to
him, Why have you done thus,
that you never called us when you
went to fight with the Midianites?
And they quarreled with him violently.

2 And he said to them, What have
I done now in comparison to you?
Is not the gleaning of the grapes of

Ephraim better than the vintage of
Jezreel?

3 For in Jezreel God has delivered
into your hands the two princes of
Midian, Oreb and Zeeb; and what
was I able to do in comparison to
you? Then their anger was abated
toward him, when he had said that.

4 ¶And Gideon came to the Jordan
and passed over, he and the three
hundred men who were with him,
pursuing, yet faint from hunger.

5 And he said to the men of Succoth, Give a few loaves of bread to
the people who are with me; for they
are faint from hunger, and, behold,
I am pursuing Zebah and Zalmunna,
kings of Midian.

6 ¶And the princes of Succoth said
to him, Are the hands of Zebah and
Zalmunna now in your hands, that
we should give bread to your army?

7 And Gideon said to them, Therefore when the LORD has delivered
Zebah and Zalmunna into my hands,
then I will tear your flesh with the
thorns of the wilderness and with
briers.

8 ¶And he went up from there to
Penuel, and the men of Penuel answered him as the men of Succoth
had answered him.

9 And he said also to the men of
Penuel, When I come again in peace,
I will break down this tower.

10 ¶Now Zebah and Zalmunna
were staying at Karkab, and their
armies with them, about fifteen thousand men, all that were left of all
the armies of the people of the east;
for there fell a hundred and twenty
thousand men that drew sword.

11 ¶And Gideon went up by the
way of them who dwell in tents on
the east of Necah and Jogbehah, and
attacked the army camp; for the army
was not on guard.

12 And Zebah and Zalmunna fled,
and he pursued them, and captured
the two kings of Midian, Zebah and
Zalmunna, and threw the whole army
into confusion.

13 ¶And Gideon the son of Joash
returned from the battle at the slope
of Hadas.

14 And he captured a young man

of the men of Succoth, and questioned him; and he wrote down for him a description of the princes of Succoth and its elders, seventy-seven men.

15 And he came to the men of Succoth and said to them, Behold Zebah and Zalmunna, about whom you upbraided me, saying, Are the hands of Zebah and Zalmunna now in your hands, that we should give bread to your servants who are faint from hunger?

16 And he dragged the elders of the city over the briers and thorns of the wilderness, and thus inflicted tortures on the men of Succoth.

17 And he broke down the tower of Penuel, and slew the men of the city.

18 ¶Then he said to Zebah and Zalmunna, What manner of men were they whom you slew at Tabor? They said to him, They were like yourself, they resembled the sons of kings.

19 And he said, They were my brothers, the sons of my mother; as the LORD lives, if you had saved them alive, I would not slay you.

20 And he said to Jether his firstborn, Arise and slay them. But the youth did not draw his sword; for he was afraid, because he was still a youth.

21 Then Zebah and Zalmunna said, Rise yourself, and fall upon us; for as the man is, so is his might. And Gideon arose and slew Zebah and Zalmunna, and took away the ornaments that were on their camels' necks.

22 ¶Then the men of Israel said to Gideon, Rule over us, both you and your son and your son's son also; for you have delivered us from the hand of Midian.

23 And Gideon said to them, I will not rule over you, neither shall my son rule over you; the LORD shall rule over you.

24 ¶And Gideon said to them, I would like to make a request of you: give me every man of you an earring of his spoil. (For they had golden earrings, since the enemies were Arabians.)

25 And they said to him, We will gladly give it. And they spread a mantle, and every man threw onto it one earring from his spoil.

26 And the weight of the golden earrings that he requested was one thousand seven hundred shekels of gold; besides ornaments, neck chains, and purple raiment that were worn by the kings of Midian, and besides the chains that were about their camels' necks.

27 And Gideon took some of them and made a little idol, and set it up in his town, Ophrah; and all Israel went astray after it there; and it became a stumbling block to Gideon and to all his household.

28 ¶Thus the Midianites were defeated before the children of Israel, so that they lifted up their heads no more. And the land was tranquil forty years in the days of Gideon.

29 ¶Then Nedo-baal the son of Joash went and dwelt in his own house.

30 And Gideon had seventy sons who were begotten by him; for he had many wives.

31 And his concubine who was in Shechem also bore him a son, whose name he called Abimeleck.

32 ¶And Gideon the son of Joash died at a good old age, and was buried in the town of his father Joash, in Ophrah of the father of Azri.

33 And it came to pass, as soon as Gideon was dead, the children of Israel turned again and went astray after Baal, and made Baal-kiama their god.

34 And the children of Israel did not remember the LORD their God, who had delivered them from the hand of all their enemies on every side;

35 Neither did they show kindness to the house of Nedo-baal, that is, Gideon, according to all the goodness that he had done to Israel.

CHAPTER 9

AND Abimeleck the son of Nedo-baal went to Shechem to his mother's brothers, and spoke to them and to all the family of the house of his mother's father, saying,

2 Speak, before all the lords of Shechem, Which is better for you, that all the seventy men, the sons of Nedo-baal, rule over you, or that one man rule over you? Remember also that I am your bone and your flesh.

3 And his mother's brothers spoke of him before all the lords of Shechem all these words; and their hearts inclined to follow Abimeleck; for they said, He is our brother.

4 And they gave him seventy pieces of silver from the house of Baal-kiama, with which Abimeleck hired vain and wanton persons, who followed him.

5 And he went to his father's house at Ophrah, and slew his brothers, the sons of Nedo-baal, seventy men, upon one stone; but Jotham the youngest son of Nedo-baal was left; for he hid himself.

6 And all the lords of Shechem gathered together, and all the people of Beth-millo, and went and made Abimeleck king over them, by the oak of Mazpiah which is in Shechem.

7 ¶And when they told it to Jotham, he went and stood on the top of mount Gerizim, and lifted up his voice and cried, and said to them, Hearken to me, O lords of Shechem, that God may hearken to you.

8 Once upon a time the trees went forth to anoint a king over them; and they said to the olive tree, Reign over us.

9 But the olive tree said to them, Should I leave my fertility, by which gods and men are honored, to be abominated for reigning over the trees?

10 And the trees said to the fig tree, Come you, and reign over us.

11 But the fig tree said to them, I am not going to leave my sweetness and my good fruit, to be abominated for reigning over the trees.

12 Then the trees said to the vine, Come you, and reign over us.

13 But the vine said to them, I am not going to leave my wine which cheers the hearts of gods and men, to be abominated for reigning over the trees.

14 Then all the trees said to the bramble, Come you, and reign over us.

15 And the bramble said to the trees, If in truth you anoint me king over you, then come and take refuge in my shade; and if not, let fire come out of the bramble and devour the cedars of Lebanon.

16 Now therefore, if you have done truly and sincerely, in that you have made Abimeleck king, and if you have dealt well with Nedo-baal and his household, and have rewarded him according to the deeds of his hands;

17 (For my father fought for you, and ventured his life afar, and delivered you from the hand of Midian;

18 And you have risen up against my father's house this day, and have slain his sons, seventy men, upon one stone, and have made Abimeleck, the son of his maidservant, king over the lords of Shechem, because he is your brother;)

19 If you then have dealt truly and sincerely with Nedo-baal and with his house this day, then rejoice in Abimeleck, and let him also rejoice in you;

20 But if not, let fire come out from Abimeleck, and devour the lords of Shechem and the lords of Millo; and let fire come out from the lords of Shechem and from the lords of Millo, and devour Abimeleck.

21 And Jotham ran away and escaped, and went to Debir, and dwelt there, the place where Abimeleck had lived before.

22 ¶When Abimeleck had reigned over Israel three years,

23 Then God sent an evil spirit upon Abimeleck and upon the lords of Shechem; and the lords of Shechem dealt treacherously with Abimeleck,

24 That the cruelty done to the seventy sons of Nedo-baal might come, and their blood be laid upon Abimeleck their brother, who slew them; and upon the lords of Shechem,

who strengthened his hands in the killing of his brothers.

25 And the men of Shechem laid an ambush against him on the top of the mountain, and they robbed all who passed by them along that way; and it was told Abimeleck.

26 And Gaal the son of Epar came with his brothers, and went over to Shechem; and the lords of Shechem put their confidence in him.

27 And they went out into the fields, and gathered their vineyards and trod the grapes, and they made a banquet and went into the house of their gods and did eat and drink, and reviled Abimeleck.

28 And Gaal the son of Epar said, Who is Abimeleck and who is Shechem that we would serve him? Is he not the son of Nedo-baal? And Zebul because he changed his allegiance served the men of Hamor the father of Shechem; why then should we serve him?

29 And would to God this people were under my command! Then I would remove Abimeleck. And he said to Abimeleck, Increase your army, and come out.

30 ¶And when Zebul the governor of the city heard the words of Gaal the son of Epar, his anger was kindled.

31 And he sent messengers to Abimeleck deceitfully, saying, Behold, Gaal the son of Epar and his brothers have come to Shechem; and, behold, they fortify the city against you.

32 Now therefore arise by night, you and the people that are with you, and lie in wait in the field;

33 And in the morning as soon as the sun is up, you must rise early, and march upon the city; and, behold, when he and the people that are with him come out against you, you may do to them as you are able to do.

34 ¶And Abimeleck and all the people that were with him rose up by night, and they laid in ambush against Shechem in four companies.

35 And Gaal the son of Epar went out and stood in the entrance of the gate of the city; and Abimeleck and the people that were with him rose up from ambush.

36 And when Gaal saw the people, he said to Zebul, Behold, there are people coming down from the top of the mountains. And Zebul said to him, You see the shadows of the mountains that look like men.

37 And Gaal spoke again and said, Behold, there are people coming down from the center of the land, and one company is coming along from the way of the house of the oak of Meaonin.

38 Then Zebul said to him, Where is now your mouth with which you said, Who is Abimeleck that we should serve him? Are not these the people whom you have despised? Go out now and fight with them.

39 And Gaal went out before the lords of Shechem and fought with Abimeleck.

40 And Abimeleck chased him, and he fled before him, and many people fell slain, even to the entrance of the gate.

41 And Abimeleck dwelt at Adomah; and Zebul expelled Gaal and his brethren, that they should not dwell in Shechem.

42 And it came to pass on the next day, that the people went out into the fields, and they told Abimeleck.

43 And he took the people and divided them into three companies, and lay in wait in the fields, and he looked, and, behold, the people were coming forth out of the city; and he rose up against them and slew them.

44 And Abimeleck and the company that was with him rushed forward, and stood in the entrance of the gate of the city; and the two other companies rushed against all the people who were in the fields, and slew them.

45 And Abimeleck fought in the city all that day; and he took the city, and he slew all the people that were in it, and he destroyed the city, and sowed it with salt.[1]

46 ¶And when all the lords of the

[1] To make the land barren.

tower of Shechem heard of it, they came to take refuge in the house of the god of the covenant.

47 And it was told Abimeleck that all the lords of the tower of Shechem were gathered together.

48 And Abimeleck went up to mount Zalmon, he and all the people that were with him; and Abimeleck took an axe in his hand and cut down a branch from the trees, and took it and laid it on his shoulder, and said to the people that were with him, What you have seen me do, make haste and do as I have done.

49 So every man cut down his branch and followed Abimeleck, and they piled them up, and then set the city on fire, so that all the men that were in the tower of Shechem died in fire, about a thousand men and women.

50 ¶Then Abimeleck went to Thebez, and encamped against Thebez and took it.

51 But there was a strong tower within the city, and thither fled all the men and women and all the lords of the city, and shut it behind themselves, and went to the top of the tower.

52 And Abimeleck advanced as far as the tower, and fought against it, and drew near to the door of the tower to set it on fire.

53 And a certain woman threw a piece of an upper millstone upon Abimeleck's head and broke his skull.

54 Then he called hastily to his young armorbearer, and said to him, Draw your sword and slay me with it, that men may not say of me, A woman slew him. So the young man thrust him through, and he died.

55 And when the men of Israel saw that Abimeleck was dead, they departed every man to his place.

56 ¶Thus God requited the wickedness of Abimeleck, which he did to his father, in slaying his seventy brothers;

57 And all the wickedness of the men of Shechem did God bring upon their heads; and upon them came the curse of Jotham the son of Nedobaal.

CHAPTER 10

AFTER Abimeleck there arose to save Israel Tola the son of Puah, the son of his uncle, a man of Issachar; and he dwelt in Shamir on mount Ephraim.

2 And he judged Israel twenty-three years, and he died and was buried in Shamir.

3 ¶And after him arose Jair, the Gileadite, and he judged Israel for twenty-two years.

4 And he had thirty sons who rode on thirty ass colts, and they had thirty towns, which are called villages of Jair to this day, which are in the land of Gilead.

5 And Jair died and was buried in Camon.

6 ¶And the children of Israel did evil again in the sight of the LORD, and served Baal and Ashtaroth and the gods of Edom, the gods of Zidon, the gods of Moab, the gods of the children of Ammon, the gods of the Philistines, and the gods of the rest of the nations, and they forsook the LORD and did not serve him.

7 And the anger of the LORD was kindled against Israel, and he delivered them into the hands of the Philistines and into the hands of the children of Ammon.

8 And from that year they vexed and oppressed the children of Israel, eighteen years, all the children of Israel who were on the other side of the Jordan in the land of the Amorites, which is in Gilead.

9 Moreover the children of Ammon crossed the Jordan to fight against Judah and also against the house of Ephraim and against Benjamin; so that Israel was exceedingly distressed.

10 ¶And the children of Israel cried to the LORD, saying, We have sinned against thee, because we have forsaken our God and have served Baal.

11 And the LORD said to the children of Israel, Did not the Egyptians, the Moabites, the children of Ammon, the Philistines,

12 The Zidonians, the Amalekites, and the Amorites oppress you; and

you cried to me, and I delivered you from their hands?

13 Yet you have forsaken me and served other gods; therefore I will save you no more.

14 Go and pray to the gods with whom you are pleased; let them become your saviors in the time of your distress.

15 ¶And the children of Israel said to the LORD, We have sinned; do thou to us whatever seems good to thee; only deliver us this day.

16 And the children of Israel put away the strange gods from among them and served the LORD; for the soul of Israel was grieved.

17 Then the children of Ammon were gathered together and encamped in Gilead. And the children of Israel assembled themselves together and encamped in Mizpeh.

18 And the people and princes of Gilead said one to another, Whosoever shall first start to fight against the children of Ammon, he shall be prince over all the inhabitants of Gilead.

CHAPTER 11

NOW Jephthah the Gileadite was a mighty man of valor, but he was the son of a harlot; and Gilead begat Jephthah.

2 And Gilead's wife bore him sons; and when his wife's sons grew up, they expelled Jephthah, saying, He shall not inherit in our father's house, because he is the son of another woman.

3 Then Jephthah fled from his brothers, and dwelt in the land of Tobtha; and there were gathered worthless men to Jephthah, and they went raiding with him.

4 ¶And it came to pass after a time, the children of Ammon made war against Israel.

5 And when the children of Ammon made war against the children of Israel, the elders of Gilead went to bring Jephthah from the land of Tobtha;

6 And they said to Jephthah, Come and be our leader, that we may fight with the children of Ammon.

7 And Jephthah said to the elders of Gilead, Did you not hate me and expel me from my father's house? And why have you come to me now when you are in distress?

8 And the elders of Gilead said to Jephthah, That is why we have come to you now, that you may go with us and fight against the children of Ammon and be the leader over all the inhabitants of Gilead.

9 And Jephthah said to the elders of Gilead, If you bring me back to fight against the children of Ammon, and the LORD deliver them before me, shall I be your chief?

10 And the elders of Gilead said to him, The LORD shall be witness between us, if we do not so according to your words.

11 Then Jephthah went with the elders of Gilead, and the people made him chief and ruler over them; and Jephthah uttered all his words before the LORD in Mizpeh.

12 ¶And Jephthah sent messengers to the king of the children of Ammon, saying, What have we against each other, that you have come against me to fight in my land?

13 And the king of the children of Ammon said to the messengers of Jephthah, Because the children of Israel took away my land when they came up out of the land of Egypt from Arnon even to Jabbok and to the Jordan, now therefore restore these lands to me peaceably.

14 And Jephthah sent letters and messengers again to the king of the children of Ammon;

15 And said to him, Thus says Jephthah, Israel did not take away the land of Moab nor the land of the children of Ammon;

16 Because when the children of Israel came up from Egypt, Israel journeyed through the wilderness as far as the Red Sea, and came to Rakim;

17 Then Israel sent messengers to the king of Edom, saying, Let me pass through your land; but the king of Edom would not listen. And they sent also to the king of Moab; but he would not consent; so Israel stayed in Rakim.

18 Then they journeyed through the wilderness, and went around the land of Edom and the land of Moab, and they encamped on the other side of Arnon, but they did not enter the territory of Moab; for Arnon was the border of Moab.

19 And Israel sent messengers to Sihon king of the Amorites, the king of Heshbon; and Israel said to him, Let us pass through your land until we come to our land.

20 But Sihon did not trust Israel to pass through his territory; so Sihon gathered all his people together and encamped at Jahaz and fought against Israel.

21 And the LORD our God delivered Sihon and all his people into the hand of Israel, and Israel destroyed the land of the Amorites.

22 And they possessed all their territory, from Arnon as far as Jabbok, and from the wilderness even to the Jordan.

23 So now after the LORD God of Israel has destroyed the Amorites from before his people Israel, are you to possess their land?

24 Will you not possess that which Chemosh your god gives you to possess? So whomever the LORD our God has destroyed from before us, their land will we possess.

25 And now are you any better than Balak the son of Zippor, king of Moab? Did he ever strive against Israel? Or did he ever fight against them?

26 While Israel dwelt in Heshbon and its villages, and in Adoer and its villages, and in all the cities that are along the banks of Arnon, three hundred years? Why did you not recover them in that time?

27 Now therefore I have not sinned against you, but you do me wrong to make war against me; let the LORD judge this day between the children of Israel and the children of Ammon.

28 But the king of the children of Ammon did not listen to the words of Jephthah which he sent him.

29 ¶Then the Spirit of the LORD came upon Jephthah, and he passed over Gilead and Manasseh, and passed over Mizpeh of Gilead; and from Mizpeh of Gilead he passed over to the children of Ammon.

30 And Jephthah vowed a vow to the LORD, and said, If thou wilt surely deliver the children of Ammon into my hands,

31 Then whosoever comes forth of the door of my house to meet me when I return in peace from the children of Ammon shall be the LORD's, and I will offer him up for a burnt offering.

32 So Jephthah passed over to the children of Ammon to fight against them; and the LORD delivered them into his hands.

33 And he smote them from Adoer, as far as the entrance of Machir, twenty cities, and as far as Abel Karmin, the plain of vineyards, with a very great slaughter. Thus the children of Ammon were defeated before the children of Israel.

34 ¶Then Jephthah came to Mizpeh to his house, and, behold, his daughter came out to meet him with timbrels and with dances; and she was his only child; besides her he had neither son nor daughter.

35 And when he saw her, he rent his clothes, and said, Alas, my daughter! You have brought me very low, and you have become today one of those that ruin me; for I have made a promise to God, and I cannot go back on it.

36 And his daughter said to him, My father, if you have made a promise to God, do to me according to that which has proceeded out of your mouth; since the LORD has taken vengeance for you on your enemies, even of the children of Ammon.

37 And she said to her father, Grant me this thing only: let me alone two months that I may go and wander on the mountains and bewail my virginity, I and my companions.

38 And he said, Go. And he sent her away for two months; and she went with her companions, and bewailed her virginity on the mountains.

39 And at the end of two months,

she returned to her father, who did with her according to his vow; and she knew no man. And it became a custom among the children of Israel,

40 That the daughters of Israel went yearly to weep and lament over the daughter of Jephthah the Gileadite four days in a year.

CHAPTER 12

THEN the men of Ephraim gathered themselves together, and went northward, and said to Jephthah, Why did you cross over to fight against the children of Ammon, and did not call us to go with you? We will burn your house over you with fire.

2 And Jephthah said to them, O men! I and my people had strife with the children of Ammon; and when I called you, you did not deliver me from their hands.

3 And when I saw that there was no one to deliver me, I risked my life, and crossed over against the children of Ammon, and the LORD delivered them into my hands; now why have you come up against me this day, to fight with me?

4 Then Jephthah gathered together all the men of Gilead and fought with Ephraim; and the men of Gilead smote the men of Ephraim, because they said, The Ephraimites dominate Ephraim and Manasseh.

5 And the Gileadites took the fords of the Jordan which belonged to Ephraim; and when any of the fugitives of Ephraim tried to cross over the passage, the men of Gilead said to him, Are you an Ephraimite? If he said, No;

6 Then they said to him, Say now Shibboleth; and he said Sibboleth; for he could not pronounce it so. Then they took him and slew him at the fords of the Jordan; and there fell at that time forty-two thousand of the Ephraimites.

7 And Jephthah judged Israel six years. Then Jephthah the Gileadite died and was buried in his city in Gilead.

8 ¶And after him Ibzan of Bethlehem judged Israel.

9 And he had thirty sons, and thirty daughters, and his thirty daughters he gave in marriage outside of his tribe, and brought in thirty daughters-in-law from outside. And he judged Israel seven years.

10 Then Ibzan died and was buried in Beth-lehem.

11 ¶And after him Elon, a Zebulunite, judged Israel; and he judged Israel ten years.

12 And Elon the Zebulunite died and was buried in Aijalon in the land of Zebulun.

13 ¶And after him Acran the son of Hillian, the Aprathonite, judged Israel.

14 And he had forty sons and thirty grandsons, who rode on seventy ass colts; and he judged Israel eight years.

15 Then Acran the son of Hillian, the Aprathonite died, and was buried in Aprathon in the land of Ephraim on the mount of the Amalekites.

CHAPTER 13

AND the children of Israel did evil again in the sight of the LORD; and the LORD delivered them into the hand of the Philistines for forty years.

2 ¶And there was a certain man of Zedah, of the family of the Danites, whose name was Manoah; and his wife was barren, and never had children.

3 And the angel of the LORD appeared to the woman and said to her, Behold, you are barren, and have borne no children; but now you shall conceive, and bear a son.

4 Now therefore beware, lest you drink wine or strong drink; and you shall not eat anything unclean.

5 For lo, you have conceived and will bear a son; and no razor shall come on his head; for the child shall be a Nazarite to God from the womb; and he will begin to deliver Israel out of the hand of the Philistines.

6 ¶Then the woman came and told her husband, saying, A man of God came to me, and his countenance was like the countenance of an angel of God, and I trembled exceedingly, and I did not ask him whence he was, nor did he tell me his name;

7 But he said to me, Behold, you have conceived, and you will bear a son; and from henceforth drink no wine nor strong drink, neither eat any unclean thing; for the child shall be a Nazarite to God from the womb to the day of his death.

8 ¶Then Manoah entreated the LORD and said, I beseech thee, O LORD, let the man of God whom thou didst send come again to us and teach us what we shall do to the child that shall be born.

9 And the LORD hearkened to the voice of Manoah; and the angel of the LORD came again to the woman as she sat in the field; but Manoah her husband was not with her.

10 And the woman made haste and ran, and told her husband and said to him, Behold, the man has appeared to me, who came to me the other day.

11 And Manoah arose and went with his wife, and came to the man and said to him, Are you the man who spoke to this woman? And he said, I am.

12 And Manoah said, Now let your words come to pass. But tell me, what is the manner by which the child is to be brought up, and what shall we do to him?

13 And the angel of the LORD said to Manoah, Of all that I said to the woman let her beware.

14 She must not eat of anything that comes of the vine, neither shall she drink wine or strong drink, nor eat any unclean thing; all that I have commanded her let her observe.

15 ¶Then Manoah said to the angel of the LORD, Let us detain you, and make ready a kid for you.

16 And the angel of the LORD said to Manoah, Though you detain me, I will not eat of your food; and if you will offer a burnt offering, you must offer it to the LORD. For Manoah did not know that he was the angel of the LORD.

17 And Manoah said to the angel of the LORD, What is your name, that when your sayings come to pass we may invoke your name?

18 And the angel of the LORD said to him, Why do you ask my name, seeing it is Glorious?

19 So Manoah took a kid with the meal offering, and offered it upon a rock to the LORD; and the angel praised the LORD; and Manoah and his wife looked on.

20 And when a flame went up toward heaven from off the rock, the angel of the LORD ascended in the flame of the altar. And Manoah and his wife looked on it, and fell on their faces to the ground and worshipped.

21 The angel of the LORD did no more appear to Manoah and to his wife. Then Manoah and his wife knew that he was an angel of the LORD.

22 And Manoah said to his wife, We shall surely die, because we have seen God.

23 But his wife said to him, If God were pleased to kill us, he would not have received a burnt offering and a meal offering from us, neither would he have showed us all these things at this time, nor would he have told us such things as these.

24 ¶And the woman bore a son, and called his name Samson; and the child grew, and the LORD blessed him.

25 And the Spirit of the LORD began to make Samson to travel with the host of Dan between Zedah and Eshtoal.

CHAPTER 14

AND Samson went down to Timnath, and saw a woman in Timnath of the daughters of the Philistines.

2 And he came up, and told his father and his mother, and said, I have seen a woman in Timnath of the daughters of the Philistines; now therefore get her for me to wife.

3 Then his father and mother said to him, Is there not a woman here among the daughters of the kinsmen of your father, or among all your people, that you are going to take a wife of the uncircumcised Philistines? And Samson said to his father, Get her for me; for she pleased me well.

4 But his father and his mother did

not know that it was of the LORD, that he might seek vengeance against the Philistines; for at that time the Philistines had dominion over Israel.

5 ¶Then Samson went down with his father and mother to Timnath, and they came to the vineyards of Timnath; and, behold, a young lion roared at him.

6 And the Spirit of the LORD came mightily upon him, and he tore the lion as one tears a kid, and he had nothing in his hand; but he did not tell his father or his mother what he had done.

7 And they went down and talked with the woman; and she pleased Samson well.

8 ¶And after a time he returned to take her, and he turned aside to see the carcass of the lion; and, behold, there was a swarm of bees in the carcass of the lion, and the honey ran out on his hands as he walked.

9 And he went to his father and mother, and gave some honey to them, and they did eat; but he did not tell them that the honey came from the carcass of the lion.

10 ¶So his father went down to the woman; and Samson made there a wedding feast for seven days; for so the young men used to do.

11 And when they saw him, there came thirty men and became his groomsmen.

12 ¶And Samson said to them, I will now put forth a riddle to you; if you can interpret it to me within the seven days of the feast and find it out, then I will give you thirty overcoats made of felt and thirty changes of garments;

13 But if you cannot interpret it to me, then you shall give me thirty overcoats made of felt and thirty changes of garments. And they said to him, Put forth your riddle, that we may hear it.

14 And he said to them, Out of the eater came forth something to eat, and out of the bitter came forth something sweet. And for three days they could not interpret the riddle.

15 But on the fourth day, they said to Samson's wife, Entice your hus-band, that he may declare to us his riddle, lest we burn you and your father's house with fire and take over his possessions.

16 And Samson's wife wept and said to him, You truly hate me and do not love me; you have put forth a riddle to my countrymen, and you have never told it to me. And he said to her, I have not told it to my father nor to my mother, and shall I tell it to you?

17 And she wept the seven days, while the feast lasted; and it came to pass on the seventh day, that he told her, because she distressed him; and she told the riddle to her countrymen.

18 And the men of the city said to him on the seventh day before the banquet, What is sweeter than honey? And what is stronger than a lion? And Samson said to them, If you had not enticed my heifer, you would not have interpreted my riddle.

19 ¶And the Spirit of the LORD came upon him, and he went down to Ashkelon, and he seized thirty of their men, and he slew them and took their garments and gave them to those who had interpreted his riddle. And his anger was kindled, and he went up to his father's house.

20 And Samson's wife, whom he loved, was given to one of his grooms-men.

CHAPTER 15

BUT it came to pass after a while, in the time of the wheat harvest, Samson visited his wife with a kid as a present; and he said, I will go in to my wife in the chamber. But her father would not let him go in.

2 And her father said, I surely thought that you had utterly hated her; therefore I gave her to your groomsman; behold, her younger sister, who is fairer than she, take her to wife instead.

3 ¶And Samson said to them, Now I shall be more blameless than the Philistines, although I am going to do them mischief.

4 So Samson went and caught three hundred foxes, and took torches and

tied tail to tail, two foxes together; and he tied a torch between each pair of foxes, between two tails.

5 And when he had set the torches on fire, he let the foxes go into the standing grain of the Philistines, and burned up both the shocks and the standing grain, and also the vineyards and olives.

6 ¶Then the Philistines said, Who has done this? And they said, Samson, the son-in-law of the Timnite, because he had taken his wife and given her to his groomsman. And the Philistines came up and burned her and her father's family with fire.

7 ¶And Samson said to them, Because you have done this, I will be avenged of you, and after that I will cease.

8 And he smote them hip and thigh with a great slaughter; and he went down and dwelt in a cave of the rock of Atmin.

9 ¶Then the Philistines went up and encamped in Judah.

10 And the men of Judah said, Why have you come up against us? And they answered, We have come up to bind Samson, to do to him as he has done to us.

11 Then three thousand men of Judah went down to the cave of the rock of Atmin, and said to Samson, Do you not know that the Philistines are rulers over us? What is this you have done to us? And he said to them, As they did to me, so have I done to them.

12 And they said to him, We have come down to bind you, that we may deliver you into the hand of the Philistines. And Samson said to them, Swear to me that you will not harm me yourselves.

13 And they said to him, No; but we will bind you and deliver you into their hands; but surely we will not kill you. So they bound him with two new chains and brought him up from the rock.

14 ¶And when he came to Lehi, the Philistines rose up to kill him; and the Spirit of the LORD came mightily upon him, and the chains that were on his arms became like flax that

has caught fire, and his bands loosed from off his hands.

15 And he found a hard jawbone of an ass, and put forth his hand and took it, and slew a thousand men with it.

16 And Samson said, With the jawbone of an ass I have made heaps upon heaps, with the jawbone of an ass I have slain a thousand men.

17 And it came to pass, when he had finished speaking, he threw away the jawbone out of his hand, and called the name of that place, the Bloody Jawbone.

18 ¶And he was very thirsty, so he called on the LORD, and said, Thou hast given this great victory into the hand of thy servant; and now shall I die of thirst and fall into the hand of the uncircumcised?

19 And the LORD God opened the hollow place that was in the jawbone of the ass, and there came water from it; and when he had drunk, his spirit returned and he revived; therefore he called the name of that place En-karna di paka di khmara, to this day.

20 And he judged Israel twenty years in the days of the Philistines.

CHAPTER 16

THEN Samson went to Gaza, and saw there a harlot, and he went in unto her.

2 And it was told the Gazites, saying, Samson has come here. And they lay in wait for him all night in the gate of the city, and were whispering all night, saying, When the morning dawns, we shall kill him.

3 But Samson slept till midnight, and arose at midnight, and took the two door-posts of the gate of the city, and lifted them up, together with the bars thereof, and put them on his shoulder and carried them to the mountain that is before Hebron.

4 ¶And it came to pass after this, he loved a woman in the valley of Sarok, whose name was Delilah.

5 And the lords of the Philistines came up to her and said to her, Entice him, and see wherein his great strength lies, and by what means we

may prevail against him, that we may bind him to disgrace him; and we will give you every one of us thirteen hundred pieces of silver.

6 ¶And Delilah said to Samson, Tell me wherein your great strength lies, and with what you might be bound, and how that you may become weak.

7 And Samson said to her, If they bind me with seven fresh bowstrings that were never dried, then I shall become weak and be like any other man.

8 Then the lords of the Philistines brought up to her seven fresh bowstrings that had never been dried, and she bound him with them.

9 Now there were men lying in wait in her inner chamber. And she said to him, The Philistines have come upon you, Samson. And he broke the bowstrings as a thread of tow is broken when it touches the fire. So his strength was not disturbed.

10 And Delilah said to Samson, Behold, you have deceived me and told me lies; now tell me with what you might be bound.

11 And he said to her, If they bind me fast with new chains that never were used, then shall I be weak and be like any other man.

12 So Delilah took new chains and bound him with them, and said to him, The Philistines have come upon you, Samson. And the men were lying in wait in the inner chamber. And he broke them from off his arms like a thread.

13 And Delilah said to Samson, Behold you have deceived me and told me lies; tell me with what you might be bound. And he said to her, If you weave the seven locks of my head into a web.

14 And she wove it with the weaver's web, and said, The Philistines have come upon you, Samson. And he awoke from his sleep, and pulled away both the weaver's loom and the web.

15 ¶And she said to him, How can you say to me, I love you, when your heart is not with me? For behold, you have deceived me these three times,

and you have not told me wherein your great strength lies.

16 And it came to pass, when she had pressed him daily with her words and urged him, his soul was vexed to death;

17 So he told her all his heart, and said to her, There has never come a razor upon my head; for I have been a Nazarite to God from my mother's womb; if I be shaven, then my strength will depart from me, and I shall become weak and be like any other man.

18 And when Delilah saw that he had told her all his heart, she sent and called for the lords of the Philistines, saying, Come up now, for he has told me all his heart. Then the lords of the Philistines came up to her, and brought the money with them.

19 And she made him sleep upon her knees; and she called for the barber, and had him shave off the seven locks of his head; and she began to overpower him, and his strength had departed from him.

20 And she said to him, The Philistines have come upon you, Samson. And he awoke from his sleep, and said, I will go out as at other times before, and I will torment them. And he did not know that the LORD had departed from him.

21 ¶And the Philistines seized him, and put out his eyes and bound him with fetters and brought him down to Gaza, and he did grind wheat in the prison house.

22 But the hair of his head began to grow again after he was shaven.

23 Then the lords of the Philistines assembled to offer a great sacrifice to Dagon their god, and to rejoice; for they said, Our god has delivered Samson our enemy into our hand.

24 And when the people saw him, they praised their god; for they said, Our god has delivered into our hands our enemy and the destroyer of our country, who slew many of us.

25 And it came to pass when their hearts were merry, they said, Call for Samson that he may make sport before us. And they called Samson out of the prison house; and he made

sport before them; and they set him between the pillars.

26 And Samson said to the lad who held him by the hand, Let me feel the pillars on which the house stands, that I may lean against them.

27 Now the house was full of men and women; and all the lords of the Philistines were there; and there were upon the roof about three thousand men and women, looking on while Samson made sport.

28 Then Samson called to the LORD, and said, O LORD God, remember me, I pray thee, and strengthen me only this once, O God, that I may be avenged of the Philistines for my two eyes.

29 And Samson took hold of the two middle pillars upon which the house stood, and he leaned against them, grasping one with his right hand and the other with his left.

30 And Samson said, Let me die with the Philistines. Then he pulled with all his might; and the house fell upon the lords and upon all the people that were therein. So the dead whom Samson slew at his death were more than those whom he slew during his life.

31 Then his brothers and all the house of his father came down and took him, and brought him up and buried him between Zedah and Eshtaol in the burying place of Menoah his father. And he had judged Israel twenty years.

CHAPTER 17

AND there was a man from mount Ephraim, whose name was Micah.

2 And he said to his mother, The eleven hundred shekels of silver which were taken from you, which you swore about, and spoke of also in my ears, behold, it was I who took the silver. And his mother said, Blessed of the LORD is my son.

3 And when he had restored the eleven hundred shekels of silver to his mother, his mother said, I have wholly consecrated the silver to the LORD from the hands of my son, to make a graven image and a molten image; now therefore restore it to me.

4 So he restored the money to his mother; and his mother took two hundred shekels of silver and gave it to the silversmith, who made it into a graven image and a molten image; and they were kept in the house of Micah.

5 And the man Micah had a house of gods, and he made an ephod and a teraphim, and consecrated one of his sons, who became his priest.

6 In those days there was no king in Israel, but every man did that which was right in his own eyes.

7 ¶Now there was a young man from Beth-lehem of Judah, whose name was Levi, and he sojourned there.

8 And the man had left the city of Beth-lehem of Judah to dwell wherever he could find a place; and he came to mount Ephraim, to the house of Micah, to obtain provisions for his journey.

9 And Micah said to him, Whence do you come? And he replied, I am a Levite of Beth-lehem of Judah, and I go to sojourn where I may find a place.

10 And Micah said to him, Dwell with me, and be to me as a father and a priest, and I will give you ten shekels of silver yearly, and your clothes and your food. So the Levite went in.

11 And the Levite was content to dwell with the man; and the young man was to him as one of his sons.

12 And Micah consecrated the Levite; and he became his priest, and was in the house of Micah.

13 Then said Micah, Now I know that the LORD will do me good, seeing that the Levite has become my priest.

CHAPTER 18

IN those days there was no king in Israel; and in those days the tribe of Dan sought for itself an inheritance to dwell in; for until that day no inheritance had fallen to them among the tribes of Israel.

2 And the Danites sent of their families five men from Zedah and from Eshtaol, to spy out the land, and to explore it; and they said to them, Go

and explore the land. And they came to mount Ephraim, to the house of Micah, and they lodged there.

3 When they were at the house of Micah, they recognized the voice of the young man, the Levite, and they turned aside there and said to him, Why did you come here? And what are you doing here?

4 And he said to them, Thus and thus has Micah dealt with me, and has hired me, and I have become his priest.

5 And they said to him, Inquire for us of God, that we may know whether the errand for which we go shall prosper.

6 And the priest said to them, Go in peace; and may the LORD prosper the errand on which you go.

7 ¶Then the five men departed and came to Laish, and saw the people who were in it, how they dwelt in tranquillity after the manner of the Zidonians, peaceful and quiet; and there was no one to do harm in the land, neither was there anyone to harass and to oppress; and they were far from the Zidonians, and had no business with any man.

8 And they came back to their brethren at Zedah and Eshtaol; and their brethren said to them, Whence did you come?

9 They said to them, Even from Laish. Now arise, let us go up against them; for we have seen the land, and, behold, it is very good; and do not hesitate, nor tarry to go and to take possession of the land.

10 When you go, you shall come against a rich people, and an extensive and arable land is before you; for the LORD has delivered it into your hands, a place where there is no lack of anything that is on the earth.

11 ¶And there went from thence of the family of the Danites, from Zedah and from Eshtaol, six hundred men armed with weapons of war.

12 And they went up and encamped at Koriath-narin, in Judah; wherefore they called that place the Camp of Dan to this day; behold, it is behind Koriath-narin.

13 And they passed on from there to mount Ephraim, and went to the house of Micah.

14 ¶Then answered the five men who had gone to spy out the land of Laish, and said to their brethren, Do you know that there is on these hills an ephod and teraphim and a graven image and a molten image? Now therefore you must consider what you have to do.

15 So they turned aside, and came to the house of the young man, Levi, even to the house of Micah, and saluted him.

16 And the six hundred men armed with weapons of war, who were Danites, stood by the entrance of the gate.

17 And the five men who had gone to spy out the land went up and entered there, and took the graven image and the ephod and the teraphim and the molten image, while the priest stood at the entrance of the gate with the six hundred men armed with weapons of war.

18 And they entered into Micah's house, and took the image, the ephod, and the teraphim, and the molten image. Then the priest said to them, What are you doing?

19 And they said to him, Hold your peace, stop talking, and come with us, and be to us a father and a priest. Which is better for you, to be a priest for one man's household, or to be a priest to a family and a tribe of Israel?

20 And the priest's heart was glad, and he took the graven image, the ephod, and the teraphim, and went with the people.

21 So they turned and departed, and put the sheep and the goods and the cattle in front of them.

22 ¶And when they were at a distance from the house of Micah, a man who was in the house beside Micah's house cried out and pursued the Danites.

23 And he shouted to the Danites, and they turned and said to Micah, What ails you, that you shout?

24 And he said to them, You have taken away the god which I made,

and also the priest, and you have gone away; and what have I left? And what is this that you say to me, What ails you?

25 And the Danites said to him, Let not your voice be heard among us, lest some angry fellows attack you, and you lose your life and the lives of your sons.

26 Then the Danites went their way; and when Micah saw that they were too strong for him, he turned and went back to his house.

27 And they took the things which Micah had made and the priest that he had, and came to Laish against the people who were rich and quiet; and they smote them with the edge of the sword, and burned the city with fire.

28 And there was no one to rescue them, because it was far from Zidon, and they had no business with any man; and the city was situated in the valley of Beth-rehob. And they rebuilt the city and dwelt in it.

29 And they called the name of the city Dan, after the name of Dan their father, who was born to Israel; but the name of the city was Laish at first.

30 ¶And the Danites set up the graven image; and Jonathan, the son of Gershon, the son of Manasseh, he and his sons were priests to the tribe of Dan until the day of the captivity of the land.

31 And they set up for themselves Micah's graven image, which he had made, all the time that the house of God was in Shiloh.

CHAPTER 19

AND it came to pass in those days, when there was no king in Israel, there was a certain Levite sojourning on the side of mount Ephraim, who took to himself a concubine from Beth-lehem of Judah.

2 And his concubine played the whore against him, and then arose and went away from him to her father's house to Beth-lehem of Judah, and remained there four whole months.

3 And her husband arose and went after her to speak lovingly to her and to bring her back, taking with him his servant and a couple of asses; and she brought him into her father's house; and when the father of the damsel saw him, he rejoiced to meet him.

4 And his father-in-law, the damsel's father, detained him; and he stayed with him three days; so they did eat and drink and lodged there.

5 ¶And on the fourth day, they rose early in the morning to depart; and the damsel's father said to his son-in-law, Strengthen yourself with a piece of bread; and after that rise and go.

6 So they sat down and did eat and drink, both of them together; and the damsel's father said to his son-in-law, If you wish you may spend the night and it will do you good.

7 And when the man rose up to depart, his father-in-law urged him to stay; and he spent the night there again.

8 And he arose early in the morning on the fifth day to depart; and the damsel's father said to him, Strengthen your heart, refresh yourself, and tarry until afternoon. And they did eat and drink both of them.

9 And when the man rose up to depart, he and his concubine and his servant, his father-in-law, the damsel's father, said to him, Behold, now the day is spent, tarry all night here; and it will do you good; and to-morrow, rise up early and go to your home.

10 But the man would not tarry that night, but he rose up and departed, and came opposite Jebus, which is Jerusalem; and there were with him two asses with burdens, and his concubine also was with him.

11 And when they were near Jebus, the day was far spent; and the servant said to his master, Come, let us turn aside to this city of the Jebusites and spend the night in it.

12 And his master said to him, We will not turn aside into a strange city that does not belong to the house of Israel; but we will pass on to Gibeah.

13 And he said to his servant, Come, let us draw near to one of

these places to lodge the night in Gibeah, or in Ramtha.

14 So they passed on and went their way; and the sun went down upon them when they were near Gibeah, which belongs to Benjamin.

15 And they turned aside there to spend the night; and they went to Gibeah, and sat down in a street of the city; for there was no man to take them into his house to spend the night.

16 ¶And, behold, there came an old man from his work out of the field at evening, and the man was also of mount Ephraim; and he sojourned in Gibeah, which belongs to Benjamin, but the men of the place were Benjamites whose deeds were exceedingly bad.

17 And the old man lifted up his eyes and saw the wayfarer in the street of the city; and the old man said to him, Where are you going? And whence do you come?

18 And he said to him, We are travelling from Beth-lehem of Judah toward the side of mount Ephraim; from thence am I; and I went as far as Beth-lehem of Judah, but now I am going to the house of the LORD, but there is no man to take us into his house.

19 And yet there is both straw and fodder for our asses; and there is bread and wine also for me and for your maidservant and for the young man, your servant; there is no lack of anything.

20 And the old man said to him, Peace be with you; anything that you may lack I will provide for you; only do not spend the night in the street.

21 So he brought him into his house, and gave fodder to his asses; and they washed their feet, and did eat and drink.

22 ¶Now as they were making their hearts merry, behold, the men of the city, certain wicked men, beset the house round about, and they beat at the door and spoke to the master of the house, the old man, saying, Bring out the man who came into your house, that we may know him.

23 And the old man, the master of the house, went out to them and said to them, No, my brethren, no, do not be so wicked; seeing that this man has come into my house, do not commit this shameful act.

24 Behold, here is my daughter, a virgin, and his concubine; I will bring them out for you, and you may humble them, and do with them what seems good to you; but to this man you shall not do any shameful thing.

25 But the men would not listen to him; so the man took his concubine and brought her outside to them; and they raped her and abused her all the night until the morning; and when dawn began to break, they let her go.

26 Then as the day was dawning, the woman came and fell down at the door of the man's house where her master was, till it was light.

27 And her master rose up in the morning and opened the door of the house and went out to go his way; and he saw his concubine lying at the door of the house, with her hands upon the threshold.

28 And he said to her, Get up, let us go. But she did not answer. Then he put her upon the ass, and the man rose up and went on to his own home.

29 ¶And when he had come to his house, he took a knife and cut his concubine in pieces, and divided her into twelve portions, and distributed them throughout all the tribes of Israel.

30 And all who saw it said, There has never been, nor seen, such a deed from the day that the children of Israel came up out of the land of Egypt until this day. So they considered it, and took counsel, and spoke out.

CHAPTER 20

THEN all the children of Israel went out, and the congregation gathered together as one man from Dan to Beer-sheba, to the land of Gilead, to the LORD in Mizpeh.

2 And the chiefs of all the families of all the people, even of all the tribes of Israel, presented themselves in the assembly of the people of God, four

hundred thousand footmen who could draw sword.

3 (Now the Benjamites heard that the children of Israel were gone up to Mizpeh.) Then said the children of Israel, Tell us, how did this wickedness happen?

4 And the Levite, the husband of the woman who was killed, answered and said to them, I came into Gibeah, that belongs to Benjamin, I and my concubine, to spend the night.

5 And the men of Gibeah rose against me, and beset me in the house during the night, and they sought to kill me; and they raped my concubine, and she died.

6 And I took my concubine, and cut her in pieces, and sent them throughout all the country of the inheritance of Israel; for they had committed sin and wickedness in Israel.

7 Behold, you are all here, O children of Israel, give an answer and counsel concerning this crime.

8 ¶And all the people arose as one man, saying, We will not any of us go to our tents, neither shall any one of us turn aside to go to his house.

9 But now this will be the thing which we shall do to Gibeah; we will draw lots against it;

10 We will take ten men of a hundred throughout all the tribes of Israel, and a hundred of a thousand, and a thousand out of ten thousand, to take provisions for the people, who cross over against Gibeah of Benjamin, to do to it according to all the wickedness which they have committed in Israel.

11 So all the men of Israel were gathered against the city, agreeing together as one man.

12 ¶And the tribes of Israel sent men through all the tribe of Benjamin, saying, What wickedness is this that has been done among you?

13 Now therefore deliver up the wicked men, who are in Gibeah, that we may put them to death, and put away evil from Israel. But the Benjamites would not listen to the voice of their brethren, the children of Israel;

14 But all the Benjamites gathered themselves together in Gibeah from their cities, to go out to battle against the children of Israel.

15 And the Benjamites were numbered in that day out of the cities twenty-six thousand men that drew sword, besides the inhabitants of Gibeah, who were numbered seven hundred chosen men.

16 Among all these people there were seven hundred chosen men who were lefthanded; every one of them could sling stones at an hairbreadth, and not miss.

17 And the men of Israel, as compared with the Benjamites, were numbered four hundred thousand men that drew sword; all these were men of war.

18 ¶And the children of Israel arose and went up to Beth-el, and inquired of God, and said, Which of us shall go up first to battle against the Benjamites? And the LORD said, Judah shall go first.

19 And the children of Israel rose up in the morning and encamped against Gibeah.

20 And the Benjamites went out of Gibeah to battle against Israel, and arrayed themselves against Israel; and the men of Israel put themselves in array to fight against them at Gibeah.

21 And the Benjamites came forth out of Gibeah, and put themselves in array against Israel, and left dead on the ground that day twenty-two thousand men of the children of Israel.

22 But the children of Israel rallied themselves, and once more set themselves in array in the same place where they had put themselves in array the first day.

23 And the children of Israel went up to Beth-el, and wept before the LORD until evening, and they asked counsel of the LORD, saying, Shall we go up again to battle against our brethren the Benjamites? And the LORD said, Go up against them.

24 And the children of Israel drew near to battle against the Benjamites on the second day.

25 And the Benjamites went out against them from Gibeah the second

day, and left dead on the ground eighteen thousand men of the children of Israel; all of these men who drew the sword.

26 ¶Then all the children of Israel, and all the people, went up and came to Beth-el, and wept and sat there before the LORD, and fasted that day until evening, and offered burnt offerings and peace offerings before the LORD.

27 And the children of Israel inquired of the LORD (for the ark of the covenant of the LORD was there in those days;

28 And Phinehas, the son of Eleazar, the son of Aaron the priest, ministered before it in those days), saying, Shall we yet again go out to battle against our brethren the Benjamites, or shall we cease? And the LORD said, Go up; for tomorrow I will deliver them into your hands.

29 So Israel set ambushes round about Gibeah.

30 Then the children of Israel went up against the Benjamites on the third day, and put themselves in array against Gibeah, as at other times.

31 And the Benjamites went out against the people, and were drawn away from the city; and they began to smite the people, and kill, as at other times, in the highways, one of which goes up to Gibeah, and the other to Beth-el through the field, about thirty men of Israel.

32 And the Benjamites said, They are defeated before us, as at first. But the children of Israel said, Let us flee, and draw them away from the city to the highways.

33 And all the men of Israel rose up out of their places, and put themselves in array at Baal-tamar; and those Israelites in ambush came forth out of their places from the cave which is in Gibeah.

34 And there came toward Gibeah ten thousand chosen men out of all Israel, and the battle was hard fought; but they did not know that disaster was near them.

35 And the LORD defeated Benjamin before Israel; and the children of Israel destroyed of the Benjamites that day twenty-five thousand, one hundred men; all of those who drew the sword.

36 So the Benjamites saw that they were defeated; and the children of Israel gave ground to the Benjamites, because they trusted in the ambushes that they had set against Gibeah.

37 And the men who were in ambush quietly made an attack against Gibeah; then the men in ambush moved forward and smote all the city with the edge of the sword.

38 Now there was an appointed signal between the men of Israel and the men in ambush, which was that they should make a great flame with smoke rise up out of the city.

39 And when the men of Israel retreated in the battle, the Benjamites killed of the men of Israel about thirty men; for they said, Surely they are defeated before us, as in the first battle.

40 But when the smoke began to rise out of the city like a pillar, the Benjamites looked behind them, and, behold, the flames of the city ascended up to heaven.

41 And when the men of Israel turned against them, the Benjamites were terrified; for they saw that disaster was upon them.

42 Therefore they fled before the men of Israel on their way to the wilderness; but the battle overtook them; and those who came out of the city first were trapped in the midst of them.

43 Thus they pursued the Benjamites and drove them away, and smote them with ease, to the east beyond Gibeah.

44 And there fell of the Benjamites eighteen thousand men; all these were men of valor.

45 And they turned and fled toward the wilderness to the rock of Rimmon; and five thousand of them fell in the highway; all men that drew the sword; and they pursued hard after them as far as Gibeon, and slew two thousand men of them.

46 So all who fell that day of Benjamin were twenty-five thousand men

that drew the sword; all these were men of valor.

47 But six hundred men turned and fled to the wilderness to the rock of Rimmon, and abode in the rock of Rimmon four months.

48 And the men of Israel turned again upon the Benjamites, and smote them with the edge of the sword, and consumed them out of the cities, both men and beasts and all that they found; also they set on fire all the cities which they found.

CHAPTER 21

NOW the men of Israel had sworn at Mizpeh, saying, None of us shall give his daughter in marriage to the Benjamites.

2 And the people came to Beth-el, and abode there till evening before God, and lifted up their voices and wept bitterly;

3 And said, O Lord God of Israel, why has this disaster come to pass in Israel, that there should be today one tribe missing from Israel?

4 And on the morrow the people rose early and built there an altar, and offered burnt offerings and peace offerings.

5 And the children of Israel said, Who is there among all the tribes of Israel that did not come up in the assembly before the Lord? For they had made a great oath concerning him who did not come up to Mizpeh before the Lord, saying, He shall surely be put to death.

6 Then the children of Israel were sorry for the Benjamites their brethren, and said, One tribe has disappeared from Israel this day.

7 And they said, What shall we do for those who are left without wives, seeing we have sworn by the Lord that we will not give them our daughters to wife?

8 ¶And they said, Which one is there of the tribes of Israel that did not come up to Mizpeh before the Lord? And, behold, there had come none to the camp from the inhabitants of Jabesh-gilead to the assembly.

9 For the people were numbered there, and behold, not one man of the inhabitants of Jabesh-gilead was found there.

10 And the people sent thither twelve thousand of the bravest men, and commanded them, saying, Go and smite the inhabitants of Jabesh-gilead with the edge of the sword, including the women and the children.

11 And this is the thing that you must do, You must utterly destroy every male and every woman that has lain with a man.

12 And they found among the inhabitants of Jabesh-gilead four hundred young virgins that had known no man by lying with him; and they brought them to the camp at Shiloh, which is in the land of Canaan.

13 Then the whole congregation sent messengers to speak to the Benjamites that were in the rock of Rimmon, and to proclaim peace to them.

14 And Benjamin came back at that time, and they gave them the women whom they had saved alive of the women of Jabesh-gilead; but there were not enough for them.

15 And the people were sorry for Benjamin, because the Lord had made a breach in the tribes of Israel.

16 ¶Then the elders of the people said, What shall we do for wives for those that remain, for all the Benjamite women have perished?

17 And they said, The remnant of Benjamin must be spared, that a tribe may not be missing from Israel.

18 Howbeit we cannot give them wives of our daughters; for the children of Israel have sworn, saying, Cursed be he who gives a wife to Benjamin.

19 Then they said, Behold, there is a feast of the Lord in Shiloh yearly in a place which is on the north side of Beth-el, on the east side of the highway that goes up from Beth-el to Shechem, south of Lebonah.

20 So they commanded the Benjamites, saying, Go and lie in wait in the vineyards;

21 And when you shall see the daughters of Shiloh come out to dance with tambourines, then come out of the vineyards and catch you every man his wife of the daughters of

Shiloh, and go to the land of Benjamin.

22 And if their parents or their brothers should come to complain before us, we will say to them, Have compassion upon them, because they did not take each man his wife with him in the war; and it is not you who gave them to them, that you should be guilty.

23 And the Benjamites did so, and they took them wives from all of those who played tambourines, whom they caught; and they returned and went to their inheritance, and rebuilt the towns, and dwelt in them.

24 And the children of Israel departed thence at that time, every man to his tribe and to his family, and they went out from thence every man to his inheritance.

25 In those days there was no king in Israel; every man did that which seemed right in his own eyes.

THE BOOK OF

RUTH

CHAPTER 1

NOW it came to pass in the days when the judges ruled, there was a famine in the land. And a certain man from Beth-lehem of Judah went to sojourn in the land of Moab, he and his wife and his two sons.

2 And the name of the man was Elimeleck, and the name of his wife Naomi, and the names of his two sons Malion and Calion, Ephrathites from Beth-lehem of Judah. And they came to the land of Moab to sojourn there.

3 And Elimeleck the husband of Naomi died; and she was left with her two sons.

4 And they took them wives of the Moabite women; the name of the one was Orpah, and the name of the other Ruth; and they dwelt there about ten years.

5 And Malion and Calion, her two sons, died; and the woman was bereft of her husband and her two sons.

6 ¶Then she started with her daughters-in-law to return from the land of Moab; for she had heard in the land of Moab that the LORD had visited his people in giving them food.

7 So she went forth out of the place where they sojourned, along with her two daughters-in-law, to return and go to the land of Judah.

8 And Naomi said to her two daughters-in-law, Return, go back to your own country and to the house of your kinsmen; may the LORD deal kindly with you, as you have dealt with me and with both of my sons who now are dead.

9 The LORD grant you favor so that you may find rest in the house of your parents. Then she kissed them; and they lifted up their voices and wept.

10 And they said to her, No, we will return with you to your land and to your people.

11 But Naomi said to them, Turn back, my daughters; why will you go with me? Will I bear sons again that they may be your husbands?

12 Turn back, my daughters, go your way; for I am too old to have a husband. If I should say, I have hope, and even if I should have a husband, and should also bear sons;

13 Would you wait for them till they were grown? Would you stay for

21

them from having husbands? No, my daughters; for I am greatly grieved for your sakes, and it grieves me more than it does you, because the hand of the LORD is gone forth against me.

14 And they lifted up their voices again and wept; and Orpah kissed her mother-in-law, and turned back and went away; but Ruth clung to her.

15 And her mother-in-law said to her, Behold, your sister-in-law has gone back to her people and to her kinsmen; return also after your sister-in-law.

16 And Ruth said to her, Far be it from me to return from following after you, and to leave you; for where you go, I will go; and where you dwell, I will dwell; your people shall be my people, and your God my God:

17 Where you die, I will die, and there will I be buried; may the LORD do so to me, and more also, if even death can separate me from you.

18 When Naomi saw that she was determined to go with her, then she ceased from urging her to go back.

19 ¶So they went together until they came to Beth-lehem of Judah. And it came to pass, when they were come to Beth-lehem, the whole city rejoiced over them, and they said, Is this Naomi?

20 And she said to them, Do not call me Naomi, but call me Bitter of Soul; for the Almighty has dealt bitterly with me.

21 For I went forth from here full, and the LORD has brought me back empty; why then call me Naomi, seeing the LORD has humbled me, and has sorely afflicted me?

22 So Naomi returned, and Ruth the Moabitess, her daughter-in-law, with her, for she was wholeheartedly willing to return with her, and they came from the land of Moab at the beginning of the barley harvest.

CHAPTER 2

AND Naomi had a kinsman of her husband's, a well-known man of wealth, of the family of Elimeleck, whose name was Boaz.

2 And Ruth the Moabitess said to her mother-in-law Naomi, Let me now go to the field and glean ears of wheat after the reapers in whose sight I may find favor. And her mother-in-law said to her, Go, my daughter.

3 So Ruth went to glean ears of wheat after the reapers; and it happened that she came upon a portion of the field belonging to Boaz, who was of the kindred of Elimeleck.

4 ¶And, behold, Boaz came from Beth-lehem, and said to the reapers, Peace be with you. And they answered him, The LORD bless you.

5 Then Boaz said to the young man who was in charge of the reapers, Whose damsel is this?

6 And the young man answered and said to him, It is the Moabite woman who came back with Naomi from the land of Moab;

7 And she said, Let me glean the ears of wheat after the reapers; so she has been gleaning from the morning until the time of rest.

8 Then Boaz said to Ruth, My daughter, have you not heard the saying, Do not glean in a field which is not yours? Now therefore stay here, and spend the night with my maidens.

9 Look at the field where they are reaping, and follow them; behold, I have charged the young men that no man shall harm you; and when you get thirsty, go and drink from the vessels which the young men have drawn.

10 Then she fell on her face to the ground, and made obeisance to him, and said, Is it because I have found grace in your eyes, that you should recognize me, seeing that I am a stranger?

11 And Boaz said to her, I have been fully informed of all that you have done for your mother-in-law after the death of your husband; and how you have left your father and mother and your family, and come to a people that you did not know before.

12 May the LORD God of Israel reward you, and may the One under whose wings you have come to take shelter recompense you.

13 Then she said to him, Because I have found favor in your sight, my

lord, and you have comforted me and have spoken kindly to your handmaid, let me become like one of your maid-servants.

14 And Boaz said to her at meal-time, Come near and eat of the bread; and he set her beside the reapers, and gave her barley-meal, and dipped bread in milk; then he gave her parched wheat, and she did eat and was satisfied, and she had some left over.

15 And when she was risen up to glean, Boaz commanded his servants, saying, Let her glean even among the sheaves, and do not harm her;

16 And they let her glean between the sheaves, and they did not harm her.

17 So she gleaned in the field until evening, and beat out what she had gleaned; and it was about an ephah of barley.

18 ¶And she took it up and went into the city; and she showed her mother-in-law what she had gleaned; and she gave her of the food which was left over after she had eaten and was satisfied.

19 And her mother-in-law said to her, Where did you glean today? Blessed be the place in which you were and the man in whose eyes you have found favor. And she told her mother-in-law where she had been, and said, The man's name in whose field I gleaned today is Boaz.

20 And Naomi said to her daughter-in-law, Blessed is the LORD, because he has not caused his kindness to cease from the living nor from the dead. And Naomi said to her, The man is near of kin to us, he is one of our nearest kinsmen.

21 And Ruth said to her mother-in-law, He said to me also, You shall keep close by my servants until all the harvest is finished.

22 And Naomi said to Ruth her daughter-in-law, Happy are you, my daughter, for you have kept close to his maidens, and no man harmed you in the field, whose owner you did not know!

23 So she kept close by the maid-servants of Boaz to glean until the end of the barley harvest and of the wheat harvest; and Ruth dwelt with her mother-in-law.

CHAPTER 3

THEN Naomi said to her, My daughter, shall I not seek rest for you, that it may be well with you?

2 And, behold, Boaz is our kins-man, with whose maidens you were; and behold, he is going to winnow barley tonight in the threshing floor.

3 Wash yourself therefore, and anoint yourself, and put on your best garments, and go down to the thresh-ing floor; but do not show yourself to him until he has finished eating and drinking.

4 And it shall be, when he lies down, that you shall remember the place where he lies, and you shall draw near and lie down near his feet; and he will tell you what you shall do.

5 And she said to her, All that you say to me I will do.

6 ¶So she went down to the thresh-ing floor, and did according to all that her mother-in-law had told her.

7 And when Boaz had eaten and drunk, and his heart was merry, he went and lay at the side of the thresh-ing floor; and while he was in deep sleep in the threshing floor, she came secretly and lifted the end of his robe and lay down near his feet.

8 ¶And it came to pass at midnight that the man woke up and was startled when he saw a woman lying at his feet.

9 And he said to her, Who are you? And she answered, I am Ruth, your handmaid; cover therefore your maid-servant with the end of your robe, for you are a near kinsman.

10 And Boaz said to her, Blessed be you of the LORD, my daughter; for you have shown more kindness in the latter days than at the begin-ning of your life in that you have not gone after young men, whether rich or poor.

11 And now, my daughter, fear not; for I will do for you all that you ask of me; for all the family of our

people know that you are a virtuous woman.

12 And now it is true that I am a near kinsman; however, there is another kinsman nearer than I.

13 Now, tarry this night and lodge here till dawn, and it shall be in the morning, if he will perform to you the part of a kinsman, well, let him do it; but if he is unwilling to do the part of a kinsman to you, then, as the LORD lives, if he does not do the part of a next of kin to you, I will do the part of a kinsman to you; then he said to her, Lie down until the morning.

14 ¶So she lay at his feet until dawn; and she rose up early in the morning while it was dark, before one could recognize another. And she said to him, Let it not be known that I came down to you to the threshing floor.

15 And Boaz said to her, Spread your mantle; and she spread it, and he measured six measures of barley, lifted it up, and laid it on her back; and she went into the city.

16 And when she came to her mother-in-law, she said to her, Who are you, my daughter? And she answered, I am Ruth, and she told her all that Boaz had done for her;

17 And how he had given her six measures of barley, and had said to her, Go not empty-handed to your mother-in-law.

18 Then her mother-in-law said to her, Sit still, my daughter, until you know the outcome; for the man will not rest until he brings the case to judgment today.

CHAPTER 4

THEN Boaz went up to the city gate and sat down there; and behold, the near kinsman of whom Boaz had spoken was passing by; and Boaz said to him, Come, sit down here. And the man said to him, What do you wish? And he sat down by him.

2 And Boaz selected ten men of the elders of the city, and seated them by him.

3 And he said to the near kinsman, Naomi is selling to me the parcel of land which belonged to our brother Elimeleck;

4 And I thought to let you know, and say to you, Buy it in the presence of those who are seated, for I am ready to speak and to purchase it in the presence of the elders of my people who are seated. And now, if you will redeem it, redeem it; but if you will not redeem it, then tell me, that I may know that you will not redeem it; then I will redeem it. And he said, I will redeem it.

5 Then Boaz said, On the day you buy the field from Naomi and from Ruth, the Moabitess, the widow of the dead, you must buy it with the intention of raising the name of the dead upon his inheritance.

6 ¶And the near kinsman said, I cannot redeem it for myself, lest I damage my own inheritance; you can redeem it yourself; because of my lack of confidence in this transaction I cannot redeem it.

7 Now this was the custom in former time in Israel concerning redeeming and the exchanging of rights to redeem which confirmed transactions: a man pulled off his shoe and gave it to another; and this was the testimonial ceremony in Israel.

8 Therefore the near kinsman said to Boaz, Buy it for yourself. And he took off his shoe.

9 ¶And Boaz said to the elders and to all the people, You are witnesses this day, that I have bought all that belonged to Elimeleck, and all that belonged to Malion and Calion, from the hand of Naomi.

10 Moreover, Ruth the Moabitess, the wife of Malion, have I taken to be my wife, to raise up the name of the dead upon his inheritance, so that the name of the dead may not be cut off and his remembrance may not be forgotten among his brethren and his family; you are witnesses this day.

11 And all the people and the elders that were at the city gate, answered, saying, We are witnesses. And they blessed him, and said to him, May the LORD make this woman who is

in your presence like Rachel and like Leah, for both of them built up the house of Israel; and may you do worthily in Ephratah, and call its name Beth-lehem.

12 And let your house be like the house of Pharez, whom Tamar bore to Judah, and may the LORD give you an offspring from this woman.

13 ¶So Boaz took Ruth, and she became his wife; and when he went in unto her, the LORD gave her conception, and she bore a son.

14 And the women said to Naomi, Blessed be the LORD, who has not left you this day without a kinsman, that his name may be famous in Israel.

15 And he shall be to you a comforter of your soul and a nourisher to your city; for your daughter-in-law,

who loves you and is better to you than seven sons, has borne him.

16 And Naomi took the child, and laid him in her bosom, and became nurse to him.

17 And the women who were her neighbors said, A son has been born to Naomi; and they called his name Obed; he is the father of Jesse, the father of David.

18 ¶Now these are the generations of Pharez: Pharez begat Hezron,

19 And Hezron begat Aram, and Aram begat Amminadab,

20 And Amminadab begat Nahshon, and Nahshon begat Shelah,

21 And Shelah begat Boaz, and Boaz begat Obed,

22 And Obed begat Jesse, and Jesse begat King David.

THE FIRST BOOK OF

SAMUEL

otherwise called

THE FIRST BOOK OF THE KINGS

CHAPTER 1

NOW there was a certain man of Ramath-dokey, of mount Ephraim, and his name was Hilkanah, the son of Jeroham, the son of Elihu, the son of Tohu, the son of Zuph, an Ephrathite;

2 And he had two wives; the name of the one was Hannah, and the name of the other Pannah; and Pannah had children, but Hannah had no children.

3 And this man used to go up out of his town yearly to worship and to sacrifice to the LORD of hosts in Shiloh. And the two sons of Eli, Hophni and Phinehas, the priests of the LORD, were there.

4 ¶And when the time came, Hil-

kanah sacrificed, and he gave to Pannah his wife, and to all her sons and her daughters, portions;

5 But to Hannah he gave a double portion; for he loved Hannah; but the LORD had shut up her womb.

6 And her rival also taunted her sorely to make her fret because the LORD had shut up her womb.

7 And Pannah did this year by year when she went up to the house of the LORD, and thus she provoked her; therefore Hannah wept and did not eat.

8 Then Hilkanah her husband said to her, Why do you weep? And why do you not eat? And why is your heart grieved? Behold, am I not better to you than ten sons?

9 ¶So Hannah rose up after she had

eaten and drunk in Shiloh, and she went up to the house of the LORD. Now Eli the priest was sitting upon a seat by the post of the temple of the LORD.

10 And she was bitter of soul, and she prayed before the LORD and wept bitterly.

11 And she made a vow, and said, O LORD of hosts, if thou wilt indeed look upon the affliction of thy maidservant, and remember me, and not forget thy handmaid, but wilt give to thy maidservant a son, then I will give him to the LORD all the days of his life, and there shall no razor come upon his head.

12 And it came to pass, as she continued praying before the LORD, that Eli watched her mouth.

13 Now Hannah spoke in her heart only, and her lips moved, but her voice was not heard; therefore Eli thought her to be drunk.

14 And Eli said to her, How long will you be drunk? Put away your wine from you.

15 Hannah answered and said to him, No, my lord, I am a woman full of grief; I have drunk neither wine nor strong drink, but have poured out my soul before the LORD.

16 Count not your maidservant in your presence a wicked woman; for out of the abundance of my sorrow and grief have I spoken hitherto.

17 Then Eli answered and said to her, Go in peace; and the God of Israel grant you the petition that you have asked of him.

18 And she said, Let your maidservant find grace in your sight. So the woman went her way, and her countenance was no more sad.

19 ¶And they rose up early in the morning and worshipped before the LORD, and returned and came to their house at Ramtha; and Hilkanah knew Hannah his wife; and the LORD remembered her.

20 And it came to pass, in due time Hannah conceived and bore a son, and called his name Samuel, saying, Because I have asked him of the LORD.

21 And the man Hilkanah and all his household went up to offer to the LORD the yearly sacrifices of his vow.

22 But Hannah did not go up; for she said to her husband, I will wait until the child is weaned, and then I will bring him, that he may appear before the LORD, and there abide forever.

23 And Hilkanah her husband said to her, Do what seems good to you; wait until you have weaned him; may the LORD establish your word. So the woman waited, and nursed her son until she weaned him.

24 ¶And when she had weaned him, she took him up with her, with a three-year old bullock and an ephah of flour and a skin of wine, and brought him to the house of the LORD in Shiloh; and the boy was very young.

25 And they slew the bullock, and brought the child to Eli.

26 Then Hannah said to Eli, I beseech you, my lord, as your soul lives, my lord, I am the woman that stood by you here, praying to the LORD for this boy.

27 I prayed and the LORD has granted me my petition which I asked of him;

28 Therefore also I have promised him to the LORD as long as he lives; for I petitioned him of the LORD. And they worshipped the LORD there.

CHAPTER 2

AND Hannah prayed and said, My heart is magnified in the LORD, my horn is exalted in my God; my mouth utters words against my enemies, because thou hast caused me to rejoice in thy salvation.

2 There is none holy like the LORD; for there is none besides thee; and there is none powerful like our God.

3 Talk no more so exceeding proudly; let not arrogancy come out of your mouths; for the LORD is a God of knowledge, and no devices can stand before him.

4 The bows of the mighty men are broken, and they that are weak are girded with strength.

5 Those who were full have hired out themselves for bread; and those who were hungry have food left over; the barren has given birth and

is satisfied; and she who has many children is lonely.

6 It is the LORD who makes men to die and makes alive; he brings down to Sheol and brings up.

7 The LORD makes poor and makes rich; he brings low and he also exalts.

8 He raises up the poor out of the dust and lifts up the needy from the dung-hill, to set them with the princes and to make them inherit the throne of glory; for the depths of the earth are protected by the LORD, and he has set the world upon them.

9 He will guard the feet of his saints, and the wicked shall be silent in darkness; for not by his own strength shall a mighty man prevail.

10 The LORD shall defeat his adversaries; out of heaven shall he thunder against them; the LORD shall judge the ends of the earth; and he shall give strength to his king and exalt the horn of his anointed.

11 And Hilkanah and his wife Hannah returned to Ramtha to his house. And the boy Samuel ministered to the LORD before Eli the priest.

12 ¶Now the sons of Eli were wicked men; they did not know the LORD.

13 They took the dues of the priests from the people, of every man who offered a sacrifice; and they made for themselves meat-forks with three prongs, and the priest's servant came, while the meat was boiling, with the three-pronged fork in his hand,

14 And he thrust it into the pot or caldron or pan or kettle; all that the meat-fork brought up the priest took for himself. Thus they did to all the Israelites who came thither to Shiloh.

15 Also before they burnt the sacrifices, the priest's servant came and said to the man who was sacrificing, Give meat to roast for the priest; for I will not accept boiled meat from you, but only raw.

16 And if the man said to him, They will surely offer sacrifices today, and then take for yourself as much as you wish; then he would say, No; you shall give it now; and if not, I will take it by force.

17 Wherefore the sin of the young men was very great before the LORD; because they offended the men who offered before the LORD.

18 ¶But the boy Samuel ministered before the LORD, and he wore a linen ephod.

19 And his mother made him a little mantle, and brought it to him from year to year when she came up with her husband to offer the yearly sacrifices of his vow.

20 ¶And Eli blessed Hilkanah and his wife, and said, The LORD give you another offspring from this woman for the child which she has dedicated to the LORD. And they went to their own home.

21 And the LORD blessed Hannah, and she conceived and bore three sons and two daughters. And the boy Samuel grew before the LORD.

22 ¶Now Eli was very old, and heard all that his sons were doing to all Israel; and how they reviled the women who prayed in the tabernacle of the congregation.

23 And he said to them, Why do you do such things? For I hear evil reports about you from all this people.

24 No, my sons; for it is not a good report that I hear; for you drive away the people of the LORD.

25 If a man sin against a man, he will seek forgiveness before the LORD; but if a man sin against the LORD, from whom shall he seek forgiveness? But they did not hearken to the voice of their father, because it was the LORD's will that they should be slain.

26 And the boy Samuel grew up, and was in favor both with the LORD and also with men.

27 ¶And there came a man of the LORD to Eli, and said to him, Thus says the LORD, I did surely reveal myself to the house of your father when they were in Egypt in the house of Pharaoh;

28 And I chose him out of all the tribes of Israel to be my priest, to offer upon my altar, to burn incense before me, and to wear an ephod; and I gave to the house of your father all the offerings made by fire of the children of Israel.

29 Why then do you deal wrongly with my sacrifices and my offerings, which I have commanded in the wilderness; and honor your sons above me, to choose the choicest of all the offerings of Israel my people?

30 Therefore thus says the LORD God of Israel, I said indeed that your house and the house of your father should minister before me for ever; but now the LORD says, Far be this from me; for those that honor me I will honor, and those that despise me shall be despised.

31 Behold, the days are coming when I will cut off your offspring and the offspring of your father, that there shall not be an old man in your house,

32 Nor him that bears rule in your habitation, in all the prosperity which God shall bring in Israel; and there shall not be an old man in your house for ever.

33 And a man of you whom I shall not cut off from my altar shall be spared to sadden you and to grieve your heart; and all the increase of your house shall die in the flower of their age.

34 And this shall be a sign to you that shall come upon your two sons, upon Hophni and upon Phinehas; both of them shall die on the same day.

35 And I will raise me up a faithful priest, according to the choice of my heart, who shall do according to that which is in my heart and in my mind; and I will build him a sure house; and he shall walk before my anointed for ever.

36 And it shall come to pass that every one who is left in your house shall come to bow down to him for a piece of silver and a loaf of bread, and shall say, Send me to one of the priests, that I may eat a piece of bread.

CHAPTER 3

AND the boy Samuel was ministering to the LORD, assisting Eli the priest. And the word of the LORD was precious in those days; there was no open vision.

2 And it came to pass at that time,

when Eli was lying down in his bed, and his eyes had begun to grow dim so that he could not see;

3 And the lamp of the LORD was not yet put out, and Samuel was lying down to sleep in the temple of the LORD, where the ark of God was.

4 And the LORD called Samuel; and he answered, Here I am.

5 And he ran to Eli and said, Here I am; for you called me. And he said, I did not call; go back and lie down. And he went and lay down.

6 And the LORD called again, Samuel. And Samuel arose and went to Eli, and said, Here I am; for you did call me. And he answered, I did not call, my son; go back and lie down.

7 Now Samuel did not yet know the LORD, neither was the word of the LORD revealed to him.

8 And the LORD called Samuel again the third time. And Samuel arose and went to Eli, and said, Here I am; for you did call me. Then Eli perceived that the LORD had called the boy.

9 Therefore Eli said to Samuel, Go back and lie down; and it shall be, if he calls you, you shall say, Speak, LORD; for thy servant hears. So Samuel went back and lay down in his place.

10 And the LORD came and stood and called twice, Samuel, Samuel. Then Samuel said, Speak, LORD; for thy servant hears.

11 ¶And the LORD said to Samuel, Behold, I will do such a thing in Israel that whoever shall hear of it, shall give heed.

12 In that day I will perform against Eli all things which I have spoken concerning his house, from beginning to end.

13 And I will show him that I will judge his house for ever for the iniquity which he knew when his sons reviled the people and he did not rebuke them.

14 Therefore I have sworn to the house of Eli that the iniquity of Eli's household shall not be purged with sacrifices nor offerings for ever.

15 ¶And Samuel lay until the morn-

ing; then he opened the doors of the house of the LORD. And Samuel feared to tell the vision to Eli.

16 Then Eli called Samuel, and said, Samuel, my son. And he answered, Here am I.

17 And he said to him, What is the thing that the LORD has said to you? Do not be afraid of me. May God do so to you, and more also, if you hide anything from me of all the things that the LORD said to you.

18 And Samuel told him everything, and hid nothing from him. And Eli said, It is the LORD; let him do what is good in his sight.

19 ¶And Samuel knew that the LORD was with him, and he did not ignore any of his words.

20 And all Israel from Dan to Beersheba knew that Samuel was to be a prophet of the LORD.

21 And the LORD continued to reveal himself by his words in Shiloh; and Samuel's words were declared throughout all Israel.

CHAPTER 4

AND the word of Samuel came to all Israel. Now Israel went out against the Philistines to battle, and encamped by the Rock of Help; and the Philistines encamped at Aphek.

2 And the Philistines put themselves in array against Israel; and when they fought, Israel was defeated before the Philistines; and there were slain on the battlefield about four thousand men.

3 ¶And when the people were come to the camp, the elders of Israel said, Why has the LORD smitten us today before the Philistines? Let us bring the ark of the covenant of the LORD of hosts out of Shiloh to us, that it may go with us and save us from our enemies.

4 So the people sent to Shiloh, and they brought from thence the ark of the covenant of the LORD of hosts, who dwells upon the cherubim; and the two sons of Eli, Hophni and Phinehas, were there with the ark of the covenant of the LORD.

5 And it came to pass, when the ark of the covenant of the LORD came into camp, all Israel shouted with a great shout, so that it re-echoed.

6 And when the Philistines heard the noise, they said, What is this noise of shouting in the camp of the Hebrews? And they learned that the ark of the LORD had come into the camp.

7 And the Philistines were afraid, for they said, God is come into the camp. And they said, Woe to us! For there has not been such a thing before.

8 Woe to us! who shall deliver us from the hands of the mighty God? This is the God who smote the whole of Egypt with all sorts of plagues and performed wonders in the wilderness.

9 Be strong, and conduct yourselves like men, O Philistines, lest you become servants to the Hebrews, as they have served you; be strong and fight with them.

10 ¶And the Philistines fought with Israel, and Israel was defeated, and they fled every man to his tent; and there was a very great slaughter in Israel; for there fell of Israel in that day thirty thousand footmen.

11 And the ark of God was taken; and the two sons of Eli, Hophni and Phinehas, were slain.

12 ¶And there ran a man of Benjamin from the battle line, and came to Shiloh the same day with his clothes rent and with earth upon his head.

13 And Eli was sitting upon a seat by the wayside watching; for his heart trembled for the ark of God. And when the man came into the city to tell of the disaster, all the city cried out.

14 And when Eli heard the noise of crying, he said, What is this noise of tumult? And the man came in hastily and told Eli.

15 Now Eli was seventy-eight years old; and his eyes were dim so that he could not see.

16 And the man said to Eli, I am he who came from the battle line, and I fled today from the battle line. And he said to him, What is the news, my son?

17 And the messenger answered and said, Israel has fled before the Philistines, and there has been also a great slaughter among the people, and your two sons also, Hophni and Phinehas, are dead, and the ark of God has been taken.

18 And it came to pass, when Eli thought of the ark of God, he fell from off the seat backward by the side of the gate, and his neck broke, and he died; for he was an old man, and heavy. And he had judged Israel forty years.

19 ¶And his daughter-in-law, Phinehas' wife, was with child; and was near to be delivered; and when she heard the news that the ark of God was taken and that her father-in-law and her husband were dead, she bowed down and travailed; for her pains came upon her.

20 And about the time of her death, the women that stood by her said to her, Fear not; for you have borne a son. But she neither answered nor did she pay attention to it.

21 And she named the child Jochabar, saying, The glory is departed from Israel; because the ark of God was taken, and because of her father-in-law and her husband.

22 And she said, The glory is departed from Israel; for the ark of God is taken.

CHAPTER 5

AND the Philistines took the ark of God, and brought it from the Rock of Help to Ashdod.

2 Then the Philistines took the ark of God, and brought it into the house of Dagon and set it by the side of Dagon.

3 ¶And when the inhabitants of Ashdod arose early the next morning, they found Dagon was fallen upon his face on the ground before the ark of the LORD. And they took Dagon and set him in his place again.

4 And when they arose early the next morning, behold, Dagon was fallen upon his face on the ground before the ark of the LORD; and the head of Dagon and both of his hands

were cut off upon the threshold; only the trunk of Dagon was left.

5 Therefore neither the priests of Dagon nor any that enter Dagon's house cross the threshold of Dagon in Ashdod to this day.

6 But the hand of the LORD was heavy upon the inhabitants of Ashdod, and he destroyed them and afflicted them with boils, both Ashdod and the territory thereof.

7 And when the men of Ashdod saw that it was so, they said, The ark of the God of Israel shall not stay with us; for his hand is heavy upon us and upon Dagon our god.

8 They sent therefore and gathered all the lords of the Philistines to them, and said, What shall we do with the ark of the God of Israel? And they answered, Let the ark of the God of Israel be returned to Gath. So they took back the ark of the God of Israel there.

9 And after they took it back, the hand of the LORD was against the city with a very great destruction; and he smote the men of the city, both small and great, and they were covered with boils.

10 ¶Therefore they sent the ark of God to Ekron. And when the ark of God came to Ekron, the Ekronites cried out, saying, They have brought the ark of the God of Israel to us, to slay us and our people.

11 So they sent and gathered together all the lords of the Philistines, and said, Send away the ark of the God of Israel, and let it return to its own place, that it may not slay us and our people. For the fear of death caused a panic that spread throughout all the city; the hand of God was very heavy there.

12 And the men who did not die were smitten with the boils; and the cry of the city went up to heaven.

CHAPTER 6

AND the ark of the LORD was in the country of the Philistines seven months.

2 And the Philistines called for the priests and the lords, saying, What shall we do with the ark of the

LORD? Tell us by what means shall we send it to its place.

3 And they said, If you send away the ark of the LORD God of Israel, do not send it away empty; but you must surely bring trespass offerings to it; then you shall be healed, and it shall be known to you why his hand is not removed from you.

4 And they said, What sort of offerings shall we bring to it? They answered, Five golden boils and five golden mice, according to the number of the lords of the Philistines; for one plague was upon you all and upon your lords.

5 Wherefore you shall make likenesses of your boils and images of the mice that are destroying the land; and you shall give glory to the God of Israel; perhaps he will remove his hand from you and from your god and from your land.

6 And you shall not harden your hearts, as the Egyptians and Pharaoh hardened their hearts, and as they mocked the Israelites and did not send them nor let them go.

7 Now therefore make a new cart, and take two milch cows upon which there has come no yoke, and tie the cows to the cart, and bring their calves home from them;

8 And take the ark of the LORD, and lay it upon the cart; and put the vessels of gold which you have brought for it as offerings, in a box by its side; and send it away, that it may go on its way.

9 And watch, for if it goes up by the way of the border which goes up to Beth-shemesh, then it is the LORD who has done us this great evil; but if not, then we shall know that it is not his hand that afflicted us, but it has happened to us by chance.

10 ¶And the men did so; and took two milch cows and tied them to the cart and shut up their calves at home;

11 And they laid the ark of God upon the cart, and the box with the mice of gold and the images of their boils.

12 And they sent out the cows by the way which is by the border of Beth-shemesh, and they went along the highway, lowing as they went, and turned not aside to the right hand nor to the left; and the lords of the Philistines went after them as far as the border of Beth-shemesh.

13 And the men of the town of Beth-shemesh were reaping their wheat harvest in the valley; and they lifted up their eyes and saw the ark, and rejoiced when they saw it.

14 And the cart came into the field of Joshua, a Beth-shemeshite, and stopped where there was a great stone; and they split the wood of the cart, and offered the cows as a burnt offering to the LORD.

15 And the Levites took down the ark of the LORD and the box that was with it in which were the vessels of gold, and put them on the great stone; and the men of Beth-shemesh offered burnt offerings and sacrifices on that day to the LORD.

16 And when the five lords of the Philistines had seen it, they returned to Ekron the same day.

17 And these are the golden boils which the Philistines had brought as offerings to God: for Ashdod one, for Gaza one, for Ashkelon one, for Gath one, for Ekron one;

18 And the golden mice, according to the number of all the cities of the Philistines, belonging to the five lords, both of the five fortified cities and of the country villages of the Perrizites, and as far as the great stone of Abel, whereon they set down the ark of the LORD, which to this day is in the field of Joshua, the Beth-shemeshite.

19 ¶And the LORD smote the men of Beth-shemesh because they worshipped the ark of the LORD, and the LORD smote five thousand and seventy men of the people; and the people mourned because the LORD had smitten many of the people with a great slaughter.

20 And the men of Beth-shemesh said, Who is able to stand before this holy LORD God? And who shall carry up from us the ark?

21 ¶So they sent messengers to the

inhabitants of Koriath-narin, saying, The Philistines have brought back the ark of the LORD; come down and take it up to you.

CHAPTER 7

AND the men of Koriath-narin came, and took up the ark of the LORD, and brought it into the house of Abinadab on the hill, and Abinadab consecrated Eleazar his son, who kept the ark of the LORD.

2 And it came to pass, from the day that the ark abode in Koriath-narin, that the time was long; for it was about twenty years; and all the house of Israel yearned after the LORD.

3 ¶Then Samuel said to all the house of Israel, If you return with all your heart to the LORD, then put away the strange gods and Ashtaroth from among you, and prepare your heart unto the LORD, and serve him only; and he will deliver you out of the hand of the Philistines.

4 So the children of Israel put away Baal and Ashtaroth, and served the LORD only.

5 And Samuel said, Gather all Israel at Mizpeh, and I will pray for you to the LORD.

6 And they gathered together at Mizpeh, and drew water and poured it out before the LORD, and fasted on that day, and said, We have sinned against the LORD. And Samuel judged the children of Israel at Mizpeh.

7 And when the Philistines heard that the children of Israel were gathered together at Mizpeh, the lords of the Philistines went up against Israel. And when the children of Israel heard it, they were afraid of the Philistines.

8 And the children of Israel said to Samuel, Do not cease to pray before the LORD our God for us, that he may save us from the hand of the Philistines.

9 ¶And Samuel took a suckling lamb and offered it for a burnt offering wholly to the LORD; and Samuel prayed before the LORD for the children of Israel; and the LORD answered him.

10 And as Samuel was offering up the burnt offering, the Philistines drew near to battle against Israel; but the LORD thundered with a great thunder on that day against the Philistines, and threw them into confusion; and they were defeated before Israel.

11 And the men of Israel went out of Mizpeh and pursued the Philistines and smote them as far as below Beth-jashan.

12 Then Samuel took a stone and set it between Mizpeh and Beth-jashan, and called its name Rock of Help, and he said, Hitherto the LORD has helped us.

13 ¶So the Philistines were defeated, and they came no more into the territory of Israel; and the hand of the LORD was against the Philistines all the days of Samuel.

14 And the cities which the Philistines had taken from Israel were restored to Israel from Ekron even to Gath, and the boundaries thereof. Thus the LORD delivered Israel from the hand of the Philistines. And there was peace between Israel and the Amorites.

15 And Samuel judged Israel all the days of his life.

16 And he went from year to year in circuit to Beth-el and Gilgal and Mizpeh, and judged Israel in all those places.

17 And he always returned to Ramtha; for there was his house, and there he judged Israel, and there he built an altar to the LORD.

CHAPTER 8

AND it came to pass, when Samuel was old, he made his sons judges over Israel.

2 Now the name of his first-born son was Joel; and the name of his second, Abiah; they were judges in Beer-sheba.

3 But his sons did not walk in his ways, but turned aside after lucre, and took bribes and perverted judgment.

4 Then all the elders of Israel gathered themselves together and came to Samuel to Ramtha,

5 And they said to him, Behold, you are old, and your sons do not walk in your ways; now give us a king to judge us like all the nations.

6 ¶But the thing displeased Samuel, when they said to him, Give us a king to judge us like all the nations. And Samuel prayed before the LORD.

7 And the LORD said to Samuel, Hearken to the voice of the people in all that they say to you; for they have not rejected you, but they have rejected me, that I should not reign over them.

8 According to all the works which they have done since the day that I brought them up out of the land of Egypt even to this day, as they have forsaken me and served other gods, so do they also to you.

9 Now therefore hearken to their voice; but testify solemnly to them, and show them the law of the king who shall reign over them.

10 ¶And Samuel told all the words of the LORD to the people who asked of him a king.

11 Then he said, This will be the law of the king who will reign over you: he will take your sons and appoint them for himself for his chariots, and to be his horsemen; and they shall run before his chariots.

12 And he will appoint for himself officers of thousands and officers of hundreds and officers of fifties and officers of tens. And they shall plow his ground and reap his harvest and make his implements of war and instruments for his chariots.

13 And he will take your daughters to be weavers and grinders and bakers.

14 And he will take the best of your fields and your vineyards and your oliveyards, and give them to his servants.

15 And he will take the tenth of your crops and of your vineyards, and give to his officers and to his servants.

16 And he will take your menservants and your maidservants, and your goodly young men and your asses, and put them to his work.

17 He will take the tenth of your sheep; and you shall be his servants.

18 And you shall cry for help in that day because of your king whom you shall have chosen for yourselves; and the LORD will not answer you on that day.

19 ¶Nevertheless the people refused to obey the voice of Samuel; and they said to him, No; but we will have a king over us,

20 That we also may be like all the nations, and that our king may judge us and go out before us and fight our battles.

21 And Samuel heard all the words of the people, and he repeated them before the LORD.

22 And the LORD said to Samuel, Hearken to their voice, and make them a king. And Samuel said to the men of Israel, Go every man to his city.

CHAPTER 9

NOW there was a man from Benjamin, whose name was Kish, the son of Abiel, the son of Zerod, the son of Bechorath, the son of Aphiah, a Benjamite, a mighty man of power.

2 And he had a son whose name was Saul, a choice young man and a goodly; and there was not among the children of Israel a more attractive person than he; he was head and shoulders higher than any of the people.

3 And the asses of Kish, Saul's father, were lost. And Kish said to Saul his son, Take now one of the servants with you, and arise, go seek the asses. And Saul arose and went, and took one of the servants with him, and they went to seek the asses of his father.

4 And they passed through mount Ephraim and through the land of Gomrey, but they did not find them; then they passed through the land of Taley, and they were not there; and they passed through the land of Benjamin, but they did not find them.

5 And when they came to the land of Sur, Saul said to the servant who was with him, Come, let us return, lest my father cease to be anxious

about the asses and begin to be concerned about us.

6 But his servant said to him, Behold, there is a man of God in this city, and he is an honorable man in the eyes of the people; all that he says comes surely to pass; now let us go there; perhaps he can tell us about the errand for which we have come.

7 Then Saul said to his servant, Behold, if we go, what shall we bring to the man of God? For the bread is spent in our bags and there are no provisions to bring a present to the man of God, because we have nothing.

8 And the servant answered his master again, and said, Behold, I have here at hand the fourth part of a shekel of silver; let us give it to the man of God, that he may tell us about our errand.

9 (Because formerly in Israel, when a man went to inquire of God, thus he said, Come, let us go to the seer; for he who is now called a prophet, before was called a seer.)

10 Then Saul said to his servant, Well said; come, let us go. So they went to the city where the man of God was.

11 ¶And as they went up the hill to the city, they found young maidens going out to draw water, and Saul said to them, Is there a seer here?

12 And they answered him and said, There is; behold, he is ahead of you; go up now quickly, for he came today to the city; for there is a sacrifice of the people today on the high place;

13 As soon as you enter the city, you shall straightway find him, before he goes up to the high place to eat; for the people will not eat until he comes, because he blesses the sacrifices; and afterwards those who are invited, eat. Now therefore go up; for today you shall find him.

14 And they went up to the city; and just as they were entering the city gate, behold, Samuel was coming out toward them to go up to the high place.

15 Now the Lord had told Samuel a day before Saul came, saying,

16 Tomorrow about this time I will send you a man from the land of Benjamin, and you shall anoint him to be a ruler over my people Israel, and he shall save my people from the hand of the Philistines; for I have seen the oppression of my people, and their cry has come to me.

17 And when Samuel saw Saul, whom the Lord had chosen, then the Lord said to Samuel, Behold the man of whom I spoke to you! This man shall reign over my people.

18 Then Saul drew near to Samuel at the gate, and said, Tell me, where is the house of the seer?

19 And Samuel answered Saul, and said, I am the seer; go up before me to the high place; for you shall eat with me today, and in the morning I will let you go, and will tell you all that is in your heart.

20 And as for your asses that were lost three days ago, do not be anxious about them, for they have been found. And on whom is all the hope of the house of Israel? Is it not on you and on your father's house?

21 And Saul answered and said to Samuel, Behold, I am a Benjamite, of the smallest of the tribes of Israel, and my family is the least of all the families of the tribe of Benjamin. Why then have you spoken thus to me?

22 And Samuel took Saul and his servant, and brought them into the house, and gave them a place at the head of those who were invited, who were about thirty persons.

23 And Samuel said to the cook, Bring the portion which I gave you, of which I said to you, Set it apart.

24 And the cook took up the shoulder and the thigh, and set them before Saul. And Samuel said, Behold that which is left! Set it before you and eat; because it has been kept for you for some time. So Saul ate with Samuel that day.

25 ¶And when they were come down from the high place into the city, Samuel conversed with Saul upon the roof.

26 And they arose at dawn, and Samuel called to Saul upon the roof,

saying, Up, that I may send you away. And Saul arose, and they went out both of them, he and Samuel.

27 And as they were going down to the end of the city, Samuel said to Saul, Tell the servant to pass on before us, but you stop where you are, that I may tell you the word of God.

CHAPTER 10

THEN Samuel took a vial of oil, and poured it upon his head and kissed him, and said to him, Behold, the LORD has anointed you to be a ruler over his inheritance.

2 When you depart from me today, behold, you will find two men at Rachel's sepulchre in the territory of Benjamin at Zelzah; and they will say to you, The asses which you went to seek are found; and, lo, your father has ceased worrying about the asses, and is concerned about you, saying, What shall I do for my son?

3 Then when you shall go on from there and you shall come to the oak of Tabor, behold, you will find there three men going up to God to Beth-el, one carrying three kids and another carrying three loaves of bread and another carrying a skin of wine;

4 And they will salute you, and give you two loaves of bread, which you shall receive from their hands.

5 After that you shall come to the hill of God where there is a garrison of the Philistines; and it shall come to pass when you arrive there at the city, behold, you will meet a company of prophets coming down from the high place with psalteries and tabrets and tambourines and timbrels before them; and they will be prophesying;

6 And the Spirit of the LORD will come upon you, and you shall prophesy with them, and you shall be changed into another man.

7 And it shall be when these signs are come to you, that you shall do whatever you wish, for the LORD is with you.

8 And you shall go down before me to Gilgal; and, behold, I will come down to you to offer burnt offerings and to make sacrifices of peace offerings; seven days you shall wait, till I come to you, and show you what you shall do.

9 ¶And it came to pass when he had turned his back to go from Samuel, God gave him another heart; and all those signs came to pass that day.

10 And when they came to Ramtha, behold, a company of prophets met him; and the Spirit of God came upon him, and he prophesied among them.

11 And it came to pass when all that knew him beforetime saw that, behold, he prophesied among the prophets, then the people said one to another, What is this that has come to the son of Kish? Is Saul also among the prophets?

12 And a man of the same place answered and said, But who is his father? Therefore it became a byword, Is Saul also among the prophets?

13 And when he had finished prophesying, he left the high place, and came home.

14 ¶And Saul's uncle said to him and to his servant, Where did you go? And they said, To seek the asses; and when we found them nowhere, we went to Samuel.

15 And Saul's uncle said to him, Tell me what Samuel said to you.

16 And Saul said to his uncle, He told us plainly that the asses were found. But of the matter of the kingdom of which Samuel had spoken, he did not tell him.

17 ¶And Samuel called the people together before the LORD at Mizpeh;

18 And he said to the children of Israel, Thus says the LORD God of Israel, I brought up Israel out of the land of Egypt and later delivered you from the hand of the Philistines and from the hand of all the kingdoms that oppressed you;

19 But you have this day rejected your God, who himself saved you from all your calamities and your tribulations; and you have said, Not so, but set a king over us. Now therefore present yourselves before the

LORD by your tribes and by your thousands.

20 And when Samuel had caused all the tribes of Israel to come near, the tribe of Benjamin was taken by lot.

21 Then when he caused the tribe of Benjamin to come near by their families, the family of Matri was taken by lot, and Saul the son of Kish was taken by lot. But when they sought him, he could not be found.

22 Therefore Samuel inquired further of the LORD, saying, Where is this man? And the LORD said to Samuel, Behold, he has hidden himself among the baggage.

23 And they ran and brought him from there; and when he stood among the people, he was head and shoulders higher than any of the people.

24 And Samuel said to all the people, Now have you seen him whom the LORD has chosen, because there is none like him among all the people? And the people shouted and said, Long live the king!

25 Then Samuel told the people the law governing the king, and wrote it in a book and laid it before the LORD. And Samuel sent all the people away, and they went every man to his house.

26 ¶And Saul also went to his house at Ramtha; [1] and there went with him a band of men whose hearts God had touched.

27 But some of the wicked men said, How shall this man save us? And they despised him and brought him no presents. But he held his peace.

CHAPTER 11

THEN Nahash the Ammonite came up and encamped against Jabesh-Gilead; and all the men of Jabesh said to Nahash, Make a treaty with us and we will serve you.

2 But Nahash the Ammonite said to them, On this condition will I make a treaty with you, when you thrust out all your right eyes, that I may make you a reproach upon all Israel.

3 And the elders of Jabesh said to him, Give us seven days respite, that

[1] Gibeah.

we may send messengers throughout all the territory of Israel; and when we see if we have a savior or not, then we will come out to you.

4 ¶Then the messengers came to Ramtha of Saul, and told these words before the people; and all the people lifted up their voices and wept.

5 And, behold, Saul was coming behind the oxen from the field; and Saul said, What ails the people that they are weeping? And they told him the words of the men of Jabesh.

6 And the Spirit of God came upon Saul when he heard these words, and his anger was kindled greatly.

7 And he took a yoke of oxen and cut them in pieces and sent them throughout all the territory of Israel by the hand of messengers, saying, Whosoever does not follow after Saul and after Samuel, so shall it be done to his oxen. And the fear of the LORD fell on the people, and they all came out as one man.

8 And when he numbered them in Bezek, the children of Israel were three hundred thousand and the men of Judah thirty thousand.

9 And they said to the messengers who had come from Jabesh, Thus shall you say to the men of Jabesh and of Gilead, Tomorrow, by the time the sun is hot, you shall be delivered. And the messengers came and told the men of Jabesh; and they were glad.

10 Therefore the men of Jabesh said, Tomorrow we will come out to you, and you shall do to us whatever seems good to you.

11 And it came to pass, on the next day, Saul divided the people in three companies; and they came into the midst of the camp in the morning watch, and slew the Ammonites until the heat of the day; and those who remained were scattered, so that no two of them were left together.

12 ¶Then the people said to Samuel, Who is he that said, Shall Saul reign over us? Bring the men that we may put them to death.

13 And Saul said, There shall not a man be put to death this day; for to-

day the LORD has wrought salvation in Israel.

14 Then Samuel said to the people, Come, let us go to Gilgal and renew the kingdom there.

15 And all the people went to Gilgal; and there they made Saul king before the LORD in Gilgal; and there they made sacrifices of peace offerings before the LORD; and there Saul and all the men of Israel rejoiced greatly.

CHAPTER 12

AND Samuel said to all Israel, Behold, I have hearkened to your voice in all that you said to me, and have made a king over you.

2 And now, behold, the king is before you; and I am old and gray-headed; and, behold, my sons are with you; and I have walked before you from my childhood to this day.

3 Behold, I am standing before you; testify against me before the LORD and before his anointed; whose ox have I taken? Or whose ass have I taken? Or whom have I defrauded? Or whom have I oppressed? Or of whose hand have I taken a bribe to look upon him with favor? Tell me, and I will restore it to you.

4 And they said to him, You have not defrauded us nor oppressed us, neither have you taken anything from any one of us.

5 And he said to them, The LORD is witness against you, and his anointed is witness this day, that you have not found anything wrong with me. And they said, He is witness.

6 ¶And Samuel said to the people, The LORD is the only God, who advanced Moses and Aaron and who brought your fathers up out of the land of Egypt.

7 Now therefore stand still that I may judge you before the LORD in all his righteous acts which he did to you and to your fathers.

8 When Jacob went into Egypt and your fathers prayed before the LORD, then the LORD sent Moses and Aaron, who brought your fathers out of the land of Egypt and made them dwell in this place.

9 And when they forgot the LORD their God, he delivered them into the hand of Sisera, general of the army of Hazor, and into the hand of the Philistines, and into the hand of the king of Moab, and they fought against them.

10 And they prayed before the LORD, and said, We have sinned, because we have forsaken the LORD our God and have served Baal and Ashtaroth; but now deliver us out of the hand of our enemies and we will serve thee.

11 And the LORD sent Deborah and Barak and Gideon and Jephthah and Samson, and delivered you out of the hand of your enemies round about you, and you dwelt in safety.

12 And when you saw that Nahash the king of the children of Ammon came against you, you said to me, No; but a king shall reign over us; yet the LORD your God was your king.

13 Now therefore behold the king whom you have chosen, and whom you have requested! And, behold, the LORD has given you a king.

14 If you will fear the LORD and serve him and obey his voice and not provoke him, then shall both you and also the king who reigns over you continue following the LORD your God.

15 But if you will not obey the voice of the LORD your God, but provoke him, then shall the hand of the LORD be against you as it was against your fathers.

16 ¶Now therefore be ready, and see this great thing which the LORD will do for you.

17 Behold, it is wheat harvest today; I will call to the LORD, and he shall send thunder and rain; and you shall know and see that your wickedness is great, in that you have asked for yourselves a king.

18 Then Samuel called to the LORD; and the LORD sent thunder and rain on that place; and all the people greatly feared the LORD and Samuel.

19 And all the people said to Samuel, Pray for your servants before the LORD your God, that we may not

die; for we have added to all our sins a great evil, in that we have asked for ourselves a king.

20 ¶And Samuel said to the people, Fear not; you have done all this wickedness; yet do not turn aside from following the LORD, but serve him with all your heart;

21 And do not turn aside after vain things which cannot deliver you; that you may not die, for they are vain things.

22 For the LORD will not forsake his people for his great name's sake; because he is pleased to make you his people.

23 Moreover as for me, far be it from me that I should sin against the LORD in ceasing to pray for you; but I will teach you the good and the right way;

24 Only revere the LORD, and serve him in truth with all your heart and with all your soul; for consider what great things he has done for you.

25 But if you shall continue to do wickedly, you shall die, both you and your king.

CHAPTER 13

AND when Saul had reigned one or two years in his kingdom over Israel,

2 He then chose for himself three thousand men of Israel; two thousand were with him in Michmash and in mount Beth-el, and a thousand were with Jonathan his son in Ramtha of Benjamin; and the rest of the people he sent every man to his house.

3 And Jonathan smote the garrison of the Philistines that was in Geba, and the Philistines heard of it. And Saul blew the trumpet throughout all the land, saying, Let the Hebrews and all Israel hear the news

4 That Saul has smitten the garrison of the Philistines and that Israel has prevailed over the Philistines. And the people were called together after Saul to Gilgal.

5 ¶And the Philistines gathered themselves together to fight with Israel, three thousand chariots, and six thousand horsemen, and people as the sand which is on the seashore in multitude; and they came up and encamped in Michmash, east of Beth-el.

6 And when the men of Israel saw them, they were afraid; so they hid themselves in caves and in holes and in rocks and in clefts and in pits.

7 And some of the Hebrews went over the Jordan to the land of Gad and Gilead. But Saul was still in Gilgal, and all the people were with him.

8 ¶And he waited seven days, according to the set time appointed by Samuel; but Samuel did not come to Gilgal; and the people were deserting Saul.

9 And Saul said, Bring here a burnt offering to me, and he offered peace offerings and burnt offerings.

10 And as soon as he had finished making the burnt offering, behold, Samuel came; and Saul went out to meet him, that he might bless him.

11 ¶And Samuel said, What have you done? And Saul said, When I saw that the people were deserting me and that you did not come within the time appointed and that the Philistines gathered themselves together at Michmash;

12 Therefore I said, The Philistines might come down against me at Gilgal, and I have not inquired of the LORD, so I ventured to offer a burnt offering.

13 And Samuel said to Saul, You have done foolishly; for you have not kept the commandment of the LORD your God, which he commanded you; for now would the LORD have established your kingdom over Israel, as he had said, I will establish you for ever.

14 But now your kingdom shall not continue; for the LORD has chosen for himself a man after his own heart, and the LORD has commanded him to be a ruler over his people, because you have not kept all the commandments that the LORD your God gave you.

15 And Samuel arose and went up from Gilgal to Ramtha of Benjamin. And Saul numbered the people that

were present with him, about six hundred men.

16 And Saul and Jonathan his son dwelt in Gibeah of Benjamin; but the Philistines encamped in Michmash.

17 ¶And raiders came out of the camp of the Philistines in three companies; one went toward the way of Ophrah to attack the land of Shual; 18 And another went toward the way of Beth-hauran; and another turned toward the way of the border that looks toward the valley of Zebaon and to the wilderness.

19 ¶Now there was no smith found throughout all the land of Israel; for the Philistines said, We do not want the Hebrews to make swords and spears;

20 But all the Israelites went down to the Philistines to sharpen every man his sickle and his ploughshare and his axe and his mattock.

21 And there was a broad file for the sickle and for the ploughshare and for mattocks and for the axe and to sharpen the goads.

22 So in the day of the battle, there was neither sword nor spear found in the hand of any of the people who were with Saul and Jonathan; but Saul and Jonathan his son had them.

23 And the garrison of the Philistines went out to the passage of Michmash.

CHAPTER 14

NOW it came to pass one day, Jonathan the son of Saul said to the young man who bore his armor, Come, let us go over to the Philistine garrison that is on the other side yonder. But he did not tell his father.

2 And Saul was staying in the outskirts of Ramtha under the pomegranate tree which is in Gibeon; and the people who were with him were about six hundred men;

3 And Ahiah, the son of Ahitub, Jochebar's brother, the son of Phinehas, the son of Eli, the LORD's priest in Shiloh, was wearing an ephod. And the people did not know that Jonathan was gone to the crossing place.

4 ¶And as he sought to cross over to the Philistine garrison, behold, there was a steep rock on one side and a steep rock on the other side; and the name of the one was Bozez, and the name of the other Siaa.

5 One crag stood out northward over against Michmash and the other southward over against Gibeah.

6 And Jonathan said to the young man who bore his armor, Come, let us cross over to the garrison of these uncircumcised; it may be that the LORD will help us; for nothing will prevent the LORD from saving by many or by few.

7 And his armorbearer said to him, Do all that is in your heart; turn aside, and go; behold, I am with you; do whatever is in your heart.

8 Then Jonathan said to him, Behold, we will cross over against these men, and we will show ourselves to them.

9 If they say to us, Stop until we come to you; then we will stand still in our place, and will not go up against them.

10 But if they say to us thus, Come up to us; then we will go up; for the LORD our God has delivered them into our hand; and this shall be a sign to us.

11 So both of them showed themselves to the garrison of the Philistines; and the Philistines said, Behold, the Hebrews are coming forth out of the holes where they had hid themselves.

12 And the men of the garrison answered Jonathan and his armorbearer, and said, Come up to us, and we will show you something. And Jonathan said to his armorbearer, Come up after me; for the LORD has delivered them into the hand of Israel.

13 And Jonathan climbed up on his hands and on his feet, and his armorbearer followed after him; and the Philistine garrison retreated before Jonathan; and his armorbearer slew with him.

14 And the first slaughter which Jonathan and his armorbearer made

was about twenty men; they cut them to pieces like stone-cutters and like men who plough a field.

15 And there was trembling in the camp, in the field, and among all the people that stood by; and the raiders also trembled and the earth quaked; and the fear of the LORD fell upon them.

16 And the watchmen of Saul in Gibeah of Benjamin looked; and, behold, the Philistine army was in confusion, going away defeated.

17 Then Saul said to the people that were with him, Take a count and see who is gone from us. And when they had mustered, behold, Jonathan and his armorbearer were not there.

18 And Saul said to Ahiah, Bring here the ark of God. For the ark of God was at that time with the children of Israel.

19 ¶And it came to pass, while Saul was talking to the priest, that the noise in the camp of the Philistines went on and increased; and Saul said to the priest, Withdraw your hand.

20 Then Saul and all the people who were with him shouted together, and they came to the battle; and, behold, every man's sword was against his fellow, and there was a very great confusion.

21 Moreover the Hebrews who were with the Philistines before that time, who had gone up with them to the camp, even they also turned to be with the Israelites and with Saul and Jonathan.

22 Likewise all the men of Israel who had hid themselves in mount Ephraim, when they heard that the Philistines fled before the Israelites, even they armed themselves and followed hard after them in the battle.

23 So the LORD saved Israel that day; then the men of Israel passed over to Beth-aon to battle.

24 ¶And Saul drew near that day and said to the people, Cursed be the man who eats food until evening, until I am avenged on my enemies. So none of the people tasted any food.

25 And they went throughout all the land and came into a forest; and, behold, there was honey in the forest on the ground.

26 And when the people were come into the forest, behold, the honey was dropping; but no one put his hand to his mouth; for the people feared the oath.

27 But Jonathan had not heard when his father adjured the people; so he put forth the end of the staff that was in his hand, and dipped it in a honeycomb, and put his hand to his mouth; and his eyes brightened.

28 Then one of the men of the people spoke and said to Jonathan, Your father has surely adjured the people, saying, Cursed be the man who eats food this day. And the people were faint with hunger.

29 Then Jonathan said, My father has troubled the land; see, how my eyes have been brightened because I tasted a little of this honey.

30 Moreover, because the people had not eaten today of the spoil of their enemies which they found, therefore there was not a greater slaughter of the Philistines.

31 We have smitten the Philistines today from Michmash to Aijalon; and the people are very faint with hunger.

32 Then the people rushed greedily on the spoil, and took sheep and oxen and calves, and slew them on the ground; and the people ate them with the blood.

33 ¶Then they told Saul, saying, Behold, the people have sinned against the LORD in eating flesh with blood. And Saul said, You have transgressed; roll a great stone to me this day.

34 And Saul said, Go round about among the people and say to them, Bring every man his ox, and every man his sheep, and slay them here, and do not sin against the LORD in eating flesh with the blood. So all the people brought every man his ox with him that night, and slew them there.

35 And Saul built there an altar to the LORD; thus he began to build his first altar to the LORD.

36 ¶And Saul said, Let us go down after the Philistines by night, and

plunder them until the morning, and let us not leave a man of them. And they said, Do whatever seems good to you.

37 And Saul said to God, Shall I go down after the Philistines? Wilt thou deliver them into the hands of Israel? But the LORD did not answer him that day.

38 And Saul said, Bring here all the families of the people; and know and see wherein this sin has been committed this day.

39 For, as the LORD lives, who saved Israel, though it be in Jonathan my son, he shall surely die. But there was no one of all the people that answered him.

40 Then Saul said to all Israel, Be you on one side, and I and Jonathan my son will be on the other side. And the people said to Saul, Do whatever seems good to you.

41 Therefore Saul said, O LORD God of Israel, give a perfect lot. And Saul and Jonathan were taken; but the people were not taken.

42 And Saul said, Cast lots between me and Jonathan my son. And Jonathan was taken.

43 Then Saul said to Jonathan, Tell me what you have done. And Jonathan told him, and said, I did taste a little honey with the end of the staff that was in my hand, and on account of that must I die?

44 And Saul said, God do so to me and more also, unless you shall surely die, Jonathan.

45 And the people said to Saul, Shall Jonathan die, who has wrought this great salvation in Israel? God forbid; as the LORD lives, there shall not a hair of his head fall to the ground; for he has saved the people of God this day. So the people delivered Jonathan and he did not die.

46 Then Saul returned from following the Philistines; and the Philistines went to their own country.

47 ¶And Saul took the kingship over Israel, and he fought against all his enemies on every side, against Moab and against the children of Ammon and against Edom and against the kingdom of Zobah and against the

Philistines; and wherever he turned he was victorious.

48 And he mobilized an army and smote the Amalekites, and delivered Israel out of the hand of those who plundered them.

49 Now these were the sons of Saul: Jonathan, Ishui, Melchi-shua, and Ashbashul; and the names of his two daughters were these: the name of the elder Nadab, and the name of the younger Malchel;

50 And the name of Saul's wife was Ahinoam, the daughter of Ahimaaz; and the name of the general of his army was Abner, the son of Ner, Saul's uncle.

51 And Kish was the father of Saul; and Ner, the father of Abner, was the son of Abiel.

52 And there was severe war against the Philistines all the days of Saul; and when Saul saw any valiant man or any strong man, he took him to himself.

CHAPTER 15

SAMUEL said to Saul, The LORD sent me to anoint you to be king over his people Israel. Now therefore hearken to the voice of the words of the LORD.

2 Thus says the LORD of hosts, I remember what Amalek did to Israel on their journey when they were coming up out of Egypt.

3 Now go and smite the Amalekites, and utterly destroy all that they have, and spare them not; but slay both men and women, young people and infants, oxen and sheep, camels and asses.

4 And Saul summoned the people to war, and he numbered them in Telaye, two hundred thousand footmen and ten thousand men of Judah.

5 And Saul came to a city of the Amalekites, and issued a directive in the valley.

6 ¶And Saul said to the Kenites, Turn aside, depart, get you down from among the Amalekites, lest I destroy you with them; for you showed kindness to all the children

of Israel when they came up out of Egypt. So the Kenites departed from among the Amalekites.

7 And Saul smote the Amalekites from Havilah as far as Shur, which is over near Egypt.

8 And he took Agag the king of the Amalekites alive, and utterly destroyed all the people with the edge of the sword.

9 But Saul and the people spared King Agag and the best of the sheep and of the oxen and of the fatlings and the stall-fed beasts and all that was good, and would not utterly destroy them; but everything that was vile and despised in their sight, that they destroyed utterly.

10 ¶Then the word of the Lord came to Samuel, saying,

11 I regret that I have made Saul king; for he has turned back from following me, and has not performed my commandments. And it grieved Samuel; and he prayed before the Lord all night.

12 And when Samuel rose early to meet Saul in the morning, it was told Samuel, saying, Saul has come to Carmel, and, behold, he has set up a dwelling place for himself, and has turned and passed on and gone down to Gilgal.

13 And Samuel came to Saul; and Saul said to him, Blessed be the Lord, who has performed his commandment.

14 And Samuel said, What then is this bleating of the sheep in my ears and the lowing of the oxen that I hear?

15 And Saul said, They have brought them from the Amalekites; for the people spared the best of the sheep and of the oxen, and brought them to sacrifice to the Lord your God; and the rest we have utterly destroyed.

16 Then Samuel said to Saul, Be still, and I will tell you what the Lord has said to me this night. And Saul said to him, Say on.

17 And Samuel said to Saul, Behold, even though you were little in your own eyes; nevertheless you were made the head of the tribes of Israel,

and the Lord anointed you king over Israel.

18 And the Lord sent you on a mission, and said, Go and utterly destroy the sinners, the Amalekites, and fight against them until they are consumed.

19 Why then did you not obey the voice of the Lord, but have spared the plunder, and have done evil in the sight of the Lord?

20 And Saul said to Samuel, I have obeyed the voice of the Lord, and have gone on the mission on which the Lord sent me, and have brought Agag the king of the Amalekites, and have utterly destroyed the Amalekites.

21 But the people took some of the spoil, sheep and oxen, the best of the things which should have been utterly destroyed, to sacrifice to the Lord your God in Gilgal.

22 And Samuel said, The Lord is not as well pleased with burnt offerings and sacrifices as with one who obeys his voice. Behold, to obey is better than sacrifices, and to hearken, than the fat of rams.

23 For divination is a rebellion, and divination is a grievous iniquity. Because you have rejected the word of the Lord, he has also rejected you from being king.

24 ¶And Saul said to Samuel, I have sinned; for I have transgressed the commandment of the Lord and your words, because I feared the people and obeyed their voice.

25 Now therefore, pardon my sin, and return with me, that I may worship the Lord.

26 And Samuel said to Saul, I will not return home with you; for you have rejected the word of the Lord, and the Lord has rejected you from being king over Israel.

27 And as Samuel turned about to go away, Saul laid hold upon the skirt of his mantle, and it tore.

28 And Samuel said to him, The Lord has torn the kingdom of Israel from you this day, and has given it to a neighbor of yours, who is better than you.

29 And also his Excellency the Lord

of Israel will not lie nor seek counsel; for he is not a human being, that he should seek counsel.

30 Then Saul said, I have sinned; yet honor me now before the elders of my people and before Israel, and return again with me, that I may worship the LORD your God.

31 So Samuel returned again with Saul, and Saul worshipped the LORD.

32 ¶Then said Samuel, Bring Agag the king of the Amalekites here to me. And Agag said, Surely death is bitter.

33 And Samuel said, As your sword has made women childless, so shall your mother be childless among women. And Samuel cut King Agag in pieces before the LORD in Gilgal.

34 ¶Then Samuel went to Ramtha; and Saul went up to his house to Ramtha of Saul.

35 And Samuel saw Saul no more until the day of his death; nevertheless, Samuel grieved for Saul; and the LORD regretted that he had made Saul king over Israel.

CHAPTER 16

AND the LORD said to Samuel, How long will you mourn for Saul, seeing I have rejected him from reigning over Israel? Fill your horn with oil, and come; I will send you to Jesse the Beth-lehemite; for I have found for myself a king among his sons.

2 And Samuel said, How can I go? If Saul hear it, he will kill me. And the LORD said to Samuel, Take a heifer with you, and say, I have come to sacrifice to the LORD.

3 And invite Jesse to the sacrifice, and I will show you what you shall do; and you shall anoint to me him whom I name unto you.

4 And Samuel did as the LORD had commanded him, and came to Bethlehem of Judah. And the elders of the town went out to meet him, and said, Is your coming peaceable?

5 And he said, Peaceably; I have come to sacrifice to the LORD; sanctify yourselves, and come with me to the sacrifice. And he sanctified Jesse

and his sons, and invited them to the sacrifice.

6 ¶And when they were come, he looked to Eliab, and said, Surely the LORD's anointed is like him.

7 But the LORD said to Samuel, Do not look on his appearance or on the height of his stature; because I have rejected him; for I do not see as man sees; for man looks on the outward appearance, but the LORD looks on the heart.

8 Then Jesse called Abinadab, and made him pass before Samuel. And he said, Neither has the LORD chosen this one.

9 Then Jesse made Shammah pass by. And he said, Neither has the LORD chosen this one.

10 And Jesse made seven of his sons pass before Samuel. And Samuel said to Jesse, The LORD has not chosen these.

11 And Samuel said to Jesse, Are these all the sons you have? And he said to him, There remains yet the youngest, and, behold, he is tending the sheep. And Samuel said to Jesse, Send and bring him here; for I will not leave till he comes here.

12 And he sent and brought him in. Now he was ruddy, with beautiful eyes, and very handsome. And the LORD said to Samuel, Arise, anoint him; for this is he.

13 Then Samuel took the horn of oil and anointed him in the midst of his brothers; and the Spirit of the LORD came upon David from that day forward. Then Samuel rose up and went to Ramtha to his house.

14 ¶But the Spirit of the LORD departed from Saul, and an evil spirit from before the LORD troubled him.

15 And Saul's servants said to him, Behold, your servants are before you;

16 Let them seek out a man who can play well on the harp; and when the evil spirit is upon you, he will play with his hands, and you shall be well.

17 And Saul said to his servants, Provide me now a man who can play well, and bring him to me.

18 Then one of the young men an-

swered and said, Behold, I have seen a son of Jesse the Beth-lehemite, who is skilful in playing and a mighty valiant man, a man of war and prudent in speech, a handsome man, and the LORD is with him.

19 ¶Wherefore King Saul sent messengers to Jesse and said, Send me David your son; he will be useful to me.

20 And Jesse took an ass laden with bread and a skin of wine and a kid of goats, and sent them by David his son to Saul.

21 And David came to Saul, and stood before him; and he loved him greatly; and he became his armorbearer.

22 And Saul sent to Jesse, saying, Let David attend me; for he has found favor in my sight.

23 And whenever the evil spirit from the LORD was upon Saul, David took a harp, and played on it; so Saul was refreshed and was well, and the evil spirit departed from him.

CHAPTER 17

NOW the Philistines gathered together their armies for battle, and were massed at the border of Judah, and they encamped between the border and Arka in Epher-samin.

2 And Saul and the men of Israel were gathered together, and encamped in the valley of Terebinth, and they set the army in array to fight against the Philistines.

3 And the Philistines stood on a mountain on the one side and Israel stood on a mountain on the other side, and the valley was between them.

4 ¶And there went out a mighty man from the camp of the Philistines, named Goliath of Gath, whose height was six cubits and a span.

5 And he had a helmet of brass upon his head, and he was armed with a coat of mail, and the weight of his coat of mail was five thousand shekels of brass.

6 And he had greaves of brass upon his legs, and a cuirass of mail between his shoulders.

7 And the staff of his spear was like a weaver's beam, and his spear's head weighed six hundred shekels of iron; and his shieldbearer went before him.

8 And he stood and cried to the armies of Israel, and said to them, Why have you come out to set your battle in array? Am I not a Philistine, and you the servants of Saul? Choose a man for yourselves, that he may come out against me.

9 If he is able to fight with me and kill me, then we will be your servants; but if I prevail against him and kill him, then you shall be our servants and serve us.

10 And the Philistine said, I have defied the armies of Israel this day; give me a man, that we may fight together.

11 When Saul and all Israel heard the words of the Philistine, they were dismayed and greatly afraid.

12 ¶Now David was the son of an Ephrathite of Beth-lehem of Judah, whose name was Jesse; and he had eight sons; and the man was old and advanced in years in the days of Saul.

13 And the three older sons of Jesse went and followed Saul to the battle; and their names were Eliab the first-born, and next to him Abinadab, and the third Shammah.

14 And David was the youngest;

15 Now David had returned from Saul, and was gone to tend his father's sheep at Beth-lehem.

16 And the Philistine drew near morning and evening, and presented himself for forty days.

17 And Jesse said to David his son, Take now for your brothers an ephah of parched wheat and ten loaves of bread, and run to the camp to your brothers;

18 And carry these ten cheeses to the commander of their thousand and inquire into the welfare of your brothers and bring the news of them to me.

19 Now Saul and all the men of Israel were in the valley of Terebinth fighting with the Philistines.

20 ¶And David rose up early in the morning and left the sheep with the keeper, and took and went as Jesse had commanded him; and he came to

the camp in the valley which goes up to the battle array, and the army shouted for the battle.

21 Then Israel and the Philistines put themselves in battle array, army against army.

22 And David put off his provisions by the side of the baggage, and ran into the army ranks, and came and saluted his brothers.

23 And while he was talking with them, behold, there came up the champion, the Philistine of Gath, Goliath by name, out of the armies of the Philistines, and spoke the same words; and David heard them.

24 And all the men of Israel, when they saw the mighty man, were afraid and fled from him.

25 And the men of Israel said, Have you seen this man who has come up? Surely to defy Israel he has come up; and it shall be that the man who kills him, the king will enrich him with great riches and will give him his daughter and make his father's house free in Israel.

26 And David said to the men who stood by him, What shall be done for the man who kills this uncircumcised Philistine and takes away the reproach from Israel? For who is this uncircumcised Philistine that he should defy the armies of the living God?

27 And the people told him the king's promises, saying, So shall it be done to the man who kills him.

28 ¶And Eliab his eldest brother heard him when he spoke to the men; and Eliab's anger was kindled against David, and he said to him, Why have you come down here? And with whom have you left those few sheep in the wilderness? I know your boldness and the evil of your heart; for you have come down to see the battle.

29 And David said, What have I done now? Behold, I was just talking.

30 ¶And he turned from him to the other side, and spoke in the same manner; and the people answered him again as they had done before.

31 And when the words which David spoke were reported to Saul, he sent for him.

32 ¶And David said to Saul, Let no man's heart fail because of him; your servant will go and fight with this Philistine.

33 And Saul said to David, You are not able to go against this Philistine to fight with him; for you are but a boy, and he has been a man of war from his youth.

34 And David said to Saul, Your servant was tending his father's sheep, and there came a lion and a bear, and took a lamb from the flock;

35 And I went out after the lion and smote him, and delivered it out of his mouth; and he growled at me, and I caught him by his beard, and I smote him and slew him.

36 Your servant slew both the lion and the bear; and this uncircumcised Philistine shall be as one of them, seeing he has defied the armies of the living God.

37 David said moreover, The LORD who delivered me from the paw of the lion and from the paw of the bear will deliver me out of the hands of the Philistine. And Saul said to David, Go, and the LORD be with you.

38 ¶And Saul armed David with his own armor and put a helmet of brass upon his head; and armed him with a coat of mail.

39 And David girded his sword upon his armor, but he was unwilling to go; for he had not tried them out. So David took them off.

40 And he took his staff in his hand, and chose five smooth stones out of the gravel, and put them into his shepherd's bag, even into his wallet, and his sling was in his hand; and he drew near to the Philistine.

41 And behold, the Philistine came and drew near to David; and his shieldbearer went before him.

42 And when the Philistine looked about and saw David, he disdained him; for he was but a youth, and ruddy, and of a fair countenance.

43 And the Philistine said to David, Am I a dog, that you come to me with a staff? And the Philistine cursed David by his gods.

44 And the Philistine said to David,

Come to me, and I will give your flesh to the fowls of the air and to the beasts of the field.

45 Then David said to the Philistine, You come against me with a sword and with a spear and with a shield; but I come against you in the name of the LORD of hosts, the God of the armies of Israel, whom you have defied.

46 This day the LORD will deliver you into my hands; and I will slay you and take your head from you; and I will give the carcasses of the host of the Philistines this day to the wild beasts of the earth and to the fowls of the air, that all the earth may know that there is a God in Israel.

47 And all this assembly shall know that the LORD saves not with sword and spear; for the battle is the LORD'S, and he will deliver you into our hands.

48 And, behold, when the Philistine came and drew near to meet David, David hastened and ran to the battle line to meet the Philistine.

49 And David put his hand in his bag and took thence a stone, and slung it and struck the Philistine in his forehead, and the stone sunk into his forehead; and he fell upon his face to the earth.

50 So David prevailed over the Philistine with a sling and with a stone, and smote the Philistine and slew him; but there was no sword in the hand of David.

51 Therefore David ran and stood over the Philistine, and took his sword and drew it out of its sheath, and slew him and cut off his head. And when the Philistines saw that their champion was dead, they fled.

52 And the men of Israel and of Judah arose and shouted, and pursued the Philistines as far as the entrance of the valley and as far as the valley of Ekron. And the slain of the Philistines fell by the way of Shaarain, even to Gath and to Ekron.

53 And the children of Israel returned from chasing the Philistines, and plundered their camps.

54 And David took the head of the Philistine and brought it to Jerusalem; but he put his armor in his tent.

55 ¶And when Saul saw David go forth against the Philistine, he said to Abner, the commander of his army, Whose son is this youth? And Abner said, As your soul lives, O king, I do not know.

56 And the king said, Inquire whose son this young man is.

57 And when David returned after he had slain the Philistine, Abner took him and brought him before Saul with the head of the Philistine in his hand.

58 And Saul said to him, Whose son are you, young man? And David said to him, I am the son of your servant Jesse the Beth-lehemite.

CHAPTER 18

WHEN David had finished speaking to Saul, the soul of Jonathan was knit to the soul of David, and Jonathan loved him as his own soul.

2 And Saul took him that day, and would not let him return to his father's house.

3 Then Jonathan and David made a covenant, because Jonathan loved David as his own soul.

4 And Jonathan stripped himself of the robe that was upon him and gave it to David, and his garments, even to his sword and his bow and his girdle.

5 ¶And David went out wherever Saul sent him and was victorious; so that Saul appointed him over the men of war, and he found favor in the sight of all the people and also in the sight of Saul's servants.

6 And it came to pass as they returned, when David came back from the slaughter of the Philistines, the women came out of all the cities of Israel, singing and dancing, to meet King Saul with tambourines, and with cymbals, and were rejoicing.

7 And the women sang as they played, and laughed, saying, Saul has slain by thousands, and David by tens of thousands.

8 And Saul was very wroth, and this

saying displeased him; and he said, They have ascribed to David ten thousands, and to me they have ascribed but thousands; and what more can he have but the kingdom?

9 And Saul began to envy David from that day forward.

10 ¶And it came to pass after some days that an evil spirit from God came upon Saul, and he prophesied in the midst of his house, and David was playing music in his presence, as at other times; and there was a javelin in Saul's hand.

11 And Saul threw the javelin; for he said, I will pin David to the wall. But David evaded it twice.

12 ¶And Saul was afraid of David, because the LORD was with him, and had departed from Saul.

13 Therefore Saul removed him from his presence, and made him a commander over a thousand; and he went out to war and came in before the people.

14 And David was a man of understanding in all his ways; and the LORD was with him.

15 And when Saul saw that he was exceedingly wise, he was afraid of him.

16 But all Israel and Judah loved David, because he went out to war and came in before them.

17 ¶And Saul said to David, Behold my elder daughter Nadab, I will give her to you to wife, but you must become a commander-in-chief for me and fight the LORD's battles. For Saul said, Let not my hand be against him, but let the hand of the Philistines be against him.

18 And David said to Saul, Who am I? And what have I done, or what is my life or my father's family in Israel, that I should be son-in-law to the king?

19 But it came to pass at the time when Nadab, Saul's daughter should have been given to David, she was given to Azriel the Meholathite to wife.

20 And Malchel Saul's daughter loved David; and they told Saul, and the thing pleased him.

21 And Saul said, I will give her to him, that she may be a hindrance to him and that the hand of the Philistines may be against him. Wherefore Saul said to David, You shall this day be my son-in-law in doing one of two things.

22 ¶And Saul commanded his servants to speak to David the son of Jesse, saying, Behold the king has delight in you, and all his servants love you; now therefore be the king's son-in-law.

23 And Saul's servants spoke these words to David. And David said, Seems it to you a light thing to be a king's son-in-law, seeing that I am a poor man and despised?

24 And the servants of Saul told him, saying, These are the words which David spoke.

25 And Saul said, Thus shall you say to David, The king does not desire any dowry, but two hundred foreskins of the Philistines, to be avenged of his enemies. But King Saul thought to make David fall by the hand of the Philistines.

26 And when the servants of Saul told David these words, it pleased David well to be the king's son-in-law; but the time had not come.

27 Wherefore David arose and went out, he and his men, and slew two hundred men of the Philistines; and David brought their foreskins and gave them to the king, that he might be the king's son-in-law. And Saul gave him Malchel his daughter to wife.

28 ¶And Saul saw and knew that the LORD was with David and that Malchel Saul's daughter loved David exceedingly.

29 And Saul was still the more afraid of David; and Saul became David's enemy thenceforth.

30 Then the princes of the Philistines went forth raiding; and it came to pass at the time they went forth raiding, David was more successful than all the servants of Saul; so that his name was highly honored.

CHAPTER 19

AND Saul told Jonathan his son and all his servants that they should kill David.

2 But Jonathan, Saul's son, was delighted much in David; and Jonathan spoke to David, saying, Saul my father seeks to kill you; now therefore take heed to yourself, and sit in a secret place and hide yourself;

3 And I will go out and stand beside my father in the field where you are, and I will speak to my father concerning you; and I will see what is on his mind, and I will tell you.

4 ¶And Jonathan spoke good of David to Saul his father, and said to him, Let not the king sin against his servant David; for he has not sinned against you, and his works are sufficient proof of his loyalty to you;

5 For he put his life at your disposal, and slew the Philistine, and the LORD wrought a great salvation for all Israel by his hand; you saw it and rejoiced; and now, why then will you sin against innocent blood, to slay David without a cause?

6 And Saul listened to the voice of Jonathan his son; and Saul swore, saying, As the LORD lives, he shall not be put to death.

7 Then Jonathan called David and told him all these things. And Jonathan brought David to Saul, and he was with him as in times past.

8 ¶And there was war again; and David went out and fought with the Philistines, and slew them with a great slaughter; and they fled before him.

9 And an evil spirit from the LORD came upon Saul as he sat in his house with his javelin in his hand; and David played the harp in his presence.

10 And Saul sought to pin David to the wall with the javelin; but he fled from Saul's presence, and Saul stuck the javelin into the wall; and David fled, and escaped that night.

11 Saul then sent messengers to David's house to watch him and to slay him in the morning; but Malchel, David's wife, told him, saying, If you do not save yourself tonight, tomorrow you will be put to death.

12 ¶So Malchel let David down through a window; and he fled and escaped.

13 And Malchel took an idol, and laid it in the bed, and put a pillow of goat's skin at the head of it, and covered it with a bedcover.

14 And when Saul sent messengers to take David, she said, He is sick.

15 And Saul sent the messengers again to see David, saying, Bring him up to me in the bed, that I may kill him.

16 And when the messengers came in, behold, there was an idol in the bed, with a pillow of goat's skin at its head.

17 And they told Saul, and Saul said to Malchel, Why have you deceived me so, and let my enemy depart, so that he has escaped? And Malchel said to Saul, He said to me, Let me go; or else I will kill you.

18 ¶So David fled and escaped, and came to Samuel at Ramtha and told him all that Saul had done to him. And he and Samuel went and dwelt in Jonath which is in Ramtha.

19 And it was told Saul, saying, Behold, David is at Jonath which is in Ramtha.

20 And Saul sent messengers to take David; and when they saw the company of the prophets prophesying and Samuel standing as a leader over them, the Spirit of God came upon the messengers of Saul, and they also prophesied.

21 And when it was told Saul, he sent other messengers, and they also prophesied. And Saul sent messengers again the third time, and they prophesied also.

22 Then he himself went to Ramtha, and came as far as the great cistern which is at the end of the town; and Saul said, Where are Samuel and David? And they said to him, Behold, they are at Jonath which is in Ramtha.

23 And he went toward Jonath in Ramtha; and the Spirit of God came upon him also; and he went on, and prophesied, until he came to Jonath in Ramtha.

24 And he stripped off his clothes and prophesied before Samuel, and lay down naked all that day and all that night. Wherefore they say, Behold, is Saul also among the prophets?

CHAPTER 20

AND David fled from Jonath, which is in Ramtha, and came and said to Jonathan, What have I done? And what is my offence? And what is my crime before your father that he seeks my life?

2 And Jonathan said to him, God forbid; you shall not die; behold, my father does nothing either great or small which he does not reveal to me; and why should my father hide this thing from me? It is not so.

3 And David swore moreover, and said, It is because your father knows that I have found favor in your eyes; therefore he has said, Let not Jonathan know this, lest he be grieved; but truly as the LORD lives, and as your soul lives, there is but a step between me and death.

4 Then Jonathan said to David, Whatever you desire, I will do for you.

5 And David said to Jonathan, Behold, tomorrow is the new moon, and I should not fail to sit in the presence of your father to eat; but let me go that I may hide myself in the field until the third day at evening.

6 If your father should miss me, then say to him, David earnestly asked leave of me that he might go to Beth-lehem his city; for there is a yearly sacrifice there for all the family.

7 If he says thus, It is well; then your servant shall have peace; but if he is displeased, then be sure that evil is determined by him.

8 Therefore you shall deal kindly with your servant; for you have brought your servant into a covenant of the LORD with you; but if there is folly in me, slay me yourself; why should you bring me to your father?

9 And Jonathan said, God forbid; for if I knew of a certainty that evil were determined by my father to come upon you, then I would come to you and tell you.

10 Then David said to Jonathan, Who shall report to me, if your father answers you roughly?

11 ¶And Jonathan said to David, Come, and let us go out into the field. So they both went out into the field.

12 And Jonathan said to David, The LORD God of Israel be a witness that I will sound my father about this time tomorrow, the third hour; and behold, if he feels good toward you, then I will send to you, and disclose it to you;

13 The LORD do so and much more to Jonathan; but if it please my father to do you harm, then I will disclose it to you, and send you away that you may go in peace; and the LORD be with you as he has been with my father.

14 And if only you will show me the kindness of God while I live, before I die;

15 And also you shall not cut off your kindness from my house for ever, when the LORD destroys the enemies of David from the face of the earth;

16 So Jonathan's house shall flourish with the house of David; and may the LORD take vengeance on David's enemies.

17 And Jonathan caused David to swear again, because he loved him; for he loved him as he loved his own soul.

18 Then Jonathan said to him, Tomorrow is the new moon; and you shall be missed, because your seat will be empty.

19 And when at the third hour you will be wanted very much, then you shall come tomorrow to the place where you hid yourself, and you shall sit down beside the same stone.

20 And I will shoot three arrows to the side of it, as though I shot at a mark.

21 And, behold, I will send a lad to go to gather up the arrows. And if I should say to the lad, The arrows are on this side of you, take them and come; then you will know and see that there is peace to you, there is no danger, as the LORD liveth.

22 But if I say thus to the lad, Behold, the arrows are beyond you; then go your way; for the LORD has sent you away.

23 And as for the matter of which you and I have spoken, behold, the LORD is between you and me forever.

24 ¶So David hid himself in the field; and when the new moon came, the king sat down to dine.

25 And the king sat upon his seat by the wall as at other times; and Jonathan went and sat upon a seat, and Abner sat by Saul's side, but David's place was empty.

26 Nevertheless Saul did not say anything that day; for he thought, Something has happened to him, or perhaps he is unclean,[1] or perhaps he has not purified himself.

27 And it came to pass on the morrow, the second day of the new moon, David's place was still empty; and Saul said to Jonathan his son, Why has not the son of Jesse come to eat, either yesterday or today?

28 And Jonathan answered and said to Saul his father, David earnestly asked leave of me to go to Bethlehem;

29 And he said, Let me go, for our family has a sacrifice in the city; and my brother has commanded me to be there; and now, if I have found favor in your eyes, let me get away and see my brothers. That is the reason he has not come to the king's table.

30 Then Saul's anger was kindled against Jonathan, and he said to him, O you rebellious son, do I not know that you are delighted in the son of Jesse to your own shame and to the shame of your mother's nakedness?

31 For as long as the son of Jesse lives upon the earth, you shall not be established, nor your kingdom. Therefore, now I will send and have him brought to me, for he shall surely die.

32 And Jonathan answered and said to Saul his father, Why should he be put to death? What has he done?

33 And Saul lifted up a javelin to smite him; whereby Jonathan knew that his father was determined to slay David.

34 So Jonathan arose from the table in fierce anger, and did not eat food the second day of the month; for he was grieved for David, because his father had determined evil against him.

35 ¶And it came to pass in the morning, Jonathan went out into the field to meet David, and a little lad was with him.

36 And he said to his lad, Run, gather up the arrows which I shoot. And as the lad ran, he shot an arrow beyond him.

37 And when the lad came to the place where Jonathan had shot the arrow, Jonathan called after the lad and said, Behold, the arrow is beyond you.

38 And Jonathan called again after the lad, saying, Make haste, quick, stay not. And Jonathan's lad gathered up the arrows and brought them to his master.

39 But the lad knew not anything; only Jonathan and David knew the matter.

40 And Jonathan gave his weapons to his lad, and said to him, Go, carry them to the city.

41 ¶And as soon as the lad was gone, David arose from beside the stone and came to Jonathan and fell on his face to the ground and bowed himself three times; and they kissed each other, and wept over each other; but David wept more.

42 Then Jonathan said to David, Go in peace, inasmuch as we have sworn both of us in the name of the LORD, saying, The LORD be between me and you and between my descendants and your descendants forever. Then Jonathan arose and went into the city.

CHAPTER 21

THEN David came to Nob, to Ahimelech the priest; and Ahimelech was afraid at meeting David, and said to him, Why have you come alone, and no man with you?

2 And David said to Ahimelech the priest, The king has entrusted me with a matter, and has said to me,

---

[1] When a person had been defiled by breaking certain ordinances he was required to purify himself before a feast. See 21:4.

Let no man know the thing for which I send you, and what I have com- manded you; and I have stationed my servants at hidden and obscure places.

3 Now therefore what provisions have you in your possession? Give me five loaves of bread in my hand, or whatever can be found.

4 And the priest answered David and said to him, There is no com- mon bread in my possession, but there is hallowed bread; you may have it if the young men have kept themselves from touching unclean things.

5 And David answered the priest and said to him, The hallowed bread has been lawful for us since yester- day and the day before, when we left, and behold, the clothes of the young men are holy, and the bread is now practically common, even though it were sanctified this day in the vessels.

6 So the priest gave him hallowed bread; for there was no bread there but the shewbread that was taken from before the LORD to be replaced by hot bread on the day when it was taken away.

7 Now a certain man of the serv- ants of Saul was there that day, de- tained before the LORD; and his name was Doeg, an Edomite, the chief of the herdsmen that belonged to Saul.

8 ¶And David said to Ahimeleck, Is there not here in your possession a sword or a spear? For I have brought neither my sword nor my javelin with me, because the king's business re- quired haste.

9 And the priest said, The sword of Goliath the Philistine, whom you slew in the valley of Terebinth, be- hold, it is here wrapped in a cloth behind the ephod; if you wish to take that, take it, for there is no other but that here. And David said, There is none like that; give it to me.

10 ¶And David arose and fled that day from fear of Saul, and went to Achish the king of Gath.

11 And the servants of Achish said to him, Is not this David, the king of the land of Israel? Did not the daugh- ters of Israel sing to one another of him in dances, saying, Saul has slain his thousands, and David his tens of thousands?

12 And David laid up these words in his heart, and was exceedingly afraid of Achish, the king of Gath.

13 So he changed his behavior in his presence, and disguised himself in their sight, and he sat at the door- post and let his spittle fall down upon his beard.

14 Then Achish said to his servants, Lo, you see the man is mad; why then have you brought him to me?

15 Do I lack good manners, that you have brought this fellow who misbehaves in my presence? Shall this fellow come into my house?

CHAPTER 22

DAVID therefore departed thence, and escaped to the cave of Ar- lam; and when his brothers and all his father's household heard it, they went down there to him.

2 And there gathered to him every man who was in distress and every man who was in debt and every man who was discontented, and he became chief over them; and there were with him about four hundred men.

3 ¶And David went thence to Miz- peh of Moab; and he said to the king of Moab, Let my father and my mother dwell with you, till I know what God will do with me.

4 And he left them with the king of Moab; and they dwelt with him all the time that David was in Mizpeh.

5 ¶And the prophet Gad said to David, Do not abide in Mizpeh; de- part and go into the land of Judah. Then David departed and came into the forest of Hiziuth.

6 ¶And when Saul heard that David was located, and the men who were with him (now Saul was staying in Gibeah under the almond tree in Ramtha, with his spear in his hand, and all his servants were standing about him);

7 Then Saul said to his servants who stood about him, Hear now, you Benjamites, will the son of Jesse give every one of you fields and vineyards, and make you all commanders of thousands and captains of hundreds;

8 And have all of you conspired against me, so that there is none to tell me about the covenant of my son with the son of Jesse; and is there none that discloses to me that my son has made a league with the son of Jesse, and is there none of you who is sorry for me, or discloses to me that my son has stirred up my servants against me to lie in wait as at this day?

9 ¶Then answered Doeg the Edomite, who was set over the servants of Saul, and said, I saw David when he came to Noh, to Ahimeleck, the son of Ahitub the priest.

10 And he inquired of God for him and gave him weapons and provisions and gave him the sword of Goliath the Philistine.

11 Then the king summoned Ahimeleck the priest, the son of Ahitub, and all his father's house, the priests that were in Noh; and all of them came to the king.

12 And Saul said, Hear now, I beseech you, son of Ahitub. And he answered, Here I am, my lord.

13 Then Saul said to him, Why have you conspired against me, you and the son of Jesse, in that you have given him bread and a sword, and have inquired of God for him, that he should rise against me to lie in wait as at this day?

14 And Ahimeleck the priest answered the king and said, And who among all your servants is so faithful as David, who is the king's son-in-law, and heeds your commands and is honored in your house?

15 Did I begin today to inquire of God for him? Far be it from me; let not the king impute anything to his servant, nor to all the house of my father; for your servant knew nothing of all this matter, less or more.

16 And the king said, You shall surely die, Ahimeleck, you and all your father's house.

17 ¶Then the king said to the guards who stood about him, Turn, and slay the priests of God; because their hand also is with David and because they knew that he fled, and

did not reveal it to me. But the servants of the king would not put forth their hands and harm the priests of God.

18 And the king said to Doeg, Turn and fall upon the priests. And Doeg fell upon the priests and slew on that day eighty-five persons who wore the linen ephod.

19 And Noh, the city of the priests, smote he with the edge of the sword, both men and women, young men and children and oxen and asses and sheep, with the edge of the sword.

20 ¶But one of the sons of Ahimeleck, the son of Ahitub, named Abiathar, escaped and fled after David.

21 And Abiathar told David that Saul had slain the priests of God.

22 And David said to Abiathar, I knew it that day when Doeg the Edomite was there that he would surely tell Saul; I myself am guilty for the death of all the persons of your father's house.

23 Abide with me; fear not; for he that seeks my life seeks your life also, but with me you shall be protected.

CHAPTER 23

THEN they told David, saying, Behold, the Philistines are fighting against Keilah and are robbing the threshing floors.

2 And David inquired of the LORD, saying, Shall I go and smite these Philistines? And the LORD said to him, Go and smite the Philistines and save Keilah.

3 And David's men said to him, We are afraid here in Judea, how much more then if we go to Keilah against the armies of the Philistines?

4 Then David inquired of the LORD again. And the LORD answered him and said, Arise, go down to Keilah; for I will deliver the Philistines into your hand.

5 So David and his men went to Keilah and fought with the Philistines and brought away their cattle and smote them with a great slaughter. So David saved the inhabitants of Keilah.

6 And it came to pass, when Abia-

thar the son of Ahimeleck fled to David to Keilah, he came down with an ephod in his hand.

7 ¶And it was told Saul that David was come to Keilah. And Saul said, God has delivered him into my hands; for he has shut himself up by entering a town that has gates and bars.

8 And Saul called all the people together to war to go down to Keilah to besiege David and his men.

9 ¶And David knew that Saul was plotting mischief against him; and he said to Abiathar the priest, Bring the ephod to me.

10 Then David said, O LORD God of Israel, thy servant has heard for certain that Saul seeks to come to Keilah to destroy the city on my account.

11 Will the men of the city deliver me and the men who are with me into the hand of Saul?

12 And the LORD said, They will deliver you; arise and go out of the city.

13 ¶Then David and his men, who were about six hundred, arose and departed from Keilah and went wherever they could go. And it was told Saul that David had fled from Keilah; and he forbore to go forth.

14 And David abode in the wilderness of Misroth, and remained in a mountain in the wilderness of Ziph. And Saul sought him every day, but God did not deliver him into his hand.

15 And David saw that Saul was come out to seek his life; and David was in the wilderness of Ziph in a forest.

16 ¶And Jonathan, Saul's son, arose and went to David in the forest, and strengthened his hands in God.

17 And he said to him, Fear not; for the hand of Saul my father shall not find you; and you shall be king over Israel, and I shall be with you, and you shall live; and even Saul my father knows that it is so.

18 And they two made a covenant in the valley before the LORD (who sits upon the cherubim). And Jonathan went to his house.

19 ¶Then the Ziphites came up to Saul at Gibeah, saying, Behold, David is hiding himself with us in Mizroth,
23

in the forest in Gibaoth, in the valley which is on the right side of the desert.

20 Now therefore, come down against us according to all the desire of your soul, and we shall deliver him into the king's hand.

21 And Saul said to them, Blessed be you of the LORD; for you have compassion on me.

22 Return and search and find the place where his haunt is and learn who has seen him there; for I am told that he is very subtle.

23 Know therefore and learn of all the lurking places where he hides himself, and return to me, to inform me with certainty, and I will go with you; and if he is in the land, I will search him out throughout all the thousands of Judah.

24 So they arose and went to Ziph before Saul; but David and his men were in the wilderness of Maon, in the plain by the side of the desert.

25 And Saul and his men went to seek David. And they told David; therefore he came down to Selah and abode in the wilderness of Maon. And when Saul heard that, he pursued David in the wilderness of Maon.

26 And Saul went on one side of the mountain and David and his men on the other side of the mountain; and David made haste to flee from Saul; for Saul and his men surrounded David and his men to take them.

27 ¶But there came a messenger to Saul, saying, Make haste and come; for the Philistines have invaded the land.

28 Wherefore Saul returned from pursuing David, and went against the Philistines; therefore they called that land the Division of Sinar.

29 ¶And David went up from thence, and dwelt in Mizroth, which is in Gibaoth.

CHAPTER 24

AND it came to pass when Saul returned from pursuing the Philistines that it was told him, saying, Behold, David is in Mizroth, which is in Gibaoth.

2 Then Saul took three thousand chosen men out of all Israel, and went to seek David and his men upon the mountains of the wild goats.

3 And he came to the sheepfolds on the way where there was a cave; and Saul went into the cave and lay down there; and David and his men were staying on the slope of the cave.

4 And the men of David said to him, Behold, this is the day of which the LORD said to you, Behold, I will deliver your enemy into your hands, that you may do to him as shall seem good in your sight. Then David arose and cut off the skirt of Saul's robe stealthily.

5 But afterward David regretted that he had cut off the skirt of Saul's robe.

6 And David said to the men who were with him, The LORD forbid that I should do this thing to my master, the LORD's anointed, to stretch forth my hand against him, because he is the anointed of the LORD.

7 So David restrained the men who were with him with these words, and did not permit them to rise against Saul. And Saul rose up out of the cave and went on his way.

8 David also arose afterward and went out of the cave and cried after Saul, saying, My lord the king. And when Saul looked behind him, David bowed with his face to the earth and did him obeisance.

9 ¶And David said to Saul, You must not listen to the words of the men who say, Behold, David seeks your hurt.

10 Behold, this day your eyes have seen how the LORD had delivered you today into my hand in the cave; and the men who were with me bade me kill you, but I had pity on you, and I said, I will not put forth my hand against my lord; for he is the LORD's anointed.

11 Moreover, turn back, and see that even the skirt of your robe is in my hand; because when I cut off the skirt of your robe I did not kill you; now you should know and see that there is neither evil nor fault in my

¹ A man of no account.

hand, and I have not sinned against you; yet you hunt me to take my life.

12 May the LORD judge between me and you, and the LORD avenge me of you; but my hand shall not be against you.

13 As it is said in the proverb of the ancients, Out of the wicked proceeds wickedness: but my hand shall not be against you.

14 After whom have you come out, O king of Israel? After whom do you pursue? After a dead dog,¹ and after a flea?

15 The LORD therefore shall be judge, and judge between me and you, and see, and plead my cause, and deliver me from your hands.

16 ¶And when David had finished speaking these words to Saul, Saul said to him, Is this your voice, my son David? And Saul lifted up his voice and wept.

17 And he said to David, You are more righteous than I; for you have rewarded me with good, whereas I have rewarded you with evil.

18 And you have showed this day how you have dealt well with me, in that the LORD had delivered me into your hands, and you did not kill me.

19 For when a man finds his enemy, and lets him go free, the LORD will reward him with good; wherefore the LORD reward you with good for what you have done to me this day.

20 And now, behold, I know well that you shall surely be king, and that the kingdom of Israel shall be established in your hand.

21 Swear now therefore to me by the LORD that you will not cut off my descendants after me and that you will not destroy my name out of my father's house.

22 So David swore to Saul. And Saul went to his home; but David and the men who were with him went up to Mizpeh.

CHAPTER 25

AND Samuel died; and all the Israelites were gathered together and mourned for him, and buried him in his grave at Ramtha. And David arose and went down to the wilderness of Paran.

2 And there was a man in Maon whose possessions were in Carmel; and the man was very wealthy; he had three thousand sheep and a thousand goats; and it came to pass, that he sheared his sheep in Carmel.

3 Now the name of the man was Nabal; and the name of his wife was Abigail; and she was a beautiful woman, and of a beautiful countenance; but the man Nabal was harsh and evil in his doings, and like a dog.

4 ¶And David heard in the wilderness that Nabal was shearing his sheep.

5 And David sent out ten young men, and said to the young men, Go up to Carmel, and go to Nabal and greet him in my name;

6 And thus shall you say to him who lives in prosperity, Peace be both to you and to your house.

7 Your shepherds were with us and we did not harm them, and they did not miss anything all the time they were in Carmel.

8 Ask your servants, and they will tell you. Now therefore let the young men find favor in your eyes; for we have come on a good day;[1] give whatever you wish to your servants and to your son David.

9 And when David's young men came, they spoke to Nabal according to all those words in the name of David.

10 ¶And Nabal answered David's servants, and said, Who is David? And who is the son of Jesse? There are many servants today who have broken away every man from his master.

11 Shall I then take my bread and my water and my meat that I have killed for my shearers, and give it to men whom I know not whence they are?

12 So David's young men turned about and came back and told David all these words.

13 And David said to the men who

were with him, Gird you on every man his sword. And they girded on every man his sword; and David also girded on his sword; and there went up after David about four hundred men; and two hundred remained with the baggage.

14 ¶But one of the young men told Abigail, Nabal's wife, saying, Behold, David sent messengers out of the wilderness to bless our master; and he railed at them.

15 But the men were very good to us and did not hurt us, and neither have they caused us to miss anything all the time that we went with them;

16 And when we were in the wilderness, they were a wall to us both by night and day, and all the time we were with them tending the sheep.

17 Now therefore know and consider what you will do; for evil is determined against our master and against all his household; and Nabal was with the shepherds.

18 ¶Then Abigail made haste, and took two hundred loaves of bread and two skins of wine and five sheep ready dressed and five measures of parched wheat and one hundred cheeses and two hundred bunches of raisins, and laid them on asses.

19 And she said to the servants, Go on before me; behold, I come after you. But she did not tell her husband Nabal.

20 And as she was riding on the ass and coming down by the covert of the mountain, behold, David and his men were coming up in her direction; and she met them.

21 Now David had said, Surely in vain have we guarded all that this fellow has in the wilderness, so that nothing was missing of all that belonged to him; and he has rewarded us evil for good.

22 The LORD do so and more also to his servant David, if I leave of all that belongs to him by morning any mature male.

23 And when Abigail saw David, she hastened and alighted from the ass, and fell before David on her

[1] When sheep are shorn, the owner prepares a banquet, and strangers and wayfarers come to eat.

face and bowed herself to the ground,
24 And fell at his feet, and said, I
beseech you, my lord, let this iniquity
be upon me, my lord; and let your
handmaid speak before you concerning this man Nabal.
25 For as his name is, so is he;
Nabal is his name, and his folly is
with him; but I, your handmaid, did
not see the young men whom my lord
sent.
26 Now therefore, my lord, as the
LORD lives, and as your soul lives, my
lord, seeing the LORD has withholden
you from coming to shed blood, now,
my lord, let your enemies and those
who seek to do evil to you be as
Nabal.
27 And now this present which your
handmaid has brought to my lord,
let it be given to the young men that
follow my lord.
28 Forgive this trespass of your
handmaid; for the LORD will certainly make for my lord a sure house;
because my lord is fighting the battles of the LORD, and evil has not
been found in you all your days.
29 Yet a man is resolved to pursue you and to seek your life; but the
life of my lord is bound in the bundle
of life with the LORD your God; but
the lives of your enemies the LORD
shall throw out of a sling.
30 And it shall come to pass, when
the LORD shall have done to my lord
according to all the good that he has
spoken concerning you, and shall
have appointed you ruler over Israel,
31 That this shall not be a grief to
you, nor an offence in your heart,
to shed blood without cause; and
when the LORD shall have dealt well
with you, then remember your handmaid.
32 ¶And David said to Abigail,
Blessed be the LORD God of Israel
who sent you this day to meet me;
33 And blessed be your advice, and
blessed be you, who have kept me
this day from coming to shed blood,
and spared my hands this day from
shedding blood.
34 For indeed, as the LORD God of
Israel lives, who has restrained me

from hurting you, if you had not
made haste and come to meet me,
surely there would not have been left
to Nabal by the morning any mature
male.
35 So David received of her hands
that which she had brought, and said
to her, Go up in peace to your house;
see, I have hearkened to your voice
and have accepted your person.
36 ¶And Abigail came to Nabal;
and, behold, he held a feast in his
house, like the feast of a king; and
Nabal's heart was merry within him,
for he was very drunk; wherefore
she told him nothing, less or more,
until the morning.
37 But it came to pass in the morning, when he had shaken off the effects of wine, that his wife told him
these things, and his heart died within him and he became paralyzed.
38 And it came to pass about ten
days after, the LORD smote Nabal
and he died.
39 ¶And when David heard that
Nabal was dead, he said, Blessed
be the LORD, who has pleaded the
cause of my reproach from the hands
of Nabal, and has kept his servant
from evil; for the LORD has returned
the wickedness of Nabal upon his
own head. And David sent and communed with Abigail, to take her to
him to wife.
40 And when the servants of David
came to Abigail at Carmel, they
spoke to her, saying, David has sent
us to you, to take you to him to
wife.
41 And she arose and bowed herself on her face to the earth, and
said, Behold, let your handmaid be
a servant to wash the feet of the
servants of my lord.
42 And Abigail hastened and arose,
and rode upon an ass with five of
her maidens who went after her; and
she went with the messengers of
David and became his wife.
43 David also took Ahinoam of
Jezreel; and both of them became his
wives.
44 ¶But Saul had given Malchel his
daughter, David's wife, to Phalti the
son of Laish, who was of Gallim.

CHAPTER 26

THEN the Ziphites came to Saul at Gibeah, saying, Behold, David is hiding himself in Gibaoth-hawilah, which is before the wilderness.

2 Then Saul arose and went down to the wilderness of Ziph, having three thousand chosen men of Israel with him, to seek David in the wilderness of Ziph.

3 And Saul encamped in Gibaoth-hawilah, which is before the wilderness by the wayside. But David abode in the wilderness, and he saw that Saul came after him in the wilderness.

4 David therefore sent out spies, and learned that Saul had come after him.

5 ¶And David arose and came to the place where Saul was encamped; and David saw the place where Saul lay, and Abner the son of Ner, the commander of Saul's army, was lying in the path, and the people were encamped round about him.

6 Then David said to Ahimeleck the Hittite and to Abishai the son of Zoriah, Joab's brother, saying, Who will go down with me to Saul's camp? And Abishai said, I will go down with you.

7 So David and Abishai came to the people by night; and, behold, Saul lay asleep in the path, with his spear lying on the ground by his bedside; and Abner and the people lay round about him.

8 Then said Abishai to David, Your God has delivered your enemy into your hands this day; now therefore let me smite him just once with this spear which is on the ground, and I will not smite him the second time.

9 But David said to Abishai, Destroy him not; for who can stretch forth his hand against the LORD's anointed, and be guiltless?

10 David said furthermore, As the LORD lives, the LORD shall smite him; or the day of his death shall come; or he will be smitten in battle and perish.

11 The LORD forbid that I should stretch forth my hand against the LORD's anointed; but now take the spear that is by his bedside, and the jug of water, and let us go.

12 So David took the spear and the jug of water from Saul's bedside; and they went away, and no man saw it nor knew it, neither awaked, for they were all asleep; because a deep sleep from the LORD had fallen upon them.

13 ¶Then David went over to the other side from Saul, and stood on the top of a hill afar off, a great space being between them;

14 And David called to the king and to Abner the son of Ner, saying, Will you not answer, Abner? Then Abner answered and said, Who are you that calls to the king?

15 And David said to Abner, Are you not a valiant man? And who is like you in all Israel? Why then have you not guarded your lord the king? For there came in one of the people today to destroy your lord the king.

16 This thing that you have done is not good. As the LORD lives, you are worthy to die, because you have not guarded your master, the LORD's anointed. And now see where the king's spear is, and the jug of water that was at his bedside.

17 And Saul heard David's voice, and said to him, Is this your voice, my son David? And David said, It is my voice, my lord, O king.

18 Then David said, Why does my lord pursue after his servant? For what have I done? Or what evil is in my hands?

19 Now therefore, let my lord the king hear the words of his servant. If the LORD has stirred you up against me, let us make an offering; but if it be of men, cursed be they before the LORD; for they have driven me out, that I should have no shelter in the inheritance of the LORD, saying, Go, serve other gods.

20 Now therefore, let not my blood fall to the earth far off from the face of the LORD; for the king of Israel has come out to seek a flea, as one who pursues a partridge in the mountain.

21 ¶Then Saul said to David, I have sinned; return, my son David; for I will no more do you harm, be-

cause my life was precious in your eyes this day; behold, I have played the fool, and have erred exceedingly.

22 And David answered and said, Behold the king's spear! Let one of the young men come over and take it.

23 The LORD renders to every man his righteousness and his faithfulness; for the LORD delivered you into my hands today, but I would not stretch forth my hand against the LORD's anointed.

24 And, behold, as your life was highly esteemed this day in my sight, so my life shall be highly esteemed in the sight of the LORD.

25 Then Saul said to David, Blessed be you, my son; you have surely done great things, and also you have surely prevailed. So David went on his way, and Saul also returned to his house.

CHAPTER 27

AND David said in his heart, Now if I should fall some day into the hands of Saul, it would not be good for me, but it is better for me that I should escape to the land of the Philistines; and Saul shall despair of seeking me any more in the territory of Israel; so I shall escape out of his hands.

2 So David arose and went over, he and the six hundred men who were with him, to Achish, the son of Maachah, king of Gath.

3 And David dwelt with Achish at Gath, he and his men and the household of David and his two wives, Ahinoam the Jezreelitess, and Abigail the Carmelitess, Nabal's wife.

4 And it was told Saul that David had fled to Gath; and he sought no more after him.

5 ¶And David said to Achish, If I have now found grace in your eyes, let the people give me a place in one of the towns in the desert, that I may dwell there; so that your servant may not dwell in the royal city with you.

6 Then Achish gave him Zinklag that day; therefore Zinklag belongs to the kings of Judah to this day.

7 And the time that David dwelt in the land of the Philistines was a full year and four months.

8 ¶And David and his men went up and made raids upon the Geshurites and the Gadolites and the Amalekites; for these nations were of old the inhabitants of the land, and they raided Geshur as far as the land of Egypt.

9 And David smote the land and left neither man nor woman alive, and he took away the sheep and the oxen and the asses and the camels and the apparel; then David returned and came to Achish.

10 And Achish said to David, Where have you made a raid today? And David said, Against the south of Judah and against the south of Jerahmel and against the south of Kailah.

11 And David spared neither man nor woman alive, to bring tidings to Gath, saying, Lest they should tell on us, saying, Thus David has done, and such was his custom all the while he dwelt in the land of the Philistines.

12 And Achish believed David, saying, He has surely displeased his people Israel; therefore he has become my servant for ever.

CHAPTER 28

AND it came to pass in those days, the Philistines gathered their armies together in the valley for war to fight with Israel. And Achish said to David, Know assuredly that you shall go out with me to the host, you and your men.

2 And David said to Achish, Surely you shall know what your servant can do. And Achish said to David, Therefore I will make you my bodyguard for ever.

3 ¶Now Samuel was dead, and all Israel had mourned over him and buried him in Ramtha in his own sepulchre. And Saul had put away the diviners and the wizards out of the land.

4 And the Philistines gathered themselves together, and came and encamped in Shechem; and Saul gathered all Israel together, and they encamped in Gilgal.

5 And when Saul saw the army of the Philistines, he was afraid, and his heart greatly trembled.

6 And when Saul inquired of the LORD, he did not answer him, either by dreams or by fire or by prophets.

7 ¶Then Saul said to his servants, Seek me a woman who has a familiar spirit, that I may go to her and inquire of her. And his servants said to him, Behold, there is a woman who has a familiar spirit at En-dor.

8 And Saul disguised himself and put on other raiment, and he went and two men with him, and they came to the woman by night; and Saul said to her, Divine for me by the familiar spirit, and bring up for me him whom I shall tell you.

9 And the woman said to him, Behold, you know what Saul has done, how he has removed those who have familiar spirits and the wizards out of the land. Why then are you laying a snare for my life to cause me to be put to death?

10 And Saul swore to her by the LORD, saying, As the LORD lives, there shall no harm come upon you for this thing.

11 Then the woman said, Whom shall I bring up to you? And he said, Bring me up Samuel.

12 And when the woman saw Samuel, she cried out with a loud voice; and she said to Saul, Why have you deceived me? For you are Saul.

13 And the king said to her, Fear not; what do you see? And the woman said to Saul, I saw gods ascending out of the earth.

14 And he said to her, What is their appearance? And she said to him, An old man is coming up; and he is covered with a mantle. And Saul perceived that it was Samuel, and he bowed with his face to the ground and made obeisance.

15 ¶And Samuel said to Saul, Why have you disturbed me to bring me up? And Saul answered, I am sore distressed; for the Philistines are making war against me, and God has departed from me, and answers me no more although I have inquired by the prophets and also by dreams; therefore I have called you, that you may tell me what I shall do.

16 Then Samuel said to Saul, Why do you ask of me, seeing the LORD has departed from you, and now he is with your neighbor David?

17 And the LORD has done to him, as he spoke by me; for he has rent asunder the kingdom out of your hand and given it to your neighbor David;

18 Because you did not obey the voice of the LORD and did not execute his fierce wrath upon Amalek, therefore the LORD has done this thing to you this day.

19 Moreover the LORD will also deliver Israel with you into the hand of the Philistines; and tomorrow you and your sons shall be with me; the LORD also shall deliver the army of Israel into the hand of the Philistines.

20 Then Saul fell straightway upon his face on the ground, and was exceedingly afraid because of the words of Samuel; and there was no strength in him; for he had eaten no bread all that day, nor all that night.

21 ¶And the woman came to Saul, and saw that he was exceedingly afraid, and said to him, Behold, your handmaid has obeyed your voice, and I have put my life in your hand, and have listened to the words which you spoke to me.

22 Now therefore, listen also to the voice of your handmaid, and let me set a morsel of bread before you; and eat, that you may have strength, because you are going on a journey.

23 But he refused, and said, I will not eat. But his servants, together with the woman, begged him; and he hearkened to their voice. So he arose from the ground and sat upon the bed.

24 Now the woman had a fatted calf in the house; and she made haste and killed it, and took flour and kneaded it and baked unleavened bread;

25 And she brought it before Saul and before his servants; and they ate. Then they rose up and went away that night.

CHAPTER 29

NOW the Philistines gathered together all their armies at Aphek; and the Israelites were encamped by the fountain which is in Jezreel.

2 And the lords of the Philistines were passing in review by hundreds and by thousands; but David and his men marched in the rear with Achish.

3 Then the princes of the Philistines said to Achish, Why are these men marching here? And Achish said to the princes of the Philistines, This is David, the servant of Saul, the king of Israel, who has been with us a year and some months, and I have found no fault in him from the day he came to me until this day.

4 But the princes of the Philistines were angry with him; and they said to him, Drive this fellow out of the camp, that he may return to his place which you have assigned him; and let him not go with us to the battle, lest he be an adversary to us there; for how could this man reconcile himself to his lord, except with our heads?

5 Is not this David, of whom the daughters of Israel sang one to another with timbrels, saying, Saul has slain his thousands, and David his tens of thousands?

6 ¶Then Achish called David and said to him, As the LORD lives, you have been upright, and your coming in and your going out with me in the battle is good in my sight; for I have not found evil in you since the day of your coming to us to this day; nevertheless you are not good in the sight of the lords.

7 Wherefore now return, and go in peace, that you may not displease the lords of the Philistines.

8 ¶And David said to Achish, But what have I done? And what have you found in your servant from the day that I have come to you until this day, that I may not go and fight against the enemies of my lord the king?

9 And Achish answered and said to David, I know that you are as good in my sight as an angel of God; but the princes of the Philistines have said, He shall not go with us to the battle.

10 Now therefore rise up early in the morning with your master's servants who came with you; and at daybreak, go on your way.

11 So David and his men rose up early in the morning to return to the land of the Philistines. And the Philistines went up to Jezreel.

CHAPTER 30

AND when David and his men were come to Zinklag on the third day, the Amalekites had raided the Negeb and Zinklag, and burned them with fire;

2 And had taken captive all the people who were in them, both the small and the great; and they put to death the men of war; and they took the spoil and went on their way.

3 ¶And David and his men came to the city, and, behold, it was burned with fire; and their wives and their sons and their daughters were taken captives.

4 Then David and the people who were with him lifted up their voices and wept until they had no more strength to weep.

5 And David's two wives were taken captive, Ahinoam the Jezreelitess and Abigail the wife of Nabal the Carmelite.

6 And David was greatly distressed; for the people spoke of stoning him, because the soul of all the people was grieved, every man for his sons and for his daughters; but David strengthened himself in the LORD his God.

7 And David said to Abiathar the priest, Ahimeleck's son, Bring me here the ephod. And Abiathar brought the ephod to David.

8 And David inquired of the LORD, saying, Shall I pursue these raiders? Shall I overtake them? And he answered him, Pursue; for you shall surely overtake them soon and deliver the captives.

9 So David went, he and the six hundred men who were with him,

and they came to the brook of Besor, and David left two hundred men there.

10 And David continued the pursuit with four hundred men; then the two hundred men who were left behind rose up and kept guard, that the raiders might not cross the brook of Besor.

11 ¶And they found an Egyptian in a field, and brought him to David, and gave him bread, and he did eat; and they gave him water to drink;

12 And they gave him two cakes of figs, and when he had eaten, his spirit revived; for he had not eaten bread nor drunk water for three days and three nights.

13 And David said to him, To whom do you belong? And where do you come from? And the young man said, I am an Egyptian, a servant of an Amalekite; and my master left me because I have been sick for three days,

14 After we returned from raiding the Negeb of Judah and the Negeb of Caleb and from Zinklag, and we burned the towns with fire.

15 And David said to him, Will you bring me down to this band of robbers? And he said to him, Swear to me by the LORD that you will neither kill me nor deliver me into the hand of my master, and I will show you this band of robbers.

16 ¶And David swore to him, and when he had brought him down, behold, they were scattered upon the ground, eating and drinking and rejoicing because of all the great spoil that they had taken from the land of the Philistines and from the land of Judah.

17 And David smote them from the morning until evening from the rear; and there escaped not a man of them, except four hundred men who rode upon camels and fled.

18 And David recovered all that the Amalekites had taken captive, and he rescued his two wives that day.

19 And they lost nothing, for David recovered all.

20 And David took all the flocks and the herds, and an abundance of other things in addition; and they said, This is David's spoil.

21 ¶And David came to the two hundred men who were left behind to guard the baggage, whom he had placed there to guard the road to Besor; and they went out to meet David and to meet the people who were with him; and when David and the people drew near, they exchanged greetings.

22 Then answered some of David's men who were evil and wicked, and said, Because they did not go with us, we will not give them any portion of the spoil which we have recovered, save that every man may take his wife and his children.

23 But David said, You shall not do thus, my brethren, with that which the LORD has given us, he who has preserved us and delivered into our hands the raiders that came against us.

24 For who will hearken to you in this matter? For as his portion is who goes down to battle, so shall his portion be who tarries by the baggage: they shall divide alike.

25 And it was so from that day forward that David made it a statute and an ordinance for Israel even to this day.

26 ¶And when David came to Zinklag, he sent some of the spoil to the elders of Judah and to their neighbors, saying, Here is a blessing for you from the spoil of the enemies of the LORD;

27 Moreover, he sent of the spoil to those who were in Beth-el and to those who were in Ramoth of the Negeb and to those who were in Ai

28 And to those who were in Adoer and those who were in Siphmoth and to those who were in Eshtemoa

29 And to those who were in Rachal and to those who were in the cities of the Jerahmeelites and to those who were in the cities of the Kenites

30 And to those who were in Hirmah and to those who were in Barbeshan and to those who were in Tanach

31 And to those who were in Hebron and to all the places in which David and his men had traveled.

CHAPTER 31

NOW the Philistines fought against Israel; and the men of Israel fled from before the Philistines, and many fell dead on mount Gilboa.

2 And the Philistines overtook Saul and his sons; and the Philistines slew Jonathan and Jeshui and Melchishua, Saul's sons.

3 And the battle was intense against Saul, and the archers overtook him with bows, and he was exceedingly afraid of the archers.

4 Then Saul said to his armorbearer, Draw your sword and thrust me through with it, lest these uncircumcised come and slay me and abuse me. But his armorbearer would not; for he was exceedingly afraid. Thereupon Saul took his sword and fell upon it.

5 And when his armorbearer saw that Saul was dead, he fell likewise upon his sword, and died with him.

6 So Saul died, and his three sons and his armorbearer and also all his servants, that same day together.

7 ¶And when the men of Israel who were on the other side of the valley of the Jordan saw that the men of Israel fled and that Saul and his sons were slain, they abandoned the cities and fled; and the Philistines came and dwelt in them.

8 And on the morrow, when the Philistines came to strip the slain, they found Saul and his three sons fallen on mount Gilboa.

9 And they cut off his head and stripped off his armor, and sent messengers to publish the news in the land of the Philistines and among the people and in the house of their idols.

10 And they put his armor in the house of Ashtaroth; and they fastened his body to the wall of Beth-jashan.

11 ¶Now when the inhabitants of Jabesh-gilead heard of that which the Philistines had done to Saul and to his sons,

12 All the valiant men arose and marched all night, and took the body of Saul and the bodies of his sons from the wall of Beth-jashan, and brought them to Jabesh and burnt them there.

13 And they took their bones and buried them under the almond tree at Jabesh, and fasted seven days.

THE SECOND BOOK OF

SAMUEL

otherwise called

THE SECOND BOOK OF THE KINGS

CHAPTER 1

NOW it came to pass after the death of Saul, when David had returned from the slaughter of the Amalekites and had abode two days in Zinklag;

2 It came to pass on the third day, that, behold, a man came out of the camp from Saul with his clothes torn and earth upon his head; and so it was that when he came to David, he fell to the earth and did obeisance.

3 And David said to him, Where do you come from? And he replied, Out of the camp of Israel have I escaped.

4 And David said to him, What is

the news? Tell me. And he answered, The people fled from the battle, and many of them also have fallen; and Saul and Jonathan his son are also dead.

5 And David said to the young man, Tell me, how did Saul and Jonathan his son die?

6 And the young man said to him, I happened by chance to be on mount Gilboa, and behold, Saul was leaning upon his spear; and lo, the chariots and horsemen overtook him.

7 And when he looked behind him, he saw me and called to me. And I answered, Here am I.

8 And he said to me, Who are you? And I answered him, I am an Amalekite.

9 Then he said to me, Stand over me and slay me; for anguish has seized me because my life is still whole in me.

10 So I stood over him and slew him, because I knew that he could not live after he had fallen; and I took the crown that was upon his head and the bracelet that was on his arm, and I have brought them here to my lord.

11 Then David took hold of his clothes and tore them; and likewise all the men who were with him;

12 And they mourned and wept and fasted until evening for Saul and for Jonathan his son and for the people of the LORD and for the house of Israel, because they had fallen by the sword.

13 ¶Then David said to the young man who told him, Where do you come from? And he answered, I am the son of a proselyte, an Amalekite.

14 And David said to him, How was it that you were not afraid to stretch forth your hand to destroy the LORD's anointed?

15 And David called one of the young men and said to him, Go near and fall upon him. And he drew near and fell upon him, and he smote him so that he died.

16 And David said to him, Your blood be upon your head; for your mouth has testified against you, for you have said, I have slain the LORD's anointed.

17 ¶And David lamented with this song of mourning over Saul and over Jonathan his son

18 (Also he commanded them to teach the children of Judah the use of the bow; behold, it is written in the book of Asher):

19 Israel was swift like a gazelle, and is slain upon her proud hills! How are the mighty fallen!

20 Tell it not in Gath, publish it not in the streets of Ashkelon; lest the daughters of the Philistines rejoice, lest the daughters of the uncircumcised exult.

21 O you mountains of Gilboa, let there be no dew, neither let there be rain upon you, nor upon the choicest fields; for there the shield of the mighty was broken, the shield of Saul, who was anointed with oil.

22 From the blood of the slain, from the fat of the mighty, the bow of Jonathan turned not back and the sword of Saul returned not empty.

23 Saul and Jonathan were lovely and pleasant in their lives, and in their death they were not divided; they were swifter than eagles, stronger than lions.

24 O daughters of Israel, weep over Saul, who clothed you in scarlet and dyed garments, who put ornaments of gold upon your apparel.

25 How are the mighty fallen in the midst of the battle! O Jonathan, upon her high places are many slain.

26 I am distressed for you, my brother Jonathan; you were very dear to me; your love to me was wonderful, passing the love of women.

27 How are the mighty fallen and the weapons of war perished!

CHAPTER 2

AND it came to pass after this, that David inquired of the LORD, saying, Shall I go up to one of the cities of Judah? And the LORD said to him, Go up. And David said, Whither shall I go up? And he said, To Hebron.

2 So David went up there, and his

two wives also, Ahinoam the Jezreelitess, and Abigail, Nabal's wife, the Carmelite.

3 And David and his men who were with him went up together, every man with his household; and they dwelt in Hebron.

4 And the men of Judah came, and there they anointed David king over the house of Judah. And they told David, saying, It was the men of Jabesh-gilead who buried Saul.

5 ¶And David sent messengers to the men of Jabesh-gilead and said to them, Blessed be you of the LORD, that you have shown this kindness to your lord, even to Saul, and have buried him.

6 And now may the LORD show kindness and truth to you; and I also will requite you this kindness, because you have done this thing.

7 Therefore now let your hands be strengthened and be valiant; for your master Saul is dead, and the house of Judah have anointed me king over them.

8 ¶But Abner the son of Ner, commander of Saul's army, took Ashbashul, the son of Saul, and brought him over to Mahanaim;

9 And made him king over Gilead and over Geshur and over Jezreel and over Ephraim and over Benjamin and over all Israel.

10 Ashbashul Saul's son was forty years old when he began to reign over Israel, and he reigned two years. But the house of Judah followed David.

11 And the time that David was king in Hebron over the house of Judah was seven years and six months.

12 ¶And Abner the son of Ner and the servants of Ashbashul the son of Saul went out from Mahanaim to Gibeon.

13 And Joab the son of Zoriah and the men of David went out and met the young men together in Gibeon; and they sat down, these young men on the one side and the other young men on the other.

14 And Abner said to Joab, Let the young men now arise and play

before us. And Joab said, Let them arise.

15 Then there arose and went over by number twelve of the men of Benjamin, who belonged to Ashbashul the son of Saul and twelve of the men of David.

16 And every man caught his fellow by the head, and thrust his sword in the other's side; so they fell down together; therefore they called that place Haklath-zadan, which is in Gibeon.

17 And there was a very fierce battle that day; and Abner was defeated, and the men of Israel, before the servants of David.

18 ¶And there were three sons of Zoriah there, Joab, Abishai, and Ashael; and Ashael was as swift of foot as a desert gazelle.

19 And Ashael pursued Abner; and he turned not to the right hand nor to the left as he followed Abner.

20 Then Abner looked behind him and said, Is that you, Ashael? And he answered, It is I.

21 And Abner said to him, Turn aside to your right hand or to your left, and seize one of the young men and take for yourself his armor. But Ashael would not turn aside from following him.

22 And Abner spoke again to Ashael, to turn from following him, saying, Turn from following me, lest I smite you and throw you on the ground; how then could I lift up my face and look at Joab your brother.

23 But he refused to turn; therefore Abner smote him with the end of the spear upon his breast, and the spear came out at his back; and he fell down there and died in the same place; and all who came to the place where Ashael fell down and died stood still.

24 Then Joab and Abishai arose and pursued Abner; and the sun went down when they came to lake Giboath which lies before Giah by the way of the wilderness of Gibeon.

25 ¶And the Benjamites gathered themselves together behind Abner, and became one company, and stood on the top of a hill.

26 Then Abner called to Joab and said, Shall the sword devour forever? Do you not know that there will be bitterness in the end? How long will it be then before you bid the people return from following their brethren?
27 And Joab said, As the LORD lives, unless you had spoken, surely in the morning I would have let the people give up every one from pursuing his brother.
28 So Joab blew the trumpet, and all the people stood still and pursued Israel no more, neither did they fight any more.
29 And Abner and his men walked all that night in the desert, and crossed the Jordan, and went toward Geshur, and they came to Mahanaim.
30 And Joab returned from following Abner; and when he had gathered all the people together and they were numbered, there were twelve wounded of David's men, and Ashael was dead.
31 But the men of David had slain of Benjamin and of Abner, three hundred and sixty men.
32 ¶And they took Ashael and buried him in the sepulchre of his father in Beth-lehem. And Joab and his men marched all night, and the day dawned upon them at Hebron.

CHAPTER 3

NOW there was a long war between the house of Saul and the house of David; but David grew stronger and stronger, and the house of Saul became weaker and impoverished.
2 ¶And sons were born to David in Hebron; and his first-born was Amnon, of Ahinoam the Jezreelitess;
3 And his second, Caleb, of Abigail the wife of Nabal the Carmelite; and the third, Absalom, the son of Maacah the daughter of Talmai king of Geshur;
4 And the fourth, Adonijah, the son of Haggith; and the fifth, Shephatiah, the son of Abital;
5 And the sixth, Ithream, by David's wife Eglah. These were born to David in Hebron.
6 ¶And it came to pass, while there was war between the house of Saul

and the house of David, Abner made himself strong for the house of Saul.
7 And Saul had a concubine, whose name was Rizpah, the daughter of Ana; and Ashbashul said to Abner, Why are you going in unto my father's concubine?
8 Then Abner was exceedingly displeased at the words of Ashbashul, and Abner said, Am I the leader of vicious men in Judah? This day I show kindness to the house of Saul your father, to his brothers and to his friends, and have not delivered you into the hand of David, and yet you charge me today with this iniquity concerning a woman?
9 So do God to Abner, and more also, if I do not perform what the LORD has spoken to David, even so will I do,
10 To transfer the kingdom from the house of Saul and to establish the throne of David over Israel and over Judah from Dan to Beer-sheba.
11 And Ashbashul could not reply to Abner, because he feared him.
12 ¶And Abner sent messengers to David, saying, Whose is the land? Now make your covenant with me, and, behold, my hand shall be with you, to bring all Israel to you.
13 ¶And David said, Well, I will make a covenant with you; but one thing I require of you, you shall not see my face, unless you first bring Malchel, Saul's daughter with you.
14 Then David sent messengers to Ashbashul Saul's son, saying, Deliver to me my wife, Malchel, whom I espoused for two hundred foreskins of the Philistines.
15 And Ashbashul sent, and took her from her husband, Palti, the son of Laish of Gallim.
16 And her husband went along with her weeping as far as Bethhurim. Then Abner said to him, Return. And he returned.
17 ¶And Abner had communication with the elders of Israel, saying, You have sought for David in times past to be king over you;
18 Now then do so; for the LORD has spoken of David, saying, By the hand of my servant David I will save

my people Israel from the hand of the Philistines and out of the hand of all their enemies.

19 And Abner also spoke in the presence of the Benjamites; and Abner went also to speak in the presence of David in Hebron. And when it seemed good in the sight of all Israel and in the sight of the whole house of Benjamin,

20 Then Abner came to David at Hebron, and twenty men with him. And David made Abner and the men who were with him a great feast.

21 And Abner said to David, I will arise and go, and will gather all Israel to my lord the king, that they may make a covenant with you and that you may reign over all that your soul desires. And David sent Abner away; and he went in peace.

22 ¶And behold, the men of David and Joab came from a raid and brought a great spoil with them; but Abner was not with David in Hebron; for he had sent him away, and he was gone in peace.

23 When Joab and all the people who were with him were come, they told Joab, saying, Abner the son of Ner came to King David, and he has sent him away and he has gone in peace.

24 Then Joab came to King David, and said to him, What have you done? Behold, Abner came to you; why have you sent him away, and he is gone from you?

25 Do you not know that Abner the son of Ner came to deceive you and to know your going out and your coming in and to know all that you are doing?

26 And when Joab was come out from the presence of David, he sent messengers after Abner, and they brought him back from the well of Sirah; but David knew it not.

27 And when Abner was returned to Hebron, Joab took him aside to a secret place within the gate to speak with him quietly, and he smote him there in his abdomen, and he died, for the blood of Ashael his brother.

28 ¶And afterward when David heard it, he said, I and my kingdom are guiltless before the LORD for ever

from the blood of Abner the son of Ner;

29 Let it rest on the head of Joab and on the head of all his father's house; and let there never fail to be in the house of Joab one who has a discharge or who is a leper or who is a beggar holding a bowl or who falls by the sword or who lacks bread.

30 So Joab and Abishai his brother slew Abner because he had slain their brother Ashael at Gibeon in the battle.

31 ¶And David said to Joab and to all the people who were with him, Rend your clothes and gird yourselves with sackcloth and mourn for Abner. And King David himself and all the people followed the bier.

32 And they buried Abner in Hebron; and the king lifted up his voice and wept at the grave of Abner; and all the people wept.

33 And the king lamented over Abner and said, Abner died like Nabal.

34 Your hands were not bound nor were your feet put into fetters; as one falls before the wicked men, so have you fallen. And all the people wept again over him.

35 And all the people tried to persuade David to eat food while it was still day, but David swore, saying, So do God to me, and more also, if I taste bread or anything else till the sun goes down.

36 And all the people took notice of it, and it pleased them; whatever the king did pleased all the people;

37 For all the people and all Israel understood that day that the king had no hand in the slaying of Abner, the son of Ner.

38 And the king said to the people, Do you not know that there is a great prince fallen this day in Israel?

39 And I am this day troubled, and as king I see that the sons of Zoriah are too hard for me; the LORD shall reward the evil doer according to his wickedness.

CHAPTER 4

WHEN Ashbashul Saul's son heard that Abner was dead in Hebron, he trembled, and all Israel was troubled.

2 And Saul's son had two men who were captains of raiding bands; the name of the one was Baana, and the name of the other Rechab, the sons of Rimmon a Beerothite of the children of Benjamin (for Beeroth also is reckoned to the Benjamites; 3 And the Beerothites fled to Gittaim and are sojourners there until this day).

4 And Jonathan, Saul's son, had a son who was lame in his feet. He was five years old when the news about Saul and Jonathan came from Jezreel, and his nurse took him up and fled; and, as she made haste to flee, he fell and became lame. And his name was Mephibosheth.

5 And the sons of Rimmon the Beerothite, Rechab and Baana, went, and came about the heat of the day to the house of Ashbashul as he was taking his noontide rest.

6 And behold, they came into the midst of the house; then those sons of wickedness took and smote him in his abdomen; and Rechab and Banna his brother escaped.

7 For when they came into the house, he was lying on his bed in his bedchamber, and they smote him and slew him and beheaded him, and took his head and fled by the way of the plain all night.

8 And they brought the head of Ashbashul to David at Hebron, and said to King David, Behold the head of Ashbashul the son of Saul your enemy, who sought your life; and the LORD has avenged our lord the king this day of Saul and of his offspring.

9 ¶And David answered Rechab and Baana his brother, the sons of Rimmon the Beerothite, and said to them, As the LORD lives, who has saved my life out of every adversity,

10 When one told me, saying, Behold, Saul is dead, thinking to have brought me good tidings, I seized him and slew him in Zinklag, instead of giving him a reward for his tidings;

11 How much more, when wicked men have slain a man in his own house upon his bed? Now I will

avenge his blood at your hands and destroy you from the earth.

12 And David commanded his young men, and they slew them, and cut off their hands and their feet, and hanged them on the hill in Hebron. But they took the head of Ashbashul and buried it in the sepulchre of Abner in Hebron.

CHAPTER 5

THEN all the tribes of Israel came to David at Hebron and said to him, Behold, we are your flesh and your bone.

2 Also in time past, when Saul was king over us, it was you who led out and brought in Israel; and the LORD said to you, You shall feed my people Israel, and you shall be a ruler over my people Israel.

3 So all the elders of Israel came to the king at Hebron; and King David made a covenant with them in Hebron before the LORD; and they anointed David king over Israel.

4 ¶David was thirty years old when he began to reign, and he reigned forty years.

5 In Hebron he reigned over Judah seven years and six months; and in Jerusalem he reigned thirty-three years over all Israel and Judah.

6 ¶And King David and his men went to Jerusalem against the Jebusites, the inhabitants of the land, who spoke to David, saying, You shall not come in here, except you destroy both the blind and the lame; [1] and they said, David cannot come in here.

7 Nevertheless David took the stronghold of Zion; the same is the city of David.

8 And David said on that day, Whosoever smites a Jebusite and whosoever strikes with a weapon blind and the lame, he is a hater of David's soul. Therefore they say, The blind and the lame shall not come into the temple.

9 So David dwelt in the fort, that is, Zion; and he called it the city of David. And David built round about the fort from within.

10 And David continued to become

greater, and the Lord God of hosts was with him.

11 ¶And Hiram king of Tyre sent messengers to David, and cedar trees and carpenters and masons; and they built David a house.

12 And David perceived that the Lord had established him king over Israel, and that he had exalted his kingdom for the sake of his people Israel.

13 ¶And David took more concubines and wives from Jerusalem, after he was come from Hebron; and there were more sons and daughters born to David.

14 And these are the names of the sons who were born to him in Jerusalem: Shammuah, Shachab, Nathan, Solomon,

15 Jocabar, Elisha, Nepheg, Naphia,

16 Elishama, Eliada, and Eliphalet.

17 ¶But when the Philistines heard that they had anointed David king over Israel, all the Philistines came up to seek David; and David heard of it, and went down to the fort.

18 The Philistines also came and encamped in the Valley of Giants.

19 And David inquired of the Lord, saying, Shall I go up against the Philistines? Wilt thou deliver them into my hands? And the Lord said to David, Go up; for I will deliver them into your hands.

20 And David came to Baal-perazim, and David defeated them there, and David said, The Lord has made a breach through my enemies before me, like the breach of waters. Therefore he called the name of that place Baal-perazim.

21 And they left their idols there, and David and his men carried them away.

22 ¶And the Philistines came up yet again and encamped in the Valley of the Giants.

23 And when David inquired of the Lord, the Lord said to him, You shall not go up; but circle behind them, and come upon them opposite Bachim.

24 And when you hear the sound of marching on the top of the moun-tain of Bachim, then you shall be-come strong; for then shall the Lord go out before you to smite the army of the Philistines.

25 And David did as the Lord had commanded him; and he smote the Philistines from Geba to the entrance of Gadar.

CHAPTER 6

AGAIN David gathered together all the young men of Israel, thirty thousand.

2 And David arose with all the people who were with him of the men of Judah and went to Geba to bring up from thence the ark of God, for at that place was invoked the name of the Lord of hosts, who dwells upon the cherubim.

3 And they set the ark of God upon a new cart, and brought it out of the house of Abinadab that was in Gibeah; and Uzzah and Ahia, the sons of Abinadab, drove the cart, walking behind it.

4 And they brought the ark of God out of the house of Abinadab which was in Gibeah, and Ahia went before the ark.

5 And David and all the house of Israel danced before the Lord waving branches of cedar trees and cypress, and played upon harps and lyres and timbrels and cornets and cymbals.

6 ¶And when they came to the threshing floors, Uzzah put forth his hand to the ark of the Lord, and took hold of it; for the oxen broke loose from the harness.

7 And the anger of the Lord was kindled against Uzzah; and the Lord smote him there because he put forth his hand to the ark; and he died there beside the ark of God.

8 And David was displeased because the Lord had stricken Uzzah; and he called the name of that place Toraetha-uzzah, and so it is called even to this day.

9 And David was afraid of the Lord that day, and he said, How shall I bring in the ark of the Lord to me?

10 So David was unwilling to bring

the ark of God with him into the city of David; but David took it aside into the house of Ober-edom the Gittite.

11 And the ark of the LORD remained in the house of Ober-edom the Gittite three months; and the LORD blessed Ober-edom the Gittite, and all his household because of the ark of the LORD.

12 ¶And it was told King David, saying, The LORD has blessed Ober-edom and all that belongs to him, because of the ark of the LORD. So David went and brought up the ark of the LORD from the house of Ober-edom into the city of David with gladness.

13 And it was so that when those who bore the ark of the LORD had gone six paces, David sacrified fat oxen.

14 And David sang praises before the LORD with all his might; and David was girded with a linen ephod.

15 So David and all the house of Israel brought up the ark of the LORD with shouting and with the sound of the trumpet.

16 And as the ark of the LORD came past the house of David, Malchel Saul's daughter looked through a window and saw King David rejoicing and dancing before the ark of the LORD; and she despised him in her heart.

17 ¶And they brought in the ark of the LORD, and set it in the midst of the tent that David had pitched for it; and David offered burnt offerings and peace offerings before the LORD.

18 And when David had finished offering the burnt offerings and peace offerings to the LORD, he blessed the people in the name of the LORD of hosts.

19 And he distributed among all the people, even among the whole multitude of Israel, both men and women, to everyone a loaf of bread and a portion of meat and a fine white loaf of bread. So all the people departed everyone to his house.

20 ¶Then David returned to go to his house. And Malchel the daughter of Saul came out to meet David, and said, How glorious was the king of Israel today, for he appeared publicly before the eyes of the handmaids of his servants, for he surely conducted himself as a vain man!

21 And David said to Malchel, It was before the LORD, who chose me rather than your father and rather than all his house, and appointed me to be a ruler over the people of the LORD, over Israel; it was because of him that I danced before the LORD.

22 And I will abase myself still more than this, and will humble myself in my own eyes; and the maidservants of whom you have spoken shall yet honor me.

23 Therefore Malchel the daughter of Saul had no child to the day of her death.

CHAPTER 7

WHEN the king dwelt in his house, and the LORD had given him rest from all his enemies,

2 The king said to Nathan the prophet, See now, I dwell in a house of cedar, but the ark of God dwells within curtains.

3 And Nathan said to the king, Go, do all that is in your heart; for the LORD is with you.

4 ¶And it came to pass that very night, the word of the LORD came to Nathan, the prophet, saying,

5 Go and tell my servant David, Thus says the LORD, You shall not build me a house for me to dwell in;

6 Because I have not dwelt in a house since the day that I brought up the children of Israel out of Egypt, to this day, but I have moved in tents.

7 In all the places where I have walked with all the children of Israel, have I spoken to any of those whom I commanded to feed my people Israel, saying, Why have you not built me a house of cedar?

8 Now therefore shall you say to my servant David, Thus says the LORD of hosts: I took you from the sheepfold, from following the sheep, to be the ruler over my people Israel;

9 And I have been with you wherever you went, and I have destroyed

all your enemies from before you, and I will make for you a great name, like the name of the great men that are on the earth.

10 Moreover I will appoint a place for my people Israel, and will plant them and make them to dwell in their own place in peace and be disturbed no more; neither shall wicked men enslave them any more, as formerly.

11 From the day that I commanded you to be a judge over my people Israel, I have given you rest from all your enemies. Also the LORD declares to you that he will make you a house.

12 ¶And when your days are fulfilled and you shall sleep with your fathers, I will raise up your offspring after you, who shall come out of your loins, and I will establish his kingdom.

13 He shall build a house for my name, and I will establish the throne of his kingdom for ever.

14 I will be like a father to him and he shall be like a son to me. If he commit folly, I will chasten him with the rod of men and with the stripes of the children of men;

15 But my mercy I will not take from him, as I took it from Saul who was king before you, and whom I put away from before me.

16 And your house and your kingdom shall be established for ever before me; your throne shall be established for ever.

17 According to all these words and according to all this vision, so did Nathan the prophet speak to David.

18 ¶Then King David went in and sat before the LORD, and he said, Who am I, O LORD God? And what is my house, that thou hast elevated me to this place?

19 And is this yet a small thing in thy sight, O LORD God, that thou hast spoken also concerning thy servant's descendants for a great while to come? Is this for the guidance of men, O LORD God?

20 And what more can thy servant David say to thee? For thou knowest thy servant, O LORD God.

21 For thy word's sake and according to thine own heart hast thou done

all these great things, to make thy servant know them.

22 Therefore thou art great, O LORD God; for there is none like thee, neither is there any God besides thee, according to all that we have heard with our ears.

23 And is there a nation on the earth like thy people Israel, whom God saved to be a people for himself and to make him a name and to do for him great and notable deeds upon the earth, as he had done in former days for thy people whom thou savedst for thyself out of Egypt, a people whose God thou art?

24 For thou hast established for thyself thy people Israel to be a people to thee for ever; and thou, O LORD, hast become their God.

25 And now, O LORD God, the word that thou hast spoken concerning thy servant and concerning his house, confirm it for ever, and do as thou hast said.

26 And let thy name be magnified for ever, and let everything be as thou hast said, O LORD of hosts, the God of Israel; and let the house of thy servant David be established before thee for ever.

27 For thou, O LORD of hosts, God of Israel, hast revealed to thy servant, saying, I will build you a house; therefore thy servant has purposed in his heart to pray this prayer before thee.

28 And now, O LORD God, thou art God and thy words are true, for thou hast promised this goodness unto thy servant;

29 Therefore now let it please thee to bless the house of thy servant, that it may continue for ever before thee; for thou, O LORD God, hast spoken it; and with thy blessing let the house of thy servant be blessed for ever.

CHAPTER 8

AND it came to pass after this that David smote the Philistines and defeated them; and David took Ramath-gema from the Philistines.

2 And he defeated the Moabites, making them lie down on the ground, and measured them with a line; and

he measured two lines to be put to death and one full line to keep alive. And so the Moabites became David's servants and brought tribute.

3 ¶Then David defeated Hadarezer, the son of Rehob, king of Zobah, as he went to have dominion at the river Euphrates.

4 And David took from him one thousand and seven hundred chariots and twenty thousand footmen; and David destroyed all the chariots, but reserved of them one hundred chariots.

5 And when the Edomites and the Arameans of Damascus came to help Hadarezer king of Zobah, David slew of the Edomites twenty-two thousand men.

6 Then David put governors in Edom and in Damascus; and the Edomites became servants to David and brought tribute. And the LORD preserved David wherever he went.

7 And David took the shields of gold that were on the servants of Hadarezer;

8 And from Tebah and from Berothai, cities of Hadarezer, King David took a great quantity of brass and brought it to Jerusalem.

9 ¶And when Toa king of Hamath heard that David had defeated all the army of Hadarezer,

10 Then Toa sent Joram his son to King David to salute him and to bless him, because he had fought against Hadarezer and defeated him; for Hadarezer was a warlike man. And Joram the son of Toa took with him vessels of silver and vessels of gold and vessels of brass; and brought them to David;

11 These also King David dedicated to the LORD, with the silver and gold that he had dedicated from all the nations which he had subdued,

12 From Edom, Moab, the Ammonites, the Philistines, the Amalekites, and from the dominion of Hadarezer, son of Rehob, king of Zobah.

13 And David fought there when he returned, after he had defeated Edom in the Valley of Salt, killing eighteen thousand men.

14 ¶And David appointed governors throughout all Edom, and all the Edomites became David's servants. And the LORD preserved David wherever he went.

15 And David reigned over all Israel, and executed judgment and justice to all his people.

16 And Joab the son of Zoriah was over the army; and Jehoshaphat the son of Ahilud was recorder;

17 And Zadok the son of Ahitub, the Gelionite, and Abiathar the son of Ahimeleck were priests, and Seraiah was the scribe;

18 And Benaiah the son of Jehoiada was over both the nobles and the laborers, and David's sons were the princes.

CHAPTER 9

AND David said, Is there yet any one left of the house of Saul, that I may show kindness to him for Jonathan's sake?

2 Now there was of the house of Saul a servant whose name was Ziba. And they called him to David, and the king said to him, Are you Ziba? And he said, I am your servant.

3 And the king said to him, Is there any one still left of the house of Saul, that I may show kindness to him for the sake of God? And Ziba said to the king, There is yet a son left to Jonathan, who is lame in his feet.

4 And the king said to him, Where is he? And Ziba said to the king, Behold, he is in the house of Machir, the son of Gammir, in Lo-debar.

5 ¶Then King David sent and took him from the house of Machir, the son of Gammir, from Lo-debar.

6 Now when Mephibosheth, the son of Jonathan, the son of Saul, was come to David, he fell on his face and did obeisance. And David said to him, Mephibosheth. And he answered, Behold your servant!

7 ¶And David said to him, Fear not; for I will surely show you kindness for Jonathan your father's sake, and I will restore to you all the land of Saul your father; and you shall eat bread at my table continually.

8 And he bowed himself and said,

What is your servant, that you should look upon me? For I am like a dead dog.

9 ¶Then the king called to Ziba and said to him, All that belonged to Saul and to all his house I have given to your master's son.

10 You therefore and your sons and your servants shall till the land for him, and you shall bring in food for your master's son, that he may eat; but Mephibosheth your master's son shall eat bread always at my table. Now Ziba had fifteen sons and twenty servants.

11 Then Ziba said to the king, Whatever my lord the king commands his servant, so shall your servant do. So Mephibosheth ate bread at the king's table, as one of the king's sons.

12 And Mephibosheth had a little son, whose name was Micha. And all who dwelt in the house of Ziba were servants to Mephibosheth.

13 So Mephibosheth dwelt in Jerusalem; for he ate continually at the king's table; and he was lame in both his feet.

CHAPTER 10

AFTER this the king of the Ammonites died, and Hanun his son reigned in his stead.

2 Then said David, I will show kindness to Hanun the son of Nahash, as his father showed kindness to me. So David sent by his servants to comfort him for his father. And David's servants came to the land of the Ammonites.

3 And the princes of the Ammonites said to Hanun their lord, Do you think that David is honoring your father, that he has sent comforters to you? Has not David rather sent his servants to you to spy out the city and to explore it and to overthrow it?

4 Wherefore Hanun took David's servants and shaved off the one-half of their beards and cut off their garments in the middle as far as their buttocks, and sent them away.

5 When they told it to David, he sent to meet them, because the men were greatly ashamed; and the king said to them, Tarry at Jericho until your beards have grown and then return.

6 ¶And when the Ammonites saw that they had acted foolishly toward David, the Ammonites sent and hired the Arameans of the son of Rehob and the Arameans of the son of Zobah, twenty thousand footmen, and of the king of Maacah a thousand men and of Ish-tob twelve thousand footmen.

7 And when David heard of it, he sent Joab and all the host of the mighty men.

8 And the Ammonites came out and set their men in battle array at the entrance of the gate of Edom the son of Rehob; and the forces of Aram the son of Zobah and Ish-tob and Maacah were by themselves in the field.

9 When Joab saw that the battle was set against him both in the front and in the rear, he selected the choice men of Israel and put them in array against Aram;

10 And the rest of the people he placed in the charge of Abishai his brother, and he put them in array against the Ammonites.

11 And he said to Abishai his brother, If the Arameans prove too strong for me, then you shall help me; but if the Ammonites prove too strong for you, then I will come and help you.

12 Be of good courage, and let us fight for the sake of our people and for the sake of the cities of our God; and the LORD will do what is good in his sight.

13 And Joab and the people who were with him drew near to battle against the Arameans, and they fled before him.

14 And when the Ammonites saw that the Arameans had fled, then they fled also before Abishai and entered into the city. So Joab returned from fighting against the Ammonites and came to Jerusalem.

15 ¶And when the Arameans saw that they were defeated before Israel, they gathered themselves together.

16 And Hadarezer sent and brought out the Arameans that were beyond

the river Euphrates; and they came to Helam; and Shobach the general of Hadarezer's army went before them.

17 And when it was told David, he gathered all Israel together and crossed the Jordan and came to Helam. And the Arameans set themselves in array against David, and David fought against them.

18 And the Arameans fled before Israel; and David destroyed one thousand and seven hundred chariots of the Arameans and slew four thousand horsemen and a great many of the people, and he smote Shobach the general of their army, who died there.

19 And when all the kings who were servants of Hadarezer saw that they were defeated before Israel, they made peace with Israel and served them. So the Arameans feared to help the Ammonites any more.

CHAPTER 11

AFTER the year expired, at the time when the king leaves the palace, David sent Joab and his servants with him and all Israel; and they besieged Rabbath. But David remained in Jerusalem.

2 ¶And it came to pass in the evening that David arose from his bed and walked upon the roof of the king's house; and he saw a woman bathing; and the woman was very beautiful to look upon.

3 And David sent and inquired about the woman. And one said, She is Bathsheba, the daughter of Ahinam, the wife of Uriah the Hittite.

4 So David sent a messenger and took her; and she came in to him and he lay with her; and that very day she had cleansed herself after her menstruation; and she returned and went to her house.

5 And the woman conceived, and sent and told David and said to him, I am with child.

6 ¶And David sent to Joab, saying, Send me Uriah the Hittite. And Joab sent Uriah to David.

7 And when Uriah came to him,

David asked of Uriah about Joab and about the people and about the war.

8 Then David said to Uriah, Go down to your house and wash your feet. And Uriah went out of the king's house, and there followed him a present from the king.

9 But Uriah slept at the door of the king's house beside all the servants of his lord, and did not go down to his house.

10 And when they told David that Uriah did not go down to his house, David said to Uriah, Behold, you have come from a journey, why then did you not go down to your house?

11 And Uriah said to David, The ark of the covenant of the LORD, and Israel, and Judah dwell in tents, and my lord Joab and the servants of my lord are encamped in the open fields; shall I then go to my house, to eat and to drink and to lie with my wife? No. As you live and as your soul lives, I will not do this thing.

12 And David said to Uriah, Remain here today also, and tomorrow I will send you away. So Uriah remained in Jerusalem that day.

13 And the next day David called him and ate before him, and he did drink, and got drunk; and in the evening he went out and slept beside the servants of his lord, but he did not go down to his house.

14 ¶And in the morning, David wrote a letter to Joab, and sent it by the hand of Uriah.

15 And he wrote in the letter, Set Uriah in the forefront of the battle, and then retire from him that he may be smitten and die.

16 So when Joab besieged the city, he assigned Uriah to a place where he knew that valiant men were.

17 And the men of the city went out and fought with Joab; and there fell some of the people of the servants of David; and Uriah the Hittite died also.

18 ¶Then Joab sent and told David all that took place in the battle;

19 And Joab charged the messenger, saying, When you have finished telling everything which took place in the battle to the king,

20 And if the king's wrath rise and he say to you, Why did you approach so near to the city to fight against it? Did you not know that they would shoot from the wall?

21 Who killed Abimeleck the son of Nedo-baal? Did not a woman cast a piece of a millstone upon him from the wall, that he died? Why did you go near the wall? Now if he should say these things to you, then you shall say to him, Your servant Uriah the Hittite is dead also.

22 ¶So the messenger went and came and told David all that Joab had charged him to say.

23 And the messenger said to David, The men prevailed against us and came out against us into the field, and we chased them back to the entrance of the city.

24 And the archers shot from the wall; and some of your servants died, O king! And your servant Uriah the Hittite is dead also.

25 Then David said to the messenger, Thus shall you say to Joab, Let not this thing displease you, for things happen this way or that way in the battle; make the battle more vigorous against the city, and take it and destroy it.

26 ¶And when the wife of Uriah the Hittite heard that her husband was dead, she mourned for her husband.

27 And when the days of her mourning were over, David sent and brought her to his house, and she became his wife and bore him a son. But the thing that David had done displeased the LORD.

CHAPTER 12

AND the LORD sent Nathan the prophet to David. And he came to him and said to him, There were two men in a certain city, the one rich and the other poor.

2 The rich man had exceedingly many flocks and herds;

3 But the poor man had nothing but one little ewe lamb which he had bought; and it lived together with him and with his children; it did eat of his food and drink from his cup and lie in his bosom, and it was to him like a daughter.

4 And there came a guest to the rich man, and he refused to take of his own herds or flocks to make a banquet for the guest who had come to him, but he took the poor man's ewe lamb and prepared it for the guest who had come to him.

5 And David's anger was greatly kindled against the man; and he said, As the LORD lives, the man who has done this thing is worthy of death;

6 And he shall restore the ewe lamb fourfold because he did this thing and because he had no pity.

7 ¶And Nathan said to David, You are the man. Thus says the LORD God of Israel, I anointed you king over my people Israel and I delivered you out of the hands of Saul,

8 And I gave you your master's daughters and your master's wives into your bosom, and I also gave you the daughters of Israel and of Judah; and if they were too few you should have told me, and I would have added to you twice that many.

9 Why have you despised the commandment of the LORD and have done that which is evil in the sight of the LORD? You have killed Uriah the Hittite with the sword and have taken his wife to be your wife and have slain him with the sword of the Ammonites.

10 Now therefore the sword shall not depart from your house for ever; because you have despised me and have taken the wife of Uriah the Hittite to be your wife.

11 Thus says the LORD, Behold, I will raise up evil against you out of your own house, and I will take your wives before your eyes and give them to your neighbor, and he shall lie with them in the broad daylight.

12 For you did it secretly; but I will do this thing in the sight of all Israel, in the daytime.

13 And David said to Nathan, I have sinned against the LORD. And Nathan said to David, The LORD also has put away your transgression; you shall not die.

14 Nevertheless, because by this deed you have made the enemies of the LORD to boast, the son also that is born to you shall surely die.

15 ¶Then Nathan went to his house. And the LORD struck the child that the wife of Uriah the Hittite bore to David, and it was very sick.

16 David therefore besought God for the child; and David fasted and went in and lay all night on the ground.

17 And the elders of his household arose and tried to raise him up from the ground, but he would not, neither did he eat bread with them.

18 And it came to pass on the seventh day that the child died. And the servants of David feared to tell him that the child was dead; for they said, Behold, while the child was yet alive, we spoke to him, and he would not listen to us; how then shall we tell him now that the child is dead? He may react violently.

19 But when David saw that his servants were whispering, David perceived that the child was dead; therefore he said to his servants, Is the child dead? And they said, He is dead.

20 Then David arose from the earth, and washed and anointed himself, and changed his garments and went into the house of the LORD and worshipped; then he came to his own house and asked for food, and they set it before him and he did eat.

21 Then his servants said to him, What is this that you have done? While the child was still alive, you were fasting and praying, but when he was dead, you did rise up and eat food.

22 David said to them, While the child was still alive, I fasted and prayed; for I said, Who knows whether God will be gracious to me, and let the child live?

23 But now he is dead, why should I fast? Can I bring him back again? I shall go to him, but he cannot return to me.

24 ¶And David comforted Bathsheba his wife, and went in to her and lay with her; and she bore a son, and

she called his name Solomon; and the LORD loved the child.

25 Then he sent for Nathan the prophet; and he named the child Jedidah because the LORD loved him.

26 ¶And Joab fought against Rabbath of the children of Ammon, and took the royal city.

27 And Joab sent messengers to David and said, I have fought against Rabbath and I have also taken the royal city.

28 Now therefore gather the rest of the people together, and come and encamp against the city and take it; lest I take the city, and it shall be called after my name.

29 So David gathered all the people together and went against Rabbath, and fought against it and took it.

30 And he took their king's crown from off his head; the weight of it was a talent of gold, and in it were precious stones; and it was set on David's head. And he brought forth the spoil of the city in great abundance.

31 And he brought forth the people who were in it, and put them in iron bands and in chains, and made them pass through the measuring line; and thus did he to all the cities of the Ammonites. Then David and all the people returned to Jerusalem.

CHAPTER 13

AND it came to pass after this, that Absalom the son of David had a sister whose name was Tamar; and Amnon the son of David loved her.

2 And Amnon was much grieved on account of his sister Tamar; for she was a virgin; and Amnon felt unable to say anything to her.

3 But Amnon had a friend whose name was Jonadab, the son of Shimeah David's brother; and Jonadab was a very wise man.

4 And he said to Amnon, O son of the king why are you so losing weight from day to day? Will you not tell me? And Amnon said to him, I love Tamar, my brother Absalom's sister.

5 And Jonadab said to him, Lie down on your bed and pretend that you are sick; and when your father

comes to see you, say to him, Let my sister Tamar come and give me food to eat and make me a couple of cakes in my sight, that I may see it and eat it from her hand.

6 ¶So Amnon lay down and pretended to be sick; and when the king came to see him, Amnon said to the king, Let Tamar my sister come and make me a couple of cakes in my sight that I may eat from her hand.

7 Then David sent for Tamar, and said to her, Go now to your brother Amnon's house and prepare food for him.

8 So Tamar went to her brother Amnon's house; and he was lying down. And she took dough and kneaded it and baked cakes.

9 And she took the cakes and placed them before him; but he refused to eat. And Amnon said, Let every one go out from the house. And they went out every man from the house.

10 And Amnon said to Tamar, Bring the food into the chamber that I may eat from your hands. And Tamar took the cakes which she had made and brought them into the chamber to Amnon her brother.

11 And when she had brought them to him to eat, he took hold of her and said to her, Come lie with me, my sister.

12 And she answered him, No, my brother, do not treat me shamefully; for no such folly ought to be done in Israel;

13 And as for me, where shall I carry my shame? And as for you, you would be reckoned as one of the fools in Israel. Now therefore, speak to the king; for he will not withhold me from you.

14 But he would not listen to her; but, being stronger than she, he forced her and lay with her and disgraced her.

15 ¶Then Amnon hated her exceedingly; so that the hatred with which he hated her was greater than the love with which he had loved her. And Amnon said to her, Arise, be gone.

16 And she said to him, So now, since you have done this great evil to

me, you send me away? But he would not listen to her.

17 Then he called his servant who ministered to him, and said to him, Put now this woman out of my house, and bolt the door after her.

18 And Tamar took ashes and put them on her head,

19 And she tore the embroidered garment which she wore; then she laid her hands on her head, and went away crying mournfully.

20 And Absalom her brother said to her, Has Amnon your brother lain with you? But hold now your peace, my sister; he is your brother; do not take this deed to your heart. So Tamar remained horrified in the house of Absalom her brother.

21 ¶But when King David heard all these things, he was exceedingly displeased.

22 And Absalom spoke to his brother Amnon neither good nor bad; for Absalom hated Amnon because he had forced his sister Tamar.

23 ¶Now from season to season, Absalom had sheepshearers in Baal-hazor, which is near Ephraim; and Absalom invited all the king's sons.

24 And Absalom came to the king and said to him, Behold now your servant has sheepshearers; let the king and his servants go with your servant.

25 And the king said to him, No, my son, let us not all now go lest we be burdensome to you. And he pressed him, but he would not go with him, but he blessed him.

26 Then said Absalom, Why should not my brother Amnon go with me? The king said to him, Why should he go with you?

27 But Absalom pressed him that he should let Amnon and all the king's sons go with him.

28 ¶Then Absalom commanded his servants, saying, Mark when Amnon's heart is merry with wine, and when I say to you, Smite Amnon and kill him, fear not; have I not commanded you? Be courageous and be valiant.

29 So the servants of Absalom did to Amnon as Absalom had commanded them. Then all the king's

sons arose, and every man mounted his mule and fled.

30 ¶And while they were on the way, the news came to David that Absalom had murdered all the king's sons and there was not one of them left.

31 Then the king arose and tore his garments and lay on the earth; and all his servants stood by with their clothes rent.

32 And Jonadab, the son of Shimeah David's brother, said to him, Let not my lord the king think that all the king's sons are dead; for Amnon alone is dead; for Absalom had been determined to do this from the day that Amnon forced his sister Tamar.

33 Now therefore let not my lord the king think that all the king's sons are dead; for Amnon alone is dead.

34 But Absalom fled. And the watchman lifted up his eyes and looked, and behold, many people were coming by the way on the side of the mountain.

35 And Jonadab said to the king, Behold, the king's sons come; as your servant said, so it is.

36 And as soon as he had finished speaking, behold, the king's sons came and lifted up their voices and wept; and the king and all his servants also wept bitterly.

37 ¶But Absalom fled, and went to Talmai, the son of Ammihud, the king of Geshur. And David mourned for his son many days.

38 So Absalom fled and went to Geshur, and was there three years.

39 And King David longed to go forth after Absalom; for he was comforted concerning Amnon, seeing he was dead.

CHAPTER 14

NOW Joab the son of Zoriah perceived that the king's heart was reconciled toward Absalom.

2 And Joab sent to Tekoah, and fetched from thence a wise woman and said to her, Pretend to be a mourner and put on mourning apparel, and do not anoint yourself with oil, but be as a woman who has been mourning many days for the dead;

3 And come to the king and speak in this manner to him. So Joab prepared the words and put them in her mouth.

4 ¶And when the woman of Tekoah came to the king, she fell on her face to the ground, and did obeisance and said, Deliver me, O my lord the king.

5 And the king said to her, What ails you? And she answered, I am indeed a widow, my husband is dead.

6 And your handmaid had two sons, and they two quarrelled together in the field, and there was none to part them, and one was stronger than the other and slew him.

7 And behold, the whole family is risen against your handmaid, and they say, Deliver to us the man who slew his brother that we may kill him for the life of his brother whom he slew; so they want to destroy the heir also; moreover they want to quench the spark of life which is left for me, that they may not leave to his father either name or family upon the earth.

8 And the king said to her, Go to your house, and I will give orders concerning you.

9 But the woman of Tekoah said to the king, My lord, O king, let this iniquity be on me and on my father's house; and the king and his throne be guiltless.

10 And the king said to her, Whosoever says anything to you, bring him to me and he shall not touch you any more.

11 Then she said, Let my lord the king remember that the LORD your God would not suffer the avengers of blood to destroy any more, wherefore let them not destroy my son. And the king said to her, As the LORD God lives, there shall not one hair of your son fall to the earth.

12 Then the woman said, Let your handmaid speak a word to the king, and he said to her, Speak.

13 And the woman said to him, Why then have you thought such a thing against the people of God? And why do you speak, O king, as one who is guilty, in that, O king, you do not bring back your lost one?

14 For we will all surely die, and we are as water that is poured upon the ground, which cannot be gathered up again; neither does God destroy a soul, but devises means that no man should go astray from him.

15 Now therefore if I have spoken this thing to my lord the king, it is because the people have made me afraid; and your handmaid said, I will now speak to the king; it may be that the king will deliver his handmaid from the hand of men,

16 That they may not destroy me and my son together from the heritage of God.

17 Then your handmaid said, The word of my lord the king shall now be confirmed and shall be like an offering; for as an angel of God, so is my lord the king to discern good and evil; therefore the LORD your God will be with you.

18 Then the king answered and said to the woman, Do not hide from me anything that I ask you. And the woman said to him, Let my lord the king now speak.

19 And the king said, Is not the hand of Joab with you in all this? And the woman answered and said to him, As your soul lives, my lord the king, I have not turned to the right hand or to the left from all that my lord the king has spoken; for it was your servant Joab who bade me, and he put all these words in the mouth of your handmaid,

20 Because he wanted to do it through me, that is why your servant Joab has done this thing; and my lord is wise, according to the wisdom of an angel of God, to know all things that are on the earth.

21 ¶And the king said to Joab, Behold now, I have done as you have said; go therefore, bring me the young man Absalom again.

22 And Joab fell on his face to the ground and did obeisance and blessed the king: and Joab said, Today your servant knows that I have found grace in your sight, my lord, O king, in that the king has fulfilled the request of his servant.

23 So Joab arose and went to Geshur and brought Absalom to Jerusalem.

24 And the king said, Let him go to his own house, but let him not be seen in my presence. So Absalom went to his own house and did not see the king's face.

25 ¶Now in all Israel there was no man so much praised for his beauty as Absalom; from the sole of his foot to the crown of his head there was no blemish in him.

26 And when he had his hair shorn (he used to cut it once a year because it was heavy on him, therefore he cut it), the hair of his head weighed two hundred shekels by the king's weight.

27 And there were born to Absalom three sons and one daughter, whose name was Tamar; she was a beautiful woman.

28 ¶So Absalom dwelt two years in Jerusalem, and saw not the king's face.

29 Therefore Absalom summoned Joab to send him to the king; but he would not come to him; and he sent a second time, but he would not come.

30 Then Absalom said to his servants, See, there is a field belonging to Joab near mine; whether it be of wheat or barley, go and set it on fire. And Absalom's servants set Joab's field on fire.

31 Then Joab arose and came to Absalom's house and said to Absalom, Why have your servants set my field on fire?

32 And Absalom answered Joab, Behold, I sent to you, saying, Come here, that I may send you to the king, to ask why I have come from Geshur. It was better for me while I was there; now I want to appear before the king and if there is any iniquity in me, let him kill me.

33 So Joab came to the king and told him the words of Absalom; and he called for Absalom, and Absalom came in before the king and bowed himself on his face to the ground before the king; and the king kissed Absalom.

CHAPTER 15

AND after this, Absalom prepared for himself chariots and horsemen, and fifty men to run before him.

2 And Absalom rose up early and stood beside the king's gate; and it was so that when any man had a case to be tried before the king, then Absalom called him to him, and said, Of what city are you? And he said, Your servant is of one of the tribes of Israel.

3 And Absalom said to him, I see your arguments are good and just; but there is no man deputed by the king to hear you.

4 Absalom said moreover, Oh that I were made a judge in the land, that every man who has a lawsuit or a cause might come to me, and I would do him justice!

5 And whenever a man arose to do him obeisance, he held him by his hand and kissed him.

6 And in this manner did Absalom to all the Israelites who came to the king for judgment; so Absalom stole the hearts of the men of Israel.

7 ¶And it came to pass after four years Absalom said to the king, Let me go and fulfil my vow which I have vowed to the LORD, in Hebron;

8 For your servant made a vow while I abode at Geshur and in Aram, saying, If the LORD will bring me again indeed to Jerusalem, then I will serve the LORD.

9 And the king said to him, Go in peace. So he arose and went to Hebron.

10 ¶But Absalom sent spies throughout all the tribes of Israel, saying, As soon as you hear the sound of the trumpet, then you shall say, Absalom reigns in Hebron.

11 And with Absalom went two hundred men from Jerusalem, but they went innocently, not knowing anything of the plot.

12 And Absalom sent for Ahithophel the Gilonite, David's counsellor, and brought him from his city, from Giloh, while he was offering sacrifices. And the conspiracy grew strong;

and the people increased continually on the side of Absalom.

13 ¶And there came a messenger to David, saying, The hearts of the men of Israel are with Absalom.

14 And David said to all his servants who were with him at Jerusalem, Arise and let us flee; for we shall not else escape from Absalom; make haste to depart, lest he overtake us suddenly and bring evil upon us and smite the city with the edge of the sword.

15 And the king's servants said to the king, Behold, your servants are ready to do whatever our lord the king wants to do.

16 So the king went forth and all his household after him. And the king left ten women who were concubines to keep his house.

17 And the king went forth and all the people after him, and they halted in a place at a distance from the city.

18 And all his servants passed on beside him; and all his noblemen and all his army and all the Gittites who had followed him from Gath passed on before the king.

19 ¶Then said the king to Ittai the Gittite, Why do you also go with us? Depart from the king; for you are a stranger, and also you were brought captive from your country.

20 You came but yesterday, and shall I trouble you today to go with us, seeing I go wherever I may? Return, and make your brethren to settle down; it will be well with you.

21 But Ittai answered the king and said, As the LORD lives and as the king lives, wherever my lord the king shall be, whether in death or life, even there will your servant be also.

22 And David said to Ittai, Go and pass over. So Ittai the Gittite passed over, and all his men and all the little ones that were with him.

23 And all the country wept with a loud voice, and all the people passed over; then the king also passed over the brook Kidron, and all the people passed over toward the way of the wilderness.

24 ¶And behold, Zadok the priest

went also and all the Levites who were with him, bearing the ark of God; and Abiathar went up and stood until all the people had finished passing over from the city.

25 Then the king said to Zadok, Carry back the ark of God into the city; perhaps I shall find favor in the eyes of the LORD, and he will bring me back again and show me both it and his habitation;

26 But if he shall say, I have no delight in you; behold, here I am, let him do to me as seems good in his sight.

27 The king said also to Zadok the priest, Return, go to the city in peace, you and your sons with you, Ahimaaz your son and Nathan the son of Abiathar.

28 See, I will wait in the plain of the wilderness until there come a man from you to inform me.

29 Zadok therefore and Abiathar carried the ark of God back to Jerusalem; and they remained there.

30 ¶And David went up by the ascent of mount Olivet and wept as he went up and had his head covered and all the people who were with him also covered their heads, and they went up on foot, weeping as they went.

31 ¶And they told David, saying, Ahithophel has conspired with Absalom. And David said, O LORD, I pray thee, nullify the counsel of Ahithophel.

32 ¶And when David came to a place where he used to worship God, behold, Hushai the Archite came to meet him with his coat torn and earth upon his head;

33 And David said to him, If you pass on with me, then you will be a burden to me;

34 But if you return to the city, say to Absalom, I am your servant, O king, as I was your father's servant hitherto. And now, I the king, want you to go and defeat the counsel of Ahithophel.

35 Behold, there are with you in the city Zadok and Abiathar the priests. Therefore it shall be that every word you hear from the king's house, you shall tell to Zadok and Abiathar the priests.

36 Behold, they have there with them their two sons Ahimaaz Zadok's son and Nathan Abiathar's son; and by them you shall send to me everything that you can hear.

37 So Hushai, David's friend, came to the city, just as Absalom entered Jerusalem.

CHAPTER 16

AND when David had passed a little beyond the place where he used to worship, behold, Ziba the servant of Mephibosheth came to meet him, with a couple of asses, laden with two hundred loaves of bread and a hundred bunches of raisins and a hundred cakes of figs and a skin of wine.

2 And the king said to Ziba, Where did you get these? Ziba said to him, The asses are to carry the burden of the king's household; and the bread and fig cakes are for the young men to eat, and the wine, that those who faint in the wilderness may drink.

3 And the king said to him, Where is your master's son? Ziba said to him, Behold he remains at Jerusalem; for he said, Today shall the house of Israel restore to me the kingdom of Saul my father.

4 Then David said to Ziba, Behold, all that belonged to Mephibosheth is given to you. And Ziba said to him, I have plenty, and I have found grace in your sight, my lord, O king.

5 ¶And when King David came to Beth-hurim, behold, there came out from there a man of the family of the house of Saul, whose name was Shimei, the son of Gera; he came forth and cursed David;

6 And he threw stones at him and at all his servants and at all his people and at all his servants who were on his right hand and on his left.

7 And thus said Shimei to David when he cursed him, Get out, get out, you bloody man, you wicked man;

8 The LORD has requited upon you

all the blood of the house of Saul, in whose stead you have reigned; and the LORD has delivered the kingdom into the hand of Absalom your son; and, behold, you have been requited for your evil, because you are a bloody man.

9 ¶Then Abishai the son of Zoriah said to David, Why should this dead dog curse my lord the king? Let me go over and take off his head.

10 And King David said to him, What is it to me and to you, O sons of Zoriah? Let him curse, it is the LORD who has told him to curse David. Therefore who can say to me, Why has this happened?

11 And David said to Abishai and to all his servants, Behold, my own son, who came forth from my loins, seeks my life; so now let this Benjamite alone, let him curse; for God has bidden him.

12 It may be the LORD will look on my affliction and requite me good for his cursing this day.

13 And as David and his servants went on the way, Shimei walked along the mountain side opposite him and cursed him as he went and threw stones at him and cast dust at him.

14 And the king and all the people who were with him arrived at their destination weary, and they refreshed themselves there.

15 ¶And Absalom and all the people who were with him and all Israel came to Jerusalem, and Ahithophel with him.

16 And when Hushai the Archite, David's friend, came to Absalom, Hushai said to Absalom, Long live the king! long live the king!

17 And Absalom said to Hushai, Is this your kindness to your friend? Why did you not go with your friend?

18 And Hushai said to Absalom, No; but whom the LORD and this people and all Israel have chosen, with him will I dwell, and his will I be.

19 And again, whom should I serve? I have no choice. As I have served in your father's presence, so will I serve before you.

20 ¶Then Absalom said to Ahitho-phel, Give me counsel, as to what we shall do.

21 And Ahithophel said to Absalom, Go in to your father's concubines, whom he has left to keep his house; and when all Israel shall hear that you have gone in to your father's concubines, then shall the hands of all who are with you be strengthened.

22 So they pitched a tent for Absalom upon the roof; and Absalom went in to his father's concubines in the sight of all Israel.

23 And the counsel of Ahithophel which he gave in those days was as if a man had inquired at the oracle of God; so was all the counsel of Ahithophel both with David and with Absalom.

CHAPTER 17

MOREOVER Ahithophel said to Absalom, Let me now choose twelve thousand men, and I will arise and pursue David this night;

2 And I will overtake him while he is weary and weak, and I will throw him into a panic, and all the people who are with him shall flee, and I will kill the king only;

3 And I will bring back all the people to you, just as those whom you sought have come back; so all the people shall be in peace.

4 And the saying pleased Absalom well, and all the elders of Israel.

5 Then Absalom said, Call now Hushai the Archite also, and let us likewise hear what he has to say.

6 And when Hushai came to Absalom, Absalom said to him, Ahithophel has spoken after this manner; shall we do what he has said? If not, you speak.

7 And Hushai said to Absalom, The counsel that Ahithophel has given is not good at this time.

8 For said Hushai to Absalom, You know well that your father and his servants are mighty men, and they are furious as a bear that devours the prey in the field; moreover, your father is a man of war, and will not spend the night with the people.

9 Behold now, he has hidden in one of the countries or in some other place; and when we attack them according to the first counsel, then the rumor will spread that there has been a great slaughter among the people who follow Absalom.

10 Even though he is valiant and his heart is as the heart of a lion, he shall utterly melt; for all Israel knows that your father is a mighty man and that those who are with him are valiant men.

11 Therefore I counsel that when all Israel is gathered to you from Dan to Beer-sheba, then you yourself march in their midst.

12 So we shall go against him in some place where he shall be found, and we will light upon him as the dew falls on the ground; and of him and of all the men who are with him there shall not be left even one.

13 Moreover, if he should enter into a city, then all Israel shall cast ropes on it, and we will drag it into the valley, and they shall leave there not even a cricket.

14 And Absalom and all the men of Israel said, The counsel of Hushai the Archite is better than the counsel of Ahithophel. For the LORD had decreed to defeat the good counsel of Ahithophel so that the LORD might bring evil upon Absalom.

15 ¶Then Hushai said to Zadok and to Abiathar the priests, Thus and thus did Ahithophel counsel Absalom and all the men of Israel; and thus and thus have I counseled.

16 Now therefore send quickly and tell David, saying, Do not spend the night in the plain of the wilderness, but pass over, lest you and all the people who are with you be destroyed.

17 Now Nathan and Ahimaaz were standing by the side of the fountain of the palace, so they might not be seen to enter the city; and a maidservant went and told them; and they went and told King David.

18 Nevertheless a lad saw them, and told Absalom; but they both went away, and came into the house of a man of Beth-hurim who had a well in his courtyard; and they went down into it.

19 And the woman took and spread a covering over the well's mouth, and put barley upon it; and the thing was not known.

20 And when Absalom's servants came to the woman at the house, they said, Where are Ahimaaz and Nathan? And the woman said to them, They have gone from here, for they wanted water; but when they could not find any, they returned to Jerusalem.

21 And after Absalom's servants had gone, they came up out of the well and went and told King David, and said to him, Arise and cross quickly over the water; for thus has Ahithophel counselled against you.

22 Then David arose and all the people who were with him and they crossed the Jordan; by early morning there was not one left who had not crossed the Jordan.

23 ¶And when Ahithophel saw that his counsel was not followed, he saddled his ass and arose and went home to his city; and he put his household in order and hanged himself and died and was buried in the sepulchre of his father.

24 And David came to Mahanaim. And Absalom crossed the Jordan, he and all the men of Israel with him.

25 ¶And Absalom had appointed Amasa over the army instead of Joab. Amasa was the son of an Israelite whose name was Ithra, who went in to Abigail the daughter of Nahash, sister of Zoriah Joab's mother.

26 So Israel and Absalom encamped in the land of Gilead.

27 ¶When David came to Mahanaim, Abishai, the son of Nahash of Rabbath of the children of Ammon, and Machir the son of Gamil of Lodebar, and Barzillai the Gileadite of Dobelin

28 Brought beds and carpets and earthen vessels and wheat and barley and parched wheat and flour and beans and lentils

29 And honey and butter and sheep and cheese of cows, and offered them to David, and to the people who were

with him, to eat; for they said, The people are hungry and weary and thirsty in the wilderness.

CHAPTER 18

AND David numbered the people who were with him, and set over them commanders of thousands and captains of hundreds.

2 And David placed a third part of the people under the command of Joab, and a third part under the command of Abishai the son of Zoriah, Joab's brother, and a third part under the command of Ittai the Gittite.

3 And the king said to the people, If we surely should flee, the enemy will not care about us; now therefore ten thousand men are enough for us; for it is better for us to receive help from the cities.

4 And the servants of David said to him, We will go forth quickly to fight against them. And the king said to them, Whatever seems good to you, do it. Then the king stood by the side of the gate, and all the people went out by hundreds and by thousands.

5 And the king commanded Joab and Abishai and Ittai, saying, Capture for me the young man Absalom alive. And all the people heard when the king gave orders to all commanders concerning Absalom.

6 ¶So the people went out into the field against Israel;

7 And there was a battle, and the people of Israel were defeated there before the servants of David, and there was a great slaughter on that day of twenty thousand men.

8 For there was a great battle which spread over the face of the country; and the wild beasts of the forest devoured more people that day than the sword devoured.

9 ¶And it happened that Absalom met the servants of David. And Absalom was riding upon a mule, and the mule went under the thick boughs of a great oak, and Absalom's head caught fast in the great oak, and he was hanging between the heaven and the earth; and the mule that was under him went away.

10 And a certain man saw it and told Joab and said, Behold, I saw Absalom hanging in an oak.

11 And Joab said to the man who told him, When you saw him, why then did you not smite him there and throw him to the ground? And I would have given you ten shekels of silver and a garment.

12 And the man said to Joab, Though you should count to me a thousand shekels of silver, I would not put forth my hand against the king's son; for in our hearing the king charged you and Abishai and Ittai, saying, Be careful not to harm the young man Absalom for my sake.

13 And if I should have done it, then I would have been guilty; and nothing would have been hidden from the king, and you yourself would have stood against me.

14 Then Joab said to him, That is not true, I will do it now myself. Then Joab took three darts in his hand and thrust them through the heart of Absalom while he was still alive and hanging from the oak.

15 And ten young men who bore Joab's armor circled about and smote Absalom and slew him.

16 And Joab blew the trumpet, and the people returned from pursuing Israel; for Joab had held back the people.

17 And they took Absalom's body and cast it into a great pit, and raised over it a great heap of large stones; and all Israel fled every man to his tent.

18 ¶Now Absalom in his lifetime had taken and set up for himself a monument in the valley of the kings; for he said, I have no son to keep my name in remembrance; and he called the monument by his own name; and it is called the work of Absalom to this day.

19 ¶Then said Ahimaaz the son of Zadok, Let me now run and bring the good tidings to the king, how the LORD has avenged him of his enemies.

20 And Joab said to him, It is not proper that you bear tidings this day,

but you may bear tidings another day; this day you shall bear no tidings because the king's son is dead.

21 Then Joab said to Cushi, Go tell the king what you have seen; and he ran.

22 Then Ahimaaz the son of Zadok said again to Joab, Why should not I too run after Cushi? And Joab said to him, Why will you run, my son, seeing no one will give you a reward for the tidings?

23 He said to him, What is the difference? Let me run. And he said to him, Run. Then Ahimaaz ran by the way of the plain, and passed Cushi.

24 Now David was sitting between the two gates; and the watchman went up to the roof over the gate to the wall, and he lifted up his eyes and looked, and saw a man running alone.

25 And the watchman called out and told the king. And the king said, If he is alone, there are tidings in his mouth. And he came apace, and drew near.

26 And the watchman drew near toward the gate, and said, Behold, another man is running alone;

27 Moreover the watchman said, I see the running of the first is like the running of Ahimaaz the son of Zadok. And the king said, He is a good man and comes with good tidings.

28 And the king called to Ahimaaz, and said to him, Have you come in peace? And he bowed before the king with his face to the earth, and said, Blessed be the LORD your God, who delivered up the men who lifted their hands against my lord the king.

29 Then the king said, Is the young man Absalom safe? And Ahimaaz answered, I saw a great army arrayed against Joab the servant of my lord the king, but I your servant knew not what was the outcome.

30 And the king said to him, Turn aside and stand here. And he turned aside and stood still.

31 And, behold, Cushi came; and he said, Tidings, my lord the king! for the LORD has avenged you this day from the hand of all those who rose up against you.

32 And the king said to Cushi, Is the young man Absalom safe? And Cushi answered, Let your enemies, my lord the king, and all who rise up against you for evil be as that young man is.

33 ¶And the king was overcome, and went up to his bedchamber and wept; and as he wept, he said, O my son Absalom, my son, my son Absalom! Would that I had died instead of you, O Absalom, my son!

CHAPTER 19

AND it was told Joab, Behold, the king is weeping and mourning for Absalom.

2 And there was mourning that day among all the people; for the people heard that day how the king was grieved for his son.

3 And the people concealed themselves as they entered into the city that day, as people who are ashamed steal away when they flee from battle.

4 But the king covered his face, and cried with a loud voice, saying, O my son Absalom, O Absalom, my son, my son!

5 And Joab came into the king's house and said to him, You have shamed this day the faces of all your servants who this day have saved your life and the lives of all your sons and your daughters and the lives of your wives and the lives of your concubines,

6 Because you have loved your enemies and hated your friends. For you have declared this day that you have neither noblemen nor servants; for this day I perceive that if Absalom were alive and all of us were dead, it would have pleased you better.

7 Now therefore arise, go out and speak comfortingly to your servants; for I swear by the LORD, if you do not go out, not a man will remain with you this night; and this will be worse for you than all the evils that have befallen you from your youth until now.

8 Then the king arose and sat in the gate. And they told all the people, saying, Behold, the king is sitting in

the gate. And all the people came before the king; for Israel had fled every man to his tent.

9 ¶And all the people were thinking in all the tribes of Israel and saying, The king delivered us from the hand of all our enemies and rescued us from the hand of the Philistines; so now let us flee from the land and from following Absalom.

10 And Absalom, whom we anointed and made king over us, is dead in battle. And they said every man to his neighbor, Why therefore hesitate to go back with the king?

11 ¶Come, therefore, let us bring him back to his house. And the words of the Israelites came to the king.

12 And the king said to them, You are my brethren and my flesh and my bones, why then are you the last to return to the king?

13 And he said to Amasa, Behold, you are my flesh and my bone. God do so to me, and more also, if you are not commander of my army permanently instead of Joab.

14 And he swayed the heart of all the men of Judah as one man; so that they sent word to the king, saying, Return you and all your servants.

15 So the king returned and came to the Jordan. And Judah came to Gilgal to meet the king and bring the king over the Jordan.

16 ¶And Shimei the son of Gera, a Benjamite, made haste and came down with the men of Judah to meet King David.

17 And Ziba the servant of Saul and his fifteen sons and his twenty servants with him crossed over and constructed a bridge over the Jordan before the king.

18 And they constructed rafts to bring over the king's household and to do whatever was good in his sight. And Shimei the son of Gera fell down before the king as he was crossing the Jordan;

19 And said to the king, Let not my lord impute iniquity to me, neither remember that which your servant did perversely the day that my lord the king went out of Jeru-

salem; let not my lord the king take it to his heart.

20 For your servant does know that I have sinned; therefore, behold, I have come this day the first of all the house of Joseph to go down to meet my lord the king.

21 But Abishai the son of Zoriah answered and said, Shall not Shimei be put to death for this, because he cursed the LORD's anointed?

22 And David said, What is it to me and to you, you sons of Zoriah, that you should this day be deceivers to me? Shall any man be put to death this day in Israel? For do I not know that I am this day king over Israel?

23 Then the king said to Shimei, You shall not die. And the king swore to him.

24 ¶And Mephibosheth the son of Jonathan, the son of Saul, came down to meet the king, and he had neither trimmed his beard nor changed his clothes, from the day the king departed until the day the king came again in peace.

25 And it came to pass, when he came to Jerusalem to meet the king, the king said to him, Mephibosheth, why did you not go with me?

26 Mephibosheth answered, My lord, O king, my servant deceived me; for I said to him, Saddle me an ass that I may ride upon it and go with my lord the king; because your servant is lame.

27 And my servant has lied about me, O my lord the king; but you, my lord the king, you are as an angel of God; do therefore what is good in your eyes.

28 For all of my father's house were worthy of death before my lord the king; yet you counted your servant among those who eat at your table. Now therefore I cannot justify myself, neither speak before my lord the king.

29 And the king said to him, You have spoken more than enough, I have already commanded that you and Ziba shall divide the fields.

30 And Mephibosheth said to the king, Yea, let him take all the produce also forasmuch as my lord the

25

king has come again in peace to his own house.

31 ¶Now Barzillai the Gileadite came down from Dobelin and went with the king to conduct him over the Jordan.

32 Now Barzillai was a very aged man, eighty years old; and he had provided the king with food while he remained at Mahanaim; for he was a very wealthy man.

33 And the king said to Barzillai, Come along with me, and I will feed you with me in Jerusalem.

34 And Barzillai said to the king, How many years have I to live, that I should go up with the king to Jerusalem?

35 I am this day eighty years old; and I cannot discern between luxury and simple living; neither can your servant taste what he eats or what he drinks. Nor can I hear any more the voice of singing men and singing women. Why then should your servant be a burden to my lord the king?

36 Your servant can hardly cross the Jordan with my lord the king; let not my lord the king recompense me with such a reward.

37 Let your servant turn back again, that I may die in my own city and be buried beside the grave of my father and my mother. But behold here is with you your servant Bimham my son; let him go over with my lord the king, and do you to him what seems good in your sight.

38 And the king said, Bimham shall go over with me and I will do to him that which seems good to you; and whatever you shall ask of me, that will I do for you.

39 And when all the people had crossed the Jordan and the king had crossed also, the king kissed Barzillai and blessed him; and he returned to his own place.

40 Then the king went on to Gilgal, and Bimham went on with him; and all the people of Judah went on with the king, and also half the people of Israel.

41 ¶And, behold, the men of Israel came to the king and said to him, Why have our brethren the men of Judah stolen you away and have brought you over the Jordan and all your household and all men of Judah with you?

42 And all the men of Judah answered and said to the men of Israel, Because the king is near of kin to us; why then are you displeased over this matter? Have we eaten at all at the king's cost? Or has he given us any gifts?

43 And the men of Israel answered the men of Judah, and said, We have ten parts in the king, and we have also more right in David than you; why then did you go ahead of us? We should have been the first to bring back the king. And the words of the men of Judah were fiercer than the words of the men of Israel.

CHAPTER 20

AND there happened to be there a wicked man, whose name was Shamoa, the son of Bichri, a Benjamite; and he blew a trumpet and said, We have no portion in David, neither have we an inheritance with the son of Jesse; every man to his tents, O Israel!

2 So all the men of Israel ceased from following David, and followed Shamoa, the son of Bichri; but the men of Judah remained loyal to the king from the Jordan to Jerusalem.

3 ¶And David came to his house at Jerusalem; and the king took the ten women his concubines whom he had left to keep his house and put them in custody and fed them, but did not go in unto them. So they were shut up to the day of their death, and were like widows.

4 ¶Then said the king to Amasa, Assemble me the men of Judah within three days, and you yourself be present.

5 So Amasa went to assemble the men of Judah; but he tarried longer than the set time which had been appointed.

6 And David said to Joab, Now Shamoa the son of Bichri will do us more harm than did Absalom; take your lord's servants and pursue him,

lest he find him fortified cities, and stay in them and incite a revolt against us.

7 And there went out after him Joab's men, the noblemen and the army and all the mighty men; and they went out from Jerusalem to pursue Shamoa, the son of Bichri.

8 When they were at the great stone which is in Gibeon, Amasa came before them. And Joab was wearing armor, and upon it was a girdle with a sword fastened upon his loins in its sheath; and as Amasa appeared, Joab placed his hand upon his sword.

9 And Joab said to Amasa, Peace be with you, my brother. And Joab took Amasa by the beard with his hand to kiss him.

10 But Amasa took no notice of the sword that was in Joab's hand; so Joab smote him with it in the middle of his body, and let out his bowels to the ground, and struck him not again; and he died. So Joab and Abishai his brother pursued Shamoa, the son of Bichri.

11 And one of Joab's men went and stood by Amasa, and said to those who passed by, To whom do you belong? Are you of the men of David who are after Joab?

12 And Amasa wallowed in his blood, lying in the highway. And when the man saw that all the people stopped to look at him, he dragged Amasa out of the highway and threw him into a field and cast a garment over him, when he saw that every one who came by him stopped.

13 When he was dragged out of the highway, all the people went on after Joab, to pursue Shamoa, the son of Bichri.

14 ¶And they went through all the tribes of Israel to Abel and to Beth-maachah and to Berin; and they went after him.

15 And they came and besieged him in Abel and in Beth-maachah, and they set ambushes against the city, and the city was in distress; and all the people who were with Joab battered the wall to throw it down.

16 ¶Then a wise woman cried out from the wall, saying, Hear, hear, and say to Joab, Come near, that I may speak to you.

17 And when he was come near to her, she said to him, Are you Joab? And he answered, I am he. Then she said to him, Hear the words of your maidservant. And he answered, I do hear.

18 Then she said, They used to say in old time, They first inquire of the prophets, then they destroy.

19 I am of those who have suffered the pangs of childbirth in Israel; you seek to destroy a child and his mother in Israel; why will you swallow up the heritage of the LORD?

20 And Joab answered and said to her, Far be it from me that I should swallow up or destroy.

21 The matter is not so; but a man of mount Ephraim, Shamoa, the son of Bichri by name, has lifted up his hand against King David; deliver him alive to me and I will depart from the city. And the woman said to Joab, Now his head shall be thrown to you over the wall.

22 Then the woman went to all the people in her wisdom. And they cut off the head of Shamoa, the son of Bichri, and threw it out over the wall to Joab. And Joab blew the trumpet, and they withdrew from the city and departed every man to his tent. And Joab returned to Jerusalem to the king.

23 ¶Now Joab was in command of all the army of Israel; and Benaiah the son of Jehoiada was in command of the freedmen and the laborers,

24 And Adoniram was in charge of the tribute, and Jehoshaphat the son of Ahilud was the recorder,

25 And Sheriah was the scribe, and Zadok and Abiathar were the priests,

26 And also Aza of Jathir was a priest to David.

CHAPTER 21

THEN there was a famine in the days of David for three years, year after year; and David inquired of the LORD. And the LORD answered, It is because of Saul and because of his bloody house, because he slew the Gibeonites.

2 So the king called the Gibeonites and said to them (now the Gibeonites were not of the children of Israel, but of the remnant of the Amorites; and the children of Israel had sworn to them, and Saul had sought to slay them in his zeal to cause the children of Israel and Judah to sin),

3 Wherefore David said to the Gibeonites, What shall I do for you? And with what shall I make an atonement to you, that you may bless the heritage of the LORD?

4 And the Gibeonites said to him, It is not silver and gold that Saul and his house owe us; neither do we wish to kill any one in Israel. And he said to them, Whatever you shall say, that will I do for you.

5 And they said to the king, The man who consumed us and planned to destroy us so that we should not remain in all the territory of Israel,

6 Let seven of his sons be delivered to us, and we will sacrifice them before the LORD in Gibeah of Saul. And the king said, I will give them.

7 But the king spared Mephibosheth, the son of Jonathan the son of Saul, because of the LORD's oath that was between them, between David and Jonathan the son of Saul.

8 But the king took the two sons of Rizpah the daughter of Ana, whom she bore to Saul, Armoni and Mephibosheth; and the five sons of Nadab the daughter of Saul, whom she bore to Azriel, the son of Barzillai the Meholathite;

9 And he delivered them to the Gibeonites, and they sacrificed them in the mountain before the LORD; and they fell all seven together, and were slain in the first days of harvest, in the beginning of barley harvest.

10 ¶And Rizpah the daughter of Ana took sackcloth and spread it under her upon the rock, from the beginning of the harvest until water dropped upon them from the heaven, and she did not let the birds of the air rest upon the bodies by day nor the wild beasts of the field by night.

11 And it was told David what Rizpah the daughter of Ana, the concubine of Saul, had done.

12 ¶And David went and took the bones of Saul and the bones of Jonathan his son from the men of Jabesh-gilead, who had stolen them from Rehab of Beth-shan, where the Philistines had hanged them, on the day the Philistines slew Saul in the mountain of Gilboa;

13 And he brought up from thence the bones of Saul and the bones of Jonathan his son; and they gathered the bones of those who were slain;

14 And they buried the bones of Saul and of Jonathan his son in the land of Benjamin in Zelzah, in the sepulchre of Kish his father; and they did all that the king commanded. And after that God was reconciled toward the land.

15 ¶Moreover the Philistines were again at war with Israel; and David went down and his servants with him to fight against the Philistines;

16 But David, Joab, and Abishai were afraid of a giant, the weight of whose breastplate was three hundred shekels of brass, and who was girded with a new sword, and had threatened to slay David.

17 But Abishai the son of Zoriah succored him and smote the Philistine and killed him. Then the servants of David swore to him, saying, You shall go out no more with us to battle, that you may not quench the lamp of Israel.

18 And it came to pass after this, that there was again war with the Philistines at Gath; then Sibbechai the Hushathite slew Saphar, who was of the sons of the giants.

19 And there was again war between Israel and the Philistines, and Elhanan the son of Malap a weaver, a Beth-lehemite, slew a brother of [1] Goliath the Philistine, the staff of whose spear was like a weaver's beam.

20 And there was again war in Gath, where there was a man of great stature, who had on each hand six fingers and on each foot six toes,

---

[1] *Brother* inserted for clarity. There might have been another Goliath.

twenty-four in number; and he also was born to the giants.

21 And when he had defied Israel, Jonathan the son of Shimeah the brother of David slew him.

22 These four were born to the giants in Gath, and fell by the hand of David and by the hand of his servants.

CHAPTER 22

AND David spoke to the LORD the words of this song on the day that the LORD had delivered him out of the hand of all his enemies and out of the hand of Saul;

2 And he said: I will love thee, O LORD my strength and my trust; the LORD is my strength and my fortress and my deliverer,

3 The mighty God in whom I trust; he is my succor and the horn of my salvation, my refuge who delivered me from the wicked men, my glorious Saviour.

4 I will call upon the LORD, and I shall be saved from my enemies.

5 For the pangs of death have compassed me, the torrents of ungodly men made me afraid;

6 The pangs of Sheol compassed me about; the snares of death lay ahead of me;

7 In my distress I called upon the LORD and cried to my God; and he did hear my voice out of his temple, and my cry did enter into his ears.

8 Then the earth shook and trembled; the foundations of the mountains quaked and burst asunder, because he was angry at them.

9 There went up a smoke because of his anger, and fire kindled out of his face; and coals were kindled by it.

10 He bowed the heavens and came down; and darkness was under his feet.

11 And he rode upon a cherub, and did fly; he flew mightily upon the wings of the wind.

12 And he made darkness his pavilion round about him, the dark waters and thick clouds of the skies.

13 Out of the brightness of his shelter he made his clouds hail and coals of fire.

14 The LORD thundered from heaven, and the most High uttered his voice, hail and coals of fire.

15 And he sent out his arrows and scattered them; he increased his lightning and discomfited them.

16 Then the channels of the sea appeared, the foundations of the world were uncovered, at thy rebuke, O LORD, at the blast of the breath of thine anger.

17 He sent from above and took me; he drew me out of many waters;

18 He delivered me from my strong enemies and from them that hated me; for they were too strong for me.

19 They fell upon me in the day of my affliction; but the LORD became my succor.

20 He relieved me from my distress; he delivered me, because he delighted in me.

21 The LORD rewarded me according to my righteousness; according to the cleanness of my hands has he recompensed me.

22 For I have kept the ways of the LORD and have not rebelled against my God.

23 For all his judgments were before me; and his statutes I have not put away from me.

24 I was blameless before him, and have kept myself from my sin.

25 Therefore the LORD has recompensed me according to my righteousness, according to the cleanness of my hands in his sight.

26 With the good man thou wilt show thyself good, with the upright man thou wilt show thyself upright.

27 With the pure thou wilt show thyself pure; and with the perverse thou wilt show thyself perverse.

28 For thou wilt save the afflicted people; and the proud ones thou wilt bring down.

29 For thou wilt light my lamp; O LORD my God, lighten my darkness.

30 For by thee I can run against a band of robbers; by the help of my God I have leaped over a wall.

31 As for God, his way is perfect; the word of the LORD is tried; he succors all who trust in him.

32 For there is no God except the LORD. And there is no one who is mighty but our God.

33 The God who has girded me with strength makes my way perfect.

34 He makes my feet like hart's feet, and makes me stand upon my high places.

35 He teaches my hands to war, and strengthens my arms like a bow of brass.

36 Thou hast also given me the shield of thy salvation, and thy right hand has helped me; thy gentleness has made me great.

37 Thou hast enlarged my steps under me, so that my feet did not slip.

38 I will pursue my enemies and will overtake them, and will not turn back until I have consumed them.

39 I will strike them that they may not arise; yea, they shall fall under my feet.

40 Thou hast girded me with strength for the battle; thou hast made them that rise up against me to be subdued under me.

41 Thou hast also made mine enemies to bend their necks to me, that I might silence those that hate me.

42 They shall cry to the LORD, but there shall be none to save them; they shall seek the LORD, but he shall not answer them.

43 I shall beat them as small as the dust which is carried by the wind; I shall tread upon them as the mire of the streets.

44 Thou hast delivered me from the strivings of the people, thou hast made me the head of the nations; a people whom I have not known shall serve me.

45 Those who give ear shall hearken to me; the sons of strangers shall be obedient to me.

46 Strangers shall halt and be restrained from their ways.

47 The LORD lives; blessed be he who gives me strength; and exalted be God my Saviour.

48 Thou art the God who has given me vengeance and hast brought down the peoples under me

49 And hast delivered me from my enemies; thou also hast exalted me over those who rose up against me; thou hast delivered me from wicked men.

50 Therefore I will give thanks unto thee, O LORD, among the nations, and I will sing praises to thy name.

51 He gives great salvation to his king and shows mercy to his anointed, to David and to his descendants for ever.

CHAPTER 23

NOW these are the last words of David. David the son of Jesse, the anointed one whose rule has been established, the one whom the God of Jacob has made the sweet psalmist of Israel said,

2 The Spirit of the LORD spoke by me and his word is upon my tongue.

3 The God of Israel said, the Mighty One of Israel spoke to me: He who governs men must be righteous, ruling over those who revere God.

4 He is like the light of the morning when the sun rises, even a morning without clouds, before dawn, a morning free from rain which makes the grass to spring up.

5 Is not my house so with God? For he has made with me an everlasting covenant, ordered in all things and sure; for it is he who fulfils all my desire and all my decrees.

6 ¶But the ungodly are all like hard thorns, for they cannot be gathered with hands;

7 But when a man comes near them, he gathers them with the handle of an axe and with iron; and they are utterly burned with fire in the same place.

8 ¶These are the names of the mighty men whom David had: seated in the first seat, in the third rank, his name was Gadho, a man who went down and slew eight hundred men in one hour.

9 Next to him was Eleazar, the cousin of Gadho, who went down with David and three other men when

the Philistines defied them and were gathered there to battle; and when the men of Israel withdrew,

10 He arose, and smote the Philistines until his hand was weary, and his hand clave to his sword; and the LORD wrought a great victory that day; and the people returned with him only to strip the slain.

11 And next to him was Shammah, the son of Agee, from the king's mountain. When the Philistines were gathered together to plunder cattle where there was a piece of ground full of lentils and the people fled from the Philistines,

12 He stood in the midst of the field and delivered the cattle and slew the Philistines; and the LORD wrought a great victory by his hand.

13 And three of the valiant men went down and came to David in the harvest time to the cave of Arlam; and the Philistines' cattle were grazing in the Plain of Giants.

14 And David was then staying in the stronghold, and the princes of the Philistines were encamped in Bethlehem.

15 And David longed for water and said, O that one would give me a drink of water from the great well which is in the city of Beth-lehem!

16 So the three valiant men broke through the camp of the Philistines and drew water out of the great well which is in the city of Beth-lehem, and took it and brought it to David; but he would not drink of it, but poured it out before the LORD.

17 And he said, Far be it from me, on account of the LORD, that I should do this; because these men went at the risk of their lives. Therefore he would not drink it. These things did these three valiant men.

18 And Abishai, the brother of Joab, the son of Zoriah, was chief of thirty men. And he lifted up his spear against three hundred and slew them.

19 And he was honored above the thirty men; therefore he became their chief and performed heroic deeds equal to thirty men.

20 And Benaiah the son of Jehoiada was a mighty man of Kabzeel who had performed good acts; he slew two mighty men of Moab and went down also and slew a lion in the midst of a forest in time of snow;

21 And he slew an Egyptian, a handsome man; and the Egyptian had a spear in his hand; but he went down against him with a staff, and seized the spear out of the Egyptian's hand and slew him with his own spear.

22 These things did Benaiah the son of Jehoiada, and he was renowned among the thirty men.

23 He performed heroic deeds equal to thirty men. And David set him over his guard.

24 Ashael, the brother of Joab, was one of the thirty;

25 Also Shammah of the king's mountain,

26 And Helez the Paltite, Ira the son of Ikkesh the Tekoite,

27 Abiezer the Anethothite, Mebunai the Hushathite,

28 Zalmon of the mount House, Mahar of Netophath,

29 Heleb the son of Baana a Netophathite, Ittai the son of Ribai of Ramtha of the children of Benjamin,

30 Benaiah the son of Pirathon of Gibeah, Hiddai of the Brooks of Gaash,

31 Abi the son of Abialemon the Gileadite, Arboth of Horim,

32 Alhana the Shaalbonite, Jonathan of the house of Nashor,

33 Shammah of the mount of Olives, Ahiam the son of Ashdad of Edri,

34 Eliphelet the son of Ahasbai the Maachathite, Eliam the son of Ahithophel the Gilonite,

35 Hezrai the Carmelite, Gadai the Arbite,

36 Negael the son of Nathan of Zobah, Baana the Gadite,

37 Zelek the Ammonite, Nahari the Beerothite, the armorbearer of Joab the son of Zoriah,

38 Hira the Ithrite, Arab of Lachish,

39 And Uriah the Hittite: the serv-

ants of David were thirty-seven in all.

CHAPTER 24

AND again the anger of the LORD was kindled against Israel, and he incited David against them and said to him, Go, number Israel and Judah.

2 So the king said to Joab the commander of the army who was with him, Go now through all the tribes of Israel, from Dan to Beer-sheba and number the people, and bring to me the sum of the number of the people.

3 And Joab said to the king, May the LORD your God add to the people a hundredfold, howsoever many they be, so that the eyes of my lord the king may see it; but why does my lord the king delight in this thing?

4 Notwithstanding the king's word prevailed against Joab and against the commanders of the army. And Joab and the commanders of the army went out from the presence of the king to number the people of Israel.

5 ¶And they crossed the Jordan and came to Sharob, which is on the right side of the city that lies in the midst of the valley of Gad and toward Eleazer;

6 Then they came to Tyre and Zidon, to the land of the Canaanites and the land of the Hittites and the land of the Jebusites,

7 And when they had gone through the whole land, they came to the land of Judah in thirty-eight days. Then they came to Dan, and circled Zidon.

8 And when they had gone through all the land, they came to Jerusalem at the end of nine months and twenty days.

9 And Joab brought the sum of the number of the people to the king; and there were in Israel eight hundred thousand valiant men who drew the sword; and the men of Judah were five hundred thousand men.

10 ¶But David's heart smote him after he had numbered the people. And David said to the LORD, I have sinned greatly in what I have done;

and now, I beseech thee, O LORD, for I have done very foolishly.

11 When David arose in the morning, the word of the LORD came to the prophet Gad, saying,

12 Go and say to David, Thus says the LORD: I will bring upon you one of three calamities; choose one of them, that I may do it to you.

13 So the prophet Gad came to David and said to him, These are the calamities which may come upon you: there shall seven years of famine come in your land, or you shall flee three months before your enemies while they pursue you, or there shall be three days of pestilence in your land. Now therefore say what answer I shall return to him who sent me to you.

14 Then David answered and said to the prophet Gad, I am greatly distressed; it is better for me to be punished by the hand of the LORD our God; for his mercies are great; let us not be punished by the hand of men.

15 ¶So the LORD sent a pestilence upon Israel from the morning until the evening; and there died of the people from Dan to Beer-sheba seventy thousand men.

16 And when the angel stretched out his hand toward Jerusalem to destroy it, the LORD restrained the angel of death who was destroying the people, and said to him, You have destroyed enough, stay now your hand. And the angel of the LORD was standing by the threshing floor of Aran the Jebusite.

17 Then David spoke to the LORD when he saw the angel who smote the people, and said to the angel, I have sinned and I have given provocation; but these innocent sheep, what have they done? Let thy hand be against me, and against my father's house.

18 ¶And Gad the prophet came that day to David and said to him, Go up and build an altar to the LORD in the threshing floor of Aran Jebusite.

19 And David went up, according to the word of Gad, as the LORD had commanded him.

20 And when Aran the Jebusite turned back and saw the king and his servants coming toward him, Aran fell down and did obeisance to the king with his face to the ground.

21 And Aran said, Why has my lord the king come to his servant? And David said to him, To buy the threshing floor from you, to build an altar to the LORD, that the plague may be stayed from the people.

22 Then Aran said to David, Let my lord the king take what seems good to him; behold, here are the oxen for the burnt offering, and the ploughshare and the yokes for fuel.

23 All these things did Aran give to King David. And Aran said to the king, May the LORD your God bless you.

24 And the king said to Aran, No, but I will surely buy it from you for a price; and I will not offer burnt offerings to the LORD my God of that which cost me nothing. So David bought the threshing floor by the garden and the oxen for fifty shekels of silver.

25 And David built there an altar to the LORD, and offered burnt offerings and peace offerings. So the LORD was entreated for the land, and the plague was stayed from Israel.

THE FIRST BOOK OF THE

KINGS

commonly called

THE THIRD BOOK OF THE KINGS

CHAPTER 1

NOW King David was old and well advanced in years; and they covered him with clothes, but he could not get warm.

2 Wherefore his servants said to him, Behold, your servants are before you, let them seek for our lord the king a young virgin; and let her wait upon the king, and let her minister to him, and let her lie in your bosom, that our lord the king may get warm.

3 So they sought for a beautiful maiden throughout all the territory of Israel, and found Abishag a Shilommite, and brought her to the king.

4 And the maiden was very beautiful, and she became the king's attendant and ministered to him; but the king knew her not.

5 ¶Then Adonijah the son of Haggith exalted himself, saying, I will be king; and he prepared for himself chariots and horsemen, and fifty men to run before him.

6 And his father had never rebuked him at any time by saying, Why have you done so? And he also was a very handsome man; and his mother bore him after Absalom.

7 And he conferred with Joab the son of Zoriah and with Abiathar the priest; and they followed Adonijah and helped him.

8 But Zadok the priest and Benaiah the son of Jehoiada and Nathan the prophet and Shimei and Rei and the mighty men who belonged to David were not with Adonijah.

9 And Adonijah sacrificed sheep and oxen and fat cattle by the great stone which is by En-kasra, and he invited

all his brothers, the king's sons, and all the men of Judah and the king's servants;

10 But he did not invite Nathan the prophet; and Benaiah, the son of Jehoiada; and David's mighty men; and Solomon his brother;

11 ¶Wherefore Nathan the prophet said to Bath-sheba the mother of Solomon, Have you not heard that Adonijah has become king, and David our lord does not know it?

12 Now therefore come, let me give you counsel, that you may save your own life and the life of your son Solomon.

13 Go and get you in to the King David and say to him, Did you not my lord, O king, swear to your handmaid, saying, Solomon your son shall reign after me, and he shall sit upon my throne? Why then does Adonijah reign?

14 And, while you are still speaking there in the presence of the king, I also will come in after you and confirm your words.

15 ¶So Bath-sheba went in to King David into the chamber; and the king was very old; and Abishag the Shilommite ministered to the king.

16 And Bath-sheba bowed and did obeisance to the king. And the king said to her, What troubles you, Bathsheba?

17 She said to him, My lord the king, you swore by the Lord your God to your handmaid, saying, Solomon your son shall reign after me and he shall sit upon my throne.

18 And now, behold, Adonijah reigns; and you, my lord the king, do not know it;

19 And he has sacrificed oxen and fat cattle and sheep in abundance, and has invited all the sons of the king and Abiathar the priest and Joab the general of the army; but Nathan the prophet; Benaiah, the son of Jehoiada; and Solomon your servant he has not invited.

20 And you, my lord, O king, the eyes of all Israel are upon you, that you should tell them who shall sit on the throne of my lord the king after him.

21 Otherwise it shall come to pass, when my lord the king shall sleep with his fathers in peace, I and my son Solomon shall be counted offenders.

22 ¶And, while she was still speaking there before the king, Nathan the prophet also came in.

23 And they told the king, saying, Behold Nathan the prophet has come. And when he was come in before the king, he bowed himself before the king with his face to the ground and did obeisance.

24 And Nathan said, My lord, O king, have you said, Adonijah shall reign after me and he shall sit upon my throne?

25 For he has gone down this day and has sacrificed oxen and fat cattle and sheep in abundance, and has invited all the king's sons and the commanders of the army and Abiathar the priest; and, behold, they are eating and drinking before him and saying, Long live King Adonijah!

26 But me, even me your servant, and Zadok the priest; and Benaiah, the son of Jehoiada; and your servant Solomon he has not invited.

27 Has this thing been done by the order of my lord the king, and you have not told your servants who should sit on the throne of my lord the king after him?

28 ¶Then King David answered and said, Call me Bath-sheba. And she came into the king's presence and stood before him.

29 And the king swore to her, and said, As the Lord lives, who has saved my soul out of all distress,

30 Even as I swore to you by the Lord God of Israel, saying, Solomon your son shall reign after me and he shall sit upon my throne, even so will I do this day.

31 Then Bath-sheba bowed with her face to the earth and did obeisance to the king, and said, Let my lord King David live for ever.

32 ¶And King David said, Call me Zadok the priest; and Nathan the prophet; and Benaiah, the son of Jehoiada. And they came before the king.

33 And the king said to them, Arise, take with you the servants of your lord, and cause Solomon my son to ride upon my own mule, and take him down to Shilokha;

34 And let Zadok the priest and Nathan the prophet anoint him there king over Israel; and blow with the trumpet, and say, Long live King Solomon.

35 Then you shall come after him, and he shall sit upon my throne; for he shall be king in my stead; I have appointed him to be king over Israel and over Judah.

36 And Benaiah the son of Jehoiada answered and said before the king, Amen; so may the LORD your God do.

37 As the LORD has been with my lord the king, even so may he be with Solomon, and make his throne greater than the throne of my lord King David.

38 So Zadok the priest and Nathan the prophet and Benaiah, the son of Jehoiada and the archers and the slingers went down and caused Solomon to ride upon King David's mule, and took him to Shilokha.

39 Then Zadok the priest and Nathan the prophet took a horn of oil out of the tabernacle and anointed Solomon. And they blew the trumpet; and all the people said, Long live King Solomon.

40 And all the people came up after him, and the people played on tambourines and rejoiced with great joy, so that the earth was shaken with their noise.

41 ¶And Adonijah and all the guests who were with him heard it as they finished eating. And when Joab heard the sound of the trumpet, he said, What is this noise of the city being in an uproar?

42 And while he was still speaking, behold, Nathan the son of Abiathar the priest came; and Adonijah said to him, Come in; for you are a valiant man, and you bring good tidings.

43 And Nathan answered and said to Adonijah, Truly our lord King David has made Solomon king.

44 And the king has sent with him

Zadok the priest; and Nathan the prophet; and Benaiah, the son of Jehoiada; and the archers; and the slingers, and they have caused Solomon to ride upon the king's mule;

45 And Zadok the priest and Nathan the prophet have anointed him king in Shilokha; and they are come up from there rejoicing, so that the whole city is rejoicing. This is the noise that you have heard.

46 And also Solomon sits on the throne of the kingdom.

47 And moreover the king's servants came to bless our lord King David, saying, May the LORD your God make the name of Solomon better than your name, and make his throne greater than your throne. And the king bowed himself upon his bed.

48 And also thus said the king, Blessed be the LORD God of Israel, who has given me a son to sit upon my throne this day, my own eyes seeing it.

49 Then all the guests who were invited by Adonijah were afraid, and rose up and went every man his way.

50 ¶And Adonijah feared because of Solomon, and arose and went and took hold of the horns of the altar.

51 And it was told King Solomon, saying, Behold, Adonijah is afraid because of you, and, lo, has taken refuge on the horns of the altar, saying, Let King Solomon swear to me this day that he will not slay his servant with the sword.

52 And Solomon said, If he will show himself to be a worthy man, there shall not a hair of his head fall to the earth; but if wickedness shall be found in him, he shall die.

53 So King Solomon sent, and they brought him down from the altar. And he came and did obeisance to King Solomon; and Solomon said to him, Go to your house.

CHAPTER 2

NOW the days of David to die drew near; and he charged Solomon his son, saying,

2 I go the way of all the earth; be

strong therefore, and show yourself a man;

3 And keep the charge of the LORD your God, and walk in his ways and keep his statutes, his commandments, his judgments, and his testimonies, as it is written in the law of Moses, that you may prosper in all that you do and succeed wherever you go;

4 That the LORD may establish his word which he spoke concerning me, saying, If your children take heed to their ways, to walk before me in truth with all their heart and with all their soul, there shall not fail you a man on the throne of Israel.

5 Now, you know also what Joab the son of Zoriah did to me, and what he did to the two commanders of the armies of Israel, to Abner the son of Ner and to Amasa the son of Jether, whom he slew and considered them as though they were in the battle, and shed their blood with the sword that was about his loins and trampled upon it with the shoes that were on his feet.

6 Do to him therefore according to your wisdom, and let not his hoary head go down to the grave in peace.

7 But show kindness to the sons of Barzillai the Gileadite, and let them be of those who eat at your table; for so they ministered to me in everything when I fled from Absalom your brother.

8 And, behold, you have with you Shimei the son of Gera, of the tribe of Benjamin, of the house of Horim, who cursed me with grievous curses on the day when I went to Mahanaim; but he came down to meet me at the Jordan and I swore to him by the LORD, saying, I will not put you to death with the sword.

9 Now therefore hold him not guiltless; for you are a wise man, and know what you ought to do to him; and bring his folly on his head; and you shall bring down his hoary head with blood to Sheol.

10 So David slept with his fathers and was buried in the city of David.

11 And the time that David reigned over Israel was forty years; seven years he reigned in Hebron, and

thirty-three years he reigned in Jerusalem.

12 ¶Then Solomon sat upon the throne of David his father; and his kingdom was firmly established.

13 ¶And Adonijah the son of Haggith came to Bath-sheba the mother of Solomon. And she said to him, Have you come in peace? And he said, In peace.

14 Then he said to her, I have something to say to you. And she said to him, Say on.

15 And he said to her, You know that the kingdom rightly was mine, and that all Israel were looking forward to me me to be king over them; but the kingdom was taken from me and is become my brother's; for it was his from the LORD.

16 And now I make one petition of you, do not refuse me. And she said to him, Say on.

17 And he said to her, Speak to King Solomon (for he will not refuse you) that he give me Abishag the Shilommite to wife.

18 And Bath-sheba said, Very well; I will speak for you to the king.

19 ¶Bath-sheba therefore went to King Solomon to speak to him for Adonijah. And the king rose up to meet her and bowed himself to her and then sat on his throne, and they brought a chair for the king's mother; and she sat on his right hand.

20 Then she said, I desire one small petition of you; do not refuse me. And the king said to her, Ask on, my mother; for I will not refuse you.

21 And she said to him, Let Abishag the Shilommite be given to Adonijah your brother to wife.

22 And King Solomon answered and said to his mother, Why do you ask Abishag the Shilommite for Adonijah? Ask for him the kingdom also; for he is my elder brother; ask even for him and for Abiathar the priest and for Joab the son of Zoriah.

23 Then King Solomon swore by the LORD, saying, God do so to me, and more also, if Adonijah have not spoken this word against his own life.

24 Now therefore, as the LORD lives, who has established me and set me on the throne of David my father, and who has made me a house as he promised, Adonijah shall be put to death this day.

25 And King Solomon sent Benaiah the son of Jehoiada, and he attacked him and slew him.

26 And to Abiathar the priest the king said, Go to Anathoth, to your own fields; for you are worthy of death; but I will not at this time put you to death because you bore the ark of the LORD before David my father and because you have been afflicted in all wherein my father was afflicted.

27 So Solomon expelled Abiathar from being priest to the LORD; that the word of the LORD might be fulfilled which he spoke concerning the house of Eli in Shiloh.

28 ¶Now when the news reached Joab that Adonijah had been slain (for Joab had been leaning toward Adonijah and he was not leaning toward Solomon), Joab fled to the tabernacle of the LORD and took refuge on the horns of the altar.

29 And it was told King Solomon that Joab had fled to the tabernacle of the LORD and had taken refuge on the horns of the altar. Then Solomon sent Benaiah the son of Jehoiada, saying, Go and attack him.

30 And Benaiah came to the tabernacle of the LORD and said to him, Thus says the king, Come forth. But he said, No, I will not go out; but I will die here. And Benaiah brought the king word, saying, Thus said Joab, and thus he answered me.

31 And the king said to him, Do to him as he has said, and attack him and kill him, that you may take away the innocent blood, which Joab shed, from me and from the house of my father.

32 And the LORD shall return his blood upon his own head, because he attacked two men more righteous and better than he and slew them with the sword, my father David not knowing of it; namely, Abner the son of Ner, commander of the army of Israel;

and Amasa the son of Jether, commander of the army of Judah.

33 Their blood shall therefore return upon the head of Joab and upon the head of his descendants for ever; but to David and to his descendants and to his house and to his throne shall there be peace for ever from the LORD.

34 So Benaiah the son of Jehoiada went up and attacked him and slew him; and he was buried in his own sepulchre in the wilderness.

35 ¶Then King Solomon appointed Benaiah the son of Jehoiada in his stead over the army; and Zadok the priest the king appointed in the place of Abiathar.

36 ¶And the king sent and called for Shimei, and said to him, Build yourself a house in Jerusalem and dwell there, and do not go forth from there hither and thither.

37 For on the day that you go out and cross the brook Kidron, you shall know for certain that you shall surely die; your blood shall be upon your own head.

38 And Shimei said to the king, The saying is good; as my lord the king has said, so will your servant do. So Shimei dwelt in Jerusalem many days.

39 And it came to pass at the end of three years that two of the servants of Shimei ran away to Achish the son of Maachah king of Gath. And they told Shimei, saying, Behold, your servants are in Gath.

40 And Shimei arose and saddled his ass, and went to Gath to Achish to seek his servants; and Shimei went and brought his servants from Gath.

41 And it was told King Solomon that Shimei had gone from Jerusalem to Gath and had returned.

42 And the king sent and called for Shimei, and said to him, Did I not make you to swear by the LORD, and witnessed against you, saying, Know for certain, on the day that you go out of Jerusalem and cross the brook Kidron, you shall surely die? And you said to me, The saying is good, so will I do.

43 Why then have you not kept the

oath of the LORD and the commandment that I have charged you with?

44 The king said moreover to Shimei, You know all the evil of which your heart is conscious that you did to David my father; therefore the LORD shall return your wickedness upon your own head;

45 And King Solomon shall be blessed, and the throne of David shall be established before the LORD for ever.

46 So the king commanded Benaiah the son of Jehoiada; and he went out and attacked him so that he died. And the kingdom was established in the hand of Solomon.

CHAPTER 3

AND Solomon became the son-in-law to Pharaoh king of Egypt, and took Pharaoh's daughter and brought her into the city of David, until he had finished building his own house and the house of the LORD and the wall of Jerusalem round about.

2 The people sacrificed only in high places, because there was no house yet built to the name of the LORD, until those days.

3 And Solomon loved the LORD, walking in the statutes of David his father; only he sacrificed and burned incense on the high places.

4 And the king went to Gibeon to sacrifice there; for that was the great high place; a thousand burnt offerings did Solomon offer upon the altar which was in Gibeon.

5 ¶Then the LORD appeared to Solomon in a vision by night; and God said to him, Ask that which I should give you.

6 And Solomon said, Thou hast shown to thy servant David my father great mercy, according as he walked before thee in truth and in faithfulness and in uprightness of heart with thee; and thou hast kept for him this great kindness that thou hast given him a son to sit on his throne as it is this day.

7 And now, O LORD God, thou hast made thy servant king in place of David my father; and I am but a little child; I know not how to go out or come in among thy people, whom thou hast chosen,

8 A great people that cannot be numbered nor counted for multitude.

9 Give therefore to thy servant an understanding heart to judge thy people and to discern between good and bad; for who is able to judge this thy so great a people?

10 And it pleased the LORD because Solomon had asked this thing.

11 And the LORD said to Solomon, Because you have asked this thing and have not asked for yourself riches, neither have you asked the lives of your enemies nor have you asked for yourself long life, but have asked for yourself wisdom to discern judgment;

12 Behold, I have done according to your words; lo, I have given you a wise and understanding heart, so that there has been none like you before you, neither shall any arise after you like you.

13 And I have also given you that which you have not asked, both riches and honor, so that there shall not be any among the kings like you all your days.

14 And if you will walk in my ways, to keep my statutes and my commandments, as your father David did walk, then I will lengthen your days.

15 And Solomon awoke; and, behold, it was a dream. And he came to Jerusalem and stood before the ark of the covenant of the LORD and offered up burnt offerings and peace offerings, and made a feast for all his servants.

16 ¶Then came there two women who were harlots to plead before King Solomon.

17 And one of them said, I beseech you, O my lord, I and this woman dwelt in one house; and I was delivered of a child with her in the house.

18 And on the third day after I was delivered, this woman was delivered also; and we were together in the house; there was no stranger with us, only we two in the house.

19 And this woman's child died in the night because she lay on it.

20 And she arose at midnight and took my son from beside me while your handmaid slept, and laid it in her bosom, and laid her dead son in my bosom.

21 And when I rose in the morning to nurse my son, behold, it was dead; but when I had examined it in the morning, behold, it was not my son which I had borne.

22 And the other woman said, It is not so; but the living is my son, and the dead is your son. And this one said, It is not so; the dead is your son, and the living is my son.

23 And the other woman said, It is not so, the living is my son and the dead is your son. Thus they argued before the king.

24 Then the king said, Bring me a sword. And they brought a sword before the king.

25 And the king said, Divide the living child in two, and give half to the one and half to the other.

26 Then the woman whose child was alive said to the king, because her affections yearned for her son, I beseech you, O my lord, give her the child alive, and in no wise slay it. But the other said, Let it be neither mine nor yours, but divide it in two.

27 Then the king answered and said, Give the child alive to the first woman and in no wise slay it; she is the mother thereof.

28 And all Israel heard of the judgment which the king had judged; and they feared the king; for they saw that the wisdom of God was in him, to do justice.

CHAPTER 4

SO Solomon was king over all Israel.

2 And these were the princes whom he had: Azariah the son of Zadok the priest;

3 Elihoreph and Ahiah, the sons of Shisha, scribes; Jehoshaphat the son of Ahilud, the recorder.

4 And Benaiah the son of Jehoiada was over the army; and Zadok and Abiathar were priests;

5 And Azariah the son of Nathan was over the governors; and Zabur, the son of Nathan, the priest, was the king's friend;

6 And Abinshar was over the household; and Adoniram the son of Abda was over the tribute.

7 ¶And Solomon had twelve governors over all Israel, who provided food for the king and his household and for the army; each month of the year it fell on one of them to supply provisions.

8 And these are their names: the son of Hur, who ruled in mount Ephraim;

9 The son of Dekar, in Makaz, and in Shaalbim, and Beth-shemesh, and Elon-beth-hanan;

10 The son of Hesed, in Raboth; to him belonged Socoth, and all the land of Hepher;

11 The son of Abinadab, in Naphatdor, who had Taphath the daughter of Solomon to wife;

12 Baana the son of Ahilud, who ruled in Taanach and Megiddo, and in all Beth-shean, which is beside Zartan, below Jezreel, from Beth-shean to Abel-meholah, as far as the other side of Nekemaam;

13 The son of Geber, in Ramoth-gilead; to him belonged the towns of Jair the son of Manasseh; to him also belonged the region of Argob, which is in Bashan, sixty great cities with walls and bronze bars;

14 Ahinadab the son of Iddo, in Mahanaim;

15 Ahimaaz was in Naphtali; he also took Basmath the daughter of Solomon to wife;

16 Baana the son of Hushai was in Asher and in Aloth;

17 Jehoshaphat the son of Paroh, in Issachar;

18 Shimei the son of Elah, in Benjamin;

19 Geber the son of Uri was in the land of Gilead, the country of Sihon king of the Amorites and of Og king of Bashan; and the governors ruled in the land.

20 ¶Judah and Israel were as many in multitude as the sand which is by the sea; they ate and drank and made merry.

21 And Solomon ruled over all the kingdoms from the river which is in the land of the Philistines as far as the border of Egypt; and his subjects brought presents and served Solomon all the days of his life.

22 ¶And Solomon's provision for one day was thirty measures of fine flour and sixty measures of meal,

23 Ten fat oxen and twenty oxen out of the pastures and a hundred sheep, besides harts and gazelles and roebucks and fatted fowls.

24 For he had dominion over all the region on this side of the river, from Tiphsah even to Azzah,[1] over all the kings on this side of the river; and he had peace on all sides round about him.

25 And Judah and Israel dwelt safely, every man under his vine and under his fig tree, from Dan even to Beer-sheba, all the days of Solomon.

26 ¶And Solomon had forty thousand stalls of horses for his chariots and twelve thousand horsemen.

27 And those governors supplied provisions for King Solomon and for all who came to King Solomon's table, every man in his month; they lacked nothing.

28 Barley also and straw for the horses and the dromedaries they brought to the place where the officers were, every man as it was his due.

29 ¶And God gave Solomon wisdom and understanding exceeding much, and largeness of heart,

30 So that Solomon's wisdom excelled the wisdom of all the people of the east and all the wisdom of the Egyptians.

31 For he was wiser than all men; than Ethan the Easterner, and Heman, and Calcol and Darda, the sons of Mahol; and his fame was in all the nations round about.

32 And he spoke three thousand proverbs; and his songs were a thousand and five.

33 And he spoke of trees, from the cedar tree that is in Lebanon even to the hyssop that springs out of the wall; he spoke also of beasts and of fowl and of creeping things and of fishes.

34 And there came men from all nations to hear the wisdom of Solomon, from all kings of the earth; and he received presents from all kings of the earth who had heard of his wisdom.

CHAPTER 5

AND Hiram king of Tyre sent his servants to Solomon; for he had heard that they had anointed him king in place of his father; for Hiram was always a lover of David.

2 And Hiram sent to Solomon and blessed him. And Solomon sent to Hiram, saying,

3 You know how David my father could not build a house to the name of the LORD his God because of the wars which were about him on every side, until the LORD put his enemies under the soles of his feet.

4 But now the LORD my God has given me rest on every side, so that there is neither adversary nor evil occurrence.

5 And, behold, I purpose to build a house to the name of the LORD my God, as the LORD spoke to David my father, saying, Your son, whom I will set upon your throne in your place, shall build a house to my name.

6 Now therefore command that they cut for me cedar trees out of Lebanon; and my servants shall be with your servants; and I will give you wages for your servants according to all that you shall ask; for you know that there is no one among us who has the skill to cut timber like the Zidonians.

7 ¶And when Hiram heard the words of Solomon, he rejoiced greatly, and said, Blessed be the LORD this day, who has given to David a wise son over this great people.

8 And Hiram sent to Solomon, saying, I have heard the things for which you have sent to me; and I will do all your desire concerning timber of cedar and timber of fir.

9 My servants shall bring them down from Lebanon to the sea, and

1 Or Gaza.

I will convey them by sea in floats to the place that you shall appoint me, and I will cause them to be discharged there, and you shall receive them from there; and you shall also accomplish my desire in giving food for my household.

10 So Hiram gave Solomon cedar trees and fir trees according to his desire.

11 And Solomon gave Hiram twenty thousand measures of wheat for food for his household and twenty thousand measures of pure oil; thus gave Solomon to Hiram year by year.

12 And the LORD gave Solomon wisdom, as he promised him; and there was peace between Hiram and Solomon always, and they two made a league together.

13 ¶And King Solomon raised a levy out of all Israel; and the levy was thirty thousand men.

14 And he sent them to Lebanon, ten thousand a month by turns; a month they were in Lebanon and two months at home; and Adoniram was in charge of the levy.

15 And Solomon had seventy thousand men who bore burdens and eighty thousand hewers of stone in the mountain,

16 Besides the chiefs of Solomon's officers who were set over the work, three thousand and three hundred, who were in charge of the people doing the work.

17 And the king commanded and they brought great stones, costly stones, and hewed stones to complete the house.

18 And Solomon's builders and Hiram's builders and the stonemasons did hew them; so they prepared stones and timber for the building of the house.

CHAPTER 6

AND it came to pass in the four hundred and eightieth year after the children of Israel were come out of the land of Egypt, in the fourth year of Solomon's reign over Israel, in the month of May, which is the second month, that he began to build the house of the LORD.

2 And the house which Solomon built for the LORD was in length sixty cubits and in breadth twenty cubits and in height thirty cubits.

3 And the porch in front of the door of the temple was twenty cubits long, the same as the breadth of the house; and ten cubits was the depth before the length of the house.

4 And for the house he made windows of narrow lights.

5 ¶And against the wall of the house he built rooms encircling the wall of the house, both of the temple and of the Holy of Holies; and he made side rooms round about.

6 The lowest chamber was five cubits broad, and the middle was six cubits broad, and the third was seven cubits broad; for outside in the wall of the house he made narrowed copings round about in order that the walls should be fastened together.

7 And the house, when it was building, was made of stones hewn before they were brought thither; so that there was neither hammer nor axe nor any tool of iron heard in the house while it was building.

8 The door of the middle chamber was on the south side of the house; and it went up with winding stairs into the middle chamber, and out of the middle into the third.

9 So he built the house and finished it; and roofed the house with beams and boards of cedar.

10 And then he built additional rooms against the whole house, five cubits high, and they were fastened to the house with timbers of cedar.

11 ¶And the word of the LORD came to Solomon, saying,

12 Concerning this house which you are building, if you will walk in my statutes and execute my judgments and keep all my commandments to walk in them, then I will perform my word with you, which I spoke to David your father;

13 And I will dwell among the children of Israel, and I will not forsake my people Israel.

14 So Solomon built the house and finished it.

15 And he covered the walls of the

house within with boards of cedar, from the floor of the house, to the rafters of the ceiling; and he covered them on the inside with wood, and he covered the floor of the house with boards of cypress.

16 And Solomon built twenty cubits in extent on the sides of the house, both the floor and the walls with boards of cedar; and he built within it the Holy of Holies.

17 And the house, that is, the inner sanctuary, was forty cubits long.

18 And the house was covered within with cedar, which was carved with buds and open flowers; all was cedar; there was no stone seen in it.

19 And the holy place he made in the inner part of the house, to set there the ark of the covenant of the LORD.

20 And the length of the holy place was twenty cubits, and the breadth was twenty cubits, and the height was twenty cubits; and he overlaid it with pure gold; and he covered the altar with gold.

21 And Solomon overlaid the house within with pure gold; and he made a doorpost in front of the sanctuary, and overlaid it with gold.

22 And the whole house he overlaid with gold, until all the house was finished; also the whole altar that was in the sanctuary he overlaid with gold.

23 ¶And within the sanctuary he made two cherubim of olive wood, each ten cubits high.

24 And five cubits was the one wing of the cherub, and five cubits the other wing of the cherub, ten cubits from the tip of the one wing to the tip of the other.

25 And the other cherub was ten cubits; both cherubim were of the same measure and the same size.

26 The height of the one cherub was ten cubits, and so was it of the other cherub.

27 And he set the cherubim within the inner house; and the wings of the cherubim were stretched forth so that the wing of one touched the one wall, and the wing of the other cherub touched the other wall; and

their wings touched each other in the middle of the house.

28 And he overlaid the cherubim with pure gold.

29 And he carved all the walls of the house round about with ornaments; and he fashioned carved ornaments and cherubim and palm trees and open flowers, within and without.

30 And the floor of the house he overlaid with gold, within and without.

31 ¶And for the entrance of the sanctuary he made doors of olive wood; the lintel and the doorposts were strongly fastened.

32 The two doors also were of olive wood; and he carved upon them figures of cherubim, and carved ornaments and palm trees and open flowers; and he overlaid them with gold, and spread gold upon the cherubim and upon the palm trees.

33 So also he made for the door of the temple, posts of olive wood, plain and square.

34 And the two doors were of fir wood; the two leaves of the one door were ornamented, and the two leaves of the other door were ornamented.

35 And he carved on them cherubim and palm trees and open flowers, and covered them with gold overlaid upon the carved work.

36 ¶And he built the inner court with three rows of hewn stone and a row of cedar beams.

37 ¶In the fourth year was the foundation of the house of the LORD laid, in the month of May;

38 And in the eleventh year, in the month Tishrin, which is the eighth month, was the house finished throughout all its parts, and according to all the fashion of it. So he was seven years in building it.

CHAPTER 7

BUT Solomon took thirteen years to build his own house and to finish it.

2 ¶He built also the house of the forest of Lebanon; its length was a hundred cubits and its breadth fifty cubits and its height thirty cubits.

upon four rows of cedar pillars, with cedar beams upon the pillars.

3 And it was covered with cedar above upon beams that lay upon forty-five pillars, fifteen in a row.

4 And there were balconies in three rows set one against another in three tiers.

5 And all the doors and posts were square, set one against another in three tiers.

6 ¶And he made a porch of pillars; its length was fifty cubits, its breadth thirty cubits; and the porch was upon the pillars, with a court in front.

7 ¶Then he made a porch for the throne where he might judge, even the porch of judgment; and covered it with cedar from the floor to the ceiling.

8 ¶And his own house where he dwelt was in another court within the porch, and was of like workmanship. Solomon also made a house like this in workmanship for Pharaoh's daughter, whom he had taken to wife.

9 All these were of costly stones, according to the measures of hewn stones, sawed with saws within and without, even from the foundation to the coping, and from the outside to the court of the temple.

10 And the foundation was of great and costly stones, some of ten cubits and some of eight cubits.

11 And above were costly stones, after the measures of hewn stones, and cedars.

12 And the great court round about was made with three rows of hewn stones and a row of cedar beams, both for the inner court of the house of the LORD and for the porch of the house.

13 ¶And King Solomon sent and brought Hiram from Tyre.

14 He was a widow's son of the tribe of Naphtali, and his father was an artist and a worker in brass; and he was filled with wisdom and understanding and cunning knowledge to fashion any work in brass. And he came to King Solomon and did all his work.

15 He cast two pillars of brass; the height of each pillar was eighteen cubits and the circumference was twelve cubits.

16 And he made two capitals of molten brass to set upon the tops of the pillars; the height of one capital was five cubits, and the height of the other was five cubits;

17 And he made carved ornaments of network and wreaths of chain work for the capitals which were upon the top of the pillars; seven for one capital and seven for the other.

18 And he made the pillars, and two rows of buds round about upon one network, to cover the capitals that were upon the top of the pillars; and he did so to the other pillar.

19 And the capitals that were upon the top of the pillars were of lily work in the porch, four cubits.

20 And the capitals that were upon the two pillars had pomegranates also above, and over against the side which was by the network; and the pomegranates were two hundred in rows round about upon the one capital; and in like manner the other capital.

21 And he made the pillars of the porch of the temple; and he set up the pillar on the right hand, and called its name Jachin; and he set up the pillar on the left hand, and called its name Boaz.

22 And upon the top of the pillars was lily work; so was the work of the pillars finished.

23 ¶Then he made a molten sea,[1] ten cubits in diameter; it was round about, and its height was five cubits and its circumference thirty cubits.

24 And under the brim of it round about there were buds encircling it, ten in a cubit, enclosing the sea; the buds were formed in two rows when it was cast.

25 It stood upon twelve oxen, three looking toward the north, three looking toward the west, three looking toward the south, and three looking toward the east; and the sea was set upon them, and their hinder parts were inward.

26 And its thickness was a hand-

[1] A large basin used for ceremonial washing.

breadth, and its brim was made like the brim of a cup, with lilies; it contained two thousand baths.[1]

27 ¶And he made ten bases of brass; four cubits was the length of one base, and four cubits its breadth, and three cubits the height of it.

28 And the work of the bases was in this manner: they had borders between panels;

29 And on the borders that were between the panels were lions, oxen, and cherubim; and upon the panels was the same, both above and below, lions and oxen; the appearance of the work was beautiful.

30 And every base had four bronze wheels and axles of brass; and the four corners thereof had a framework under the laver joined to it, framework molten, beautiful work.

31 And the opening of the base within was a cubit; and its opening was round like the work of the base, a cubit and a half; and also upon the opening of it were engravings with borders foursquare, not round.

32 And under each border were four wheels; and the axletrees of the wheels were joined to the base; and the height of a wheel was a cubit and a half.

33 And the work of the wheels was like the work of a chariot wheel; their axletrees and their spokes and their rims and their hubs were all cast.

34 And there were four supports at the four corners of one base; and the supports were part of the very base itself.

35 The supports and the frame of the base were half a cubit; and on the top of the base there was a rim; and the top of the base, its axletrees, and its borders were of the same.

36 And on the plates of the axletrees and on its borders he engraved cherubim, lions, and palm trees round about.

37 After this manner he made the ten bases: all of them were of one casting, one measure, and one size.

38 ¶Then he made ten lavers of brass; one laver held forty baths; and every laver was four cubits; and

upon every one of the ten bases one laver.

39 And he put five bases on the right side of the house and five on the left side of the house; and he set the sea on the right side of the house, toward the south.

40 ¶And Hiram made the lavers and the pots and the cauldrons and the large hanging pots. So Hiram finished all the work that King Solomon made in the house of the LORD;

41 The two pillars, and the two bowls of the capitals that were on the top of the two pillars; and the two networks to cover the two bowls of the capitals which were upon the top of the pillars;

42 And four hundred pomegranates for the two networks, two rows of pomegranates for each network to cover the two bowls of the capitals that were upon the pillars;

43 And the ten bases and the ten lavers upon the bases;

44 And the one sea and the twelve oxen under the sea;

45 And the pots and the cauldrons and the hanging pots; and all the vessels of ministration which Hiram made for King Solomon for the house of the LORD were of Corinthian brass.

46 In Kakar which is in the plain of Jericho by the side of the Jordan did the king cast them, in the clay ground between Succoth and Zarthan.

47 And Solomon made all sorts of vessels, exceeding many; there was no limit to the weighing of the brass which King Solomon used for the house of the LORD;

48 And he made all the vessels that pertained to the house of the LORD: the altar of gold, and the table of gold whereupon the shewbread was,

49 And the candlesticks of pure gold, five on the right side and five on the left before the sanctuary, the snuffers, and the lamps, and the tongs of gold,

50 And the bowls, and the saucers, and the basons, and the spoons, and the censers of pure gold; and the hinges of pure gold, both for the

---

[1] A *bath* is about ten gallons.

doors of the inner house, the most holy place, and for the doors of the house of the temple.

51 Thus was ended all the work that King Solomon made in the house of the LORD. And Solomon brought in the things which David his father had dedicated; the silver and the gold and the vessels, and placed them among the treasures of the house of the LORD.

CHAPTER 8

THEN Solomon assembled all the tribes of Israel, all the heads of the tribes, and the chiefs of the fathers, to him in Jerusalem to bring up the ark of the covenant of the LORD out of the city of David, which is Zion.

2 And all the men of Israel assembled themselves to King Solomon at the feast in the month of the harvest, which is the seventh month.

3 And all the tribes of Israel came, and the priests took up the ark of the LORD.

4 And they brought it up to the temple of the LORD, and brought the tabernacle of the congregation and all the holy vessels that were in the tabernacle, and the priests and the Levites of Israel went up with them.

5 And King Solomon and all the congregation of Israel that were assembled to him were with him before the ark, sacrificing sheep and oxen that could not be counted or numbered for multitude.

6 And the priests brought in the ark of the covenant of the LORD to its place, into the temple, to the inner house, the Holy of Holies, under the wings of the cherubim.

7 For the cherubim spread forth their wings over the holy place, and the cherubim covered the ark and its staves above.

8 And the staves were so long that the ends of them were seen from the holy place before the inner house, but they were not seen outside; and there they are to this day.

9 There was nothing in the ark except the two tablets of stone, which Moses had put there at Horeb when the LORD made a covenant with the children of Israel when they came out of the land of Egypt.

10 And when the priests came out of the holy place, a cloud filled the house of the LORD,

11 So that the priests could not stand to minister because of the cloud; for the glory of the LORD had filled the house of the LORD.

12 ¶Then Solomon said, O LORD, thou hast said that thou wouldst dwell in the thick darkness.

13 And I have surely built thee a house to dwell in, a settled place for thee to abide in for ever.

14 Then the king turned his face about and blessed all the congregation of Israel; and all the congregation of Israel stood;

15 And he said, Blessed be the LORD God of Israel, who spoke with his mouth to David my father, and has with his hands fulfilled his promise, saying,

16 Since the day that I brought forth my people Israel out of Egypt, I chose no city out of all the tribes of Israel to build a house, that my name might be therein; but I chose David to be over my people Israel.

17 And it was in the heart of David my father to build a house for the name of the LORD God of Israel.

18 But the LORD said to David my father, Whereas it was in your heart to build a house to my name, you did well that it was in your heart.

19 Nevertheless you shall not build the house to my name; but your son who shall come forth out of your loins, he shall build the house to my name.

20 Now the LORD has performed the word that he spoke, and I have risen up in the place of David my father and sit on the throne of Israel, as the LORD promised, and have built a house to the name of the LORD God of Israel.

21 And I have set there the ark of the covenant of the LORD, which he made with our fathers when he brought them out of the land of Egypt.

22 ¶And Solomon stood before the altar of the LORD in the presence of all the congregation of Israel, and spread forth his hands toward heaven and prayed;

23 And he said, O LORD God of Israel, there is no one like thee in heaven above or on earth beneath, who keepeth covenant and mercy with thy servants who walk before thee in truth with all their heart and with all their soul;

24 Who hast kept with thy servant David my father what thou didst promise him; thou didst speak with thy mouth, and hast fulfilled it with thy hand, as it is this day.

25 Therefore, now, O LORD God of Israel, keep with thy servant David my father what thou didst promise him, saying, There shall not fail you a man in my sight to sit on the throne of Israel; if only your sons take heed to their way, to walk before me in truth as you have walked before me.

26 And now, O LORD God of Israel, let thy word be confirmed, which thou hast sworn to thy servant David my father.

27 But will God indeed dwell on the earth? Behold, the heaven and the heaven of heavens cannot contain thee; how much less this house that I have built?

28 But turn toward the prayer of thy servant, and to his supplication, O LORD my God, to hearken to the supplication and to the prayer which thy servant prays before thee this day;

29 That thine eyes may be open upon this house day and night, even toward this place of which thou hast said, My name shall be there; that thou mayest hearken to the prayer which thy servant prays before thee for this place.

30 And hearken thou to the supplication of thy servant and of thy people Israel, when they pray before thee in this place; and hear thou, O our God, from thy dwelling place in heaven, and forgive.

31 ¶If any man sins against his neighbor and an oath be laid upon him to cause him to swear and he

comes and swears before thine altar in this house;

32 Then hear thou in heaven, and do, and judge thy servants, condemning the wicked, and bring his transgressions upon his head, and vindicating the righteous to reward him according to his innocence.

33 ¶When thy people Israel are defeated in the battle before the enemy because they have sinned before thee, and shall turn again to thee and confess thy name and pray and make supplication to thee in this house;

34 Then hear thou in heaven and forgive the sin of thy servants and of thy people Israel, and bring them back to the land which thou gavest to their fathers.

35 ¶When the heavens are shut up and there is no rain because they have sinned against thee; and they shall come and pray in this place and confess thy name and turn from their sins, when thou dost afflict them;

36 Then hear thou in heaven and forgive the sins of thy servants and of thy people Israel, when thou teach them the good way wherein they should walk, and give thy rain upon the land which thou hast given to thy people for an inheritance.

37 ¶And when there is famine in the land, if there is pestilence, blasting, mildew, locust, or when there are caterpillars; or when their enemy besieges them in one of their cities; whatsoever sickness, or whatsoever plague may be;

38 Whatsoever prayer and whatsoever supplication be made by any man or by all thy people Israel, who shall know every man the trouble of his own heart, and shall spread forth his hands before thee in this house;

39 Then hear thou in heaven thy dwelling place, and forgive, and do, and give to every man according to his ways, whose heart thou knowest (for thou, even thou only, knowest the hearts of all the children of men);

40 That they may reverence thee all the days that they live on the face of the land which thou gavest to their fathers.

41 Moreover concerning a stranger

who is not of thy people Israel, but comes from a far country for thy name's sake

42 (When they shall hear of thy great name and of thy strong hand and of thy stretched out arm), when he shall come before thee and pray in this house;

43 Hear thou in heaven thy dwelling place, and do according to all that the stranger calls to thee for; that all the peoples of the earth may know thy name, to worship thee, as do thy people Israel; and that they may know that this house which I have built is called by thy name.

44 ¶When thy people go out to battle against their enemies, by whatever way thou shalt send them, and shall pray to the LORD toward the city which thou hast chosen and toward the house that I have built for thy name;

45 Then hear thou in heaven their prayer and their supplication, and maintain their cause.

46 When they sin against thee (for there is no man who does not sin), and thou be angry with them and deliver them to the enemy so that they carry them away captives to the land of their enemies, far or near;

47 Yet if they shall reckon it in their heart in the land to which they have been carried captives, and repent and make supplication to thee in the land of their captivity, saying, We have sinned and have done perversely, we have committed wickedness;

48 And so return to thee with all their heart and with all their soul, in the land of their enemies who carried them away captive, and pray to thee according to the religion of their own land, which thou gavest to their fathers, the city which thou hast chosen and the house which I have built for thy name;

49 Then hear thou in heaven, thy dwelling place, their prayer and their supplication, and maintain their cause,

50 And forgive thy people who have sinned against thee and all their transgressions wherein they have transgressed against thee, and give

them compassion in the presence of those who carried them captive, that they may have compassion on them;

51 For they are thy people and thine inheritance, whom thou didst bring forth out of Egypt, from the midst of the furnace of iron;

52 That thine eyes may be open to the supplication of thy servants and to the supplication of thy people Israel, to hearken to them in all that they call for unto thee.

53 For thou didst separate them from among all the people of the earth, to be thine inheritance, as thou didst speak through Moses thy servant, when thou didst bring our fathers out of Egypt, O LORD God.

54 And it came to pass, when Solomon had finished praying all this prayer and supplication unto the LORD God, he arose from before the altar of the LORD, from kneeling with his hands spread up to heaven.

55 And he stood and blessed all the congregation of Israel with a loud voice, saying,

56 Blessed be the LORD God, who has given rest to his people Israel, according to all that he promised; there has not failed one word of all his good promises which he promised by the hand of Moses his servant.

57 The LORD our God be with us, as he was with our fathers; let him not leave us nor forsake us;

58 That he may incline our heart unto him, to walk in all his ways and to keep his commandments and his statutes and his judgments, which he commanded our fathers.

59 And let these my words wherewith I have made supplication before the LORD be near to the LORD our God day and night, that he maintain the cause of his servant and the cause of his people Israel day by day;

60 That all the people of the earth may know that the LORD is God and that there is none else.

61 Let your heart therefore be perfect with the LORD our God, to walk in his ways and to keep his commandments, his covenant, his judgments, and his laws, as at this day.

62 ¶And the king and all Israel with

him offered sacrifice before the
LORD.

63 And Solomon offered a sacrifice
of peace offerings before the LORD,
twenty-two thousand oxen and a hundred and twenty thousand sheep.
So the king and all the children of
Israel dedicated the house of the
LORD.

64 The same day the king consecrated the interior of the court that
was before the house of the LORD;
for there he offered burnt offerings
and meal offerings and the fat of the
peace offerings; because the bronze
altar that was before the LORD was
too little to receive the burnt offerings and the meal offerings and the
fat of the peace offerings.

65 And Solomon made a feast on
that day, and all Israel with him, a
great congregation, from the entrance
of Hamath to the entrance of the
river of Egypt, before the LORD our
God, seven days and seven days, even
fourteen days.

66 On the eighth day the people
sent a delegation and blessed the king,
and went to their tents joyful and
glad of heart for all the goodness that
the LORD had done for David his
servant and for Israel his people.

CHAPTER 9

AND when Solomon had finished
the building of the house of the
LORD and the king's house and all
Solomon's desire which he was
pleased to do,

2 Then the LORD appeared to him
the second time, as he had appeared
to him at Gibeon.

3 And the LORD said to him, I have
heard your prayer and your supplication that you have made before me;
and I have hallowed for me this
house which you have built to put
my name there for ever; and my eyes
and my heart shall be there perpetually.

4 And as for you, if you will walk
before me, as David your father
walked in integrity of heart and in
uprightness, to do according to all
that I have commanded you, and will

keep my statutes and my judgments;

5 Then I will establish the throne
of your kingdom over Israel for ever,
as I promised to David your father,
saying, There shall not fail you a man
upon the throne of Israel.

6 But if you shall indeed turn from
following me, you or your children,
and will not keep my commandments
and my statutes which I have set before you, but go and serve other gods
and worship them;

7 Then I will destroy Israel from
the face of the land which I have
given them; and this house which I
have hallowed for my name will I
cast out of my sight; and Israel shall
be a proverb and a byword among all
peoples;

8 And this house shall be in ruins;
every one that passes by it shall be
astonished and shall hiss; and they
shall say, Why has the LORD done
thus to this land and to this house?

9 And they shall answer, Because
they forsook the LORD their God, who
brought forth their fathers out of the
land of Egypt, and have taken hold
upon other gods, and have worshipped
them and served them; therefore the
LORD has brought upon them all this
evil.

10 ¶And it came to pass at the end
of twenty years, when Solomon had
built the two houses, the house of the
LORD and the king's house

11 (Now Hiram the king of Tyre
had furnished Solomon with cedar
trees and fir trees and gold, according to all his desire), that then King
Solomon gave Hiram twenty towns
in the land of Galilee.

12 And Hiram came out from Tyre
to see the cities which Solomon had
given him; and they did not please
him.

13 And he said, What kind of cities
are these which you have given me,
my brother? And he called them the
land of Cabuli to this day.

14 And King Hiram sent to King
Solomon one hundred and twenty
talents of gold.

15 ¶And this is the portion of tribute which King Solomon levied to
build the house of the LORD and his

own house. And he also built the wall of Jerusalem and Millo and Hazor and Megiddo and Gezer.

16 For Pharaoh king of Egypt had gone up and conquered Gezer and burned it with fire and slain the Canaanites who dwelt in the city and given it as a present to his daughter, Solomon's wife.

17 And Solomon built Gezer and Beth-hauran the lower

18 And Baalath and Tadmor in the land of the wilderness

19 And all the cities for storage that Solomon had, and the cities for the chariots and cities for the horsemen and whatsoever Solomon desired to build in Jerusalem and in Lebanon and in all the land of his dominion.

20 And all the people who were left of the Amorites, the Hittites, the Perizzites, the Hivites, and the Jebusites, who were not of the children of Israel,

21 Their children who were left after them in the land, whom the children of Israel were not able to destroy utterly, Solomon made slaves and tributaries to this day.

22 But of the children of Israel Solomon made no slaves; because they were his men of war and his servants and his princes and his mighty men and commanders of his chariots and his horsemen.

23 These were the superintendents who were over Solomon's work, five hundred and fifty, who had charge of the people and who supervised the work.

24 ¶But Pharaoh's daughter came up out of the city of David to the house which Solomon had built for her; then he built Millo.

25 ¶And three times in a year did Solomon offer burnt offerings and peace offerings upon the altar, and he burned incense upon it before the LORD. So he finished the house of the LORD.

26 ¶And King Solomon built a ship in Ezion-geber, which is beside Eloth, on the shore of the Red Sea, in the land of Arwad.

27 And Hiram sent his servants in the ship, seamen who had knowledge of the sea, with the servants of Solomon.

28 And they came to Ophir and took from there gold, four hundred and twenty talents, and brought it to King Solomon.

CHAPTER 10

AND when the queen of Sheba heard of the fame of Solomon and the name of the LORD, she came to try him out with proverbs.

2 And she came to Jerusalem with a very great train, with camels bearing spices and very much gold and precious stones; and when she was come to Solomon, she tested him with all that was in her heart.

3 And Solomon answered all her questions; there was nothing hidden from the king which he did not tell her.

4 And when the queen of Sheba had seen all Solomon's wisdom and the house that he had built

5 And the food of his table and the order in which his servants sat and the attendance of his ministers and their apparel, and his cupbearers and their clothing and his burnt offerings which he offered in the house of the LORD, she was greatly overcome.

6 And she said to the king, It was a true report that I heard in my own land of your sayings and of your wisdom.

7 Howbeit I did not believe the words until I came, and my own eyes had seen it; and, behold, the half was not told me; your wisdom and prosperity exceed the report which I heard.

8 Happy are your wives, happy are these your servants, who stand continually before you and hear your wisdom.

9 Blessed be the LORD your God, who has delighted in you and has set you upon the throne of Israel; because the LORD loved Israel for ever, therefore he has made you king, to do judgment and justice.

10 And she gave King Solomon one hundred and twenty talents of gold and a very great amount of spices and precious stones; and there came

no more such abundance of spices as these which the queen of Sheba gave to King Solomon.

11 And the ships also of Hiram, that brought gold from Ophir, brought in from Ophir a great amount of sandalwood and precious stones.

12 And the king made of the sandalwood ornaments for the house of the Lord and for the king's house, harps also and psalteries for singers; never before nor since came such sandalwood to this day.

13 And King Solomon gave to the queen of Sheba all that she desired, and whatsover she asked for, besides that which he gave her of his royal bounty. So she turned and went to her own land, she and her servants.

14 ¶Now the weight of gold that came to Solomon in one year was six hundred and sixty-six talents,

15 Besides that which came from the craftsmen and from the traffic of merchants and from all the kings of the Arabs and from the governors of the land.

16 ¶And King Solomon made two hundred shields of pure gold; six hundred minas of gold went into each shield;

17 And three hundred round shields of pure gold; and three hundred minas went into each shield; and the king put them in the house of the forest of Lebanon.

18 ¶Moreover the king made a great throne of ivory, and overlaid it with gold from Ophir.

19 The throne had six steps, and the top of the throne was round behind; and there were arm rests on either side at the place of the seat, and two lions stood on either side of the seat.

20 And twelve lions stood there on the one side and on the other upon the six steps; there was not the like in any kingdom.

21 ¶And all King Solomon's drinking vessels were of gold, and all the vessels of the house of the forest of Lebanon were of pure gold; silver was counted as nothing in the days of Solomon.

22 For the king had at sea a navy of ships of Tarshish with the navy of Hiram; once every three years came the navy from Tarshish, bringing silver and gold, ivory, apes and peacocks.

23 So King Solomon exceeded all the kings of the earth in riches and in wisdom.

24 ¶And all the kings of the earth sought to see the face of Solomon and to hear the wisdom which God had put in his heart.

25 And they brought every man his present, vessels of gold and vessels of silver, garments, armor, spices, horses, fancy chariots, and mules, year by year.

26 ¶And Solomon gathered together chariots and horsemen; and he had a thousand and four hundred chariots and twelve thousand horsemen, and he left some of the chariots in the cities and kept others with the king in Jerusalem.

27 And King Solomon made silver to be as plentiful in Jerusalem as stones, and he made cedar as abundant as sycamore trees that are on the plain.

28 ¶And Solomon had horses brought out of Egypt, and the king's merchants received a commission on the goods they bought.

29 And a chariot was delivered from Egypt for six hundred shekels of silver, and a horse for a hundred and fifty; and so for all the kings of the Hittites and for the kings of Aram, they brought many gifts with their own hands.

CHAPTER 11

BUT King Solomon loved many foreign women, as well as the daughter of Pharaoh, women of the Ammonites, Moabites, Edomites, Zidonians, and Hittites;

2 Of the nations concerning which the Lord had said to the children of Israel, You shall not mix with them, neither shall they mix with you, lest they turn away your heart after their gods; Solomon clung to these in love.

3 And he had seven hundred wives, princesses, and three hundred concu-

bines; and his wives turned away his heart.

4 For it came to pass, when Solomon was old, that his wives turned away his heart after other gods; and his heart was not perfect with the LORD his God, as was the heart of David his father.

5 For Solomon went after Ashtaroth the goddess of the Zidonians, and after Chemosh the god of the Moabites, and after Malcom the god of the Ammonites.

6 And Solomon did evil in the sight of the LORD, and went not fully after the LORD, as did David his father.

7 Then Solomon built a high place for Chemosh the god of Moab, on the mountain that is before Jerusalem, and for Malcom the god of the Ammonites.

8 And likewise did he for all his foreign wives, who burned incense and sacrificed to their gods.

9 ¶And the LORD was angry with Solomon, because his heart was turned from the LORD God of Israel, who had appeared to him twice,

10 And had commanded him concerning this thing, that he should not go after other gods; but he kept not that which the LORD commanded him.

11 Therefore the LORD said to Solomon, Forasmuch as you have done this, and you have not kept my covenant and my statutes and my commandments, which I have commanded you, I will surely rend the kingdom from you and will give it to your servant.

12 Nevertheless, in your days I will not do it for David my servant's sake; but I will rend it out of the hand of your son.

13 However I will not rend away all the kingdom; but will give one tribe to your son for David my servant's sake and for Jerusalem's sake, the city which I have chosen.

14 ¶And the LORD stirred up an adversary against Solomon, Hadad the Edomite; he was of the royal family in Edom.

15 For when David destroyed Edom, and Joab the commander of the army went up to bury the slain, he slew every male in Edom

16 (For Joab and all Israel with him remained there six months, until he had slain every male in Edom);

17 But Hadad fled, he and certain Edomites from among his father's servants into Egypt, Hadad being yet a little boy.

18 They set out from Midian and came to Paran; and they took men with them out of Paran and went into Egypt, to Pharaoh king of Egypt, who gave him a house and food, and said to him, Dwell with me; and gave him land.

19 And Hadad found great favor in the sight of Pharaoh, so that he gave him to wife the sister of his own wife, the sister of Tahpenes the queen.

20 And the sister of Tahpenes bore him Genubath his son, whom Tahpenes weaned in Pharaoh's house; and Genubath was in Pharaoh's household among the sons of Pharaoh.

21 And when Hadad heard in Egypt that David slept with his fathers and that Joab the commander of the army was dead, Hadad said to Pharaoh, Let me depart that I may go to my own country.

22 But Pharaoh said to him, What have you lacked with me that, behold, you seek to go to your own country? And he answered, Nothing; but do let me go.

23 ¶God also stirred up against Solomon another adversary, Hidron the son of Eliadah, who had fled from his lord Hadarezer king of Zobah;

24 And he gathered men to him, and became captain over a band, when David slew the people of Zobah; and they went to Damascus and dwelt in it, and Hadad reigned in Damascus.

25 And he was an adversary to Israel all the days of Solomon, because of the evil which he did; and Hadad oppressed the children of Israel and reigned over Aram [1] (Syria).

26 ¶And Jeroboam the son of Nebat, an Ephrathite of Zedda, Solomon's servant, whose mother's name

[1] At this time the King of Aram was an Edomite.

was Zoriah, a widow, even he lifted up his hand against King Solomon.

27 And this was the reason why he lifted up his hand against King Solomon. When Solomon built Millo and repaired the breaches of the city of David,

28 The man Jeroboam was a mighty man of valour; and Solomon, seeing that the young man was valiant, made him ruler over all the charge of the house of Joseph.

29 And it came to pass at the time when Jeroboam went out of Jerusalem that the prophet Ahijah the Shilonite encountered him on the road; and Ahijah had clad himself with a new garment; and the two of them were alone in a field;

30 And Ahijah caught the new garment that was on him, and tore it into twelve pieces;

31 And he said to Jeroboam, Take for yourself ten pieces; for thus says the LORD God of Israel, Behold, I will rend the kingdom out of the hand of Solomon, and will give ten tribes to you

32 (But he shall have one tribe for my servant David's sake and for Jerusalem's sake, the city which I have chosen out of all the tribes of Israel);

33 Because he has forsaken me and has worshipped Ashtaroth the goddess of the Zidonians, and Chemosh the god of the Moabites, and Malcom the god of the Ammonites, and has not walked in my ways and has not done that which is right in my eyes and has not kept my statutes and my judgments, as did David his father.

34 Nevertheless I will not take the whole kingdom out of his hand; but I will make him a ruler all the days of his life for David my servant's sake, whom I chose because he kept my commandments and my statutes;

35 But I will take the kingdom out of his son's hand and will give it to you, ten tribes.

36 And to his son I will give one tribe, that David my servant may have an heir always before me in Jerusalem, the city which I have chosen for myself to put my name there.

37 And I will give it to you, and you shall reign according to all that your soul desires, and you shall be king over Israel.

38 And if you shall hearken to all that I command you and will walk in my ways and do what is right in my sight and keep my statutes and my commandments, as David my servant did, I will be with you, and build you a sure house, as I built for David my servant, and will give Israel to you.

39 And for this I will afflict the descendants of David, but not for ever.

40 Solomon sought therefore to kill Jeroboam. And Jeroboam arose and fled to Egypt, to Shishak king of Egypt, and was in Egypt until the death of Solomon.

41 ¶And the rest of the acts of Solomon and all that he did and his wisdom, behold, they are written in the Book of the Acts of Solomon.

42 And the time that Solomon reigned in Jerusalem over all Israel was forty years.

43 And Solomon slept with his fathers and was buried in the city of David his father; and Rehoboam his son reigned in his stead.

CHAPTER 12

AND Rehoboam went to Shechem; for all Israel were come to Shechem to make him king.

2 And when Jeroboam the son of Nebat, who was yet in Egypt, heard of it (for he had fled from the presence of King Solomon, and Jeroboam dwelt in Egypt)

3 Then they sent and called him. And Jeroboam and all the people of Israel came, and spoke to Rehoboam, saying,

4 Your father made our yoke harsh; now therefore lighten some of the grievous service of your father, and his heavy yoke which he put upon us, and we will serve you.

5 And he said to them, Depart yet for three days, then come again to me. So all the people departed.

6 ¶And King Rehoboam consulted

with the old men who had stood before his father while he was still alive, and said to them, How do you advise that I may answer the people?

7 And they said to him, If you will be a servant to this people this day and will serve them and answer them and speak good words to them, then they will be your servants for ever.

8 But he forsook the counsel which the old men had given him and consulted with the young men who were grown up with him and who stood before him;

9 And he said to them, What counsel do you give, that we may answer the people who have spoken to me, saying, Make the yoke which your father did put upon us lighter?

10 And the young men who were grown up with him spoke to him, saying, Thus shall you speak to the people who have said to you, Your father made our yoke heavy, but make you it lighter for us; thus shall you say to them, My little finger is thicker than my father's thumb.

11 And now whereas my father laid a heavy yoke upon you, I will add to your yoke; my father has chastised you with whips, but I will chastise you with knouts.

12 ¶So Jeroboam and all the people came to Rehoboam the third day, as the king had commanded them, saying, Come to me again the third day.

13 And the king answered the people harshly, and forsook the old men's counsel that they gave him;

14 And spoke to them according to the counsel of the young men, saying, My father made your yoke heavy, but I will add to your yoke; my father also chastised you with whips, but I will chastise you with knouts.

15 Wherefore the king did not listen to the people; for the stirring of strife was from the LORD, that the LORD might perform his saying which he spoke by his servant Ahijah the prophet, the Shilonite, unto Jeroboam the son of Nebat.

16 ¶So when all Israel saw that the king did not listen to them, the people answered the king, saying, We have no portion in David, neither have we inheritance in the son of Jesse; to your tents, O Israel; now see to your own house, David. So Israel departed unto their tents.

17 And the children of Israel dwelt in their cities; but Judah made Rehoboam the son of Solomon king over them.

18 Then King Rehoboam sent Adoniram, who was over the tribute; and all Israel stoned him with stones, and he died. Therefore King Rehoboam made haste to ride in his chariot to flee to Jerusalem.

19 So Israel has rebelled against the house of David to this day.

20 And when all Israel heard that Jeroboam had returned, they sent and called him to the congregation and made him king over all Israel; there was none that followed the house of David but the tribe of Judah only.

21 ¶And when Rehoboam was come to Jerusalem, he assembled all the house of Judah and the tribe of Benjamin a hundred and eighty thousand chosen men of war to fight against the house of Israel, to bring the kingdom again to Rehoboam the son of Solomon.

22 But the word of the LORD came to Shemaiah the prophet of God, saying,

23 Speak to Rehoboam, the son of Solomon, king of Judah, and to all the house of Judah and Benjamin, and to the remnant of the people, saying,

24 Thus says the LORD: You shall not go up, nor fight against your brethren the children of Israel; return every man to his house; for this thing is from me. They hearkened therefore to the word of the LORD, and returned according to the word of the LORD.

25 ¶Then Jeroboam built Shechem in mount Ephraim and dwelt therein; and went out from thence, and built Penuel.

26 And Jeroboam said in his heart, Now the kingdom will return to the house of David;

27 If this people go up to do sacri-

fices at the house of the LORD in Jerusalem, then shall the heart of this people turn again to their lord, even to Rehoboam king of Judah, and they shall kill me and return to Rehoboam king of Judah.

28 So the king took counsel, and made two calves of gold, and said to all Israel, It is too much for you to go up to Jerusalem; behold your gods, O Israel, who brought you up out of the land of Egypt!

29 And he set the one in Beth-el, and the other he put in Dan.

30 And this thing became a sin; for the people went to worship before the one, even unto Dan.

31 And he made a temple of idols, and made priests from among the people who were not of the sons of Levi.

32 And Jeroboam made a feast in the eighth month, on the fifteenth day of the month, like the feast that is in Judah, and he went up to the altar to offer sacrifices. So did he in Beth-el, sacrificing to the calves that he had made; and he appointed in Beth-el priests for the temples of idols which he had made.

33 And he went to the altar which he had made in Beth-el, on the fifteenth day of the eighth month, even in the month which he had devised of his own heart; and made a feast to the children of Israel; and he went up to the altar to burn incense.

CHAPTER 13

AND, behold, there came a prophet out of Judah by the word of the LORD to Beth-el; and Jeroboam was standing by the altar to burn incense on the fifteenth day of the month, according to the feast which was in Judah. And he burned incense on the altar.

2 And the prophet cried against the altar by the word of the LORD, and said, O altar, altar, hear the word of the LORD, thus says the LORD: Behold, a son shall be born to the house of David, Josiah by name; and upon you he shall offer the priests of the temples of idols who burn incense

upon you, and men's bones shall be burnt upon you.

3 And he gave a sign the same day, saying, This is the sign which the LORD has sent me: Behold, the altar shall be rent, and the ashes that are upon it shall be poured out.

4 And when the king heard the saying of the prophet of God which he had cried against the altar in Beth-el, the king, standing at the altar, put forth his hand, saying, Lay hold on him. And his hand which he put forth against him, dried up, so that he could not draw it back again to him.

5 The altar also was broken, and the ashes which were upon it poured out, according to the sign which the prophet of God had given by the word of the LORD.

6 And the king answered and said to the prophet of God, Pray for me before the LORD your God, and entreat for me that my hand may be restored to me. And the prophet of God prayed before the LORD, and the king's hand was restored to him, and it became as it was before.

7 And the king said to the prophet of God, Come home with me to eat and I will give you presents.

8 And the prophet of God said to him, If you give me half your house, I will not go home with you, neither will I eat bread nor drink water in this place.

9 For so it was charged me by the word of the LORD, saying, Eat no bread, and drink no water, nor return again by the way that you came.

10 So he went by another way, and did not return by the way that he came to Beth-el.

11 ¶Now there dwelt an old prophet in Beth-el; and his sons came and told him all the works that the prophet of God had done that day in Beth-el; and the words which he had spoken to the king, them they told also to their father.

12 And their father said to them, Which way did he go? And his sons showed him the way by which the prophet of God went, who came from Judah.

13 And he said to his sons, Saddle

me the ass. So they saddled him the ass; and he rode on it,

14 And went after the prophet of God, and found him sitting under an oak; and he said to him, Are you the prophet of God who came from Judah? And he said, I am.

15 Then he said to him, Come home with me and eat bread.

16 And he answered, I cannot return with you nor go to your house; neither will I eat bread with you, nor drink water in this place;

17 For so it was said to me by the word of the LORD, You shall not eat bread nor drink water there, nor return again by the same way that you came.

18 He said to him, I am a prophet also as are you; and an angel spoke to me by the word of the LORD, saying, Bring him back with you into your house, that he may eat bread and drink water. But he lied to him.

19 So he went back with him, and did eat bread in his house and drank water.

20 ¶And as they sat at the table, the word of the LORD came to the prophet who brought him back;

21 And he cried to the prophet of God who came from Judah and said to him, Thus says the LORD, Because you have disobeyed the word of the LORD and have not kept the commandment which the LORD your God commanded you,

22 But have come back and have eaten bread and drunk water in the place of which the LORD said to you, You shall not eat bread, nor drink water; therefore your corpse shall not come into the sepulchre of your fathers.

23 ¶And after the two prophets had eaten bread and had drunk, they saddled the ass for the prophet of God.

24 And when he was gone, a lion met him by the way and slew him; and his corpse was cast in the way, and the ass stood beside, and the lion also stood by the corpse.

25 And, behold, men passed by and saw the corpse cast in the way and the ass standing beside it, and the lion also standing beside the corpse; and

they came and told it in the city where the old prophet dwelt.

26 And when the prophet who brought him back from the way heard of it, he said, It is the prophet of God who disobeyed the word of the LORD; therefore the LORD has delivered him to the lion, which has torn him and slain him, according to the word of the LORD, which he spoke to him.

27 And he said to his sons, Saddle me the ass, and they saddled it.

28 And he went and found the corpse cast in the way, and the ass and the lion standing beside the corpse; the lion had not eaten the corpse nor torn the ass.

29 And the prophet took up the corpse of the prophet of God, and laid it upon the ass and brought it back to the city where the old prophet dwelt, to mourn over him and to bury him.

30 And he laid his corpse in the grave; and he mourned over him, saying, Alas, my brother! Alas, my brother!

31 And after he had buried him, he said to his sons, When I die, bury me in the sepulchre wherein the prophet of God is buried; lay my bones beside his bones;

32 For the saying which he cried out by the word of the LORD against the altar in Beth-el and against all the temples of idols which are in the cities of Samaria shall surely come to pass.

33 ¶After this thing Jeroboam did not turn from his evil way, but made again from among the people priests for the temples of idols; whosoever would become a priest, he offered an offering and thus became the priest of the temple of idols.

34 And this thing became a sin to the house of Jeroboam, even to cut it off, and to destroy it from off the face of the earth.

CHAPTER 14

AT that time Abijah the son of Jeroboam fell sick.

2 And Jeroboam said to his wife,

Arise and disguise yourself, that people may not know that you are the wife of Jeroboam; and go to Shiloh; behold, Ahijah the prophet is there, who told me that I should be king over this people.

3 And take with you ten loaves of bread and dried fruits and a pot of honey, and go to him; he shall tell you what shall become of the child.

4 And Jeroboam's wife did so, and arose and went to Shiloh, and came to the house of Ahijah. But Ahijah could not see; for his eyes were dim because of his age.

5 ¶And the LORD said to Ahijah, Behold, the wife of Jeroboam is coming to you, to ask word of you concerning her son, for he is sick; thus and thus shall you say to her; for it shall be, when she comes in, behold, she has disguised herself.

6 And when Ahijah heard the sound of her feet, as she came in at the door, he said, Come in, wife of Jeroboam; why do you disguise yourself? For I am sent to you with heavy tidings.

7 Go, tell Jeroboam, Thus says the LORD God of Israel: Forasmuch as I exalted you from among the people and made you ruler over my people Israel,

8 And tore the kingdom away from the house of David and gave it to you; and yet you have not been like my servant David, who kept my commandments and followed me with all his heart, to do that only which was right in my sight;

9 But you have done more evil than all who were before you; for you have gone and made for yourself molten gods, to provoke me to anger, and have cast me behind your back;

10 Therefore, behold, I will bring evil upon the house of Jeroboam, and will cut off from Jeroboam every male and him that possesses authority in Israel, and I will glean after the house of Jeroboam as they glean the vines of the vineyard when the gathering of the grapes is over.

11 Him that dies of Jeroboam in the city shall the dogs eat; and him that dies in the field shall the fowls of the air eat; for the LORD has spoken it.

12 Arise therefore, go to your own house; and when your feet enter into the city, the child shall die.

13 And all Israel shall mourn for him and bury him; for he only of Jeroboam shall come to the grave, because in him there is found some good thing in the sight of the LORD God of Israel in the house of Jeroboam.

14 Moreover the LORD shall raise up for himself a king over Israel who shall cut off the house of Jeroboam from that day.

15 And henceforth the LORD shall smite Israel as a reed is shaken by the wind, and he shall uproot Israel out of this good land which he gave to their fathers, and shall scatter them beyond the river (Euphrates), because they have made for themselves idols and have provoked the LORD to anger.

16 And he shall deliver Israel up because of the sins of Jeroboam, who did sin and caused Israel to sin.

17 ¶Then Jeroboam's wife arose and departed and came to Tirzah; and when she came to the threshold of her house, the child died;

18 And all Israel mourned over him, and buried him, according to the word of the LORD which he spoke by his servant Ahijah the prophet, the Shilonite.

19 And the rest of the acts of Jeroboam, how he warred and how he reigned, behold, they are written in the Book of the Chronicles of the Kings of Israel.

20 And the days which Jeroboam reigned over Israel were twenty-two years; and Jeroboam slept with his fathers, and Nadab his son reigned in his stead.

21 ¶And Rehoboam the son of Solomon reigned over Judah. Rehoboam was forty-one years old when he began to reign, and he reigned seventeen years in Jerusalem, the city which the LORD did choose out of all the tribes of Israel, to put his name there. And his mother's name was Naamah, an Ammonitess.

22 And Judah did evil in the sight of the LORD, and they provoked him to indignation in everything that their fathers had done and in their sins which they had committed.

23 For they also built for themselves high places and statues and idols on every high hill and under every green tree.

24 And there were also Sodomites in the land; and they did according to all the abominations of the nations which the LORD had destroyed before the children of Israel.

25 ¶And it came to pass in the fifth year of King Rehoboam, Shishak king of Egypt came up against Jerusalem;

26 And he took away the treasures of the house of the LORD and the treasures of the king's house; he even took away all the shields of gold which Solomon had made.

27 And King Rehoboam made in their stead shields of brass, and committed them into the hands of the chiefs of the guard who kept the door of the king's house.

28 And it was so, when the king went into the house of the LORD, the guards bore them and brought them back into the guard chamber.

29 ¶Now the rest of the acts of Rehoboam and all that he did, behold, they are written in the Book of the Chronicles of the Kings of Judah.

30 And there was war between Rehoboam and Jeroboam all their days.

31 And Rehoboam slept with his fathers and was buried in the city of David. And Abijah his son reigned in his stead.

CHAPTER 15

NOW in the eighteenth year of King Jeroboam the son of Nebat, Abijah reigned over Judah.

2 He reigned for three years in Jerusalem. And his mother's name was Maacah, the daughter of Abedshalom.

3 And he walked in all the sins of his father, which he had committed before him; and his heart was not perfect with the LORD his God, like the heart of David his father.

27

4 Nevertheless for David's sake did the LORD God give him an heir in Jerusalem, to set up his son after him and to establish him in Jerusalem;

5 Because David did that which was right in the sight of the LORD his God and did not turn aside from anything that he commanded him all the days of his life, except in the matter of Uriah the Hittite.

6 And there was war between Abijah the son of Rehoboam and Jeroboam all the days of their lives.

7 Now the rest of the acts of Abijah and all that he did, behold, they are written in the Book of the Chronicles of the Kings of Judah.

8 And Abijah slept with his fathers; and they buried him in the city of David; and Asa his son reigned in his stead.

9 ¶And in the twentieth year of Jeroboam king of Israel, Asa reigned over Judah.

10 And he reigned forty-one years in Jerusalem, and his mother's name was Maacah, the daughter of Abedshalom.

11 And Asa did that which was right in the sight of the LORD, as did David his father.

12 And he put the Sodomites out of the land and removed all the idols that his fathers had made.

13 Moreover he removed Maacah his mother from being queen, because she used to make a feast to her idol, and Asa destroyed her idol and burned it at the brook Kidron.

14 But the high places he did not remove; nevertheless Asa's heart was perfect with the LORD his God all his days.

15 And he brought the things which his fathers had dedicated and the things which he himself had dedicated into the house of the LORD, silver and gold and vessels.

16 ¶And there was war between Asa and Baasha king of Israel all their days.

17 And Baasha king of Israel went up against Judah and built Ramtha, and did not permit any to go out or come in to Asa king of Judah.

18 Then Asa took all the silver and

the gold that were left in the treasures of the house of the LORD, and the treasures of the king's house, and delivered them into the hand of his servants; and Asa king of Judah sent them to Bar-hadad, the son of Tabrimon, the son of Hezion, king of Aram, who dwelt in Damascus, saying,

19 There is a league between me and you and between my father and your father; behold, I have sent to you a present of silver and gold; come and break your league with Baasha king of Israel, that he may withdraw from me.

20 So when Bar-hadad heard from Asa, he sent the commanders of his armies against the cities of Israel and destroyed Ijon and Dan and Abel-beth-maacah and all the towns that are in all the land of Naphtali.

21 And when Baasha heard of it, he left off building Ramtha and dwelt in Tirzah.

22 Then King Asa made a proclamation throughout all Judah; none was exempted; and they carried away the stones of Ramtha and its timber with which Baasha had built it; and King Asa built with them Geba of Benjamin, and Mizpeh.

23 The rest of the acts of Asa and all his might and all that he did and the cities which he built, behold, they are written in the Book of the Chronicles of the Kings of Judah. But in the time of his old age he was diseased in his feet.

24 And Asa slept with his fathers and was buried with his fathers in the city of David his father; and Jehoshaphat his son reigned in his stead.

25 ¶And Nadab the son of Jeroboam began to reign over Israel in the second year of Asa king of Judah, and he reigned over Israel two years.

26 And he did evil in the sight of the LORD, and walked in the way of his father and in his sins wherewith he made Israel to sin.

27 ¶And Baasha the son of Ahijah, of the house of Issachar, conspired against him and slew him in Gath, which belonged to the Philistines; for

Nadab and all Israel laid siege to Gath.

28 So Baasha slew him in the third year of Asa king of Judah, and reigned in his stead.

29 And when he reigned, he smote all the house of Jeroboam; he left not to Jeroboam any that breathed, until he had destroyed him, according to the saying of the LORD which he spoke by his servant Ahijah the prophet, the Shilonite;

30 Because of the sins of Jeroboam the son of Nebat which he sinned and which he made Israel sin, by his great provocation with which he provoked the LORD God of Israel to anger.

31 ¶Now the rest of the acts of Nadab and all that he did, behold, they are written in the Book of the Chronicles of the Kings of Israel.

32 And there was war between Baasha and Asa the king of Judah all their days.

33 In the third year of Asa king of Judah, Baasha the son of Ahijah began to reign over all Israel in Tirzah, twenty-four years.

34 And he did evil in the sight of the LORD, and walked in the ways of Jeroboam, the son of Nebat, and in his sins wherewith he made Israel to sin.

CHAPTER 16

THEN the word of the LORD came to Jehu the son of Hanan against Baasha, saying,

2 Thus says the LORD: Forasmuch as I have exalted you out of the dust and made you a ruler over my people Israel and you have walked in the ways of Jeroboam and have made my people Israel to sin to provoke me to anger with the evil work of their hands;

3 Behold, I will pluck out one by one the posterity of Baasha and the posterity of his house, and I will make his house like the house of Jeroboam the son of Nebat.

4 Him that dies of Baasha in the city shall the dogs eat; and him that dies in the fields shall the fowls of the air eat.

5 Now the rest of the acts of Baasha, and all that he did and all his might, behold, they are written in the Book of the Chronicles of the Kings of Israel.

6 So Baasha slept with his fathers and was buried in Tirzah; and Elah his son reigned in his stead.

7 And also by the prophet Jehu the son of Hanan the word of the LORD came against Baasha and against all his house, because of all the evil that he had done before the LORD, in provoking him to anger with the works of his hands, in being like the house of Jeroboam, and because he killed him.

8 ¶In the twenty-sixth year of Asa king of Judah, Elah the son of Baasha began to reign over Israel in Tirzah, two years.

9 And his servant Zimri, commander of the half of the horsemen, conspired against him as he was in Tirzah, drinking old wine in the house of cedar which he had built in Tirzah.

10 And Zimri went in and smote him and killed him, in the twenty-seventh year of Asa king of Judah, and reigned in his stead.

11 ¶And when he began to reign, as soon as he sat on his throne, he slew all the house of Baasha; he left him not one male child, neither of his kinsfolks nor of his friends.

12 Thus Zimri destroyed all the house of Baasha, according to the word of the LORD which he spoke against Baasha by Jehu the prophet

13 For all the sins of Baasha and the sins of Elah his son which they committed and made Israel to sin in provoking the LORD God of Israel to anger with their idols.

14 Now the rest of the acts of Elah and all that he did, behold, they are written in the Book of the Chronicles of the Kings of Israel.

15 ¶In the twenty-seventh year of Asa king of Judah, Zimri reigned seven days in Tirzah. And the people were encamped against Gath, which belonged to the Philistines.

16 And the people who were encamped heard the news that Zimri had conspired, and had also slain the king; wherefore all Israel made Omri, the commander of the army, king over Israel that day in the camp.

17 And Omri went up from Gath, and all Israel with him, and they besieged Tirzah.

18 And when Zimri saw that the city was taken, he went into the shrine of the king's house and burned the king's house over him with fire, and died,

19 Because of the sins which he committed in doing evil in the sight of the LORD, in walking in the ways of Jeroboam the son of Nebat, and the sins which he did to make Israel sin.

20 Now the rest of the acts of Zimri and the treason that he wrought, behold, they are written in the Book of the Chronicles of the Kings of Israel.

21 ¶Then the people of Israel were divided into two parts: half of the people followed Tibni the son of Ginath to make him king, and half followed Omri.

22 But the people who followed Omri prevailed against the people who followed Tibni; so Tibni died and Omri reigned.

23 ¶In the thirty-first year of Asa king of Judah, Omri began to reign over Israel, and reigned for twelve years; six years he reigned in Tirzah.

24 And he bought the hill of Samaria from Shemer for one talent of silver, and he built on the hill, and called the name of the city which he built after the name of Shemer, the owner of the hill of Samaria.

25 ¶But Omri did evil in the sight of the LORD, and did worse than all the kings who were before him.

26 And he walked in all the ways of Jeroboam the son of Nebat and in his sins wherewith he made Israel to sin, to provoke the LORD God of Israel to anger with their idols.

27 Now the rest of the acts of Omri, and all that he did and all his might, behold, they are written in the Book of the Chronicles of the Kings of Israel.

28 So Omri slept with his fathers

and was buried in Samaria; and Ahab his son reigned in his stead.

29 ¶And in the thirty-eighth year of Asa king of Judah, Ahab the son of Omri began to reign over Israel; and Ahab the son of Omri reigned over Israel in Samaria twenty-two years.

30 And Ahab the son of Omri did evil in the sight of the LORD above all who were before him.

31 And as though it had been a light thing for him to walk in the sins of Jeroboam the son of Nebat, he went and took to wife Jezebel the daughter of Ethbaal king of the Zidonians, and went and served Baal and worshipped him.

32 And he erected an altar for Baal in the house of Baal which he had built in Samaria.

33 And Ahab served idols; and Ahab did more to provoke the LORD God of Israel to anger than all the kings of Israel who were before him.

34 ¶In his days did Ahab build the accursed place, Jericho; he finished it with the death of Abiram, his firstborn, and set up its gates with the death of his younger son Shacob, according to the word of the LORD, which he spoke by Joshua the son of Nun.

CHAPTER 17

AND Elijah the Tishbite, who was of the inhabitants of Gilead, said to Ahab, As the LORD God of Israel lives, before whom I stand, there shall not be dew nor rain these years but according to my word.

2 And the word of the LORD came to him, saying,

3 Depart from here and turn eastward and hide yourself by the brook of Cherith that is before the Jordan.

4 And you shall drink from the brook; and I have commanded the ravens to feed you there.

5 So he went and did according to the word of the LORD; for he went and dwelt by the brook of Cherith that is before the Jordan.

6 And the ravens brought him bread and meat in the morning, and bread and meat in the evening; and he drank from the brook.

7 But after a while the brook dried up because there had been no rain in the land.

8 ¶And the word of the LORD came to him, saying,

9 Arise, go to Zarephath, which belongs to Zidon, and dwell there; behold, I have commanded a widow there to feed you.

10 So he arose and went to Zarephath. And when he came to the gate of the city, behold, the widow was there gathering sticks; and he called to her and said, Bring me a little water in a vessel, that I may drink.

11 And as she was going to fetch it, he called to her and said, Bring me a morsel of bread in your hand.

12 And she said, As the LORD your God lives, I have nothing but a handful of flour in a pot and a little oil in a cruse; and, behold, I am gathering a few sticks, that I may go in and bake it for me and my son, that we may eat it and die.

13 And Elijah said to her, Fear not; go and do as you have said; but first make a little cake and bring it to me, and afterward make for yourself and your son.

14 For thus says the LORD God of Israel, The pot of flour shall not be spent, and the cruse of oil shall not diminish, until the day that the LORD sends rain upon the earth.

15 And she went and did according to the saying of Elijah; and she and he and her household did eat many days.

16 And the pot of flour was not spent, neither did the cruse of oil diminish, according to the word of the LORD, which he spoke by Elijah.

17 ¶And it came to pass after these things that the son of the woman, the mistress of the house, fell sick; and his sickness was so sore that there was no breath left in him.

18 And she said to Elijah, What have I done to you, O prophet of God? Are you come to me to call my trespasses to remembrance and to slay my son?

19 And Elijah said to her, Give me

your son. And he took him from her bosom, and carried him up into the upper chamber where he abode, and laid him upon his own bed.

20 And he cried to the LORD and said, O LORD God, why hast thou also brought misfortune upon this widow with whom I sojourn, by slaying her son?

21 Then he stretched himself upon the boy three times and cried to the LORD and said, O LORD my God, let this boy's soul return to him again.

22 And the LORD heard the voice of Elijah; and the soul of the boy returned into him again, and he revived.

23 And Elijah took the boy and brought him down from the upper chamber into the house, and delivered him to his mother; and Elijah said to her, See, your son lives.

24 ¶And the woman said to Elijah, Now I know that you are a prophet of God and that the word of the LORD in your mouth is truth.

CHAPTER 18

AND it came to pass after many days, that the word of the LORD came to Elijah in the third year, saying, Go, show yourself to Ahab; and I will send rain upon the earth.

2 And Elijah went to show himself to Ahab. And there was a severe famine in Samaria.

3 And Ahab called Obadiah, who was the steward of his household. (Now Obadiah revered the LORD greatly;

4 For when Jezebel slew the prophets of God, Obadiah took a hundred prophets, and hid them by fifty in a cave, and fed them with bread and water.)

5 And Ahab said to Obadiah, Go through the land, to all fountains of water and to all brooks; perhaps we may find grass to save the horses and mules alive, that we may not lose all the beasts.

6 So they divided the land between them to pass throughout it; Ahab went one way by himself, and Obadiah went another way by himself.

7 ¶And as Obadiah was on the way,

behold, Elijah met him; and he recognized him, and fell on his face and said, Is that you, my lord Elijah?

8 And he answered him, It is I; then he said to him, Go, tell your lord, Behold, Elijah is here.

9 And Obadiah said, What sin have I committed, that you would deliver your servant into the hand of Ahab, to slay me?

10 As the LORD your God lives, there is no nation or kingdom whither my lord has not sent to seek you; and when they said, He is not here, he took an oath of the kingdoms and nations, that they had not found you.

11 And now you say to me, Go, tell your lord, Behold, Elijah is here.

12 And as soon as I am gone from you, the Spirit of the LORD will take you up and carry you whither I know not; and so when I come and tell Ahab, and he cannot find you, he shall slay me; but I your servant have revered the LORD from my youth.

13 Has it not been told my lord what I did when Jezebel slew the prophets of God, how I took a hundred of the prophets of the LORD and hid them by fifty in a cave and fed them with bread and water?

14 And now you say to me, Go, tell your lord, Behold, Elijah is here; and he shall slay me.

15 And Elijah said, As the LORD of hosts lives, before whom I stand, I will surely show myself to him today.

16 So Obadiah went to meet Ahab, and told Ahab; and Ahab went to meet Elijah.

17 ¶And when Ahab saw Elijah, Ahab said to him, Are you he who troubles Israel?

18 And Elijah said to him, I have not troubled Israel; but it is you and your father's house, in that you have forsaken the commandments of the LORD and have followed Baal.

19 Now therefore send and gather to me all Israel at mount Carmel and the prophets of Baal four hundred and fifty and the prophets of the idols four hundred and fifty who eat at Jezebel's table.

20 So Ahab sent to all the children of Israel, and gathered the prophets together to mount Carmel.

21 Then Elijah came near to all the people, and said, How long will you halt between two opinions? If the LORD is God, follow him, but if Baal is god, then follow him. And the people answered him not a word.

22 Then Elijah said, I, even I only, remain a prophet of the LORD; but Baal's prophets are four hundred and fifty men.

23 Let them therefore give us two bullocks; and let them choose one bullock for themselves, and cut it in pieces and lay it on wood and put no fire under; and I will prepare the other bullock and cut it in pieces and lay it on wood and put no fire under it;

24 And you call on the name of your gods, and I will call on the name of the LORD my God; and the God who answers by fire, he is God. And all the people answered and said, You have spoken well.

25 Then Elijah said to the prophets of Baal, Choose for yourselves one bullock, and prepare it first; for you are many;

26 And they took the bullock which was given them and prepared it and called on the name of Baal from morning even until noon, saying, O Baal, answer us. But there was no voice nor any that answered. And they cut themselves [1] upon the altar which they had made.

27 And when it was noon, Elijah mocked them and said, Cry with a loud voice; for he is a god; perhaps he is meditating or he is busy or he is on a journey, or perhaps he is asleep and must be awakened.

28 And they cried with a loud voice and they cut themselves after their custom with daggers and lances, until their blood gushed out upon them.

29 And when midday was past, they prophesied until the time of the offering of the evening sacrifice, but there was no voice nor any to answer nor any to listen. Then Elijah said to the prophets of the idols, Now you can move, so that I may prepare my burnt offerings. And they moved aside.

30 And Elijah said to all the people, Come near to me. And all the people came near to him. And he repaired the altar of the LORD that was broken down.

31 And Elijah took twelve stones, according to the number of the tribes of the sons of Jacob, to whom the word of the LORD came, saying, Israel shall be your name;

32 And with the stones he built an altar in the name of the LORD; and he made a trench about the altar, as great as would contain two measures of seed.

33 And he put the wood in order and cut the bullock in pieces and laid it on the wood and said, Fill four jars with water and pour it on the burnt offering and on the wood.

34 And he said, Do it the second time. And they did it the second time. And he said, Do it the third time. And they did it the third time.

35 And the water ran round about the altar; and they filled the trench also with water.

36 And at the time of the offering of the evening sacrifice, Elijah the prophet came near and said, O LORD God of Abraham, of Isaac, and of Israel, let it be known this day that thou art God in Israel and that I am thy servant and that I have done all these things at thy word.

37 Answer me, O LORD, answer me, that all this people may know that thou art the LORD God and that thou hast turned their perverse heart back again.

38 Then the fire of the LORD fell, and consumed the burnt offering and the wood and the stones and the dust, and licked up the water that was in the trench.

39 And when all the people saw it, they fell on their faces; and they said, The LORD, he is God; the LORD, he is God.

40 And Elijah said to them, Seize the prophets of Baal, and let not one of them escape. And they seized them;

[1] Pagan priests inflicted injuries to their bodies when they prayed vehemently.

and Elijah brought them down to the brook Kishon and slew them there.

41 ¶And Elijah said to Ahab, Go up, eat and drink; for there is a rushing sound of heavy rain.

42 So Ahab went up to eat and to drink. And Elijah went up to the top of Carmel; and he bent himself down upon the earth, and put his face between his knees;

43 And said to his servant, Go up now, and look toward the sea. And he went up and looked, and said, There is nothing. And Elijah said to him, Go again seven times.

44 And at the seventh time, he said, Behold, there is a little cloud like a man's hand rising out of the sea. And he said to him, Go up, say to Ahab, Mount your horse, and get down before the rain stops you.

45 And while he busied himself here and there, the heavens were black with clouds and wind, and there was a great rain. And Ahab rode, and went to Jezreel.

46 And the hand of the LORD was on Elijah; and he girded up his loins and ran before Ahab till he entered Jezreel.

CHAPTER 19

AND Ahab told Jezebel all that Elijah had done, and how he had slain all the prophets of Baal and the prophets of the shrines with the sword.

2 Then Jezebel sent a messenger to Elijah, saying, So let the gods do to me, and more also, if I do not make your life as the life of one of them by tomorrow about this time.

3 And Elijah was afraid, and he arose and fled for his life, and came to Beer-sheba, which belongs to Judah, and left his disciple there.

4 ¶But he himself went a day's journey into the wilderness, and came and sat down under an oak tree; and he requested for himself that he might die, and said, It is enough for me; now, O LORD, take away my life; for I am not better than my fathers.

5 Then he lay down and slept soundly under the oak tree; and, be-

hold, an angel touched him and said to him, Arise and eat.

6 And he looked, and, behold, there was at his head a cake baked on the coals and a cruse of water. And he did eat and drink, and lay down again.

7 And the angel of the LORD came again the second time and touched him and said, Arise, eat and drink; because the journey is too great for you.

8 And he arose, and did eat and drink, and went in the strength of that food forty days and forty nights as far as Horeb the mount of God.

9 ¶And he entered into a cave and lodged there; and, behold, the word of the LORD came to him, and he said to him, What are you doing here, Elijah?

10 And he said, I have been very zealous for the LORD God of hosts; for the children of Israel have forsaken thy covenant, thrown down thine altars, and slain thy prophets with the sword; and I, even I only, am left; and they seek my life, to take it away.

11 And he said, Go forth and stand upon the mount before the LORD. And, behold, the LORD passed by, and a great and strong wind rent the mountains and broke in pieces the rocks before the LORD; but the LORD was not in the wind; and after the wind an earthquake; but the LORD was not in the earthquake:

12 And after the earthquake a fire; but the LORD was not in the fire; and after the fire a still small voice.

13 And when Elijah heard it, he wrapped his face in his mantle and went out and stood at the entrance of the cave. And, behold, there came a voice to him, and said to him, What are you doing here, Elijah?

14 And he said, I have been very zealous for the LORD God of hosts, because the children of Israel have forsaken thy covenant, thrown down thine altars, and slain thy prophets with the sword; and I, even I only, am left; and they seek my life, to take it away.

15 And the LORD said to him, Go,

return on your way to the wilderness of Damascus; then go and anoint Hazael to be king over Aram; [1]

16 And Jehu the son of Jamshi you shall anoint to be king over Israel; and Elisha the son of Shaphat of Abel-meholah you shall anoint to be prophet in your place.

17 And it shall come to pass, that him who escapes from the sword of Hazael shall Jehu slay; and him who escapes from the sword of Jehu shall Elisha slay.

18 Yet I have left me seven thousand in Israel, all the knees which have not bowed to Baal, and every mouth that has not kissed him.

19 ¶So he departed thence and found Elisha the son of Shaphat, who was plowing, and twelve ploughs were ahead of him, and he was one of the twelve; and Elijah came up to him and cast his mantle upon him.

20 And he left the plough and the oxen and went after Elijah and said to him, Let me kiss my father and my mother, and then I will follow you. And he said to him, Go back again; for what have I done to you?

21 And he returned back from him, and took a yoke of oxen and slew them and boiled their meat with wood from the yokes of the oxen and gave it to the people, and they ate. Then he arose and went after Elijah and ministered to him.

CHAPTER 20

AND Bar-hadad the king of Edom [2] gathered all his army together; and there were thirty-two kings with him, and horses and chariots; and he went up and besieged Samaria and fought against it.

2 And he sent messengers to Ahab king of Israel, and said to him, Thus says Bar-hadad,

3 Your silver and your gold are mine; and the most attractive of your wives and your children are mine also.

4 And the king of Israel answered and said, According to your word,

my lord, O king, I am yours, and all that I have.

5 And the messengers came again, and said, Thus says Bar-hadad, Although I sent to you at first, saying, You shall deliver to me your silver and your gold and your wives and your children;

6 Yet I will send my servants to you tomorrow at about this time, and they shall search your house and the houses of your servants; and whatsoever pleases them, they shall take in their hands and bring back.

7 Then the king of Israel called all the elders of the land and said to them, Know, and see how this man seeks mischief; for he sent to me for my wives and for my children and for my silver and for my gold; and I denied him not.

8 And all the elders and all the people said to him, Do not hearken to him, nor consent.

9 Wherefore he said to the messengers of Bar-hadad, Tell my lord the king, All that you did send for to your servant at the first I will do; but this thing I cannot do. And the messengers departed and brought him word again.

10 And Bar-hadad sent to him and said, The gods do so to me, and more also, if the dust of Samaria in handfuls shall suffice for all the people who are with me.

11 And the king of Israel answered and said, Let him talk; nevertheless, the one who ties a knot is not more able than the one who can untie it.

12 And when Bar-hadad heard this message as he was drinking, he and the kings in the pavilions, he said to his servants, Set yourselves in array against the city.

13 ¶And, behold, a prophet drew near to Ahab king of Israel and said to him, Thus says the Lord, Have you seen all this great army? Behold, I will deliver it into your hands this day; and you shall know that I am the Lord.

14 And Ahab said, By whom? And he said to him, By the young men and

[1] Syria was a name later given by the Greeks; derived from Sur (Tyre).
[2] King James, *Syria.* Apparently Syria and Edom were united at this time.

by the princes of the city. Then he said, Who shall begin the battle? And he answered, You.

15 Then he numbered the young men and the princes of the city, and they were two hundred and thirty-two; and after them he numbered all the people, even all the children of Israel, being seven thousand.

16 And they went out at noon, but Bar-hadad was drinking old wine in the pavilions, he and the kings, the thirty-two kings who were come to help him.

17 And the young men and the princes of the city went out first; and Bar-hadad sent out men, and they told him, saying, There are men come out of Samaria.

18 And he said, Whether they have come out for peace, take them alive; or whether they have come out for war, take them alive.

19 So these young men and these princes came out of the city, and the army followed them.

20 And they slew every one his man; and the Arameans fled; and Israel pursued them; and Bar-hadad the king of Aram escaped in chariots with horsemen.

21 And the king of Israel went out and destroyed the horses and chariots, and slew the Arameans with a great slaughter.

22 ¶And, behold, the prophet of God came near to Ahab king of Israel, and said to him, Go, strengthen yourself, and know, and see what you have to do; for at the beginning of the year[1] the king of Aram will come up against you.

23 And the servants of the king of Aram said to him, Their god is a god of the mountains; this is why they triumphed over us; but let us fight against them in the plain, and surely we shall triumph over them.

24 And do this thing: Remove the kings, every one from his command, and put officers in their places;

25 And number for yourself an army like the army that you have lost, horse for horse and chariot for chariot; and we will fight against them in

the plain, and surely we shall be stronger than they. And he hearkened to their voice, and did so.

26 And it came to pass at the beginning of the year, that Bar-hadad gave orders to the Arameans, and went up to Aphek to fight against Israel.

27 And the children of Israel were mustered and set in array against them, like two little flocks of goats; but the Arameans filled the country.

28 ¶And a prophet of God drew near to Ahab the king of Israel, and said to him, Thus says the LORD, Because the Arameans have said, The LORD is a god of the mountains, but he is not a god of the valleys, therefore I will deliver all this great army into your hands, and you shall know that I am the LORD.

29 So they encamped, one over against the other, seven days. And on the seventh day the battle was joined; and the children of Israel slew of the Arameans a hundred thousand footmen in one day.

30 But the rest fled to Aphek, into the city; and there a wall fell upon twenty-seven thousand men that were left. And Bar-hadad fled and came into the city into an inner chamber.

31 ¶And his servants came near and said to him, Behold now, we have heard that the kings of Israel are merciful kings; let us put sackcloth upon our heads and gird ropes on our loins and go out to the king of Israel; perhaps he will spare our lives.

32 So they put sackcloth on their heads and girded ropes on their loins, and went to the king of Israel and said to him, Your servant Bar-hadad says, Let me live. And the king said, Is he still alive? He is my brother.

33 Now Bar-hadad was a soothsayer, and the men surmised and quickly caught his meaning, and they said, Behold your brother, Bar-hadad. Then he said, Go, bring him. Then Bar-hadad came forth to him; and Ahab caused him to sit with him in the chariot.

34 And Bar-hadad said to him, The cities which my father took from your father, I will restore; and I will

---

[1] Spring.

make a market place for you in Damascus, as my father made in Samaria. Then Ahab said, I will send you away with a covenant. So he made a covenant with him and sent him away.

35 ¶And a certain man of the sons of the prophets said to his neighbor according to the word of the LORD, Strike me. But the man refused to strike him.

36 Then he said to him, Because you have not obeyed the voice of the LORD your God, behold, as soon as you are departed from me, a lion shall slay you. And as soon as he departed from him, a lion found him and slew him.

37 Then he found another man and said to him, Strike me. And the man struck him, and wounded him.

38 So the prophet departed and waited for the king by the way, and disguised his face with ashes.

39 And, behold, as the king was passing by, he cried to the king and said, Your servant went out into the midst of the battle; and, behold, a man turned aside, and brought a soldier to me, and said, Keep this man; if by any means he be missing, then shall your life be for his life, or else you shall pay a talent of silver.

40 And as your servant was busy here and there, he was gone. And the king of Israel said to him, So shall your judgment be; you yourself have decided it.

41 And he hasted and wiped off the ashes from his face; and the king of Israel realized that he was of the prophets.

42 And he said to him, Thus says the LORD, Because you have let go out of your hand a man whom I appointed to utter destruction, therefore your life shall go for his life and your people for his people.

43 Then the king of Israel went to his house sad and displeased, and came to Samaria.

CHAPTER 21

AND it came to pass after these things that Naboth the Jezreelite had a vineyard in Jezreel, beside the palace of Ahab king of Samaria.

2 And Ahab spoke to Naboth, saying, Give me your vineyard that I may have it for a vegetable garden, because it is near to my house; and I will give you for it a better vineyard than it; or, if it seem good to you, I will give you its worth in money.

3 And Naboth said to Ahab, The LORD forbid that I should give you the inheritance of my fathers.

4 And Ahab went to his house sad and displeased because of the word which Naboth the Jezreelite had spoken to him; for he had said, I will not give you the inheritance of my fathers. And he laid him down on his bed and turned away his face and would eat no food.

5 ¶But Jezebel his wife came to him and said to him, Why is your spirit so sad, that you refuse to eat food?

6 And he said to her, Because I spoke to Naboth the Jezreelite, and said to him, Give me your vineyard for money; or else, if it please you, I will give you another vineyard for it, better than it; but he answered, I will not give you my vineyard.

7 And Jezebel his wife said to him, Are you really king over Israel? Arise, and eat bread, and let your heart be merry; I will give you the vineyard of Naboth the Jezreelite.

8 So she wrote a letter in Ahab's name and sealed it with his ring, and sent the letter to the elders and to the nobles who dwelt in the city with Naboth.

9 And she wrote in the letter, saying, Proclaim a fast and set Naboth on high among the people;

10 Then bring two wicked men and set them opposite him, and let them testify against him, saying, Naboth has reviled God and the king. And then take him out, and stone him, that he may die.

11 And the men of his city, even the elders and the nobles who dwelt in the city with Naboth, did as Jezebel had sent to them and as it was written in the letter which she had sent to them.

12 They proclaimed a fast and set Naboth on high among the people.

13 And they brought two wicked men, and seated them opposite him; and the wicked men witnessed against Naboth, saying, Naboth reviled God and the king. Then they took him outside the city and stoned him, so that he died.

14 Then they sent to Jezebel, saying, Naboth has been stoned, and he is dead.

15 ¶And when Jezebel heard that Naboth was dead, Jezebel said to Ahab, Arise, take possession of the vineyard of Naboth the Jezreelite, which he refused to give you for money; for Naboth is not alive but dead.

16 And when Ahab heard that Naboth was dead, Ahab rose up to go down to the vineyard of Naboth the Jezreelite, to take possession of it.

17 ¶And the word of the Lord came to Elijah the Tishbite, saying,

18 Arise, go down to meet Ahab king of Israel, who is in Samaria; behold, he is in the vineyard of Naboth the Jezreelite, for he has gone there to possess it.

19 And you shall say to him, Thus says the Lord: Behold, you have killed, and, behold, you have also taken possession; thus says the Lord, In the place where dogs licked the blood of Naboth shall dogs lick your blood, even yours.

20 And Ahab said to Elijah, Have you found me, O my enemy? And he answered, I have found you because you have exalted yourself to do evil in the sight of the Lord.

21 Behold, I will bring evil upon you, and will pluck one by one your posterity, and will cut off from Ahab every male child and every one who has authority in governing Israel;

22 And I will make your house like the house of Jeroboam the son of Nebat and like the house of Baasha the son of Ahijah for the provocation wherewith you have provoked me to anger and made Israel to sin.

23 And of Jezebel also the Lord spoke, saying, The dogs shall eat Jezebel in the inheritance which is in Jezreel.

24 Anyone belonging to Ahab who dies in the city shall the dogs eat; and anyone who dies in the field shall the fowls of the air eat.

25 ¶But there was none like Ahab, who thought to do evil in the sight of the Lord, whom Jezebel his wife incited.

26 And he did very abominably in following idols, just as the Amorites had done, whom the Lord destroyed before the children of Israel.

27 And when Ahab heard these words, he tore his clothes and put sackcloth upon his body and fasted and lay in sackcloth and walked barefooted.

28 And the word of the Lord came to Elijah the Tishbite, saying,

29 Have you seen how Ahab has humbled himself before me? Because he has humbled himself before me, I will not bring the evil in his days; but in his son's days will I bring the evil upon his house.

CHAPTER 22

AND three years passed without war between Aram and Israel.

2 And it came to pass in the third year, that Jehoshaphat the king of Judah came down to Ahab the king of Israel.

3 And the king of Israel said to his servants, Do you know that Ramath-gilead belongs to us, and how long shall we keep still and not take it out of the hand of the king of Aram?

4 And he said to Jehoshaphat, Will you go with me to battle to Ramath-gilead? And Jehoshaphat said, I will go as you go, my people as your people and my horses as your horses.

5 And Jehoshaphat said to the king of Israel, Enquire, I pray, for the word of the Lord this day.

6 Then the king of Israel gathered the prophets together, about four hundred men, and said to them, Shall I go to Ramath-gilead to battle or shall I forbear? And they said, Go up; for the Lord will deliver the Arameans into the hand of the king.

7 And Jehoshaphat said, Is not here a prophet of the Lord that we might enquire of him?

8 And the king of Israel said to

Jehoshaphat, There is yet one man by whom we may enquire of the LORD; his name is Micah the son of Imlah; but I hate him, for he does not prophesy good concerning me, but evil. And Jehoshaphat said, Let not the king say so.

9 Then the king of Israel called a eunuch and said, Make haste and bring here Micah the son of Imlah.

10 And the king of Israel and Jehoshaphat the king of Judah were seated each on his throne, clothed with robes of different colors, at the entrance of the gate of Samaria; and all the prophets were prophesying before them.

11 And Zedekiah the son of a Canaanitish woman made for himself horns of iron; and he said, Thus says the LORD: With these you shall pierce the Arameans, until you have destroyed them.

12 And all the prophets prophesied so, saying, Go up to Ramath-gilead and you will triumph; for the LORD shall deliver them into your hands, O king.

13 And the messenger who went to call Micah spoke to him, saying, Behold now the words of the false prophets with one accord have predicted favorably concerning the king; let your word be like the word of one of them, and you also predict favorably.

14 And Micah said, As the LORD lives, whatsoever the LORD says to me, that will I speak.

15 ¶So he came to the king. And the king said to him, Micah, shall we go to Ramath-gilead to battle or shall we forbear? And he answered him, Go up and be victorious; for the LORD shall deliver them into your hand, O king.

16 And the king said to him, How many times shall I adjure you that you tell me nothing but that which is true in the name of the LORD?

17 And Micah said, I saw Israel scattered upon the mountains like sheep that have no shepherd; and the LORD said, These have no master; let them return every man to his own house in peace.

18 And the king of Israel said to Jehoshaphat, Did I not tell you that he would not prophesy good concerning me, but evil?

19 And Micah said, Hear therefore the word of the LORD; I saw the LORD sitting on his throne, and all the host of heaven standing by him on his right hand and on his left.

20 And the LORD said, Who shall persuade Ahab that he may go up and fall at Ramath-gilead? And one said in this manner and another said in that manner.

21 And there came forth a spirit, and stood before the LORD, and said, I will persuade him.

22 And the LORD said to him, By what means? And he said, I will go forth, and will be a lying spirit in the mouth of all his prophets. And he said to him, You shall persuade him and prevail also; go forth and do so.

23 Now therefore, behold, the LORD has put a lying spirit in the mouth of all these your prophets, and the LORD has spoken evil concerning you.

24 But Zedekiah the son of the Canaanitish woman went near and struck Micah on his cheek and said to him, Which way has the Spirit of the LORD departed from me and spoken to you?

25 And Micah said to him, Behold, you shall see in that day, when you shall go into an inner chamber to hide yourself.

26 Then the king of Israel said, Take Micah and deliver him to Amon the governor of the city and to Joash the king's son;

27 And say, Thus says the king: Put this fellow in the prison and feed him with bread of affliction and with water of affliction until I come in peace.

28 And Micah said, If you return in peace, then the LORD has not spoken by me. And he said, Hear, all you people.

29 So the king of Israel and Jehoshaphat the king of Judah went up to Ramath-gilead.

30 And the king of Israel said to

Jehoshaphat, I will disguise myself and enter into the battle; but you put on your robes. And the king of Israel disguised himself and went into the battle.

31 But the king of Aram commanded the thirty-two captains of his chariots, saying, Fight neither with small nor great, save only with the king of Israel.

32 And when the captains of the chariots saw Jehoshaphat, they thought he was the king of Israel. And they turned aside to fight against him; and Jehoshaphat cried out.

33 And when the captains of the chariots saw that he was not the king of Israel, they turned back from pursuing him.

34 And a certain man drew his bow toward him at a venture and smote the king of Israel between the joints of the breastplate; wherefore the king said to the driver of his chariot, Turn around and carry me out of the army; for the pangs of death have come upon me.

35 And the battle grew fiercer that day; and the king was standing in the chariot facing the Arameans, and died that evening; and the blood ran out of his wound into the hollow of his chariot.

36 And at sunset a herald proclaimed throughout the army, saying, Go, every man to his city and every man to his own country.

37 ¶So the king died and was brought to Samaria; and they buried him in Samaria.

38 And they washed the chariot on the hill of Samaria; and they washed his armor; and the dogs licked up his blood, according to the word of the LORD which he spoke.

39 Now the rest of the acts of Ahab and all that he did and the ivory house which he built and all the cities that he built, behold, they are written in the Book of the Chronicles of the Kings of Israel.

40 So Ahab slept with his fathers; and Ahaziah his son reigned in his stead.

41 ¶And Jehoshaphat the son of Asa began to reign over Judah in the fourth year of Ahab king of Israel.

42 Jehoshaphat was thirty-five years old when he began to reign; and he reigned twenty-five years in Jerusalem. And his mother's name was Arubah the daughter of Shilhi.

43 And he walked in all the ways of Asa his father; he did not turn aside from doing that which was right in the sight of the LORD; nevertheless he did not remove the temples of idols; for the people still offered sacrifices and burned incense on the high places.

44 And Jehoshaphat made peace with the kings of Israel.

45 Now the rest of the acts of Jehoshaphat and all the might that he showed and how he warred, behold, they are written in the Book of the Chronicles of the Kings of Judah.

46 And the remnant of the Sodomites, which remained in the days of his father Asa, he removed from the land.

47 There was then no king who reigned in Edom.

48 Jehoshaphat built ships at Tarshish to go to Ophir for gold; but they did not go; for the ships were broken at Ezion-geber.

49 Then Ahaziah the son of Ahab said to Jehoshaphat, Let my servants go with your servants in the ships. But Jehoshaphat would not consent.

50 ¶And Jehoshaphat slept with his fathers, and was buried with his fathers in the city of David his father; and Joran his son reigned in his stead.

51 ¶Ahaziah the son of Ahab began to reign over Israel in Samaria in the seventeenth year of Jehoshaphat king of Judah, and he reigned two years over Israel.

52 And he did evil in the sight of the LORD, and walked in the ways of his father and in the ways of his mother and in the ways of Jeroboam the son of Nebat who made Israel sin;

53 For he served Baal and worshipped him and provoked to anger the LORD God of Israel, according to all that his father had done.

THE SECOND BOOK OF THE

KINGS

commonly called

THE FOURTH BOOK OF THE KINGS

CHAPTER 1

THEN Moab rebelled against Israel after the death of Ahab.

2 And Ahaziah fell down from the balcony of his upper chamber in Samaria, and was injured; so he sent messengers and said to them, Go, inquire of Baal-zebub the god of Ekron whether I shall recover from this injury.

3 But the angel of the LORD said to Elijah the Tishbite, Arise, go up to meet the messengers of the king of Samaria and say to them, Is it because there is no God in Israel that you are going to inquire of Baal-zebub the god of Ekron?

4 Now therefore thus says the LORD: You shall not come down from the bed on which you are lying, but you shall surely die. And Elijah departed.

5 ¶And when the messengers returned to Ahaziah, he said to them, Why have you turned back?

6 And they said to him, A man came up to meet us and said to us, Go, turn again to the man who sent you and say to him, Is it because there is no God in Israel that you are sending to inquire of Baal-zebub the god of Ekron? Therefore thus says the LORD: You shall not come down from the bed on which you are lying, but you shall surely die.

7 And he said to them, What manner of man was he who came up to meet you and told you these words?

8 And they answered him, He was a hairy man and girt with a girdle of leather about his loins. And he said to them, It is Elijah the Tishbite.

9 Then he sent to him a captain of fifty with his fifty. And he went up to him; and he was sitting on top of a mountain. And he said to him, O prophet of God, the king says, Come down.

10 And Elijah answered and said to the captain of fifty, If I am a prophet of God, then let fire come down from heaven and consume you and your fifty. And there came down fire from heaven and consumed him and his fifty.

11 Again he sent to him another captain of fifty with his fifty. And he spoke to him, saying, O prophet of God, thus says the king, Come down quickly.

12 And Elijah answered and said to him, If I am a prophet of God, then let fire come down from heaven and consume you and your fifty. And the fire of God came down from heaven and consumed him and his fifty.

13 ¶And he sent again to him the third time a captain of fifty with his fifty. And the captain of fifty went up and fell on his knees before Elijah and besought him and said to him, O prophet of God, let my life and the lives of these fifty servants of yours who are standing before you be precious in your sight.

14 For behold, there came fire down from heaven and consumed the two captains of the former fifties with their fifties; therefore let now my life be precious in your sight.

15 And the angel of the LORD said to Elijah, Go down with him; be not afraid of him. And he arose and went down with him to the king.

410

16 And he said to him, Thus says the LORD: Because you have sent messengers to inquire of Baal-zebub the god of Ekron, is it because there is no God in Israel to inquire for his word? Therefore you shall not come down from the bed on which you are lying, but you shall surely die.

17 ¶So he died according to the word of the LORD which Elijah had spoken. And Joram, his brother, reigned in his stead in the second year of Joram the son of Jehoshaphat king of Judah, because he had no son.

18 Now the rest of the acts of Ahaziah and all which he did, behold, they are written in the Book of the Chronicles of the Kings of Israel.

CHAPTER 2

AND it came to pass, when the LORD was about to take Elijah up to heaven by a whirlwind, Elijah and Elisha had departed from Gilgal.

2 And Elijah said to Elisha, Wait for me here, for the LORD has sent me to Beth-el. And Elisha said, As the LORD lives, and as your soul lives, I will not leave you. So they went down to Beth-el.

3 And the sons of the prophets who were at Beth-el came forth to Elisha and said to him, Do you know that today the LORD will take away your master from over you? And he said, Yes, I also know it; hold your peace.

4 And Elijah said to Elisha, Wait for me here; for the LORD has sent me to Jericho. And he said, As the LORD lives, and as your soul lives, I will not leave you. So they came to Jericho.

5 And the sons of the prophets who were in Jericho drew near to Elisha and said to him, Do you know that today the LORD will take away your master from over you? And he answered, Yes, I also know it; hold your peace.

6 And Elijah said to Elisha, Wait for me here; for the LORD has sent me to the Jordan. And he said, As the LORD lives, and as your soul lives, I will not leave you. And they two went on.

7 And fifty men of the sons of the prophets went and stood to watch from afar; and they two stood by the Jordan.

8 Then Elijah took his mantle and wrapped it together and struck the waters of the Jordan, and they were divided half hither and half thither, so that they two crossed on dry ground.

9 ¶And when they had crossed, Elijah said to Elisha, Ask what I shall do for you before I am taken away from you. And Elisha said, Let a double portion of your spirit be upon me.

10 And he said, You have asked too much; nevertheless, if you see me when I am taken from you, it shall be so to you; but if not, it shall not be so.

11 And it came to pass, as they still went on and talked, behold, there appeared a chariot of fire and horses of fire, and separated the two; and Elijah went up by a whirlwind into heaven.

12 ¶And Elisha saw it and he cried, saying, My father, my father, the chariot of Israel and the horsemen thereof. And he saw him no more; and he took hold of his own clothes and tore them in two pieces.

13 Then he took up the mantle of Elijah that had fallen from him, and went back and stood by the bank of the Jordan;

14 And he took the mantle of Elijah that had fallen from him, and struck the waters and said, O LORD, the God of my lord Elijah! And when he also had struck the waters of the Jordan, they parted half hither and half thither; and Elisha went over.

15 And when the sons of the prophets who came to watch at Jericho saw him, they said, The spirit of Elijah rests on Elisha. And they came to meet him, and bowed themselves to the ground before him.

16 ¶And they said to him, Behold now, there are with your servants fifty strong men; let them go and seek your master, lest peradventure the Spirit of the LORD has taken him up and cast him upon one of the

mountains or into one of the valleys. And he said, You shall not send.

17 And when they urged him till he was embarrassed, he said, Send. So they sent therefore fifty men; and they sought him for three days, but found him not.

18 And when they came back to him (while he tarried at Jericho), he said to them, Did I not say to you, Do not go?

19 ¶And the men of the city said to Elisha, Behold, the situation of the city is pleasant, as our lord sees; but the water is bad and the ground is barren.

20 And he said, Bring me a new cruse and put salt in it. And they brought it to him.

21 And he went forth to the spring of water and cast the salt in there, and said, Thus says the LORD: I have healed these waters; there shall not be from thence any more death or barren land.

22 So the waters were healed to this day, according to the saying of Elisha which he spoke.

23 ¶And he went up from thence to Beth-el; and as he was going up along the way, there came forth little boys out of the city and mocked him, saying, Go up, you bald head, go up, you bald head.

24 And he turned back and saw them and cursed them in the name of the LORD. And there came forth two she-bears out of the forest, and tore forty-two of the boys.

25 And he went from thence to mount Carmel, and from there he returned to Samaria.

CHAPTER 3

NOW Joram the son of Ahab began to reign over Israel in Samaria in the eighteenth year of Jehoshaphat king of Judah, and he reigned twelve years.

2 And he did evil in the sight of the LORD; but not like his father and like his mother; for he put away the statue of Baal which his father had made.

3 Nevertheless he clung to the sins of Jeroboam the son of Nebat, who made Israel sin; he did not turn aside from them.

4 ¶Now Mesha king of Moab was a sheepmaster, and he used to bring up to the king of Israel a hundred thousand fat lambs and a hundred thousand rams, with their wool.

5 But it came to pass, when Ahab was dead, the king of Moab rebelled against the king of Israel.

6 ¶And King Joram went out of Samaria at the same time and numbered all Israel.

7 Then he went on and sent to Jehoshaphat king of Judah, saying, The king of Moab has rebelled against me; come with me, let us go to war against Moab. And Jehoshaphat said, I will go up as you go, my people as your people and my horses as your horses.

8 And he said to him, Which way shall we go up? And he answered, By the way of the wilderness of Edom.

9 So the king of Israel went with the king of Judah and the king of Edom, and traveled seven days' journey; and there was no water for the army and for the people who were with them.

10 And the king of Israel said, Alas! truly for this the LORD has called these three kings together, to deliver them into the hand of Moab!

11 But Jehoshaphat said, Is there not here a prophet of the LORD, that we may inquire of the LORD by him? And one of the king of Israel's servants answered and said, Here is Elisha the son of Shaphat, who used to pour water on the hands of Elijah.

12 And Jehoshaphat said, The word of the LORD is with him. So the king of Israel and Jehoshaphat and the king of Edom went down to him.

13 And Elisha said to the king of Israel, What have I to do with you? Go to the prophets of your father and to the prophets of your mother. And the king of Israel said to him, Truly for this the LORD has called these three kings together, to deliver them into the hand of Moab.

14 And Elisha said, As the LORD of hosts lives, before whom I stand, were it not that I regard the presence of

Jehoshaphat the king of Judah, I would not look toward you nor see you.

15 But now bring me a minstrel. And it came to pass, when the minstrel played, the hand of the LORD came upon him.

16 And he said, Thus says the LORD: Let this valley be made full of cisterns.

17 For thus says the LORD: You shall not see wind, neither shall you see rain; yet this valley shall be filled with water, that you may drink, both you and your cattle and your beasts.

18 And this is but a small thing in the sight of the LORD; he will deliver the Moabites also into your hands.

19 And you shall destroy every fortified city and every choice city, and shall fell every good tree and pollute all the springs of water and mar every good piece of land with stones.

20 And it came to pass in the morning, when the sacrifice was offered, that, behold, there came water by the way of Edom, and the land was covered with water.

21 ¶And when all the Moabites saw that the kings were come up to fight against them, they called out all that were able to gird themselves with the sword and stood on the border.

22 And they rose up early in the morning, and the sun shone upon the water, and the Moabites saw the water on the other side as red as blood;

23 And they said, This is blood; the kings are surely slain, and they have killed one another; now therefore, Moab, to the spoil.

24 And when they came to the camp of Israel, the Israelites rose up and smote the Moabites, so that they fled before them; but they continued attacking them, and they devastated Moab.

25 And they destroyed the cities, and on every good piece of land cast every man his stone and filled it; and they polluted every spring of water and felled all the good trees, till the stones in the walls of the capital city were left demolished; and the slingers surrounded it and destroyed it.

26 ¶And when the king of Moab saw that the battle was too sore for him, he took with him seven hundred men who drew swords, to break through to the king of Edom; but he could not.

27 Then he took his eldest son who was to reign in his stead and offered him as a burnt offering upon the wall. And there was great indignation against Israel; and kings departed from Moab and returned to their own country.

CHAPTER 4

NOW a certain woman of the wives of the sons of the prophets cried to Elisha, saying, Your servant my husband is dead; and you know that your servant did fear the LORD; and the creditor has come to take my two sons to be his bondmen.

2 And Elisha said to her, What shall I do for you? Tell me, what have you in the house? And she said, Your handmaid has nothing in the house except a pot of oil.

3 Then he said to her, Go, borrow for yourself vessels from the houses of all your neighbors, even empty vessels; borrow not a few.

4 And then go in, and shut the door upon you and upon your sons, and pour out into all these vessels; and the vessel which is full bring up to me.

5 So she went from him, and entered her house and shut the door upon herself and upon her sons who brought the vessels to her; and she poured out.

6 And when the vessels were full, she said to her son, Bring me more vessels. But her son said to her, There are no more vessels. And the oil stopped.

7 Then she came and told the prophet of God. And he said, Go, sell the oil, and pay your debt, and live, you and your sons, on what is left over.

8 ¶And it came to pass on the morrow, Elisha went and came to Shiloh, where was a wealthy woman; and she constrained him to eat food. So that

whenever he passed by, he turned in there to eat food.

9 And she said to her husband, Behold now, I perceive that the prophet of God is a holy man who passes by us continually.

10 Let us make for him a little upper room, and let us set for him there a bed and a table and a chair and a candlestick, so that when he comes to us, he shall turn in there.

11 And it happened on a certain day, he came there, and he turned in to the upper room and lay there.

12 And he said to Gehazi his servant, Call this Shilomite woman. And when he had called her, she stood before him.

13 And he said to her, Behold, you have shown us all this respect; what is to be done for you? Is there anything to be spoken on your behalf to the king or to the commander of the army? And she answered, I dwell among my own people quite well.

14 Then he said, What shall I do for her? And Gehazi said to him, Verily she has no son and her husband is old.

15 And he said, Call her. And when he had called her, she stood in the door.

16 And he said to her, About this season, you will be with child, and shall embrace a son. And she said, No, my lord, O prophet of God, do not lie to your handmaid.

17 And the woman conceived and bore a son; at the season that Elisha had said to her, she was with child.

18 ¶Now when the child had grown, he went out on a certain day to his father who was with the reapers.

19 And he said to his father, Oh, my head, my head! And his father said to a servant, Take him up and carry him to his mother.

20 And when he had taken him and brought him to his mother, he sat on her knees till noon and then died.

21 And she went up and laid him on the bed of the prophet of God, and shut the door upon him and went out.

22 Then she called to her husband and said, Send me one of the servants and one of the asses, that I may go hastily to the prophet of God.

23 And he said to her, Why will you go to him today? It is neither new moon nor sabbath. But the Shilomite gave orders;

24 And they saddled an ass for her, and she said to the servant, Drive fast; do not stop to dismount me unless I tell you.

25 So she went to the prophet of God at mount Carmel. And when the prophet of God saw her afar off, he said to Gehazi his disciple, Behold, there is the Shilomite:

26 Run now to meet her, and say to her, Is it well with you? Is it well with your husband? Is it well with the child? And she answered, It is well.

27 And when she came to the prophet of God to the mountain, she caught hold of his feet; but Gehazi came near to remove her. And the prophet of God said to him, Let her alone; for her soul is in bitter anguish; and the LORD has hidden it from me and has not told me.

28 Then she said, Did I ask a son of my lord? Did I not say to you, Do not ask a son for me?

29 Then he said to Gehazi, Gird up your loins and take my staff in your hand and go. If you meet any man, do not salute him; and if any man salutes you, do not answer him; and lay my staff upon the face of the child.

30 And the mother of the child said, As the LORD lives and as your soul lives, I will not leave you. And he arose and followed her.

31 And Gehazi went on before them and laid the staff upon the face of the child; but there was neither voice nor hearing. Therefore he returned to meet Elisha, and told him, saying, The child is not awake.

32 And when Elisha was come into the house, behold, the child was dead and lying upon his bed.

33 He went in therefore and shut the door upon the two of them, and prayed unto the LORD.

34 And he went up and lay upon the child and put his mouth upon his mouth, and his eyes upon his eyes,

and his hands upon his hands; and he stretched himself upon him, and the flesh of the child became warm.

35 Then he returned, and walked to and fro in the house; and went up and stretched himself upon him; and the child sneezed seven times, and the child opened his eyes.

36 And Elisha called Gehazi and said to him, Call this Shilomite. So he called her. And when she was come to him, he said to her, Take up your son.

37 Then she went in and fell at his feet and bowed herself to the ground and took up her son and went out.

38 ¶And Elisha returned to Gilgal; and there was a famine in the land; and the sons of the prophets were sitting before him; and he said to his disciple, Set on the great pot, and cook pottage for the sons of the prophets.

39 And one of them went out into the field to gather herbs and found a wild vine in the field and gathered from it his lap full of wild gourds, and came and put them into the pot of pottage; for he did not know what they were.

40 So he poured out for the men to eat. And as they were eating of the pottage, they cried out and said, O prophet of God, there is death in the pot. And they could not eat of it.

41 But he said, Take meal and cast it into the pot; and he said, Pour out for the people, that they may eat. And there was no harm in the pot.

42 ¶And there came a certain man from the city of giants, and brought the prophet of God bread of the first fruits, twenty loaves of barley and new wheat rubbed from the ears in a cloth. And he said, Give to the people, that they may eat.

43 And his servant said, What, should I set this before a hundred men? And Elisha said to him again, Give them to the people, that they may eat; for thus says the LORD, They shall eat and shall leave some.

44 So he set it before them, and they did eat and left some, according to the word of the LORD.

CHAPTER 5

NOW Naaman, general of the army of the king of Aram, was a great man with his master, and honorable, because by him the LORD had given deliverance to Aram; and Naaman was a valiant man, but he was a leper.

2 And the Arameans had gone out raiding, and had brought away captive out of the land of Israel a little maid; and she waited on Naaman's wife.

3 And she said to her mistress, Blessed would be my lord if he would go to the prophet who is in Samaria! for he would immediately cure him of his leprosy.

4 And they went in and told her lord, saying, Thus and thus said the maid who is from the land of Israel.

5 And the king of Aram said to him, Come, go, I will send a letter to the king of Israel. And he departed and took with him ten talents of silver and six thousand pieces of gold and ten changes of garments.

6 And he brought the letter to the king of Israel, and this was written in it: In the hour when this letter reaches you, behold, I have sent to you Naaman my servant that you may heal him of his leprosy.

7 And when the king of Israel had read the letter, he tore his clothes and said, Am I God, to kill and to make alive, that this man sends me a man to heal him of his leprosy? Wherefore consider, and see how he is seeking to pick a quarrel with me.

8 ¶And when Elisha the prophet of God had heard that the king of Israel had torn his clothes, he sent to the king, saying, Why have you torn your clothes? Let him come now to me, and he shall know that there is a prophet in Israel.

9 So Naaman came with his horses and with his chariots, and stood at the door of the house of Elisha.

10 And Elisha sent a messenger to him, saying, Go and wash in the Jordan seven times, and your flesh shall come again to you and you shall be clean.

11 But Naaman was angry, and went away and said, Behold, I thought, He will surely come out to me and stand and call on the name of the LORD his God and wave his hand over the place, and I will recover from the leprosy.

12 Are not Amnan and Pharpar, rivers of Damascus, better than all the waters of Israel? I will go and wash in them and be clean. So he turned and went away in a rage.

13 And his servants came near and spoke to him and said, Our lord, if the prophet had told you to do some great thing, you would have done it; but behold, he has told you to do a small thing. Go and wash, and be clean. And he listened to them and did so.

14 And he went down and washed seven times in the Jordan, according to the saying of the prophet of God; and his flesh came again like the flesh of a little child, and he was clean.

15 ¶And he returned to the prophet of God, he and all his company, and came and stood before him, and said to him, Behold, now I know that there is no God in all the earth but in Israel; now therefore, take this blessing from your servant.

16 But Elisha said, As the LORD lives, before whom I stand, I will receive none. And he urged him to take it; but he refused.

17 And Naaman said, Shall there not then be given to your servant two mules' burden of earth? For your servant will henceforth offer neither burnt offerings nor sacrifices to any other god but to the LORD.

18 In this matter may the LORD forgive your servant, when my master goes into the house of Rimmon to worship there; I am the king's aide and I worship also in the house of Rimmon; and when I worship in the house of Rimmon, the LORD pardon your servant in this matter.

19 And he said to him, Go in peace. So he departed from him a little way.

20 ¶Then Gehazi the disciple of Elisha the prophet of God, said, Behold, my lord has spared Naaman the Aramean, in not accepting from him that which he brought; but, as the LORD lives, I will run after him, and take something from him.

21 So Gehazi ran after Naaman. And when Naaman saw him running after him, he alighted from his chariot to meet him and said to him, Is all well?

22 And he said, All is well. My master has sent me, saying, There have just now come to me from mount Ephraim two men of the sons of the prophets; give them a talent of silver and two changes of garments.

23 And Naaman said, I am willing; take two talents. And he urged him and bound two talents of silver in two pieces of cloth, with two changes of garments, and he gave them to two of his servants; and they carried them before him.

24 And when they came to a secret place, he took them from their hand and put them in the house; and he sent the men away and they departed.

25 But he went in and stood before his master. And Elisha said to him, Where have you been, Gehazi? And he said, Your servant went nowhere.

26 And he said to him, My heart told me when the man alighted from his chariot to meet you. Is it a time to gain money and to gain garments and oliveyards and vineyards and sheep and oxen and menservants and maidservants?

27 The leprosy therefore of Naaman shall cleave to you and to your descendants for ever. And he went out from his presence a leper as white as snow.

CHAPTER 6

AND the sons of the prophets said to Elisha, Behold now, this place wherein we dwell with you is too small for us.

2 Let us go to the Jordan and cut from there every man a beam, and let us make a place for us to dwell there. And he said, Go.

3 And one of them answered and said, If you please, go with your servants. And he answered, I will go.

4 So he went with them. And when

they came to the Jordan, they cut down trees.

5 But as one of them was felling a beam, the axehead fell into the water; and he cried and said, I beseech you, my lord! it was borrowed by your servant.

6 And the prophet of God said to him, Where did it fall? And he showed him the place. And he cut off a stick and thrust it in there; and it stuck in the hole of the axehead.

7 And he said, Take it up to you. And he put out his hand and took it.

8 ¶Then the king of Aram warred against Israel, and took counsel with his servants, saying, In such and such a place shall we lie in wait.

9 And the prophet of God sent to the king of Israel, saying, Beware that you do not pass this place; for the Arameans are lying in wait.

10 And the king of Israel sent to the place of which the prophet of God told him and warned him about it, not once nor twice.

11 Therefore the heart of the king of Aram was sore troubled because of this thing; and he called his servants and said to them, Will you not show me who of us is for the king of Israel?

12 And one of his servants answered, and said, None of us, my lord O king; but Elisha, the prophet who is in Israel, tells the king of Israel the thing that you plan in your bedchamber.

13 ¶And he said, Go and see where he is, that I may send and take him. And it was told him, saying, Behold, he is in Dothan.

14 Therefore he sent there horsemen and chariots and a great army; and they came by night and surrounded the city.

15 And when the servant of the prophet of God arose early and went out, behold, an army surrounded the city both with horses and chariots. And his servant said to him, Alas, my master! what shall we do?

16 And he said to him, Fear not; for those who are with us are more than those who are with them.

17 And Elisha prayed to the LORD and said, O LORD, open his eyes that he may see. And the LORD opened the eyes of the young man; and he saw; and, behold, the mountain was full of horses and chariots of fire round about Elisha.

18 And when they came down to him, Elisha prayed to the LORD and said, Smite this people with dimness of vision. And he smote them with dimness according to the word of Elisha.

19 ¶And Elisha said to them, This is not the way, neither is this the city; follow me, and I will bring you to the man whom you seek. But he led them to Samaria.

20 And when they were come into Samaria, Elisha said, O LORD, open the eyes of these men, that they may see. And the LORD opened their eyes, and they saw; and, behold, they were in the midst of Samaria.

21 And the king of Israel said to Elisha when he saw them, My father, shall I slay them? Shall I slay them?

22 And he answered, You shall not slay them; would you slay those whom you have taken captive with your sword and with your bow? Set bread and water before them, that they may eat and drink and go to their master.

23 So he prepared for them a great banquet; and when they had eaten and drunk, they went to their master. So the raiders of Aram came no more across the border of Israel.

24 ¶And it came to pass after this, that Bar-hadad king of Aram gathered all his army, and went up and besieged Samaria and fought against it.

25 And there was a great famine in Samaria, as they besieged it, until an ass's head was sold for eighty pieces of silver and the fourth part of a cab [1] of dove's dung for five pieces of silver.

26 And as the king of Israel was passing by upon the wall, there cried a woman to him, saying, Help me, my lord, O king.

27 And he said to her, Let the

[1] About a pint, dry measure.

Lord help you; whence shall I help you? Out of the threshing floor or out of the wine press?

28 And the king said to her, What troubles you? And she said to him, This woman said to me, Give your son, that we may eat him today, and we will eat my son tomorrow.

29 So we cooked my son and ate him; and I said to her on the next day, Give your son, that we may eat him; but she had hidden her son.

30 ¶And when the king heard the words of the woman, he tore his clothes as he walked upon the wall, and the people looked, and behold, he was wearing sackcloth within upon his flesh.

31 Then he said, May God do so and more also to me, if the head of Elisha the son of Shaphat shall remain on him this day.

32 But Elisha was sitting in his house and the elders were sitting with him; and the king sent a messenger; but before the messenger came to him, he said to the elders, Do you see how this son of a murderer has sent to take away my head? Look, when the messenger comes, shut the door and push him outside, because the sound of his master's feet is behind him.

33 And while he was still speaking with them, the messenger came to him; and he said, Behold, this evil is from the Lord; why should I pray to the Lord any longer?

CHAPTER 7

THEN Elisha said, Hear the word of the Lord; thus says the Lord: Tomorrow about this time a measure of fine flour shall be sold for a shekel and two measures of barley for a shekel in the gate of Samaria.

2 Then the king's aide answered and said, If the Lord should make windows in heaven, could this thing be? And Elisha said to him, Behold, you will see it with your eyes, but you shall not eat of it.

3 ¶Now there were four leprous men sitting at the entrance of the gate; and they said to one another, Why do we sit here until we die?

4 If we say, We will enter into the city, the famine is severe in the city, and we shall die there; and if we still sit here, we die also. Now therefore come and let us go to the camp of Aram; if they save us alive, we shall live; and if they put us to death, we shall but die.

5 So they rose up early in the twilight to go to the camp of Aram; and when they were come to the uttermost part of the camp, behold, there was no man there;

6 For the Lord had made the army of Aram hear the noise of horses and the noise of chariots and the noise of a great army; and they said to one another, Lo, the king of Israel has hired against us the king of the Egyptians and the king of the Hittites to come upon us.

7 Wherefore they arose and fled in the twilight, and left their tents, their horses, and their asses, even their camp as it was, and they fled for their lives.

8 And when these lepers came to the uttermost part of the camp, they went into a tent and ate and drank and took from there silver and gold and clothing, and went and hid it; then they came again and entered into another tent and carried booty from there also and went and hid it.

9 Then they said one to another, We are not doing right; this day is a day of good tidings, and how long shall we remain silent? If we wait until the morning light, some mischief will come upon us; now therefore come, let us go and tell the king's household.

10 So they came and called to the doorkeepers of the city; and they told them, saying, We went to the camp of Aram, and behold, there was no man there, neither voice of man, but horses tied and asses tied and tents as they were.

11 And the doorkeepers called out and told it to the king's household within.

12 ¶And the king arose in the night and said to his servants, I will now tell you what the Arameans have done to us. They know that we are hungry;

therefore they have gone out of the camp to hide themselves in the field, saying, When they come out of the city, we shall capture them alive and then get into the city.

13 And one of his servants answered and said, Let some horsemen take five of the horses that remain; if they are captured, let them be considered a loss like all the army of Israel that has perished; therefore let us send and see.

14 So two couples of horsemen mounted, and the king sent them after the army of Aram, saying, Go and see.

15 And they went after them as far as the Jordan; and, lo, all the road was full of garments and vessels which the Arameans had left behind in their haste. And the messengers returned and told the king.

16 And the people went out and plundered the camp of Aram. So a measure of fine flour was sold for a shekel and two measures of barley for a shekel, according to the word of the LORD.

17 ¶And the king placed his aide in charge of the gate; and the people trod upon him at the gate and he died, as the prophet of God had said when he came down as a messenger to him.

18 And it came to pass as the prophet of God had foretold to the king, saying, A measure of fine flour for a shekel and two measures of barley for a shekel shall be sold tomorrow at this time in the gate of Samaria.

19 But that mighty man had answered the prophet of God and said, If the LORD should make windows in heaven, could this thing be? And the prophet had said, Behold, you shall see it with your eyes, but you shall not eat of it.

20 And so it happened to him; for the people trod upon him in the gate and he died.

CHAPTER 8

THEN Elisha said to the woman whose son he had restored to life, Arise and go, you and your household, and sojourn wherever you can; for the LORD has called for a famine; and it shall come upon the land for seven years.

2 So the woman arose and did according to the word of the prophet of God; and she went with her household and sojourned in the land of the Philistines seven years.

3 And at the end of the seven years, when the woman returned from the land of the Philistines, she went forth to cry to the king for her house and for her field.

4 And the king talked with Gehazi the servant of the prophet of God, saying, Tell me all the great things that Elisha has done.

5 And while he was telling the king how Elisha had restored a dead body to life, behold, the woman whose son he had restored to life cried to the king for her house and for her field. And Gehazi said, My lord, O king, this is the woman and this is her son whom Elisha restored to life.

6 And when the king asked the woman, she told him. So the king appointed to her a certain officer and said to him, Restore all that was hers and all the produce of her field from the day that she left the land even until now.

7 ¶And Elisha came to Damascus; and Bar-hadad the king of Aram was sick; and it was told him, saying, The prophet of God has come here.

8 And the king said to Hazael, Take a present with you and go to meet the prophet of God, and inquire of the LORD by him, saying, Shall I recover of this disease?

9 So Hazael went to meet him and took a present with him, even of every good thing of Damascus, forty camels' burden, and came and stood before him and said to him, Your son Bar-hadad king of Aram has sent me to you, saying, Shall I recover of this disease?

10 And Elisha said to him, Go, say to him, You shall surely recover; but the LORD has shown me that he shall surely die.

11 Then the prophet of God wept.

12 And Hazael said, Why does my

lord weep? And Elisha said to him, Because I know the evil that you will do to the children of Israel: their strongholds you will set on fire, their young men you will slay with the sword, and you will dash their children against the ground and rip up their women with child.

13 And Hazael said, But what, is your servant a dog, that he should do this terrible thing? And Elisha answered, The LORD has shown me that you shall be king over Aram.

14 So Hazael departed from Elisha and came to his master; and his master said to him, What did Elisha say to you? And he answered, Thus he said to me: You shall surely recover.

15 And on the morrow, Hazael took a thick cloth and dipped it in water and spread it on the king's face, so that he died; and Hazael reigned in his stead.

16 ¶And in the fifth year of Joram the son of Ahab king of Israel, Joram the son of Jehoshaphat, king of Judah, began to reign.

17 He was thirty-two years old when he began to reign; and he reigned eight years in Jerusalem.

18 And he walked in the way of the kings of Israel, as did the house of Ahab; for the sister of Ahab was his wife; and he did evil in the sight of the LORD.

19 Yet the LORD would not destroy Judah for David his servant's sake, as he promised to him that he would give an heir to his children all the days.

20 ¶In his days Edom revolted from under the hand of Judah and set up a king over themselves.

21 So Joram went over to Zair, and all the chariots with him; and he rose by night to smite the Edomites who had surrounded him and his commanders with chariots; but the people fled to their tents.

22 So Edom revolted from under the hand of Judah even to this day. Then Libnah revolted at the same time.

23 And the rest of the acts of Joram and all that he did, behold, they are written in the Book of the Chronicles of the Kings of Judah.

24 And Joram slept with his fathers and was buried with his fathers in the city of David; and Ahaziah his son reigned in his stead.

25 ¶In the eleventh year of Joram the son of Ahab king of Israel, Ahaziah the son of Joram king of Judah began to reign.

26 Ahaziah was twenty-two years old when he began to reign; and he reigned one year in Jerusalem. And his mother's name was Athaliah, the daughter of Omri king of Israel.

27 And he walked in the way of the house of Ahab, and did evil in the sight of the LORD, as did the house of Ahab; for he was the son-in-law of the house of Ahab.

28 ¶And he went with Joram the son of Ahab to war against Hazael the king of Aram at Ramath-gilead; and the Arameans wounded Joram.

29 And Joram the son of Ahab went back to be healed in Jezreel of the wounds which the Arameans had inflicted on him at Ramath, when he fought against Hazael king of Aram. And Ahaziah the son of Joram king of Judah went down to see Joram the son of Ahab in Jezreel, because he was sick.

CHAPTER 9

THEN Elisha the prophet called one of the sons of the prophets and said to him, Gird up your loins and take this flask of oil in your hand and go to Ramath-gilead;

2 And when you get there, look for Jehu the son of Jimshi, and go in and make him arise up from among his brethren, and bring him into an inner chamber;

3 Then take the flask of oil and pour it on his head, and say to him, Thus says the LORD, I have anointed you king over my people Israel. Then open the door and flee, and do not tarry.

4 ¶So the young prophet went to Ramath-gilead.

5 And when he came in, behold, the commanders of the army were sitting; and he said, I have an errand to you,

O commander. And Jehu said, To which of us? And he said to him, To you, O commander.

6 And he arose and went into an inner chamber; and he poured the oil on his head, and said to him, Thus says the LORD God of Israel, I have anointed you king over the people of the LORD, even over Israel.

7 And you shall smite the house of Ahab your master, that I may avenge the blood of my servants the prophets and the blood of all the servants of the LORD, at the hand of Jezebel.

8 For I will destroy the whole house of Ahab, and I will cut off from Ahab every male and every one in authority in Israel;

9 And I will make the house of Ahab like the house of Jeroboam the son of Nebat and like the house of Baasha the son of Ahijah;

10 And the dogs shall eat Jezebel in the inheritance of Naboth in Jezreel, and there shall be none to bury her. And he opened the door and fled.

11 ¶Then Jehu came forth to the servants of his lord; and they said to him, Is all well? Why did this mad fellow come to you? And he said to them, You know the man, and his folly.

12 And they said to him, You are lying; tell us now. And he said to them, Thus and thus he spoke to me, saying, Thus says the LORD: I have anointed you king over Israel.

13 Then they hastened and took every man his garment and put it under him on the top of the stairs and blew with trumpets, saying, Jehu is king.

14 So Jehu the son of Jimshi conspired against Joram. (Now Joram was holding Ramath-gilead, he and all Israel with him because of Hazael king of Aram.

15 But King Joram had returned to be healed in Jezreel of the wounds which the Arameans had inflicted on him when he fought against Hazael king of Aram.) And Jehu said, If it please you, let no one go forth nor escape out of the city to tell it in Jezreel.

16 So Jehu rode in a chariot and went to Jezreel; for Joram lay there. And Ahaziah king of Judah had come down to see Joram the son of Ahab who was sick in Jezreel.

17 And the watchman was standing on the tower of Jezreel, and he saw the chariot of Jehu as it was coming, and the watchman said, I see chariots. And Joram said, Take a chariot and send it to meet them, and let him say, Is it peace?

18 So there went a horseman to meet him and said to him, Thus says the king: Is it peace? And Jehu said, What have you to do with peace? Turn behind me. And the watchman told, saying, The messenger came to them, but he did not return.

19 Then he sent out a second horseman, who came to them and said, Thus says the king, Is it peace? And Jehu answered, What have you to do with peace? Turn behind me.

20 And the watchman told, saying, The messenger came to them, but he did not return; and the driving is like the driving of Jehu the son of Jimshi; for he drives furiously.

21 And Joram said, Make ready. And they made ready chariots. And Joram king of Israel and Ahaziah king of Judah went out, each in his chariot, and they went to meet Jehu and they met him in the field of Naboth the Jezreelite.

22 And when Joram saw Jehu, he said, Is it peace, Jehu? And Jehu answered, What peace, so long as the whoredoms of your mother Jezebel and her witchcrafts are so many?

23 Then Joram turned back and fled, and said to Ahaziah, There is treachery, O Ahaziah!

24 And Jehu drew a bow with his full strength, and smote Joram in his back, and the arrow went out at his heart, and he sank down in his chariot.

25 Then Jehu said to Bar-dekar his mighty man, Take him up, and cast him into the field of Naboth the Jezreelite; for I remember how when you and I were driving together after Ahab his father, and the LORD said this thing against him;

26 Surely I have seen yesterday the

blood of Naboth and the blood of his sons, says the LORD; and I will require you in this field, says the LORD. Now therefore take him up and cast him into the field, according to the word of the LORD. So they cast him into the field of Naboth the Jezreelite.

27 ¶But when Ahaziah the king of Judah saw this, he fled by the way of the garden house. And Jehu pursued him, and said, Slay him also, and they slew him in his chariot at the ascent of the mound, which is by Nebleam. And he fled to Megiddo, and died there.

28 And his servants took him and carried him (in a chariot) to Jerusalem, and buried him in his sepulchre with his fathers in the city of David.

29 And in the eleventh year of Joram the son of Ahab, Ahaziah began to reign over Judah.

30 ¶And when Jehu was come to Jezreel, Jezebel heard of it; and she painted her eyelids with kohl, and adorned her head, and looked out a window.

31 And as Jehu entered in at the gate, she said, Is it peace, you Zimri, murderer of his master?

32 And he lifted up his face to the window, and said, Who is on my side? And there looked out at him two or three eunuchs.

33 And he said, Throw her down. So they threw her down; and some of her blood was sprinkled on the wall, and the horses entered and trod her under foot.

34 Then he went in to eat and drink, and he said, See now to this cursed woman, and bury her; for she is a king's daughter.

35 And they went to bury her; but they found no more of her than her skull and her feet and the palms of her hands.

36 And when they returned, they told him, and he said, This is the word of the LORD which he spoke by his servant Elijah the Tishbite, saying, In the field of Jezreel shall dogs eat the flesh of Jezebel;

37 And the corpse of Jezebel shall be as refuse upon the face of the field of Jezreel; and there will be none to bury her, so that they shall not say, This is Jezebel.

CHAPTER 10

AND Ahab had seventy sons in Samaria. And they were brought up by the nobles of the city. And Jehu wrote a letter and sent it to Samaria, to the princes of Jezreel, to the elders, and to those who brought up Ahab's children, saying,

2 Now as soon as this letter reaches you, seeing your master's sons are with you and there are with you chariots and horses, fortified cities also, and weapons;

3 Whichever seems to you good and best of your master's sons, set him on his father's throne and fight for your master's house.

4 But when they heard the letter, they were exceedingly afraid and said, Behold, two kings could not stand before Jehu; how then shall we stand before him?

5 So the overseer of the royal household, the governor of the city, the elders, and those who brought up the children, sent to Jehu, saying, We are your servants and will do all that you shall bid us; we will not make any man king over us; do whatever is good in your eyes.

6 Then he wrote to them a second letter, saying, If you are mine, and if you will hearken to my voice, then take the heads of your master's sons and bring them to me to Jezreel by this time tomorrow. Now the king's sons were seventy persons, and the nobles of the city brought them up.

7 And as soon as the letter reached them, they took the king's sons and slew them, seventy persons, and put their heads in baskets and sent them to him in Jezreel.

8 ¶And there came a messenger, and told him, saying, They have brought the heads of the king's sons. And he said, Lay them in two heaps at the entrance of the gate until morning.

9 And in the morning, he went out and said to all the people, You are righteous; I conspired against my

master and slew him; but who slew all these?

10 Know now that there shall fall to the earth nothing of the word of the LORD, of all which the LORD spoke concerning the house of Ahab; for the LORD has done that which he spoke by his servant Elijah.

11 So Jehu slew all that remained of the house of Ahab in Jezreel, and all his great men and his kinsfolks and his priests, until he left him none remaining.

12 ¶And he arose and departed and came to Samaria. And on the way he destroyed the houses of idols.

13 Then Jehu met with the brothers of Ahaziah king of Judah and said to them, Who are you? And they answered, We are the brothers of Ahaziah; and we have come down to salute the sons of the king and the sons of the queen.

14 And he said, Take them alive. And they took them alive and slew them and threw them into the pit of Beth-akar, forty-two persons; and he left none of them.

15 ¶And when he was departed from there, he found Jonadab the son of Rechab coming to meet him; and he blessed him, and said to him, Is your heart right, as my heart is with your heart? And Jonadab answered, It is, it is. And he said to him, Give me your hand. And he gave him his hand; and he took him up with him into the chariot.

16 And he said to him, Come with me and see my zeal for the LORD. So he made him ride in his chariot.

17 And when he came to Samaria, he slew all that remained to the house of Ahab in Samaria, till he had destroyed them, according to the saying of the LORD which he spoke to Elijah.

18 ¶Then Jehu gathered all the people together and said to them, Ahab served Baal a little; but Jehu shall serve him much.

19 Now therefore invite to come to me all the prophets of Baal, all his priests, and all who serve him; let none be missing; for I have a great sacrifice to make to Baal; whoever is missing, he shall not live. But Jehu

did it deceitfully, with the intent to destroy the worshippers of Baal.

20 And Jehu said, Invite all the assembly to come to Baal. And they invited them;

21 And Jehu sent through all Israel; and all the worshippers of Baal came, so that there was not a man left who did not come. And they came into the house of Baal; and the house of Baal was full from one end to the other.

22 And he said to him who was over the vestry, Bring out vestments for all the worshippers of Baal. And he brought them forth vestments.

23 Then Jehu and Jonadab, the son of Rechab, went into the house of Baal and said to the worshippers of Baal, Search, and see that there be here with you none of the servants of the LORD, but the worshippers of Baal only.

24 And when they went in to offer sacrifices and burnt offerings, Jehu had posted three hundred and eighty men outside by the door, and said, If any of the men whom I have delivered into your hands escape, his life shall be for the life of him.

25 And as soon as he had made an end of offering the burnt offerings, Jehu said to the guards and to the mighty men, Go in and slay them; let none of them come forth. And they smote them with the edge of the sword; and the guards and the mighty men cast them out, and went to the city of the house of Baal.

26 And they brought forth the statue of Baal out of the house of Baal and burned it with fire.

27 And they broke down the image of Baal and demolished the house of Baal and made it a public toilet-room to this day.

28 Thus Jehu destroyed Baal out of Israel.

29 ¶But as for the sins of Jeroboam the son of Nebat, who made Israel to sin, Jehu did not depart from them, especially the worship of the golden calves that were in Beth-el and in Dan.

30 And the LORD said to Jehu, Because you have done well in my

sight, and have done to the house of Ahab according to all that was in my heart, your sons even to the fourth generation shall sit on the throne of Israel.

31 But Jehu did not try to walk in the law of the LORD God of Israel with all his heart; and he did not depart from the sins of Jeroboam the son of Nebat, who made Israel sin.

32 ¶In those days the LORD began to bring distress in Israel; and Hazael smote them in all the territory of Israel,

33 From the Jordan eastward, all the land of Gilead and of Gad and of Reuben and of Manasseh, from Adoer, which is by the river Arnon, even Gilead and Mathnin.

34 Now the rest of the acts of Jehu and all that he did and all his might, behold, they are written in the Book of the Chronicles of the Kings of Israel.

35 And Jehu slept with his fathers; and they buried him in Samaria. And Jehoahaz his son reigned in his stead.

36 And the time that Jehu reigned over Israel in Samaria was twenty-eight years.

CHAPTER 11

AND when Athaliah the mother of Ahaziah saw that her son was dead, she arose and destroyed all the royal heirs.

2 But Jehosheba, the daughter of King Joram, sister of Ahaziah, took Joash the son of Ahaziah and stole him from among the king's sons who were slain; and she hid him and his nurse in her bedchamber; thus she hid him from Athaliah, so that he was not slain.

3 And he was hidden with her in the house of the LORD six years. And Athaliah reigned over the land.

4 ¶And in the seventh year Jehoiada the priest sent and brought the captains of hundreds and the guards and the runners, and had them come to him into the house of the LORD and stationed them there, and made a covenant with them and took an oath of them and showed them the king's son.

5 And he commanded them, saying, This is the thing that you shall do: a third part of you who enter in on the sabbath shall keep guard of the king's house;

6 And a third part shall be at the gate of Kersa; and a third part at the gate of the house of the guards; so shall you keep the watch of the house, that it be in perfect order.

7 And two parts of all you that go off duty on the sabbath, even they shall keep the watch of the house of the LORD together with the king's house;

8 And you shall surround the king, every man with his weapons in his hand; and whosoever comes within range, let him be slain; and you be with the king as he goes out and as he comes in.

9 And the captains of the hundreds did according to all that Jehoiada the priest commanded them; and they took every man his men who were to be on duty on the sabbath, with those who were to be off duty on the sabbath, and came to Jehoiada the priest.

10 And the priest gave to the captains of hundreds King David's spears and shields, which were in the house of the LORD.

11 And the guards stood, every man with his weapons in his hand, from the right side of the temple to the left side of the temple and they surrounded the altar and the king's house.

12 And they brought forth the king's son and put the royal crown upon his head, and they anointed him and made him king; and they clapped their hands and said, Long live the king!

13 ¶And when Athaliah heard the noise of the uproar of the people as they rejoiced, she came to the people into the temple of the LORD.

14 And when she looked, behold, the king stood by the pillar, as was the custom of the kings, and the princes and the trumpeters were standing before the king, and all the people of the land were rejoicing, and blowing with trumpets; and

Athaliah tore her clothes and cried, 'Treason! Treason!

15 But Jehoiada the priest commanded the captains of hundreds and the officers of the army, and said to them, Take her forth outside the ranks; and whosoever follows her shall be slain with the sword. For the priest had said, Let her not be slain in the house of the LORD.

16 So they made room for her; and she went by the way of the horses' entrance to the king's house; and there she was slain.

17 ¶And Jehoiada the priest made a covenant between the LORD and the king and the people, that they should be the LORD's people; between the king also and the people.

18 And all the people of the land went into the house of Baal and demolished his altars and broke his images in pieces and slew Mattan the priest of Baal before the altar. And the priest appointed officers over the house of the LORD.

19 And he took the captains of the hundreds and the guards and the runners and all the people of the land; and they brought down the king from the house of the LORD, and came by the way of the gate of the guard to the king's house. And he sat on the throne of the kings.

20 And all the people of the land rejoiced, and the city was quiet; and they slew Athaliah with the sword in the king's house.

21 Joash was seven years old when he began to reign.

CHAPTER 12

IN the seventh year of Jehu Joash began to reign; and he reigned forty years in Jerusalem. And his mother's name was Zobah of Beersheba.

2 And Joash did that which was right in the sight of the LORD all his days wherein Jehoiada the priest instructed him.

3 But the temples of idols were not taken away; the people still sacrificed and burned incense on the high places.

4 ¶And Joash said to the priests, All the money of the dedicated things which is brought into the house of the LORD, even the money which every man gives for the salvation of his soul, the money which every man thinks in his heart to bring into the house of the LORD,

5 Let the priests receive it, every man from him who has decided to give; and let them spend it for the repairing of the house, wherever a breach to be repaired shall be found in it.

6 But it was so, that even in the twenty-third year of King Joash the priests had not repaired the breaches of the house.

7 Then King Joash called for Jehoiada the priest and the other priests, and said to them, Why have you not repaired the breaches of the house? Now therefore you shall not receive money from those who give it to you, but deliver it for the repair of the house.

8 So the priests agreed not to receive any more money from the people, nor to repair the breaches of the house.

9 But Jehoiada the priest took a chest and bored a hole in the lid of it and set it beside the altar, on the right side as one comes into the house of the LORD; and the priests who kept the door put therein all the money that was brought into the house of the LORD.

10 And when they saw that there was much money in the chest, the king's scribe and the high priest came up, and they counted and bound in bags the money that was found in the house of the LORD.

11 And they gave the money tied in bags to those who did the work, who had the oversight of the house of the LORD; and they gave it to the carpenters and to the builders who worked upon the house of the LORD,

12 And to the masons and the stonecutters, and to buy timber and hewed stones for the repair of the breaches of the house of the LORD, and for all that was spent to repair the house.

13 But there were not made for the house of the LORD bowls of silver,

snuffers, braziers for incense, trumpets or any vessels of gold or vessels of silver, of the money that was brought into the house of the LORD;

14 But they gave that to the workmen, and repaired with it the house of the LORD.

15 Moreover they did not ask an accounting from the men to whom they delivered the money to give it to the workmen; for they dealt faithfully in paying out the repair money.

16 The money from the trespass offerings and the money from the sin offerings was not brought into the house of the LORD; it was the priests'.

17 ¶Then Hazael king of Aram went up and fought against Gath and took it; and Hazael set his face to go up to Jerusalem.

18 And Joash king of Judah took all the hallowed things that Jehoshaphat and Joram and Ahaziah, his fathers, kings of Judah, had dedicated, and his own hallowed things and all the gold that was found in the treasures of the house of the LORD and in the king's house, and sent it to Hazael king of Aram; and he went away from Jerusalem.

19 ¶And the rest of the acts of Joash and all that he did, behold, they are written in the Book of the Chronicles of the Kings of Judah.

20 And the servants of Joash arose and made a conspiracy and slew Joash in the house of Millo, as he was going down to Silla.

21 It was Jozachar the son of Shimeath and Jehozabar the son of Shomer, his servants, who smote him so that he died; and they buried him with his fathers in the city of David; and Amaziah his son reigned in his stead.

CHAPTER 13

IN the twenty-third year of Joash the son of Ahaziah king of Judah, Jehoahaz the son of Jehu began to reign over Israel in Samaria, and he reigned seventeen years.

2 And he did that which was evil in the sight of the LORD and followed in the sins of Jeroboam the son of

Nebat, who made Israel sin; he did not turn aside from them.

3 ¶And the anger of the LORD kindled against Israel, and he delivered them into the hand of Hazael king of Aram and into the hand of Bar-hadad the son of Hazael, all their days.

4 And Jehoahaz prayed before the LORD, and the LORD hearkened to him; for he saw the suffering of Israel, because the king of Aram oppressed them.

5 (And the LORD gave Israel a saviour, so that they went out from under the hand of Aram; and the children of Israel dwelt securely in their tents as beforetime.

6 Nevertheless they did not depart from the sins of Jeroboam the son of Nebat, who made Israel sin, but walked in them; and also the idol worship remained in Samaria.)

7 There was not left much of an army to Jehoahaz but fifty horsemen and ten chariots and ten thousand footmen; for the king of Aram had destroyed them and had made them like the dust under his feet.

8 ¶Now the rest of the acts of Jehoahaz and all that he did and his might, behold, they are written in the Book of the Chronicles of the Kings of Israel.

9 And Jehoahaz slept with his fathers; and they buried him in Samaria; and Jehoash his son reigned in his stead.

10 ¶In the thirty-seventh year of Joash king of Judah, Jehoash the son of Jehoahaz began to reign over Israel in Samaria and he reigned thirteen years.

11 And he did that which was evil in the sight of the LORD; he did not turn aside from the sins of Jeroboam the son of Nebat, who made Israel sin; but he walked therein.

12 And the rest of the acts of Jehoash and all that he did and his might and how he fought against Amaziah king of Judah, behold, they are written in the Book of the Chronicles of the Kings of Israel.

13 And Jehoash slept with his fathers; and Jeroboam his son sat

upon his throne; and Jehoash was buried in Samaria with the kings of Israel.

14 ¶Now Elisha was fallen ill of the sickness of which he was to die. And Jehoash the king of Israel came down to him and wept in his presence and said, O my father, my father, the chariots of Israel and the horsemen thereof!

15 And Elisha said to him, Take a bow and arrows. And he took a bow and arrows.

16 And he said to the king of Israel, Put your hand upon the bow. And he put his hand upon it; and Elisha put his hands upon the king's hands.

17 And he said, Open the window to the east. And he opened it. Then Elisha said, Shoot. And he shot. And he said, The arrow of the LORD's deliverance and the arrow of the deliverance from Aram; for you shall smite the Arameans in Aphek till you have consumed them.

18 And he said to him, Take an arrow. And he took it. And he said, Strike upon the ground. And he struck three times and stopped.

19 And the prophet of God was angry with him and said, You should have struck five or six times; then you would have smitten the Arameans till you would have consumed them; whereas now you shall smite Aram but three times.

20 ¶And Elisha died and they buried him. And bands of the Moabites invaded the land that very year.

21 And it came to pass as they were burying a man, behold, a band of raiders was seen; and they cast the man into the sepulchre of Elisha; and when the man was let down and touched the bones of Elisha, he revived and stood up on his feet.

22 ¶But Hazael king of Aram oppressed Israel all the days of Jehoahaz.

23 And the LORD was gracious to them and had compassion on them, and returned to them, because of his covenant with Abraham, Isaac, and Jacob, and would not destroy them, neither did he cast them from his presence as yet.

24 So Hazael king of Aram died; and Bar-hadad his son reigned in his stead.

25 Then Jehoash the son of Jehoahaz took again from Bar-hadad the son of Hazael the cities which he had taken from Jehoahaz his father by war. Three times did Jehoash defeat him, and restored the cities to Israel.

CHAPTER 14

IN the second year of Jehoash the son of Jehoahaz king of Israel, Amaziah the son of Joash king of Judah, began to reign.

2 He was twenty-five years old when he began to reign, and he reigned twenty-nine years in Jerusalem. And his mother's name was Jehoaddan of Jerusalem.

3 And he did that which was, right in the sight of the LORD, yet not like David his father; he did according to all things that Joash his father did.

4 But the temples of idols he did not remove, and the people still were sacrificing and burning incense on the altars on the high places.

5 ¶And it came to pass, as soon as the kingdom was firmly in his hand, he slew his servants who had slain King Joash his father.

6 But the children of the murderers he did not kill, according to that which is written in the Book of the Law of Moses, wherein the LORD commanded, saying, The fathers shall not be put to death for the children, nor the children be put to death for the fathers; but every man shall be put to death for his own sin.

7 He slew of Edom in the valley of Salt twenty thousand, and destroyed Selah by war, and called the name of it Nakthael, which is its name to this day.

8 ¶Then Amaziah king of Judah sent messengers to Jehoash, the son of Jehoahaz son of Jehu, king of Israel, saying, Come let us look one another in the face.[1]

9 And Jehoash the king of Israel sent to Amaziah king of Judah, saying, The thistle that was in Lebanon sent to the cedar that was in Lebanon,

[1] Let us settle our troubles by war.

saying, Give your daughter to my son to wife; and there passed by a wild beast that was in Lebanon and trod down the thistle.

10 You have indeed smitten Edom, and your heart has lifted you up; glory in this, and tarry at your house; for why should you stir up trouble, so that you should fall, even you, and Judah with you?

11 But Amaziah would not listen to him. So Jehoash king of Israel and Amaziah king of Judah went up and they faced each other at Beth-shemesh, which belongs to Judah.

12 And Judah was defeated before Israel; and they fled every man to his tent.

13 And Jehoash king of Israel captured Amaziah king of Judah at Bethshemesh, and he entered Jerusalem and broke down the wall of Jerusalem from the gate of Ephraim to the corner gate, four hundred cubits.

14 And he took all the gold and silver and all the vessels that were found in the house of the LORD and in the treasures of the king's house, and hostages, and returned to Samaria.

15 ¶Now the rest of the acts of Jehoash and all that he did and his might and how he fought with Amaziah king of Judah, behold, they are written in the Book of the Chronicles of the Kings of Israel.

16 And Jehoash slept with his fathers and was buried in Samaria with the kings of Israel; and Jeroboam his son reigned in his stead.

17 ¶And Amaziah the son of Joash king of Judah lived after the death of Jehoash son of Jehoahaz king of Israel fifteen years.

18 And the rest of the acts of Amaziah, behold, they are written in the Book of the Chronicles of the Kings of Judah.

19 Now they made a conspiracy against him in Jerusalem; and he fled to Lachish; but they sent after him to Lachish and slew him there.

20 And they brought him on horses; and he was buried in Jerusalem with his fathers in the city of David.

21 ¶Then all the people of Judah took Uzziah, who was sixteen years old, and made him king instead of his father Amaziah.

22 He built Elath and restored it to Judah, and after that the king slept with his fathers.

23 ¶In the fifteenth year of Amaziah the son of Joash king of Judah, Jeroboam the son of Jehoash, the son of Jehoahaz king of Israel, began to reign in Samaria, and he reigned forty-one years.

24 And he did that which was evil in the sight of the LORD; he did not turn aside from all the sins of Jeroboam the son of Nebat, who made Israel sin, and he walked in them.

25 He restored the frontier of Israel from the entrance of Hamath as far as the sea of the plain, according to the word of the LORD God of Israel which he spoke by his servant Jonah, the son of Matai, the prophet, who was of Gath-hepher.

26 For the LORD saw the affliction of Israel, that it was very bitter; for there was no one in power, and there was no one to help Israel.

27 And the LORD did not say that he would blot out the name of Israel from under heaven; but he saved them by the hand of Jeroboam the son of Jehoash, the son of Jehoahaz.

28 ¶Now the rest of the acts of Jeroboam and all that he did and his might, how he warred, and how he recovered Damascus and Hamath to Israel, behold, they are written in the Book of the Chronicles of the Kings of Israel.

29 And Jeroboam slept with his fathers, and was buried with his fathers, with the kings of Israel; and Zachariah his son reigned in his stead.

CHAPTER 15

IN the twenty-seventh year of Jeroboam king of Israel, Uzziah the son of Amaziah king of Judah, began to reign.

2 He was sixteen years old when he began to reign, and he reigned fifty-two years in Jerusalem. And his mother's name was Jechoaniah of Jerusalem.

3 And he did that which was right in the sight of the LORD, according

to all that his father Amaziah had done;

4 But the temple of idols he did not remove; the people still sacrificed and burned incense on the high places.

5 ¶And the LORD smote the king, so that he was a leper to the day of his death, and he dwelt in a house in seclusion. And Jotham the king's son was over the house, judging the people of the land.

6 Now the rest of the acts of Uzziah and all that he did, behold, they are written in the book of the Chronicles of the Kings of Judah.

7 So Uzziah slept with his fathers; and they buried him with his fathers in the city of David; and Jotham his son reigned in his stead.

8 ¶In the thirty-eighth year of Uzziah king of Judah, Zachariah the son of Jeroboam reigned over Israel in Samaria six months.

9 And he did that which was evil in the sight of the LORD, as his father had done; he did not turn aside from the sins of Jeroboam the son of Nebat, who made Israel sin.

10 And Shallum the son of Jabesh conspired against him and smote him before the people and killed him, and reigned in his stead.

11 And the rest of the acts of Zachariah, behold, they are written in the Book of the Chronicles of the Kings of Israel.

12 Thus was fulfilled the word of the LORD which he spoke to Jehu, saying, Your sons shall sit on the throne of Israel to the fourth generation. And so it came to pass.

13 ¶Shallum the son of Jabesh began to reign in the thirty-ninth year of Uzziah king of Judah; and he reigned a full month in Samaria.

14 For Menahem the son of Gadi went up from Tirzah and came to Samaria and smote Shallum the son of Jabesh in Samaria, and slew him and reigned in his stead.

15 Now the rest of the acts of Shallum and the conspiracy which he made, behold, they are written in the Book of the Chronicles of the Kings of Israel.

29

16 ¶Then Menahem smote Tiphsah and all who were in it and the territory thereof from Tirzah; because they did not open the gate to him, therefore he smote it; and he ripped up all the women in it that were with child.

17 In the thirty-ninth year of Uzziah king of Judah, Menahem the son of Gadi began to reign over Israel and he reigned ten years in Samaria.

18 And he did that which was evil in the sight of the LORD; he did not turn aside all his days from all the sins of Jeroboam the son of Nebat, who made Israel sin.

19 And Pul the king of Assyria came against the land; and Menahem gave Pul a thousand talents of silver to help him and to confirm the kingdom in his hand.

20 And Menahem levied taxes upon Israel, even on all wealthy men of the land, each man fifty shekels of silver, to give to the king of Assyria. So the king of Assyria turned back and stayed not there in the land.

21 ¶And the rest of the acts of Menahem and all that he did, behold, they are written in the Book of the Chronicles of the Kings of Israel.

22 And Menahem slept with his fathers; and Pekahiah his son reigned in his stead.

23 ¶In the fiftieth year of Uzziah king of Judah, Pekahiah the son of Menahem began to reign over Israel in Samaria, and he reigned two years.

24 And he did that which was evil in the sight of the LORD; he did not turn aside from the sins of Jeroboam the son of Nebat, who made Israel sin.

25 But Pekah the son of Romaliah, his mighty man, conspired against him and slew him in Samaria in the palace of the king's house; he took with him Argob and Lani and fifty men of the Gileadites, and he killed him and reigned in his stead.

26 And the rest of the acts of Pekahiah and all that he did, behold, they are written in the Book of the Chronicles of the Kings of Israel.

27 ¶In the fifty-second year of Uzziah king of Judah, Pekah the son of

Romaliah began to reign over Israel in Samaria, and he reigned twenty years.

28 And he did that which was evil in the sight of the LORD; he did not turn aside from the sins of Jeroboam the son of Nebat, who made Israel sin.

29 In the days of Pekah king of Israel, Tiglath-pileser king of Assyria came and took Ijon, Abel, Mehola, and all Beth-maachah, and Niah, Kedesh, Hazor, Gilead, and Galilee, and all the land of Naphtali, and carried the people captive to Assyria.

30 And Hoshea the son of Elah made a conspiracy against Pekah the son of Romaliah, and smote him and slew him and reigned in his stead in the second year of Jotham the son of Uzziah.

31 And the rest of the acts of Pekah and all that he did, behold, they are written in the Book of the Chronicles of the Kings of Israel.

32 ¶In the second year of Pekah the son of Romaliah king of Israel, Jotham the son of Uzziah king of Judah, began to reign.

33 He was twenty-five years old when he began to reign, and he reigned sixteen years in Jerusalem. And his mother's name was Jerusha, the daughter of Zadok.

34 And he did that which was right in the sight of the LORD, according to all that his father Uzziah had done.

35 ¶But the temple of idols he did not remove; the people sacrificed and burned incense still on the high places. He built the upper gate of the house of the LORD.

36 ¶Now the rest of the acts of Jotham and all that he did, behold, they are written in the Book of the Chronicles of the Kings of Judah.

37 In those days the LORD began to provoke against Judah Rezin the king of Aram[1] and Pekah the son of Romaliah.

38 And Jotham slept with his fathers, and was buried with his fathers in the city of David; and Ahaz his son reigned in his stead.

[1] The modern name is Syria.

CHAPTER 16

IN the eighteenth year of Pekah the son of Romaliah, Ahaz the son of Jotham king of Judah began to reign.

2 Ahaz was twenty years old when he began to reign, and he reigned sixteen years in Jerusalem, and he did not do that which was right in the sight of the LORD his God, and thus was unlike David his father.

3 But he walked in the way of the kings of Israel, and also made his son to pass through the fire, according to the custom of the Gentiles whom the LORD had destroyed from before the children of Israel.

4 And he sacrificed and burned incense on the high places and on the hills and under every green tree.

5 ¶Then Rezin king of Aram, and Pekah the son of Romaliah king of Israel came up to Jerusalem to war against it; but they could not fight against it.

6 At that time Rezin king of Aram recovered Elath for Aram, and drove Judah from Elath; and the Arameans came to Elath and dwell there to this day.

7 So Ahaz sent messengers to Tiglath-pileser king of Assyria, saying, I am your servant and your son; come up and save me from the hands of the king of Aram and from the hands of the king of Israel, who are risen up against me.

8 And Ahaz took the silver and gold that was found in the house of the LORD and in the treasures of the king's house, and sent it as a present to the king of Assyria.

9 And the king of Assyria listened to him; so the king of Assyria went up against Damascus and took it and carried its people captive to Kir, and he slew Rezin.

10 ¶And when King Ahaz went to Damascus to meet Tiglath-pileser king of Assyria, he saw an altar that was in Damascus; and King Ahaz sent to Urijah the priest the fashion of the altar and the pattern of it, according to all the workmanship thereof.

11 So Urijah the priest built an altar according to all that King Ahaz had sent from Damascus; and Urijah the priest made it before King Ahaz came from Damascus.

12 And when the king was come from Damascus, King Ahaz saw the altar; and the king drew near to the altar and went up to it,

13 And burned his burnt offerings and his meal offerings, and poured his drink offerings and sprinkled the blood of his peace offerings upon the altar.

14 And the altar of brass, which was before the LORD, he removed from the forefront of the house, from between the altar and the house of the LORD, and put it on the north side of the altar.

15 And King Ahaz commanded Urijah the priest, saying, Upon the great altar burn the morning burnt offering and the evening meal offering and the king's burnt offering and his meal offering, with the burnt offerings of all the people of the land and their meal offerings and their drink offerings; and sprinkle upon it all the blood of the burnt offerings and all the blood of the sacrifices; and the bronze altar shall be for me to inquire of the LORD.

16 Thus did Urijah the priest, according to all that King Ahaz commanded him.

17 ¶And King Ahaz cut off the borders of the bases and removed the lavers from off them; and took down the sea from off the bronze oxen that were under it and put it upon a pavement of stones.

18 And the shelter for the sabbath which they had built in the house of the LORD and in the entrance of the outer gate, he turned round the house of the LORD because of the fear of the king of Assyria.

19 ¶Now the rest of the acts of Ahaz and all that he did, behold, they are written in the Book of the Chronicles of the Kings of Judah.

20 And Ahaz slept with his fathers and was buried with his fathers in the city of David; and Hezekiah his son reigned in his stead.

CHAPTER 17

IN the twelfth year of Ahaz king of Judah, Hoshea the son of Elah began to reign in Samaria over Israel, and reigned nine years.

2 And he did that which was evil in the sight of the LORD, but not as the kings of Israel who were before him.

3 ¶Against him came up Shalmaneser king of Assyria; and Hoshea became his servant and brought him tribute.

4 And the king of Assyria found conspiracy in Hoshea; for he had sent messengers to So king of Egypt, and did not bring up tribute to the king of Assyria, as he had been doing year by year; therefore the king of Assyria shut him up and bound him in prison.

5 ¶Then the king of Assyria came up against the whole land, and went up to Samaria and besieged it three years.

6 ¶In the ninth year of Hoshea, the king of Assyria took Samaria, and carried Israel away to Assyria and placed them in Halah and in Habor by the river of Gozan, the cities of Media.

7 For so it was, that the children of Israel had sinned against the LORD their God, who had brought them up out of the land of Egypt from under the hand of Pharaoh king of Egypt and had worshipped other gods,

8 And walked in the statutes of the nations whom the LORD had destroyed from before the children of Israel,

9 And the children of Israel had spoken words that were not right against the LORD their God, both they and their kings; and they built them temples of idols in all their cities, from the tower of the watchmen to the fortified city.

10 And they set up for themselves statues and idols on every high hill and under every green tree;

11 And there they burned incense on all the high places, as did the nations whom the LORD destroyed from before them; and wrought wicked things to provoke the LORD to anger:

12 For they served idols, of which the LORD had said to them, You shall not do this thing.

13 Yet the LORD testified against Israel and against Judah by all his servants the prophets and by all the seers, saying, Repent from your evil ways and keep my commandments and my statutes, according to all the law which I commanded your fathers and according to that which I sent to them by my servants the prophets.

14 But they would not hearken, but were stubborn more than were their fathers who did not believe in the LORD their God.

15 And they rejected my covenants, and my statutes which I commanded to their fathers and the testimonies which I testified against them; and they followed vanity and gained nothing, and they followed the nations concerning whom the LORD had commanded them that they should not do like them.

16 And they left all the commandments of the LORD their God and made for themselves molten images, even two calves, and they sacrificed to the idols and worshipped all the stars and served Baal.

17 And they caused their sons and their daughters to pass through the fire and used divinations and sorcery, and they purposed to do all manner of evil in the sight of the LORD to provoke him to anger.

18 Therefore the LORD was very angry with Israel, and removed them out of his sight; there was none left but the tribe of Judah only.

19 Also the children of Judah did not keep the commandments of the LORD their God, but walked in the statutes of Israel who had done that which is evil in the sight of the LORD and provoked him to anger all the days.

20 And the LORD rejected all the descendants of Israel and despised them, and delivered them into the hand of spoilers, until he had cast them out of his sight.

21 For the house of Israel had seceded from the house of David; and they made Jeroboam the son of Ne-

bat king over themselves; and Jeroboam caused Israel to go astray from following the LORD, and made them sin great sins.

22 For the children of Israel walked in all the sins of Jeroboam which he did; they departed not from them

23 Until the LORD removed Israel out of his sight, as he had declared by all his servants the prophets. So was Israel carried away out of their land to Assyria, where they are to this day.

24 ¶And the king of Assyria brought people from Babylon and from Cuth and from Ava and from Hamath and from Sepharvim, and settled them in the cities of Samaria instead of the children of Israel; and they possessed Samaria, and dwelt in the cities thereof.

25 And at the beginning of their dwelling there, they did not reverence the LORD; therefore the LORD sent lions against them, which slew some of them.

26 Therefore they told the king of Assyria, saying, The nations which you have carried captive and placed in the cities of Samaria do not know the religion of the god of the land; therefore he has sent lions against them, and, behold, they slay them because they do not know the religion of the god of the land.

27 Then the king of Assyria commanded, saying, Take there one of the priests whom you have carried away from there; and let him go and dwell there, and let him teach them the religion of the god of the land.

28 Then one of the priests whom they had carried away from Samaria came and dwelt in Beth-el, and taught them how they should worship the LORD.

29 Nevertheless every nation served gods of their own, and put them in the houses of idols which had been made in Samaria, every nation in their cities wherein they dwelt.

30 And the men of Babylon served Succoth-benoth and the men of Cuth served Nergal and the men of Hamath served Ashima,

31 And the Avites served Jibzah and

Tartak, and the Sepharvites burned their children in fire to Ardammeleck and Amalek, the gods of Sepharvim.

32 So they worshipped the LORD, and made for themselves of their own people priests of the high places, who served for them in the houses of idols on the high places.

33 They worshipped the LORD and served their own gods after the manner of the nations. So the children of Israel were carried away out of their land

34 To this day, because they forsook the LORD and did according to the manner of the nations; they do not revere the LORD, neither do they according to the covenant or according to the ordinance or according to the law and commandment which the LORD commanded the children of Jacob, whom he named Israel;

35 With whom the LORD had made a covenant, and charged them, saying, You shall not revere other gods nor worship them nor serve them nor sacrifice to them;

36 But you must serve the LORD, who brought you up out of the land of Egypt with great power and with an outstretched arm, him shall you serve and him shall you worship and to him shall you sacrifice.

37 And the covenants and the ordinances and the laws and the commandments which he wrote for you, you shall observe to do for evermore; and you shall not revere other gods.

38 And the covenant that I have made with you, you shall not forget; neither shall you worship the gods of the Gentiles.

39 But the LORD your God you shall worship; and he shall deliver you out of the hand of all your enemies.

40 However they did not hearken, but they did according to their former customs.

41 So these nations also who dwelt in Samaria worshipped the LORD and served their graven images, also their children and their children's children; as did their fathers, so do they to this day.

CHAPTER 18

NOW in the third year of Hoshea son of Elah king of Israel, Hezekiah the son of Ahaz king of Judah began to reign.

2 He was twenty-five years old when he began to reign; and he reigned twenty-nine years in Jerusalem. His mother's name was Ahi, the daughter of Zechariah.

3 And he did that which was right in the sight of the LORD, according to all that David his father had done.

4 ¶He removed the high places and broke the images and cut down the idols and broke in pieces the bronze serpent that Moses had made; for the children of Israel had gone astray after it, and until those days they did burn incense to it; and they called it Nehushtan.

5 He trusted in the LORD God of Israel, so that after him there was none like him among all the kings of Judah nor among those who were before him.

6 For he held fast to the LORD and turned not aside from following him, but kept his commandments, according to all that the LORD commanded Moses.

7 And the LORD was with him; and wherever he went forth he conquered; and he rebelled against the king of Assyria and served him not.

8 He smote the Philistines as far as Gaza and the borders thereof, from the tower of the watchmen to the fortified city.

9 ¶In the fourth year of King Hezekiah, which was the seventh year of Hoshea son of Elah king of Israel, Shalmaneser king of Assyria came up against Samaria and besieged it.

10 And at the end of three years he took it, even in the sixth year of Hezekiah; that is, in the ninth year of Hoshea king of Israel, Samaria was taken.

11 And the king of Assyria carried away Israel to Assyria and put them in Halah and in Habor by the river of Gozan, the cities of Media,

12 Because they did not obey the voice of the LORD their God, but

transgressed his covenant and all that Moses the servant of the LORD commanded them, and would not hearken nor do them.

13 ¶Now in the fourteenth year of King Hezekiah, Sennacherib king of Assyria came up against all the fortified cities of Judah, and took them.

14 And Hezekiah king of Judah sent to the king of Assyria at Lachish, saying, I have offended; return from attacking me; and whatever tribute you lay on me I will bear. And the king of Assyria imposed upon Hezekiah king of Judah three hundred talents of silver and thirty talents of gold.

15 And Hezekiah gave him all the silver that was found in the house of the LORD and in the treasures of the king's house.

16 At that time Hezekiah stripped off the gold from the doors of the temple of the LORD and from the pillars which Hezekiah king of Judah had overlaid, and gave it to the king of Assyria.

17 ¶Then the king of Assyria sent Tartan and the Rab-shakeh [1] and Rabsisak from Lachish to King Hezekiah with a great army to Jerusalem. And they came up against Jerusalem, and when they were come up they stood by the ascent of the conduit of the upper pool, which is in the highway of the palace's field.

18 And when they had called to the king, there came out to them Eliakim the son of Hilkiah, who was the steward of the household, and Shebna the scribe and Joah the son of Asaph the recorder.

19 Then the Rab-shakeh said to them, Speak now to Hezekiah, Thus says the great king, the king of Assyria: What confidence is this in which you trust?

20 You have said that you are a good speaker and that you have counsel and strength for war. Now on whom do you trust, that you have rebelled against me?

21 Now, behold, you have trusted upon the staff of the broken reed, even on Egypt, on which if a man leans, it will go into his hand and pierce it; so is Pharaoh king of Egypt to all who trust in him.

22 But if you say to me, We trust in the LORD our God; is it not he whose high places and whose altars Hezekiah has removed, and has said to Judah and Jerusalem, You shall worship before a single altar in Jerusalem?

23 Now therefore, make an alliance with my lord the king of Assyria, and I will give you two thousand horses, if you have riders to set upon them.

24 How then will you refuse the request of one of the least nobles of my master's servants and put your trust in the Egyptian to give you chariots and horsemen?

25 And now perhaps you think that I have come up without the LORD against this land to destroy it? The LORD said to me, Go up against this land and destroy it.

26 Then said Eliakim, the son of Hilkiah, and Shebna and Joah to Rab-shakeh, Speak to your servants in the Aramaic; for we understand it; and do not speak to us in the Jews' language [2] in the presence of the people who are on the wall.

27 But the Rab-shakeh said to them, It was not to you and to your master that my master has sent me to speak these words, but to the men who are sitting on the wall, that they may not eat their own dung and drink their own urine with you.

28 Then the Rab-shakeh stood and cried with a loud voice in the Jews' language, and spoke, saying, Hear the word of the great king, the king of Assyria;

29 Thus says the king: Let not Hezekiah deceive you; for he shall not be able to deliver you out of my hands;

30 Neither let Hezekiah make you trust in the LORD, saying, The LORD will surely deliver us, and this city shall not be delivered into the hand of the king of Assyria.

31 Do not hearken to Hezekiah; for thus says the king of Assyria: Make an agreement with me by a present,

---

[1] Aramaic, an army general.

[2] The literary language was Aramaic.

and come out to me, and then eat every one of you of his own vine and of his own fig tree and drink every one the waters of his own cistern,

32 Until I come and take you away to a land like your own land, a land of many kinds of fruit trees, a land of grain and vineyards, a land of olive trees and of fatness and of honey, that you may live and not die; and do not listen to Hezekiah, and let not Hezekiah deceive you, saying, The LORD will deliver us.

33 Has any of the gods of the nations been able to deliver his land out of the hand of the king of Assyria?

34 Where are the gods of Hamath and of Arpad? Where are the gods of Sepharvim, Dena, and Ivah? Have they delivered Samaria out of my hands?

35 Who are there among all the gods of these nations that have delivered their country out of my hands, that the LORD should deliver Jerusalem out of my hands?

36 But the people held their peace, and answered him not a word; for the king had commanded, saying, Do not answer him.

37 Then came Eliakim the son of Hilkiah, the steward of the household, and Shebna the scribe and Joah the son of Asaph the recorder to Hezekiah with their clothes torn and told him the words of the Rab-shakeh.

CHAPTER 19

AND when King Hezekiah heard it, he tore his clothes and covered himself with sackcloth and went into the house of the LORD.

2 And he sent Eliakim, the steward of the household, and Shebna the scribe and the elders of the priests, covered with sackcloth, to Isaiah the prophet the son of Amoz.

3 And they said to him, Thus says Hezekiah: This day is a day of distress and of rebuke and of anger; for the children have come to the birth, and there is no strength in the mother to bring forth.

4 It may be the LORD your God will hear the words of the Rab-shakeh, whom his master, the Assyrian king has sent to reproach the living God; and will rebuke him for the words which the LORD your God has heard; therefore beseech and pray for the remnant that is left.

5 So the servants of King Hezekiah came to Isaiah the prophet.

6 ¶And Isaiah said to them, Thus shall you say to your master: Thus says the LORD, Do not be afraid of the words that you have heard, with which the ambassadors of the king of Assyria have blasphemed me.

7 Behold, I will send a blast [1] upon him, and he shall hear a rumor and shall return to his own land; and I will cause him to fall by the sword in his own land.

8 ¶So the Rabshakeh returned and found the king of Assyria warring against Libnah; for he had heard that he had departed from Lachish.

9 And when he heard it said concerning Tarhak king of Ethiopia, Behold, he is come out to fight against you, he sent messengers again to Hezekiah, saying,

10 Thus shall you say to Hezekiah king of Judah: Do not let your God in whom you trust deceive you, saying, Jerusalem shall not be delivered into the hands of the king of Assyria.

11 Behold, you have heard what the kings of Assyria have done to all lands by destroying them utterly; and shall you be delivered?

12 Have the gods of the nations delivered them which my fathers have destroyed, such as Gozan, Haran, and Rezeph, and the inhabitants of Eden who were in Thelasar?

13 Where is the king of Hamath, and the king of Arpad, and the king of Sepharvim, and of Dena, and Ivah?

14 ¶And Hezekiah received the letters from the hand of the messengers, and read them; and Hezekiah went up into the house of the LORD and spread them before the LORD.

15 And Hezekiah prayed before the LORD and said, O LORD God of Israel,

[1] Aramaic, a spirit; a deadly wind.

who sits upon the cherubim, thou art
the God, even thou alone, over all
the kingdoms of the earth; thou hast
made the heaven and the earth.

16 O LORD, incline thine ear and
hear; open thine eyes, O LORD, and
see; and hear all the words of Sennacherib, who hath sent messages to
reproach the living God.

17 Of a truth, O LORD, the kings
of Assyria have destroyed the nations
and their lands,

18 And have burned their gods in
fire; for they were no gods, but the
works of men's hands, wood and
stone; therefore they have burned
them.

19 Now therefore, O LORD our
God, save us from his hands, that all
the kingdoms of the earth may know
that thou art the LORD God, even
thou alone.

20 ¶Then Isaiah the son of Amoz
sent to Hezekiah, saying, Thus says
the LORD God of Israel: That which
you have prayed to me concerning
Sennacherib king of Assyria I have
heard.

21 This is the word that the LORD
has spoken concerning him: The virgin the daughter of Zion despises you
and laughs you to scorn; the daughter of Jerusalem shakes her head behind you.

22 Whom have you reproached and
blasphemed? And against whom have
you raised your voices and lifted up
your eyes on high? Even against the
Holy One of Israel.

23 By your messengers you have reproached the LORD and have said,
With the multitude of my chariots I
will go up to the height of the mountains, to the sides of Lebanon, and
will cut down the tall cedar trees
thereof and the choice fir trees thereof; and I will enter into the extreme
limits of the forest of Carmel.

24 I will dig and drink strange
waters, and with the hoofs of my
horses I will dry up all the great
rivers.

25 Have you not heard long ago
how I have done it, and of the days
of old how I prepared it? And now
I have brought it to pass, that you

lay waste fortified cities into ruinous
heaps;

26 Therefore their inhabitants became weak, they were defeated and
confounded, and became like the
grass of the field and like the green
herb, like the grass on the housetops,
and like tender grass blasted before
it is grown up.

27 But I know your dwelling place
and your coming in and your going
out and your rage against me.

28 Because you have dared and
raged against me, and your blasphemy
has come to my ears, therefore I will
put a hook in your nose and a bit
in your lips, and I will turn you back
by the way by which you came.

29 And this shall be a sign to you:
you shall eat this year that which
grows of itself, and in the second year
that which springs of the same; and
in the third year sow and reap and
plant vineyards and eat the fruits
thereof.

30 And the remnant that is left of
the house of Judah shall increase, they
shall again take root downward and
bear fruit upward.

31 For out of Jerusalem shall go
forth a remnant, and they that escape
out of the mount of Zion; the zeal of
the LORD of hosts shall do this.

32 Therefore thus says the LORD
concerning the king of Assyria: He
shall not enter this city nor shoot an
arrow there nor come before it with
shields nor lay an ambush against it.

33 But by the way that he came,
by the same shall he return, and shall
not enter this city, says the LORD.

34 For I will abide in this city and
save it for my own sake and for my
servant David's sake.

35 ¶And it came to pass that night,
the angel of the LORD went out and
slew in the camp of the Assyrians a
hundred and eighty-five thousand; and
when the survivors arose early in the
morning, they looked, and behold,
their comrades were all dead.

36 So Sennacherib king of Assyria
departed, and went and returned and
dwelt at Nineveh.

37 And as he worshipped in the
house of Nisroch his god, Adram-

meleck and Sharezer his sons slew him with the sword; and they escaped into the land of Armenia. And Sarhaddom his son reigned in his stead.

CHAPTER 20

IN those days Hezekiah became sick to death. And Isaiah the prophet the son of Amoz came to him and said to him, Thus says the LORD: Set your house in order; for you shall die, you shall not live.

2 Then Hezekiah turned his face to the wall and prayed to the LORD, saying,

3 I beseech thee, O LORD, remember now how I walked before thee in truth and with a perfect heart, and have done that which is good in thy sight. And Hezekiah wept bitterly.

4 And before Isaiah was gone out into the middle court, the word of the LORD came to him, saying,

5 Turn again and tell Hezekiah the ruler of my people, Thus says the LORD, the God of David your father: I have heard your prayer, I have seen your tears; behold, I will heal you; on the third day you shall go up to the house of the LORD.

6 And I will add to your days fifteen years; and I will deliver you and this city out of the hands of the king of Assyria; and I will defend this city and deliver it for my own sake and for my servant David's sake.

7 And Isaiah said, Let them take a cake of figs and lay it on the boil and he shall recover.

8 ¶And Hezekiah said to Isaiah, What shall be the sign that the LORD will heal me, and that I shall go up into the house of the LORD the third day?

9 And Isaiah said, This is the sign that you shall have from the LORD, that the LORD will do the thing that he has spoken: shall the shadow go forward ten degrees or backward ten degrees?

10 And Hezekiah answered, It is an easy thing for the shadow to go down ten degrees; not so, but let the shadow turn backward ten degrees.

11 And Isaiah the prophet cried to the LORD, and he brought the shadow ten degrees backward, by which it had gone down on the dial of Ahaz.

12 ¶At that time Merodach-baladan, the son of Baladan, king of Babylon, sent letters and presents to Hezekiah; for he had heard that Hezekiah had been sick and was healed.

13 And Hezekiah rejoiced with them, and showed them all his treasure house, the silver, the gold, the spices, the precious ointments, and all the house of his armor, and all that was found in his treasures; there was nothing in his house nor in all his dominion that Hezekiah did not show them.

14 ¶Then came Isaiah the prophet to King Hezekiah and said to him, What did these men say to you? And from whence did they come to you? And Hezekiah said, They have come to me from a far country, even from Babylon.

15 And he said, What have they seen in your house? And Hezekiah answered, They have seen all the things that are in my house; I left nothing in my treasure house that I did not show them.

16 Then Isaiah said to Hezekiah, Hear the word of the LORD.

17 Behold, the days are coming when all that is in your house and that which your fathers have laid up in treasure to this day shall be carried to Babylon; nothing shall be left for you, says the LORD.

18 And of your sons that shall issue from you, whom you shall beget, shall they take away; and they shall be eunuchs in the palace of the king of Babylon.

19 Then Hezekiah said to Isaiah, Good is the word of the LORD which you have spoken. But would that peace and justice shall be in my day!

20 ¶And the rest of the acts of Hezekiah and all his might and how he made a pool and a conduit and brought water into the city, behold, they are written in the Book of the Chronicles of the Kings of Judah.

21 And Hezekiah slept with his fathers; and Manasseh his son reigned in his stead.

CHAPTER 21

MANASSEH was twelve years old when he began to reign, and he reigned fifty-five years in Jerusalem. And his mother's name was Hephzibah.

2 And he did that which was evil in the sight of the LORD, according to the abominations of the nations which the LORD destroyed from before the children of Israel.

3 For he built up again the high places which Hezekiah his father had destroyed; and he erected altars for Baal and made idols, as Ahab king of Israel had done; and worshipped all the host of heaven and served them.

4 And he built an altar in the house of the LORD, of which the LORD had said, In Jerusalem will I put my name.

5 And he built altars for all the host of heaven in the two courts of the house of the LORD.

6 And he caused his son to pass through the fire, and used divinations and practiced augury and appointed men with familiar spirits and wizards; he wrought much which was evil in the sight of the LORD, to provoke him to anger.

7 And he set up the image and the idol that he had made in the house of the LORD, in the house of which the LORD said to David and to Solomon his son, In this house and in Jerusalem, which I have chosen out of all the tribes of Israel, will I put my name for ever;

8 Neither will I make the feet of Israel move any more out of the land which I gave to their fathers, only if they will observe to do everything that I have commanded them and all the laws that my servant Moses commanded them.

9 But they did not hearken; and Manasseh seduced them, and they did more evil than did the nations whom the LORD destroyed before the children of Israel.

10 ¶And the LORD spoke by his servants the prophets, saying,

11 Because Manasseh, the son of Hezekiah, king of Judah has done these abominations and has done more wickedly than all that the Amorites did, who were before him, and has made Judah also sin with his idols;

12 Therefore thus says the LORD God of Israel: Behold, I am bringing such evil upon Judah and upon Jerusalem that whoever hears of it, both his ears shall tingle.

13 And I will stretch over Jerusalem the line of Samaria and the plummet of the house of Ahab; and I will smite Jerusalem and destroy it because of all the abominations which Manasseh had done in Judah.

14 And I will forsake the remnant of my inheritance and deliver them into the hand of their enemies; and they shall become a prey and be trampled under the feet of all their enemies,

15 Because they have done that which was evil in my sight and have provoked me to anger since the day their fathers came forth out of Egypt, even to this day.

16 Moreover Manasseh shed very much innocent blood, till he had filled Jerusalem from one end to another, besides his sins wherewith he made Judah sin, in doing that which was evil in the sight of the LORD.

17 ¶Now the rest of the acts of Manasseh and all that he did and the sins that he sinned, behold, they are written in the Book of the Chronicles of the Kings of Judah.

18 And Manasseh slept with his fathers and was buried in the garden of his own house, in the garden of the treasury; and Amon his son reigned in his stead.

19 ¶Amon was twenty-two years old when he began to reign, and he reigned two years in Jerusalem. And his mother's name was Meshullemeth, the daughter of Haduz of Jotbath.

20 And he did that which was evil in the sight of the LORD, as his father Manasseh had done.

21 And he walked in all the ways that his father walked and served the idols that his father served and worshipped them;

22 And he forsook the LORD God

of his fathers, and walked not in the way of the LORD.

23 ¶And the servants of Amon conspired against him and slew him in his own house.

24 And the people of the land slew all those that had conspired against King Amon; and the people of the land made Josiah his son king in his stead.

25 Now the rest of the acts of Amon and all that he did, behold, they are written in the Book of the Chronicles of the Kings of Judah.

26 And they buried him in his sepulchre in the garden of the treasury; and Josiah his son reigned in his stead.

CHAPTER 22

JOSIAH was eight years old when he began to reign, and he reigned thirty-one years in Jerusalem. And his mother's name was Jedidah, the daughter of Azariah of Boscath.

2 And he did that which was right in the sight of the LORD, and walked in all the way of David his father, and did not turn aside to the right hand or to the left.

3 ¶Now in the eighteenth year of King Josiah, the king sent Shaphan the son of Alaziah, the son of Meshullam, the scribe, to the house of the LORD, saying,

4 Go up to Hilkiah the high priest that he may deliver the silver which has been brought into the house of the LORD, which the keepers of the door have collected from the people;

5 And let them deliver it into the hand of the workmen who have the oversight of the house of the LORD: and let them give it to the doers of the work which is in the house of the LORD, to repair the breaches of the house,

6 To the carpenters and to the builders and masons, and to buy timber and hewn stone to repair the house of the LORD.

7 However there was no accounting made with them of the money that was delivered into their hands, because they dealt faithfully.

¹ See 2 Ch. 34:22.

8 ¶And Hilkiah the high priest said to Shaphan the scribe, I have found the book of the law in the house of the LORD. And Hilkiah gave the book of the law to Shaphan the scribe and he read it.

9 And Shaphan the scribe came to the king, and brought the king word again, saying, Your servants have delivered the money that was found in the house, and have delivered it into the hand of the workmen who have the oversight of the house of the LORD.

10 And Shaphan the scribe spoke to the king, saying, Hilkiah the priest has given me a book. And Shaphan read it before the king.

11 And when the king had heard the words of the book of the law, he tore his clothes.

12 And the king commanded Hilkiah the priest and Ahikam the son of Shaphan and Achbor the son of Micah and Shaphan the scribe and Ashaiah a servant of the king, saying,

13 Go, inquire of the LORD for me and for all the people and for all Judah concerning the words of this book that has been found; for great is the wrath of the LORD that is kindled against us, because our fathers have not hearkened to the words of this book, to do according to all that which is written in it.

14 So Hilkiah the priest and Ahikam and Achbor and Shaphan and Ashaiah went to Huldi the prophetess, the wife of Shallum the son of Tikvah, the son of Hadhas, the keeper of the weapons (now she dwelt in Jerusalem studying the Law ¹), and they talked with her.

15 ¶And she said to them, Thus says the LORD God of Israel: Tell the man who sent you to me,

16 Thus says the LORD: Behold, I will bring evil upon this country and upon its inhabitants, even all the words of the book which the king of Judah has read,

17 Because they have forsaken me and have burned incense to other gods and have provoked me to anger with all the works of their hands;

therefore my wrath shall be kindled against this place and I shall destroy you, says the LORD.

18 But to the king of Judah who sent you to inquire of the LORD, thus shall you say to him: Thus says the LORD God of Israel concerning the words which you have heard:

19 Because your heart was sad and you trembled before the LORD when you heard what I spoke against this country and against its inhabitants, that they should become a desolation and a curse, and have torn your clothes and wept before me; I also have heard you, says the LORD.

20 Behold, therefore, I will gather you to your fathers, and you shall be gathered into your grave in peace; and your eyes shall not see all the evil which I will bring upon this country. And they brought the king word again.

CHAPTER 23

AND the king sent and they gathered to him all the elders of Judah and of Jerusalem.

2 And the king went up to the house of the LORD, and all the men of Judah and all the inhabitants of Jerusalem with him, and the priests and the prophets and all the people, both small and great; and he read before them all the words of the book of the covenant which was found in the house of the LORD.

3 ¶And the king stood by a pillar and made a covenant before the LORD, to walk after the LORD and to keep his commandments and his testimonies and his statutes with all their heart and all their soul, to perform the words of this covenant that were written in this book. And all the people agreed to the covenant.

4 Then the king commanded Hilkiah the high priest and the priests of the second order and the keepers of the doors to bring forth out of the temple of the LORD all the vessels that were made for Baal and for the idols and for all the host of heaven; and he burned them outside Jerusalem in the fields of Kidron, and carried their ashes to Beth-el.

5 And he slew the priests whom the kings of Judah had ordained to burn incense on the high places in the cities of Judah and in the places round about Jerusalem, and those also who burned incense to Baal, to the sun and to the moon and to the planets and to all the host of heaven.

6 And he brought out the idol from the house of the LORD, outside Jerusalem, to the brook Kidron and burned it at the brook Kidron, and ground it to dust and cast the dust of it upon the graves of the common people.

7 And he destroyed the houses of the Sodomites which were in the house of the LORD, and the houses of the women who wove hangings for the idols.

8 And he brought all the priests out of the cities of Judah and defiled the high places where the priests had burned incense in them, from Dan to Beer-sheba, and destroyed the shrine which was at the entrance of the gate of Salvation which was on a man's left hand at the gate of the city.

9 Nevertheless the priests of the high places did not come up to the altar of the LORD in Jerusalem, but they did eat of the unleavened bread with their brethren.

10 And he destroyed the high places which the kings of Judah had made in Taphath, which is in the valley of Bar-hannom, that no man might make his son or his daughter to pass through the fire to Amlech.

11 And he slew the horses which the kings of Judah had given to the sun, at the entrance of the house of the LORD, by the chamber of Nathan the king's eunuch, which was in the suburbs, and burned the chariot of the sun with fire.

12 And the altar that was on the top of the upper chamber of Ahaz, which the kings of Judah had made, and the altars which Manasseh had made in the two courts of the house of the LORD, did the king beat down, and broke them down from thence and cast the dust of them into the brook Kidron.

13 And the high places that were before Jerusalem, which were on the right hand of the mount of Corruption, which Solomon the king of Israel had built for Ashtoreth, the goddess of the Zidonians, and for Chemosh, the idol of Moab, and for Malcom, the idol of the children of Ammon, did King Josiah destroy.

14 And he broke in pieces the images and cut down the idols and filled their places with the bones of men.

15 ¶Moreover the altar that was at Beth-el and the high places which Jeroboam the son of Nebat, who made Israel sin, had made, both that altar and the high place he demolished, and burned the high place and ground it to dust and burned the idols.

16 And as Josiah returned, he saw the sepulchres that were there on the mount, and he sent and took the bones out of the sepulchres and burned them upon the altar and defiled it, according to the word of the LORD which the prophet of God proclaimed, who predicted these things.

17 Then the king said, What monument is that which I see? And the men of the city said to him, It is the sepulchre of the prophet of God, who came from Judah and proclaimed these things that you have done against the altar of Beth-el.

18 And he said, Let him alone; let no man touch his sepulchre, and let no man move his bones, so his bones spared the bones of the prophet who came from Samaria from being burned.

19 And all the temples also of idols that were in the cities of Samaria, which the kings of Israel had made to provoke the LORD to anger, Josiah removed, and did to them according to all the acts that he had done in Beth-el.

20 And he slew all the priests of the high places, who burned incense upon the altars and burned men's bones upon them, and he returned to Jerusalem.

21 ¶And the king commanded all the people, saying, Keep the passover to the LORD your God, as it is written in the book of this covenant.

22 Surely no such a passover had been kept from the days of the judges who judged Israel nor in all the days of the kings of Israel nor of the kings of Judah,

23 Like that in the eighteenth year of King Josiah, when this passover was kept to the LORD in Jerusalem.

24 ¶Moreover the men with familiar spirits and the wizards and the images and the idols and all the abominations that were seen in the land of Judah and in the streets of Jerusalem did Josiah put away, that he might perform the words of the law which were written in the book that Hilkiah the priest found in the house of the LORD.

25 And like unto him was there no king before him, who turned to the LORD with all his heart and with all his soul and with all his might, according to all that which is written in the law of Moses; neither after him arose there any like him.

26 ¶Nevertheless the LORD did not turn from the fierceness of his great wrath wherewith his anger was kindled against Judah because of all the provocations with which Manasseh had provoked him.

27 And the LORD said, I will remove Judah also out of my sight, as I have removed Israel, and I will cast off this city Jerusalem which I have chosen, and the house of which I said, My name shall be there.

28 Now the rest of the acts of Josiah and all that he did, behold, they are written in the Book of the Chronicles of the Kings of Judah.

29 ¶In his days Pharaoh the Lame, king of Egypt went up against Mabog which is by the river Euphrates; and King Josiah went to meet him, to fight against him; and Pharaoh said to him, I have not come against you, turn aside from me; but Josiah did not listen to him; so Pharaoh smote him at Megiddo, when he saw him there.

30 And his servants carried him in a chariot dead from Megiddo, and brought him to Jerusalem and buried him there in his own sepulchre. And the people of the land took Jehoahaz the son of Josiah and anointed him

and made him king in his father's stead.

31 ¶Jehoahaz was twenty-three years old when he began to reign; and he reigned three months in Jerusalem. And his mother's name was Hamutal, the daughter of Jeremiah of Libnah.

32 And he did that which was evil in the sight of the LORD, just as Manasseh had done.

33 And Pharaoh the Lame, king of Egypt put him in bands at Diblath in the land of Hamath, when Pharaoh took over Jerusalem; and levied on the land a tribute of one hundred talents of silver and ten talents of gold.

34 And Pharaoh the Lame made Eliakim the son of Josiah king in the place of Josiah his father, and changed his name to Jehoiakim, and he took Jehoahaz away, and brought him to Egypt and he died there.

35 And Jehoiakim gave the silver and gold to Pharaoh; but he taxed the land to give the money as he was commanded by Pharaoh; he exacted silver and gold from the people of the land, of every one according to his means, to give it to Pharaoh the Lame.

36 ¶Jehoiakim was twenty-five years old when he began to reign; and he reigned eleven years in Jerusalem. And his mother's name was Zebudah, the daughter of Peraiah of Ramtha.

37 And he did that which was evil in the sight of the LORD, according to all that his fathers had done.

CHAPTER 24

IN his days Nebuchadnezzar king of Babylon came up against Jerusalem, and Jehoiakim became his servant three years; then he turned and rebelled against him.

2 And the LORD stirred up against him bands of the Chaldeans and bands of Edomites and bands of Moabites and bands of the children of Ammon, and sent them against Judah to destroy it, according to the word of the LORD which he spoke by his servants the prophets from the mouth of the LORD.

3 And there came a fierce wrath against Judah, to remove them out of his sight on account of the sins of Manasseh and all that he had done, 4 And also for the innocent blood that he had shed; for he filled Jerusalem with innocent blood, which the LORD would not pardon.

5 ¶Now the rest of the acts of Jehoiakim and all that he did, behold, they are written in the Book of the Chronicles of the Kings of Judah.

6 So Jehoiakim slept with his fathers; and Jehoiachin his son reigned in his stead.

7 And the king of Egypt did not again come out of his land; for the king of Babylon had taken all that had belonged to the king of Egypt, from the river of Egypt to the river Euphrates.

8 ¶Jehoiachin was eighteen years old when he began to reign, and he reigned three months in Jerusalem. And his mother's name was Nehushta, the daughter of Eliathan of Jerusalem.

9 And he did that which was evil in the sight of the LORD, according to all that his father had done.

10 ¶At that time Nebuchadnezzar king of Babylon came up against Jerusalem and the city was besieged.

11 And Nebuchadnezzar king of Babylon came against the city, and his servants were besieging it.

12 And Jehoiachin the king of Judah went out to the king of Babylon, he and his mother and his servants and his princes and his eunuchs; and the king of Babylon took him with him in the eighth year of his reign.

13 And he carried out from there all the treasures of the house of the LORD and the treasures of the king's house, and he cut in pieces all the vessels of gold which Solomon king of Israel had made for the temple of the LORD, as the LORD had said.

14 And he carried away all Jerusalem and all the princes and all the mighty men of valour, even ten thousand captives, and all the guardsmen and all the guard; and he left none except the poorest people of the land.

15 And he carried away Jehoiachin to Babylon and the king's mother and

the king's wives and his eunuchs and the princes of the land he carried into captivity from Jerusalem to Babylon.

16 And all the men of might, even seven thousand, and guardsmen and the guard of a thousand and all the men who were trained for war, even them the king of Babylon brought captive to Babylon.

17 ¶Then the king of Babylon made Mattaniah the king's uncle king in his stead and changed his name to Zedekiah.

18 Zedekiah was twenty-one years old when he began to reign and he reigned eleven years in Jerusalem. And his mother's name was Hamutal, the daughter of Jeremiah of Libnah.

19 And he did that which was evil in the sight of the LORD, according to all that Jehoiakim had done.

20 So the anger of the LORD was against Judah and against Jerusalem, until he cast them out from his presence, and Zedekiah rebelled against the king of Babylon.

CHAPTER 25

AND in the ninth year of his reign, in the tenth month, on the tenth day of the month, Nebuchadnezzar king of Babylon came, he and all his army against Jerusalem, and pitched against it and built forts against it round about.

2 And the city was besieged till the eleventh year of King Zedekiah.

3 And in the eleventh year of King Zedekiah, on the ninth day of the fifth month, the famine was severe in the city and there was no bread for the people of the land.

4 ¶And the city was breached, and all the men of war fled by night by the way of the gate between the two walls, which is by the king's garden (now the Chaldeans were round about the city), and they went by the way of the plain.

5 And the army of the Chaldeans pursued the king and overtook him in the plains of Jericho; and all his army was scattered from him.

6 So they took the king and brought him up to the king of Babylon at

Diblath; and he pronounced judgment against him.

7 And the king of Babylon slew the sons of King Zedekiah before his eyes, and put out the eyes of Zedekiah, and bound him with fetters and carried him to Babylon.

8 ¶In the fifth month, on the seventh day of the month, which is the nineteenth year of Nebuchadnezzar king of Babylon, came Nebuzara-dan, the commander of the guard, a servant of the king of Babylon, to Jerusalem;

9 And he burned the house of the LORD and the king's house; and all the houses of Jerusalem and all the houses of the princes he burned with fire.

10 And all the army of the Chaldeans who were with the commander of the guard broke down the walls of Jerusalem round about.

11 Now the rest of the people who were left in the city and the deserters who had gone over to the king of Babylon, with the remnant of the multitude, Nebuzara-dan, the commander of the guard, carried away to Babylon.

12 But Nebuzara-dan, the commander of the guard, left some of the poor of the land to be vinedressers and husbandmen.

13 And the pillars of brass that were in the house of the LORD and the bases and the bronze sea that was in the house of the LORD the Chaldeans broke in pieces, and took all the brass and carried it to Babylon.

14 And the pots and the cauldrons and the large hanging pots and the snuffers and the spoons and all the vessels of brass with which they ministered, they took away.

15 And the censers and the bowls, which were of gold and silver, and the cups, the commander of the guard took away.

16 The two pillars, one sea, and the bases which King Solomon had made for the house of the LORD; the weight of the brass of all these vessels was beyond calculation.

17 The height of one pillar was eighteen cubits, and the capital upon it was of brass; and the height of the

capital was three cubits; and the carved ornaments and pomegranates upon the capital round about, all of brass; and the second pillar was likewise with carved ornaments, all of brass.

18 ¶And the commander of the guard took Sheriah the chief priest and Zephaniah the second priest and the three keepers of the door;

19 And out of the city he took an officer who was in charge of the men of war and five men of those who were in the king's presence, who were found in the city, and the scribe and the commander of the army who mustered the people of the land, and sixty men of the people of the land who were still in the city;

20 And Nebuzara-dan, the commander of the guard, took these, and brought them to the king of Babylon at Diblath;

21 And the king of Babylon smote them, and slew them at Diblath in the land of Hamath. So Judah was carried away captive out of their land.

22 ¶And as for the people who remained in the land of Judah, whom Nebuchadnezzar king of Babylon had left, he appointed over them Gedaliah the son of Ahikam, the son of Shaphan, ruler.

23 And when all the commanders of the armies, they and their men, heard that the king of Babylon had made Gedaliah ruler, they came to Gedaliah at Mizpah, even Ishmael the son of Nethaniah and Johanan the son of Korah and Sheriah the son of Tanhumeth and Tobia and Jaazaniah the son of Maachat, they and their men.

24 And Gedaliah swore to them and to their men, and said to them, Fear not the Chaldeans; dwell in the land and serve the king of Babylon; and it shall be well with you.

25 But in the seventh month, Ishmael the son of Nethaniah, the son of Ishmael of the royal seed came, and ten men with him, and smote Gedaliah, that he died, and also the Jews and the Chaldeans that were with him at Mizpeh.

26 And all the people of the land, both small and great, and all the commanders of the armies, arose and went to Egypt; for they were afraid of the Chaldeans.

27 ¶And in the thirty-seventh year of the captivity of Jehoiachin king of Judah, in the twelfth month, on the twenty-seventh day of the month, Aolmerodach king of Babylon in the first year that he began to reign honored Jehoiachin king of Judah and brought him out of the prison;

28 And he spoke kindly to him, and set his throne above the thrones of the kings who were with him in Babylon;

29 And changed his prison garments; and he did eat bread continually before him all the days of his life.

30 And his allowance was a continual allowance given him by the king of Babylon, a portion for every day, all the days of his life.

THE FIRST BOOK OF THE

CHRONICLES

CHAPTER 1

ADAM, Sheth, Enosh,
2 Kenan, Mahalalael, Jered,
3 Enoch, Methuselah, Lamech,

4 Noah, Shem, Ham, and Japheth.
5 ¶The sons of Japheth: Gomer, Mongolia, Madai, Javan, Tubal, Meshech, and Tiras.

6 And the sons of Gomer: Ashchenaz, Diphar, and Togarmah.
7 And the sons of Javan: Elishah, Tarshish, Kittim, and Doranim.
8 ¶The sons of Ham: Cush, Mizraim, Put, and Canaan.
9 And the sons of Cush: Seba, Havilah, Sabta, Raamah, and Sabachtha. And the sons of Raamah: Sheba and Daran.
10 And Cush begat Nimrod; and he began to be a mighty man in the earth.
11 And Mizraim begat Ludim, Jaabim, Lehabim, Naphtuhim,
12 Pathrusim, and Casluhim (of whom came the Philistines and Capedocians).
13 And Canaan begat Zidon his first-born and Heth and
14 The Jesubites and the Amorites and the Girgasites
15 And the Hivites and the Arkites and the Sinites
16 And the Arvadites and the Zemarites and the Hamathites.
17 ¶The sons of Shem: Elam, Asshur, Arphahshar, Lud, Aram, Uz, Hul, Gather, and Meshech.
18 And Arphahshar begat Shelah, and Shelah begat Eber.
19 And to Eber were born two sons; the name of the one was Peleg, because in his days the earth was divided, and his brother's name was Joktan.
20 And Joktan begat Almodad, Sheleph, Hazarmoth, and Jerah,
21 Hadoram, Uzal, Diklah,
22 Ebal, Abimael, Sheba,
23 Ophir, Havilah, and Jobab. All these were the sons of Joktan.
24 ¶Shem, Arphahshar, Shelah,
25 Eber, Peleg, Reu,
26 Serug, Nahor, and Terah;
27 Abram; the same is Abraham.
28 The sons of Abraham: Isaac and Ishmael.
29 ¶These are their generations: The first-born of Ishmael, Nebaioth; then Kadar, Arbal, and Mibsam,
30 Mishma, Romah, Massa, Hadad, Temna,
31 Nator, Naphish, and Kedemah. These are the sons of Ishmael.
32 ¶The sons of Kenturah, Abraham's concubine: she bore Zimran, Jokshan, Maran, Midian, Ishbak, and Shuah. And the sons of Jokshan: Sheba and Daran.
33 And the sons of Midian: Ephah, Epher, Henoch, Abida, and Eldaah. All these were the sons of Kenturah.
34 And Abraham begat Isaac. The sons of Isaac: Esau and Israel.
35 ¶The sons of Esau: Eliphaz, Reuel, Jeush, Elam, and Korah.
36 The sons of Eliphaz: Teman, Omar, Zoph, Gatham, Kenaz, Timna, and Amalek.
37 The sons of Reuel: Nahath, Zerah, Shammah, and Mizzah.
38 And the sons of Seir: Lotan, Shobal, Zibeon, Anah, Doshan, Ezar, and Dishan.
39 And the sons of Lotan: Horar and Homam; and Timna was Lotan's sister.
40 The sons of Shobal: Anon, Manahath, Ebal, Shaphar, and Onam. And the sons of Zibeon: Ana, and Annah.
41 The son of Annah: Dishon. And the sons of Dishon: Hamran, Ashkan, Ithran, and Cheran.
42 The sons of Ezer: Calhan, Zimran, and Jakan. The sons of Dishon: Uz, and Aram.
43 ¶Now these are the kings that reigned in the land of Edom before any king reigned over the children of Israel: Bela the son of Beor, and the name of his city was Dihab.
44 And when Bela died, Jobab the son of Zerah of Bozrah reigned in his stead.
45 And after him Husham of the land of Teman reigned in his stead.
46 And when Husham died, Hadad the son of Bedad, who defeated the Edomites in the fields of Moab, reigned in his stead; and the name of his city was Gewith.
47 And when Hadad died, Samlah of Masrekah reigned in his stead.
48 And when Samlah died, Shaul of Rehoboth by the river reigned in his stead.
49 And when Shaul died, Baal-hanan the son of Abcor reigned in his stead.
50 And when Baal-hanan died, He-

dad reigned in his stead; and the name of his city was Pao; and his wife's name was Mehetabel, the daughter of Matred, the daughter of Mezahab.

51 ¶Hadad died also. And the princes of Edom were prince Timnah, prince Anwa, prince Jetheth,

52 Prince Aholibamah, prince Elah, prince Pinon,

53 Prince Kenaz, prince Teman, prince Mibzar,

54 Prince Magdiel, prince Giram. These are the princes of Edom.

CHAPTER 2

THESE are the sons of Israel: Reuben, Simeon, Levi, Judah, Issachar, Zebulun,

2 Dan, Joseph, Benjamin, Naphtali, Gad, and Asher.

3 ¶The sons of Judah: Er, Onan, and Shelah; these three were born to him of Bathshua the Canaanitess. And Er, the first-born of Judah, was wicked in the sight of the LORD; and he slew him.

4 And Tamar his daughter-in-law bore him Pharez and Zerah. All the sons of Judah were five.

5 The sons of Pharez: Hezron and Hamul.

6 And the sons of Zerah: Zimri, Ethan, Haman, Calcol, Darda; five of them in all.

7 And the son of Carmi: Achar, the troubler of Israel, who transgressed in the thing dedicated.

8 And the son of Ethan: Azariah.

9 The sons of Hezron that were born to him: Rahmael, Ram, and Salbai.

10 And Ram begat Amminadab; and Amminadab begat Nahshon, prince of the children of Judah;

11 And Nahshon begat Salma; and Salma begat Boaz;

12 And Boaz begat Obed; and Obed begat Jesse;

13 ¶And Jesse begat his first-born Eliab, and Abinadab the second, and Shimma the third,

14 Nathanael the fourth, Darai the fifth,

15 Ozem the sixth, Eliho the seventh, and David the eighth,

16 Whose sisters were Zuriah and Abigail. And the sons of Zuriah: Abishai, Joab, and Ashail, three.

17 And Abigail bore Amasa; and the father of Amasa was Jether.

18 ¶And Caleb the son of Hezron begat Jedioth of Arubah his wife, and these were her sons: Asher, Jobab, and Adon.

19 And when Arubah died, Caleb took to him Ephrath, who bore him Hur.

20 And Hur begat Uri, and Uri begat Bezaliel.

21 ¶And afterward Hezron went in to the daughter of Machir the father of Gilead, whom he married when he was sixty years old; and she bore him Segub.

22 And Segub begat Jair, who had twenty-three towns in the land of Gilead.

23 And after that Hezron was dead in Caleb's land, Ephrath, then his wife, bore him Eshtawir the father of Tekoa.

24 And the sons of Jerahmeel the first-born of Hezron were Aram the first-born and Banah, Aran, and Azam their sister.

25 ¶Jerahmeel had also another wife, whose name was Atarah; she was the mother of Onam.

26 And the sons of Aram the first-born of Jerahmeel were Maaz, Nabin, and Aotar.

27 And the sons of Onam were Sabai, and Jada. And the sons of Sabai: Nadab and Abishur.

28 And the name of the wife of Abishur was Abihail, and she bore him Ahban and Molid.

29 And the sons of Nadab: Seled and Pelarim; but Seled died without children.

30 And the son of Pelarim was Isaiah. And the son of Isaiah: Shushan; and the son of Shushan: Ahlai.

31 And the sons of Jehoiada the brother of Sabai: Jether and Jonathan; and Jether died without children.

32 And the sons of Jonathan: Lapath and Aoza. These were the sons of Jerahmeel.

33 ¶Now Shushan had no sons, but daughters. And Shushan had a son-

in-law from Mizra, whose name was Jardaha.

34 And Shushan had given him his daughter to wife; and she bore him Attai.

35 And Attai begat Nathan, and Nathan begat Dabir,

36 And Dabir begat Ephil, and Ephil begat Jobab,

37 And Jobab begat Jehu, and Jehu begat Azariah,

38 And Azariah begat Helez, and Helez begat Eleasah,

39 And Eleasah begat Samsai, and Samsai begat Shallum,

40 And Shallum begat Elkamiah, and Elkamiah begat Elishama.

41 ¶Now the sons of Caleb the brother of Jerahmeel were Elishmai his first-born, who was the father of Ziph;

42 And the sons of Mareshah the father of Hebron were Korah, Tappuah, Rakim, and Shema.

43 And Shema begat Raham, the father of Jorkoam; and Jorkoam begat Samai.

44 And Auphnah, Caleb's concubine, bore Horan,

45 And Horan begat Gozan.[1]

46 And the son of Shammai was Maon; and Maon was the father of Bethzur.

47 And the sons of Jahdai: Regem and Jotham and Gesham and Pelet and Ephah and Shaaph.

48 Maachah, Caleb's concubine, bore Sheber and Tirhanah.

49 She bore also Shaaph the father of Madmannah, Sheva the father of Machbenah, and the father of Gibea; and the daughter of Caleb was Achsa.

50 ¶These were the sons of Caleb the son of Hur, the first-born of Ephratah: Shobal, who was born in Kirjath-narin;

51 Samla, who was born in Bethlehem; and Abi, who was born in Gader.

52 And sons were born to Shobal in Kirjath-narin; namely, Atroth, Jobal, Hazri,

53 Sepharvim, Netophath, Samla, Shemothim, Shechab, and Hama;

54 All these sons were born to Shobal in Kirjath-narin.

55 And the families of the scribes which dwelt at Jabez: the Tirathites, the Shimeathites, and Suchathites. These are the Kenites that came of Hemath, the father of the house of Rechab.

CHAPTER 3

NOW these were the sons of David that were born to him in Hebron: the first-born Hamnon, by Ahinoam the Jesreelitess; the second Caleb, by Abigail the Carmelitess;

2 The third Abshalom, the son of Maachah the daughter of Talmai king of Geshur; the fourth Adonijah, the son of Haggith;

3 The fifth Shephatiah, the son of Abital; the sixth Ithream, by Eglah his wife.

4 These six sons were born to him in Hebron, where he reigned for seven years and six months; and in Jerusalem he reigned thirty-three years.

5 Now these are the names of the sons that were born to him in Jerusalem: Shimea, Shecob, Nathan, and Solomon,

6 Ibhar, Elishama, Eliadah,

7 Eliphelet, Nogah, Nepheg,

8 Nephig, and Elishama.

9 These were all the sons of David, and Tamar was their sister.

10 ¶And Solomon's son was Rehoboam, Abijah was his son, Asa his son, Jehoshaphat his son,

11 Joram his son, Ahaziah his son, Joash his son,

12 Amaziah his son, Uzziah his son, Jotham his son,

13 Ahaz his son, Hezekiah his son, Manasseh his son,

14 Amon his son, Josiah his son.

15 And the sons of Josiah were: his first-born Johanan, the second Jehoiakim, the third Zedekiah, the fourth Shallum.

16 And the sons of Jehoiakim: Jeconiah his son, Zedekiah his son.

17 ¶And the sons of Jeconiah: Ashrashtiel his son,

---

[1] Some of the verses missing in the Eastern text of Chronicles are supplied from the King James version.

18 Malcom his son, Peraiah his son, Shaazar his son, Nekamiah his son, Shimei and Shaua his sons, and Nedabiah his son.

19 And the sons of Nedabiah were Zerubbabel and Shemei; and the sons of Zerubbabel: Meshullam and Hananiah, and Selkath was their sister;

20 And Hashubah, Jehoael, Beria, and Hasadiah.

21 And the sons of Hananiah: Pelatiah and Jesaiah; Arphaiah his son, Arnon his son, and Aobiah the son of Jesaiah.

22 And the son of Shechaniah: Shemaiah; and the sons of Shemaiah: Hattush, Negael, Azariah, and Hezekiah;

23 And the sons of Neariah: Elioenai, Hezekiah, and Azrikam, three.

24 Also Hodaiah, Eliashib, Pelaiah, Jacob, Johanan, Delaiah, and Anan.

CHAPTER 4

THESE are the sons of Judah: Pharez, Hezron, Carmi, Hur, and Shobal.

2 And Lana the son of Shobal begat Nahath; and Nahath begat Ahumai and Lahad. These are the families of Rehoboam.

3 And these are the sons of Aminadab: Ahizareel, Neshmah, and Dibash.

4 Pegoael and Hoshiah, these are the sons of Hur, the first-born of Ephratah, whose father was of Bethlehem.

5 ¶And Ashur the father of Tekoa had two wives.

6 And one of them bore Ahiram, Ephaor, Teman, and Hereshtar. These were the sons of one of them.

7 And the sons of Helah were, Zereth and Jezoar and Ethnan.

8 And Coz begat Anub and Zobebah and the families of Aharhel the son of Harum.

9 ¶And one of them was dear to his father and to his mother, so they called his name Our Eyes.

10 And they said to him, The LORD shall surely bless you and enlarge your territory, and his hand shall be with you and shall deliver you from evil, that it may not have power over you, and he shall grant you that which you request of him.

11 ¶And Caleb the brother of Ahijah begat Mehir, who was the father of Eshton.

12 And Eshton begat Tehiah, and Ropha begat Paseah, and Paseah begat Tehiah, and Tehiah begat Jazir.

13 These were the sons of Caleb the son of Jophaniah. The name of his first-born was Elah, and the name of the second was Naam, and the name of the third was Kenaz, and the name of the fourth was Ashiph, and the name of the fifth was Jamoael, and the name of the sixth was Jahrob.

14 These are the sons of Caleb the son of Jophaniah.

15 And the sons of Ezra were Jether, and Mered and Epher and Jalon; and she bore Miriam and Shammai and Ishbah the father of Eshtomoa.

16 And his wife Jehudijah bore Jered the father of Gedor and Heber the father of Socho and Jekuthiel the father of Zanoah. And these are the sons of Bithiah the daughter of Pharoah, which Mered took.

17 And the sons of his wife Hodiah the sister of Nahom, the father of Keilah the Garmite, and Eshtemoa the Maahathite.

18 And the sons of Shimon were, Annon and Rinnah, Benhanan, and Tilon. And the sons of Ishi were Zoheth and Benzoheth.

19 The sons of Shelah the son of Judah were Er, the father of Lecah, and Laadah the father of Mareshah, and the families of the house of them that wrought fine linen, of the house of Ashbea.

20 And the sons of Uriah's wife, the sister of Nahom the father of Keilah, were Zemri, Eshtemoa, Maachat, Eshtma, and Ashimon.

21 And the sons of Ashimon were Ammon, Domiah, Zerah, and Shelah.

22 These are the sons of Judah: Jemoael, Jamin, Ahar, Jachin, Zahar, Jarib, Zerah, and Saul.

23 These are the sons of Shelah.

24 The sons of Simeon were Mibsam his son, Mishma his son,

25 Shemati his son, Hamuel his son,

26 Zaccai his son, Shimei his son.
27 And Shimei had sixteen sons and six daughters; but his brothers had not many children, neither did all their family multiply until the children of Judah came to dwell with them.

28 And they dwelt with them in the towns of Beersheba, in Moladah, and in Darath-Shuah.

29 And in Bilhah, Ezem, and Tolad, 30 Bansel, Hirmah, Hazar-gadah, Heshmon, Hethpelet, and Zinglag,

31 And in Marmeranah and Samsalah. These were their cities until the reign of David.

32 And their villages were Akim, Ekin, Rimmon, Athchen, and Ashan, five cities;

33 And all the villages that were round about the same cities of Arkites.

34 These were the cities of their habitations, and they became very famous

35 And were situated in beautiful locations, and peace and tranquillity reigned round about them.

36 These were the names of the princes who were there in their families and in the house of their fathers.

37 And they came to the entrance of Geder, as far as the east side of the valley, to seek pasture for their flocks.

38 And they found good and rich pasture, and the land was wide and good, and tranquillity and peace there reigned;

39 For they who dwelt in it were the first settlers.

40 And these written by name came in the days of Hezekiah king of Judah, and destroyed their tents utterly

41 And polluted all the springs of water which were there to this day and dwelt in their places, because there was good pasture for their flocks.

42 And some of them and some of the sons of Simeon, five hundred men, went to mount Gebel. These are the names of the men who went as their leaders: Pelatiah, Metitha, Rephaiah, and Uzziel, the four sons of Ishi.

43 And they smote the rest of the Amalekites that escaped, and have dwelt in their place to this day.

1 Genesis 49:10.

CHAPTER 5

NOW the sons of Reuben the first-born of Israel (for he was the first-born of his father; but, because he defiled his father's bed, his birthright was given to the sons of Joseph his brother, the son of Israel; and upon his two sons came the blessings more than all the tribes of Israel.

2 For from Judah shall come forth Messiah the King,[1] but the blessings shall be given to Joseph),

3 The sons of Reuben, the first-born of Israel were Hanoch, Pallu, Hezron, and Carmi.

4 The sons of Carmi: Shemaiah his son, Doag his son, Shimei his son,

5 Micah his son, Uriah his son, Balah his son,

6 Abdaiah his son, whom Tiglath-pileser king of Assyria carried away captive; he was the prince of the tribe of Reubenites.

7 And his brethren by their families, when the genealogy of their generations was reckoned: Azrael, their chief, and Zechariah, second in rank,

8 And Bela and the son of Uzai, the son of Shema, the son of Joel, who dwelt in Adoer and as far as Nebo and the plain of Meon,

9 And eastward he inhabited as far as the border of the desert from the river Euphrates, because their cattle were multiplied in the land of Gilead.

10 And in the days of Saul they made war against the Arabians, the inhabitants of Sekah, and were delivered into their hands; and they dwelt in their tents throughout all the east land of Gilead.

11 ¶And the children of Gad dwelt opposite them, in the land of Mathnin as far as the border of Siba and Salcah.

12 Joel was their chief, and he judged them and taught them good scriptures.

13 These are the sons of Abihail, the son of Khuri, the son of Zerah, the son of Gilead, the son of Machir,

14 The son of Abdael, the son of Eli, chiefs of the house of their fathers.

15 And they dwelt in Mathnin and its villages.

16 All these were reckoned by genealogies in the days of Jotham king of Judah, and in the days of Jeroboam king of Israel.

17 ¶The Reubenites, the Gadites, and the half tribe of Manasseh, valiant men, able to bear sword and shield and to shoot with bow, and skilled in war, were forty-four thousand six hundred and sixty-six.

18 All of these went out to war and fought against the inhabitants of Sekah.

19 And they were delivered into their hands, for they prayed to the LORD in the battle, and he heard their voice because they put their trust in him.

20 And they carried away abundant goods and cattle: fifty thousand camels, two hundred and fifty thousand sheep, two thousand asses, and a hundred thousand persons.

21 For many fell slain in the battle of those who dwelt in tents. And the remnant stayed in their tents.

22 And the children of the half tribe of Manasseh dwelt in the land of Mathnin, as far as the plain of mount Hermon and as far as Har, and there they multiplied and became great.

23 ¶These were the heads of the house of their fathers: Apha, Shob, Eldaa, Azriel, Adomiah, Uriah, and Hezaiel,

24 All mighty men of valour, famous men, and heads of the house of their families.

25 ¶And they transgressed against the God of their fathers, and went astray after the gods of the people of the land, whom God destroyed before them.

26 And the God of Israel stirred up the spirit of Tiglath-pileser king of Assyria, and he carried them away, even the tribe of Reuben and the tribe of Gad and the half tribe of Manasseh, and brought them to Halah and Habor, and to the river Gozan, cities of Media. And they still dwell there to this day.

CHAPTER 6

THE sons of Levi: Gershon, Kohath, and Merari.

2 And the sons of Kohath: Amram, Izhar, Hebron, and Uzziel.

3 And the children of Amram: Moses, Aaron, and Miriam. And the sons of Aaron: Nadab, Abihu, Eleazar, and Ithamar.

4 ¶Eleazar begat Phinehas, Phinehas begat Abishua,

5 And Abishua begat Abikar, and Abikar begat Uzzi,

6 And Uzzi begat Zerahiah, and Zerahiah begat Maro,

7 And Maro begat Amariah, and Amariah begat Ahitub,

8 And Ahitub begat Zadok, and Zadok begat Ahimaaz,

9 And Ahimaaz begat Azariah, and Azariah begat Johanan,

10 And Johanan begat Azariah (it was he who ministered in the priestly office in the temple that Solomon built in Jerusalem),

11 And Azariah begat Amariah, and Amariah begat Ahitub,

12 And Ahitub begat Zadok, and Zadok begat Shallum,

13 And Shallum begat Hilkiah, and Hilkiah begat Azariah,

14 And Azariah begat Seraiah, and Seraiah begat Zadok,

15 And Zadok was carried away captive when the LORD carried away Judah and Jerusalem by the hand of Nebuchadnezzar.

16 ¶The sons of Levi: Gershon, Kohath, and Merari.

17 And these are the names of the sons of Gershon: Libni and Shimei.

18 And the sons of Kohath were Amram, Izhar, Hebron, and Uzziel.

19 The sons of Merari: Mahli and Moshi. And these are the families of the Levites according to their fathers.

20 Of Gershon: Libni his son, Nahath his son, Zimmah his son,

21 Joah his son, Iddo his son, Jathor his son.

22 The sons of Kohath: Amminadab his son, Korah his son, Assir his son,

23 Hilkanah his son, Akinsaph his son,

24 Tahath his son, Uriel his son, Uzziah his son, and Shaul his son.

25 And the sons of Hilkanah: Amasai and Ahimoth.

26 As for Hilkanah, the sons of Hilkanah: Zoph his son, Nahath his son, Zerah his son, Shamla his son, Mari his son,

27 Eliab his son, Gadhiel his son, Hilkanah his son.

28 And the sons of Samuel: Joel his first-born, and the name of his second son Abijah.

29 The sons of Merari: Mahli, Libni his son, Shimei his son, Uzza his son,

30 Shimea his son, Ashaiah his son.

31 These are all of those whom David appointed to minister in the house of the LORD at the place where the ark stood.

32 And they ministered before the LORD in the tabernacle of the congregation with great singing, until Solomon built the house of the LORD in Jerusalem; and then he appointed them to their office according to their order.

33 And these are the ministers and their sons: of the sons of the Kohathites, of the family of the Levites, Haman, and Joel the son of Samuel,

34 The son of Hilkanah, the son of Jeroham, the son of Eliel, the son of Taho,

35 The son of Zuph, the son of Hilkanah, the son of Hamath, the son of Moshi,

36 The son of Hilkanah, the son of Joel, the son of Azariah, the son of Zephaniah,

37 The son of Tahath, the son of Assir, the son of Akhsiph, the son of Korah,

38 The son of Izhar, the son of Kohath, the son of Levi, the son of Israel.

39 And his brother Asaph, who stood on the right hand of Asaph the son of Berachiah, the son of Shimea,

40 The son of Michael, the son of Measiah, the son of Malchiah,

41 The son of Ethi, the son of Zerah, the son of Ariah,

42 The son of Ethan, the son of Zimmah, the son of Shimei,

43 The son of Joha, the son of Gershon, the son of Levi.

44 And their brethren the sons of Merari stood on the left hand: Ethan, the son of Kishi, the son of Amar, the son of Malluch,

45 The son of Hashabiah, the son of Amaziah,

46 The son of Hilkiah, the son of Nator,

47 The son of Mahli, the son of Moshi, the son of Merari, the son of Levi.

48 Their brethren also the Levites were appointed to all manner of service of the tabernacle of the house of the LORD.

49 ¶But Aaron and his sons offered upon the altar of burnt offerings and upon the altar of incense, and were appointed for all the work of the Holy of Holies, and to make an atonement for Israel, according to all that Moses the servant of God had commanded.

50 And these are the sons of Aaron: Eleazar his son, Phinehas his son, Abishua his son,

51 Bakki his son, Uzzi his son, Zerahiah his son,

52 Maro his son, Amariah his son, Ahitub his son,

53 Zadok his son, Ahimaaz his son.

54 ¶Now these are the names of the cities which they were assigned for the families throughout their boundaries, to the sons of Aaron, of the family of the Kohathites; for theirs was the first lot.

55 And they gave them Hebron in the land of Judah, and its suburbs round about it;

56 But all the fields of the city, and those which were round about it, they gave to Caleb the son of Jophaniah.

57 And to the sons of Aaron they gave all the cities of refuge, and to the priests, Hebron with its suburbs, Libnah with its suburbs, Jattir with its suburbs, Lehem with its suburbs, Eshtemoa with its suburbs,

58 Debir with its suburbs, Ashan with its suburbs,

59 Atrah with its suburbs, and Bethshemesh with its suburbs;

60 And out of the tribe of Benjamin,

Geba with its suburbs, Alemeth with its suburbs, and Anathoth with its suburbs. All their cities throughout their families were thirteen cities.

61 And to the sons of Kohath, who inherited out of the tribe of Manasseh, were given ten cities in number;

62 And to the sons of Gershon according to their families out of the tribe of Issachar and out of the tribe of Asher and out of the tribe of Manasseh and out of the tribe of Nahptali in Mathnin, thirteen cities.

63 To the sons of Merari were given by lot, according to their families, out of the tribe of Reuben and out of the tribe of Dan and out of the tribe of Zebulun, twelve cities.

64 And the children of Israel gave to the Levites these cities with their suburbs.

65 And they gave by lot out of the tribe of the children of Judah and out of the tribe of the children of Simeon and out of the tribe of the children of Benjamin, these cities, which are called by the name of the families of the Kohathites.

66 Moreover they had other cities and their territory out of the tribe of Ephraim.

67 And they gave to them, of the cities of refuge, Shechem with its suburbs in mount Ephraim and Gezer with its suburbs,

68 Beth-horon with its suburbs,

69 Aijalon with its suburbs, and Gath-rimmon with its suburbs;

70 And out of the half tribe of Manasseh: Anath with its suburbs, Jablin with its suburbs, for the inheritance of the families of the sons of Kohath;

71 And to the sons of Gershon were given out of the half tribe of Manasseh, Golan in Mathnin with its suburbs and Ashtor with its suburbs;

72 And out of the tribe of Issachar: Rakim with its suburbs, Deberath with its suburbs,

73 Elam with its suburbs;

74 And out of the tribe of Asher: Mashal with its suburbs and Abron with its suburbs

75 And Akik with its suburbs and Dahab with its suburbs;

76 And out of the tribe of Naphtali: Rakim in Galilee with its suburbs and Hammon with its suburbs and Koriathaim with its suburbs.

77 To the family of Merari, who inherited out of the tribe of Zebulun, were given Armoni with its suburbs, Tabor with its suburbs;

78 And on the other side of the Jordan by Jericho, on the east side of the Jordan, were given them out of the tribe of Reuben: Bozer in the wilderness with its suburbs, Mepophat with its suburbs, Jahaz with its suburbs.

79 Kedemoth with its suburbs, Mephaath with its suburbs,

80 Ramoth with its suburbs, Mahlam with its suburbs,

81 Jazer with its suburbs, and Heshbon with its suburbs.

CHAPTER 7

NOW the sons of Issachar were Tola, Puah, Shob, and Shimron, four.

2 The sons of Tola: Uzzi, Rephaiah, Joel, Lahmai, Jibsam, and Samuel, heads of their father's house; these were the sons of Tola. They were valiant men of might in their families and their generations, whose number was in the days of David twenty-two thousand and six hundred.

3 And the son of Uzzi: Izarhan; and the sons of Izarhan: Malchael, Obadiah, Joel, and Ishoa, four, all of them chief men.

4 And with them by their generations, according to their father's house, were valiant men of war, thirty-six thousand men; for they had many wives and sons.

5 And their brethren, all the families of Issachar, were valiant men of might, reckoned in all by their genealogy, eighty-seven thousand.

6 ¶These are the names of the sons of Benjamin: Bela, Akbar, Ashbel, Gera, Naaman, Ahai, Arosh, Maphai, Hitim, and Adar.

7 And the sons of Bela: Ezbon, Uzzi, Uzzaiel, Jermoth, and Azri, five; heads of the house of their fathers, valiant men of valour; and were reckoned by their genealogy, twenty-two-thousand and thirty-four.

8 And the sons of Akbar: Zemora, Joash, Eliezer, Elioenai, Omri, Jermoth, Abijah, Anathoth, and Alamoth. All these were the sons of Akbar.

9 And their number, according to their genealogy by their generations, heads of the house of their fathers, valiant men, was twenty-two thousand and two hundred.

10 And the son of Ashcol: Bilhan; and the sons of Bilhan: Joash, Benjamin, Ehud, Chenanah, Zethan, Tarshish, and Ahishahar.

11 All these were the sons of Ashcol, according to the heads of their fathers, mighty men of valour, seventeen thousand and two hundred soldiers, fit to go out in the army for battle;

12 Shaphan, also, and Huphis, the sons of Aod, of the children of Hoshah.

13 ¶The sons of Naphtali: Jahziel, Guni, Jezer, and Shallum, the sons of Bilhah.

14 ¶The sons of Manasseh: Asarchiel, whom his concubine bore him; she also bore Machir the father of Gilead;

15 And Machir took to wife the daughter of a prince, whose sister's name was Maachah; and the name of his eldest brother was Zelophehad; and Zelophehad had no sons but daughters.

16 And Maachah also the mother of Machir bore a son, and she called his name Peresh; and the name of his brother was Sheresh;

17 And the son of Ulam: Rakim, and the son of Rakim, Baran. These were the sons of Gilead, the son of Machir, the son of Manasseh.

18 And his sister Maachah bore Ashhor and Abiezer,

19 And Shemirah, Elenon, Shem, and Etham.

20 ¶And the sons of Ephraim: Shuthelah, Bachar his son, Tahath his son, Eladah his son, and Ahath his son,

21 ¶And Zabor his son, Shuthelah his son and Lazar his son, whom the men of Gath who were born in the land slew because they came down to take away their wealth.

22 And Ephraim their father mourned many days, and his brethren came to comfort him.

23 ¶And he went in to his wife, and she conceived and bore a son, and she called his name Beriah, because misfortune had befallen his house.

24 (And her daughter escaped in lower and upper Beth-horon.)

25 And all those who escaped were healed by her daughter; for she was a woman physician, and she healed the sick.

26 And she also healed Edan the son of Ammihud,

27 Of the sons of Nun, the father of Hosea.[1]

28 ¶And their possessions and habitations were: Beth-el and its towns and Shechem and its towns and Anath and its towns;

29 And by the borders of the children of Manasseh, Beth-sechem and its towns, Taanach and its towns, Megiddo and its towns, and Dor and its towns. In these cities dwelt the children of Joseph the son of Israel.

30 ¶The sons of Asher were Imnah, Ishuah, Ishuai, Beriah, and their sister Sarah.

31 And the sons of Beriah: Hepher and Malchiel, who is the father of Birzavith.

32 And Hepher begat Phelet, Shomer, Hotham, and Shua their sister.

33 And the sons of Phelet: Pasach, Bimhal, and Ashvath. These are the sons of Phelet: Arah, and Hananaiel.

34 And the sons of Shamer: Ahi, Rohgah, Jehubbah, and Aram.

35 And the sons of his brother Helem: Zophah and Imna and Shelesh and Amal.

36 The sons of Zophah: Suah and Harnepher and Shual and Beri and Imrah,

37 Bezer and Hod and Shamma and Shilshah and Ithran and Beera.

38 And the sons of Jether: Jophaniah, and Pispah and Ara.

39 And the sons of Ulla: Arah and Haniel and Rezia.

[1] Or Joshua.

40 These were the sons of Asher, heads of their father's house, according to their generations, valiant men, chiefs of the princes. Their number was reckoned in the army for battle, twenty-six thousand men.

CHAPTER 8

NOW Benjamin begat Bela his first-born, Akbar the second, Ashcol the third,

2 Gera the fourth, Naaman the fifth,

3 Ahai the sixth, Arosh the seventh,

4 Mathim the eighth, Hasim the ninth,

5 And Adar the tenth.

6 And the sons of Bela were Abdo, Gerah and Abihud,

7 Abishua, Naaman, and Ahiah,

8 And Saphim, Hupham, and Ahiram.

9 And these are the sons of Abihud;

10 These are the heads of their fathers by their families, and they were carried captive to the plain of Naaman.

11 And he begat of his wife Harash, Hobab,

12 Zebiah, and Malcom, and Manasseh, Seriah, Jarmanah, and Zebaz;

13 These were his sons, heads of the fathers.

14 And Mahshim begat Hobat and Elipaleg.

15 The sons of Elipaleg: Eber, Mishlam, and Shamer,

16 Who built Eio and Lod, with the hamlets thereof;

17 And he became the chief of the fathers over the inhabitants of Gath;

18 And Shishak and Jeremoth,

19 And Zebadiah, Azor, and Adai,

20 And Mancel, Anshephi, Ebron, and Zabdai,

21 And Henani, Henaniah, Aulam, Anatoth, Peraiah,

22 Phael, and the children of Shishak, and Shimirah.

23 These were the heads of the fathers, by their generations; these were the men who dwelt in Jerusalem at first.

24 And in Gibeon dwelt the father of Gibeon, whose wife's name was Maachah,

25 And his first-born son Abron, also Kish, Bela, and Nadab,

26 And Good, Ahib, Ezabar, and Mikloth.

27 And Mikloth begat Maa.

28 And these also dwelt with their brethren in Jerusalem, opposite them.

29 And Mir begat Kish, and Kish begat Saul, and Saul begat Jonathan, Malchishua, Jashui, and Ashbashul.

30 And the son of Jonathan was crippled in his feet, and Jashui had a son whose name was Merib-baal, and Merib-baal begat Micah.

31 And the sons of Micah were Pithon, Melech, Tarea, Ahor, and Aran.

32 And Ahor begat Jehoiadah; and Jehoiadah begat Alemoth, Azmaveth, and Zimri; and Zimri begat Moza,

33 And Moza begat Canaaniah, and Canaaniah begat Zopa, Elasah his son, and Azel his son.

34 And Azel had six sons, whose names are these: Azri his first-born, Kim his second, Ishmael his third,

35 And Sheadiah, Obadiah, and Hanan. All these were the sons of Azel.

36 And the sons of Eshek his brother were Ulam the first-born, Jehush the second, and Eliphelet the third.

37 And the sons of Ulam were mighty men of valour, archers,

38 And they instructed their sons and their sons' sons,

39 One hundred and fifty.

40 All these are of the tribe of the sons of Benjamin.

CHAPTER 9

SO all Israel and Judah were considered wicked, for they were carried captive to Babylon because of their wickedness.

2 ¶Now the first inhabitants who dwelt in their possessions in their cities were the Israelites, the priests, the Levites, and the proselytes.

3 And in Jerusalem dwelt some of the children of Judah and of the children of Benjamin and of the children of Ephraim and of Manasseh:

4 Zori the son of Ammihud, the son of Omri, the son of Imri, the son of

Benjamin, of the descendants of Pharez the son of Judah.

5 And of the land of the Shilonites: Asaiah the first-born, and Bezaiah his brother.

6 And of the descendants of Zerah: Jeuel, and their brethren, six hundred and ninety.

7 And of the descendants of Benjamin: Sallu the son of Meshullam, the son of Hodiah, the son of Jahbanah,

8 And Jocaniah the son of Jeroham. These were the descendants of Uzzi the son of Machir and Meshullam the son of Reuel, the son of Jocaniah;

9 And their brethren, according to their generations, nine hundred and ninety-nine. All these were valiant men, captains over hundreds according to their fathers' houses.

10 ¶And of the priests: Jonadab, Jodaiah, and Zachim,

11 And Azariah the son of Hilkiah, the son of Meshullam, the son of Zadok, the son of Maro, the son of Ahitub, whose house was situated opposite the house of the LORD.

12 And Azariah the son of Jeroham, the son of Pashur, the son of Malchijah, and Mansai the son of Adiel, the son of Johanan, the son of Meshullam, the son of Meshraoth, the son of Immer;

13 And their brethren, heads of the house of their fathers, one thousand seven hundred and sixty; very able men for the work of the service of the house of the LORD.

14 And of the Levites: Shemaiah the son of Hashum, the son of Azrikam, the son of Hashabiah,

15 Of the descendants of Merari: Jarhum the son of Hadush, the son of Alal, and Mattaniah the son of Micah, the son of Zabdai, the son of Asaph;

16 And Obadiah the son of Shemaiah, the son of Cala, the son of Jerithun; and Berechiah the son of Asaph, the son of Hilkanah, who dwelt in Ramtha.[1]

17 And the porters were Shallum, Jacob, Talan, Hamnon, Ahihom, and Shallum,

1 Or Rama.

18 Who hitherto waited in the king's gate eastward; they were the porters in the companies of the descendants of Levi.

19 And Shallum the son of Kora, the son of Akhsiph, the son of Korah, and his brethren and the members of his father's house were over the work and over the keepers of the gates of the tabernacle; and their fathers, who were over the host, were the keepers of the exit and of the entrance.

20 And Phinehas the son of Eleazar was ruler over them in time past, and the LORD was with him.

21 And Zechariah the son of Meshallum was porter of the door of the tabernacle of the congregation.

22 All those who were chosen to be porters in the gates were two hundred and twelve. These were reckoned by their genealogy, whom David and Samuel the prophet appointed to their set office.

23 For they appointed them and their sons to keep the gates of the house of the LORD and the house of the tabernacle of the congregation, as guards.

24 The gates were open toward the four directions, toward the east, west, north, and south.

25 And their brethren who kept the watch in their generation did not enter into the temple except once every seven days from time to time,

26 For these Levites were in their set office, and were in charge of four gates in the four directions; and stood on guard, and were over the work and over the treasuries of the house of the LORD.

27 ¶And they lodged round about the house of the LORD, because upon them was the duty of guarding the gates.

28 And certain of them had charge of inspecting all the vessels of service, which were counted every morning when they were brought in and when they were taken out.

29 And some of the Levites were appointed over the vessels and over all the instruments of the sanctuary,

over the altar and the vessels, the wine, the oil, the frankincense, and the pure spices.

30 And some of the sons of the priests prepared the incense for the censers, and the gifts were given by the Levites.

31 And Mattithiah, one of the Levites, who was the first-born of Shallum, was intrusted with the office of the mysterious rites.

32 And also some of the descendants of Kohath were over their brethren and over the shewbread, to prepare the meal every sabbath.

33 And these are the ministers, chiefs of the fathers of the Levites, who kept the watch in the chambers round about the temple, because they were over the work day and night.

34 These were chiefs of the fathers of the Levites, according to their generations; and these dwelt in Jerusalem.

35 ¶And in Gibeon dwelt the father of Gibeon, and the name of his first-born son was Joel, and the name of his wife was Maachah;

36 And his second son was Abron; then Zur, Kishon, Baal, Ner, and Nadab,

37 And Gedor, Ahiah, Zechariah, and Mikloth.

38 And Mikloth begat Shimaez. And they also dwelt with their brethren in Jerusalem, opposite their brethren.

39 And Ner begat Kish; and Kish begat Saul; and Saul begat Jonathan and Malchishua and Jeshui and Ashbashul.

40 And Jeshui had a son, whose name was Merib-baal: and Meribbaal begat Micah.

41 And the sons of Micah were Pithon, Melech, and Ahaz.

42 And Ahaz begat Jezaniah; and Jezaniah begat Alemoth; and Alemoth begat Zimri; and Zimri begat Moza;

43 And Moza begat Canaaniah; and Rephaiah his son, Azel his son, and Eleasah his son.

44 And Azel had six sons, whose names are these: Uzzi his first-born, Kim his second, Ashmah, Shadiah, Obadiah, and Hanan. These were the sons of Azel.

CHAPTER 10

NOW the Philistines fought against Israel; and the men of Israel fled from before the Philistines, and many fell slain on mount Gilboa.

2 And the Philistines overtook Saul and his sons; and the Philistines slew Jonathan and Jeshui and Malchishua, the sons of Saul.

3 And the battle went sore against Saul, and the archers who were skilled in shooting with bows found him; and when Saul saw them, he was sore afraid of them.

4 Then Saul said to his armourbearer, Draw your sword, and thrust me through with it, before these uncircumcised come and slay me and torment me. But his armourbearer would not; for he was sore afraid. So Saul took his own sword and fell on it.

5 And when his armorbearer saw that Saul was dead, he fell likewise on his sword, and died with him.

6 So Saul died and his three sons and his armourbearer, and all his mighty men died on that day together.

7 And when all the men of Israel who were on the other side of the valley and on the other side of Jordan saw that Israel had fled and that Saul and his sons were slain, they forsook the cities and fled; and the Philistines came and dwelt in them.

8 ¶And it came to pass on the morrow, when the Philistines came to strip the slain, they found Saul and his three sons fallen on mount Gilboa.

9 And they cut off their heads, stripped them of their armour, and sent them to the land of the Philistines, throughout the towns and cities and provinces, to carry the good tidings to their idols and to their people;

10 And they put their garments and their armour in the house of their idols, and hanged their bodies by the wall of Beth-jashan.

11 ¶Now when the inhabitants of

Jabesh-gilead heard all that the Philistines had done to Saul,

12 They arose, all the valiant men, and went all the night, and took away the body of Saul and the bodies of his sons from the wall of Beth-jashan, and brought them to Jabesh and burned them there; then they took their bones and buried them under the oak in Jabesh, and fasted seven days.

13 ¶So Saul died because of the transgression which he committed against the LORD, and because of the command of the LORD, which he kept not,

14 And also because he consulted men who had familiar spirits, and did not inquire of the LORD his God. Therefore his kingdom was given to David the son of Jesse.

CHAPTER 11

THEN all Israel gathered themselves to David to Hebron, saying, Behold, we are your blood and your flesh always;

2 And moreover in times past, even when Saul was king over us, it was you that led and brought in Israel; and the LORD your God said to you, You shall feed my people Israel, and you shall be ruler over all the tribes of Israel.

3 Wherefore all the elders of Israel came to the king to Hebron; and King David made a covenant with them in Hebron before the LORD; and they appointed David king over Israel. Thus the words of Samuel the prophet were confirmed, which he spoke in the name of the LORD.

4 ¶Then David and all Israel went to Jerusalem (which was formerly called Jebus) where the Jebusites were, the inhabitants of the land.

5 And the inhabitants of Jebus said to David, You shall not come in here. Nevertheless David gathered all the people together and took the city of Zion, which is called the city of David.

6 And David said, Whoever smites a Jebusite person first shall be chief

and commander of the army. So Joab the son of Zeruiah went up first, and King David appointed him chief and commander of the army.

7 And David dwelt in the city of Zion; therefore they called it the city of David.

8 And David built the city round about, even from Millo, which is outside; and David gave the east side of the city to the rest of the people who were in the villages.

9 So David became greater and greater; and the LORD of hosts was with him.

10 ¶These are the chiefs of David's mighty men, who strengthened themselves with him in his kingdom and helped him to be made king over all Israel, according to the word of the LORD which he spoke concerning Israel.

11 And this is the number of the mighty men whom David had: seated in the first rank, chief of thirty men, Gedho, a valiant man; he lifted up his spear and slew three hundred men in one hour.

12 And after him was Eleazar his uncle's son, of the city of Dakhokh, who was over three hundred men.

13 He was with David at Pasi-demaya, when the Philistines were fighting there, where there was a field of barley; and the people fled from before the Philistines.

14 And they set themselves in the midst of the field, and delivered it and slew the Philistines; and the LORD wrought a great victory.

15 ¶Now three of the thirty chieftains went down to David, into the cave of Arlam; and the host of the Philistines was encamped in the valley of Gabarey.[1]

16 And David dwelt then in the tent, and the garrison of the Philistines was then at Bethlehem.

17 And David longed, and said, Oh that one would give me a drink of water from the great cistern of Bethlehem that is at the gate of the city!

18 And as soon as three men heard it, they broke through the camp of the Philistines, and went and drew

[1] Giants.

water out of the cistern of Bethlehem that was by the gate of the city, and took it and brought it to David; but David would not drink of it, but poured it out in the presence of the LORD,

19 And said, The LORD forbid that I should do this thing in the presence of my God; for these men went forth with the jeopardy of their lives. Therefore he would not drink it. These things did these three valiant men.

20 ¶And Abishai the brother of Joab was chief of thirty; for he lifted up his spear against three hundred and slew them, and he was highly honored, promoted to be over thirty men.

21 He was more honorable than the thirty men, and he became their chief and fought like thirty men.

22 Benaiah the son of Jehoiada, a valiant man of the province of Kabzeel who had done good deeds; he slew the two mighty men of Moab; also he went down and slew a lion in the midst of a forest on a snowy day.

23 And he slew an Egyptian, a man of great stature, five cubits high; and in the Egyptian's hand was a spear like a weaver's beam; and he went down against him with a staff, and took the spear out of the Egyptian's hand and slew him with his own spear.

24 These things did Benaiah the son of Jehoiada, and was more renowned than the three valiant men.

25 And he was honorable among the three valiant men, for he fought like three mighty men; and David set him over his bodyguard and over the chiefs of the army;

26 ¶Also the valiant men of the army were: Ashail the brother of Joab, Elhanan his uncle's son of Bethlehem,

27 Shammoth of the mount, King Helez the Pelonite,

28 Ira the son of Ikkes of Tekoa, Abiezer of Anathoth,

29 Sabbai the Hushathite, Ilai the Ahohite,

30 Maharai the Netophathite, Heled the son of Baanah the Netophathite,

31 Ithai the son of Ribai of Gibeah, of the Benjamites, Benaiah the Pirathonite,

32 Hadai of the brooks of Gaash, Abiel the Arbathite,

33 Uzban the Marhomite, Elipha the Shaalbonite,

34 The sons of Shem the Gizonite, Jonathan the son of Shage of mount Carmel,

35 Ahiram the son of Sacim of mount Beta, Elipon the son of Ur of Begarthon,

36 Hepher the Mecherathite, Ahijah the Hasarite,

37 Hezro the Carmelite, Lazar the Aobite,

38 Joel the brother of Nathan, Machad the Gaddite,

39 Zelek the Ammonite, Mahrai the Berothite, the armorbearer of Joab the son of Zuriah,

40 Ira the Ithrite, Garab the Ithrite,

41 Uriah the Hittite, Zabad the son of Ahlai,

42 Adina the son of Shara the Reubenite, of the house of Reubenites, and he was a captain over thirty men,

43 Hanan the son of Maachah, and Azrai the Anathotite,

44 Jehoshaphat the Ashterathite, Shama and Emael the sons of Hotham the Aroerite,

45 Jediael the son of Shimri, and Joha his brother,

46 Amozoth and Anael, Moham, Mozel, Ribai and his son Ashua; Ahmael and Jathmah the Moabites,

47 Eliel, Jathmah, Ober, Lasiel, and Ashkir.

CHAPTER 12

NOW these are all the mighty men of David, who stood by him in the battle, and they came with David to the city of Zinklag, when he fled from Saul the son of Kish; and they were among the mighty men who stood before David. If David had wished, they would have slain Saul the son of Kish, for they were mighty men of war, but David would not permit them to slay Saul.

2 They held the bows with their left hand and the swords with their right, and their bows were filled with

arrows, but David was unwilling to slay Saul, because he was the chief, the prince of the tribe of Benjamin.

3 These are the names of the mighty men who were with David: Ahiezer and his son Joash; Joel of Macsite; Shemaiah the Gibeathite; Pelet and Berachiah, the sons of Arboth; and Jehu the Anatothite;

4 And Shemaiah the Gibeonite, who was captain over thirty men, and fought equal to all of them; and Jeremiah, Nahaziel, Zabor, Azar,

5 Gadai, Jermoth, Bealiah, Shemariah, Shephatiah, Habar,

6 Elkanah, Jesiah, Azariel, Shebnah, Asaph,

7 Joah and Zechariah, the sons of Jeroham of Gadar.

8 And those of the tribe of the Gadites separated themselves to David to go out with him to the stronghold in the wilderness; mighty men and men of stature and fit for battle, who could handle sword and shield, whose faces were like the faces of lions, and who were swift for war upon the mountains:

9 Ezra the chief of the mighty men, Obadiah the second, Eliab the third,

10 Ashur the fourth, Jeremiah the fifth,

11 Athar the sixth, Eliel the seventh,

12 Johanan the eighth, Elzabad the ninth,

13 Jeremiah the tenth, Shepatiah the eleventh.

14 These were of the descendants of Gad, commanders of the army; one of them was captain over a hundred, and the others were over a thousand.

15 These are they who crossed the Jordan in the month of Nisan,[1] when it had overflowed all its banks; and they put to flight all the army that was encamped in the valley, both toward the east and toward the west. And these are the numbers of the commanders of the army who gathered together and came to David to Hebron to give him the kingdom of Saul, so that the word of Samuel the prophet might be fulfilled, who spoke by the command of the LORD.

[1] April, the first month.

16 And there came some of the children of Benjamin and Judah to the camp to David.

17 And David went out to meet them and blessed them, and said to them, If you have come peaceably to me to help us, then may the LORD grant you a double portion of that which you have in your heart; but if you have come to betray me and to deliver me to my adversaries, seeing that I have not sinned against you and there is no wrong in my hands, the God of my fathers knows it, and he will rebuke whoever is wrong among us.

18 Then the spirit of might came upon Amasa, the son of Jatar, chief of the thirty, and he answered and said to David, Come on, David, come on, O son of Jesse! I am also with you, peace be to you, be not afraid, and peace will be given to you from your helpers; for your God is your helper in every hour. Then David received them, and made them captains of the army.

19 And some of the men of the tribe of Manasseh went over to David when he went to war with the Philistines against Saul to battle; but they would not go with Saul to war to help him, because they hated him, for they had gone and made a secret treaty with the princes of the Philistines, saying, Let us go first and fall on Saul our master;

20 And as he goes to Zinklag, we will besiege him and capture him alive. These are their names: Ada, Zabor, Jediael, Michael, Elihu, and Jozabad, commanders of thousands of the house of Manasseh.

21 And they helped David when he went against the band of raiders; for they were all mighty men of valor and commanders over all the army, and they did as they pleased through him.

22 For every day they went into the presence of David to eat food before him, for he loved them exceedingly.

23 ¶And of the children of Judah who bore sword and spear were six

thousand and eight hundred mighty men of war.

24 And of the children of Simeon, mighty men of valor for the war, eight thousand and seven hundred.

25 And of the children of Levi, four thousand and six hundred.

26 And Jehoiada was the leader of the family of the Aaronites, and with him were three thousand and seven hundred;

27 And Zadok, a young man mighty of valour, and of his father's house and his brothers, twenty-two officers.

28 And of the children of Benjamin, the kindred of Saul, three thousand; for until the day in which Saul was slain, they guarded the house of Saul.

29 And of the children of Ephraim, twenty thousand and eight hundred, mighty men of valour, famous throughout the house of their fathers.

30 And of the half tribe of Manasseh, eighteen thousand, who were renowned, and they came first to make David king.

31 And of the children of Issachar, men who had understanding in their times, who did good and upright deeds before the LORD; their chiefs were two hundred; and all their brethren did whatever they were commanded.

32 And of the tribe of Zebulun, such as went forth to battle, expert in war, with all weapons of war, fifty thousand, who were ready to fight against those whose loyalty was doubtful concerning the kingdom of David.

33 And of the children of Naphtali, a thousand officers; and with them were thirty-seven thousand men with shield and spear.

34 And of the Danites, expert in war, twenty-eight thousand and six hundred.

35 And of Asher, such as went forth to battle, valiant men of war, forty thousand.

36 And of the other side of the Jordan, of the Reubenites and of the Gadites and of the half tribe of Manasseh, armed with all manner of weapons of war, one hundred and twenty thousand.

37 All these mighty men of war went to battle with a perfect heart, and came to Hebron to make David king over all Israel; and also all the rest of the chiefs of Israel came with a sincere heart to make David king over Israel.

38 And they were there with David for three days, eating and drinking; for their brethren had prepared for them.

39 Now these were the names of the tribes who supplied them with food, who were near them:

40 The tribes of Issachar and Zebulun and Naphtali brought bread on asses and on camels and on mules, also flour and raisins and baskets of grapes and wine and oil and sheep and oxen in abundance; for there was great joy in Israel.

CHAPTER 13

AND David consulted with the commanders of thousands and of hundreds, and with all the leaders and governors of Israel.

2 And David said to all the assemblies of Israel, If it seems good to you, let us beseech the LORD our God to repair the breaches of our brethren who reside in all towns of Israel, and settle with them priests and Levites in their cities and suburbs;

3 So that they may gather themselves and come to us, and pray before the LORD our God and beseech him because of our sins; for we did not pray before him in the days of Saul.

4 And all the assemblies said that they would do so.

5 So David gathered all Israel together, from the river of Egypt even to the entrance of Hamath,[1] to bring the ark of the LORD from Koriathnarin.

6 And David went up, and all Israel, to Koriath-narin, which belongs to the tribe of Judah, to bring up from there the ark of the LORD God who dwells upon the high cherubim, which are known by his name.

7 And they placed the ark of the LORD in a new cart, and carried it out

¹ Antioch.

of the house of Abinadab; and Uzza and his brothers drove the cart.

8 And David and all Israel played before the LORD with all their might, and with singing and with harps and with psalteries and with cymbals and with timbrels.

9 ¶And when they came to the threshing floor of Remin, Uzza put forth his hand to hold the ark; for the oxen ran toward the threshing floor.

10 And the anger of the LORD was kindled against Uzza, and he smote him there because he put forth his hand to the ark; and he died there before the ark.

11 And David was displeased because the LORD had smote Uzza; wherefore that place is called Toretha-di-Uzza to this day.

12 And David was afraid of the LORD that day, saying, How can I bring the ark of God home to me?

13 So David was unwilling to bring the ark home to the city of David. And David commanded it be carried to the house of Ober-edom the Gittite.

14 And the ark of the LORD remained in the house of Ober-edom the Gittite three months. And the LORD blessed the house of Ober-edom the Gittite and all that he had.

CHAPTER 14

NOW Hiram king of Tyre [1] sent messengers to David, and timber of cedars, with masons and carpenters, to build a house for him.

2 And David perceived that the LORD had chosen him to be king over Israel, for his kingdom was exalted because of his people Israel.

3 ¶And David took more wives in Jerusalem, after he had come from Hebron, and there were born to him more sons and daughters.

4 Now these are the names of the children who were born to him in Jerusalem: Shammua, Shocob, Nathan, and Solomon,

5 Ibhar, Elisha, Eliphalet,

6 Nogah, Nepheg, and Naphia,

[1] Sur.

31

7 And Elishama, Eliada, and Eliphalet.

8 ¶And when the Philistines heard that David was anointed king over all Israel, all the Philistines went up to seek David. And David heard of it, and went out against them.

9 And the Philistines came and encamped in the valley of giants.

10 And David inquired of the LORD, saying, Shall I go up against the Philistines? And wilt thou deliver them into my hands? And the LORD said to him, Go up; for I will deliver them into your hands.

11 So they came up to the valley of Toretha, and David smote them there. Then David said, The LORD has broken in upon my enemies before me like the breaking forth of waters; therefore they called the name of that place the valley of Toretha.

12 And when they had left their idols there, David gave a commandment to his mighty men, saying, Burn them with fire and scatter their ashes to the wind.

13 And the Philistines came up again and encamped in the valley of giants.

14 Therefore David inquired again of God; and God said to him, You shall not go up after them; but turn away from them, and go attack them from the front.

15 And it shall be, when you hear the sound of howling in the top of the mountain, then you shall go out to battle; for the LORD has gone forth before you to smite the army of the Philistines.

16 And David therefore did as the LORD commanded him; and they smote the army of the Philistines from Gibeon even to Gadar.

17 And the fame of David went out into all lands; and the LORD brought the fear of him upon all the nations.

CHAPTER 15

AND David built citadels for himself in the city of David, and also built a place for the ark of the LORD and for the instruments of the tabernacle.

2 Then David commanded the Levites to carry the ark of the LORD and the instruments of the tabernacle; for the Levites the LORD had chosen to minister and to carry the ark of the LORD, and to look after it for ever.

3 And David gathered all Israel together to Jerusalem, to bring up the ark of the LORD to the place which he had built for it.

4 And David assembled the descendants of Aaron and the Levites:

5 Of the sons of Kohath, Uriel the elder and his brethren, a hundred and twenty;

6 Of the sons of Merari, Ashiel the elder and his brethren, two hundred and twenty;

7 Of the sons of Gershon, Joel the elder and his brethren, a hundred and thirty;

8 Of the sons of Elizaphan, Shemaiah the elder and his brethren, two hundred;

9 Of the sons of Hebron, Eliab the elder and his brethren, eighty;

10 Of the sons of Uzziel, Amminadab the elder and his brethren, a hundred and twelve.

11 Then David called for Zadok the priest and Abiathar, and for the Levites, for Uriel, Amsah, Joel, Asaiah, Shemaiah, Uriel, and Amminadab,

12 And said to them, You are the chiefs of the fathers of the Levites; sanctify yourselves, both you and your brethren, that you may bring up the ark of the LORD God of Israel to the place which has been built for it before,

13 So that the LORD our God may not smite us because we did not seek him after the due order.

14 So the priests and the Levites sanctified themselves to bring up the ark of the LORD God of Israel.

15 And the Levites carried the ark of the LORD upon their shoulders with the poles thereon, as Moses had commanded according to the word of the LORD.

16 And David spoke to the elders of the Levites to appoint their brethren to be singers with instruments of music, psalteries and harps and cymbals, sounding by raising up their voices in joy.

17 So the Levites appointed Heman the son of Joel; and of his brethren, Asaph the son of Berechiah; and of the sons of Merari their brethren, Ethan the son of Kushaiah;

18 And with them their brethren of the second order, Zechariah the son of Neaiel, Jehiel, Eliab, Benaiah, Asa, Mattitha, Elipheleu, Mikiaho, Oberedom, and Jeiel.

19 Now these were all those who stood by the gates and sang: Heman, Asaph, and Ethan.

20 These were all who played with the instruments of brass to minister in the service: Azariah, Aziel, Jehiel, Unni, Eliab, Maasiah, and Benaiah;

21 And those who sang songs: Mattitha, Mikiaho, Ober-edom, Uzzael, and Uzzanaiah; these played with harps every day at three o'clock and at nine o'clock.

22 And Benaiah, chief of the Levites, played every day in the booth, for they had prepared a place for him.

23 And Berechiah and Hilkanah looked after the ark, providing for it what was needed.

24 And Shebaniah, Jehoshaphat, Nathanael, Amasai, Zechariah, Benaiah, and Eliezer, the priests, did blow with the trumpets before the ark of the LORD; and Ober-edom and Ahiah looked after the ark.

25 ¶So David and the elders of Israel and the commanders of thousands went to bring up the ark of the covenant of the LORD from the house of Ober-edom to the city of David with great joy.

26 And it came to pass when the LORD helped the Levites who carried the ark in which was the covenant of the LORD that they sacrificed seven bullocks and seven rams.

27 And David was clothed with robes of fine linen, and all the Levites who bore the ark were also clothed with robes of fine linen; and David wore upon his linen garments an ephod of fine linen.

28 Thus David and all Israel brought up the ark in which was the covenant of the LORD, with songs and with sound of straight trumpets and curved trumpets and shouting.

29 ¶And it came to pass as the ark in which was the covenant of the LORD reached the city of David, Michal the daughter of Saul looked out a window and saw David dancing and playing, and she despised him in her heart.

CHAPTER 16

SO they brought the ark of the LORD and set it in its place in the tent that David had pitched for it; and they offered burnt offerings and peace offerings before the ark of the LORD.

2 And when David had finished offering the burnt offerings and the peace offerings, he blessed the people of Israel in the name of the LORD of hosts.

3 And he distributed to all the people of Israel, both men and women and young men and the little ones, to every one a loaf of bread, a portion of meat, and a fine white loaf. Then all the people went away, every one to his own house.

4 ¶And he appointed certain of the Levites to minister before the ark of the LORD and to invoke and to thank and to praise the LORD God of Israel:

5 Asaph the chief, and second to him Zechariah, also Jeiel, Jehiel, Mattitha, Eliab, Benaiah, Asaph, Amminadab, Asaph, Nahaziel, and Asaph.

6 These were all the priests who sounded with trumpets continually before the ark of the LORD.

7 ¶Then on that day David delivered this psalm, both he and the chiefs of all the priests and the Levites to praise the LORD, in the company of Asaph and his brethren. These are the headings of the songs which David sang on that day before the ark of the LORD:

8 Give thanks to the LORD, call upon his name, make known his deeds among the peoples.

9 Sing to him, give thanks to him, tell of all his wondrous works.

10 Glory in his holy name; let the heart of those who seek the LORD rejoice.

11 Seek the LORD and his strength, pray before him continually.

12 Remember his marvellous works that he has done, his wonders and the judgments of his mouth,

13 O you descendants of Abraham his servant, children of Jacob, his chosen ones.

14 He is the LORD our God; his laws are in all the earth.

15 Be mindful of his covenant for ever, the word which he commanded to a thousand generations,

16 Even his oath to Abraham and the covenant which he made with the sons of Isaac;

17 And he has confirmed the same to Jacob for a law, and to Israel for an everlasting covenant,

18 Saying, To you I will give the land of Canaan, the lot of your inheritance;

19 When you were but few, even a few in numbers and strangers in it.

20 And when you were carried away captive from nation to nation and from kingdom to another kingdom,

21 He permitted not the rulers to harm you, yea, he chastened kings for your sakes,

22 Saying, Touch not my anointed ones and do my prophets no harm.

23 Sing to the LORD, all the earth; show forth from day to day his salvation.

24 Declare his glory among the nations;

25 For great is the LORD, and greatly to be praised; and he is to be revered above all kings.

26 For all the gods of the Gentiles are images; but the LORD made the heavens.

27 Glory and majesty are in his presence; strength and greatness are in his sanctuary.

28 Give thanks to the LORD, O families of the peoples, give thanks before the LORD due to his glory and strength.

29 Give thanks to the LORD with the honor due to his name; bring offer-

ings, and give thanks before him with the prayer of your mouth; worship the LORD with holy songs.

30 Tremble before him, all the earth; the world also shall be stable, that it be not moved.

31 Let the heavens be glad, and let the earth rejoice; and let men say among the nations, The LORD reigns.

32 Let the sea roar and the fulness thereof; let the fields rejoice, and all that is therein.

33 Then shall the trees of the forest sing praises at the presence of the LORD because he comes to judge the earth. He shall judge the world with justice, and reprove the peoples in faithfulness;

34 Say also, O give thanks to the LORD; for he is good; for his mercy endures for ever.

35 Save us, O LORD, save us and gather us together, and bring us back from among the nations, that we may give thanks to thy holy name, and glory in thy praises.

36 Blessed be the LORD God of Israel for ever and ever. Then all the people shall say, Amen; and with a pleasant and pure mouth, let them praise their God.

37 ¶So he left there before the ark of the covenant of the LORD, Asaph and his brethren, to minister before the LORD continually, each man working in his appointed day;

38 And Ober-edom with his brethren, sixty-eight; Ober-edom the junior, the son of Jotham, and Haso. All of these were keepers of the outer gates;

39 And Zadok the priest, and his brethren the priests, these were all priests who ministered before the tabernacle of the LORD with a great joy in the town of Gibeon,

40 To offer burnt offerings to the LORD upon the altar of the burnt offering continually morning and evening, and to do according to all that is written in the law of the LORD, which he gave by the hand of Moses to teach to the children of Israel;

41 And these are the names of the men who stood up singing praises: Haman, Ariton, and the rest of the

righteous men whose names were not expressed by name, to give thanks to the LORD because his mercy endures for ever;

42 And these righteous men gave thanks not with the instruments of singing, neither with the tambourines nor with the timbrels nor with the curved trumpets nor with the straight trumpets nor with the cymbals, but with a pleasant mouth and with pure and perfect prayer and with righteousness and with purity to the LORD God of hosts, the God of Israel.

43 Then David dismissed the people, and they went every man to his own house; and David returned to bless his household.

CHAPTER 17

NOW it came to pass when David dwelt in his house, David said to Nathan the prophet, Behold, I dwell in a house which is covered with the beams of cedars, but the ark of the covenant of the LORD is resting in the midst of the tent of hair of goats.

2 Then Nathan said to David, Go and do all that is in your heart.

3 ¶And it came to pass that same night, the word of the LORD came to Nathan the prophet, saying,

4 Go and thus say to my servant David, You shall not build me a house to dwell in;

5 For I have not dwelt in a house since the day that I brought up Israel out of Egypt to this day; but I moved from tent to tent.

6 Behold, wherever I have walked with all Israel, did I speak a word to any of the judges of Israel whom I commanded to judge my people Israel, saying, Why have you not built me a house which is covered with cedars?

7 Now therefore thus shall you say to my servant David, Thus says the LORD of hosts: I took you from the sheepfold, even from following the sheep, that you should be king over my people Israel;

8 And I have been with you wheresoever you went and have destroyed your enemies from before

you, and I have made you a great name, like the name of the great men who are on the earth.

9 I will also appoint a place for my people Israel and will cause them to settle, and they shall dwell in their place and shall be moved no more; neither shall the wicked men carry them captive any more, as formerly.

10 And since the day that I made you a judge over my people Israel, I have given you rest from all your enemies. Moreover the LORD has declared to you that the kingdom is established for ever.

11 ¶And it shall come to pass when your days are fulfilled that you shall go to be gathered with your fathers, I will raise up your offspring after you, who shall come out of your loins, and I will establish him in your kingdom.

12 He shall build a house to my name, and I will establish the throne of his kingdom for ever.

13 I will be his father and he shall be my son; and I will not take my mercy away from him, as I took it from Saul, who was before you.

14 But I will make him a ruler in my house and in my kingdom for ever; and his throne shall be established for evermore.

15 According to all these words and according to all this vision, so did Nathan speak to David.

16 ¶And King David came and sat before the LORD and said, Who am I in thy presence, O LORD God, and what is my house, that thou hast brought me to this eminence?

17 And yet this was a small thing in thine eyes, O LORD God; for thou hast also spoken of thy servant's house for a great while to come; for all the men who worship thee with all their heart, thou bringest out of the darkness into the light, O LORD God.

18 What more can David boast to speak before thee? For the works of thy servant are known, O LORD God.

19 For thou knowest that which is in the heart of thy servant, that thou hast done for him all this greatness in making great thy servant.

20 Therefore I know, O LORD God, there is none like thee and there is no God besides thee, according to all that we have heard with our ears.

21 And what other nation on earth is united like thy people Israel? For thou didst reveal thyself from heaven and saved them, and for their sakes thou didst perform great and terrible wonders and brought severe plagues upon the Egyptians until thou didst bring them out from among them.

22 For thy people Israel thou didst make thine own people for ever; and thou, O LORD, didst become their God.

23 Therefore now, O LORD, let the word that thou hast spoken concerning thy servant and concerning his house be established for ever, and do as thou hast said.

24 And let thy works be established for ever, and thy name be magnified in the world for ever, so that the people shall say, The LORD of hosts is the God of Israel; and let the house of David thy servant be established before thee for ever.

25 For thou, O my God, hast revealed the secret to thy servant, and hast said to him, Build for yourself a house; therefore thy servant has set in his heart to pray before thee this prayer.

26 And now, O LORD, thou art God, and all thy words are true, with which thou hast promised this goodness to thy servant;

27 Now therefore reveal thyself to bless the house of thy servant, that it may be before thee for ever; for thou, O LORD God, hast spoken, and of thy blessing shall all the houses of righteous men be blessed for ever.

CHAPTER 18

AND after these things it came to pass that David smote the Philistines and destroyed them, and took the power from the hand of the Philistines, and took Gath and the small villages that were round about it out of the hand of the Philistines.

2 And he smote Moab; and the Moabites became David's servants and brought tribute.

3 ¶Then David slew Hadarezer the king of Nisibin, as he went to establish his dominion by the river Euphrates.

4 And David took from him a thousand chariots and seven thousand horsemen, and David hamstrung all the chariot horses, but reserved of them a hundred chariots.

5 And when the Edomites and the Arameans of Damascus came to help Hadarezer king of Nisibin, David slew of the Edomites twenty-two thousand men.

6 Then David appointed governors in Damascus, and the Arameans became David's servants and brought tribute. Thus the LORD preserved David wheresoever he went.

7 And David took the shields of gold that were hanging on the horses of the servants of Hadarezer, and brought them to Jerusalem.

8 Likewise from Tibhath and from Berothi, cities of Hadarezer, David took very much brass, wherewith Solomon made the bronze sea and the pillars of brass and the oxen of brass and the vessels of brass in abundance.

9 ¶Now Pul, king of Hamath, heard that David had smitten the whole army of Hadarezer, king of Nisibin;

10 And he sent Jehoram his son to David to inquire of his welfare and to congratulate him because he had fought against Hadarezer and killed him (for Hadarezer was a valiant warrior) and Jehoram had with him all manner of vessels of gold and silver and brass.

11 ¶Some of these also King David dedicated to the LORD, together with the silver and the gold that he had captured from all the nations which he had subdued: from the Edomites, from the Moabites, from the children of Ammon, from the Philistines, and from the Amalekites.

12 Moreover Abishai the son of Zuriah brother of Joab slew the Edomites in the valley of salt, eighteen thousand men.

13 ¶And David appointed governors over the Edomites, and all the Edomites became David's servants.

Thus the LORD preserved David wherever he went.

14 ¶So David reigned over all Israel and executed justice and righteousness to all the people.

15 And Joab the son of Zuriah was over all the army; and Jehoshaphat the son of Ahilud was recorder.

16 And Zadok the son of Ahitub and Ahimelek the son of Abiathar were the priests; and Seriah was scribe;

17 And Benaiah the son of Jehoiadah was over the archers and the slingers; and the sons of David were princes of the realm.

CHAPTER 19

NOW it came to pass after this that Nahash the king of the children of Ammon died, and his son Hanun reigned in his stead.

2 And David said, I will show kindness to Hanun the son of Nahash, just as his father showed kindness to me. So David sent messengers to comfort him concerning his father. So David's servants came into the land of the children of Ammon to Hanun to comfort him.

3 But the princes of the children of Ammon said to Hanun their lord, Do you think that David really did honor your father when he was alive and that he has truly sent comforters to you? It is for the purpose of spying the city and knowing the entrances and the exists that David has sent his servants to us.

4 So Hanun took David's servants and shaved half of their beards and half of their heads and cut off their garments in the midst as far as their buttocks, and sent them away.

5 And when they had told David, he sent men to meet them, for the men were greatly ashamed. And the king said to them, Remain at Jericho until your beards have grown, and then return.

6 ¶And when the children of Ammon saw that they had made themselves odious to David's servants, Hanun and the children of Ammon sent a thousand talents of silver to hire for themselves chariots and

horsemen from Aram-nahrin,[1] from Haran, from Nisibin, and from Edom.

7 So they hired thirty-two thousand horsemen, and the king of Haran, the king of Edom, the king of Aram-nahrin, and the king of Nisibin, and all their armies; who came and encamped before Medeba. And the children of Ammon gathered themselves together from their cities and came to battle.

8 And when David heard of it, he sent Joab and all the army of the mighty men.

9 And the children of Ammon came out and set the battle in array before the gate of the city; and the kings who had come to them and their armies were encamping by themselves in the fields.

10 Now when Joab saw that the battle was fierce against him in front and in the rear, he chose some of all the valiant men of Israel and arrayed them against the Arameans.

11 And the rest of the people he placed under the command of Abishai his brother, and they pitched battle against the children of Ammon.

12 And he said to him, If the Arameans are too strong for me, then you shall come to my help; but if the children of Ammon are too strong for you, then I will come to help you.

13 Be of good courage, and let us be strong for the sake of our people and for the sake of the cities of our God; and let the LORD do that which is good in his sight.

14 So Joab and the people who were with him drew near against the Arameans to battle, and they fled before him.

15 And when the children of Ammon saw that the Arameans had fled, they likewise fled before Abishai his brother, and entered into the city. Then Joab returned to Jerusalem.

16 ¶And when the Arameans saw that they had been defeated before Israel, they sent messengers and brought out the Arameans who were beyond the river; and they came to Hilam, and Shobach the commander

of the army of Hadarezer went before them.

17 And it was told David; and he gathered all Israel and came against them, and set the battle in array against the Arameans and fought with them.

18 And the Arameans fled before Israel; and David slew of the Arameans seven thousand men who fought in chariots and four thousand footmen, and killed there Shobach the commander of the army of Hadarezer.

19 And when the servants of Hadarezer saw that they had been defeated before Israel, they made peace with David and served him; and the Arameans were not willing to help the children of Ammon any more.

CHAPTER 20

AND it came to pass that in the next year, at the time when kings go out to battle, Joab mobilized the armed forces and came and encamped against the land of the children of Ammon and took some of the towns, and came and besieged Rabbath their capital city. But David remained at Jerusalem. And Joab captured Rabbath and destroyed it.

2 And David took the crown of their king from off his head, and he weighed it and found it to weigh a talent of gold, and there were precious stones in it; and David set it upon his head; and he brought also much spoil out of the city.

3 And he brought out the people who were in it, and bound them with chains, iron bands, locks and fetters. And thus David did bind all of them, and did likewise to all men who were found in the cities of the children of Ammon; but he did not kill any one of them; and he brought them and settled them in the villages of the land of Israel. Then David and all the people returned to Jerusalem.

4 ¶And it came to pass after this that there arose war at Gaza with the Philistines; then Sibbechai the Hushathite slew Sippai, who was one of the descendants of the giants.

5 And there was war again with the

---

[1] Mesopotamia.

Philistines; and Elhanan the son of Jair slew Lahmi of the descendants of the giants, who was the brother of Goliath the mighty man of Gath, whose spear staff was like a weaver's beam.

6 And there was again war at Gath, where there was a man of great stature, who had six fingers on each hand and six toes on each foot, twenty-four in number; he also was the son of a giant.

7 But when he defied Israel, Jonathan the son of Shimea David's brother slew him.

8 These four were born to the giants in Gath; and they fell by the hand of David and by the hand of his servants.

CHAPTER 21

THEN Satan stood up against Israel and provoked David to number Israel.

2 So David said to Joab the son of Zuriah and to the princes of the people, Go, number the people of Israel from Beersheba even to Dan, and come back to me, that I may know the number of the people.

3 And Joab said to King David, May the LORD make his people a hundred times so many more as they are, and let the eyes of my lord the king see it, for they are all his servants; why then should our lord the king require this thing?

4 Nevertheless the king's word prevailed against Joab. Wherefore Joab departed and went throughout all Israel and came back to Jerusalem.

5 ¶And Joab gave the sum of the number of the people to David. And the total number of the children of Israel was one million and one hundred thousand footmen who drew the sword; and the tribe of Judah was four hundred and seventy thousand men who drew the sword.

6 But the Levites, the priests, and the tribe of Benjamin were not counted among them; for the king's word was abominable to Joab, and Joab was unwilling to number them.

7 And the LORD was displeased with this thing, because David had numbered Israel.

8 And David said to the LORD, I have sinned greatly in that I have done this thing; but now, take away the iniquity of thy servant; for I have done very foolishly.

9 ¶And David arose early in the morning, and the word of the LORD came to Gad, the prophet, saying,

10 Go and tell David, saying, Thus says the LORD: I offer you three disasters; choose one of them, that I may do it to you.

11 So Gad the prophet came to David and said to him, Thus says the LORD: Choose for yourself

12 Either three years of famine in the land or three months to be defeated before your enemies while they shall pursue you and rule over you or else three days the sword of the LORD in Israel. Now therefore advise what answer you will give to him who sent me to you.

13 And David said to Gad, I am in a great distress; let me be delivered into the hands of the LORD; for his mercies are very great; but let me not be delivered into the hand of men.

14 ¶So the LORD sent pestilence upon Israel; and there fell of Israel seventy thousand men.

15 And the LORD sent an angel to Jerusalem to destroy it; and as he was destroying it, the LORD saw and considered it and averted the disaster, and said to the angel that destroyed, You have destroyed a great many, stay now your hand. And the angel of the LORD stood by the threshing floor of Aran the Jebusite.

16 And David lifted up his eyes and saw the angel of the LORD standing between heaven and earth, having a drawn sword in his hand stretched out over Jerusalem. Then David and the elders of Israel, who were with him clothed in sackcloth, fell upon their faces.

17 And David said to the LORD, Is it not I who commanded the people to be numbered? Even I it is who have sinned, and the folly which I have committed is great; but as for these innocent sheep, what have they done? Let thy hand, O LORD my God, be against me and against my father's

house; but let the plague cease from the people.

18 ¶Then the angel of the LORD said to Gad the prophet, Go and say to David that David should go up and build an altar to the LORD in the threshing floor of Aran the Jebusite.

19 And David went up at the saying of Gad which he spoke in the name of the LORD.

20 And David saw the angel who was destroying the people, that he had stayed his hand and was destroying no more.

21 And as David came to Aran, Aran turned and saw David and went out of his threshing floor, and bowed himself to David with his face to the ground.

22 Then David said to Aran, Give me the place of this threshing floor, that I may build on it an altar to the LORD; you shall give it to me for money at a good price, that the plague may be stayed from the people.

23 And Aran said to David, Take it to you, and let my lord the king do that which is good in his eyes; and I will give you oxen also for burnt offering and the threshing instrument for wood and the wheat for the meal offering; everything which is needed I shall give it all.

24 But King David said to Aran, Far be it, but I will surely buy it with money for the full price; for I will not take that which is yours and offer a burnt offering to the LORD without cost.

25 So David bought from Aran that place of the threshing floor for fifty shekels.

26 And David built there an altar to the LORD, and offered burnt offerings and peace offerings of lambs, and prayed before the LORD and he answered him, and fire came down from heaven and consumed the burnt offerings that were upon the altar.

27 And the LORD commanded the angel; and he put back his sword again into its sheath.

28 ¶At that time when David saw that the LORD had answered him in the threshing floor of Aran the Jebu-site, then he offered there many sacrifices.

29 And he pitched there before the LORD the tabernacle which Moses had made in the wilderness when the children of Israel went forth out of Egypt.

30 At that time David was exceedingly afraid, and could not go to pray before the LORD for he was afraid because of the sword of the angel of the LORD.

CHAPTER 22

THEN David said, This is the house of the LORD God and this is the altar of the burnt offerings for Israel.

2 And David commanded to gather together all the proselytes who were in the land of Israel, to make some of them stonecutters to hew stones for the house of the LORD;

3 And to make some of them blacksmiths to forge iron to make axes and hatchets for hewing stones. And David prepared bars of iron, and brass in abundance without weight;

4 Also cedar trees in abundance; for the Tyrians and the Sidonians brought much cedar wood to David.

5 And David said, Solomon my son is still a small boy, and concerning him it is said in the book that he will build a house to the LORD which will be exceedingly magnificent, of fame and of glory throughout all countries; I will therefore prepare everything necessary for it while I am living. So David prepared everything that was needed for the house, and lacked nothing.

6 ¶Then he called for Solomon his son and said to him,

7 You shall build a house for the LORD God of Israel;

8 For he has sent to me by a prophet, saying, You have shed blood abundantly and have made great wars; you shall not build a house to my name because you have shed much blood upon the earth in my sight.

9 Behold, a son shall be born to you who shall be a man of peace; and I will give him rest from all his enemies round about; for his name

shall be Solomon, and there shall be peace and quietness to Israel in his days.

10 He shall build a house for my name; and he shall be to me like a son, and I will be to him like a father; and I will establish the throne of his kingdom over Israel for ever.

11 Now, my son, the LORD be with you, so that you may prosper, and build the house of the LORD your God, as he has said to me.

12 Only may the LORD give you wisdom and understanding, and give you charge concerning Israel, that you may keep the law of the LORD your God, just as he has commanded you.

13 Then you shall prosper if you take heed to observe these commandments and the statutes and judgments just as the LORD charged Moses to teach Israel, then you will be strong and of good courage; fear not, nor be dismayed.

14 Now, behold, I have prepared for you everything necessary for the building of the house of the LORD. I have prepared for you a hundred thousand talents of gold, a million talents of silver; and brass and iron without weight; no man knows its weight, for it is in abundance; timber also and stones I have prepared; and you may add thereto.

15 Moreover there are workers with you in abundance, stonecutters, masons, and carpenters,

16 Cunning men for every manner of work; of gold, silver, brass, and iron in abundance. Be strong therefore and be doing, and the LORD will help you.

17 ¶David also commanded all the elders of Israel, saying, You must help Solomon my son.

18 For behold, the LORD your God is with you; and he will help you and relieve you on every side. Behold he has delivered all the inhabitants of the land into your hand, and the land is subdued before the LORD and before his people.

19 Now set your heart and your soul to pray before the LORD your God; arise therefore, and build the sanctuary of the LORD God, and bring there the ark in which is the covenant of the LORD our God, and the holy vessels of the LORD our God; and build the house because of his great name by which we are known.

CHAPTER 23

WHEN David was old and full of days, he made Solomon his son king over Israel.

2 ¶And he gathered together all the elders of the priests and the Levites.

3 Now the Levites were numbered from the age of thirty years and upward; and their number by their polls, man by man, was thirty-eight thousand.

4 Of them David appointed overseers over the work of the house of the LORD, twenty-four men over every thousand workers; and judges and scribes, six men over each hundred workers

5 To look after the building, to carry on their work, to oversee the resources and the work, and to give an accounting of wealth and the alms which they had distributed to the poor.

6 And David appointed administrators and managers over the poor and needy, to provide and distribute to the poor; one person over each ten, and they lacked nothing. And David appointed them all in their courses according to the sons of Levi; namely, Gershon, Kohath, and Merari.

7 ¶Of the Gershonites were Laadan and Shimei.

8 The sons of Ladan: his first-born was Nahliel, and then Jotham and Joel, three.

9 And the sons of Shimei: Shelomoth, Haziel, and Aran, three. These were the chiefs of the fathers of Shimei.

10 And the sons of Shimei were, Nahat, Zabda, Jeush, and Beriah. These were the four sons of Shimei.

11 And Nahat was his first-born, Zabda the second; but Jeush and Beriah did not have many sons; therefore they were included in their father's family as one.

12 The sons of Kohath: Amram, Izhar, Hebron, and Uzziel, four.

13 The sons of Amram: Aaron and Moses; and Aaron was chosen to minister in the Holy of Holies, he and his sons for ever, to burn incense before the LORD, to minister to him, and to bless in his name for ever.

14 Now as for Moses the prophet of God, his sons were named among the tribe of Levi.

15 The sons of Moses were Gershon and Eliezer.

16 The son of Gershon was Samuel his first-born.

17 And the son of Eliezer was Arhimah his first-born. And Eliezer had no other sons; but the son of Arhimah was Ribbi his first-born.

18 And the son of Izhar was Shelomith his first-born.

19 The sons of Hebron: Joda his first-born, Amariah the second, Nahzaiel the third, and Nakmaiel the fourth.

20 The sons of Uzziel: Micah his first-born and Shoh the second.

21 ¶The sons of Merari: Mahli and Mushi. The sons of Mahli: Eleazar and Kish.

22 And Eleazar died, and had no sons, but daughters; and the sons of Kish took them for wives in marriage.

23 The sons of Mushi: Mahli, Eder, and Jeremoth, three.

24 ¶These were the sons of Levi after the house of their fathers, even the chiefs of the fathers, as they were counted by number of names by their polls, who were overseers over the work for the service of the house of the LORD, from the age of twenty years and upward.

25 For David said, The LORD God of Israel has given rest to his people, and he dwells in Jerusalem for ever;

26 And he also said to the Levites that they should carry the tabernacle and all the vessels for the service thereof.

27 For by the last words of David the Levites were numbered from twenty years old and upward,

28 Because he appointed them to the office to help the sons of Aaron to be overseers in the house of the LORD, over those who sound with straight and curved trumpets, and over the chambers in which the holy vessels of the LORD were stored;

29 And over the shewbread and the fine flour for meal offering and the unleavened cakes and over all those who sing and offer thanks,

30 And that they might arise every morning to thank and praise the LORD, and likewise at evening,

31 And to offer burnt offerings to the LORD on the sabbaths, in the new moons, and on the days of set feasts, by number, according to the order commanded to them, continually before the LORD,

32 And that they should have charge of the vessels of the tabernacle of the congregation and charge of the vessels of the sanctuary and charge of the sons of Aaron their brethren when they were needed to minister in the house of the LORD.

CHAPTER 24

NOW these are the divisions of the sons of Aaron. The sons of Aaron were Nadab and Abihu, Eleazar and Ithamar.

2 But Nadab and Abihu died during the lifetime of their father Aaron, and had no children; therefore Eleazar and Ithamar executed the priest's office.

3 And David divided them, both Zadok of the sons of Eleazar and Ahimelech of the sons of Ithamar, according to their offices in their service.

4 And there were more chief men found of the sons of Eleazar than of the sons of Ithamar; and thus he divided them. Among the sons of Eleazar there were sixteen chief men of the house of their fathers and eight of the sons of Ithamar, according to the house of their fathers.

5 Thus he divided them by lot, both families alike; for they were chief priests of the sanctuary and authorities over the priests, both of the sons of Eleazar and of the sons of Ithamar.

6 And Shemaiah the son of Nethaniel the scribe, one of the Levites, recorded them before King David and

the elders of Israel and Zadok the priest and Ahimelech the son of Abiathar and before the chiefs of the fathers of the priests and of the Levites, one principal family being taken for Eleazar and one taken for Ithamar.

7 Now the first lot fell to Jehoiadah, the second to Jedaiah,

8 The third to Haram, the fourth to Seorim,

9 The fifth to Malchijah, the sixth to Mijamin,

10 The seventh to Akkoz, the eighth to Abijah,

11 The ninth to Elishah, the tenth to Shecaniah,

12 The eleventh to Eliashib, the twelfth to Elikrab,

13 The thirteenth to Huppah, the fourteenth to Ahaziah,

14 The fifteenth to Baglah, the sixteenth to Immer,

15 The seventeenth to Ahaziah, the eighteenth to Pazin,

16 The nineteenth to Pethahiah, the twentieth to Ezekiel,

17 The twenty-first to Jachin, the twenty-second to Gamul,

18 The twenty-third to Delaiah, and the twenty-fourth to Maadiah.

19 These are their numbers according to their service, to come into the house of the LORD, according to their ordinances, as prescribed for them by the counsel of Aaron their father, as the LORD God of Israel had commanded him.

20 ¶And the rest of the sons of Levi were these: of the sons of Amram, Shubael; of the sons of Shubael, Jehdeiah and Rehabiah.

21 Of the sons of Rehabiah: his first-born was Jeshua, then

22 Zahor and Salmoth. Of the sons of Salmoth: Nahath,

23 Jeremiah, Hezaiel, and Neshamim.

24 Of the sons of Uzziel: Michah; of the sons of Michah: Shamir and Jeshua.

25 Of the sons of Jeshua: Zechariah.

26 The sons of Merari were Mahli and Mushi; the son of Jaaziah, Beno.

27 ¶The sons of Merari by Jaaziah: Beno and Shoham and Zaccur and Ibri.

28 Of Mahli came Eleazar, who had no sons.

29 Of Kish: the son of Kish was Jerahmeel.

30 The sons also of Mushi: Mahli and Eder and Jerimoth. These were the sons of the Levites, after the house of their fathers.

31 These likewise cast lots over against their brethren the sons of Aaron in the presence of David the king, and Zadok and Ahimelech, and the chief of the fathers of the priests and Levites, even the principal fathers, over against their younger brethren.

CHAPTER 25

MOREOVER David and the princes of the tribes set aside for the service of the sons of Asaph, Haman and Jeruthun, the sons of Azram his son. These are the Levites according to the families of their fathers. These likewise cast lots over their brethren the sons of Aaron in the presence of David the king and Zadok and Ahimelech and the chiefs of the fathers of the priests and Levites. The younger and the elder brother were reckoned alike in numbering; and the number of the workmen according to their service was,

2 Of the sons of Asaph: Zaccuri, Joseph, Nethaniah, and Israel. And the sons of Asaph whom the king placed under the direction of Jeruthun as singers.

3 Of the sons of Jeruthun: Azariah, Isaiah, Hashabiah, Mattithiah, and Jeruthun, six, under the direction of their father Jeruthun, who sang with harps and gave thanks to the LORD.

4 Of Heman: the sons of Heman, Bukkiah, Mattaniah, Uzziel, Shebuel, and Jerimoth, Hananiah, Hanani, Eliathah, Giddalti, and Romamtiezer, Joshbekashah, Mallothi, Hothir, and Mahazioth.

5 All these were the sons of Heman the king's seer in the words of God, to lift up the horn. And God gave to Heman fourteen sons and three daughters.

6 All these were under the hands of their father for song in the house of the LORD, with cymbals, psalteries,

and harps for the service of the house of God, according to the king's order to Asaph, Jeruthun, and Heman.

7 So the number of them, with their brethren who were instructed in the songs of the LORD, was two hundred and eighty-eight.

8 ¶And they cast lots for their courses, as well the younger as the elder, the pupil as the teacher.

9 Now the first lot fell for Asaph to Joseph; the second to Gedaliah, who with his brethren and his sons were twelve;

10 The third to Zori, he, his sons, and his brethren were twelve;

11 The fourth to Nazri, he, his sons, and his brethren were twelve;

12 The fifth to Nethaniah, he, his sons, and his brethren were twelve;

13 The sixth to Bukkiah, he his sons, and his brethren were twelve;

14 The seventh to Lasrael, he, his sons, and his brethren were twelve;

15 The eighth to Isaiah, he, his sons, and his brethren were twelve;

16 The ninth to Mattaniah, he, his sons, and his brethren were twelve;

17 The tenth to Shimei, he, his sons, and his brethren were twelve;

18 The eleventh to Azaiel, he, his sons, and his brethren were twelve;

19 The twelfth to Hashabiah, he, his sons, and his brethren were twelve;

20 The thirteenth to Shubael, he, his sons, and his brethren were twelve;

21 The fourteenth to Mattithiah, he, his sons, and his brethren were twelve;

22 The fifteenth to Jeremoth, he, his sons, and his brethren were twelve;

23 The sixteenth to Hananiah, he, his sons, and his brethren were twelve;

24 The seventeenth to Elishab, he, his sons and his brethren were twelve;

25 The eighteenth to Hanani, he, his sons, and his brethren were twelve;

26 The nineteenth to Malloth, he, his sons, and his brethren were twelve;

27 The twentieth to Eliab, he, his sons, and his brethren were twelve;

28 The twenty-first to Jattir, he, his sons, and his brethren were twelve;

29 The twenty-second to Rabbi, he, his sons, and his brethren were twelve;

30 The twenty-third to Mahazioth, he, his sons, and his brethren were twelve;

31 The twenty-fourth to Roman, he, his sons, and his brethren were twelve;

CHAPTER 26

CONCERNING the divisions of the porters whom David the king appointed as guards: Meshele-miah of the sons of Joseph.

2 And Meshelemiah had seven male children: namely, Zechariah his first-born, Jediael the second, Zechariah the third, Nathanael the fourth,

3 Elam the fifth, Johanan the sixth, Jadie the seventh.

4 Moreover, the sons of Ober-edom were Shemaiah his first-born, Jeho-zabad the second, Joah the third, Sha-bar the fourth, and Matlal the fifth,

5 Gemaiel the sixth, Issachar the seventh, Pali the eighth; for the LORD blessed him.

6 Also to Shemaiah his son were sons born, who ruled over the house of their fathers; for they were mighty men of valour.

7 The sons of Shemaiah: Gathael, Cadhael, Obedael, and Zechariah, the mighty man, and Elijah and Sema-chiah.

8 All these were of the sons of Ober-edom, they and their sons and their brethren, able men with strength for the service of the sanctuary, sixty-two sons of Ober-edom.

9 And Meshelemiah's eldest son had sons, mighty men, eighteen.

10 Also Hasah, of the children of Merari, had sons, mighty men; his eldest son died, and his father made the second the chief, but he did not call him by the name of the eldest.

11 Hilkiah the second, Tebaliah the third, Zechariah the fourth; all the sons and brethren of Hasah were thirteen.

12 Among these were the divisions of the porters, even among the chief

men, having watch one opposite another, to minister in the house of the LORD.

13 ¶And they cast lots, the least as well as the great, according to the house of their fathers, for every gate.

14 And the lot eastward fell to Shelemiah. Then for Zechariah his son, a wise counsellor, they cast lots; and his lot came out northward.

15 To Ober-edom southward; and to his sons the porches.

16 To Shuppim and Hasah the lot fell westward, as far as the gate which is made in the road that goes up, watch opposite watch.

17 Eastward were six Levites, northward four a day, southward four a day, and for the porches two by two.

18 At Parbar westward, four at the road and two at Parbar.

19 These are the divisions of the porters among the sons of Korah and among the sons of Merari.

20 And of the Levites, Ahijah was over the storehouses of the house of God and over the storehouses of the dedicated things.

21 The sons of Laadan: of the descendants of Gershon, Laadan, chiefs of the fathers, even of Laadan the Gershonite, was Nahli.

22 The sons of Nahli: Zetham and Joel his brother who were over the storehouses of the house of the LORD.

23 Of the Amramites and the Izharites, the Hebronites and the Uzzielites,

24 Samuel the son of Gershon, the son of Moses, was chief in charge of the storehouses.

25 And his brother Eliezer, Rehabiah his son and Isaiah his son and Joram his son and Zichri his son and Shelomith his son.

26 This Shelomith and his brothers were in charge of all storehouses of the dedicated things, which David the king, the chiefs of the fathers, the commanders of the thousands and the hundreds, and the commanders of the army had dedicated.

27 From spoils won in battles they dedicated some to maintain the house of the LORD.

28 And all that Samuel the seer and Saul the son of Kish and Abner the son of Ner and Joab the son of Zuriah had dedicated; and whoever had dedicated anything, it was under the charge of Shelomith and of his brothers.

29 ¶Of the Izharites: Chenaniah and his sons were for the secular business of Israel, as scribes and judges.

30 And of the Hebronites: Hashabiah and his brethren, men of valour, one thousand and seven hundred, were officers over the Israelites on this side of Jordan westward, in charge of all the business of the LORD and in the service of the king.

31 Among the Hebronites was Neriah the chief, even among the Hebronites, according to the generations of their fathers. In the fortieth year of the reign of David they were sought for, and there were found among them mighty men of valour at Jazer of Gilead.

32 And his brethren, men of valour, were two thousand and seven hundred chiefs of the fathers, whom King David made chiefs over the Reubenites, the Gadites, and the half tribe of Manasseh, for every matter pertaining to God and the affairs of the king.

CHAPTER 27

NOW the children of Israel after their number, the chiefs of the fathers and the commanders of thousands and of hundreds, and their governors who served the king in all matters of the divisions, those who came in and went out month by month throughout all the months of the year under every division were twenty-four thousand.

2 Over the first division for the first month was Shaabam the son of Zabdiel; and in his division were twenty-four thousand.

3 He was of the descendants of Perez; he was the chief of all the commanders of the army for the first month.

4 And over the division of the second month was David the Ahohite, and of his division was Mikloth also

the governor; in his division were twenty-four thousand.

5 The third commander of the army for the third month was Benaiah the son of Jehoiada, the chief priest; and in his division were twenty-four thousand.

6 This is the Benaiah, who was mighty among the thirty, and in command of the thirty officers; and in his division was Mizbar his son.

7 The fourth commander for the fourth month was Ashael the brother of Joab, and Zebadaiel his son after him; and in his division were twenty-four thousand.

8 The fifth commander for the fifth month was Shamhuth the Nezrahite; and in his division were twenty-four thousand.

9 The sixth commander for the sixth month was Ira the son of Ikkesh the Tekoite; and in his division were twenty-four thousand.

10 The seventh commander for the seventh month was Helez the Pelonite, of the descendants of Ephraim; and in his division were twenty-four thousand.

11 The eighth commander for the eighth month was Sibbecai the Hushathite, of the Zarites; and in his division were twenty-four thousand.

12 The ninth commander for the ninth month was Abiezer the Anatothite, of the Benjamites; and in his division were twenty-four thousand.

13 The tenth commander for the tenth month was Maharai the Netophathite, of the Zarhites; and in his division were twenty-four thousand.

14 The eleventh commander for the eleventh month was Benaiah the Pirathonite, of the descendants of Ephraim; and in his division were twenty-four thousand.

15 The twelfth commander for the twelfth month was Heldai the Netophathite, of Othniel; and in his division were twenty-four thousand.

16 ¶Furthermore over the tribes of Israel were these: the prince of the Reubenites was Eliezer the son of Zichri; of the Simeonites, Shephatiah the son of Maachah;

17 Of the Levites, Hashabiah the son of Kemuel; of the Aaronites, Zadok;

18 Of Judah, Elihu, one of the brothers of David; of Issachar, Omri the son of Michael;

19 Of Zebulun, Ishmaiah the son of Obadiah; of Naphtali, Jerimoth the son of Azriel;

20 Of the Ephraimites, Hoshea the son of Azariah; of the half tribe of Manasseh, Joel the son of Peraiah;

21 Of the half tribe of Manasseh in Gilead, Iddo the son of Zechariah; of Benjamin, Jaasiel the son of Abner;

22 Of Dan, Azariel the son of Jeroham. These were the princes of the tribes of Israel.

23 ¶But David did not number those twenty years old and under because the LORD had said he would increase Israel like the stars of the heavens.

24 Joab the son of Zuriah began to number, but he did not finish because there came wrath upon Israel for this, neither was the number put in the account of the chronicles of David.

25 ¶And over the king's treasures was Azmaveth the son of Gediel; and over the storehouses in the fields, in the cities, and in the villages, and in the castles was Jonathan the son of Uzziah;

26 And over those who did the work of the field for tilling of the ground was Ezri the son of Chelub;

27 And over the vineyards was Shimei the Ramathite; over the increase of the vineyards for the wine cellars was Zabdi the Shiphmite;

28 And over the olive trees and the sycamore trees that were in the low plains was Baalhanan the Gederite; and over the stores of oil was Joash;

29 And over the herds that fed in Sharon was Shitrai the Sharonite; and over the herds that were in the valleys was Shaphat the son of Adlai;

30 Over the camels was Abel the Ishmaelite; and over the asses was Judah the Meronothite;

31 And over the flocks was Jaziz the Hagerite. All these were overseers

of the substance which was King David's.

32 Also Jonathan David's beloved friend was a counsellor, a man of understanding, and a scribe; and Hananiel the son of Hachmoni was with the king's sons;

33 And Ahithophel was the king's counsellor; and Hushai the Archite was the king's friend;

34 And after Ahithophel was Jehoiada the son of Benaiah, and Abiathar; and Joab was the general of the king's army.

CHAPTER 28

AND David assembled all the princes of Israel, the princes of the tribes and the commanders of the divisions that ministered to the king and the commanders of the thousands and the captains of hundreds and the stewards of all the substance and herds of the king and of his sons, with the officers and with the mighty men of valour; and they all came to Jerusalem.

2 Then he said to them, Hear me, my brethren and my people: I had it in my heart to build a house of rest for the ark of the covenant of the LORD and for a dwelling place of our God, and I had made ready everything for the building of the house;

3 But the LORD said to me, You shall not build a house for my name because you are a man of war and have shed much blood.

4 However the LORD God of Israel chose me from all my father's house to be king over Israel for ever; for he has chosen out of the house of Judah to be the king; and of the tribe of Judah, the house of my father; and among the sons of my father he chose me to be king over Israel;

5 And of all my sons (for the LORD has given me many sons), he has chosen Solomon my son to sit upon the throne of the kingdom of the LORD over Israel.

6 And he said to me, Solomon your son, he shall build my house and my courts; for I have chosen him to be my son, and I will be a father to him.

7 Moreover I will establish the throne of his kingdom for ever if he continues to keep my commandments and my judgments as at this day.

8 Now therefore in the sight of all Israel the people of the LORD and in the presence of the LORD our God, keep and seek for all his commandments; and you shall possess this land for ever and leave it for an inheritance for your children after you for ever, and it shall not be destroyed.

9 ¶And you, Solomon my son, know everything that the LORD our God has commanded us, and serve him with a perfect heart and with a willing mind; for the LORD knows everything that is in the heart and understands all the imaginations of the thoughts of men; if you seek him, he will be found by you; but if you forsake him, he will cast you off for ever.

10 Know now and take heed; for the LORD has chosen you to build a house for the sanctuary of the name of the LORD; be strong, be valiant, and do it.

11 ¶Then David gave to Solomon his son the pattern of the porch and the measurements of the house and of its treasuries and of the upper chambers thereof and of the inner porticos thereof and of the outer porticos thereof and of the upper porticos thereof and of the lower porticos thereof;

12 And the pattern of the treasury and of the chambers for the service of the house of the LORD and the chambers of the cooks and the chambers of the butlers and the chamber of those in charge of the lamps;

13 Also for the divisions of the priests and the Levites, and for all the work of the service of the house of the LORD, and for all the vessels of service in the house of the LORD.

14 He gave of gold by weight for things of gold, for all vessels of all manner of service; silver also for all instruments of silver by weight, for all instruments of every kind of service;

15 And the place for the candlestick of gold and for their lamps of gold and the wicks thereof and the ornaments thereof and the vessels of

oil thereof. David recorded everything, and gave it to Solomon his son;

16 And tables of silver and tables of gold; dishes of silver and dishes of gold;

17 Also large spoons, flesh hooks, and bowls of silver; the gold of these vessels could not be weighed;

18 And for the altar of incense refined gold by weight; and gold for the pattern of the chariot of the cherubim that spread out their wings and covered the ark of the covenant of the LORD.

19 All this, said David, the LORD made me understand in writing by his hand upon me, even all the works of this pattern.

20 Then David said to Solomon his son, Be strong and of good courage, and do it; fear not, nor be dismayed; for the LORD God is with you; he will not fail you, nor forsake you, until you have finished all the work for the service of the house of the LORD.

21 And, behold, the divisions of the priests and of the Levites, I have given them authority over all the service of the house of the LORD; and they are with you, and shall be in charge of all the service; and they will do the work with skill, all the workmanship which is necessary for the service of the house of the LORD. And, behold, I have appointed over them authorities and overseers, so that they may seek and render all manner of service which is necessary.

CHAPTER 29

MOREOVER David the king said to all the assemblies of Israel, This Solomon my son is still a small boy, and yet the LORD has chosen him out of all my sons, because he is wise and has understanding, and this work which is given to him is not small, but it is great; for such a task has never been given to any man; now therefore be strong and of good courage, because the work belongs to the LORD our God.

2 Now I have provided with all my might and with all my wealth everything which is necessary for the house of the LORD my God: the gold for things to be made of gold, the silver for things of silver, the brass for things of brass, the iron for things of iron, and wood for things of wood; and cedars for things of cedar; precious stones and pearls.

3 Moreover, everything which is necessary for the house I have provided of my own sacrifices; I have also provided money for the expenses of the house of my God of my own sacrifices;

4 One million talents of gold, of fine gold, and two million talents of silver, to overlay the walls of the house:

5 The gold for things of gold, and the silver for things of silver, and for all manner of work to be made by craftsmen, so that the work may be completed in its month, and that no work should be left undone, but be finished in its due time, according to the expenses thereof.

6 ¶Then the chiefs of the fathers and the princes of the tribes of Israel and the commanders of thousands and of hundreds and the overseers of the 'king's work gathered together

7 And gave for the service of the house of the LORD five thousand gold talents and fine tin for the pipes two hundred thousand talents and silver twenty thousand talents and of Corinthian brass seventy thousand talents and one hundred thousand talents of iron.

8 Moreover they gave silver and gold, offering them willingly to the treasury of the house of the LORD by the hand of Gershon the treasurer.

9 Then all the people of Israel rejoiced in all these gifts because David offered them with perfect heart willingly before the LORD; and David also rejoiced with great joy. Therefore David sang great praises to the LORD.

10 ¶Wherefore David blessed LORD before all the assemblies of Israel; and David said, Blessed be thou, O LORD God of Israel our father, for ever and ever.

11 For thine, O LORD, is the greatness and the power and the glory and

the beauty and the majesty and the honor; for thou art the ruler over all that is in the heaven and on the earth; thine is the kingdom, O LORD, and the wisdom and the might and the knowledge.

12 Both riches and honor come of thee, and thou rulest over all; and in thy hand is power and might; and in thy hand is to make great and to give strength to all creations which thou hast created.

13 Even now, O LORD our God, we thank thee and praise thy glorious name.

14 But who am I and what is my people, because all my teachers have taught me that thy way of life has helped us, and thou art our hope, O LORD our God.

15 For we are like the proverb of vapor and of the potter,[1] and we are sojourners before thee and a small people in the world, but thou didst rule over our fathers of old, and thou didst command them by which way they should walk and live.

16 And to thee we offer praise, O LORD our God, that thou mightest save us from all those who harm us, for the nations reproach us, saying, Where is your God, whom you serve?

17 I know also, my God, that thou triest the heart, and hast pleasure in uprightness. As for me, in the uprightness of my heart I have sung all these praises; and now I have seen that thy people who are present here praise thee with a great joy, saying,

18 O LORD God of Abraham, Isaac, and of Israel, our fathers kept all these things which thou hast promised us for ever, and now turn away our heart from evil, that we may not sin before thee, and prepare our hearts to worship thee.

19 And I David answered and said thus: O LORD my God, give to Solomon my son a perfect heart, to keep thy commandments, thy testimonies, and thy statutes, and to do all these things which I have commanded, and to build the temple for which I have made provision; for thy great

name will be hallowed and praised in the world which thou hast created, in the presence of those who worship thee.

20 ¶Then David said to all the people of Israel, Now bless the LORD your God. And all the people blessed the LORD God of their fathers, and bowed down and worshipped the LORD, and they also blessed King David.

21 And they offered sacrifices to the LORD and offered burnt offerings to the LORD, and on the next day they sacrificed a thousand bullocks and a thousand rams and a thousand lambs, with their drink offerings, and sacrificed in abundance for all Israel;

22 And they did eat and drink before the LORD on that day with great gladness. And they made Solomon the son of David king, and appointed Zadok to be the priest.

23 Then Solomon sat on the throne of the kingdom of the LORD as king instead of David his father, and prospered; and all Israel obeyed him.

24 And all the mighty men and all the sons of King David submitted themselves to Solomon his son.

25 And the LORD magnified Solomon exceedingly in the sight of all Israel, and bestowed upon him such royal majesty as had not been on any king of Israel who had been before him.

26 ¶Thus David the son of Jesse made Solomon his son king over all Israel.

27 Now the time that David reigned over all Israel was forty years; he reigned seven years in Hebron and thirty-three years he reigned in Jerusalem, over all Israel and Judah.

28 And David the son of Jesse died in a good old age, full of days and great in worldly riches and honor; and Solomon his son reigned in his stead.

29 Now the acts of David the king from first to last, behold, they are written in the book of Samuel the prophet and in the book of Nathan the prophet and in the book of Gad the prophet,

[1] Vapor appears and disappears, and a potter breaks his vessels and remakes them.

30 With all his reign and his might and the times that passed over him and over Israel and over all the kingdoms of the countries. David did that which was good in the presence of the LORD, and he transgressed not against anything that he commanded him all the days of his life.

THE SECOND BOOK OF THE

CHRONICLES

CHAPTER 1

AND Solomon the son of David was strengthened in his kingdom, and the LORD his God was with him and exalted him exceedingly above all the kings of the earth.

2 Then Solomon spoke to all Israel, to the commanders of thousands and of hundreds, and to the judges, and to all the princes, the chiefs of the fathers.

3 So Solomon and all the people who were with him went to a great banquet that was at the town of Gibeon; for there was the tabernacle of the congregation of the LORD, which Moses the servant of the LORD had made in the wilderness.

4 But David had brought up the ark of the LORD from Koriath-kaproney to the place which David had prepared for it; for he had pitched a tent for it in Jerusalem.

5 Moreover the bronze altar that Bezaliel the son of Uri, the son of Hur, had made was placed before the tabernacle of the LORD; and Solomon and the whole congregation of Israel went to it.

6 And Solomon went up there to the bronze altar before the LORD, which was at the tabernacle of the congregation, and offered a thousand burnt offerings upon it.

7 ¶That night the LORD appeared to Solomon in a vision and said to him, Ask what I shall give you.

8 And Solomon said to the LORD, Thou hast shown great mercy to David my father, and hast made me to reign in his stead.

9 Now, O LORD my God, let thy promise to David my father be established; for thou hast made me king over this people, like the dust of the earth in multitude.

10 Give me now wisdom and knowledge, that I may go out and come in before this people; for who can judge this thy people that is so great?

11 And the LORD said to Solomon, Because this was in your mind, and you have not asked riches, honor, nor the life of your enemies, neither have you asked for long life; but have asked wisdom and knowledge for yourself that you may judge my people over whom I have made you king;

12 Also the things for which you have not asked will I grant to you. And I will give you wisdom and knowledge, wealth, riches, and honor, such as none of the kings have had that have been before you, neither shall there any after you have the like.

13 ¶Then Solomon came from his journey to the great banquet that was at the town of Gibeon, east of Jerusalem, from before the tabernacle of the congregation, and reigned over all Israel.

14 And Solomon gathered chariots and horsemen; and he had a thousand and four hundred chariots and twelve thousand horsemen, which he placed in the chariot cities, and some of them with the king in Jerusalem.

15 And the king made silver in Jerusalem as plenteous as stones, and he made cedar as the sand that is by the sea for abundance.

16 And the king's merchants purchased horses for Solomon from Egypt and from the city of the Apelites for a price.

17 And they went up and bought a chariot from Egypt for six hundred shekels of silver, and a horse for a hundred and fifty; and so through the king's merchants they brought horses for all the kings of the Hittites and for the kings of Aram.

CHAPTER 2

AND Solomon commanded to build a temple for the name of the LORD and a house for his kingdom.

2 And Solomon appointed seventy thousand men to bear burdens and eighty thousand stone cutters in the mountain and three thousand and six hundred to oversee them.

3 ¶And Solomon sent to Hiram king of Tyre, saying, As you showed great kindness to David my father, and sent him cedars to build him a house to dwell in,

4 Behold, I am building a house to the name of the LORD my God, to dedicate it to him and to burn before him sweet incense and to light a lamp continually and to offer burnt offerings morning and evening, on the sabbaths and on the new moons and on the solemn feasts of the LORD our God. This is an ordinance for ever to Israel.

5 And the house which I am about to build is very great, for our God is greater than all kings.

6 But who is able to build him a house, seeing the heaven and heaven of heavens cannot contain him? Who am I then, that I should build him a house or burn sweet incense before him?

7 Now therefore, send me a man skilled to work in gold and in silver and in brass and in iron and in purple and in fine linen and in crimson and in blue, and who has the skill to engrave with the skilled men who are with me in Judah and in Jerusalem, whom David my father did provide.

8 Send me also cedar trees, fir trees, and algum [1] timber out of Lebanon; for I know that your servants know how to cut cedar timber in Lebanon; and, behold, my servants shall be with your servants

9 And shall bring me timber in abundance; for the house which I am about to build will be very great and wonderful.

10 And I will provide carpenters who are skilled in woodwork, and will give provisions to your servants, twenty thousand measures of wheat and twenty thousand measures of barley and twenty thousand baths of wine and twenty thousand baths of oil.

11 ¶Then Hiram the king of Tyre answered in writing which he sent to Solomon, saying, Because the LORD has loved his people, he has made you king over them.

12 Hiram said moreover, Blessed be the LORD God of Israel, who created heaven and earth, who has given to David a wise son, endued with prudence and understanding, who has set his mind to build a house for the LORD and a house for his kingdom.

13 And now I have sent to you a skilful man, endued with understanding, even Hiram,

14 Who is the son of a widow of the house of Dan, and his father was a skilful man; he knows how to work in gold and in silver, in brass, in iron, in stones, in timber, in purple, in blue, in fine linen, in crimson and other red materials, also how to make any manner of keys for the doors, and to devise every kind of craft which shall be assigned to him from the LORD, with your craftsmen and with the craftsmen of our lord David your father.

15 Now therefore the wheat and the barley, the oil and the wine which my lord has promised to his servants, let him send them;

16 And we will cut cedar trees out of Lebanon, as many as you wish; and we will bring them to you in floats by

[1] Probably sandalwood.

sea to Joppa; and you shall carry them up to Jerusalem.

17 ¶Then Solomon gathered together all the proselytes who were in the land of Israel, after the numbering of them which David his father had done; and there were found a hundred and fifty-three thousand and six hundred.

18 And King Solomon set seventy thousand of them to be bearers of burdens and eighty thousand to be stonecutters in the mountain and three thousand and six hundred overseers to make the people work.

CHAPTER 3

THEN Solomon began to build the house of the LORD in Jerusalem on mount Moriah, in the place which David his father had prepared in the threshing floor which he had bought from Aran the Jebusite.

2 And he began to build the temple in the second month of the fourth year of his reign.

3 ¶Now these are the measurements which Solomon measured for the building of the house of the LORD: The length of the house by the measure of the sanctuary was sixty cubits, and its height thirty cubits, and its breadth twenty cubits.

4 And he made a porch in the front thereof; the length of it was the same as the breadth of the house, twenty cubits, and its height twenty cubits; and he overlaid it within with pure gold.

5 And the greater house he ceiled with cypress wood, which he overlaid with fine gold, and he carved on it the likeness of palm trees and flowers.

6 And he adorned the house with precious stones for beauty; and he overlaid all of it with fine gold.

7 He overlaid also the house, from the front of the porch and its walls and its door posts, with fine gold, and he carved on it the likeness of palm trees and flowers.

8 And he made the sanctuary of the holy of holies; its length was the same as the breadth of the house, twenty cubits, and its breadth twenty cubits; and he overlaid it with fine

gold, amounting to six hundred talents.

9 And he also overlaid the altar with fine gold.

10 In the most holy house he made two cherubim of solid material, and overlaid them with gold.

11 ¶And the wings of the cherubim were twenty cubits long; one wing of the one cherub was five cubits, reaching to the wall of the house; and the other wing was likewise five cubits, reaching to the wing of the other cherub.

12 And one wing of the other cherub was five cubits, reaching to the wall of the house; and the other wing was five cubits also, joining to the wing of the other cherub.

13 The wings of these cherubim were spread forth twenty cubits; they stood on their feet and their faces were inward.

14 ¶And he made the veil of blue and purple and crimson and fine linen, and wrought cherubim on it, and placed the ark in it.

15 Also he made in front of the great house two pillars, eighteen cubits long, and the capitals that were on the top of each of them were five cubits high.

16 And he made chains, fifty cubits long, and put them on the tops of the pillars; and made a hundred pomegranates, and put them on the chains.

17 And he set up the two pillars in front of the temple, one on the right hand and the other on the left; and he called the name of that which he set on the right hand, Jachin, and the name of that on the left, Boaz.

CHAPTER 4

MOREOVER he made an altar of brass, twenty cubits its length and twenty cubits its breadth and ten cubits its height.

2 ¶And he made a molten sea of ten cubits from brim to brim, round in shape, and five cubits its height and thirty cubits its circumference.

3 And it stood upon twelve oxen, three facing north, three facing south, three facing west, and three facing east; and the sea was set above them, and their hinder parts were inward.

4 And the thickness of it was a handbreadth, and its brim was round like the brim of a cup, very beautiful.

5 And he made also ten poles, and put five on the right hand and five on the left, to carry with them the altar of burnt offering.

6 ¶And he made ten lavers of brass, and put five on the right hand and five on the left, so that the priests might wash their hands and their feet in them.

7 And he made ten candlesticks of gold according to their specifications, and set them in the temple, five on the right hand and five on the left.

8 He made also ten tables, and placed them in the temple, five on the right side and five on the left. And he made a hundred basins of fine gold.

9 ¶Furthermore he made a large court for the priests and for the Levites, and overlaid the doors and the bars with brass.

10 And he set the sea on the right side of the north end, over against the south.

11 And Hiram made the pots, and the shovels, and the basins. And Hiram finished the work that he was to make for King Solomon for the house of God;

12 To wit, the two pillars and the knobs and the capitals which were on the top of the two pillars, and the two wreaths to cover the two knobs of the capitals which were on the top of the pillars;

13 And four hundred pomegranates on the two wreaths; two rows of pomegranates on each wreath, to cover the two knobs of the capitals which were upon the pillars.

14 He made also bases, and lavers made he upon the bases;

15 One sea, and twelve oxen under it.

16 The pots also and the shovels and the fleshhooks and all their instruments did Hiram make for King Solomon, for the house of the LORD, of bright brass.

17 In the plain of Jordan did the king cast them, in the clay ground between Succoth and Zeredathah.

18 Thus Solomon made all these vessels in great abundance; for the weight of these vessels of brass that Solomon made could not be found out.

19 ¶And Solomon made all the vessels that were for the house of God, the golden altar also, and the tables whereon the shewbread was set;

20 Moreover the candlesticks with their lamps,[1] that they should burn after the manner before the oracle, of pure gold;

21 And the flowers and the lamps and the tongs made he of gold, and that perfect gold;

22 And the snuffers and the basins and the spoons and the censers, of pure gold; and the entry of the house, the inner doors thereof for the most holy place, and the doors of the house of the temple, were of gold.

CHAPTER 5

THUS all the work that Solomon made for the house of the LORD was finished; and Solomon brought in all the things which David his father had dedicated; and the silver and the gold and all the vessels he put in the treasures of the house of the LORD.

2 ¶Then Solomon assembled at Jerusalem all the elders of Israel and all the heads of the tribes, the chiefs of the fathers of the children of Israel, to bring up the ark of the covenant of the LORD from the city of David, which is Zion.[2]

3 Wherefore all the men of Israel assembled themselves to King Solomon at Jerusalem in the feast of tabernacles, which is in the seventh month.[3]

4 And all the elders of Israel came; and the priests took up the ark.

5 And they brought up the ark of the LORD and the tabernacle of the congregation and all the holy vessels that were in the tabernacle, these did the priests and the Levites bring up.

---

[1] According to ordinance.   [2] From the old city to the temple.   [3] August.

6 And King Solomon and all the people of Israel that were assembled to him before the ark sacrificed sheep and oxen which could not be counted nor numbered for multitude.

7 Then the priests brought in the ark of the covenant of the LORD, and put it in its place, into the most holy place under the wings of the cherubim:

8 For the cherubim spread forth their wings over the place of the ark, and the cherubim covered the ark and the poles thereof above.

9 And the poles were so long that the ends of the poles were seen from underneath the ark within the house, but they were not seen from the outside. And there they remain to this day.

10 There was nothing in the ark except the two stone tablets which Moses had put there, which he brought from mount Sinai. This is the same covenant which the LORD made with the children of Israel when they came out of the land of Egypt.

11 ¶And it came to pass, when the priests were come out of the holy place (for all the priests who were present there entered into the holy place;

12 Also the Levites, who were the singers, all of them of Asaph, of Heman, of Jeruthun, with their sons and their brethren, being arrayed in white linen, having cymbals and psalteries and harps, stood at the east end of the altar, and with them an hundred and twenty priests sounding with trumpets):

13 That the trumpeters and singers were as one, to make one sound to be heard in praising and thanking the LORD; and when they lifted up their voice with the trumpets and cymbals and instruments of music, and praised the LORD, saying, For he is good; for his mercy endures for ever; that then the house was filled with a cloud, even the house of the LORD,

14 So that the priests could not stand to minister because of the cloud; for the house of the LORD was filled with the brightness of his glory.

CHAPTER 6

THEN Solomon said, O LORD, thou hast declared that thou wouldst dwell in the thick darkness.

2 But I have built a house of habitation for thee, and a place for thy dwelling for ever.

3 Then the king turned his face and blessed the whole congregation of Israel; and all the congregation of Israel stood.

4 And he said, Blessed be the LORD God of Israel, who spoke with his own mouth to David my father, and with his word has fulfilled that which he had promised, saying,

5 Since the day that I brought forth my people out of the land of Egypt, I chose no city among all the tribes of Israel to build a house in, that my name might be there;

6 But I have chosen Jerusalem that my name might be there; and I have chosen David to be king over my people Israel.

7 Now it was in the heart of David my father to build a house for the name of the LORD God of Israel.

8 But the LORD said to David my father, Forasmuch as it was in your heart to build a house for my name, you did well in that it was in your heart;

9 Nevertheless you shall not build the house for my name, but your son who shall come forth out of your loins, he shall build the house for my name.

10 The LORD therefore has performed his word that he has spoken; for I have risen up in the place of David my father, and I sit on the throne of Israel, as the LORD promised, and I have built the house for the name of the LORD God of Israel.

11 And I have prepared a place for the ark, wherein is the covenant of the LORD that he made with our fathers when he brought them forth out of the land of Egypt.

12 ¶And Solomon stood up before the altar of the LORD in the presence of all the congregation of Israel, and spread forth his hands toward heaven;

13 For Solomon had made a bronze

platform, five cubits long, five cubits wide, and two cubits high, and had set it in the midst of the court; and he went up and stood upon it, and knelt down upon his knees in the presence of all the people of Israel and spread forth his hands in prayer toward heaven,

14 And prayed and said, O LORD God of Israel, there is no one like thee; thou art the LORD who dwellest in heaven above, and thy will is carried out upon the earth below; who keepest covenant and showest mercy to thy servants who walk before thee uprightly with all their hearts;

15 Thou who hast kept with thy servant David my father that which thou hast promised him; and thou didst speak with thy mouth, and hast fulfilled it with thy will, as it is this day.

16 Now therefore, O LORD God of Israel, keep with thy servant David my father the promise which thou hast made to him, saying, There shall not fail you a son in my sight to sit upon the throne of Israel; if only your children take heed to their way to walk in my law, as you have walked before me.

17 Now then, O LORD God of Israel, let thy words be confirmed which thou hast spoken to thy servant David.

18 For in truth the LORD has made his dwelling place with his people Israel on the earth. Behold, heaven and the heaven of heavens cannot contain thee; how much less this house which I have built!

19 Have regard therefore to the prayer of thy servant and to his supplications, O LORD my God, to hearken to the prayer and the supplication which thy servant prayeth before thee this day;

20 That this house may remain in thy presence, that thou mayest hearken to the prayer of whosoever may come to pray before thee in this house day and night, the place of which thou hast said that thou wouldst put thy habitation there.

21 Hearken therefore to the prayer of thy servant, and of thy people Israel, which they shall pray before thee in this place; hear thou from thy dwelling place, even from heaven; and when thou hearest, forgive.

22 ¶If a man should offend his neighbor, and it is decreed upon him that he should take an oath, and he should come and swear before thy altar in this house;

23 Then hear thou his prayer, even from heaven, and do, and judge thy servants, by requiting the wicked, by bringing his guilt upon his own head; and by justifying the righteous, by rewarding him according to his righteousness.

24 ¶And if thy people Israel are defeated before the enemy because they have sinned against thee, and shall return to thee and confess thy great name, and pray and make supplication before thee in this house;

25 Then hear thou from the heavens and forgive the sins of thy people Israel and bring them again to the land which thou gavest to them and to their fathers.

26 ¶And when the heaven is shut up and there is no rain, because they have sinned against thee; yet if they pray before thee in this place, and confess thy great name and turn from their sins when thou dost afflict them;

27 Then hear thou from heaven their prayer, and forgive the sins of thy servants and of thy people Israel when thou hast taught them the good way in which they should walk; and send rain of blessing upon the land which thou hast given to thy people for an inheritance.

28 ¶If there is famine in the land, if there is pestilence or blasting or mildew or locusts or caterpillars; if their enemies besiege them in the cities of their land; whatsoever trouble or whatsoever sickness there be;

29 Then what prayer or what supplication soever shall be made of any man or of all thy people Israel, when every one shall declare his own grief, and shall come and spread forth his hands in this house;

30 Then hear thou from heaven their prayer and forgive their sins, and render to every man according to all his ways, whose heart thou know-

est (for thou only knowest the hearts of all the children of men),

31 That they may revere thee, to walk before thee in thy ways so long as they live in the land which thou gavest to their fathers.

32 ¶Moreover concerning the stranger who is not of thy people Israel, but comes from a far country for thy great name's sake and thy mighty hand and thy stretched out arm; if they come and pray before thee on that day in this house;

33 Then hear thou from thy dwelling place, even from heaven, and do according to all that the stranger prays before thee, so that all the peoples of the earth may know thy name and worship before thee, as do thy people Israel, and that they may know that this house which I have built is called by thy name.

34 If thy people go out to war against their enemies by the way that thou shalt send them, and they pray to thee towards this land which thou hast given to their fathers, or towards this city which thou hast chosen for thyself, or towards the house which I have built for thy name;

35 Then hear thou from the heavens their prayer and their supplication, and plead their cause.

36 If they sin against thee (for there is no man who does not sin), and thou be angry with them and deliver them over to their enemies, and they carry them away captives to a land far off or near;

37 Yet if they pray before thee, and repent in the land to which they were carried captive, saying, We have sinned, we have provoked thee to anger and have dealt wickedly;

38 If they return to thee with all their heart and with all their soul in the land of their captivity to which they were carried captive, and pray toward their land which thou gavest to their fathers and toward the city which thou hast chosen for thyself and toward the house which I have built for thy name;

39 Then hear thou from the heavens, even from thy dwelling place, their prayer and their supplication,

and maintain their cause, and forgive thy people who have sinned against thee.

40 Now, O my God, let thy eyes be open and let thy ears be attentive to the prayer that is made in this place.

41 Now therefore arise, O LORD God, into thy resting place, thou and the ark of thy strength; let thy priests, O LORD God, be clothed with salvation, and let thy righteous men rejoice in thy goodness.

42 O LORD God, turn not away the face of thy anointed one; remember the mercies of David thy servant.

CHAPTER 7

NOW when Solomon had made an end of praying, the fire came down from heaven and consumed the burnt offerings and the wood; and the glory of the LORD filled the house.

2 And the priests could not enter into the house of the LORD because the glory of the LORD had filled the LORD's house.

3 And when all the children of Israel saw how the fire came down and the glory of the LORD filled the house, they bowed themselves with their faces to the ground upon the pavement and worshipped, and said to each other, Praise the LORD, for he is good; for his mercy endures for ever.

4 ¶Then the king and all the people offered sacrifices before the LORD.

5 And King Solomon offered a sacrifice of twenty-two thousand oxen and a hundred and twenty thousand sheep; so the king and all the people dedicated the house of the LORD.

6 And the priests waited on their offices; the Levites also with instruments of music praised the LORD, and this is what they said in their praises, in the songs of David, Give thanks to the LORD, for he is good; for his mercy endures for ever; and the priests sounded with curved and straight trumpets, and all the people of Israel stood.

7 Moreover Solomon consecrated the middle of the court that was before the house of the LORD; for there he offered burnt offerings and the fat of the peace offerings, because the

bronze altar which Solomon had made was too small to hold the burnt offerings and the meal offerings and the fat:

8 ¶Also at that time Solomon kept the feast seven days, and all Israel with him, a very great congregation, from Hamath to the river of Egypt the people were assembled before the LORD our God.

9 Seven days were given for the feast and seven days for the dedication of the house; the extent of both occasions was fourteen days.

10 And on the fifteenth day of the month of Tishrin the king dismissed the people; and the people blessed the king and departed to their towns, glad and merry in heart, and giving thanks and praises for all the goodness that the LORD had shown to David his servant and to Solomon his son and to Israel his people.

11 And it came to pass that King Solomon finished building the house of the LORD and the king's house; and all that Solomon had reasoned in his mind to make in the house of the LORD and in the king's house he successfully accomplished.

12 ¶And the LORD appeared to Solomon that night and said to him, I have heard your prayer and have chosen this place to myself for a house of sacrifice.

13 If I shut up the heavens so that there is no rain, or if I command the locusts to devour the land, or if I send pestilence among my people;

14 If my people who are called by my name shall humble themselves and pray and seek my face and turn from their wicked ways; then I will hear from heaven and will forgive their sins and will heal their land.

15 And even now my eyes shall be open and my ears attentive to the prayer that is made in this place.

16 For now I have chosen this house for myself, that my glory may be in it for ever, and that my good works and my will shall be done in the midst of it perpetually.

17 And as for you, if you will walk before me as David your father walked, with innocence of heart and uprightness, to do everything that I have commanded you and to observe my commandments and my statutes;

18 Then I will establish the throne of your kingdom for ever, as I have covenanted with David your father, saying, There shall not fail you a son in my presence to sit on the throne of Israel.

19 But if you turn away from my ways, both you and your children, and shall not keep my commandments and my statutes which I have set before you, and shall go and serve the idols of the nations and worship them;

20 Then I will scatter you out of this land which I have given you; and this house, which I have sanctified for my name, I will uproot out of my sight, and Israel shall be a proverb and a byword among all nations.

21 And this house shall be in ruins, and every one passing by shall stand and shake his head in amazement, and say, Why has the LORD done thus to this great city and to this house?

22 And they will say, Because they forsook the covenant of the LORD God of their fathers, who brought them forth out of the land of Egypt, and they went and revered the gods of the Gentiles and served them and worshipped them; therefore the LORD has brought all this evil upon them.

CHAPTER 8

AND it came to pass at the end of twenty years, wherein Solomon had built the house of the LORD and the royal palace,

2 That Solomon rebuilt the cities which Hiram had given to him, and caused the children of Israel to dwell in them.

3 And Solomon went to Hamath and besieged it, and destroyed it.

4 And he built Tadmor, which had been laid waste like the wilderness, and all the store-cities;

5 Also he built Beth-hauran the upper and Beth-hauran the lower;

6 And built all the store-cities that Solomon had and all the chariot cities and the cities for the horsemen and all that Solomon desired to build in

Jerusalem and in Lebanon and throughout all the land of his dominion.

7 ¶As for all the people who were left of the Amorites, the Hittites, the Perizzites, the Hivites, and the Jebusites, who were not of Israel,

8 But of their descendants, who were left after them in the land, whom the children of Israel could not destroy, these Solomon made servants for himself, and workers and tributaries to this day.

9 But of the children of Israel Solomon made no servants in his kingdom, for they were men of war and the commanders of his chariots and his horsemen.

10 And these were the governors and overseers of King Solomon, even two hundred and fifty, who exercised authority over the people, who did the work.

11 ¶And Solomon brought up the daughter of Pharaoh out of the city of David to the house which he had built for her; for he said, No wife shall dwell with me in the house of David king of Israel, because the place in which the ark of the LORD has come is holy.

12 ¶Then Solomon offered burnt offerings to the LORD, and peace offerings upon the altar of the LORD which he had built before the porch,

13 Even after a certain rate every day, offering according to the commandment of Moses, on the sabbaths and on the solemn feasts, three times in the year, in the feast of unleavened bread, and in the feast of the fasting, and in the feast of tabernacles.

14 ¶And he appointed, according to the order of David his father, the courses of the priests to their service, and the Levites to their charges, to praise and minister before the priests, as the duty of every day required; and the porters also by their courses, to guard the doors every day; for so had David the king of Israel, whom the LORD had made king, commanded.

15 And he did not depart from all that King David had commanded him concerning the priests and the Levites and concerning all the service of the house.

16 Thus all the work of Solomon was set in order from the day the foundations of the house of the LORD were laid until all its work was finished.

17 ¶Then Solomon went to Eziongeber, the town which is opposite Eloth, at the seaside in the land of Edom.

18 And Hiram sent his servants by ships, skilful mariners, who knew how to pilot ships in the sea, and they went with the servants of Solomon to the city of Ophir, and took from there four hundred talents of gold, and brought them to King Solomon.

CHAPTER 9

AND when the queen of Sheba heard of the fame of Solomon, she came to test Solomon with enigmas. And she came to Jerusalem with a very great company, and camels bearing spices and gold in abundance and precious stones; and when she was come to King Solomon, she told him all that was in her heart.

2 And King Solomon told her every secret that was in her heart; and there was nothing hidden from the king which he could not tell her.

3 And when the queen of Sheba had seen the wisdom of Solomon and the house that he had built

4 And the food of his table and the seating of his servants and the attendance of his ministers and their apparel, his cupbearers also and their apparel, and the sacrifices that he offered in the house of the LORD, there was no more spirit left in her to see more.

5 And she said to King Solomon, It was a true report which I heard in my own land of your acts and of your wisdom;

6 Howbeit I did not believe their words until I came and my eyes had seen it; and, behold, the half of the greatness of your wisdom was not told me; for you exceed the report which I heard.

7 Happy are these your servants,

who stand continually before you and hear your wisdom.

8 Blessed be the LORD your God, who has chosen you and set you on the throne of the kingdom of Israel; because the LORD loved Israel, he has made you king over them for ever, to do judgment and justice.

9 And she gave the king a hundred and twenty talents of gold, and of spices great abundance, and precious stones; there were no such spices in the world as those which the queen of Sheba gave to King Solomon.

10 And the servants also of Hiram and the servants of King Solomon brought gold from Ophir.

11 And they also brought algum wood for stools for the house of the LORD and for the house of King Solomon, and harps for singers, and there were none such seen before in the land of Judah.

12 And King Solomon gave to the queen of Sheba all that she asked, besides that which he had already given, and he told her all that was in her heart. So she turned and went away to her own land, she and her servants.

13 ¶Now the weight of gold that came to Solomon in one year was six hundred and sixty-six talents of gold,

14 Besides the taxes from the cities and the traffic which the merchants brought. And all the kings of Arabia and the governors of the land brought silver and gold to Solomon.

15 ¶And King Solomon made two hundred shields of fine gold; six hundred shekels of fine gold went into each shield.

16 And he made three hundred shields of fine gold; three hundred shekels of fine gold went to the handle of each shield. And the king put them in the House of the Forest of Lebanon.

17 Moreover the king made a great throne of ivory, and overlaid it with pure gold.

18 And there were six steps to the throne, and the rim of the throne encircled from behind it, with armrests on each side of the seat, and two lions standing behind the armrests.

19 And twelve lions stood there, on the one side and on the other side upon the six steps. There was not the like ever made in any kingdom.

20 ¶And all the vessels of the service of King Solomon were of gold, and all the vessels of the king's treasuries were of pure gold; silver was not accounted as anything in the days of Solomon.

21 For the king had ships that went to Tarshish with the servants of Hiram; once every three years the ships of Tarshish came loaded with silver and gold, elephants, apes, and peacocks.

22 Thus King Solomon excelled all the kings of the earth in riches and wisdom.

23 ¶And all the kings of the earth sought the presence of Solomon to hear the wisdom that the LORD had put into his heart.

24 And they brought every man his present, vessels of silver and vessels of gold and garments, myrrh and spices, horses and mules, a fixed amount year by year.

25 ¶And Solomon had four thousand stalls for horses and chariots, and twelve thousand horsemen, whom he placed in the chariot cities and with the king at Jerusalem.

26 ¶And Solomon ruled over all the kings from the river Euphrates to the land of the Philistines, and to the border of Egypt.

27 And King Solomon made silver as plentiful in Jerusalem as stones, and he made cedar trees as the sand that is by the sea in abundance.

28 And they brought to Solomon horses from Egypt and from all lands.

29 ¶Now the rest of the acts of Solomon, first and last, are they not written in the book of Nathan the prophet and in the prophecy of Ahijah the Shilonite and in the visions of Iddo the seer against Jeroboam the son of Nebat?

30 And Solomon reigned in Jerusalem forty years over all Israel.

31 And Solomon slept with his fathers, and they buried him in the city of David his father; and Rehoboam his son reigned in his stead.

CHAPTER 10

AND Rehoboam went to Shechem; for to Shechem were all Israel come to make him king.

2 And it came to pass, when Jeroboam and all Israel heard it,

3 They came and said to Rehoboam the son of Solomon,

4 Your father made our yoke grievous; now therefore lighten somewhat the harsh rule of your father and his heavy yoke that he put upon us, and we will serve you.

5 And he said to them, Go away and come again to me after three days. And the people departed.

6 ¶And King Rehoboam took counsel with the old men who had served Solomon his father while he was yet alive, saying, What counsel do you give me to return an answer to this people?

7 And they spoke to him, saying, If you will answer kindly to this people, and please them and speak good words to them, they will be your servants for ever.

8 But he forsook the counsel which the old men gave him, and took counsel with the young men who were brought up with him and stood before him.

9 And he said to them, What advice do you give me that we may return answer to this people who have spoken to me, saying, Lighten the yoke which your father did put upon us, and we will serve you?

10 And the young men who were brought up with him in the streets [1] spoke to him, saying, Thus shall you say to the people who have spoken to you, saying, Your father made our yoke heavy, but you make it somewhat lighter for us; thus shall you say to them, My little finger is thicker than my father's thumb.

11 And now, whereas my father put a heavy yoke upon you, I will add to your yoke; my father chastised you with whips, but I will chastise you with scorpions.

12 So Jeroboam and all the people came to Rehoboam on the third day, as the king had bade them, saying, Come again to me on the third day.

13 And the king answered them with harsh words; and King Rehoboam forsook the counsel of the old men,

14 And spoke to them according to the advice of the young men, saying, My father made your yoke heavy, but I will add to your yoke; my father chastised you with whips, but I will chastise you with scorpions.

15 So the king did not listen to the people; for the decree had been made by God, that the LORD might perform the word of Ahijah the prophet the Shilonite concerning Jeroboam the son of Nebat.

16 ¶And when all Israel saw that the king would not listen to them, the people answered the king, saying, We have no portion in David, nor an inheritance in the son of Jesse; return every man to his house, O Israel; and now, David, see to your own house. So Israel went to their houses.

17 But as for the children of Israel who dwelt in the cities of Judah, Rehoboam reigned over them.

18 Then King Rehoboam sent Adoniram, who was in charge of tribute; and the children of Israel stoned him with stones, that he died. But King Rehoboam hastily got up into his chariot to flee to Jerusalem.

19 So Israel rebelled against the house of David to this day.

CHAPTER 11

AND when Rehoboam came to Jerusalem, he assembled of the house of Judah and Benjamin a hundred and eighty thousand chosen men who drew sword, and who were warriors, to fight against Israel to restore the kingdom to Rehoboam the son of Solomon.

2 But the word of the LORD came to Shemaiah, saying,

3 Speak to Rehoboam the son of Solomon, king of Judah, and to the house of Benjamin and to all Israel and to the rest of the people, saying,

4 Thus says the LORD: You shall not go up, nor fight; return every man

[1] His former playmates.

to his house, for this thing is done of me. And they obeyed the word of the LORD, and returned, to go every man to his house.

5 ¶And Jeroboam built Shechem on the mountain of the tribe of the house of Ephraim, and dwelt in it; and went out from there and built Penuel.

6 And Jeroboam said in his heart, Now shall the kingdom return to the house of David;

7 If this people go up to offer sacrifices in the house of the LORD in Jerusalem, then shall the heart of this people turn again to their LORD, and they shall kill me and restore the kingdom to Rehoboam the son of Solomon.

8 Therefore the king took counsel and made two calves of gold, and said to the people, It is too much for you to go up to Jerusalem, why should you go up to Jerusalem and come down? Then he said, These are your gods, O Israel, who brought you up out of the land of Egypt.

9 And he set the one in Beth-el, and the other he put in Dan.

10 And this thing became a sin; for the people went to worship before the calf, even to Dan. And this thing became a sin to all the house of Jeroboam, to be uprooted and destroyed from the earth.

11 At that time Abijah the son of Jeroboam fell sick; and Jeroboam said to his wife, Arise and disguise yourself, and be as a simple woman, that you may not be known to be the wife of Jeroboam; and go to Shiloh; behold, there is Ahijah the prophet, who told me that I should be king over this people.

12 Go to him; he shall tell you what shall become of this child.

13 And the LORD said to Ahijah, Behold, the wife of Jeroboam is coming to ask a thing of you concerning her son; for he is sick; thus and thus shall you say to her; for it shall be, when she comes in, that she will disguise herself.

14 And it came to pass, when Ahijah heard the sound of her feet as she came in at the door, he said to

¹ Verses 18 to 23 are not in the Eastern text.

her, Come in, wife of Jeroboam; why have you disguised yourself? For I am sent to tell you harsh words.

15 Go, tell Jeroboam, Thus says the LORD God of Israel: I have exalted you from among the people and made you king over my people Israel,

16 And took the kingdom away from the house of David and gave it to you; and yet you have not been like my servant David, who kept my commandments and who walked in my statutes with all his heart to do that which was right in my presence;

17 But you have done evil above all kings who were before you; for you have gone and made for yourself idols of the nations, and images to blaspheme before me, and have cast my worship behind your back.

18 ¶And Rehoboam took to him Mahalath the daughter of Jerimoth, the son of David, to wife, and Abihail the daughter of Eliab the son of Jesse,¹

19 Which bare him children; Jeush, and Shamariah and Zaham.

20 And after her he took Maachah the daughter of Absalom, which bore him Abijah and Attai and Ziza and Shelomith.

21 And Rehoboam loved Maachah the daughter of Absalom above all his wives and his concubines (for he took eighteen wives and sixty concubines; and begat twenty-eight sons, and sixty daughters).

22 And Rehoboam made Abijah the son of Maachah the crown prince, to be ruler among his brethren; for he thought to make him king.

23 And he dealt wisely, and dispersed all of his children throughout all the countries of Judah and Benjamin unto every fortified city; and he gave them food in abundance. And he desired many wives.

CHAPTER 12

AND it came to pass when Rehoboam had established the kingdom and had strengthened himself, he forsook the law of the LORD, and all Israel with him.

2 And it came to pass that in the

fifth year of King Rehoboam, Shishak king of Egypt came up against Jerusalem, because they had transgressed against the LORD,

3 With twelve hundred chariots and sixty thousand horsemen; and the people were without number that came with him out of Egypt; the Lubims, the Sukkiims and the Ethiopians.

4 And he took the fenced cities which pertained to Judah, and came to Jerusalem.

5 ¶Then came Shemaiah the prophet to Rehoboam and to the princes of Judah that were gathered together at Jerusalem because of Shishak, and said unto them, Thus says the LORD: You have forsaken me, and therefore have I also left you in the hand of Shishak.

6 Whereupon the princes of Israel and the king humbled themselves; and they said, The LORD is righteous.

7 And when the LORD saw that they humbled themselves, the word of the LORD came to Shemaiah, saying, They have humbled themselves; therefore I will not destroy them, but I will grant them some deliverance; and my wrath shall not be poured out upon Jerusalem by the hand of Shishak.

8 Nevertheless they shall be his servants, that they may know my service, and the service of the kingdoms of the countries.

9 So Shishak king of Egypt came up against Jerusalem, and took away the treasures of the house of the LORD and the treasures of the king's house; he took all; he carried away also the shields of gold which Solomon had made.

10 Instead of which King Rehoboam made shields of brass, and committed them to the hands of the chief of the guard that kept the entrance of the king's house.

11 And when the king entered into the house of the LORD, the guard came and fetched them, and brought them again into the guard chamber.

12 And when he humbled himself, the wrath of the LORD turned from him, that he would not destroy him altogether; and also in Judah things went well.

13 ¶So King Rehoboam strengthened himself in Jerusalem, and reigned; for Rehoboam was forty-one years old when he began to reign, and he reigned seventeen years in Jerusalem, the city which the LORD had chosen out of all the tribes of Israel to put his name there. And his mother's name was Naamah an Ammonitess.

14 And he did evil before the LORD, for he did not prepare his heart to worship the LORD and to seek him with all his heart.

15 Now these are the acts of Rehoboam, first and last, to do evil before the LORD God of Israel. And there were wars between Rehoboam the son of Solomon and Jeroboam the son of Nebat continually.

16 And Rehoboam slept with his fathers, and was buried in the city of David; and Abijah his son reigned in his stead.

CHAPTER 13

IN the eighteenth year of King Jeroboam the son of Nebat Abijah began to reign over the tribe of Judah.

2 He reigned three years in Jerusalem. His mother's name was Maachah the daughter of Uriel of Ramtha.

3 And Abijah mobilized an army of valiant men of war, four hundred thousand young men, who took upon themselves to go and fight against Jeroboam the son of Nebat. And Jeroboam also had mobilized an army, and he came to fight against him with eight hundred thousand young men, being mighty men of valour.

4 ¶And Abijah stood up upon mount Zemaraim, which is in the border of mount Ephraim, and said, Hear me, O Jeroboam the son of Nebat, and all Israel;

5 Perhaps you know that the LORD God of Israel gave the kingdom over Israel to David for ever, even to him and to his sons by a covenant pertaining to the kingship.

6 Yet Jeroboam the son of Nebat,

the servant of Solomon the son of David, rose up and rebelled against his lord.

7 And he gathered to him certain wicked men, the children of iniquity, and he prevailed against Rehoboam the son of Solomon, when Rehoboam was young and not advanced in years and did not know what to say, and did not comfort the people concerning the heavy yoke which Solomon his father had laid upon them.

8 And even now what can you say? You went away and renounced the kingdom of the house of David and went and served dead gods. And I reign over a single tribe, but you over many tribes, and there are with you golden calves which Jeroboam the son of Nebat made for you.

9 And you have cast out the priests the sons of Aaron and the Levites, and have made priests for yourselves of the people of the land. And whosover comes to offer an offering, you take from him a young bullock and seven rams, and he becomes a priest of them that are not gods.

10 But as for us, we have not forsaken the LORD our God, and the priests, who minister to the LORD, are the sons of Aaron, and the Levites serve as they should;

11 They offer to the LORD every morning and every evening burnt offering and sweet incense, and set the shewbread in order upon the pure table; and the candlestick of gold with its lamps, and a boy having charge of the lamps lights them every evening; thus we have charge of the ordinances of the LORD our God;

12 But you have forsaken him and have gone after dead gods, and you serve them and worship them; and have forsaken the LORD God of your fathers, therefore you shall not prosper in the world.

13 But Jeroboam caused an ambush to come about behind them; so they were before Judah, and the ambush was behind them.

14 And when Judah looked back, behold, the battle was before and behind; and they cried unto the LORD,

and the priests sounded with the trumpets.

15 And it came to pass when the men of the house of Judah shouted, the LORD defeated Jeroboam the son of Nebat and all Israel before Judah and Abijah.

16 And the children of Israel fled before Judah;

17 And Abijah slew them with a great slaughter; so there fell slain of Israel five hundred thousand young men.

18 Thus the children of Israel were defeated at that time, and the children of Judah prevailed, because they said, We rely upon the LORD God of our fathers.

19 And Abijah pursued Jeroboam, and took some great cities from him, Beth-el with its pastures, Shelah with its pastures, and Ephron with its pastures.

20 Neither did Jereboam recover strength again in the days of Abijah; and the LORD struck Jeroboam, and he died.

21 ¶But Abijah became strong, and he married fourteen wives, and there were born to him twenty-two sons and sixteen daughters.

22 And the rest of the acts of Abijah and his ways, behold, are written in the poems of the prophet Iddo.

CHAPTER 14

SO Abijah slept with his fathers, and they buried him in the city of David; and Asa his son reigned in his stead. In his days the land was quiet for ten years.

2 And Asa did that which was good and right in the presence of the LORD his God;

3 For he demolished the altars of the strange gods and the shrines, and broke down the images and cut down the groves;

4 And he said to Judah, Come, let us pray before the LORD God of our fathers.

5 Also he uprooted out of all the cities of Judah the shrines on the high places and the idols; and his kingdom was quiet in his days, and he had no enemies on all his borders.

6 ¶And he built fenced cities in Judah; for the land had rest, and there was no one who made war against him in those years, because the LORD had given him rest.

7 Therefore he said to Judah, Come, let us build these cities, and surround them with walls and towers, gates, and bars, while the land is still quiet of wars; because we have sought the LORD our God, and he also has sought us and he has given us rest from all those who are round about us, and has comforted us and delivered us.

8 And Asa had an army of mighty men of valour that bore swords and spears out of the tribe of Judah, three hundred thousand, and out of Benjamin, that bore breastplate and drew bows, two hundred and eighty thousand; all these were mighty men of valour.

9 ¶And there came out against them Zerah the Ethiopian with a large army of a million men and thirty thousand chariots, and came to Mareshah.

10 Then Asa went out against him, and he fought against him in the valley of Mareshah.

11 And Asa prayed before the LORD his God and said, Thou art our LORD, thou art the help of thy people; and when thou dost deliver a great army in the hands of a small force, then all the inhabitants of the earth shall know that it is good to rely on thee; help us, O LORD our God, because in thy name we have come against this great army. O LORD our God, delay not thy might from us.

12 And when Asa had finished praying, the angel of the LORD routed the Ethiopians before Asa and before Judah; and the Ethiopians fled.

13 And Asa and the people that were with him pursued them as far as Gedar; and there fell of the Ethiopians so many that they could not be numbered; for they were defeated before the LORD and before his armies; and they took and carried away very much spoil.

14 And they smote all the cities round about Gedar, for the fear of the LORD came upon them; and they plundered all the cities; for there was exceeding much spoil in them.

15 They also carried away the tents of the Arabians and carried away sheep and camels in abundance, and brought them to Jerusalem.

CHAPTER 15

AND the Spirit of the LORD came upon Azariah the son of Azor;

2 And he went out to meet Asa and said to him, Hear me, Asa, and all Judah and Benjamin: The LORD is with you for ever and ever; and if you seek him, he will be found by you; but if you forsake him, he will forsake you.

3 Now for a long time Israel has not served their God in truth and has not accepted the teaching of their priests and would not obey their laws; therefore they were delivered into the hand of their enemies.

4 But when in their distress they prayed to the LORD God of Israel and sought him, he was found by them.

5 And in those early times when we did not worship our God, there was no peace to him that went out, nor to him that came in, because of great misfortune that came upon all the inhabitants of the land.

6 And we were scattered in every nation and people, and in towns and cities,

7 Because we had forsaken our God and would not listen to the voice of his servants, the prophets; so he rewarded us according to our works.

8 And when Asa heard these words of Azariah the son of Azor the prophet, he took courage and removed the idols from all the land of Judah and Benjamin and from the cities which he had taken in the land of Ephraim, and he repaired the altar of the LORD that was in the front of the porch of the LORD.

9 And he gathered all Judah and Benjamin and the proselytes with them out of Ephraim and Manasseh and out of Simeon; for they gathered together and came to him out of Is-

33

rael in abundance when they saw that the LORD his God was with him.

10 So they gathered themselves together at Jerusalem in the third month, in the fifteenth year of the reign of Asa.

11 And the same day they offered to the LORD of the spoil which they had brought, seven hundred oxen and six thousand sheep.

12 And they entered into a covenant to pray to the LORD God of their fathers with all their heart and with all their soul;

13 And that whosoever would not pray to the LORD God of Israel should be put to death, whether small or great, whether man or woman.

14 And they swore to the LORD with a loud voice, and with sounding of curved and straight trumpets.

15 And all Judah rejoiced at this report which they heard; for they sought him with all their heart and prayed to him with all their soul; and he was found by them, and he delivered them from all their enemies round about.

16 ¶And also Maachah the mother of Asa he removed from being queen-mother, because she had a feast to her idols; and Asa cut down her idols and burned them at the brook Kidron.

17 But the altars on the high places were not taken away out of Israel; nevertheless the heart of Asa was perfect in the worship of the LORD his God all the days of his life.

18 ¶And he brought into the house of the LORD the things that his father had dedicated and that he himself had dedicated, silver and gold and vessels.

19 And there was no more war until the thirty-fifth year of the reign of Asa.

CHAPTER 16

IN the thirty-sixth year of the reign of Asa, Baasha king of Israel came up against Judah and built Ramtha, that he might let none go out or come in to Asa king of Judah.

2 Then Asa brought silver and gold out of the treasures of the house of the LORD and of the king's house, and sent them to Bar-hadad king of Aram, who dwelt in Damascus, saying,

3 There is a league between me and you, as there was between my father and your father; behold, I have sent you silver and gold; go, break your league with Baasha king of Israel, that he may withdraw from me.

4 And Bar-hadad hearkened to King Asa, and sent the commanders of his armies against the cities of Israel; and they came and encamped against the cities of Israel; and they took Ijon, Abel, and Beth-maacah, and all the store cities of Naphtali.

5 Then when Baasha heard of it, he stopped building Ramtha, and let his work cease.

6 Then Asa the king gathered together all Judah; and they carried away the stones of Ramtha and its timber with which Baasha was building; and King Asa built with them Ramtha of Benjamin and the town of Mizpah.

7 ¶And at that time Hanan the prophet came to Asa king of Judah and said to him, Because you have relied on the king of Aram and not relied on the LORD your God, therefore the army of Aram will flee.

8 And they will go and become strong, both they and the Ethiopians and the kings that are with them, and will become great armies with very many chariots and horsemen, but when you seek the LORD your God, he will deliver them into your hands.

9 For the eyes of the LORD run to and fro throughout the whole earth; therefore, be strong, and let your heart be perfect towards his worship, and understand all his wonders; for the LORD your God will fight for you.

10 Then Asa was wroth with the seer, and put him in prison because he reported things which he did not see and made the heart of the people tremble; therefore Asa kept himself aloof from the people at that time.

11 ¶And, behold, the acts of Asa, first and last, lo, they are written in the Book of the Kings of Judah and Israel.

12 And Asa was diseased in his feet

in the thirty-ninth year of his reign, and was laid in his house.

13 ¶And Asa slept with his fathers, and died in the forty-first year of his reign.

14 And they buried him in his own sepulchre in the city of David, and they laid him on a bier which was filled with many kinds of spices, and they made a very great burnt offering for him.

CHAPTER 17

AND Jehoshaphat his son reigned in his stead, and strengthened himself against Israel.

2 And he placed mighty men in all the fortified cities of Judah, and appointed governors in the land of Judah and in the cities of Ephraim which Asa his father had taken.

3 And the LORD was with Jehoshaphat because he walked in the first ways of his father David and did not pray to images;

4 But he prayed to the LORD God of his father and walked in his commandments and kept his statutes, and did not do according to the ways of Israel.

5 Therefore the LORD established the kingdom in his hand; and all Judah brought presents to Jehoshaphat and he had riches and honor in abundance.

6 And his heart was strengthened in the ways of the LORD; moreover he uprooted the altars and the high places which were within the territory of Judah.

7 ¶Also in the third year of his reign he sent and called his princes and the commanders of the armies, even to Obadiah, Zechariah, Nathanael, Melachiah, to teach in the cities of Judah.

8 And with them were the Levites, even Shemaiah, Nethaniah, Zechariah, Ashaiel, Natorah, Jonathan, Adonijah, and Tobiah. These were all Levites, and with them were Elishama and Jehoram, priests.

9 And they taught in all the land of Judah, having the book of the law of the LORD with them, and went

about throughout all the cities of Judah and taught the people.

10 ¶And the fear of the LORD fell upon all the kingdoms of the lands that were round about Judah, so that they made no war against Jehoshaphat.

11 Also some of the cities of the Philistines brought Jehoshaphat presents, silver, and poll tax; and the Arabians brought him flocks, seven thousand and seven hundred rams, and seven thousand and seven hundred he-goats, yearly.

12 ¶And Jehoshaphat grew exceedingly rich; and he built in Judah castles and store cities.

13 And he had much business in the cities of Judah; and the men of war, mighty men of valour, were in Jerusalem.

14 And this is the number of them according to the house of their fathers. Of Judah, the commanders of thousands: Adino the chief, and with him mighty men of valour, three hundred thousand.

15 And next to him was Johanan the commander, and with him two hundred and eighty thousand valiant men.

16 And next to him was Shemai the son of Zerah, with whom the LORD was pleased, and with him two hundred thousand valiant men.

17 And of Benjamin: Eliada, a mighty man of valour, and with him, armed with bow and shield, two hundred thousand.

18 And next to him was Jehozabad, a mighty man, and with him a hundred and eighty thousand ready for the war.

19 These were all who served King Jehoshaphat, besides those whom the king put in the fortified cities throughout all the land of Judah.

CHAPTER 18

NOW Jehoshaphat had riches and honor in abundance, and he made an alliance with Ahab.

2 And after two years he went down to Ahab in Samaria. And Ahab killed sheep and oxen for him in abundance, and for the armed forces

that were with him, and advised him to go up to Ramath-gilead.

3 And Ahab king of Israel said to Jehoshaphat king of Judah, Will you go up with me to Ramath-gilead? And he answered him, I will go up as you do; and my people are as your people; and my horses as your horses, and we will go with you to war.

4 ¶And Jehoshaphat said to the king of Israel, Inquire, I pray, for the word of the LORD today.

5 Therefore the king of Israel gathered together of the prophets four hundred men, and said to them, Shall we go to Ramath-gilead to battle or shall I forbear? And they said to him, Go up; for the LORD will deliver your enemies into your hands.

6 But King Jehoshaphat said, Is there not here a true prophet of the LORD, that we may inquire of him?

7 And the king of Israel said to Jehoshaphat, There is yet one man by whom we may inquire of the LORD; but I hate him; for he never prophesies good concerning me, but always evil. His name is Micaiah the son of Imla. And Jehoshaphat said, Let not the king say so.

8 And the king of Israel called for one of the officers and said to him, Bring quickly Micaiah the son of Imla.

9 And the king of Israel and Jehoshaphat the king of Judah were sitting each man on his throne, clothed in their robes, and they sat at the entrance of the gate of Samaria; and all the false prophets were prophesying before them.

10 And Zedekiah the son of a Canaanitish woman had made for himself horns of iron,[1] and he said, Thus says the LORD: With these you shall pierce the Arameans until they are cut off and destroyed.

11 And all the prophets prophesied so, saying, Go up to Ramath-gilead, and triumph: for the LORD will deliver your enemies into your hands, O king.

12 And the messenger who went to call Micaiah spoke to him, saying, Behold, the words of the false prophets have declared good to the king

[1] A head-dress.

with one accord; let your words, therefore, be pleasant like one of theirs, and you also prophesy good.

13 And Micaiah said, As the LORD God lives, what my God puts into my heart, that will I speak.

14 And when he was come to the king, the king said to him, Micaiah, shall we go to Ramath-gilead or shall I forbear? And he said to him, Go up and triumph, and they shall be delivered into your hands.

15 And the king said to him, How many times shall I adjure you that you say nothing but the truth to me in the name of the LORD?

16 Then he said, I saw all Israel scattered upon the mountains as sheep that have no shepherd; and the LORD said, These have no king; let them return therefore every man to his house in peace.

17 And the king of Israel said to Jehoshaphat, Did I not tell you that he would not prophesy good concerning me, but evil?

18 Then Micaiah said, Therefore hear the word of the LORD: I saw the LORD sitting upon his throne, and all the host of heaven standing on his right hand and on his left.

19 And the LORD said, Who shall entice Ahab king of Israel, that he may go up and be slain at Ramath-gilead? And one said, I will entice him after this manner, and another said, I will entice him after that manner.

20 Then there came out a spirit, and stood before the LORD and said, I will entice him, and the LORD said to him, With what?

21 And he said, I will go out, and be a lying spirit in the mouth of all his prophets. And the LORD said, You shall entice him, and you shall also prevail; go out, and do according to what you have said.

22 Now therefore, behold, the LORD has put a lying spirit in the mouth of these your prophets, and the LORD has decreed evil against you.

23 Then Zedekiah the son of the Canaanitish woman came near and struck Micaiah on his cheek, and said to him, Since when did the Spirit of

the LORD depart from me to speak to you?

24 And Micaiah said, Behold, you shall see on that day when you shall go into an inner chamber to hide yourself.

25 Then the king of Israel said, Take Micaiah, and carry him back and detain him in the house of Amon the governor of the city and in the house of Joash the king's son;

26 And say, Thus says the king: Put this fellow in the prison, and feed him with bread of affliction and with water of affliction until I return in peace.

27 And Micaiah said, If you certainly return in peace, then the LORD has not spoken by me. And he said, Hear, all you people.

28 So Jehoshaphat the king of Judah and Ahab the king of Israel went up to Ramath-gilead.

29 And the king of Israel said to Jehoshaphat, I will put on my armor, and go and stand in the battle array; and you put on your armor. So the king of Israel put on his armor, and went and stood in the battle array.

30 Now the king of Aram had commanded the captains of the chariots that were with him, thirty-two in number, saying, Fight not with small or great, but only with the king of Israel.

31 And it came to pass when the captains of the chariots saw Jehoshaphat, they said, It is the king of Israel. Therefore they came against him to fight him; but Jehoshaphat cried out and the LORD helped him; and he turned them away from him.

32 And it came to pass when the captains of the chariots saw that it was not the king of Israel, they turned back from pursuing him.

33 And a certain man shot an arrow unwittingly towards him, and smote the king of Israel between the joints of his breastplate; therefore he said to his chariot man, Turn your hand and carry me out of the host; for I am grievously wounded.

34 And the battle grew fiercer that day; but the king of Israel was seated in the chariot fighting against the Arameans until the evening, and at sunset he died.

CHAPTER 19

AND at the evening Jehoshaphat the king of Judah returned to his house in peace to Jerusalem.

2 And Jehu the son of Hanan the seer went out to meet him, and said to King Jehoshaphat, Should you go to help the ungodly, and love those who hate the LORD? Therefore the LORD is angry with you.

3 But I believe good reports have been heard about you, in that you have not shed innocent blood in the land and have prepared your heart to pray before the LORD in truth.

4 And Jehoshaphat dwelt at Jerusalem; and he went out again among the people from the city of Beer-sheba to mount Ephraim, and brought them back to worship the LORD God of their fathers.

5 ¶And he appointed judges in the land throughout all the fortified cities of Judah and the great cities.

6 And he said to the judges, Take heed what you do; for you judge not for man, but for the LORD our God.

7 Therefore be courageous and judge righteously, so that the LORD may be with you for ever; take heed and do it; for there is no iniquity with the LORD our God nor respect of persons nor taking of bribes.

8 ¶Moreover in Jerusalem also Jehoshaphat appointed men of the Levites and of the priests and of the chiefs of the fathers of the children of Israel for the judgment of the LORD; then he returned to Jerusalem.

9 And he charged them, saying, Thus shall you do in reverence of the LORD, in faithfulness and with a perfect heart.

10 And whatsoever case shall come to you of your brethren who dwell in your cities, between bloodshed and bloodshed, between law and commandment, between statutes and ordinances, you shall warn them so that they may not be guilty before the LORD, and thus he become angry with them and with their brethren; this do, and you shall not be guilty.

11 And, behold, I have appointed priests over you, that they may judge just and faithful judgments according to the commandment of the LORD. And Zechariah the son of Shemiah declared to all the people of Judah all the commandments of the king; he also declared to the scribes and the Levites, repeating everything before them, saying, Deal courageously, and the LORD will help you for ever.

CHAPTER 20

AND it came to pass after this, the children of Moab and the children of Ammon, with the mighty men of war, came against Jehoshaphat to battle.

2 Then there came messengers and told Jehoshaphat, saying, A great army has come against you from beyond the Red Sea; and, behold, they are encamping in Jericho, which is En-gad.

3 And Jehoshaphat feared, and he raised up his face to pray before the LORD and proclaimed a fast for all the inhabitants of Judah. And he said to them, Gather yourselves together and come let us beseech the LORD our God.

4 And all the inhabitants of Judah gathered themselves together, even from far off cities, and they came to beseech the LORD.

5 ¶And Jehoshaphat stood in the midst of the assembly of Judah in the house of the LORD, which is in Jerusalem, before the new court,

6 And he prayed and said, O LORD God of our fathers, thou art the God in heaven, and thou art ruler over all the kingdoms of the world, and thine is power and might, and now I stand before thee praying.

7 And thou art our God, who didst destroy the inhabitants of this land before thy people Israel and gavest it to the descendants of Abraham thy friend for ever.

8 And they have dwelt in it, and have built in it a sanctuary for thy name, saying,

9 Now, because there is a sanctuary among us, no evil shall come upon us, nor the sword nor judgment nor pestilence nor famine; and we shall come and stand before this house and before thee (for thy name has been invoked in this house), and we will pray before thee in this house, and thou wilt hear our prayer and save us.

10 And now, behold, the children of Ammon, of the mount of Gabel, and of Moab, with whom thou wouldst not let Israel mix when thou didst bring them out of the land of Egypt, and thou hadst removed the yoke of the Egyptians from them,

11 Behold, now they reward us; they are coming to drive us out of thy possession, which thou hast given us to inherit.

12 O our God, make thyself known and judge them, for we have no strength to stand before them; bring upon them the sword of thy judgment, for we do not know what to do; but our eyes are upon thee.

13 And all Judah stood before the LORD with their little ones, their wives, their sons, and their daughters.

14 ¶Then upon Hazaiel the son of Zechariah, the son of Benaiah, the son of Jehoiadah, the son of Mattaniah, a Levite of the sons of Asaph, came the spirit of might from before the LORD, and he was standing before the people of Israel;

15 And he said, Hearken, all Judah and inhabitants of Jerusalem and King Jehoshaphat, thus says the LORD your God: Be not afraid nor dismayed because of this great army; for the battle is not yours, but God's.

16 Hasten, go down against them; behold, they are coming up early in the morning; and you shall find them in the cliff of the valley, before the wilderness. They are coming up to fight against you.

17 And in that hour, stand still and see the salvation that the LORD will do for you, O Judah and the inhabitants of Jerusalem; fear not, nor be dismayed; tomorrow go out against them; for the LORD God will help you.

18 Then Jehoshaphat bowed his head with his face to the ground and worshipped; and all Judah and the

inhabitants of Jerusalem fell before the LORD, worshipping the LORD.

19 And the Levites of the descendants of the Kohathites and of the descendants of the Korhites stood up to praise the LORD God of Israel with a loud voice,

20 ¶And they rose early in the morning and went forth into the wilderness of Tekoa; and as they went forth, Jehoshaphat stood and said, Hear me, O Judah and inhabitants of Jerusalem: Believe in the LORD your God, so you shall be established; believe in his prophets, and you shall be delivered.

21 Then he stood in the midst of the people and said, Come, let us give thanks to the LORD, and give praise to the excellency of his holiness, as he is going forth before our armies to fight for us against our enemies. And they said, Give thanks to the LORD, for he is good; for his mercy endures for ever. Then the hills began to give praise and the mountains began to rejoice.

22 ¶And when they began to sing and to praise, the LORD set ambushments against the children of Ammon, Moab, and mount Seir, which were come against Judah; and they were smitten.

23 For the children of Ammon and Moab stood up against the inhabitants of mount Seir, utterly to slay and destroy them: and when they had made an end of the inhabitants of Seir, every one helped to destroy another.

24 And when Judah came toward the watchtower in the wilderness, they looked to the multitude, and, behold, they were dead bodies fallen to the earth, and none had escaped.

25 And when Jehoshaphat and the people of Israel came to take away the spoil from them, they found among them an abundance of booty: riches, bridles, horses, and precious jewels, and they took for themselves whatever they desired.

26 ¶And it came to pass after three days, when they were through taking the spoil, because it was so much,

¹ Valley of Blessing.

they assembled themselves on the fourth day in the valley of Borktha; ¹ for there they blessed the LORD God; therefore the name of that place was called the valley of Borktha to this day.

27 Then all the men of Judah returned to Jerusalem with Jehoshaphat at their head, for they were returning to Jerusalem rejoicing; for the LORD had made them rejoice over their enemies.

28 And they came to Jerusalem with songs, harps, lyres, and curved and straight trumpets, to the house of the LORD.

29 And the fear of the LORD fell on all the kingdoms of those countries when they heard that the LORD had fought against the enemies of Israel.

30 So the realm of Jehoshaphat was quiet; for the LORD gave him rest on all sides.

31 ¶And Jehoshaphat reigned over Judah; he was thirty-five years old when he began to reign, and he reigned twenty-five years in Jerusalem. And his mother's name was Arubah the daughter of Shilhi.

32 And he walked in all the ways of Asa his father, and did not turn aside from them, doing that which was right in the sight of the LORD.

33 However the shrines on the high places were not removed; for as yet the people had not prepared their hearts to the God of their fathers.

34 Now the rest of the acts of Jehoshaphat, first and last, behold, they are written in the sayings of Jehu the son of Hanan, which are written in the Book of the Kings of Israel.

35 ¶And after this Jehoshaphat king of Judah joined himself with Ahaziah king of Israel, who did very wickedly, more than all the kings of Israel.

36 And he joined himself with him to make ships to go to Tarshish; and they made the ships in Ezion-gaber.

37 Then Eliezer the son of Jehoshaphat's uncle prophesied in the city of Mareshah against Jehoshaphat, saying, Because of your partnership with Ahaziah, the LORD has confused all

your works. And the ships were damaged and were not able to go to Tarshish.

CHAPTER 21

NOW Jehoshaphat slept with his fathers, and was buried with his fathers in the city of David. And Jehoram his son reigned in his stead.

2 And he had brothers, the sons of Jehoshaphat, and these are their names: Azariah, Nahjaiel, Zechariah, Azariah, Malchael, and Shephatiah; all these were the sons of Jehoshaphat king of Judah.

3 And their father gave them great gifts of silver and of gold, and many other gifts, with fortified cities in Judah; but the kingdom gave he to Jehoram because he was his first-born.

4 Now when Jehoram was risen up to the kingdom of his father, he strengthened himself and slew all his brothers in the battle and also slew some of the elders of Israel.

5 ¶Jehoram was thirty-two years old when he began to reign, and he reigned eight years in Jerusalem.

6 And he walked in the ways of the kings of Israel, as did the house of Ahab; for Ahab's sister was his wife; and he did that which was evil in the presence of the LORD.

7 However the LORD would not destroy the house of David, because of the covenant that he had made with David and because he had promised to give an heir to him and to his sons for ever.

8 ¶In his days the Edomites revolted from under the dominion of Judah, and made themselves a king.

9 Then Jehoram crossed over the Jordan with his princes, and all his chariots with him; and he rose up by night and smote the Edomites who had surrounded him and the captains of the chariots.

10 So the Edomites revolted from the dominion of Judah to this day. At the same time also did the Edomites who dwelt in Libnah revolt from his rule, because Jehoram had forsaken the LORD God of his fathers.

11 Moreover he made shrines on high places in the mountains of Judah and caused the Nazarites of Jerusalem to drink wine and scattered the house of Judah.

12 ¶And there was brought to him a letter from Elijah the prophet, saying, Thus says the LORD God of David your father: Because you have not walked in the ways of Jehoshaphat your father nor in the ways of Asa king of Judah,

13 But have walked in the ways of the kings of Israel and have caused Judah and the inhabitants of Jerusalem to go astray with the whoredoms of the house of Ahab, and also have slain your brothers, your father's sons, who were better than yourself;

14 Behold, the LORD will smite you with a great plague, together with your people, your children, your wives, and all your goods;

15 And you yourself shall die with a severe sickness; and you shall be consumed with a great torment until your bowels fall out because of your sickness. And you shall be tormented for many years.

16 ¶Moreover the LORD stirred up against Jehoram the spirit of the Philistines and of the Arabians who dwelt near the Ethiopians;

17 And they came up against Judah and smote it, and carried away all the substance that was found in the king's house, and his sons also and his wives; so that no son was left to him except Ahaziah his youngest son.

18 ¶And after all this he was smitten in his bowels with an incurable disease.

19 And it came to pass that in the process of time, after the end of two years, the word of the prophet was fulfilled, his bowels fell out because of his sickness; so he died of sore disease. And his people did not honor him with a funeral according to the manner they had done for his fathers.

20 He was thirty-two years old when he began to reign, and he reigned eight years in Jerusalem, and his departure was not regretted. And he was buried in the city of David his father, but not in the sepulchres of the kings.

CHAPTER 22

THEN the inhabitants of Jerusalem made Ahaziah his youngest son king in his stead; for raiders had come to the camp and slain all the eldest. So Ahaziah the son of Jehoram king of Judah reigned.

2 Twenty-two years old was Ahaziah when he began to reign, and he reigned one year in Jerusalem. His mother's name was Athaliah the daughter of Omri.

3 And he walked in the ways of the house of Ahab, for he was the son of Ahab's sister.

4 He also committed many sins and did evil in the sight of the LORD like the house of Ahab; for they were his counsellors after the death of his father to his destruction,

5 ¶Because he walked after their counsel, and went with Joram the son of Ahab king of Israel to war against Hazael king of Aram at Ramath-gilead; and the Arameans smote Joram.

6 And he returned to be healed in Jezreel because of the wounds which he had received at Ramtha, when he fought with Hazael king of Aram. And Ahaziah went down to see Joram the son of Ahab in Jezreel because he was sick.

7 And the destruction of Ahaziah was determined by God, who decreed that he should go to Joram; for when he was come, he went out with Joram to meet Jehu the son of Jamshi, whom the LORD had anointed to destroy the house of Ahab.

8 And when Jehu was executing judgment upon the house of Ahab, he found the princes of Judah and the sons of the brothers of Ahaziah who ministered to Ahaziah and slew them.

9 And he sought Ahaziah and he caught him (for he was hiding in Samaria) and brought him to Jehu; and when they had slain him, they buried him; for they said, He is the son of Jehoshaphat, who sought the LORD with all his heart. So the house of Ahaziah had no one with power to rule over the kingdom.

10 ¶Now when Athaliah the mother of Ahaziah saw that her son was dead, she arose and destroyed all the king's sons of the house of Judah.

11 But Jehoshabeath, the daughter of the king, stole Joash the son of Ahaziah from among the king's sons who were about to be slain, and hid him and his nurse in her bedchamber. So Jehoshabeath, the daughter of King Jehoram, the wife of Jehoiadah the priest (for she was the sister of Ahaziah), hid him from Athaliah so that she did not slay him.

12 And he was hid with her in the house of the LORD six years; and Athaliah reigned over the land.

CHAPTER 23

AND in the seventh year Jehoiadah strengthened himself and took the captains of hundreds, Azariah the son of Jeruham and Ishmael the son of Johanan and Azariah the son of Obed and Shemiah the son of Ido and Elishaphat the son of Zichri, and they made a covenant together.

2 And they went about in Judah and gathered the Levites from all the cities of Judah and the chiefs of the fathers of Israel, and they came to Jerusalem.

3 And all the congregation made a covenant in the presence of the king in the house of the LORD. And Jehoiadah said to them, Behold, the king's son shall reign over you, as the LORD has spoken to David his servant.

4 This is the thing that you shall do: a third part of you who enter the temple on the sabbath, of the priests and of the Levites and of the porters shall be on guard;

5 And a third part shall be at the king's house; and a third part at the cook's gate; and all the people shall be on guard in the court of the house of the LORD.

6 But let no one enter the house of the LORD except the priests and the Levites; they shall enter, for they are holy; but all the people shall keep watch over the house of the LORD.

7 And the Levites shall surround the king, every man with his weapons in his hand; and whosoever else enters

the inner house shall be put to death; but you be with the king when he comes in and when he goes out.

8 So the Levites and all Judah did according to all that Jehoiadah the priest had commanded, and every man took his men who were to keep watch on the sabbath, with those who were to go out on the sabbath; for Jehoiadah the priest had dismissed them from their duties.

9 Moreover Jehoiadah the priest delivered spears and bucklers and shields to the captains of hundreds that had been King David's, which were in the house of the LORD.

10 And all the people stood up, every man having his weapon in his hand, from the right side of the temple to the left side of the temple, along by the altar and the temple, and by the king round about.

11 Then they brought out the king's son and put the crown on his head, and gave him the sceptre and made him king. And Jehoiadah and his sons anointed him and said, Long live the king!

12 ¶Now when Athaliah heard the noise of the people rejoicing and praising the LORD, she came to the king into the house of the LORD;

13 And she looked, and, behold, the king stood by the pillar according to the rite of the kings, and the people were sounding with curved and straight trumpets before the king; and all the people were rejoicing and blowing trumpets, and the singers accompanied with instruments of music. Then Athaliah tore her clothes and said, Treason! Treason!

14 Then Jehoiadah the priest commanded the captains of hundreds who were set over the army and said to them, Take her out of the ranks, and whosoever follows her, let him be slain with the sword. For the priest said, Do not slay her in the house of the LORD.

15 Then they made a passage for her, and she went into the entrance of the horse gate, and she was put to death there.

16 ¶And Jehoiadah made a covenant between himself and all the people,

and between himself and the king, that they should be the LORD's people.

17 Then all the people went to the house of Baal and demolished it, and broke his altars and his images in pieces, and slew the priest of Baal before the altar.

18 Also Jehoiadah appointed officers in the house of the LORD, and the priests and the Levites, whom David had divided into groups, to be in charge of the house of the LORD, to offer burnt offerings to the LORD, as it is written in the law of Moses, with rejoicing and with singing, as it was ordained by David.

19 And he set the porters at the gates of the house of the LORD so that no one who was unclean in anything should enter in.

20 And he took the captains of hundreds and the governors of the people and all the people of the land, and they came through the high gate of the king's house and set the king upon the throne of the kingdom.

21 And all the people of the land rejoiced, sounding with trumpets, after they had slain Athaliah with the sword.

CHAPTER 24

JOASH was seven years old when he began to reign, and he reigned forty years in Jerusalem. His mother's name was Zibiah of the city of Beer-sheba.

2 And Joash did that which was right in the sight of the LORD all the days of Jehoiadah the priest.

3 And Jehoiadah the priest took for him two wives; and he begat sons and daughters.

4 ¶And it came to pass after this that Jehoiadah determined in his heart with Joash secretly to restore the house of the LORD and to repair everything that was needed in it.

5 And Jehoiadah the priest gathered together the priests and the Levites and said to them, Go out to the cities of Judah and gather from all the cities of Israel silver and gold to repair the house of your God from year to year, and see that you hasten the matter.

6 And the king called for Jehoiadah the chief priest and said to him, Why have you not required the Levites to go and bring in from Judah and from Jerusalem the gifts that were prescribed by Moses the servant of the LORD and summon the congregation of Israel for the feast of the tabernacle of the assembly?

7 For Athaliah taught wickedly, and had broken up the house of the LORD; and also given all the dedicated things that were in the house of the LORD for the worship of the idols.

8 And at the king's commandment, they made a chest, and set it outside the gate of the house of the LORD.

9 And they made a proclamation throughout Judah and Jerusalem to bring in to the LORD the portion that Moses the servant of the LORD laid upon Israel in the wilderness.

10 And all the princes and all the people rejoiced, and brought in gifts and took the chest and put it in its place and cast into it until it was full.

11 And when they saw that there was much money in the chest, then the king's scribe and the overseer of the high priest's house came and counted the money, and put it into bags.

12 And they gave it to those who did the work of the service of the house of the LORD, and hired masons and carpenters to repair the house of the LORD, and also workers in iron and brass to restore the house of the LORD.

13 So the workmen wrought, and the work was perfected by them, and they set the house of God in order and strengthened it.

14 And when they had finished it, they brought the rest of the money before the king and Jehoiadah, whereof were made vessels for the house of the LORD, even vessels to minister and to offer withal, and spoons, and vessels of gold and silver. And they offered burnt offerings in the house of the LORD continually all the days of Jehoiadah.

15 ¶But Jehoiadah grew old, and was full of days when he died; a hun-

dred and thirty years old was he when he died.

16 And they buried him in the city of David among the kings, and they said, Such shall be rewarded to him who does good in Israel. And he also had contributed greatly to the house of the LORD.

17 Now after the death of Jehoiadah came the princes of Judah, and made obeisance to the king. Then the king listened to them.

18 And they left the house of the LORD God of their fathers, and went and served images and idols; and wrath came upon Judah and Jerusalem because they committed this sin.

19 Yet God sent prophets to them to bring them back from their ways, but they would not listen, so the prophets testified against them, but they would not give ear.

20 And the Spirit of the LORD came upon Zechariah the son of Jehoiadah the priest, and he went up and stood above the people and said to them, Thus says the LORD: Why do you transgress the commandments of the LORD, that you cannot prosper? Because you have forsaken my way, I will also forsake you.

21 And they conspired against him, and stoned him with stones at the commandment of the king in the court of the house of the LORD.

22 Thus Joash the king did not remember the kindness which Jehoiadah his father had done to him, but he slew his sons after him. And when his sons were about to be slain, they said, May the LORD see and avenge it.

23 ¶And it came to pass at the end of the year, the army of Aram came up against him; and they came to Judah and Jerusalem, and destroyed all the princes of the people, and sent all their spoil to the king of Damascus.

24 For the army of Aram came with a small company of men, and the LORD delivered a very great army into their hand because they had forsaken the LORD God of their fathers. So what Joash had done was condemned by the judges.

25 And when they were departed from him (for they left him in a state

of severe illness), his own servants conspired against him for the blood of the sons of Jehoiadah the priest, and slew him on his bed, and he died; and they buried him in the city of David his father, but they did not bury him in the sepulchres of the kings.

26 And these are the names of those who conspired against him: Zaccor the son of Shimeath an Ammonitess and Jehozabad the son of Netoroth a Moabitess.

27 ¶And his sons also and many other people conspired against him. And the rest of the sins which he committed in the house of the LORD, behold, they are written in the poems of the Book of the Kings. And Amaziah his son reigned in his stead.

CHAPTER 25

AMAZIAH was twenty-five years old when he began to reign, and he reigned twenty-nine years in Jerusalem. And his mother's name was Jehoaddan of Jerusalem.

2 And he did that which was right in the sight of the LORD, but not with a perfect heart.

3 ¶Now it came to pass when the kingdom was strengthened in his hand, he slew his servants who had killed the king his father.

4 But he did not slay the children of the murderers, because so it is written in the book of the law of Moses, where the LORD commanded, saying, The fathers shall not die for the children, neither shall the children die for the fathers, but every man shall die for his own sin.

5 ¶Then Amaziah gathered Judah together and appointed over them commanders of thousands and captains of hundreds, according to the houses of their fathers, throughout all Judah and Benjamin; and he numbered them from twenty years old and above, and found that they were three hundred thousand young men, able to go forth to war, that could draw sword and handle shield.

6 He hired also a hundred thousand mighty men of valour from Israel for a hundred talents of silver.

7 But there came a prophet of the LORD to him, saying, O king, let not all the army of Israel go with you; for the LORD is not with all Israel, neither with all the house of Ephraim.

8 You are to engage in a great battle, and the LORD will cause you to fall before your enemies because you have not praised the LORD, for he is the helper and one who exalts.

9 And Amaziah said to the prophet of the LORD, What folly have I committed in giving the hundred talents to the men of Israel? And the prophet of God said to him, The LORD your God is able to give you much more than this, double what you have given.

10 Then Amaziah separated the men that had come to him from Ephraim, to go home again; wherefore his anger was greatly kindled against Israel. And he sent them back home in his great anger.

11 ¶And Amaziah strengthened himself and led forth his people, and went to the valley of salt and slew ten thousand of the men of mount Gebal.

12 And another ten thousand left alive, the children of Judah captured and brought to the top of the rocks, and all of them came bound in chains.

13 ¶And the valiant men whom Amaziah had carried captive when he went to war, he set over the cities of Judah, and over Samaria, and over the towns of the Gentiles; and they smote three thousand men of the towns and took much spoil.

14 ¶Now it came to pass after Amaziah was come from slaughter of the Edomites, they brought to him the gods of the men of mount Gebal, and he set them up before him and worshipped before them and burned incense to them.

15 Therefore the anger of the LORD was kindled against Amaziah, and he sent to him a prophet, who said to him, Why have you prayed before the gods of the Gentiles, which could not deliver their own people out of your hands?

16 And it came to pass, as the prophet conversed with him, he said to him, The worship of wooden idols has been taken up by the kings.

Then the prophet withdrew from him, and said to him, Woe to you! for, behold, the LORD has determined to destroy you because you have done this and have not listened to my counsel.

17 ¶Then Amaziah king of Judah took counsel, and sent to Joash, the son of Jehoahaz, the son of Jehu, king of Israel, saying, Come, let us face each other in battle.

18 But Joash king of Israel sent to Amaziah king of Judah, saying, The thistle that is in Lebanon sent to the cedar that is in Lebanon, saying, Give your daughter to my son to wife; and there passed by a wild beast that was in Lebanon and trampled down the thistle.

19 Surely, because you have defeated the Edomites, your heart has lifted you up to boast; keep your dignity and stay at home; why should you stir up trouble, that you should fall, even you and all Judah with you?

20 But Amaziah would not listen; then Joash king of Israel and Amaziah king of Judah went up

21 And confronted each other in battle, at the town of Beth-shemesh, which is in the border of the land of Judah.

22 And Judah was defeated before Israel; and they fled every man to his tent.

23 And Joash the king of Israel captured Amaziah king of Judah in the town of Beth-shemesh, and brought him to Jerusalem, and broke down the wall of Jerusalem from the gate of Ephraim to the corner gate, four hundred cubits.

24 And he took all the silver and the gold and all the vessels that were found in the house of God, together with the vessels that were kept by Ober-edom, and the treasures of the king's house and the vessels of the king's house and the vessels of gold, and returned to Samaria.

25 ¶And Amaziah the son of Joash king of Judah lived after the death of Joash son of Jehoahaz king of Israel fifteen years.

26 Now the rest of the acts of Amaziah, first and last, behold, they are written in the Book of the Kings of Judah and Israel.

27 ¶Now from the time that Amaziah turned away from following the LORD, his servants made a conspiracy against him in Jerusalem; and he fled to Lachish; but they sent to Lachish after him, and slew him there.

28 And his servants brought him upon horses, and buried him with his fathers in the city of David.

CHAPTER 26

THEN all the people of Judah took Uzziah his son, who was sixteen years old, and made him king instead of his father Amaziah.

2 He built Eloth, and restored it to Judah after the king slept with his fathers.

3 Uzziah was sixteen years old when he began to reign, and he reigned fifty-two years in Jerusalem. His mother's name was Jeconiah of Jerusalem.

4 And he did that which was right in the sight of the LORD, according to all that his father David did.

5 And he prayed before the LORD in the days of Zechariah, who taught him in the worship of the LORD, and the LORD prospered all his ways.

6 And he went forth and made war against the Philistines, and broke down the wall of Gath and the wall of Gaza and the wall of Ashdod.

7 And God helped him against the Philistines and against the Arabians that dwelt in Gurbaal and the Mehunims.

8 And his fame spread as far as the land of Egypt; for he continued to fight.

9 Moreover Uzziah built towers in Jerusalem at the corner gate and at the western gate, and fortified them with iron bars.

10 He also built many towers in the cities which he had, and he built for himself many castles; for he had much wealth; and had farmers and workers both in the plains and on the mountains, because he had much cattle.

11 Moreover Uzziah had an army of mighty men that went out to war.

Their number was thirty-two thousand and six hundred.

12 And the others who dwelt in the open country were three hundred thousand; and the men who were girded with sword were seven thousand and five hundred,

13 Who stood up every day guarding the king.

14 And Uzziah prepared for them, throughout all the host, shields and spears and helmets and breastplates and bows and slings to cast stones.

15 And his fame spread throughout all the lands, until he became very rich.

16 ¶But when he became very rich, his pride was lifted up exceedingly, so he transgressed against the LORD his God and went into the temple of the LORD to burn incense upon the altar of incense.

17 And Azariah the priest went in after him and said to him,

18 It is not your place, O king, nor have you the right to burn incense upon the altar.

19 Then immediately King Uzziah's anger kindled against the priests, and he commanded to put them out of the sanctuary; and in that hour the leprosy went forth out of the sanctuary and fell on the forehead of King Uzziah as he entered to burn incense in the house of the LORD.

20 And Azariah the chief priest, and all the priests, turned toward him, and, behold, he hastened to go out because he knew that the LORD had smitten him.

21 And Uzziah the king was a leper to the day of his death, and dwelt in a house in solitude, being a leper; for he had blasphemed against the house of the LORD; and Jotham his son was over the king's house, judging the people of the land.

22 ¶Now the rest of the acts of Uzziah, first and last, behold, they are written by Isaiah the prophet, the son of Amoz.

23 So Uzziah slept with his fathers, and they buried him in the cemetery, not in the burial place which belonged to the kings; for they said, He is a leper; and Jotham his son reigned in his stead.

CHAPTER 27

JOTHAM was twenty-five years old when he began to reign, and he reigned sixteen years in Jerusalem. His mother's name was Jerushah, the daughter of Zadok.

2 And he did that which was right in the sight of the LORD, according to all that his father Uzziah had done; howbeit he neglected to enter into the temple of the LORD, and the people were still corrupt.

3 He built the upper gate of the house of the LORD, and completed the wall and improved it.

4 Moreover he built cities in the land of Judah, and in the forests he built castles and towers.

5 ¶He fought also with the Ammonites, and prevailed against them. And the Ammonites gave him that year a hundred talents of silver and ten thousand measures of wheat and ten thousand measures of barley. The Ammonites gave to him the same amount in the second year and in the third year.

6 So Jotham became mighty because he established his ways before the LORD his God.

7 ¶Now the rest of the acts of Jotham and all his wars and his ways, behold, they are written in the Book of the Kings of Israel and Judah.

8 He was twenty-five years old when he began to reign, and reigned sixteen years in Jerusalem.

9 ¶And Jotham slept with his fathers, and they buried him in the city of David; and Ahaz his son reigned in his stead.

CHAPTER 28

AHAZ was twenty-five years old when he began to reign, and he reigned sixteen years in Jerusalem; and he did not do that which was right in the sight of the LORD his God, like David his father;

2 But he walked in the ways of the kings of Israel, and also made altars for the idols.

3 Moreover he burned incense in great valleys, and passed his son through the fire, according to the cus-

tom of the nations whom the LORD had destroyed from before the children of Israel.

4 And he sacrificed also and burned incense upon the altars and on high places and under every beautiful tree.

5 Therefore the LORD God delivered him into the hand of the king of Aram; and he smote him with a great slaughter, and carried away a great multitude of people captive and brought them to Damascus. And he was also delivered into the hand of the king of Israel, who smote him with a great slaughter.

6 ¶For Pekah the son of Romaliah slew from the army of the king of Judah a hundred and twenty thousand in one day, all valiant men, because they had forsaken the LORD God of their fathers.

7 And Zichri, a mighty man of Ephraim slew Maasiah the king's son and Azrikai the governor of the palace and Elkanah who was next to the king.

8 And the children of Israel carried away captive of their brethren two hundred thousand and their sons and their daughters, and also took away much spoil from them, and brought the spoil to Samaria.

9 But a prophet of the LORD was there, whose name was Ado; and he went out before the army that came to Samaria, and said to them, Behold, because the LORD God of our fathers was angry with Judah, he has delivered them into your hands, and you have slain them and had no pity on them.

10 And now you purpose to make them menservants and maidservants to yourself, and even now you know that you have committed this sin in the presence of the LORD your God.

11 Now hear me, therefore, and send back those whom you have taken captive from your brethren, lest the fierce wrath of the LORD come upon you.

12 Then certain of the chiefs of the Ephraimites, Azariah the son of Johanan and Berechiah the son of Mekariah, stood up against them who came from the war,

13 And said to them, You shall not bring these captives here, that we may not sin again against the LORD our God; you intend to add more to our trespass and to our sins; for our sins are exceedingly great.

14 So they sent back all the captives to Jerusalem. But again they dealt deceitfully with the LORD.

15 And the men who were expressed by name [1] rose up, and took the captives, and with the spoil clothed all that were naked among them, and arrayed them and shod them, and gave them to eat and to drink, and anointed them, and carried all the feeble of them upon asses, and brought them to Jericho, the city of palm trees, to their brethren; then they returned to Samaria.

16 ¶At that time King Ahaz asked the king of Assyria to help him,

17 For until this time the Edomites came and smote Judah and carried away captives.

18 And the Philistines also had come and besieged the cities of the low country, and of the south of Judah, and had captured the town of Beth-shemesh and the town of Ajalon and the town of Azoroth and Shob with its villages and Timnah with its villages and Geram with its villages.

19 For the LORD brought Judah low because of the sins of Ahaz king of Judah; for he increased iniquity in Judah and transgressed grievously against the LORD.

20 And Tiglath-pilezer king of Assyria came against him, and encamped against him and distressed him greatly.

21 And King Ahaz took away the vessels that were in the house of the LORD and the vessels that were in the houses of former kings and in the houses of rich men, and gave them to the king of Assyria, that he might not harm him in the time of his distress.

22 ¶But they transgressed still more against the LORD: this same King Ahaz.

[1] The chiefs.

23 For he sacrificed to the gods of Damascus, saying, You are my gods and my lords; to you will I offer worship and to you will I make sacrifice; thus he was a stumbling block to Judah, he sinned and caused all the people of Judah to sin.

24 And Ahaz gathered together all the vessels of the house of the LORD, and cut in pieces the vessels that were in the house of the LORD, and shut up the inner and the outer doors of the house of the LORD, and he made for himself altars in every corner of Jerusalem.

25 And in every village and hamlet of Judah he made an altar to serve other gods.

26 ¶Now the rest of the acts of Ahaz and all his ways, first and last, behold, they are written in the Book of the Kings of Judah and Israel.

27 And Ahaz slept with his fathers, and they buried him in Jerusalem; for they did not bring him into the sepulchres of the kings of Judah; and Hezekiah his son reigned in his stead.

CHAPTER 29

HEZEKIAH began to reign when he was twenty-five years old, and he reigned twenty-nine years in Jerusalem. And his mother's name was Ani, the daughter of Zechariah.

2 And he did that which was right in the sight of the LORD, just as David his father had done.

3 ¶In the first year of his reign, in the first month, he opened the doors of the house of the LORD, and repaired them.

4 And he brought in the priests and the Levites, and gathered them together into the court of the sanctuary,

5 And said to them, Hear me, O Levites, sanctify now yourselves and sanctify the house of the LORD God of our fathers, and remove your evil works from your mind,

6 So that we may not do according to that which our fathers have done, for they did evil in the sight of the LORD our God, and have forsaken him and have turned away their faces from the habitation of the LORD, and turned their backs.

7 Also they have shut up the doors of the porches and put out the lamps, and have not burned incense nor offered burnt offerings upon the altar of the God of Israel.

8 Therefore the wrath of the LORD came upon Judah and Jerusalem, and he has delivered them to curse, to desolation, and to sword, as you see with your own eyes.

9 For, lo, our fathers have fallen by the sword, and our sons and our daughters and our wives are in captivity for this.

10 And even now, because we have gone astray from following the LORD our God and have forsaken the covenant which he gave to our fathers, therefore he also has forsaken us.

11 My sons, be not now negligent; for the LORD has chosen you to stand before him, to serve him and to minister unto him and burn incense.

12 ¶Then the Levites arose, Mahath the son of Amasai and Joel the son of Azariah, of the sons of the Kohathites; and of the sons of Merari, Kish the son of Abdi and Azariah the son of Jehalelel; and of the Gershonites, Joah the son of Zimmah and Eden the son of Joah;

13 And of the sons of Elzaphan, Shimri and Jeiel; and of the sons of Asaph, Zechariah and Mattaniah;

14 And of the sons of Heman, Jehiel and Shimei; and of the sons of Jeruthun, Shemaiah and Uzziel.

15 And they gathered their brethren, and sanctified themselves, and came, according to the commandment of the king by the words of the LORD to cleanse the house of the LORD.

16 And the priests went into the inner part of the house of the LORD, to cleanse it, and brought out all the uncleanness that they found in the temple of the LORD into the court of the house of the LORD. And the Levites took it to carry it out into the brook Kidron.

17 Now they began on the first day of the first month to sanctify, and on the eighth day of the month came they to the porch of the LORD; so

they sanctified the house of the LORD in eight days, and in the sixteenth day of the first month they made an end.

18 Then they went in to Hezekiah the king, and said, We have cleansed all the house of the LORD and the altar of burnt offering with all the vessels thereof, and the shewbread table with all the vessels thereof.

19 Moreover all the vessels which King Ahaz in his reign did cast away in his transgression have we prepared and sanctified, and, behold, they are before the altar of the LORD.

20 ¶Then Hezekiah the king rose early and gathered the elders of Jerusalem, and went up to the house of the LORD.

21 And they brought to him seven bullocks, seven rams, seven lambs, and seven he-goats for an atonement for the kingdom and for Judah and for the sanctuary. And he commanded the priests, the sons of Aaron, to offer them on the altar of the LORD

22 And to kill the bullocks, and commanded the priests to receive the blood and sprinkle it on the horns of the altar;

23 And to bring forth the he-goats before the LORD and before the king and before the congregation of Israel, and to lay hands upon them;

24 And that the priests should kill them and sprinkle their blood upon the horns of the altar to make an atonement for all Israel; for the king had commanded that all Israel should bring burnt offerings and sacrifices.

25 And he set the Levites in the house of the LORD with cymbals, with psalteries, and with the songs of David, and with the songs of Gad the prophet of King David and of Nathan the prophet of King David; for David used to sing the songs of the LORD his God as they were sung by the mouth of the prophets.

26 And the Levites stood singing the songs of David, and the priests sounded with curved and straight trumpets.

27 Then Hezekiah commanded to offer the burnt offerings upon the altar. And when the burnt offerings began, Hezekiah also began to sing the songs of the LORD, according to the songs of David king of Israel.

28 And all the congregation of Israel worshipped and sang songs and sounded with the curved and straight trumpets until the burnt offerings were finished.

29 And when they had made an end of offering, the king and all that were present with him knelt and worshipped.

30 Moreover Hezekiah the king and the princes commanded the Levites to sing praises to the LORD with the words of David and of Asaph the prophet. And they sang praises with gladness, and they bowed down and worshipped.

31 Then Hezekiah answered and said, Now you have consecrated yourselves to the way of the LORD; come near and bring sacrifices and thank offerings into the house of the LORD. And the people brought in sacrifices and thank offerings; everything which their hearts desired, they brought in.

32 And the number of the burnt offerings which the people brought was seventy bullocks, a hundred rams, and two hundred lambs; all these were for a burnt offering to the LORD.

33 And the consecrated things were six hundred oxen and three thousand sheep.

34 But the priests were too few, so that they could not slay all the burnt offerings; therefore their brethren, the Levites, helped them until the work was finished, and after this the priests sanctified themselves; for the Levites were meek in their hearts to sanctify themselves more than the priests.

35 And also the burnt offerings were in abundance, with the fat of the peace offerings and of the lambs for the burnt offerings. So the service of the house of the LORD was set in order.

36 And Hezekiah rejoiced, and all the people of Israel, because the service of the temple was accomplished; for the thing was done promptly.

CHAPTER 30

AND Hezekiah sent to all Israel and Judah, and wrote letters also to Ephraim and Manasseh, that they should come to the house of the LORD at Jerusalem to keep the passover to the LORD God of Israel.

2 For the king and his princes and all the congregation of Israel who were in Jerusalem had taken counsel to celebrate the passover to the LORD God of Israel in the second month.

3 For they could not keep it at the appointed time because the priests had not sanctified themselves, neither had the instructors of the people gathered themselves together to Jerusalem.

4 And the thing pleased the king and all the people of Israel.

5 So they confirmed a decree to carry it out; and they made a proclamation throughout all Israel from Beer-sheba even to Dan that they should come to celebrate the passover to the LORD God of Israel at Jerusalem; for they were exceedingly rich.

6 So the couriers went with the letters from the king and his princes throughout all Israel and Judah, and by the command of the king, saying, O you children of Israel, turn again to the LORD God of Abraham, Isaac, and Israel, and he will return to the remnant of you who have escaped from the hands of the king of Assyria.

7 And be not like your fathers and like your brethren who trespassed against the LORD God of our fathers so that he gave them up to desolation, as you see.

8 Now do not be stiffnecked as your fathers were, but enter into the sanctuary which he has sanctified for ever, and serve the LORD your God, that the fierceness of his wrath may turn away from you.

9 Because he has revealed himself to you, your children, and your brethren; and he shall grant you compassion before those who carry you captive, and shall bring you back to this land; for the LORD your God is gracious and merciful, and will not turn away his face from you when you return to him.

10 So the couriers of King Hezekiah passed from village to village throughout the land of Ephraim and Manasseh and as far as Zebulun;

11 But some of the wicked men, who were in the tribe of Asher, the tribe of Ephraim, the tribe of Manasseh, and the tribe of Zebulun, laughed them to scorn and mocked them.

12 Nevertheless the rest of the men of these tribes humbled themselves and came to Jerusalem with the tribe of Judah. And the hand of God was upon them to give them one heart to do the commandment of the king and of his princes, according to the word of the LORD.

13 ¶And there assembled at Jerusalem many people to celebrate the feast of unleavened bread in the second month, a very great congregation.

14 And they arose and demolished the altars that were in Jerusalem, and they destroyed all the shrines of idols and cast them into the brook Kidron.

15 Then they celebrated the passover on the fourteenth day of the second month; and the priests and the Levites sanctified themselves and brought in burnt offerings to the house of the LORD.

16 And they stood in their places after their manner, as it is written in the law of Moses the prophet of the LORD; the priests sprinkled the blood which they received from the hand of the Levites.

17 For there were many in the congregation of Israel who had not sanctified themselves; therefore the Levites had charge of the killing of the passover lambs, and they saw that every one was clean, to sanctify him to the LORD;

18 For there were a great many people in the assembly of Israel, from Ephraim, Manasseh, Issachar, and Zebulun, the four tribes, who had not cleansed themselves, yet they ate the passover unlawfully. But Hezekiah prayed for them, saying, May the good LORD pardon all the people of Israel,

19 For we have prepared our hearts to pray to the LORD God of our fathers, and sanctification would not purify us any more.

20 And the LORD hearkened to the voice of Hezekiah, and healed the people.

21 And the children of Israel that were present in Jerusalem kept the feast of unleavened bread seven days with great gladness; and the Levites and the priests praised the LORD day by day, singing songs of praise.

22 And Hezekiah spoke to all the Levites who were singing good songs before the LORD; and they ate throughout the feast seven days, offering peace offerings and making confession to the LORD God of their fathers.

23 And the whole assembly stayed over to celebrate another seven days; and they kept the other seven days with gladness.

24 For Hezekiah king of Judah gave to the assembly seven thousand of the choicest oxen, large and small, and also gave to the assembly of Israel a thousand of the choicest bullocks, and ten thousand sheep; and a great number of priests sanctified themselves.

25 And all the congregation of Judah, with the priests and the Levites, and all the congregation that came out of Israel, and the proselytes who came out of the land of Israel, and those who dwelt in Judah, rejoiced.

26 So there was great joy in Jerusalem; for since the time of Solomon the son of David king of Israel, there had been nothing like this in Jerusalem.

27 ¶Then the priests and the Levites arose and blessed the people of Israel; and the LORD heard their voice, and their prayer came up to his holy dwelling place, even to heaven.

CHAPTER 31

NOW when all this was finished, all Israel who were present went out to the cities of Judah, and broke the images in pieces and cut down the leopard statues and demolished the shrines and the altars that were in Judah and Benjamin and in Ephraim and Manasseh, until they had utterly destroyed them all. Then the Israelites returned, every man to his possession; and they entered in peace into their own cities.

2 ¶And Hezekiah appointed the times of serving of the priests and the Levites according to their divisions, every man according to his service, the priests and the Levites for burnt offerings and for peace offerings, to minister and to give thanks and to praise in the gates of the temple of the LORD.

3 And the king gave of his own substance oxen for the morning and evening burnt offerings, and the burnt offerings for the sabbaths and for the new moons and for the set feasts, as it is written in the law of the LORD.

4 Moreover he commanded the people who dwelt in Jerusalem to give the portion due to the priests and the Levites, that they might be encouraged in the law of the LORD.

5 ¶And as soon as the commandment was published in Israel, they brought the first fruits of grain, wine, oil, and of their cattle, and of the produce of the field; and the tithe of all things they brought in abundantly.

6 And the children of Israel and Judah who dwelt in the cities of Judah also brought in gifts and offered them to the LORD their God. And they brought in tithes upon tithes of grain, of wine, and of their cattle, and of the produce of the field. They brought the tithes and consecrated them to the LORD their God.

7 In the third month they began to lay the foundation of the tithe supplies, and in the seventh month Hezekiah took it and distributed it among the priests and the Levites.

8 And when Hezekiah and the princes saw that the tithe of the priests was so abundant, they blessed the LORD and prayed for Israel.

9 Then Hezekiah prayed for the priests and for the Levites concerning the abundance of the tithe.

10 And he called for Azariah the chief priest of the house of Zadok

and said to him, This tithe is ready for you, to be eaten, because it has been brought into the house of the LORD, now you can eat and be filled, and what is left of it, give it to the poor and to the fatherless, for the LORD has blessed his people and has given them this abundance. And what is left, give it to all the people of Israel.

11 ¶Then Hezekiah commanded that storehouses be prepared in the house of the LORD; and they prepared them,

12 And they brought in the tithes and the dedicated things faithfully; over them Cononiah the Levite was overseer and Shimei his brother was the next.

13 And Nehiel, Uzziah, Nahath, Ashail, Jerimoth, Jozabar, Eliel, Ismachiah, Matah, Benaiah, and Shemiah his brother were overseers under the hand of Cononiah, at the command of Hezekiah the king and Azariah the ruler of the house of the LORD.

14 And Kariah the son of Imnah the Levite, the porter of the east gate, was over the freewill offerings of the LORD and over the most holy things.

15 And next to him were Eden, Benjamin, Jeshua, Shemaiah, Amariah, and Shecaniah, in the cities of the priests, in their set office, to distribute portions to their brethren, to the great and small alike;

16 Besides that which is due to the males from three years old and upward, even to every one who entered into the house of the LORD, their daily portion for their service in their duties according to their divisions;

17 And oil and wine were given to the priests and the Levites according to the house of their fathers, from twenty years old and upward, in their charges by their divisions;

18 And oil was given for their lanterns, to their wives, their sons, and their daughters, and to all the congregation of Israel, for in their set office they sanctified themselves faithfully.

19 For the sons of Aaron the priest were holy, their flesh was holy, and they never touched women; and they went about in every village and suburb, men whose names were well known, to give portions to all the males among the priests and to all that were reckoned by the genealogies among the Levites.

20 ¶And thus did Hezekiah throughout all Judah, and he did that which was good and right, and walked in truth before the LORD.

21 And in every work that he began to do in the house of the LORD, and in the law and in the commandments, to seek his God, he did it with all his heart and prospered.

CHAPTER 32

AFTER these things and the faithful acts which Hezekiah did, Sennacherib king of Assyria came and invaded Judah and encamped against the fortified cities, and said to their inhabitants, Give me a pledge and come to me.

2 And when Hezekiah saw that Sennacherib king of Assyria and his armies had come to fight against Jerusalem,

3 He took counsel with his princes and his mighty men to conceal the waters of the fountains which were outside the city; and they did help him.

4 So there was gathered a great multitude of the people of Israel together, who concealed all the fountains and the great brooks that ran through the midst of the land, saying, Lest the king of Assyria come and find much water.

5 They also strengthened themselves and built up one wall opposite the other and polluted the canal which David had constructed. And Hezekiah made weapons, shields, and spears in abundance.

6 And he set captains of war over the people, each one over ten, and gathered them together to him in the market place of the city, and spoke to all of them, saying,

7 Be strong and courageous; do not be afraid nor dismayed in the pres-

ence of the king of Assyria, nor in the presence of all the armies that have come with him; for there is more with us than with him:

8 With him is an arm of flesh; with us is the LORD our God to help us and to fight our battles. And the people were encouraged with the words of Hezekiah king of Judah.

9 ¶After this Sennacherib king of Assyria sent Rab-shakey together with his servants, and they came to Jerusalem (but he himself was besieging Lachish, and all his commanders with him) to all the people of Judah that were in Jerusalem, saying,

10 Thus says Sennacherib king of Assyria: On whom are you trusting, that you remain in Jerusalem during the siege?

11 Hezekiah is deceiving you that he may give you over to die by famine and by thirst, and moreover he is misleading you, saying, The LORD our God shall deliver us out of the hands of the king of Assyria.

12 Has not the same Hezekiah removed his high places and altars, and commanded Judah and the inhabitants of Jerusalem, saying, You shall worship before one altar and burn incense upon it?

13 Perhaps you know what I and my fathers have done to all the people of other lands? And the gods of nations of those lands were not able to deliver their lands out of my hand.

14 Who is there among all the gods of those nations that my fathers utterly destroyed that was able to deliver his people out of my hand, that the LORD should be able to deliver you out of my hand?

15 Now therefore do not let Hezekiah deceive you nor make you to trust in this, and do not believe him; for your God will not be able to deliver you out of my hand; for all nations and kingdoms have not been able to deliver their cities out of my hand, and out of the hands of my fathers; your God also will not be able to deliver you out of my hand.

16 And his servants spoke these things before the LORD God of Israel

¹ Aramaic or Hebrew dialect spoken by the Jews.

and in the presence of his servant Hezekiah.

17 And he wrote letters to revile the LORD God of Israel, and to speak to the people of Israel, saying, As the gods of the nations of these lands were unable to deliver their cities out of my hand, so shall not the God of Hezekiah be able to deliver his city out of my hand.

18 Then they cried with a loud voice in the Jewish language ¹ to the people who were seated on the wall of Jerusalem, to frighten them and to trouble them, that they might capture the wall of the city.

19 And they spoke in the name of the gods of the people of the earth and also in the name of the God of Jerusalem, imploring him to reward them according to the work of their hands.

20 Then Hezekiah and Isaiah the son of Amoz, the prophet, prayed because of this, and the LORD heard the voice of their prayer.

21 ¶And the LORD sent an angel from before him, who smote all the mighty men of valour and the kings and the princes who were in the camp of the king of Assyria. So the king of Assyria returned in disgrace to his own land. And when he came into the house of his gods, his sons, who came forth of his own loins, slew him there with the sword.

22 Thus the LORD saved Hezekiah and the inhabitants of Jerusalem from the hands of Sennacherib the king of Assyria and from the hand of all of those who invaded their borders.

23 And many of the children of Israel brought gifts to the LORD to Jerusalem, and gave presents to Hezekiah king of Judah, so that he was exalted before all nations.

24 ¶In those days Hezekiah was sick to death, and he prayed before the LORD and said, Thou hast performed mighty miracles for me and thou hast rewarded me according to the works of my hands.

25 And the sickness of Hezekiah was due to the pride of his heart; therefore the wrath of the LORD came

upon him and upon Judah and Jerusalem.

26 But Hezekiah humbled himself for the pride of his heart, both he and the inhabitants of Jerusalem, so that the wrath of the LORD did not come upon them in the days of Hezekiah.

27 ¶And Hezekiah had exceeding great wealth and honor; and he made for himself treasuries for silver and for gold and for precious stones and for spices and for shields and for all manner of pleasant vessels;

28 Storehouses also for the increase of grain and wine and oil; and stalls for all kinds of beasts;

29 And folds for herds and for flocks, and for oxen and other beasts; for the LORD had given him very much substance.

30 This same Hezekiah also buried the outlet for the waters of the upper spring and brought it straight down to the western cistern of the city of David. And Hezekiah prospered in all his works.

31 ¶And he sought the law of the LORD, as it was given in the land, and the LORD knew all that was in his heart.

32 ¶Now the rest of the acts of Hezekiah, and his goodness and his excellent ways, behold, they are written in the prophecy of Isaiah the prophet, the son of Amoz, and in the Book of the Kings of Judah and Israel.

33 And Hezekiah slept with his fathers, and they buried him in the city of David; and all Judah and the inhabitants of Jerusalem did him honor at his death, and they returned to Jerusalem. And Manasseh his son reigned in his stead.

CHAPTER 33

MANASSEH was twelve years old when he began to reign, and he reigned fifty-five years in Jerusalem;

2 And he did that which was evil in the sight of the LORD, according to the works of the nations which the LORD had destroyed before the children of Israel.

3 ¶For he built again the altars which Hezekiah his father had broken down, and he built shrines for the idols and made images of leopards, and worshipped them.

4 Moreover he worshipped all the host of heaven in the two courts of the house of the LORD.

5 And he built altars for all the host of heaven in the two courts of the house of the LORD.

6 And he also caused his son to pass through the fire in the great valley; and he practiced augury and soothsaying and sorcery, and inquired of the Chaldeans and of familiar spirits; and he did much evil in the sight of the LORD, to provoke him to anger.

7 And he set the image of the idol which had four faces, which he had made, in the house of the LORD, of which the LORD had said to David and to Solomon his son, In this house and in Jerusalem, which I have chosen for myself out of all the tribes of Israel, will I put my name for ever;

8 Neither will I any more remove the children of Israel from this land which I have given to their fathers; if only they will take heed to do all that I have commanded them, according to the whole law and my statutes and my ordinances which my servant Moses commanded them.

9 So Manasseh caused Judah and the inhabitants of Jerusalem to go astray and to do evil works like the nations which the LORD had destroyed before the children of Israel.

10 And the LORD spoke to Manasseh and to his people; but they would not hearken.

11 ¶Therefore the LORD brought against them the commanders of the army of the king of Assyria, who captured Manasseh alive and bound him with chains and carried him to Babylon.

12 But when he was in distress, he prayed before the LORD his God and reverenced greatly the LORD God of his fathers,

13 And he prayed before the LORD, and he heard his voice and heard his prayer, and brought him back to Jerusalem into his kingdom. Then Manasseh knew that the LORD was God.

14 Now after this he built an outer

wall to the city of David on the west side of the brook of Gihon to the entrance of the fish gate, and encircled the whole of Jerusalem with an outer wall and raised it up a very great height, and he appointed commanders of the army in all the fortified cities of Judah.

15 And he took away the strange gods and the idols out of the house of the LORD, and all the altars that he had built in the mount of the house of the LORD and in Jerusalem, and cast them out of the city.

16 And he built an altar to the LORD, and sacrificed upon it burnt offerings and peace offerings and thank offerings, and commanded Judah to keep the feast to the LORD God of Israel;

17 And not to sacrifice again to strange gods, nor to offer burnt offerings to them, but before the LORD their God only.

18 ¶Now the rest of the acts of Manasseh and his prayer to his God and the words of the prophets who prophesied concerning him in the name of the LORD God of Israel, behold, they are written in the Book of the Kings of Israel and Judah.

19 His prayer, also, and how the LORD heard his voice, and all his sins and his iniquity, and the places on which he built altars and appointed priests, and the shrines he built for the idols, behold, they are written among the sayings of Hanan the prophet.

20 ¶So Manasseh slept with his fathers, and they buried him in his own house, in the garden of the treasury; and Amon his son reigned in his stead.

21 ¶And Amon was twenty-two years old when he began to reign, and he reigned two years in Jerusalem.

22 And he did that which was evil in the sight of the LORD, as Manasseh his father had done; for Amon sacrificed to all the images and idols which Manasseh his father had made and worshipped them;

23 And he did not humble himself before the LORD his God, for Manasseh humbled himself before the LORD his God; but Amon committed sins more and more.

24 And his servants conspired against him and slew him in his own house.

25 ¶But the people of the land slew all those who had conspired against King Amon; and the people of the land made Josiah his son king in his stead.

CHAPTER 34

JOSIAH was eight years old when he began to reign, and he reigned thirty-one years in Jerusalem.

2 And he did that which was right in the sight of the LORD, and walked in the ways of David his father, and he turned neither to the right hand nor to the left.

3 ¶For in the eighth year of his reign, while he was still a little boy, he began to pray to the LORD the God of David his father; and in the twelfth year he began to purge Judah and the inhabitants of Jerusalem. Moreover he began to demolish altars, idols, carved images, and idol temples,

4 And the decorations, necklaces, bells, and all the trees that were made for idols, he broke in pieces and ground them to dust and scattered their ashes upon the graves of those who had sacrificed to them.

5 And the bones of the priests who served them, he dug out of their graves and brought them and burned them, and cleansed Judah and Jerusalem.

6 And so did he in the cities of Manasseh and Ephraim and Simeon and Naphtali, in their streets round about.

7 And when he had broken down the altars and smashed in pieces the images, and ground them into dust and scattered it throughout all the land of Israel, he returned to Jerusalem.

8 ¶Now in the eighteenth year of his reign, when he had purged the land of Israel and his own house, he sent for Shaphan the son of Azaliah and Maasiah the scribe of the city,

and said to them, Go, repair the house of the LORD your God.

9 And when they came to Hilkiah the high priest, they delivered the money that was brought into the house of the LORD, which the Levites the keepers of the doors had collected from Manasseh and Ephraim and from all the remnant of Israel and from all Judah and Benjamin and from all the inhabitants of Jerusalem.

10 And they delivered it into the hands of the workmen who had the oversight of the house of the LORD, and they gave it to the workmen who did the work in the house of the LORD, to repair and to plaster the house;

11 And they gave it also to the carpenters and to the masons and to those who bought precious stones and timber for the repairing and for the plastering of the house which the kings of Judah had destroyed.

12 And the men did the work of the sanctuary faithfully; and the overseers over them were Nahat and Obadiah, the Levites, of the sons of Merari; and Zechariah and Shallum, of the sons of the Kohathites, and the singers and the Levites who played with the instruments of music,

13 And all those who did the work in any manner of service; and of the Levites there were scribes and officers and porters who acted as overseers.

14 ¶And when they carried out the money that had been brought into the house of the LORD, Hilkiah the priest found a book of the law of the LORD given by Moses.

15 And Hilkiah the priest said to Shaphan the scribe, I have found the book of the law in the house of the LORD. And Hilkiah the priest gave the book to Shaphan.

16 And Shaphan the scribe told the king what Hilkiah had told him, and brought him word, saying, All that you have committed to your servants, they do.

17 And they have spent the money for the repair of the house of the LORD, and have given account to the overseers and to the workmen.

18 Then Shaphan the scribe told the king, saying, Hilkiah the priest has given me a book. And Shaphan read it before the king.

19 And it came to pass when the king had heard the words of the law, he tore his clothes.

20 Then the king commanded Hilkiah and Ahikam the son of Shaphan and Abchor the son of Micah and Shaphan the scribe and Asaiah the steward of the king's household, saying,

21 Go, pray before the LORD for me and for the people of Israel and Judah concerning the words of this book that is found; for great is the wrath of the LORD that is poured out upon us, because our fathers have not hearkened to the words of the LORD to do after all that is written concerning us in this book.

22 So Hilkiah and those whom the king had appointed, went to Huldi the prophetess, the wife of Shallum the son of Tikvah, the son of Hisdah the keeper of the vessels (now she dwelt in Jerusalem in meditation) and they spoke to her according to the king's command.

23 ¶And she said to them, Thus says the LORD God of Israel: Tell the man who sent you to me,

24 Thus says the LORD: Behold, I will bring evil upon this place and upon its inhabitants, even all the curses that are written in the book which they have read before the king of Judah,

25 Because they have forsaken me and have worshipped other gods and have provoked me to anger with the works of their hands; therefore my wrath shall be poured out upon this place, and shall not be quenched.

26 And as for the king of Judah, who sent you to inquire of the LORD, so shall you say to him: Thus says the LORD God of Israel concerning the words which you have heard:

27 Because your heart was humbled, and you did tremble before the LORD when you heard these things which I will bring against this place and against its inhabitants, and have humbled yourself before me and have rent

your clothes and wept before me; I have heard you also, says the LORD.

28 Therefore, I will gather you to your fathers, and you shall be gathered to your grave in peace, and your eyes shall not see all the evil that I will bring upon this place and upon its inhabitants. So they brought back the word to the king.

29 ¶Then the king sent and gathered together all the elders of Judah and Jerusalem.

30 And the king went up into the house of the LORD, and all the men of Judah and the inhabitants of Jerusalem and the priests and the Levites and all the people, great and small; and he read before them all the words of the book of the covenant that was found in the house of the LORD.

31 And the king stood in his place and made a covenant before the LORD, to walk after the LORD and to keep his commandments and his statutes and his testimonies, with all his heart and with his whole soul, to perform the words of the covenant which are written in this book.

32 And he caused all who were present in Jerusalem and Benjamin to stand to it. And the inhabitants of Jerusalem did according to the covenant of the LORD God of their fathers.

33 And Josiah took away all the abominations which the LORD had destroyed before the children of Israel, and he made all the people who were found in Israel to serve the LORD their God. And they did not go astray from following the LORD God of their fathers.

CHAPTER 35

MOREOVER Josiah kept a passover to the LORD in Jerusalem; and he celebrated the feast on the fourteenth day of the first month.

2 And he set the priests in their charges, and appointed them over the service of the house of the LORD,

3 And he said to the Levites who dwelt in all Israel, Sanctify yourselves to the LORD, and put the holy ark in the house which Solomon the son of David king of Israel did build; for you have no longer to carry it upon your shoulders; serve now the LORD your God and his people Israel,

4 And prepare your hearts and the heart of your fathers, according to the writing of David, king of Israel, and according to the writing of Solomon his son,

5 And stand in the holy place according to the divisions of the families of your fathers and of your brethren the people, and after the divisions of the families of the Levites,

6 And kill the passover and sanctify yourselves and prepare the hearts of your brethren, that they may do according to the word of the LORD by the hand of Moses.

7 Then Josiah gave to the people sheep, lambs, and kids of the goats, all for the passover offerings, for all that were present, to the number of thirty thousand, and three thousand bullocks; these were of the king's substance.

8 And his princes gave willingly to the people and to the priests and to the Levites; Hilkiah and Zechariah and Nehiel, rulers of the house of the LORD, gave to the priests for the passover offerings two thousand and six hundred sheep and three hundred oxen.

9 Conaniah, also, and Shemaiah his nephew and Hashabiah and Jadiel gave to the Levites for passover offerings five thousand sheep and five hundred oxen.

10 So the service was prepared, and the priests stood in their places and the Levites in their courses,

11 And they killed the passover according to the king's command, and the priests sprinkled some of the blood,

12 And the Levites flayed the victims and gave the burnt offerings to the divisions of the families of the people, to offer to the LORD, as it is written in the law of Moses. And so they did every morning.

13 And they roasted the passover with fire according to the ordinance; but the other holy offerings they cooked in pots and in caldrons and in pans, and divided them speedily among all the people.

14 And afterward they prepared for themselves and for the priests, because the priests the sons of Aaron were busied in offering the burnt offerings and the fat until the Levites were through; then the Levites prepared for themselves and for the priests the sons of Aaron, who ministered.

15 And the singers the sons of Asaph were in their place, according to the commandment of David, and Haman and Jerithon, the king's seers; and the porters remained at every gate; they might not depart from their service; for their brethren the Levites served them.

16 So all the service of the LORD was prepared the same day, to keep the passover and to offer burnt offerings upon the altar of the LORD, according to the commandment of King Josiah.

17 And the children of Israel who were present kept the passover at that time, and the feast of the unleavened bread seven days.

18 And there was no passover like to that kept in Israel from the days of Samuel the prophet; neither did all the kings of Israel keep such a passover as Josiah kept, and the priests and the Levites and all Judah and Israel who were present in Jerusalem.

19 In the eighteenth year of the reign of Josiah was this passover kept.

20 ¶After all this, when Josiah had prepared the affairs of the temple, Pharaoh the lame king of Egypt came up to fight against Mabog [1] by Euphrates; and Josiah went out against him.

21 But he sent ambassadors to him, saying, What have I to do with you, O king of Judah? I am not coming against you this day, O king of Judah; for indeed I have not come to fight against you. The LORD has told you to frighten me; cease from meddling with God, who is with me, that he may not destroy you.

22 Nevertheless Josiah would not turn his face from him; for he had gone to fight with him. And he did not listen to the words of Pharaoh the lame; for Josiah did not know that it was from the LORD, so he went forth to fight against him in the plain of Megiddo.

23 Then Pharaoh the lame shot two arrows at Josiah; and the king said to his servants, Take me away; for I am severely wounded.

24 So his servants took him out of the chariot, and put him into his own royal chariot; and they brought him to Jerusalem, and he died and was buried in the sepulchres of his fathers. And all Judah and Jerusalem mourned for Josiah.

25 ¶And Jeremiah lamented for Josiah, saying, All righteous men and righteous women, weep in your lamentations for Josiah. And he made them an ordinance in Israel, to this day; and, behold, these lamentations are written in the Book of Lamentations.

26 Now the rest of the acts of Josiah and his goodness, according to that which is written in the law of the LORD,

27 And his deeds, first and last, behold, they are written in the Book of the Kings of Israel and Judah.

CHAPTER 36

THEN the people of the land took Jehoahaz the son of Josiah, and made him king in his father's stead in Jerusalem.

2 And Jehoahaz was twenty-three years old when he began to reign, and he reigned three months in Jerusalem.

3 And the king of Egypt deposed him,

4 And he made Eliakim his brother king over Judah and Jerusalem, and changed his name to Jehoiakim. And Pharaoh the lame took Jehoahaz his brother and carried him to Egypt, and he died there.

5 ¶Jehoiakim was twenty-five years old when he began to reign, and he reigned eleven years in Jerusalem; and he did that which was evil in the sight of the LORD his God.

6 Against him came up Nebuchadnezzar king of Babylon, and bound

[1] Charchemish in Western texts. Perhaps the later name.

him in chains to carry him to Babylon.

7 Nebuchadnezzar also carried away some of the vessels of the house of the LORD to Babylon and put them in his temple in Babylon.

8 Now the rest of the acts of Jehoiakim and the abominations which he did, behold, they are written in the Book of the Kings of Israel and Judah; and Jehoiachin his son reigned in his stead.

9 ¶Jehoiachin was eighteen years old when he began to reign, and he reigned three months and ten days in Jerusalem; and he did that which was evil in the sight of the LORD.

10 And when the year was expired, Nebuchadnezzar king of Babylon sent a force against him and brought him to Babylon. both him and the precious vessels of the house of the LORD, and made Zedekiah his brother king over Judah and Jerusalem.

11 ¶Zedekiah was twenty-one years old when he began to reign, and he reigned eleven years in Jerusalem.

12 And he did that which was evil in the sight of the LORD his God, and did not humble himself before Jeremiah the prophet, who prophesied from the mouth of the LORD.

13 And he also rebelled against Nebuchadnezzar, who had made him swear by the name of the LORD; but he stiffened his neck and hardened his heart and would not pray before the LORD God of Israel.

14 ¶Moreover all the chiefs of the priests and of the Levites and the people transgressed very much after all the abominations of the nations, and polluted the house of the LORD which he had hallowed in Jerusalem.

15 And the LORD God of their fathers sent to them by his messengers, giving useful advice in advance; because he had compassion on his people and on the flock that he had chosen;

16 But they laughed at the messengers of the LORD and despised their words and mocked his prophets until the wrath of the LORD arose against his people, till there was no remedy.

17 Therefore he brought up against them the king of the Chaldeans, who slew their young men with the sword in the house of their sanctuary and who had no compassion upon young men or virgins, nor upon the old men, nor upon babies; he delivered them all into his hand.

18 And all the vessels of the house of the LORD, great and small, and the treasures of the house of the LORD and the treasures of the king and of his princes, all these he brought to Babylon.

19 And they burned the house of the LORD and broke down the walls of Jerusalem and burned all its palaces with fire and destroyed all the costly vessels thereof.

20 And those who had escaped from the sword he carried away captive to Babylon, where they became servants to him and to his sons until the LORD delivered the kingdom to the Persians;

21 To fulfil the word of the LORD by the mouth of Jeremiah the prophet until the land had enjoyed its sabbaths, all the days that it lay desolate until the seventy years were completed.

22 ¶Now in the first year of Cyrus king of Persia, that the word of the LORD spoken by the mouth of Jeremiah the prophet might be fulfilled, the LORD stirred up the spirit of Cyrus king of Persia, that he made a proclamation throughout all his kingdom and put it also in writing, saying,

23 Thus says Cyrus king of Persia: All the kingdoms of the earth has the LORD God of heaven given me; and he has charged me to build him a house in Jerusalem, which is in Judah. Who is there among you of all his people with whom the LORD his God is pleased? Let him go up, and let him come to me.

www.ingramcontent.com/pod-product-compliance
Lightning Source LLC
Chambersburg PA
CBHW020810100426
42814CB00001B/13